AND THE
DEAD
SHALL RISE

AND THE
DEAD
SHALL RISE

*The Murder of Mary Phagan
and the Lynching of Leo Frank*

STEVE ONEY

PANTHEON BOOKS, NEW YORK

Library of Congress Cataloging-in-Publication Data

Oney, Steve, 1954–
And the dead shall rise : the lynching of Leo Frank / Steve Oney.
p.   cm.
Includes bibliographical references and index.
ISBN 0-679-42147-5
1. Phagan, Mary, d. 1913.   2. Murder—Georgia—Atlanta—Case studies.
3. Frank, Leo, 1884–1915.   4. Lynching—Georgia—Marietta—Case studies.
5. Trials (Murder)—Georgia—Atlanta—Case studies.   I. Title.

HV6534.A7O54 2003   364.15'23'09758231—dc21   2003048274

www.pantheonbooks.com

Book design by M. Kristen Bearse

Printed in the United States of America
First Edition

2   4   6   8   9   7   5   3   1

To Madeline Stuart,
who believed in me

"When we dream about those who are long since forgotten or dead, it is a sign that we have undergone a radical transformation and that the ground on which we live has been completely dug up: then the dead rise up, and our antiquity becomes modernity."

—FRIEDRICH NIETZSCHE,
Mixed Opinions and Maxims

Contents

AND THE
DEAD
SHALL RISE

April 26, 1913

That morning, thirteen-year-old Mary Phagan, after eating a breakfast of cabbage and wheat biscuits, devoted herself to getting dressed. First, she donned stockings and garters, then a store-bought violet dress and gunmetal-gray pumps. Two bows in her auburn hair and a blue straw hat adorned with dried red flowers atop her head completed the outfit. Mary wanted to look nice, for Saturday, April 26, 1913, marked a special occasion—Confederate Memorial Day. Around 11:45, with a silvery mesh purse and an umbrella (the skies were misting rain) in her hands, she boarded the English Avenue trolley headed to downtown Atlanta, where the annual parade would soon begin.

Well turned out or not, Mary would have been one of the prettiest girls in any crowd. Eyes blue as cornflowers, cheeks high-boned and rosy, smile beguiling as honeysuckle, figure busty (later, everyone acknowledged that "she was exceedingly well-developed for her age"), she had undoubtedly already tortured many a boy. There was simply something about her—a tilt to the chin, a dare in the gaze—that projected those flirtatious wiles that Southern girls often employ to devastating effect.

As her correspondence with her country cousin and friend Myrtle Barmore illustrates, Mary could be a handful. On December 30, 1912, she wrote:

Well, Myrt I don't know what to think of you for not coming [to lunch on Christmas day]. I think that was a poor excuse. When I come up there I'll give you what you need. Me and Ollie [her sister] & Mama & Charles & Joshua [her brothers] went out at Uncle Jack Thurs. and taken dinner. "But gee" how we did eat. Had fresh "hog." I don't know when I can get to come. Mama is getting where she will not let me go anywhere. "But gee" I am going to save my money and go West. Gee I will have some time . . . When I come there, we will have some time "kid."

Yet despite her beauty and airy hopes (many inspired by the movies, which she attended frequently and followed in such magazines as *Photo*

Lore), Mary Phagan was unlikely to escape drab and impoverished environs. She lived in Atlanta's Bellwood section, no one's vision of a beautiful
wood. Northwest of downtown, the neighborhood was bordered on one
side by the Exposition Cotton Mill and its adjacent factory-owned village,
Happy Hollow, on another by the clanging sheds of the Atlantic Steel Mill
and on a third by an expanse of crookedly carpentered "nigger shacks." In
homage to its bare-knuckled ward politics, the community was called "the
bloody fifth."

Like most Bellwood people, Mary was a hillbilly. Her father, a farmer
named William Joshua Phagan, had died of the measles in 1899 a few
months before her birth in Alabama. Around 1900, Mary's widowed
mother, Fannie, carried the children back to the family's ancestral home
near Marietta in Cobb County, twenty miles northwest of Atlanta.

At one time, Phagan had been a fine name around Marietta. During the
1890s, the patriarch—William Jackson—had stood in the traces behind his
own mules on his own land snug against the Blue Ridge mountains that rim
Cobb County. But the old man had accompanied his son to Alabama, and
after the boy's death, there he remained. When Fannie Phagan and her
brood returned to Georgia, they moved in with her people, the Bentons, in
the Sardis section, a rural area several miles outside Marietta.

In 1907, the family relocated again—this time to the dingy mill town of
Eagan, a tiny place encysted in the southern Atlanta suburb of East Point.
There, the widow Phagan opened a boardinghouse. The clan didn't move to
Georgia's capital until 1912, when Fannie remarried. Her new husband,
John W. Coleman, toiled intermittently at the Exposition mill but was
presently employed by the municipal sanitation department.

That, down deep, Mary Phagan cleaved tight to her struggling family can
be seen in the lines of a poem entitled "My Pa," which she'd recently copied
from *Successful Farmer* magazine and presented to her stepfather:

> *My pa ain't no millyunaire, but, Gee! He's offul smart!*
> *He ain't no carpenter, but he can fix a feller's cart . . .*
> *My pa ain't president becoz, he says, he never run,*
> *But he could do as well as any president has done . . .*
> *My pa ain't rich, but that's becoz he never tried to be;*
> *He ain't no 'lectrician, but one day he fixed the*
> *telephone for me . . .*
> *My pa knows everything, I guess, an' you bet I don't care*
> *'Coz he ain't president or rich as any millyunaire!*
> *Whenever things go wrong, my pa can make 'em right, you see;*
> *An' if he ain't rich or president, my pa's good enough fer me!*

Like many girls her age, Mary had quit school to help out at home. In 1909, at the age of ten, she'd hired on part-time at a textile mill. In 1911, she'd taken a steady job at a paper manufacturer. In 1912, she'd moved to her current position at the National Pencil Factory, where she was paid ten cents an hour to run an apparatus called a knurling machine that inserted rubber erasers into the metal tips of nearly finished pencils.

Tough as times had been for the Phagans, the family was no worse off than most Atlantans in the early twentieth century. During these years, refugees from Georgia's hardscrabble tenant farms poured into the city, driven from the flatlands by the fluctuating price of cotton, from Appalachia by a rocky soil unkind to seed and plow. Figures compiled by the United States Census Bureau show that between 1900 and 1910 Atlanta nearly doubled in size. Many of the new arrivals toiled in the mills, chief among them the Fulton Bag and Cotton Mill, whose factory-owned village, Cabbagetown, spread out in row after identical clapboard row east of downtown. For these thousands of souls, the average workweek lasted 66 hours, and pay fell 37 percent below that earned by northern workers. In a city whose cost of living was exceeded among other American cities only by Boston's, a wage of ten or fifteen cents an hour did not go far. In 1911, Atlanta's *Journal of Labor* reported four thousand requests for assistance; in 1912, five thousand.

There were other problems as well. Over half of Atlanta's school children—both white and Negro—suffered from anemia, enlarged glands, heart disease or malnutrition. Death rates were abnormally high for citizens of all ages. (In 1905, 2,414 of every 100,000 Atlantans died; the national average was 1,637.) And there wasn't much indication that things would get better soon. More than 50,000 Atlantans lived with no plumbing. To service its 10,800 "earth closets," as the newspapers called them, the city provided just fifteen horse-drawn honey wagons. Moreover, the capital's physicians possessed no means of isolating and then combating infections, as Georgia was among only a handful of states yet to set up a department of vital statistics.

Nonetheless, Atlanta's crackers—as country folk come to town were known generally—and its lintheads—as millworkers were known specifically—did not spend their time in despair. On April 1, they'd staged their own musicale—the first annual Atlanta Fiddler's Convention—at the Municipal Auditorium. The master of ceremonies was Colonel Max Poole, a one-armed Confederate veteran from Oxford, Georgia, who played by cradling a bow under his stub, while the featured performer was Fiddlin' John Carson, a Cabbagetown resident and future RCA recording star who toted his 1714 Stradivarius reproduction in a feed sack. The Scotch-Irish reels the fiddlers favored—"Trail of the Lonesome Pine," "Annie Laurie,"

"Hop Light, Ladies" — could sure enough move a crowd. By closing night of the three-day festival, Momma and 'em were clogging in the aisles.

The spirit of Atlanta's crackers was independent to the point of contrariness and a little bit hellish. No matter how bad things got, folks weren't likely to complain unless, of course, their dignity was threatened, which was exactly what the city's industrialists, by relying increasingly on child laborers, were now doing.

Rarely, if ever, had Atlantans been as conscious of the difficult lives to which so many of their children had been reduced as on April 26, 1913. THINKS GEORGIA TREATS LITTLE TOILERS WORST, declared the headline in the afternoon's *Atlanta Georgian* over an article pointing out that "Georgia is the only state that allows children ten years old to labor eleven hours a day in the mills and factories, and is worse in that respect than North Carolina, where the age limit is twelve years." Even more damning, the piece detailed how just a few months earlier a group of Georgia factory owners had banded together to kill a bill in the state senate that would have raised the legal working age to fourteen.

The *Georgian*'s story was but the latest in a series of attacks by the newspaper on exploitative factory owners. William Randolph Hearst, its publisher since he purchased the sheet a year before, had pursued the issue relentlessly. His campaign, while intended to win readers, was not entirely disingenuous. The press baron's wife, Millicent, was obsessed with the "little girl in the mill town [who] is not receiving a living wage." And his chief correspondent and ponderous moral conscience, Arthur Brisbane, was a fanatic on the subject. Earlier in the spring, Brisbane had filed a long, probably apocryphal piece about a Georgia mill owner so depraved that he refused to release his employees during daylight to attend the burial of one of their tiny coworkers. Entitled "A Funeral by Lamplight," the story was set in "a squalid room at midnight," where "a coffin rests on trestles" and children in "all stages of emaciation" moaned and sobbed.

Hearst was not alone in calling attention to the plight of Atlanta's underage workforce. Elsewhere in the city on this spring Saturday, others were speaking out just as forcefully. During a Confederate Memorial Day sermon delivered at the downtown Oakland Cemetery, Dr. Charles Lee, a first cousin of General Robert E. Lee, stood on a platform at the base of the Sleeping Lion, the Confederacy's Tomb of the Unknown, and told a rain-soaked audience of a thousand:

Our principles were not defeated when we surrendered at Appomattox. The wars are not over. There are other enemies, bitter ones, that must be fought — emigration, labor, the double standard of child labor and white slavery. Our fathers would face these and defeat them had they the youth and vitality that was once theirs, and it behooves us to do it for their sake, if nothing else.

Meantime across town at the Wesley Chapel, the Southern Sociological Conference was convening. Among the convocation's goals was the formulation of tactics to put an end to "the awful curse" of child labor. Attended by some one thousand educators, pastors and social workers (many of them Negro), the affair was chaired by Alexander J. McKelway, regional secretary of the National Child Labor Committee, an organization best known as the sponsor of the photographer Lewis Hine, whose portraits of begrimed little coal miners and millworkers had alerted America to the Dickensian dilemma of its urchin wage earners.

The three-day Atlanta assembly was not devoted solely to the topic of child labor. Also on the agenda were such subjects as "Race Problems" and "Organized Charities." In fact, the convention was something of a referendum on the myriad problems affecting the city's poor. Yet in the end, the fiercest stir was created by the remarks of Owen R. Lovejoy, general secretary of the National Child Labor Committee, who promised the multitude: " 'Thy Kingdom come' means the coming of the day when child labor will be done away with, when every little tot shall have its quota of sunlight and happiness."

How this vision could be realized was a subject of great debate. Ideas involving everything from labor unions to legislation, and ranging from the utopian to the revolutionary, vied for attention. At the radical end of the spectrum could be heard alarming notions inspired by the fact that many of Atlanta's factories, among them the Fulton Bag and Cotton Mill, were Jewish-owned. At first such talk was discouraged. In fact, when Dr. Edwin M. Poteat, the president of the Baptist-endowed Furman University in Greenville, South Carolina, began to denounce Jews for their purported crimes against workers, Alexander McKelway cut him off in mid-diatribe. But Poteat literally walked his text over to the Baptist Tabernacle. There, after telling a packed house that "in America today, the immediate conflict is between the bosses and the people," he lit into the faith that he believed had produced a disproportionate share of the oppressors. "The Jewish race lost its divine commission when it rejected Jesus as the Saviour," he thundered. "Up to that time, it had been the leader in religion. Every great idea contributed to the thought of the world came from the Jews. In fact, the Jews were chosen of God, but they rejected the stone that is the keystone of the arch." Then, for good measure, Poteat flayed the Catholics: "The Catholic church has no place in America. The priest is 2,000 years out of date. The nation cannot and will not submit to the encroachments of the despot, even in religion."

Considering the many outcries on the topic of child labor, one Georgian was conspicuously silent on April 26, 1913. In his heyday, Thomas E. Watson had been the state's most relentless advocate for the workingman, leading a quarter-century-long campaign against the forces of rapacious capitalism. To "The Sage of McDuffie County," factories were the "soulless" locus of modern evil, dynamos studded by "a hundred dull red eyes, indicative of the flames within which were consuming the men, women, and children, the atrocious sacrifice to an insatiable god!"

Rail-thin, redheaded and possessed of galvanizing rhetorical skill, Watson was equal parts stem-winding stump speaker, defense lawyer, poet, popular historian, sentimental defender of the Old South and seer of an unlikely New South. Early on, he had divined that the strangest but truest allies in the region were poor white farmers and Negroes, and with these groups—each victimized by Dixie's elites—as his constituency, he had ascended to the United States Congress.

But since the mid-1890s, when leaders of a rival political faction stuffed the ballot box to deny him reelection to the House of Representatives from Georgia's predominantly rural tenth district, Watson had been in decline. His troubles had increased in 1896 after the Populist Party's national ticket—William Jennings Bryan for president, Watson for vice president—went down to defeat. By the early 1900s, the self-proclaimed friend of "Old Man Peepul" had abandoned his black supporters and become, after his own overwrought fashion, a muckraker, pillorying "the Standard Oil crowd" and various sleek plutocrats and plunderers in the pages of *Tom Watson's Magazine.* Eventually, these targets proved unsatisfying, and in the teens, the agrarian rebel focused his guns on the insidious foreigner behind it all. Week after week in a new publication, the *Jeffersonian,* he explored innovative ways to excoriate that "fat old dago" who cohabited with "voluptuous women"—the Pope.

Ultimately, the United States government indicted Watson for violating postal laws against sending obscenity through the mail. His trial was scheduled to begin in May. While he retained power as a behind-the-scenes kingmaker, in terms of his own electability he was, as he put it, "in the Valley of the Shadow," and friends and critics alike speculated as to his mental stability. He no longer seemed capable of mustering the initiative to take on genuine far-ranging injustice. "Your Uncle T.E.W.," as Watson often referred to himself in print, simply wasn't there for his poor little nieces, Atlanta's factory girls.

Due to a shortage of sheet brass at the pencil factory, the week ending April 26, 1913, had not been a good one for Mary Phagan. Ordinarily, she was scheduled to work fifty-five hours. During the past six days, however, she'd been needed only for two abbreviated shifts. The sealed envelope awaiting her in her employer's office safe contained just $1.20. Still, it was something, which was why after she got off her trolley in downtown Atlanta, she walked not to Peachtree Street, where the parade was forming, but to 37 South Forsyth Street, where she worked.

The building that housed the National Pencil Company was four stories in height, a full city block in length. Situated just below a ribbon of railroad tracks that formed an unofficial border between Atlanta's commercial and industrial districts, the place bore scant resemblance to the squat brick and frame constructions surrounding it. Banner Sheet Metal, Southern Belting, Keystone Type Foundry, Schenck Brothers Machine Shop and the local John Deere distributor were all of a piece, drab and close to the ground. Only this bulky interloper a door up from the northwest corner of Forsyth and Hunter broke the pattern.

Yet what ultimately set the old Venable Building—so named for its original owners—apart was its architecture. Granite facade dominated by a series of somber arches that repeated themselves on each succeeding floor, main entry topped by a fan-shaped brass transom bearing a bas-relief image of the sun, upper levels punctuated by clusters of sash windows that seemed to glower from beneath beetling stone brows, the structure was a passable example of the ponderous style that had flourished throughout New England during the gilded age: Richardsonian Romanesque. Initially operated as a hotel—the Granite Hotel, logically enough—the edifice had been designed to dignify. Instead, it intimidated. Around noon, Mary Phagan went inside.

Twenty-nine-year-old Leo Max Frank, the superintendent of the National Pencil Company, had spent most of the morning of April 26, 1913, in his factory office working on the books. Saturdays were invariably the same for him: triplicate invoices on each job (white sheet to the purchaser, pink to the majority stockholder for serial recording, yellow to the alphabetical file), lading bills, commission forms for the salesmen and distributing agents, and a financial report balancing the costs of labor, machinery and materials (lead, wood, rubber, paint) against earnings.

In spite of the sheet-brass shortage, it had been a busy week at the National Pencil Company. Though output had been depressed—2,719½ gross of new pencils—inventory had more than met demand, enabling the factory to dispatch 4,374 gross of pencils to the freight yards, most destined for the shelves of such five-and-dime stores as F. W. Woolworth and S. H. Kress, others special-ordered and headed to such coveted customers as

"Cadillac" and "Packard." This embarrassment of pencils had generated an avalanche of paperwork, all of it landing on the factory superintendent's desk.

Leo Frank was not an ugly man, but he was quite decidedly no blandly handsome Georgia boy. It wasn't hard to see his delicate, small-boned, distinctly Hebraic face as the flesh-and-blood articulation of a mechanical drawing—jaw long and angular, chin sharply squared off, nose a draftsman's triangle rising from elliptical cheeks. His features, however, were not pure geometry. Full-lipped and sensual, his mouth was too pretty. His eyes, magnified by thick-lensed wire-rimmed spectacles, bulged perceptibly. At five feet six inches and 120 pounds, he appeared just the sort to relish the task of tabulating figures. And he did—yet not only for the work's sake. By applying "scientific methods" to the manufacturing of pencils, he was ascending to the top of Atlanta's German-Jewish aristocracy.

Since arriving in Georgia nearly five years earlier, Frank had enjoyed a propitious rise. The Texas-born, Brooklyn-reared factory superintendent was the product of good German-Jewish stock. His recently retired father, Rudolph, though he made his living in the new world as a salesman, had trained in Dusseldorf as a physician. His mother, Rae (short for Rachel), had stayed at home raising Leo and his younger sister, Marian. Meantime, his uncle—Confederate veteran Moses Frank—was a globe-trotting Atlanta-based magnate who owned a substantial percentage of National Pencil Company stock and whose address was generally the best hotel in whatever city he was visiting. Young Frank did not, however, owe his position solely to this influential patron. Well educated—drafting studies at Pratt Institute, an engineering degree from Cornell University—Leo had apprenticed with two northern concerns: B. F. Sturtevant in Hyde Park, Massachusetts, and the National Meter Company in New York. He had also traveled to Germany to learn the pencil business at Eberhard-Faber.

More important, Frank had married well. Twenty-three-year-old Lucille Selig Frank was the granddaughter of Levi Cohen, cofounder of Atlanta's reform synagogue, the Temple. Emil Selig, Lucille's father, worked for the family's thriving business—West Disinfecting ("Largest Manufacturer of Disinfectant in the World," trumpeted the ads). Through his new connections, Frank had forged relationships with numerous leading lights of the wandering Southern tribe. One brother-in-law, Alexander E. Marcus, ran a stylish Atlanta haberdashery, while Lucille's Athens, Georgia, cousins, the Michael brothers, owned the college town's flagship department store. Even Leo's lone Christian relative through intermarriage cut an important figure in the business world. Charles Ursenbach, a Lutheran and Frank's other brother-in-law, operated the glove and cosmetic concessions at Atlanta's most fashionable women's clothing salon, J. P. Allen, one of the city's few importers of Parisian couture.

As the newly elected president of Gate City Lodge No. 144 of the B'Nai Brith, Frank was among his faith's most visible representatives. With five hundred members, the chapter sponsored dances, violin and vocal recitals, and lectures, and in late March, its leaders had pulled off a coup. They had persuaded their national executive committee to select Atlanta as the site for the B'Nai Brith's 1914 convention.

Outside of work, Frank's world was one of culture and privilege. Atlanta's German-Jewish section centered along Washington Street, several blocks south of Georgia's impressive domed capitol. It was a leafy old neighborhood of magnolia trees and pavered sidewalks lined by stone walls, and its residences—many two-storied and gabled, most embraced by porches—bespoke substance and poise. While a few of the wealthier sorts reared here had already moved to fancier purlieus such as Inman Park (a Frederick Law Olmsted–inspired Victorian subdivision) or Druid Hills (a verdant enclave of mock-Tudor estates clustered around a new country club), most of the city's leading Jewish families remained in the section or at the very least visited once a week to attend services at the Temple on South Pryor Street or charitable events at the Hebrew Orphans' Home on Georgia Avenue, a Moorish castle whose onion-domed spires rose above the neighborhood in exotic foreign counterpoint to the slender church steeples that spiked the sky all around it.

The men and women whose lives were closely tied to the Washington Street area were an impressive lot. There were, for instance, the Riches, three of whose sons had founded the eponymous department store that was Atlanta's preeminent retailer. Then there were the Montags, whose patriarch—Mister Sig—not only controlled a majority share of National Pencil Company stock but owned a paper-manufacturing empire that bore the family name. Without Joseph Hirsch—a millionaire clothing merchant, city council member and health care activist—Grady Hospital, the town's first medical facility to provide reliable service for the indigent, would not have gotten off the ground. Without Henry Alexander, a young lawyer who filed the Atlanta Art Association's incorporation documents, the High Museum would not have come into being. Without Mayer Wolfsheimer, a butcher and gourmet food purveyor, a tin of caviar would not have been available to the capital's epicureans. And Oscar Elsas, president of the Fulton Bag and Cotton Mill, employed more people than anyone else in town. Then there was Victor Hugo Kriegshaber. Proprietor of a construction supply firm and an officer of the Atlanta Loan & Savings Company, Kriegshaber would soon assume the presidency of the Chamber of Commerce.

Presiding over this thoroughly assimilated minority was a rabbi who could well have been called the great assimilator. David Marx had come to Atlanta in 1895 at the age of twenty-three. When he'd arrived, he discovered a Jewish community that, though well established (according to a 1911 magazine article, Caroline Haas, daughter of banker Joseph Haas, was the "first white female child" to enter life in Atlanta), still clung to tradition. While the Hebrew Benevolent Congregation had been organized in 1867, its directors had heretofore hired only German-born rabbis. With Marx, a New Orleans native, the capital's Jews finally eschewed the old ways of the old world. Within five years of his appearance, Marx had abolished the bar mitzvah, ordered the removal of hats in the Temple and endorsed the Reform Union prayer book. Marx also shed rabbinical garb in favor of a business suit, repudiated Zionism and inaugurated Sunday services that outdrew the traditional Friday-evening and Saturday-morning services combined.

By 1913, not only was Marx's ministry a popular success but the rabbi was himself a celebrity. Guest columnist for the *Atlanta Journal,* frequent speaker in both the statehouse and the pulpits of the capital's churches, he had even started what would become an Atlanta tradition—ecumenical Thanksgiving services held at the Temple but conducted by Presbyterian, Baptist and Unitarian pastors.

The lone segment of the populace that David Marx ignored was comprised of the orthodox Jews who had just begun to immigrate to Atlanta. While the influx of Russians and Poles into the South was but a trickle compared to the floodtide pouring into New York, enough of them had settled in Georgia's capital to support several synagogues and import customs that evoked the Gypsy world across the water. As Eli Evans points out in *The Provincials,* a study of Southern Jewry: "The Germans . . . shook their heads at the newcomers—they wore skullcaps in public, spoke in an embarrassing language called Yiddish, lived on the poor side of town and trucked with the Negroes as customers." So while Harry Epstein, the longtime rabbi of an orthodox congregation, would later scoff, "Marx would have been an excellent Presbyterian minister; he knew little about the Talmud and they taught absolutely nothing in the Sunday school," such criticism mattered little to the Temple crowd, whose sights were set not on Jerusalem but on somewhere closer to home. Again according to Evans: "He [Marx] was trying to say to . . . Christian neighbors, 'Look—we're not the kind of Jews you think we are—we're just like you.' When members of the congregation said, 'He made us proud to be Jews,' they were referring not to pride in the teachings of Judaism but pride in his acceptance by the gentile community, which they assumed to represent acceptance for themselves."

Still, there would always be territory from which all Jews—even those resembling Presbyterians—would be barred, and in Atlanta, the line was drawn north of Tenth Street and east of the Ansley Park neighborhood at the front gate of the Piedmont Driving Club. Though the dashing Aaron Haas—a legendary Confederate blockade runner—was among the club's founders, by the turn of the century this haughty social preserve had become a restricted bastion of WASPdom, the exclusive domain of those Bourbon-cured old families that preferred to hold their high teas and debut their daughters among their own kind. Hence in 1905, Victor Kriegshaber, Walter Rich and a few others had formed the Standard Club, which in just eight years had become the foremost social institution in the Jewish life of Atlanta. Now, at dusk, the city's Christian peerage repaired to its sanctum, the Jews to theirs, and Atlanta came to be known—at least to the Jews—as "a five o'clock town." Yet while Rabbi Marx's followers went their own way at sunset, during business hours, there was nowhere they could not go, nothing they could not become, for like their gentile counterparts, they practiced moneyed Atlanta's one true faith: free enterprise.

Whatever the difficulties facing Atlanta's poor, its powerful and wealthy citizens saw the spring of 1913 as the moment the city was joining, in the *Journal*'s words, "the permanent rank of the nation's metropolises." Towering over Atlanta's skyline was a handful of shining new high-rises. While some of the structures housed luxurious hostelries such as the Georgian Terrace and Winecoff, the largest of them—the Hurt, Candler and Grant—were frankly and beautifully office buildings. Real estate speculators had become the city's most affluent citizens, men capable of paying $357,000 for prime commercial lots, as one did on Saturday, April 26, then crowing that such purchases were bargains.

It was a time not only of expansion but of newfangled rages. Atlanta's Pierce-Arrow dealer had recently signaled the end of the horse-and-buggy era by torching twenty-five phaetons, victorias and sulkies in a public bonfire. The more daring debs were wearing "cubist gowns" and affecting a "cubist walk" in line with the ideas of futurist painters. A bookstore in the best shopping district was displaying prints of a French nude, "September Morn," that had been banned in Boston. And in several weeks, the *Atlanta Georgian* would kick off a campaign to raise the city's population from its current 173,713 to 500,000 by 1920.

That many of these newcomers might be Yankees was fine with Atlanta's elite, for unlike their impoverished kin, the hard-charging sorts who reigned in Georgia's capital had long ago struck the Stars and Bars. In 1886,

Henry Grady, the forward-looking editor of the *Atlanta Constitution,* told investment-minded members of New York's New England Society: "We have . . . put business above politics . . . We have reduced the commercial rate of interest from 24 to 6 percent, and are floating 4 percent bonds. We have learned that one northern immigrant is worth fifty foreigners." In the wake of these remarks, the city's leaders had never looked back.

Deeply mulched in hyperbole, Atlanta—which after all had not been incorporated until 1845 and consequently never did bear much resemblance to such older southern cities as Richmond or Charleston—had become a place where influence as opposed to reverence, hustle as opposed to charm composed the coin of the realm. For "live-wire boosters" who wanted to strike it rich, it offered untold attractions. The textile and steel industries were the most obvious allure. Yet the city would never truly sully itself with the dust of the loom or the fire of the smelter. No, its destiny rode the rails—the L & N, the Southern, the Atlanta and West Point—that connected it to the North and West and made it a center of transportation, sales and distribution.

If one man could have been said to embody Atlanta's progressive temperament in 1913, he was Georgia's governor-elect, John M. Slaton, linked by blood to a tradition of high-mindedness and by marriage to one of the city's great fortunes. His father was the longtime superintendent of Atlanta's public schools. His wife, the former Sallie Grant, was heiress to a $2 million estate conceived in property, built by railroads and compounded in bonds.

John and Sallie Slaton inhabited the highest stratum of Atlanta society. At forty-six, Georgia's new chief executive moved effortlessly from courthouse to boardroom to garden reception to the Paces Ferry Dancing Club, where he was an avid turkey trotter. As a lawyer, he represented many of the city's biggest businesses—among them, the Fulton Bag and Cotton Mill. And as a politician, he consistently catered to corporate interests. Observed the *Constitution:* He "not only has never known the bitterness of defeat but [has] not even had to feel the twinge of a single temporary setback in a uniformly brilliant career."

If possible, the new first lady was an even more dazzling figure. Though she had experienced profound grief (her first husband committed suicide), Sallie Slaton had retained the grace and style of a celebrated belle while maturing into a patroness of the arts. Educated at the Ballard Seminary, where a smitten professor composed a piano trilogy whose component pieces sang the pink of her lips ("Anemone"), the blue of her eyes ("The Blue Bells") and the white of her brow ("The Lily of the Valley"), she now devoted her talents to the Atlanta Players Club, where she was soon to portray Lady Augusta Bracknell in a production of Oscar Wilde's *The Importance of Being Earnest*. Sallie Slaton's charms were so universally acknowledged that even the often piquant Polly Peachtree—the *Georgian*'s pseudonymous gossip columnist—offered an unqualified endorsement: "I frankly and freely confess myself her ardent admirer. Her beauty and wit will make the executive mansion during her husband's administration the most brilliant state court in all these United States."

On April 26, 1913, the story making the rounds was that John Slaton and Luther Z. Rosser, arguably Atlanta's fiercest litigator, were merging their law practices into the new firm of Rosser, Brandon, Slaton & Phillips. While the Rossers were also pillars of Atlanta's patrician class, Rosser was in demeanor and style Slaton's antithesis. As the blunt instrument the city's powerful engaged to demolish those who stood in their way, he had acquired a reputation for charging outlandish fees and employing brusque courtroom tactics. He was presently earning the unheard-of sum of $100,000 a year representing, among others, the Georgia Railway and Electric Company (predecessor of the Georgia Power Company), which was embroiled in a battle in Rabun County, high in the Blue Ridge. The utility's officers wanted to open a $5 million generating station in the mouth of pristine Tallulah Gorge, but resistance from those claiming the project would despoil "one of the greatest scenic wonders of the world" was furious and had found its voice in an Appalachian widow whose husband, General James Longstreet, had been a Confederate hero. It was Rosser's job to make sure that neither this fiery opponent nor the hallowed specter she invoked stood in the way of lights for Atlanta's streets or power for her factories.

As news of Slaton and Rosser's impending affiliation was bruited about Atlanta, the principals refused to confirm the reports. However, the governor-elect, back in town following a preliminary trip north to acquaint financiers in Boston and on Wall Street with business opportunities in Georgia, did consent to reflect on the excitement that had not only precipitated the partnership but was invigorating both finance and fashion in the city. "Whereas once Georgia was largely attractive to agricultural interests," Slaton told a reporter, "it is now attractive to manufacturers who wish to harness her natural resources and reap profits in assured safety." One of the greatest of these natural resources was, of course, the state's supply of child laborers. Far from being frowned upon by industrial barons, the practice was advocated for both its economic advantages and its supposed benefits for the children. As no less a personage than Asa G. Candler, president of Atlanta's quintessential enterprise, the Coca-Cola company, had recently stated: "The most beautiful sight that we see is the child at labor; as early as he may get at labor the more beautiful, the more useful does his life get to be." In this, the National Pencil Company—whose 170-member workforce consisted largely of teenage girls—was perfectly in step.

On April 26, 1913, dramatic proof of Atlanta's new status as a seat of commerce and culture could be found at the Municipal Auditorium. There, at 8 P.M., Arturo Toscanini, the conductor of New York's Metropolitan Opera Company, would raise his baton; Enrico Caruso, the fabled tenor, would take the stage in the role of Mario Cavaradossi; and a stylishly attired 6,433 would settle back in their seats for the season's grand finale performance of Giacomo Puccini's *Tosca*.

During the previous week—"A Week of Wonders," proclaimed one headline writer—Atlantans had celebrated the company's record-breaking Southern engagement (seven shows, a $91,000 gate) with elegantly catered cocktail parties, sumptuous late-night suppers in the ballrooms of Peachtree Street's hotels, and elaborate entertainments at the Piedmont Driving Club. The festivities had been spirited in so many senses of the word that the *Constitution*'s editorial cartoonist had approvingly caricatured the city on the paper's front page as a red-nosed dandy in top hat and tails clutching a champagne glass from which half-notes and clef signs bubbled in giddy profusion.

Leo Frank, however, avoided the dizzying round of opera-related festivities that were attracting most Atlantans of his station. In fact, Saturday afternoon, while his wife and her mother enjoyed the Met's matinee production of Gaetano Donizetti's *Lucia di Lammermoor,* Frank remained at the office. The women missed Caruso, but the atmospherics were just as transporting as those that would suffuse the evening show. The fashions were just as smart. The diva, Frieda Hempel, just as inspired. And the illusion that the host city had been transformed into Manhattan on the Chattahoochee just as blinding.

As for the vast majority of Atlantans, at the exact moment the curtain was rising for the Met's matinee, they were packing five and six deep on both sides of Peachtree Street to watch the Confederate Memorial Day parade.

First, a police honor guard cleared the way for the grand marshal and various dignitaries, most notably outgoing governor Joseph M. Brown, a leading citizen of Marietta. Next, a brass band set an appropriately martial tone for the companies of United States infantrymen, Georgia national guardsmen, military academy cadets, Boy Scouts, Odd Fellows and Knights of Pythias. The stage, of course, was being set for the thin gray line, and soon enough, the ragged formation of five hundred stooped veterans—many in their patched butternuts, a few hoisting faded regimental banners—straggled into view. "The majority of them," noted the *Journal,* "were afoot, walking not so alertly as they did a few years ago. Some were riding, having come to the day of life when exertion must be spared, [although] the flash in their eyes showed that they had not forgotten the times, half a century ago, when music bade them farewell as they went to battle."

The climactic scene in the afternoon's pageantry belonged to the young—battalion after battalion of white-uniformed elementary school students, each group accompanied by a drum corps. Stretched out over seven blocks, the four thousand children marched proudly, orderly, only occasionally capitulating to urges from the crowd to give the rebel yell.

Mary Phagan, however, never saw these dashing boys, never heard their high-pitched cries of resurgent insurrection.

TWO

Look Out, White Folks

They found her around 3:30 Sunday morning at the rear of the National Pencil Factory basement. Partially hidden behind a partition that closed off a storage shed running nearly the length of one side of the place, she lay on her left shoulder, arms folded beneath her torso, face pressed into a trash-filled depression, head pointed toward Forsyth Street, toward the front. While her dress was hitched up around her knees and a shoe was missing, not until they turned her over could they appreciate the savage and perverse nature of the crime.

Caught in the beam of Call Officer W. F. Anderson's flashlight, the girl's battered visage mesmerized even as it appalled: right eye purple and puffy, cheeks bruised and badly scratched and, most severe, scalp jaggedly gashed open just above the left ear. These wounds, however, had apparently not caused death. Twisted around the girl's neck and tied in a slipknot in back was a seven-foot length of ¾-inch wrapping cord. Girdling the noose were two strips of cloth torn from her skirt, but such a clumsy, not to mention curious, bit of handiwork could not obscure the signs of strangulation. A trenchlike scar where twine had cut into flesh was plainly visible. Meanwhile, the poor thing's thickly swollen tongue protruded far over her lower lip, and blood had bubbled from her mouth and ears.

Later, the responding officers would agree that the most chilling aspect of all was the color of the body. When Newt Lee, the plant's Negro night watchman, had phoned in the alarm, he'd said: "A white woman has been killed up here." The girl, though, was black as pitch. Her features—even her eye sockets and nostrils—were caked with soot, and her mouth was choked with cinders. After fishing a scrap of paper from the debris upon which her head so rudely rested, Sergeant R. J. Brown, the morning watch commander, tried to wipe away the grime. "I rubbed the dirt and trash from her face," the sergeant would subsequently remember, "and then I said that she was a white girl, [but] the others said that she was colored."

The initial attempts to determine the victim's race—indeed, the initial attempts to determine much of anything—were not made easier by the surroundings. From the factory lobby, there were only two ways into the basement—an elevator (metal door shut, car parked somewhere above) and a wooden plank ladder that descended from a tiny scuttle hole. Some 200 feet long, the rock-walled, earthen-floored cavity was narrow as a catacomb and just as dark. The single permanent source of illumination, a flickering gas jet at the front of the room, had been turned so low it reminded Newt Lee of a lightning bug. Details—a boiler and toilet on one side, the storage shed on the other—emerged as indefinite, ghostlike masses. Intensifying the eerie gloom was the almost stifling odor. Over the years, so many tons of sawdust and parings had been swept down here from the manufacturing departments above that, like a cavernous pencil sharpener, the chamber reeked of cedar and lead.

Though the men from headquarters never admitted they were frightened by this veritable tomb, they were surely unsettled—and that, too, was at first a factor. After all, they'd been rousted from the dull and sleepy station house and raced through the empty predawn streets at a 40-mile-per-hour clip. Newt Lee had met them at the building's front door, ushered them across the lobby and pointed to the scuttle hole. After clambering, one by one, into inky blackness, the men had proceeded blindly—the only sound was the "crunch crunch" of shoes striking the shavings-and-coal-slag-carpeted soil—until the Negro, who toted a smoky lantern, had brought them to a halt with the warning: "Look out, white folks, you'll step on her." And they might have. As Anderson subsequently remarked, "I did not see the body until I reached it."

The officers ascertained the girl's color with surprising ease. Anderson simply lowered one of her stockings: milky thigh, milky calf. She was white. Based on the signs of a scuffle near the body, the men speculated that the girl's slayer had pinned her face against the ground where, as she'd gasped for breath, the grinds and ashes that were everywhere had adhered to her skin, pitting and tarring it. As for the obvious question—how had Newt Lee known she was not black—the officers initially didn't pursue it, for in determining the victim's race, they discovered lurid evidence suggesting that another crime had preceded the murder.

While examining the girl's legs, Anderson noticed that the belts attaching corset to garters were unfastened and that her underpants had been ripped up the crotch. Sergeant Brown, in language that would prove too graphic for the newspapers, subsequently described what the men saw: "By raising the skirt a bit, you could see in between the mouth of the vagina, close to the privates, and it had blood on it and blood on the drawers . . . It would flow on its own accord . . . You could see it run from her stomach, this blood coming from her privates."

To everyone clustered around the corpse, the significance of the crimson discharge was self-evident. The girl, in the euphemistic terminology of the age, had been "outraged" or "criminally assaulted." And this is how it would initially be reported, yet the last word on the subject of whether she had been raped—whether she had, in fact, been mutilated—would not be uttered for a long time, if ever.

So far as the officers could decipher the language of the dead, the victim had spoken. After making a couple of last assessments—icy hands and stiffening joints indicated she had evidently expired hours earlier—the men began combing the basement for clues.

Taking into account the group's makeup, the search was surprisingly thorough. Though Sergeant Brown, 49, was a twenty-year veteran of the Atlanta Police; Call Officer Anderson, 31, was a ten-year man; and Sergeant L. S. Dobbs, another 49-year-old, also had two decades under his belt, the others were civilians. W. W. "Boots" Rogers—an erstwhile Fulton County officer, future bailiff and full-time swell—was along merely because he'd chauffeured the party to the scene. And as for a young *Atlanta Constitution* reporter named Britt Craig, he was there, according to his account, because he'd been waiting at headquarters for a ride home; but, according to all others, he'd been passed out drunk in Boots's machine.

The first item these men found was the victim's missing shoe poking out of a garbage pile near the boiler. Next, they located a bloodstained handkerchief several feet behind the body. Then, at the very rear of the cellar, up a gently inclined service ramp, they noticed that a sliding wooden door opening onto an alley had been tampered with. Though the door was closed, an iron staple had been pried from it, rendering the hasp and lock useless. Finally, they spotted a trail leading back from the elevator, suggesting that the remains had been dragged the length of the basement.

The most significant discoveries, however, were made almost literally under the dead girl's nose. It was there that Sergeant Dobbs, using a cane to rake through the rubbish, dug up the first of two bewildering messages. Eventually, the "murder notes," as they'd come to be known, would be judged the case's most enigmatic pieces of evidence. But on this Sunday morning, they did no more than focus suspicion on Newt Lee.

After ruminating a minute on the first of the notes—which was scrawled on a sheet of lined white paper that had been detached from a gummed book lying nearby—Dobbs started to read aloud:

he said he wood love me land down play like the night witch did it but that long tall black negro did boy his slef

Yet before the sergeant could finish reciting this gumbo—in fact, just as he pronounced the words "night witch"—Lee blurted something out. Later, Newt would contend he said only that someone was trying to "put it off on" him, but the officers would remember differently, claiming he declared: "White folks, that's me."

A few minutes after Lee's outburst, Sergeant Dobbs found the other note. This one, which also had been buried in the refuse near the dead girl's head, was jotted across a yellow National Pencil Co. order sheet atop which was printed the plant address and phone number and blank lines for date and invoice information. Like its counterpart, the second communiqué seemed to implicate Newt:

mam that negro hire down here did this i went to make water and he push me down that hole a long tall negro black that hoo it wase long sleam tall negro i wright while play with me

Up to this point, the officers had held their doubts about Lee in check. The Negro—who was in his mid-50s and thus born into slavery—had comported himself with the requisite docility and humility. As one writer would subsequently describe him: "Lee [is] a black, ignorant, corn-field, pot-likker-fed darky. His head is flat as a ballroom floor. His big frame is slightly bent, not from weakness but from the natural laziness of his type. [He] is beyond doubt a white man's nigger." Accordingly, the men had patronized the night watchman. But once the notes were aired, Dobbs immediately accused him of committing the crime.

"You did this or you know who did it," the sergeant charged.

Lee, though he'd begun to shake, denied any connection with the murder. Then, with the officers surrounding him, he told his story, one he repeated without substantive variation several days later at the coroner's inquest:

[At] almost three o'clock . . . I wanted to go into the basement on my rounds. So . . . I went down the ladder and went back to the toilet. I set the lantern on the floor against the side of the toilet. I came out of the toilet and stepped up a few feet. I don't know just how far. I looked to see if the back door was all right and to see if there was any fire [a much dreaded hazard at the factory] in the basement. Then I saw the body. I thought it was something some devilish boys had put there to scare me. I went over and saw it was a body and I got scared. Then I called the police.

Though Lee's narrative seemed believable, and while in it he managed to explain how he'd determined the girl was white (her hair was simply too straight to belong to any Negress), he did not satisfy the officers. To begin with, he swore that when he saw the victim, she was lying faceup, not down, as when the men arrived. Moreover, he couldn't say anything to persuade them that his response to the initial note wasn't incriminating. Then there was the undeniable fact that, like the "black negro" alluded to in each missive, he was ebony-complected. Finally, regardless of what he said, he was still a colored man in a filthy cellar where a white girl lay dead and bleeding from between the legs—which was reason enough for the police to hand-cuff him and lead him away.

With the arrest of Newt Lee, the officers repaired to the factory's second-floor offices and telephoned Chief of Detectives Newport A. Lanford, who in turn alerted two of his best men, John Black and John Starnes. Then they notified Bloomfield's Funeral Home, just a few blocks away on Pryor Street, and in due course the undertaker arrived. Following a hasty exami-nation, Will Gheesling placed the remains in his wicker basket and carried them out the back door to the alley, where his hearse was waiting. Soon thereafter, Detective Starnes appeared on the scene and, during a tour of the basement, discovered more clues. First, in the trash pile where Sergeant Dobbs and company had found the missing shoe, he located a blue straw hat. Then, he noticed that the sliding wood door was covered with bloody fingerprints and that a metal pipe that had apparently been used as a crow-bar was leaning against a nearby wall.

Even as the official investigation was beginning, an equally important task was in progress in the nearly deserted city room of the *Atlanta Constitution*.

Regardless of the fact that he'd been delivered to his biggest scoop in a state of questionable sobriety, Britt Craig was not an alcoholic hack. Quite to the contrary, this 19-year-old son of a respected newspaper family (Craig's father edited a North Georgia weekly) was one of the *Constitu-tion*'s rising stars. True, Craig wasn't going to win many awards for writing. His prose was marred by bad puns, and his accuracy was spotty. However, he possessed two highly valued attributes in newsmen: luck and pluck. Craig often came up with the stories his rivals didn't. Typical of the reporter was a stunt he pulled when assigned to cover the Salon du Bon Ton lingerie show at Atlanta's premier department store, Rich's. After sequestering himself in a cranny rigged with a strategically placed mirror above the mod-els' runway, he proceeded to spy on Mademoiselle Barboure's lace-frilled, bone-corseted beauties as they paraded before an otherwise exclusively female audience. " 'Figuratively' speaking," he enthused in the next day's editions, "there's not a greater show in town." Craig, in other words, was an ingenious scamp who habitually popped up in unlikely spots.

Exactly what measures Craig took to get his story of the murder into a Sunday-morning extra aren't known, but the job couldn't have been easy. Not only did he have to pound out his piece, but he had to awaken editors and they in turn had to order pressmen back to work. However, there were compelling reasons for such exertions, and they could be summed up in one name: William Randolph Hearst. Craig knew that if he didn't move quickly, the newshawks whom the press baron had imported to beef up the *Atlanta Georgian* would poach his exclusive, so he moved, and by 6:30 A.M., the *Constitution*'s special edition was on the streets. In length, Britt's account was actually modest—a boxed page-one item played next to a report on the Metropolitan Opera's triumphant grand finale. (The paper buried the Confederate Memorial Day chestnut inside.) Yet in impact, it was enormous. Here was the germ of the tale—a girl found dead in the bowels of a child-labor factory—that would set the believers in Atlanta's past against the apostles of its future.

That the news reached the two Atlanta families it would most directly affect before vendors began hawking the *Constitution*'s extra was due in large part to the efforts of Boots Rogers.

As it so happened, Rogers had a 16-year-old sister-in-law named Grace Hicks who worked at the pencil factory. While the detectives had been surveying the crime scene and Britt Craig had been writing his story, Boots had sped to Grace's home on McDonough Boulevard south of town, fetched her and raced to Bloomfield's. There, the Hicks girl identified the victim as Mary Phagan. Uncertain how to contact Mary's parents, Boots's sister-in-law then called a mutual friend, 16-year-old Helen Ferguson, who worked at the plant and lived in Bellwood. Young Helen had been close to Mary, so close, in fact, that she knew the girl's stepfather—unlike the hero of the poem "My Pa"—could not afford a telephone. She would have to carry the sad message to the modest frame house at 146 Lindsay Street herself.

Ever since her daughter failed to appear for Saturday supper, Fannie Coleman had been racked with worry. Around seven that evening, her husband journeyed into the city, hoping that Mary had lost herself at the movies. For nearly three hours, John W. Coleman stood at the edge of the Bijou lobby, examining every face, failing to spot the one he so desperately sought. Around ten, he returned home, but he ventured right back out, now knocking on the neighbors' doors. The new prayer was that the girl, who'd planned to take the trolley to Marietta on Sunday to visit her country cousins, had, on a whim, left early. If so, she probably would have called one of the several Bellwood families who allowed the clan to use their phones. Yet, of course, no one had heard a thing. The police, when eventually contacted, were also still in the dark. With nowhere to turn, the couple had done what anxious parents do—they'd waited up. At daybreak, Helen Ferguson appeared, spoke but a sentence and Fannie Coleman—widowed before Mary's birth and now bereft of the child William Joshua Phagan never knew—collapsed. The family physician would soon be summoned to administer a sedative.

Even as word of their loss was reaching John and Fannie Coleman, the indefatigable Boots Rogers was barreling to a halt in front of the ash-green, two-story East Georgia Avenue home where Leo and Lucille Frank lived with Lucille's parents. Unlike at the dead girl's house, where the ensuing tableau of sorrow and lamentation, no matter how searing, was predictable, the scene that unfolded here was ambiguous and open to wildly subjective interpretations.

Accompanying Boots was Detective John Black. At 40, Black was big and bearish with suety jowls, a slab of a nose and rheumy eyes. Rarely seen without a porkpie hat he wore pushed far back on his head, he more closely resembled a railroad dick than a celebrated detective, and until four years earlier, he had worked as a cooper at the Atlanta Brewing and Ice Company. But appearances aside, Black was a bulldog of an investigator who'd already made a reputation for himself by solving a couple of headline-making cases and sending several men to the gallows. Suspicious by nature, he was the instinctive sort, and this morning, his instincts told him something was wrong.

To say that Black had a hunch about Leo Frank is putting it too strongly, but ever since he and his colleague John Starnes had debriefed the responding officers back at the pencil plant around 5:30, he had entertained doubts. What piqued his curiosity wasn't anything the factory superintendent had done but something the men said he hadn't done. During the flurry of telephone activity following Newt Lee's arrest, an operator had connected Call Officer Anderson to Frank's home. For what had seemed like an eternity, the policeman remained on the line waiting for someone to pick up. Nothing. And that was not the first call to the superintendent's residence that had gone unanswered this morning. According to the night watchman, after he'd located the body, he, too, had tried and failed to reach Frank. In marked contrast, the men had experienced no difficulties raising such company officials as the majority stockholder, Sig Montag.

Admittedly, not picking up the phone was no offense, and besides, John Black believed old Newt was as guilty as he was dusky. Yet there was enough here to convince the detective to approach Leo Frank warily and to wait for the right moment before unveiling a critical bit of intelligence. By day's end, the name Mary Phagan would be on a thousand tongues, but before it became too widely circulated, the investigator wanted to see how one man in particular responded upon hearing it.

When Black rang the Seligs' bell, Lucille Frank, wearing a heavy blue housecoat, appeared and ushered the detective and Boots into the parlor. Her husband, she said, was still getting dressed but would be right down.

For five or six minutes—the amount of time that had passed since he *had* answered the phone—Leo Frank had known that a policeman was coming to see him. The prospect disconcerted him, but then, anyone else who'd received the wake-up call John Starnes had given the factory superintendent might have been disconcerted. At 50, Starnes was widely regarded as the detective department's most "immaculate attaché." Slender, stern-faced, mustachioed and usually clad in a smart suit and bowler, he could have passed as the head teller at a downtown bank. Generally, Starnes was "suave and polite," yet this morning when speaking to Frank, he had been abrupt and evasive, for like Black, he was aware of the earlier effort to contact the factory superintendent, and it didn't sit well with him. While specific aspects of the detective's conversation with Frank would subsequently be debated, both parties were in accord as to its basic drift:

> "Is this Mr. Frank, superintendent of the National Pencil Company?" Starnes had begun.
> "Yes, sir."
> "I want you to come down to the factory right away."
> "What's the trouble? Has there been a fire?"
> "No, a tragedy," Starnes had replied vaguely. "I'll send a car for you."

John Black and Boots Rogers had been waiting only a minute or two when Frank entered the room through a portiere that separated the front of the house from a hall linking it to both the kitchen and a staircase that led to the second floor. By all accounts, the factory superintendent was in an agitated state when he greeted his visitors. Dressed in a freshly pressed pleated shirt, blue trousers and suspenders (the only missing pieces were collar and tie), he paced restlessly across the parlor, wringing his hands and firing questions so fast that he apparently didn't leave Black time to answer: "Has anything happened at the factory? . . . Did the night watchman report anything to you? . . . I dreamt I heard the phone ring around four o'clock."

Evidently, Black's reply to this barrage was a curt "Mr. Frank, you had better put your clothes on, and let us go to the factory." Subsequently, the detective would remember it this way:

> His voice was hoarse and trembling and nervous and excited. He looked to me like he was pale . . . He seemed to be nervous in handling his collar. He could not get his tie tied, and talked very rapid.

Boots Rogers would echo these impressions:

> Mr. Frank seemed to be extremely nervous. His questions were jumpy . . .
> His voice was a refined voice . . . kind of lady-like . . . He was rubbing his
> hands . . . He seemed to be excited.

Yes, no one challenged the fact that Leo Frank was upset this Sunday
morning, but as to what that meant and whether Black, and earlier Starnes,
had anything to do with provoking it was another matter. From almost any
perspective, these fiercely unforthcoming men couldn't have helped but
inspire anxiety. They were obstinately mute. Later, Frank would recollect:

> I asked them what the trouble was and the man who I afterwards found
> out was Detective Black hung his head and didn't say anything.

In short, one man rattled on, the other two kept quiet. One man gestured
and gesticulated, the other two hunkered down. Only once—when someone suggested a cup of coffee to relax them all—did there seem to be a
chance for the parties to talk to instead of past each other. Yet far from
achieving its desired effect, this idea gave rise to an enduring misunderstanding. The disagreement hinged on who actually proposed the plan.
According to Lucille Frank and Boots, it was Lucille, but according to
Black, it was Leo. Innocuous as this seems, the detective's version, which
would gain the greater credence, was eventually cited as evidence of an
attempt on the factory superintendent's part to avoid the inevitable. And as
for the coffee itself, none was ever served, as Black argued that Frank
needed something stronger. "I think a drink of whisky would do him good,"
he cracked, sending Lucille scurrying to find a bottle. Eventually, she came
back empty-handed, saying her father, who suffered from indigestion, had
polished off the last of their liquor the previous night.

Black and Rogers had been at the Franks' home for some ten minutes,
and as yet had offered no satisfactory explanation for why they'd come. As
it turned out, their reticence was about to end, but when and where they
told Frank that a girl had been found murdered in the factory basement and
that her name was Mary Phagan became grounds for yet another dispute.
As Frank would subsequently put it:

> Now at this point . . . Mr. Rogers and Mr. Black differ with me on the place
> where the conversation occurred—I say, to the best of my recollection, it
> occurred right there in the house in front of my wife; they say it occurred
> just as I left the house in the automobile; but be that as it may, this is the
> conversation: They asked me did I know Mary Phagan, and I told them

I didn't. They then said to me, "Didn't a little girl with long hair hanging down her back come up to your office yesterday sometime for her money—a little girl who works in the tipping plant?" I says, "Yes, I do remember such a girl coming up to my office, that worked in the tipping room, but I didn't know her name was Mary Phagan" . . . and I finished dressing, and as they had said they would bring me right away back, I didn't have breakfast, but went right on with them in the automobile.

Though Rogers and Black would indeed differ with Frank—later, Boots vividly recalled that Frank and Black were sitting in his backseat when the detective broke the news, adding that Frank then offered up a worrisomely complete list of reasons why he couldn't have known Mary Phagan—the disagreement ultimately did not bear out Black's worst suspicion, for it wasn't as if the superintendent betrayed a knowledge of the child's identity before the detective mentioned it. However, the fact that the men could not later agree on the place where the conversation occurred suggests that by the time they departed for town, they weren't seeing anything in the same light.

Bloomfield's mortuary was a rambling one-story frame building halfway between the state capitol and the factory. This was the group's first stop. Will Gheesling met the men in his reception room, then led them down a long passageway. After opening a door at the end of the corridor, the undertaker briefly disappeared into darkness, leaving Boots and Frank at the threshold, with Black just behind them and a wild-haired man who'd entered the establishment in the party's wake behind Black. A second passed, Gheesling switched on a brilliant electric lamp and there, laid out on a circular cooling table, was Mary Phagan's body, her face turned toward a far wall. To make sure everyone could see, Gheesling pulled down the sheet that covered the corpse, then slipped his hands beneath the girl's head, lifting it up like a battle trophy. Which gave rise to a critical disagreement: Did Frank look, or did he recoil in revulsion and guilty fear?

John Black and Boots Rogers were positive that the plant manager turned away. As Boots would later recollect:

Mr. Gheesling caught the face of the dead girl and turned it over towards me. I looked then to see if anybody followed me and I saw Mr. Frank step from outside of the door into what I thought was a closet. There was a little single bed in there. I didn't see Frank look at the corpse. I don't remember that Mr. Frank ever followed me in this room . . . he could not have seen her face because it was lying over towards the wall . . . His general manner made me think that he was nervous.

Not surprisingly, Frank would subsequently disagree:

> I stood right in the door, leaning up against the right facing . . . Mr.
> Gheesling . . . removed the sheet which was covering the body, and took
> the head in his hands, turned it over, put his finger exactly where the
> wound in the left side of the head was located—put his finger right on it; I
> noticed the hands and arms of the little girl were very dirty—blue and
> ground with dirt and cinders, the nostrils and mouth—the mouth being
> open—nostrils and mouth just full of sawdust and swollen, and there was a
> deep scratch over the left eye on the forehead; about the neck there was
> twine . . . and also a piece of white rag. After looking at the body, I identi-
> fied that little girl as the one that had been up shortly after noon the day
> previous and got her money from me.

Gheesling, contending that his position behind the body blocked his sight line, claimed he couldn't tell what Leo Frank did, but there was one other impartial observer—the wild-haired man who'd followed the party into the funeral home. This was the *Atlanta Journal*'s 20-year-old police reporter, Harold W. Ross. The hard-drinking, chain-smoking son of a Boulder, Colorado, mining engineer, Ross had dropped out of high school his sophomore year to take a reporting job on the *Salt Lake City Tribune*. Before arriving in Atlanta, he'd gypsied across the country, hopping from newspaper to newspaper, acquiring an education and a skepticism that generally doesn't come until far later in life. Although he was already experimenting with the first-person plural style that would one day become the talk of another town, he wasn't a graceful writer, yet he did pay exceptional attention to detail. Truth be told, he could be tediously precise. In short, Ross was already very much the man who in 1925 would found *The New Yorker*.

On this early morning, Ross—whose city editor had read the *Constitution*'s extra—was charged with the unenviable job of coming up with a new angle the *Journal* could get into Monday's editions. Thus he'd raced to Bloomfield's. Later, he'd recall that he "saw Leo M. Frank as he looked upon the mutilated and abused body of Mary Phagan in the morgue three hours after her remains had been found."

Not that Ross was the final authority on the matter. No, the conflicting accounts remained unreconciled, although the police version would gain wider acceptance and have a greater impact. To John Black, Frank was simply more shaken than the admittedly upsetting circumstances warranted.

By 7:45 A.M. Sunday—the hour Boots and Black arrived at the National Pencil Factory with Frank—a crowd had gathered out front, but the men passed quickly through the onlookers. At the door, they were met by 47-year-old N. V. Darley, a coworker the superintendent had asked his wife to call. In charge of plant personnel, Darley was one of Frank's closest associates. The party thus complete, the men continued into the lobby, ascended a set of stairs, then disappeared through another door.

Frank's office occupied a front corner of the building's second floor, adjacent to the packing room. A hundred feet or so farther back, through a set of swinging metal doors, was the plating department. The metal department— where spare parts were lathed, eraser tips fabricated, sheet brass stored and Mary Phagan had worked—was also on this level. Yet despite their proximity to these operations, the superintendent's quarters were protected from the dirt and din by an elevator lobby and an anteroom dominated by a massive cast-iron safe and staffed on weekdays by runners and a secretary.

It was in the anteroom that the men—now joined by Detective Starnes and a handcuffed Newt Lee—set up operations. The first order of business was to make sure that Mary Phagan was indeed the girl the superintendent had paid the previous day. This fact, Frank declared, could be easily determined, and after working the safe combination and extracting the factory payroll ledger, he opened the book and ran a finger down a page until he stopped and said: "Yes, Mary Phagan worked here. She was here yesterday to get her pay. I will tell you about the exact time she left. My stenographer left about twelve o'clock, and a few minutes after she left the office boy left and then Mary came in and got her money and left."

Next, someone suggested that Frank should see the spot where the body had been found. Apparently, the factory superintendent chose this moment to again request a cup of coffee, in Black's mind confirmation that he was stalling, but the detectives said there was no time, so the party trooped to the elevator lobby, a shabby room that was the plant's crossroads. On one side of this L-shaped space, the lift stopped. On another, stairs led down to the street level and up to the manufacturing floors. Also, the time clocks that employees had to punch twice daily were here, as was the cashier's window where on Fridays and Saturdays pay envelopes were distributed. And not only money flowed from this chamber. Mounted on a far wall was the fuse box that controlled the building's power. Since electricity was shut off on Sundays, Frank needed to throw the switch inside the box if the group was to take the elevator to the basement.

Frank experienced no trouble performing this task—however, when one of the men asked him why the fuse box wasn't kept locked, he launched into a wordy explanation involving insurance rates and a recent edict from the fire inspector that struck Starnes and Black as overly detailed.

The lift itself was a cantankerous contraption primarily used to transport freight. Once the motor coughed to life, the passengers filed on, and Frank gave a tug at a steel cable that dangled from the top of the car and served as a stop and start button, but the cable wouldn't budge. Later, he'd recall:

> It seemed to be caught, and I couldn't move it . . . it seemed like the chain which runs down in the basement had slipped a cog and gotten out of gear and needed somebody to force it back.

To the detectives, it appeared as if Frank—whose exertions were painful to witness—was too upset to operate the device. As even the sympathetic N. V. Darley would subsequently remember:

> When we started down the elevator, Mr. Frank was nervous, shaking all over. I can't say positively as to whether his whole body was shaking or not, but he was shaking.

Finally, Darley—who was a heavyset sort and, as Frank said, "a great deal stronger"—grabbed the cable, gave it a swift yank, and the men were on their way, dropping into the basement where the car settled firmly and, to everyone's disgust, malodorously, against the ground. Indeed, the instant the lift hit bottom, a fresh, powerful stench wafted up from beneath the men. It was a stench they would never forget. Yet any chance to submit the offending substance to a scientific examination had been squandered hours earlier when a 35-year-old patrolman had failed to collect it as evidence.

Around daybreak, R. M. Lassiter, whose beat included Forsyth Street, had given the plant cellar a complete once-over. The first thing he'd spotted was the trail running from a point just in front of the elevator pit all the way back to the area where the child had been found. Like the responding officers, Lassiter believed that the body—which aside from the head contusions was covered with abrasions on its left arm and leg—had been dragged over the path. Lassiter's other discoveries, however, didn't avail themselves of easy analysis. In the elevator pit itself—which like everything else in the basement was full of waste and debris—he'd turned up a trove of items that simply did not belong together. To wit: the victim's black umbrella, a big ball of red knitting twine and "a fresh mound of human excrement that looked like someone had dumped naturally." Lassiter had removed the first two articles but left the third in its place, and it was this pile that the car carrying Frank and the detectives mashed, unleashing the noxious scent.

Other than acknowledging the fact that someone had stunk up the place, the men who first breathed in the aroma paid no attention to, nor were they curious about, its source, proceeding, instead, directly toward the back of the cellar—in the process further trampling the potentially telltale trail, destroying any opportunity to take footprints later. After examining the spot where the body had been located, Frank accompanied the officers to various other sites where clues had been discovered. Upon seeing how the back door had been jimmied, the superintendent expressed concern that if the opening wasn't secured, someone could break in, so he and Darley zipped upstairs, grabbed hammer and nails, then zipped back. It was at this juncture that Frank removed his jacket and for the benefit of Darley — who in the past had chided him regarding his penchant for brown suits — mentioned the fact that for a change, he was in blue. While intended to break the tension, the line only raised eyebrows and was filed away by Black and Starnes, who wondered why Frank was calling attention to the fact. Yet this reaction was mild compared to that which greeted the superintendent's awkward effort to perform the rudimentary task at hand. Apparently, he could not make the hammer hit the nails, and once again, Darley had to take over.

The door sealed up, the men returned to the second-floor offices, where they found Atlanta's chief of detectives waiting. At 51, Newport A. Lanford was stout and hale with a great graying walrus mustache. He had been with the force for 25 years, and though his florid complexion and too-puffy eyes hinted at base appetites and dubious connections, he was nonetheless a fixture, a harrumphingly reassuring presence.

With Lanford on the scene, anxieties began to ease. During the course of the next twenty minutes, Frank and Darley toured the detective chief around the factory, spending much of that time on the third and fourth floors amidst the German-engineered equipment that transformed rough cedar slats into sleek writing implements. The men also peered into dressing rooms, storage bins and the second-story metal department where Mary Phagan had toiled. They saw nothing out of the ordinary. Their last stop was at the time clocks. Here, Black and Starnes — with Newt Lee in tow — rejoined the party. The night watchman was required as one of his duties to punch in every half hour of his shift, indicating the completion of each round. After obtaining the Negro's time slip from the night just ended, Frank eyeballed it and proclaimed everything in order. Between 6 P.M., when Lee had reported to work, and 3 A.M., he'd hit all his marks. This fact agreed upon, Frank initialed Lee's slip, writing "Removed 8:26" across it. The superintendent then placed the slip in the safe, shut the door and turned the lock.

For now, the detectives were satisfied and only wanted Frank to do them the last favor of examining the murder notes, which had been taken to the station house. So after walking back out to Forsyth Street, the men once again piled into Boots's car — Black, Starnes and Lee riding in back; Darley and Frank up front with Frank perched on his friend's lap — and were soon racing east on Decatur Street toward headquarters. The trip was uneventful save for the fact that to a soul, everyone noticed the superintendent could not stop shivering.

At the station house, the officers quickly ascertained that the murder notes were not available for examination. As a critic of the Atlanta police would later phrase it, they had been "borrowed," apparently by the *Journal*'s Harold Ross, who during his time in town acquired a reputation for being light-fingered around newsworthy documents. That the authorities let the notes—as yet undusted for fingerprints or examined by any experts— out of their hands was, of course, a disaster. Yet in Lanford's office Sunday, no one voiced any concern about the missing evidence, and after a brief and apparently cordial discussion, the detective chief informed the factory superintendent that he was free to go.

From the station house, Frank—joined by Darley—walked back to Bloomfield's, evidently to see the body, but Dr. J. W. Hurt, the county physician, was conducting his postmortem, so the men proceeded on to the Montag Paper Company, which was in the general vicinity, hoping to find Mister Sig. But Montag had not come in. So Frank caught a trolley car for the Washington Street section he and his superior both called home. After stopping at Montag's residence and talking to him briefly, Frank returned to East Georgia Avenue. It was 10:45 A.M. and at last he got his cup of coffee.

Despite the fact that Chief Lanford and his men were discomfited by Leo Frank's twitchy behavior, as of Sunday morning they did not regard the superintendent as a suspect. In fact, the detectives—their ranks now swelled by such local legends as "two-fisted" Pat Campbell, a 46-year-old son of Castle Carn, Donegal County, Ireland—believed that the murder of Mary Phagan was a "Negro crime" and that the Negro who did it was Newt Lee. Buttressing this conviction was an experiment Sergeant L. S. Dobbs had conducted back at the factory. While his colleagues had been busy with Frank, Dobbs had dragooned a black man who worked at a Forsyth Street livery stable, ordered him to lie in the exact spot where the dead girl had been found and then instructed Lee to repeat the steps he'd taken that led to the discovery of the body. Thus the night watchman had again descended the ladder, walked to the toilet, squatted, placed his lantern at his feet and gazed into darkness. To Dobbs, the exercise confirmed what he'd thought from the start: the globe of Newt's light was so smudged that "unless one looked directly at the body it could not have been seen from the toilet." Dobbs believed the night watchman was lying.

All day Sunday, investigators incessantly grilled Lee. Yet even as the detectives worked Newt over, other angles began to develop, one predicated on the notion that while a Negro may have committed the murder, it was at a white man's bidding. The event that inspired the officers to make this leap was the late-morning arrival of Edgar L. Sentell at Chief Lanford's office. A 21-year-old grocery store clerk and longtime acquaintance of Mary Phagan, Sentell had read Britt Craig's story and believed himself to be in possession of a vital clue. Around 12:30 Saturday night, as he'd been walking home from work, he said he'd seen the "tired and angry" victim being shepherded along Forsyth Street by an erstwhile streetcar conductor named Arthur Mullinax. Though the part of town where Sentell claimed to have spotted the girl was dark, illuminated only by the intermittent lights of cheap fruit-and-water stands, the flickering flame of a peanut roaster here and there and the dull glow of the city lamps, he was certain that his eyes hadn't failed him, for he said that when he'd called out, "Hello, Mary," she had replied, "Hello, Edgar."

Sentell's story so impressed the investigators that late Sunday evening an officer picked up the 24-year-old Mullinax at his girlfriend's house and brought him to headquarters. While Mullinax proclaimed his innocence, he was an excellent suspect. For one thing, he not only admitted having known Mary Phagan, he confessed he'd been enamored of her. The two had appeared in the Western Heights Baptist Church's 1912 Christmas production of *Snow White,* Mary playing the title role and Mullinax a blackface part. At the station house, Mullinax told a reporter: "I couldn't keep my eyes off her. She noticed it, and while I was standing near her, she remarked that I looked good with my face blacked. I turned to her and replied that 'I'd keep my face blacked all the time, then.' " Moreover, when Sentell appeared to identify Mullinax, he pointed an accusing finger at him and in the presence of a half-dozen policemen announced: "That's the man who was with the girl last night. There's not a doubt about it." With that, Mullinax, a doe-eyed cracker Casanova, was booked and jailed. The charge — suspicion of murder.

While the detectives believed that in Lee and Mullinax they had two strong suspects, they were also looking into another possibility. Sunday afternoon, one E. S. Skipper appeared at headquarters to say that on Saturday night he'd seen a girl answering the description of Mary Phagan walking on a street near the pencil factory in the company of three young men. What attracted his attention, Skipper said, was that the girl "was reeling slightly, as though affected by drugs or narcotics, and was weeping." Soon, officers were scouring the city for the unidentified youths.

Around three in the afternoon, Leo Frank returned to town to visit Bloomfield's. There, hundreds of mourners — the majority of them strangers who'd read Britt Craig's scoop—had congregated. In fact, the line snaked around the block. Eventually, ten thousand people (nearly double the number who had attended the Metropolitan Opera's final performance) would file by. Many, of course, came to grieve for Mary Phagan, but more came to peer into the open white casket in which the victim reposed, her throat—despite Gheesling's efforts—necklaced by the violet indentation of the noose.

Frank stayed at the funeral home long enough to pay his respects and speak to a few employees—among them Darley and the factory office boy, Alonzo Mann—then proceeded to headquarters. The *Journal* had returned the murder notes, and the detectives wanted Frank to look at them. Apparently, the superintendent could make nothing of them, so he dropped back by the plant, where another crowd had gathered.

Yet for most of the day's dwindling hours, Frank sought refuge in Atlanta's Jewish enclave. First, he and Lucille dropped by the Carl Wolfsheimers' and talked about the murder with a group of friends who'd assembled for a postopera party, among them the couple's Athens, Georgia, in-laws, Julian and Philip Michael; Virginia Silverman; May Lou Liebman; and Julian Loeb. Then it was on to Alexander Marcus's, and from there, to Charlie Ursenbach's, where such familiar faces as Harold Marcus and Ben Wiseberg were present. Come dusk, Frank found himself alone and strolled through the verdant neighborhood. Down Bass, up Washington and over to Georgia he walked, all the while keeping the spires of the Hebrew Orphan's Home in view. Later at home—where the Seligs were hosting a bridge party attended by the Lippmans, the Wolfsheimers and the Strauses—Frank caught up with the morning's newspapers. As cards were shuffled and rubbers dealt, he sat to the side and read. In Europe, Austria was preparing to invade Montenegro, while in New York, medical researchers were working on a tuberculosis serum. Locally, sports fans were overjoyed that after a weeklong holdout, Ty Cobb—the Georgia Peach—had signed a $12,500 contract with the Detroit Tigers. Immersed in such accounts of events great and small, Frank betrayed no hint of disquiet within, no apprehension regarding the storm gathering without.

THREE

Extra, Extra

O f all the images Atlantans could have awakened to that Monday morning, few could have been more ghoulishly titillating than the one of Mary Phagan stripped down the center of the *Atlanta Georgian*'s front page. As McLellan Smith, in 1913 a Hearst reporter, would recall years later: "We sent a photographer to the undertaker's and got a picture of her on the slab." The *Georgian*'s death likeness was not, however, everything it seemed to be. Or, to put it precisely, it was more than it seemed to be. One didn't have to scrutinize the shot too closely to notice the disconcerting fact that its deceased subject was holding her skirts in her left hand as if quite alive and about to curtsy. Then there was the coy caption: "Photograph of Mary Phagan showing her in street dress." The image, in short, was a composite fabricated by cutting the head off the shot of the victim and pasting it atop a shot of another, more animate girl's torso. In any of the dozen or so American metropolises whose citizens were used to the excesses of Hearst journalism, such a production would not have raised the collective pulse rate. Indeed, at the *New York Journal,* Hearst's flamboyant flagship, the doctored morgue mug shot was a speciality of the house. But in Atlanta, where Hearst had only recently set up shop, this sort of thing had never before been seen, and folks couldn't plunk down their two cents fast enough.

Monday's *Georgian* devoted five pages to the murder. For starters, the sheet made a spectacle of the Phagan family's grief. Beneath such headlines as MRS. COLEMAN PROSTRATED BY CHILD'S DEATH, various members of the clan spoke searingly of their loss. Lamented the poor thing's uncle, D. R. Benton of Marietta: "She was just a little playful girl without a bad thought in her mind, and she has been made victim of the blackest crime that can be perpetuated [*sic*]." And her mother added: "The poor baby. If you only could have seen her. She looked so beautiful and so young and so bright! She said she was only going to see the parade before she came home. And now look!" Fannie Coleman then invoked the issue of child labor, making her daughter a martyr to the cause the *Georgian* had been flogging for months. "I'm so sorry for other young girls working everywhere," she was quoted as saying. "To think that they're all open to the same things and there is nothing to protect them." From a woman so distraught that on Sunday morning she'd been sedated, it seemed an improbable utterance, but in the incantatory realm of Hearst journalism, if a dead girl could be depicted holding her skirts, a mourning mother could serve as an editorial mouthpiece.

Exploding amidst these lachrymose accounts were the sharper reports of other Hearst ordnance. NEIGHBORS OF SLAIN GIRL CRY FOR VENGEANCE, boomed one headline. GIRL'S GRANDFATHER VOWS VENGEANCE, boomed another. The desire for retribution conveyed by such headlines was spelled out in the texts they topped. One of the sternest blasts was delivered by a twelve-year-old playmate of the victim: "I'd help lynch the man that killed poor Mary," pledged Vera Epps. "If they'd let me, I'd like to hold the rope that choked him to death." Yet it was the patriarch, William Jackson Phagan (now returned from Alabama), who spoke most vehemently, and the reporter the *Georgian* assigned to tell his story—a 23-year-old would-be Theodore Dreiser named Herbert Asbury—stirringly evoked the scene:

> Standing with bared head in the doorway of his Marietta home, with tears falling unheeded down his furrowed cheeks, W. J. Phagan cried to heaven for vengeance for the murder of his granddaughter, fourteen-year-old [*sic*] Mary Phagan, and vowed that he would not rest until the murderer had been brought to justice.
>
> In a silence unbroken save by the sound of his own sobs and the noise of the gently falling rain, the old man lifted his quavering voice in a passionate plea for the life of the wretch who had lured the little girl into the darkness of a deserted building and strangled her to death. It was an infinite grief—the grief of an old and broken man—that Mr. Phagan expressed when, with hands outspread imploringly, he invoked divine aid in bringing the murderer of the child to justice.
>
> "By the power of the living God," prayed the old man, his voice rising high and clear above the patter of the rain and the roar of a passing train, "I hope the murderer will be dealt with as he dealt with that innocent child. I hope his heart is torn with remorse in the measure that his victim suffered pain and shame; that he suffers as we who loved the child are suffering. No punishment is too great for the brute who foully murdered the sweetest and purest thing on earth—a young girl. Hanging cannot atone for the crime he has committed."

Asbury's account pulsated with heartbreaking details. But in truth, it had been submitted to what was known at the *Georgian* as "a little laboratory work"—the facts had been improved upon. Years later, Asbury would confess his sins. Yes, he did speak to William Jackson Phagan, and yes, the bereaved man did beseech the Lord, but in writing the piece, Asbury felt it lacked Hearstian punch. Which is why he invented the atmospherics. "It wasn't raining," Asbury admitted, "although it might well have been."

One of the most sensational items to appear in Monday's *Georgian*— certainly one whose repercussions would reverberate powerfully during the coming days, influencing the initial direction of the investigation—was a two-column line drawing displayed prominently atop page two. Headlined "Who Is This Man?" the sketch depicted a tall, slender, black-haired 25-year-old wearing a straw boater, blue suit and tan shoes. Based on the description grocery store clerk Edgar L. Sentell had given the police Sunday that resulted in the arrest of Arthur Mullinax, the illustration offered Atlantans a possible suspect, and notwithstanding the fact that Mullinax was behind bars, every slender, black-haired fellow in town now became the object of stares and whispers.

The *Georgian* also offered the populace the incentive to take matters into its own hands. Festooned above Monday's front-page masthead was the banner: "$500 REWARD." This was the sum the Hearst organization said it would pay for "EXCLUSIVE Information Leading to the Arrest and Conviction of the Murderer." At a time when well-compensated Atlantans earned only $200 a month and most took home less (at ten cents an hour, Mary Phagan would have needed a year and a half to earn $500), the mention of such an extravagant figure was intoxicating. In effect, the bounty served to deputize the entire city, and by late Monday, the officers working the case would be spending more time following dubious tips than developing legitimate leads.

Just how many extras the *Georgian* published Monday is disputed— surviving copies confirm at least eight, but estimates go as high as 20. (The *New York Journal* printed 40 extras the day after the sinking of the American battleship *Maine* in the Havana harbor in February 1898.) Regardless, nearly every hour from 8:00 A.M. on, a new edition of the *Georgian* rolled off the presses at 20 East Alabama Street and within minutes was in the hands of newsboys:

NEW STRANGLING ARREST, screamed the Afternoon Edition.

ARRESTED AS GIRL'S SLAYER, echoed the Home Edition.

GANTT ARRESTED AS SLAYER OF GIRL, TELLS STORY TO GEORGIAN, promised the Night Extra, in a line that referred to a new suspect.

By dark, Atlanta was awash in these extras—or pinks, as they were sometimes called because their streamers were printed in scarlet ink that lent everything a sizzling urgency. Not since William Tecumseh Sherman had the city experienced such a bombardment. As Herbert Asbury would later note: "Our paper was in modern parlance, a wow. It burst upon Atlanta like a bomb and upon the *Constitution* and *Journal* like the crack of doom."

For proprietor William Randolph Hearst, Monday's *Georgian* was a combination fiftieth birthday and tenth wedding-anniversary present. That evening, Hearst and his wife celebrated both occasions with a dinner dance—the menus were engraved on a scroll of tin with a photograph of the couple on top—at their 30-room apartment (the largest in Manhattan) in the Clarendon Building at West End Avenue and Eighty-sixth Street. Among the 50 friends in attendance were Elbert H. Gary, the president of U.S. Steel, and Joseph Duveen, the art dealer who was helping Hearst acquire the treasures of Europe that would fill the castle he would soon build in San Simeon, California. Hearst's reaction to the gift his Atlanta editors bestowed upon him on this occasion was undoubtedly favorable, for their handling of the Phagan murder was an homage to the master— himself.

By 1913, America's journalistic wildcat was at the height of his power. His empire stretched from San Francisco (the *Examiner*) and Los Angeles (also the *Examiner*) on the West Coast to Boston (the *American*) and New York (the *Journal*) on the East with vital points (Chicago, Detroit, Baltimore) in between.

At their best, the Hearst newspapers were vigorous trustbusters, newsprint knights errant that jousted with the railroad and steel monopolies and championed the little man. They were also stylishly written, featuring the sort of syndicated stars (Ambrose Bierce, Damon Runyon) that only Hearst could afford. Moreover, the papers pioneered the use of bold headlines and photography. The Chief, as the publisher was known, knew how to get readers' attention.

At their worst, however, the Hearst newspapers encouraged recklessness. "In a strict sense," notes W. A. Swanberg in his tough-minded biography *Citizen Hearst,* they "were not newspapers at all. They were printed entertainment and excitement—bombs exploding, firecrackers popping, victims screaming, flags waving, cannons roaring, houris dancing, and smoke rising from the singed flesh of executed criminals." Deceit, gore, petty vendettas, self-aggrandizing bombast—all were ingredients in the formula. "To be a Hearst reporter," adds the biographer, "required talents unsought by sober journals—a lively imagination, a fictional sense that could touch up news stories with vivid glints, balanced by a subtle understanding of how far one could go without being accused of fakery."

The most infamous example of the Hearst style had, of course, occurred in 1898 when his martial vaporings kindled the Spanish-American War.

Motivated by a desire to score a circulation victory for the *New York Journal* against the rival *New York World,* the Chief had let neither fact nor caution stand in his way. After receiving a cable from Frederic Remington (ultimately remembered for his cowboy sculpture but at the time Hearst's man in Havana) telling him, "Everything is quiet. There is no trouble here. I wish to return," Hearst had imperially rejoined: "Please remain. You furnish the pictures and I'll furnish the war." And he had. After the sinking of the *Maine,* the Chief had ignored any evidence that the disaster might have been an accident, running out saber-rattling banner after saber-rattling banner. Typical was the double-deck headline atop a February 17 edition:

THE WARSHIP *MAINE* WAS SPLIT IN TWO
BY AN ENEMY'S SECRET INFERNAL MACHINE

The *Journal* had pounded home the point until an initially cautious President William McKinley ordered in the troops. In Swanberg's verdict, rendered sixty years after the fact, "Hearst's coverage of the *Maine* disaster still stands as the orgasmic acme of ruthless, truthless newspaper jingoism." The Chief, however, wasn't worried about history's judgment. For him the key point was this: Before hostilities started, the *Journal*'s circulation hovered at 800,000; afterward, it stood at 1,250,000.

Though Hearst was in many ways to the American manor born—scion of a wealthy California family (his silver-mining father made his first fortune in the Comstock lode, his second at Anaconda); San Francisco–bred; Harvard-educated; initiated into journalism not as an ink-stained wretch but as proprietor of the going concern, the *San Francisco Examiner,* that his father gave him—he remained, oddly, an outsider. Most observers of the day contended that he was lonely, but more probably, his remove was the product of immense egocentricity, with its accompanying feeling of superiority. As with many such American originals, Hearst believed the only house where he could feel truly at home stood at 1600 Pennsylvania Avenue, and since 1900—when he'd used his papers to launch a run for the Democratic nomination—he'd been seeking the presidency. In the process, Hearst had proved himself to be a man of mutable loyalties. In 1908, rebuffed by the Democrats, he'd formed a third party (the Independent) and dictated a ticket beholden to himself. In 1912, he'd swung around to the Republicans, pursuing an endorsement from former president Theodore Roosevelt by offering the old Rough Rider the ultimate bully pulpit as columnist for the Hearst papers. Rejected by the GOP, Hearst had of late returned to the Democratic fold, his presidential yearnings unabated— which was why he'd acquired the *Atlanta Georgian.*

Throughout Hearst's decade-long pursuit of the presidency, he'd courted several powerful Georgians he believed could deliver the key to a Democratic nomination—the Solid South. The first object of his blandishments was the firebrand Tom Watson. Not only did Hearst puff Watson's populist effusions in the *New York Journal;* his trusted adjutant, Arthur Brisbane, invited "the Sage" to Manhattan, took him to lunch at Delmonico's and offered him command of Hearst's new morning paper, the *New York American,* at $10,000 a year. The Sage, however, would not leave Dixie, so the Chief's attentions drifted to John Temple Graves, the *Georgian*'s founding editor and a Watson protégé. Graves was only too happy to answer Hearst's call, and for the rest of his career he'd do his bidding, editing the *American,* running for vice president in 1908 on the Independent ticket and, in 1912, acting as his agent during negotiations to buy the *Georgian.*

On February 5, 1912, when William Randolph Hearst's purchase of the *Georgian* was announced, the paper seemed an unlikely vehicle for someone who aspired to the highest office in the land.

The *Georgian* had been launched a mere six years earlier by the real estate developer Fred Seely, yet despite its owner's profession, the sheet was anything but forward-looking. Under Graves's stewardship, the *Georgian*'s editorial columns advocated reactionary populism while its news columns were often used to cast stones at such local powers as Coca-Cola. In a boomtown like Atlanta, these positions ran counter to the prevailing winds. Moreover, the *Georgian* was boring, its front page usually cluttered with bland wire-service accounts from distant lands. The most exciting feature in Hearst's new acquisition was the Saturday "Poultry, Pet and Livestock" tabloid, which carried "Bill Zimmer's Hen Call" column and photographs ("By Our Chicken Expert") of pullet after pulchritudinous pullet. With a circulation of 38,000, the *Georgian* was Atlanta's weakest daily.

The dominant voices in Georgia journalism in 1912 belonged to the morning *Atlanta Constitution,* the mouthpiece of the New South, and the evening *Atlanta Journal,* which, as its masthead proclaimed, Covered Dixie Like the Dew. Though separately owned and of varying circulations (the *Journal,* thanks to its strong rural following, reported an audited circulation of 52,000; the *Constitution,* just 41,405), the papers were in many ways similar. Each boosted Atlanta's metropolitan aspirations. Each devoted countless inches to the doings of the capital's social elite. And each, it went without saying, purveyed the stereotypic view of Negroes.

Yet there were differences, in both style and substance. The *Constitution* was by far the breezier and less formal of the two. It was the brassy voice of Dixie's city of big shoulders—cotton broker for the world, cola maker, player with railroads and the South's freight handler. It took chances, followed hunches. The *Journal,* on the other hand, was more conservative and literary; it still used honorifics—"Mr." Slaton—and in 1912, it unveiled a Sunday magazine. Like Harold Ross, its reporters took obsessive care with the facts.

There were, of course, sharper distinctions between the papers, for this was the age of partisan journalism. The *Constitution,* published and edited by Clark Howell, was with a few reservations the organ of Governor Joseph Brown. The *Journal,* published by James Gray, was with no reservations the organ of its founder, United States Senator Hoke Smith, Brown's rival. As a consequence, the sheets fought continuously, the battles intensifying during Georgia's Democratic primaries. The *Constitution* supported the railroads (Brown was connected with the Western and Atlantic line), while the *Journal* supported reform. (Smith had been a personal injury lawyer before entering politics and had campaigned against the railroads' grip on the South.)

Despite the fractiousness of these disputes, they were, in any final analysis, family feuds. The Clark Howells and James Grays, the Hoke Smiths and Joseph Browns—in fact, all the men who ran Atlanta's newspapers—were, if not brothers in blood, brothers in the same larger faith. They'd attended the University of Georgia, dated girls from Athens's Lucy Cobb Institute—a rigorous finishing school on whose ornately carved verandas many a romance had bloomed—married each other's sisters and cousins and buried each other's fathers. Thus, while they might spar in print and hate for life, the clashes—save for those involving the unfettered Tom Watson—rarely threatened what was, at heart, a rigidly ordered world, one rooted in common lineage and preserved by mutual interests. Sons of the true South, their bonds went deeper than factional politics.

Within a month after purchasing the *Georgian,* William Randolph Hearst had utterly transformed the paper. Overnight, the stale features, stodgy layouts and irrelevant wire-service stories from faraway locales disappeared, replaced by 120-proof Hearst journalism. Every day, the *Georgian*'s redesigned front page played up a jarring local crime story, and if there were no jarring local crimes, the editors would pull together a dozen unrelated items from the police blotter and run them beneath the banner CRIME WAVE SWEEPS CITY. Inside, a host of new columnists—most writing under flashy noms de plume—made their debuts. In her "Chatter of Society" column, Polly Peachtree—a Dixified Cholly Knickerbocker—broadcast bits of gossip while chronicling tea parties. Meantime, in her "Advice to the Lovelorn" department, Beatrice Fairfax—as the syndicated Marie Manning was known—salved the wounds of the heartsick in a warm and winning style. Mixed into this stew were Hearst's famed cartoons (among them, the popular *Barney Google*), alliteratively titled sports departments

("Jolts and Jars in the Squared Circle," "Bunts and Bingles of the Baseball World"), original artwork and so many photographs that the paper sometimes resembled a picture gallery.

Simultaneously, the *Georgian* inaugurated an editorial stance that, while remaining true to the sheet's combative roots, managed to throw a bone to Atlanta's ruling elites. Hearst had been in possession but a week when the paper began assailing the very symbol of patrician hegemony—the Georgia Railway and Electric Company. Beneath the page-one screamer "This Is Why Atlanta's Electricity Must Be Cheaper," the paper charged the utility with gouging consumers. Yet in the same edition that kicked off the campaign, the editorial page boomed: "Be An Optimist and Hitch Your Wagon to the Star of Atlanta's Destiny." Beneath this caption, Atlantans were urged to boost more loudly, to cheer "new skyscrapers and roads" and "the real estate and population boom."

The hand orchestrating the *Georgian*'s journalistic balancing act belonged to Keats Speed, erstwhile managing editor of the *New York Journal* and, equally important, a native of Kentucky. Speed, in Asbury's estimation, "was familiar with the South and Georgia; he knew exactly what the people would accept." To enable the editor to do the job, Hearst had imported what even fifty years later one old-time Georgia newsman termed "the finest staff of any paper in the country." City editor Mike Clofine was a *New York Journal* alum. Police reporter William Flythe, a native Georgian, would be in Atlanta just two years, then move on to cover the Mexican revolution. Photographers Johnny Brown and Matty Mathewson were on loan from the *Chicago American*. A few holdovers from the old *Georgian* remained, among them the insightful political editor James B. Nevin and a silver-tongued feature writer from Marietta named O. B. Keeler. But by and large, everyone involved was a hired gun.

One of the most talented of these hired guns was that journalistic rainmaker Herbert Asbury. During the 1920s, Asbury would write such roguish books as *The Gangs of New York,* while contributing frequently to the nation's leading magazines.

"Hearst Comes to Atlanta," Asbury's 1926 account for the *American Mercury* of the *Georgian*'s coverage of Mary Phagan's murder and all that followed offers the only insider's view of how Hearst journalism transformed a hideous crime into a conflagration. Equal parts reportage and indictment ("Had not Hearst owned the *Georgian,*" asserts Asbury, "the story probably would have died a natural death"), the piece is unsparing in its assessments, including those of its author. But it is most unsparing in its judgment of a newly arrived editor.

Several weeks before the Phagan murder, the Chief, believing that Keats Speed had put the *Georgian* on sound Hearstian footing, recalled the editor to New York. The evidence—most especially, a 22,000 circulation gain—boded well. Furthermore, Hearst had used his acquisition to form a friendship with a rising political star he could envision aiding his presidential ambitions in the South: Governor-elect John Slaton. (Just days before the Phagan killing, in fact, Hearst had feted the Slatons at his New York apartment.) The situation seemed in hand, and the Chief turned the reins over to Foster Coates.

By 1913, the 53-year-old Coates—known behind his back as "Curser" and regarded as one of the most profane men in a business of profane men—had become Hearst's roving surrogate. One month he was in Los Angeles, the next San Francisco, the next New York. Yet despite having graduated to management, Coates remained, at heart, the greatest page-one editor of his day, the virtual headline wizard who as managing editor of Joseph Pulitzer's *World* in 1898 had gone one-on-one with the Chief during the circulation war that sparked the shooting war in Havana. (It was a Coates screamer that became the conflict's rallying cry: REMEMBER THE *MAINE*.) Whatever gains the *Journal* made following the sinking of the American battleship, the *World* matched (Pulitzer sold five million papers the week the battleship exploded), and Coates deserved much of the credit. Or, in Pulitzer's view, the blame. Pulitzer valued the circulation victories Coates was winning but was offended by the editor's methods, and once the Spanish-American War ended, he ordered his pressmen to melt the cases of three-inch lead type with which Coates had worked his magic. For the editor, it was a harsh rebuke, one that William Randolph Hearst, who'd recognized a kindred spirit when he read him, used to his advantage. For the Chief, men like Coates were invaluable, and he wooed and ultimately won him by appealing to both his vanity and his checkbook. Within days of going to work for the *Journal,* Coates was tooling around Manhattan in a sporty new $1,700 automobile.

Curser Coates enjoyed the perks of power, and upon arriving in Atlanta, he settled in at the luxurious Georgian Terrace Hotel on Peachtree Street and Ponce de Leon Avenue in one of the capital's plushest enclaves. It was there, on Sunday morning, April 27, that he read Britt Craig's scoop in the *Constitution*'s extra and, in Asbury's words, "saw the possibilities immediately." By noon, as the staffs of the *Journal* and *Constitution,* again quoting Asbury, "slumbered peacefully in church or otherwise wasted the Sabbath," every last *Georgian* reporter was hard at work in the newspaper's Alabama Street newsroom.

For Coates, it was 1898 all over again. Suddenly, he was back at the helm of a great newspaper atop a breaking story. Telephones ringing, typewriters clattering, adrenaline surging—this was what newsmen lived for. This was also—for someone who had literally just stepped off the train—an environment conducive to rashness and foolhardiness. Even as he was caught up in Coates's machinations, Herbert Asbury was alarmed. Where Speed had realized from the start that "the *Georgian* couldn't do many of the things that the *Journal* did," Asbury would later write, Coates, "knowing little if anything of the South or the Southern temperament, thought the *Georgian* could do these things and more." And what made it all so explosive was that the journalistic shock troops at Coates's command had been sitting around for months bored out of their minds by life in what to Hearst may have been a critical stop on his way to Washington but to them was a provincial outpost. "We played the case harder," Asbury would declare, "than any Hearst paper had ever played such a case anywhere."

By the time the *Georgian* hit the streets Monday, it was too late for the *Constitution* to recover. Only 24 hours earlier, the morning paper had owned the Phagan story, but now it belonged to Hearst. Even the *Georgian*'s straight news pieces were better—not that this was so surprising. To practice the sort of journalistic cubism preferred by Hearst, a newspaperman first had to master the just-the-facts approach. To distort, one had to report, and this the *Georgian*'s hardened veterans did. All of which left the *Constitution* in a bad position. While the sheet scored a couple of coups— among them a family snapshot of little Mary strolling beneath her umbrella and an X-marks-the-spot photo of the corner of the factory basement where the body had been discovered—it otherwise paled in comparison, devoting just a column and a half to the murder on its front page and only three columns inside.

In its first Monday edition, the *Journal* published less on the crime than the *Constitution,* but by late afternoon, it had rallied. The *Journal*'s editors topped the front page of their final edition with a four-column picture of Mary Phagan—bows in her hair, eyes sparkling—that presented the girl as the embodiment of Southern womanhood. Additionally, they ran a shot of the pencil factory building with cutouts showing where the body had been found and an inset offering an enlarged view of the sliding back door. They also ran a photograph of one of the murder notes that Harold Ross had "borrowed" Sunday morning.

Yet for all of that, the *Journal*'s performance faded when compared to any edition of the *Georgian*. The afternoon paper simply didn't have the goods. "They couldn't verify half the *Georgian*'s stories sufficiently to rewrite them for subsequent editions," noted Asbury. Not that the *Journal* didn't try to rewrite the *Georgian*. Beneath the headline "GOD'S VENGEANCE WILL STRIKE BRUTE WHO KILLED HER," SAYS GRANDFATHER

OF MARY PHAGAN, the paper published a toned-down version of Asbury's article about William Jackson Phagan. But it wasn't the same. Gone was the roaring train. Gone were the tears running down the old man's face. And gone was the rain. What was left—like most of what ran in the *Journal*—was factual, but for now the facts weren't selling. On this April Monday, Atlanta had surrendered to William Randolph Hearst.

FOUR

Onward, Christian Soldiers

etween 6:30 and 7:00 on Monday morning, just as the *Georgian*'s first extra was rolling off the presses, an 18-year-old National Pencil Company machinist named R. P. Barrett noticed a suspicious red spot on the factory's metal department floor near a women's dressing room some twenty feet from Mary Phagan's workstation. Fan-shaped, four or five inches in diameter and haloed by a few smaller crimson spatterings, the spot appeared to be blood. Additionally, it seemed as if someone had tried to hide it. "It looked like some white substance had been wiped over it," Barrett would later testify. "It looked like it had been smeared with a coarse broom." Whether this substance was potash or a soapy lubricant called Haskoline—both of which were stored nearby—Barrett couldn't determine, but after a janitor told him that neither the spot nor the white grease had been there Friday afternoon, he summoned Lemmie Quinn, a foreman, who in turn notified the police.

With that, Barrett prepared to start his day. At quitting time Friday, he had left a piece of unfinished work in a bench lathe that faced the metal department wall about ten feet past the dead girl's machine. Powered by pulleys that descended from the ceiling, the lathe was controlled by an L-shaped steel handle that extended at a right angle from its front edge. When Barrett turned the handle, he observed something more startling than the red spot—six or eight strands of auburn hair that he would swear weren't "there on Friday, for I had used that machine up to 5:30." Once again, he alerted Quinn.

By now, the plant had begun to fill with workers, and many flocked to the scene of Barrett's discoveries. Soon, Detective John Starnes and several officers appeared, trailed by a gaggle of reporters. As the crowd looked on, 14-year-old Magnolia Kennedy, a metal department employee, tiptoed to the lathe, stared intently and exclaimed: "It's Mary's hair. I know it."

Hard upon the Kennedy girl's pronouncement came another dramatic verdict, this one from a more authoritative figure—Police Chief James Litchfield Beavers. Testifying to the thrall in which the crime held Atlanta, the chief had come to the factory to assure himself—and the city—that the investigation was progressing. After an officer chipped up several pieces of the red-stained floor, Beavers pulled a bottle of alcohol from his pocket and submitted one of the specimens to a rudimentary test. When the discoloration did not dissolve as it would have had it been oil or paint, when it in fact turned scarlet, he announced that it was blood.

Thus the idea that Mary Phagan had been attacked on the factory's second floor took hold at the outset. The *Georgian* gave the theory its unqualified blessing, reporting that "blood stains leading from the lathe showed the manner in which the fiend had dragged the body of his victim to the basement." So, too, did the more sober *Journal,* which proclaimed that "investigations [this] morning proved that Mary Phagan was murdered in the metal room and that her body was lowered in the elevator to the basement."

At the very hour the police and the press were determining that Mary Phagan had been slain in the general vicinity of Leo Frank's office, another group of detectives was pursuing the man who at this juncture appeared to be the best suspect—a recently discharged pencil company bookkeeper named James Milton Gantt.

The detectives' suspicions regarding Gantt—a Marietta native who'd been reared in the same Sardis section where little Mary had spent her early childhood—had been whetted by a report that the 26-year-old bookkeeper was enamored of the girl. Among the sources for this information were several of the factory's female laborers, day watchman E. F. Holloway and evidently Leo Frank. More crucial, however, was the news that Gantt had appeared at the plant Saturday at six P.M. just as Newt Lee and Frank were locking up. After advising the superintendent—who'd fired him when the factory cash box had tallied $2 short a few weeks earlier—that he'd left two pairs of shoes upstairs, Gantt had been granted admittance to the building, where he'd remained some twenty minutes, phoning an unidentified woman before emerging with his size elevens. Detectives had actually begun looking for Gantt on Sunday, but it wasn't until Monday morning, when he was spotted leaving a bar across the street from the plant, that they caught a break. While Gantt managed to board a Marietta-bound trolley before officers closed in, they alerted the Cobb County sheriff, and around noon Deputy J. B. Hicks arrested him.

Gantt—who when apprehended was reportedly carrying a suitcase packed for a long trip—was rushed back to Atlanta, where he informed detectives that though he had dropped by the factory Saturday evening, he was home in bed by ten P.M. and hadn't seen Mary Phagan in weeks. Yet according to Gantt's sister, with whom he roomed and to whom the officers had already spoken, the bookkeeper hadn't been home in nearly a month.

Mrs. F. C. Terrell told the police that she'd actually been worried about her brother because she'd not received a single letter from him during the period. Gantt's alibi seemingly destroyed, the investigators began to weave circumstances into theory, the theory being that the bookkeeper had murdered the girl sometime during the day Saturday, then used his six P.M. visit to the plant to recruit Newt Lee to hide her body. Late Monday afternoon, according to the *Constitution,* "a squad of detectives and criminal experts pulled off their coats, rolled their sleeves, and prepared for a determined siege, which they vowed would not end until they had been convinced that Gant [*sic*] was either guilty or innocent."

It was while R. P. Barrett was making his discoveries and the officers were searching for James Gantt that Detective John Black, accompanied by a young investigator named B. B. Haslett, reappeared at Leo Frank's home to escort the factory superintendent back downtown. Though this second encounter between Black and Frank was less tense than the first—the detectives waited patiently while Frank ate breakfast—Black was no more forthcoming regarding the purpose of the visit. In fact, as the men walked into the city, strolling east on Georgia Avenue, north on Capitol, then east on Decatur toward police headquarters at 175 Decatur, Black was as taciturn as ever. In response to Frank's persistent queries, Haslett finally replied: "Well, Newt Lee has been saying something."

What Newt Lee—during the course of several Sunday-night and early-Monday-morning sweatings—had been saying was that when he'd arrived at work on Saturday at four P.M. just as Frank had instructed on Friday, the superintendent had anxiously ordered him away. "He was rubbing his hands," Lee would later tell the coroner's inquest. "He told me to go back out in town and not to get back later than six o'clock." Newt said he'd answered that he would rather curl up in the building and take a nap but Frank had objected, hustling him off with the words: "Go out and have a good time." Just before six, Newt had returned, followed closely by Gantt, whose appearance had further upset Frank. According to Lee, the superintendent had been reluctant to let the dismissed bookkeeper inside, informing him that his shoes had been swept out by the janitor—a contention that was quickly disproved. At seven, Lee said, Frank had phoned him from home to ask if things were all right. It was, he added, the first time his boss had ever called him.

Not that Haslett was going to tell Frank any of this. "Chief Lanford will tell you when you get down there," he responded when the factory superintendent continued to press him, and the group marched on in silence.

Once the men reached the station house, they headed to the third-floor offices of Newport Lanford, but the detective chief had gone out. So for the next hour, Frank waited in an anteroom, talking with various officers. About 9:30, Herbert Haas, of counsel to the pencil company, and Sig Montag appeared. And at 10:00, Luther Rosser, the lawyer to Atlanta's corporate elite and the new partner of governor-elect John Slaton, arrived. Rosser's presence was interpreted by many as an indication that Mister Sig believed Frank to be in serious straits, but there was also another explanation. Haas's wife was expecting, and he'd evidently asked his colleague, who occasionally handled some of the pencil company's affairs, to back him up in case he needed to make a sudden departure.

"Hello boys, what's the trouble?" Rosser inquired by way of greeting, whereupon Haas began explaining. During this huddle, Lanford returned, beckoned Frank into his office and shut the door.

Though the detective chief and the superintendent were alone for just a few seconds, it was time enough for Rosser to take umbrage.

Standing at six feet and weighing 220 pounds with a massive, balding snapping turtle of a head, 53-year-old Luther Rosser was the embodiment of Atlanta's fierce moneyed might. An old hand at the game of badgering and buffeting who discarded all rules laid down by polite society and was thus of great utility to polite society, Rosser was uncowed, unbowed and unrepentant. Even in matters of dress, he was obstinate, usually appearing before the bar—and everywhere else, for that matter—sans cravat. Friends viewed his refusal to wear a tie as a harmless idiosyncracy. In a story still told years later, his grandson delighted in recalling that Rosser wouldn't make an exception when arguing a case before the United States Supreme Court. ("If it's clothes they want," he reportedly roared at a fellow lawyer prior to a joint appearance before the high tribunal, "you give it to them. If it's law they want, I'll give it to them.") Yet Rosser's disdain for neckwear was no mere quirk. It was, instead, a defining gesture, the adamant signature of an adamant soul.

In brief, no detective chief was going to shut a door in Rosser's face, and following Frank's disappearance, he flew into a rage, bellowing to a guard: "I am going into that room. That man is my client." Soon thereafter, Lanford admitted the lawyer, but he would not forget the outburst. In fact, he would always wonder why Rosser had thrown a fit on behalf of someone who at this point had not been charged with anything.

The sequence in which events unfolded in Lanford's office was never made clear, but early on, Frank handed Lanford Newt Lee's time slip—the card the superintendent had initialed Sunday morning after a glance indicated the night watchman had clocked in at all the appropriate intervals. Then, Frank made a stunning announcement: After studying the slip more carefully, he said, he'd realized that his first assessment had been wrong.

Lee had actually missed three punches, meaning that on three occasions between 6 P.M. Saturday and 3 A.M. Sunday, the night watchman's where-abouts could not be accounted for.

On the heels of this astonishing about-face, the chief, believing any sub-sequent revelations should be part of the sworn record, asked Frank if he would make a statement, to which Rosser assented. Accordingly, the super-intendent sat down at a table across from the detective department's secre-tary, a mustachioed notary public named C. Gay February.

Frank's deposition took the form of a straightforward chronology of his version of the events of Saturday, April 26. He reiterated that he'd been alone in his office when Mary Phagan "came in between 12:05 and 12:10, maybe 12:07, to get her pay envelope," adding: "I paid her and she went out of the office. It was impossible to see the direction she went in when she left. My impression was that she just walked away. I didn't pay any particular attention." At 1:10, he said he'd decided to go to lunch, but since he in-tended to bolt the Forsyth Street door (making ingress to or egress from the factory impossible), he had to alert two laborers—Arthur White and Harry Denham—who were on the fourth floor servicing some equipment. White's wife, who'd dropped by to visit, was with the men. As a consequence, he said he'd dashed upstairs. After White and Denham told him they weren't done, he'd agreed to let them remain in the locked-up plant. Immediately there-after, Mrs. White exited, and he followed. At 3:00, he said, he'd returned to find White and Denham almost finished. At 3:15, the workers clocked out, although he recalled that White had ducked into the office and asked for a $2 loan. He said he'd responded: "What's the matter; we just paid off." When the worker replied that his wife had "robbed him," he said he'd given him the money.

Now came the part Frank's auditors were awaiting, the part about which Lee had been talking:

> On Friday night I told [Newt] after I give him the keys, "You had better come around early tomorrow because I may go to the ball game" [the Atlanta Crackers were playing the Nashville Vols at 4 P.M. at Ponce de Leon Park], and he come early because of that fact. I told him to come early, and he came 20 minutes to 4. I figured I could leave about 1 o'clock and would not come back, but it was so cold I didn't want to risk catching cold [at the game] and I come back to the factory as I usually do. He come in and I said, "Newt, you are early," and he said, "Yes, sir," . . . I told him he could go out; he got there so early and I was going to be there.

From here, Frank shifted seamlessly to the other critical topic, the 6 P.M. encounter with the discharged bookkeeper:

When I went out, talking to Newt Lee was J. M. Gantt, a man I had fired about two weeks previous. Newt told me he wanted to go up to get a pair of shoes he left while he was working there, and Gantt said to me, "Newt don't want me to go up," and he said, "You can go with me, Mr. Frank," and I said, "That's all right, go with him Newt," and I went on home, and I got home about 6:25. Nothing else happened; that's all I know . . . I tried to telephone [Newt] when I got home [but] I didn't get an answer . . . at 7 o'clock . . . I called him and asked him if Gantt got his shoes and he said yes, he got them, and I said is everything all right and he said yes, and the next thing I knew they called me at 7:30 the next morning.

To the police officers, Frank's recounting seemed at once mystifyingly detailed and frustratingly vague. They pressed him to clarify certain facts. "Why, it's preposterous," interceded Luther Rosser. "A man who would have done such a deed must be full of scratches and marks and his clothing must be bloody." Whereupon the superintendent stood and stripped. As Frank would later describe it:

I . . . showed them my underclothing and my top shirt and my body, I bared it to them all that came within the range of their vision. I had everything open to them, and all they had to do was to look and see it.

Frank's torso was, indeed, unblemished. But his lawyers didn't believe the display convinced the lawmen. Hoping to vanquish all doubts, Herbert Haas urged Frank to take John Black and B. B. Haslett to his home and let them examine the laundry. So around noon, the group returned to Georgia Avenue. At the house, the men trooped upstairs to Leo and Lucille's bedroom. There, Frank dumped the contents of his laundry bag onto the bed, then stood aside as the detectives pawed "every article of clothing that I had discarded that past week." Finding no bloodstains, Black and Haslett departed and Frank, feeling that they were satisfied, joined Lucille and her parents in the parlor. Soon the Negro cook, Minola McKnight, served dinner, and life resumed its familiar rhythms.

Though calm may have returned to 68 East Georgia Avenue Monday afternoon, at the Decatur Street headquarters of the Atlanta police, pandemonium reigned, and it had little to do with hair and blood samples, fired bookkeepers or Leo M. Frank. Now that the news of Mary Phagan's death had been widely broadcast, now that the scent of reward money was in the air, everyone, it seemed, was advancing a solution to the crime. As the *Georgian*—failing to acknowledge its role in fomenting the chaos—described the situation: "All day was a ceaseless procession going into the detectives' offices and another coming out. The officers were harrassed as much as they were aided."

Most of the tipsters arrived bearing variations of two related and much publicized theories—the tall, thin man scenario advanced by Edgar Sentell and the reeling, drug-addled girl scenario advanced by E. S. Skipper. Charlie Hall, director of the city sanitation department's motor division, said he'd seen a girl being dragged along Forsyth Street on Saturday night by a tall, thin man. R. B. Pyron, a telegraph operator, said he'd seen a sobbing girl in a touring car stopped at a downtown railroad crossing at roughly the same hour. John R. Phillips, the manager of a Forsyth Street hotel, said a man who resembled James Gantt had tried to register at his establishment that evening in the company of an underage girl. Most dramatic, an unidentified man said he'd observed a woman and two men mistreat a crying girl near the pencil plant late Saturday. The woman had reportedly told the girl: "Come along dearie, don't create a scene. You'll attract the cops." To which the girl had reportedly replied: "I don't care. I don't care."

Even at the time, many of these leads must have been recognizable as manifestations of either communal shell shock or Hearst-induced avarice, yet none of them could be discounted and some were compelling. The hotel manager who said he had turned away the couple on Saturday evening had come forward only after checking at Bloomfield's mortuary to assure himself that the body lying in state belonged to the young lady who'd called at his concern.

As report after report flowed into the station house, detectives began seriously entertaining the notion that Mary Phagan, after receiving her pay Saturday afternoon, had been accosted on Atlanta's streets, if not by an acquaintance such as Mullinax or Gantt, then by some as yet unidentified man who'd used drugs to seduce her or by so-called white slavers who lured girls into prostitution. As the *Journal* reported: "Police are making two random investigations: One is that Mary Phagan was the victim of a white slave plot. The other is that she was taken for an automobile ride before her murder and was drugged or made drunk."

How officers hoped to reconcile either of these possibilities with the clues they'd thus far accumulated is uncertain. At this point, the case lay before them in dozens of pieces, none of which fit together. If, as the police suspected, Mary Phagan had been waylaid on the streets of Atlanta, why had her assailant brought her back to the pencil factory's second floor to kill her? If, as Mullinax's girlfriend was now maintaining, young Arthur had spent Saturday night with her, why was Edgar Sentell so certain he'd seen the ex-streetcar conductor squiring little Mary along Forsyth Street that evening? The reverse of this question could be asked about Gantt. If, as the bookkeeper swore, he was home in bed at the time, why would his sister contend she hadn't seen him in a month? As for Newt Lee, the *Journal* flatly declared: "The police place no belief in his protestations of innocence." Then there was Leo Frank, whose behavior on Sunday morning had seemed overly agitated, whose change of heart regarding Lee's time slip provoked skepticism and whose account of his Saturday activities also inspired doubts. And as for the murder notes, all anyone could say about them was summed up in a *Georgian* headline: "Strange Notes Increase Mystery." No wonder that come Tuesday, the *Constitution* would report: "All day Monday, detectives worked diligently for evidence which would throw light upon the killing, and when night came they were baffled."

The headquarters of the Atlanta Police Department dominated a section of Decatur Street lined by pawnshops whose Russian Jewish proprietors lived upstairs or in the rear, wagon yards crowded with mule carts and swarming with raw-boned old boys just in from the hills, Chinese laundries, tintype studios, Irish near-beer saloons, Greek pastry shops, Italian delicatessens boasting such delectable fare that they were frequented each season by the Met's visiting stars and—most ubiquitously—fish markets and grills that catered solely to Negroes and lent the byway its piscatory cognomen: Mullet Avenue. In 1913, this thoroughfare, if not as legendary as Peachtree Street, was much more vibrant, the throbbing aorta that pulsed the blood of every race, class and creed into the burgeoning capital of the New South. As a writer for the *Journal* magazine described it:

> Decatur Street is a kaleidoscope of light, noise and bustle from dawn to dawn. No hour is too early for the fish and "hot dogs" to be sold, or for a dusky thief to pawn a watch or dispose of a little "blind tiger" [illegal whisky]; no time too late for a black mammy to buy a red cotton dress or a Jew to auction off ten pairs of number twelve shoes . . . Here, bearded mountaineers . . . brush shoulders with laborers fresh from the Old Country . . . The Yankee spieler cries his wares and the Confederate veteran buys 'em, and through it all negroes, yellow, black and brown thread their laughing, shiftless way, types of the south which could be seen in no other city in the land in all their native picturesqueness. Decatur Street is the melting pot of Dixie.

The station house building, an immense Victorian-Gothic affair erected in 1893, consisted of two three-story redbrick wings radiating from a seven-story central tower that emerged from an arched marble portal and bulked upward toward an observation deck surrounded by columns and guarded by gargoyles. For a department that was at once righteous yet rascally, moralizing yet draconian, there could have been no more fitting home.

Just as Atlanta's other municipal services—especially those regulating public health and sanitation—were unprepared for the many problems bred by the city's emergence as a metropolis, so, too, was its police department. With few exceptions, the squad's 313 members were country boys who had received no formal training. (Until 1931, recruits were issued a badge, revolver, blackjack and Sam Brown belt and, after a week of instruction, became full-fledged policemen.) Similarly, the force was ill-equipped and essentially unmotorized. Chief Beavers was chauffeured around in a limousine and a motorcycle division had been formed, but by day officers patrolled on horseback, by night on bicycle. The force did employ a Bertillon technician (an expert in the archaic system that used skull and hand measurements for identification purposes), but it had yet to invest in a fingerprint lab. Perhaps most tellingly, the department maintained no precincts in outlying districts, relying instead on a network of "lockboxes" for warehousing prisoners who couldn't be readily transported downtown. These hexagonal cast-iron booths—freezing in winter, sweltering in summer—were located in all parts of the city and called to mind nothing so much as the pillories of Salem Common.

Exacerbating the force's operational shortcomings was a departmentwide predisposition to brutality. Much of the violence was directed at Negroes. (In 1915, the force arrested 11,787 blacks as opposed to just 5,486 whites). Since 1909, the police had beaten at least one Negro to death, and since 1911, they had failed to solve the murders of seventeen Negro women. (Since 1900, it must be added, three officers had been killed in the line of duty by black toughs.)

Had the Atlanta Police Department been merely befuddled by change, its men merely inclined to pistol-whip the random Negro wrongdoer, it would be misleading to dwell on these failings, for in 1913, most other big-city law enforcement agencies were just as mired in the past, just as mean and, in the South, just as hostile to blacks. Yet the force was also plagued by another demon: institutional corruption.

One particular incident had exposed Detective Chief Newport A. Lanford and his officers to damning scrutiny and would cast an instructional light on the techniques they brought to bear in the Phagan case. On a November night in 1910, Detective Robert A. Wood, believing himself to be unobserved, attacked one Ivan Wimbush east of headquarters. After knocking Wimbush, who was white and had done nothing illegal but was regarded around the station house as a disreputable character, to the ground, Wood clubbed him across the face, drew his pistol and crouched as if preparing to fire. How far the detective intended to go is unknown, although Wimbush later swore that Wood would have killed him had not two bystanders interceded. While the detective termed these Samaritans "rounders," they were in actuality reporters, one from the *Journal,* the other from the *Constitution,* and as it turned out they'd seen everything and were still watching during the booking procedure at headquarters when Wood again hit Wimbush, this time under the unblinking gaze of a captain and two patrolmen.

For all its ugliness, the Wimbush beating probably would not have created a stir had it not been for what happened afterward. At first, only Wood and several others were involved in the cover-up, falsifying an attempted murder charge against their prisoner, then seeking a high bail in order to keep him out of sight. But the judge who conducted the preliminary hearing, having received reports of what had transpired, dismissed the allegations, reprimanded Wood and demanded an investigation. At which point, as the *Georgian* phrased it, "the [full] machinery of the police department" was put to work. With Newport Lanford's knowledge, C. Gay February, the secretary who would take Leo Frank's statement, concocted an affidavit asserting that the *Journal* and *Constitution* reporters were not present during the attack. Numerous officers signed the document. Meanwhile, a statement attesting to Wimbush's bad character was also prepared and forwarded to a prostitute for her signature.

Not surprisingly, Atlanta's newspapers soon exposed the goings-on, and after a week of headlines, the city's police commission convened a hearing. At this session, the men who'd signed the false affidavits confessed, the captain and patrolmen who'd stood by while Wimbush was beaten were disciplined and Wood was suspended. Chief Lanford avoided punishment, although a year later, editorial writers were still demanding his head. In response, the detective chief—with a bravura suggesting he'd lined up assurances from on high—called for an investigation, and the police commission appointed what would be dubbed the "whitewash committee." In August 1911, Lanford was exonerated. Lamented the *Constitution:* "The investigating committee was made up of members who are evidently ready to give the detective department a clean bill of health, without even a perfunctory inquiry."

In the wake of the Wimbush incident, it's small wonder that Atlantans could often be heard to say that the police "could frame up anything on you." Yet the force's savage predilections—evident as they would become in the Phagan investigation—were, in truth, on the wane, retreating under the onslaughts of a new puritanical regime that sought to rid the city of vice and make it a paragon of municipal virtue. The department's moralizing angels, in short, were ascendant, and they would exert as powerful an influence on the Phagan probe as their darker twin.

To understand how the Atlanta police force became a regiment of Christian soldiers and how Chief James L. Beavers—a dapper man who shaded his fine nose and neatly clipped mustache beneath the brim of a smart blue kepi—became a fierce and terrible archangel, one must first understand that since Reconstruction, Atlanta had boasted the most raffish houses of prostitution south of New York or east of New Orleans and that they'd operated with the consent of the police and to the financial benefit of top city officials.

At least fifty in number, the majority of these brothels were located in a neighborhood known as the "restricted district" on Mechanic Street west of the ornate towers of Atlanta's principal port of entry—Terminal Train Station. This section's overlord was a dashing rogue named Charles C. Jones. Typically identified in the papers as a "sporting man," Jones navigated easily among Atlanta's elite. He owned the Rex, an elegant establishment snug against Peachtree Street's Candler Building. There, amid the crack of pool balls, the city's tippling businessmen discussed politics and deals. In a sense, the Rex was Jones's cover, not that he made any secret of his other line of merchandise. Everybody knew, and while not everybody approved, anyone who protested would risk insulting Jones's benefactor—Atlanta mayor Jimmy Woodward.

Jones and Woodward were, at first blush, unlikely allies. While the suave Jones was a friend of the mighty, Woodward was a devoted union man, an ex-printer who had risen through ward politics to the mayor's office in 1898. In subsequent years, he'd been reelected, defeated and in 1912 reelected again. Woodward, however, had a weakness: he was a falling-down drunk. Since 1900, reports of Woodward's jags, which tended to occur in public and feature bawdy ladies, had become a staple in Atlanta's newspapers, and while the voters had been tolerant, the mayor had tried their souls. As a columnist for a North Georgia weekly observed after one of Woodward's benders prompted hearings: "It seems that Atlanta's mayor—Mr. Woodward—has been having a high old time in that city, judging from the testimony given against him during the investigation, getting drunk and making calls on lewd women. Very nice rooster for a mayor."

The restricted district did not depend solely on the mayor's largesse. Some police officers received payoffs to look the other way. More important, numerous disinterested Atlanta judges, doctors and editors believed the district performed a vital function. As the *Georgian* observed: "There are many who say that [if] women are driven from a 'regulated' and supervised restricted district [they] will drift into residence districts and good citizens will be living next door to disreputable resorts and in the same apartment houses with objectionable characters without knowing it until the disorder becomes flagrant." In short, the district was a necessary evil, a bulwark against those goatish demons that if not exorcised by fallen women would spend themselves beneath respectable roofs.

There was, of course, dissenting opinion, most of it originating along moral lines but some of it arising from a growing awareness that the women who worked in the district came primarily from poor families and that their subjugation by the likes of Charles C. Jones was the final indignity in a process that began when they were dislocated from the good earth and forced to toil in factories. In the Men and Religion Forward Committee, this position had found its champion. The group, which included not only Bible-thumping jackdaws but high-church divines and wealthy capitalists (principally John J. Eagan, owner of the American Cast Iron and Pipe Company of Birmingham, and Marion Jackson, an Atlanta lawyer), had been looking for a way, in one member's words, "to join with others in bringing the power of the gospel to bear upon the active personal and social troubles of [the] community." In February 1912, Jackson and Eagan had attended a convention of like-minded souls in New York. There, the men had heard the fiery activist Jane Addams—author, mistress of Chicago's Hull House and the most influential social worker of the day—address the evils of prostitution and the economic causes underlying it. Suddenly, the path became clear.

On June 15, 1912, Atlanta's Men and Religion Forward Committee inaugurated its campaign against "The Houses in Our Midst." The campaign took the form of prominent weekly ads in all of the city's newspapers. The ads challenged citizens to shut down the restricted district, pointing out the links between the vice lords and the politicians ("Woodwardism," the pox was termed) and citing figures showing that prostitution spread venereal disease to wives and unborn children.

By mid-September, the campaign against "The Houses In Our Midst," while prompting the formation of a special vice committee, had produced no results. The restricted district was so insulated that when the vice committee—a member of which was said to own one of the brothels—issued its report, it didn't acknowledge that the district even existed. Yet far from being discouraged, the Men and Religion Forward Committee stepped up its attacks. Soon, a drawing of a gorilla wearing a visored police cap labeled "Protected Vice," wielding a billy club labeled "Public Indifference," and clutching a naked young girl against his hairy thigh began topping the ads. The illustration—captioned "The White Slave"—was, considering its purpose, oddly alluring. The swell of the child's bosom and the curvature of her bottom could just as easily have spoken to the satyr as to the prig. But the message was plain enough not to be lost on its intended audience: Chief James Litchfield Beavers.

The Men and Religion Forward Committee knew its man. At 47, the slightly built Beavers was equal parts bluenose and warrior. Known to friends as "Litch," he had been raised a pious Presbyterian in Clayton County a few miles south of Atlanta. A 23-year department veteran, he'd worked his way up from patrolman to sergeant to captain. Only Woodwardism had slowed his steady climb. Referring broadly to the setback, the *Georgian* noted: "When the Woodward administration went into office, heads were lopped off freely. Sergeant Beavers went back in the ranks." Beavers's rise, however, had merely been delayed, and during one of Woodward's descents into the bottle, he'd resumed his ascent, becoming chief in 1911.

On the morning of September 24, 1912, Beavers sent out notices giving landlords of the houses in Atlanta's midst five days to shut down and prostitutes an equal amount of time to vacate. Reported the *Georgian:* "The action of Chief Beavers came with the suddenness of a thunderclap, and its effect was cyclonic."

By the next day, Atlanta was in an uproar. On the one hand, the district's advocates were furious. Jimmy Woodward, campaigning for reelection, declared: "It was a bad mistake to scatter those people over the city in respectable neighborhoods. The social evil question should be handled with good common sense, not fanaticism." Yet members of the Men and Religion Forward Committee were ecstatic, amending that day's "Houses in Our Midst" ad to proclaim: "Thank God for a man who dares to do his duty. The credit should be given to Chief Beavers." Soon, clergymen were canvasing the restricted district, offering girls opportunities to make an "honest living" and boasting of a $10,000 fund set up for that purpose. Meanwhile, Charles C. Jones was also touring the neighborhood, distributing $100 bills to his madams and brandishing a list of alleged brothels in other parts of town that he claimed had been ignored by Beavers because they paid graft to the police.

That a deadly battle had been joined became apparent two days after the crackdown when a madam named Nellie Busby was found in one of the district's houses with a knife plunged into her heart. "Dramatic Suicide Marks Clean-Up," boomed the headline, yet the woman's demise was suspicious. Not only did officers discover an untouched meal and an unopened bottle of beer sitting on the table in her room, but by her body, they found a note that challenged all credulity:

> This is the end. They have ordered me to close my house, and I have nowhere to go. I might as well die . . . Tell Chief B. to go to hell. He's the cause of this.

Who killed Nellie Busby was a mystery, yet the answer to the question of why was obvious—money. Just how lucrative the houses in Atlanta's midst were is uncertain, but in a city whose railroads poured thousands of salesmen into Terminal Station daily, such a business surely produced a windfall—and the women were only part of it. Since 1908, when Georgia outlawed the sale of alcoholic beverages, Atlanta had been dry. While barkeeps could sell near-beer, no one could legally sell whisky. (No one, that is, except proprietors of licensed locker clubs, which usually catered to the rich and included such elegant dives as the Piedmont Driving Club.) There were, however, myriad illegal "blind tigers." Generally, these speakeasies took the form of back rooms frequented by Negroes and crackers. Yet they also included the restricted district's houses. Charles C. Jones was both whoremaster and bootlegger. So while members of the Men and Religion Forward Committee may have viewed Beavers as a crusader, men like Jones viewed him as a threat to a distillery of illicit profits, and they would not have shed a tear had Nellie Busby's death been laid at his doorstep.

Oddly enough, one of the few Atlantans who stood above the fray was the one who started it—Chief Beavers. In interviews, he was relaxed and confident. "I'm enforcing the law, that's all," he told reporters. "The law plainly says that such places shall not exist. I intend to wipe them out." If Charles Jones defied him, he vowed to lead demolition teams into the district and raze it. Thanks to the support of the Men and Religion Forward Committee, Beavers believed he could back up such talk. And he could. Within the allotted period, the houses of Mechanic Street were shuttered.

The effects of Beavers's action were immense but contradictory. The most immediate beneficiary was the chief himself. By the time of Mary Phagan's murder, he was among the most visible law enforcement officials in America. At the 1913 convention of the International Association of Police Chiefs in Washington, D.C., Beavers delivered a much quoted address detailing the interests he'd battled and boasting that in the months since the district's demise, crime in Atlanta had decreased "fully one-third." Back home, however, many remained skeptical. Not only had Woodward been reelected over a pro-Beavers candidate, but the papers were brimming with stories alleging that prostitutes had infested "good" neighborhoods. In a widely reported incident, two preachers in town for a convention claimed they were accosted ten times in one night by streetwalkers.

Yet despite such incidents, the Atlanta Police Department was generally viewed as a crusading force that had stood up against vice. That this holy aura had little more to do with justice than the disreputable practices for which 175 Decatur Street was also renowned was not a subject of much discussion.

Whatever confusion had paralyzed the Atlanta police on Monday regarding the Phagan investigation had by late Tuesday morning been replaced by a newfound certitude. Around 11:30, Detectives John Black and B. B. Haslett arrested the man they were now convinced had committed the crime—Leo Frank. The officers took Frank into custody at the pencil factory, giving him just enough time to grab a pocketful of cigars and say goodbye to his employees, many of whom were in tears, before packing him into the chief's limousine and rushing him to headquarters. There, a mob of photographers and reporters was waiting. As he was being whisked inside, Frank made a brief statement:

> I am not guilty. Such an atrocious crime has never entered my mind. I am a man of good character and I have a wife. I am a home-loving and God-fearing man. They will discover that. It is useless to detain me, unless for investigation and for information I might be able to give.

Then he disappeared into 175 Decatur Street.

The detectives' certitude had been born in an increasingly febrile environment. Tuesday morning, the *Constitution* had upped the reward ante and put Chiefs Beavers and Lanford on notice. In a biting editorial headlined $1,000 REWARD, the sheet declared:

> The detective force and the entire police authority of Atlanta are on probation in the detection and arrest of this criminal with proof. To justify the confidence that is placed in them and the relation they are assumed to hold toward law and order, they must locate this arch-murderer.
>
> All Atlanta, shocked at a crime that has no local parallel in sheer horror and barbarity, expects the machinery of the law to be sufficient to meet the call made upon it. If ever the men who ferret out crime and uphold the law in Atlanta are to justify their function it must be in apprehending the assailant and murderer of Mary Phagan.
>
> Fidelity to oath and pride of reputation should be sufficient incentive to the detectives to insure their solution of this mystery, but as an added incentive . . .
>
> The Constitution offers **$1,000 . . .**

Not to be outdone, the *Georgian* saw the *Constitution*'s bet and raised it, sparking a fund drive that by midday had brought the reward total to $1,800—$100 of which had been donated by none other than Charles C. Jones.

Meanwhile, in Marietta Tuesday morning, remarks made at Mary Phagan's funeral—which the *Georgian* covered in an extra available on Atlanta's streets almost instantaneously—put even more pressure on the police. The ceremony was conducted in a weathered wood-frame Baptist church that perched atop a raw, red-clay bank. The Phagans—mother Fannie, sister Ollie, brothers Joshua, Charlie and Benjamin and stepfather John W. Coleman—were consumed by grief. Indeed, the family was so overwrought that pallbearers had to be picked at random on the grounds. As the white, carnation-banked casket was carried in, the choir sang "Nearer My God to Thee," and from that time on the incessant sound of muffled sobbing filled the air.

Yet for all the soulful lamentations, the obsequies were dominated by cries for retribution. The Reverend T.T.G. Linkous, ordained in the hardshell Christian denomination and the Phagans' pastor during their years in the little mill town of Eagan, prefaced his remarks by praying that "we may not hold too much rancor in our hearts—we do not want vengeance." But once the preacher caught fire, such pleas vanished in an eruption of sulphurous gustings:

> We pray for the police and the detectives of the city of Atlanta. We pray that they may perform their duty and bring the wretch that committed this act to justice. We pray that the authorities apprehend the guilty party or parties and punish them to the full extent of the law. Even that is too good for the imp of Satan that did this. Oh, God, I cannot see how even the devil himself could do such a thing. I believe in forgiveness. Yet I do not see how it can be applied in this case. I pray that this wretch, this devil, be caught and punished according to the man-made God-sanctioned laws of Georgia.

At the cemetery, the angry talk subsided. As the Reverend Linkous, himself now holding back tears, looked heavenward, the first shovelful of dirt hit the casket and Mary's mother fell to her knees, crying: "Goodbye, Mary. Goodbye. It's too big a hole to put you in. It's so big, and you were so little."

The *Georgian,* of course, retailed all these sad details, but it headlined the most incendiary angle, the one aimed directly at 175 Decatur Street: PASTOR PRAYS FOR JUSTICE AT GIRL'S FUNERAL.

No single development had persuaded Chiefs Beavers and Lanford that Leo Frank had murdered Mary Phagan. Instead, to the cumulative weight of Sunday's suspicions and Monday's misgivings had been added several last factors that tipped the scales against the superintendent. First, by Tuesday the police had all but dropped charges against two men who just the day before had seemed prime suspects. One of them—handsome Arthur Mullinax—had been the victim of a case of mistaken identity. Not only had Mullinax's sweetheart provided her beau with a convincing alibi, but his accuser had proved to be a myopic meddler. Edgar Sentell, who'd claimed to have spotted Mullinax escorting Mary along Forsyth Street Saturday night, had received a medical discharge from the navy three weeks earlier

due to poor eyesight. James M. Gantt had also been victimized by a misleading source—his sister. Despite Mrs. F. C. Terrell's assertion that she
hadn't seen her brother in a month, he had, as he'd insisted, been home the
night of the crime. Frightened and according to her husband not well,
Gantt's sister, hoping to keep the family out of the matter, had lied to officers. Though vexing aspects of Gantt's story—his attraction to little Mary,
his Monday trip to Marietta—were left unresolved, he would soon be freed.

So two key suspects had been eliminated. But it wasn't the diminishing
of the ranks so much as what the diminishing suggested that had further
pointed the finger at Frank. It was now plain that reports placing Mary Phagan on Atlanta's streets Saturday night were fictitious, that in truth, after
receiving her wages, she'd never left the pencil factory. Unless some new
figure appeared upon the stage, Frank was and would remain the last
person to admit having seen the girl alive.

Equally important in hardening the case against Frank had been a late-
Monday afternoon meeting at the National Pencil Company offices be-
tween Frank and assistant factory superintendent N. V. Darley and Harry
Scott, second in command of the Atlanta branch of the Pinkerton Detective
Agency.

Frank had arranged the get-together almost as soon as John Black and
B. B. Haslett had finished searching through his dirty laundry. He had
phoned a trusted coworker, assistant superintendent Herbert Schiff, and
instructed him to engage a private investigator, "preferably a Pinkerton
detective." Later, Frank would assert that his only motivation had been a
desire to "assist the city detectives in ferreting out the crime, as an evidence
of the interest in this matter which the National Pencil Company was taking." Frank's rationale may have been as stated, but measured against the
Pinkerton firm's reputation, it rang somewhat hollow. By 1913, the detective agency that had come to prominence protecting presidents and battling
black-hatted hombres had evolved into an ex-officio standing army for
American business. Supplier of strikebreakers and infiltrator of unions, the
firm specialized not so much in investigating crimes as in safeguarding
industry. The Pinkertons were just the people a company official hoping to
stave off scandal would have specified.

Yet where Frank may have harbored a hidden agenda, Scott brought
with him an undeniable conflict of interests. A college-educated Pennsyl-
vanian who before moving to Atlanta in 1911 had worked in the agency's
Philadelphia branch, Scott was smooth-shaven, pudgy and could even have
been termed baby-faced were it not for his sharp nose and button eyes. But
while the 27-year-old detective looked the part of the archetypal Pinkerton
operative and thus the antithesis of the rough old cobs at headquarters, he

was closely tied to the police. Private investigators operating in the city were required to submit duplicate copies of their reports to the department, even if the documents implicated a client. This much Scott would reveal to Frank. What he would not reveal, however, was that his allegiance to the force went deeper than the statutes required, that indeed, one of his best friends, someone with whom he often worked in tandem, was the individual who from the outset had believed Frank guilty: Detective John Black.

It would have been hard to find men at greater cross purposes than the ones who'd sat across from each other Monday afternoon in Frank's office. As Scott would later testify, Frank had opened the conversation by confiding: "John Black [seems] to suspect me of the crime." That said, the superintendent had repeated his version of events. Generally speaking, this was the same narrative he'd given the police, but it did contain several new wrinkles, each of which had an influence on the investigation.

First, Frank—according to Scott's account—had gone out of his way to implicate James Gantt. As the Pinkerton operative would subsequently testify:

> He [Frank] stated during our conversation that Gantt knew Mary Phagan very well, that he was familiar and intimate with her. He seemed to lay special stress on it at the time. He said that Gantt had paid a good deal of attention to her.

To Scott, Frank's familiarity with Gantt's interest in little Mary raised a troubling question: How could a man who on Sunday had told John Black that he did not know the victim have by Monday become an expert on her suitors?

Second, Frank had provided Scott with a newly discovered piece of information: On the day of the crime, an unidentified Negro had been spotted in the factory. As the superintendent would later put it:

> I told him [Scott] something which Mr. Darley had that afternoon communicated to me, viz.: that Mrs. White had told him that on going into the factory at about 12 o'clock noon on Saturday, April 26th, she had seen some negro down by the elevator shaft. Mr. Darley had told me this and I just told it to Mr. Scott.

Scott would subsequently confirm that Frank had apprised him of this news, but at the time, the Pinkerton man had either accorded it no importance (he didn't mention it in his report) or deemed it inconvenient, and for weeks, the possibility that an unknown party had been lurking in the building would go unexamined by the police.

Following an hour's discussion, Frank and Darley had given Scott the grand tour. Through the metal department, down the scuttle hole, into the basement, out the back door, up the alley and around to the Forsyth Street entrance the three had walked. As darkness fell, they'd stood in front of the building, discussing the Pinkerton Agency's rates. After agreeing on a deal, Frank returned to 68 East Georgia Avenue for the last evening he'd ever spend at home. As for Scott, it is uncertain where he passed Monday night, but what is certain is that before he saw Frank again, he'd seen John Black and that when Black and Haslett arrived at the factory to arrest Frank, Scott was with them.

Of all the elements that had persuaded the detectives that Frank was the culprit, however, none had been more important than the shifting view of Newt Lee's role in the affair. By Tuesday morning, the police had pegged the night watchman as both Frank's accomplice and his patsy.

As best as can be determined, the notion that Lee and Frank were in cahoots had first been articulated late Monday by one of Newt's former employers, T. Y. Brent. The police, hoping that Brent could help them bridge the gap between the night watchman's denials of guilt and their certainty that he had been involved, had allowed him to assist in quizzing Lee. Near the interrogation's conclusion, Brent had experienced an epiphany:

> "I know what's the trouble," Brent had exclaimed. "Someone you are faithful to killed that girl. You know all about it. I wouldn't be surprised if you didn't have a hand in it yourself. You don't want to tell because you want to shield whoever murdered her. I'm going to tell you this — it's just a question of loyalty or your neck. You can't keep but one."
>
> "Yessir, Mr. Brent; that's a fact. I know that," Lee had replied.
>
> [Lee's] lips were trembling and he shifted nervously. His questioners waited eagerly for an expected confession. The negro checked himself and recovered but the police are confident of their suspicion.

In a predawn grilling Tuesday, Detective John Black had revisited the issue. "We know you did not do the murder," he had assured Lee. "We know you are guiltless of the whole affair. But we know that you know exactly who did it and that you are protecting that person."

Tuesday's *Journal* had intensified the detectives' need to make the connection between Frank and Lee by linking Lee to the case's greatest mystery—the authorship of the murder notes. The paper had engaged several bank officials to study the missives. While none of these men were trained experts, the *Journal,* taking its cues from the *Georgian,* had not let such shortcomings stand in its way, unequivocally proclaiming in a front-page screamer:

THREE HANDWRITING EXPERTS SAY
NEGRO WROTE THE TWO NOTES FOUND BY BODY OF GIRL

Beneath these lines, the sheet reported:

Through its own investigations the *Atlanta Journal* has proven conclusively that Newt Lee, the negro night watchman for the National Pencil company, either himself mistreated and murdered pretty Mary Phagan, or that he knows who committed the crime and is assisting the perpetrator to conceal his identity.

Locked in this negro's breast is the key to the murder mystery that has shocked the entire south.

Dovetailing with the investigators' evolving theory that Lee was trying to protect Frank was the simultaneously evolving theory that Frank was trying to implicate Lee. This idea had first occurred to the police Monday morning after the superintendent reversed himself regarding the punches on Lee's time slip. But from there, it had gone underground, burrowing through a maze of unknown influences, not emerging until late Tuesday morning, minutes before Frank's arrest, when in one of the case's most bizarre turns, Detective Black had located yet another critical and enigmatic piece of evidence.

Around 11 A.M. Tuesday, Black had let himself into Newt Lee's apartment at 40 Henry Street in a neighborhood near the Bellwood section where the Phagan family resided. Lee lived alone in the back of a shotgun house whose front rooms were occupied by several unrelated Negro tenants. In a metal trash drum Lee had transformed into a wardrobe, the lawman found an exceedingly suspicious item—a bloody linen shirt. The shirt was soaked to the armpits, and from the beginning, everything about it had seemed wrong. The goriest stains, for instance, were on the inside and appeared to have been purposely applied, as if the shirt had been mopped over a butcher's block. Moreover, the shirt looked freshly pressed, as if it had not been worn in weeks. All of which, the detective subsequently claimed, led him to conclude the shirt was a plant. Though Black never revealed how he decided Frank had planted it, an officer of the court would later assert:

Frank was trying to point suspicion at Newt Lee . . . He wanted his own house searched so that when the officers had gone through it and nothing had been found there, he could tell them to go and search Newt Lee's

house ... this shirt was a plant and Frank's request was a ruse to get the
police to search his house and then Newt Lee's house and thus throw suspicion on the negro. The shirt was a part of the scheme.

Whether or not any of this was so, Black—after dropping the shirt off at
Decatur Street and intimating to the reporters gathered out front that there
had been a major break in the case—had picked up Haslett and Harry Scott
and raced to the factory.

Frank's arrest, then, was the culmination of a journey that after beginning
in the ambiguities of Sunday morning had proceeded along a road that
had only grown curiouser and curiouser. Yet just because the superintendent was now in custody did not mean that the journey was at an end. In
fact, Frank was barely through the station house doors before Black and
Scott rushed him to Lanford's third-floor office. There, with Lanford and
Beavers looking on, the detectives produced a bundle of butcher's paper in
which they'd wrapped the just discovered shirt. Hoping to catch Frank off
guard, the men pulled out a tiny bit of the shirt—a sleeve or the tail—and
asked him if he recognized the fabric. As Frank subsequently recalled the
moment:

> They showed me a little piece of material of some shirt, and asked me if I
> had a shirt of that material. I looked at it and told them I didn't think I ever
> had a shirt of that description.

The reaction to Frank's answer went unreported, but he wasn't the only one
subjected to the test. Presently Newt Lee was dragged in. After perusing the
fabric, Newt said it resembled that of one of his shirts, whereupon the lawmen ripped open the package, releasing, as Frank later put it, a "distinct
odor of blood," and Lee confirmed that the garment indeed belonged to
him.

Moments after Lee identified the shirt, a commotion broke out in the
stairwell leading to Lanford's office between an officer who'd been posted
on the steps with orders to let no one pass and Luther Rosser, who, upon
learning of Frank's arrest, had raced to Decatur Street. Forced to retreat to
the lobby and phone upstairs, the lawyer, once he'd been granted passage,
upbraided the man he held responsible.

"I've got my opinion of how a chief of police should conduct himself,"
Rosser snorted upon greeting Beavers. "I had a perfect right to be admitted
by that policeman downstairs. He told me he had orders to keep me down
from here. He even called me by my name."

"I've got my opinion, too, of how a police department should be run," Beavers fired back. "I did not give instructions to keep you from this office. I ordered that the crowd be kept away." On that note, the clash—the second in as many days between the police hierarchy and Frank's lawyer—ended.

When the interrogation resumed, Black ceded the floor to Scott, a turn of events that was too much for Frank to bear. "You're acting mighty funny," the superintendent snapped, expressing anger for the first time. "You were hired by me, if you remember! Why should you ask me such questions?"

To which Scott coolly responded: "I was put on the case by my superiors. They were employed to catch the murderer. That was what I was instructed to do. If you are the murderer, then it's my duty to convict you."

Near the end of the session, Lucille Frank—accompanied by her father and her brother-in-law Alexander Marcus—arrived at the station house. Denied admittance to Chief Lanford's office, the three were shown to a lobby desk. There, they waited. While Lucille maintained her composure long enough to express her belief in Leo's innocence to newsmen, she soon broke down. Later, she would recollect:

> I was humiliated and distressed by numerous people, maybe newspaper reporters, maybe somebody else, snapshotting me with hand cameras. I was besieged for interviews, and made thoroughly miserable in many ways.

At some point, word reached Frank that Lucille was downstairs "weeping bitterly." Hoping, as he'd subsequently put it, to protect his wife from the "humiliation and harsh sight" of seeing him under arrest, he sent a message to her conveying his belief that he would soon be freed and asking her to return home, which she did. Her visit, brief as it was, made the papers, but it stuck in few memories. What was almost universally remembered, though, was the fact that two weeks would pass before Lucille again visited her husband.

Shortly after Lucille departed, the interrogation came to a halt, and all involved spilled into the detectives' bullpen. According to the *Journal,* Rosser "made light of the evidence against his client," claiming that the "police could hold him no longer than he, Mr. Rosser, was willing for them to."

However, Detectives Black and Scott, talking to reporters on the other side of the room, made it sound as if Frank would not be released anytime soon. In joint remarks, the two flatly announced:

> We have sufficient evidence to convict the murderers of Mary Phagan. The mystery is cleared.

Whereupon Frank, so nervous and agitated that he could not stand without support, was led away.

As darkness fell, Black and Scott, their boasts notwithstanding, knew there was much to be done. Though the detectives claimed they had the evidence to convict, that was far from so. Somehow, they had to make the cases against Frank and Lee mesh, or, barring that, firm up a case against one or the other.

Initially, it was Lee upon whom the authorities exerted their powers of persuasion. As yet unrepresented by counsel, exhausted after three days of interrogation and terrified, old Newt was starting to wobble, and the detectives—or, more precisely, their surrogates—went after him with the cruel ingenuity Southern white men reserved for recalcitrant Negroes.

Sometime after sunset, one Francis E. Wright—a salesman who had no connection to the case but believed himself to possess a knack for making blacks open up—was admitted to Lee's cell. After identifying the visitor as a minister, Detective Black and Agent Scott walked away, although along with a *Constitution* reporter, they stayed in earshot.

"Newt," Wright began, "you haven't got long on this earth—only a few days. They're going to get you. They've already got you. What little time you've been allotted for life, you'd better put to good advantage."

With that, Wright implored Lee to talk:

> There isn't but one thing to do. Tell all you know and cleanse your soul. If you die with a lie on your lips, you'll drop straight to perdition.

Wright paused, then produced the texts with which he intended to induce a confession. The first was a copy of an extra the *Georgian* had published late in the afternoon topped by a page-one banner declaring:

LEE'S GUILT PROVED!

Though Hearst's troops, in an uncharacteristic moment of restraint, had couched the screamer within the qualifying embrace of quotation marks, such a nicety was lost on Lee, who with increasing distress reread the line. Meanwhile, Wright pulled out his second text—a Bible. At the sight, the Negro, who was handcuffed to a chair, lunged forward, fell to his knees, and kissed the book's cover. Then, he plaintively vowed: "I swear 'fore God I didn't do it."

That was good enough for Wright. After collecting his props, the counterfeit preacher emerged from Lee's cell and announced: "He's innocent as a babe." The investigators, however, weren't convinced. If the Lord was an insufficient truth serum, they'd try a stronger one. Which was evidently why one Walter Graham, identified only as a "young white man," was allowed to take a derringer into a cell next to Lee's and fire it into the ceiling. Again, the same result. As the *Journal* related: "Lee was badly frightened by the report, but when visited shortly afterwards by the detectives he had not weakened."

It was nearly midnight when Black and Scott decided that the only way to reach a resolution was to bring Lee and Frank together. So the detectives descended from the building's central bank of cell blocks to the private room adjacent to Lanford's office where Frank—due to the fact that he could afford to pay an off-duty officer to stand guard—was being held under the equivalent of house arrest. As Frank would subsequently recall, he'd just turned back the covers of his cot to go to bed when Black and Scott arrived and asked if they could talk with him. Frank agreed, accompanying the men to a nearby room. There, he said, they made their proposal:

> In that room was detective Scott and detective Black and myself . . . They said: "Mr. Frank, you have never talked alone with Newt Lee. You are his boss and he respects you . . . We can't get anything more out of him. See if you can." I says: "All right, I understand what you mean; I will do my best," because I was only too willing to help. Black says: "Now put it strong to him, and tell him to cough up and tell all he knows. Tell him that you are here and that he is here and that he better open up and tell all he knows about the happenings at the pencil factory that Saturday night, or you will both go to hell." Those were the detectives' exact words.

The detectives' exact words would later become a topic of dispute, but what is indisputable is that on the heels of Frank's conversation with Black, Lee was placed in the room with him—Black and Scott standing just outside the door.

According to Frank, his conversation with Newt was to the point but unproductive:

> They put Newt Lee into a room and handcuffed him to a chair. I spoke to him at some length in there, but I couldn't get anything additional out of him . . . Remembering the instructions Mr. Black had given me I said: "Now, Newt, you are here and I am here, and you had better open up and tell all you know, and tell the truth and tell the full truth, because you will get us both into lots of trouble if you don't tell all you know," and he answered me like an old Negro: "Before God, Mr. Frank, I am telling you the truth and I have told you all I know." And the conversation ended right there.

According to Black and Scott, however, things went differently. They said that while eavesdropping, they heard Frank—following a series of denials by Lee and using language that was all his own—tell his employee that if he kept it up "they'd both go to hell." Moreover, they said that it was not Lee but Frank who seemed on the defensive. As Scott would subsequently assert:

> They were together there for about ten minutes alone. When ten minutes was up, Mr. Black and I entered the room and Lee hadn't finished his conversation with Frank and was saying, "Mr. Frank it is awful hard for me to remain handcuffed to this chair," and Frank hung his head the entire time the negro was talking to him, and finally in about thirty seconds, he said, "Well, they have got me too." After that we asked Mr. Frank if he had gotten anything out of the negro and he said, "No, Lee sticks to his original story." Mr. Frank was extremely nervous at that time. He was very squirmy in his chair, crossing one leg after the other and didn't know where to put his hands; he was moving them up and down his face, and he hung his head a great deal of the time the negro was talking . . .

The conflicting versions of what happened during the headquarters encounter between Frank and Lee would never be reconciled, but the session's effect upon the detectives would be readily apparent. Henceforth, their interest in Lee would diminish, leaving Frank as the lone suspect.

FIVE

A Good Name, a Bad Reputation

The idea that the National Pencil Company was a business whose grindingly mechanistic surface masked a luridly bawdy core arose Monday morning after a group of officers making yet another sweep through the factory basement discovered what appeared to be a trysting place. Enclosed in the shallow plywood-walled storage shed that ran nearly the length of the cellar's south side and behind which Mary Phagan's body had been secreted, this dank, filthy compartment housed an improvised cot fashioned from wooden boxes and covered with crocus bags. Impressed into the sawdust floor surrounding the cot were numerous female footprints, a sight that briefly led the police to entertain the notion that Mary Phagan had been lured here, assaulted and then murdered. Even after abandoning this theory in favor of the one holding that the girl had been killed upstairs in the metal department, the lawmen continued to assert that the basement room was connected with the crime. As the *Journal* was soon asking in an insinuating front-page teaser: "Was Factory Used as Rendezvous?"

Tuesday morning, before such possibilities could be sufficiently explored, the *Georgian* rushed into print with a story intimating that not only were employees conducting assignations in the factory's basement but they'd adorned their hideaway with decorative touches befitting a bordello. Beneath the headline NUDE DANCERS' PICTURES ON WALLS, Hearst's minions reported:

> Pictures of Salome dancers in scanty raiment and of chorus girls in different postures adorned the walls of the National Pencil Company plant. They had been clipped from a theatrical and prize-fighting magazine. A more melodramatic stage setting for a rendezvous or for the committing of a murder could hardly have been obtained.

Once again, the *Georgian* was in all likelihood exercising dramatic license. In fact, Leo Frank's friends would later contend that the only art on the premises consisted of a chaste calendar-girl illustration hanging in the superintendent's office, and no other Atlanta paper would pick up the pinup tale. Yet the larger point—that the plant provided a gamy setting for venery— was never really contested. Indeed, R. P. Barrett, the machinist who'd spotted the hair and bloodstains in the metal department, would tell the coroner's inquest that he'd "frequently" heard that the building was used for "immoral purposes." Meanwhile, V. F. Schenck, proprietor of the neighboring Schenck Brothers' Metal Shop, would testify that "frolics were secretly held in the place."

The National Pencil Company's emerging bad reputation could also be linked to its location. Though South Forsyth Street was lined primarily by reputable small manufacturers, and while it was paralleled two blocks to the east by luminous Peachtree Street, it was intersected two blocks to the south by a thoroughfare that conjured an altogether different image. Mitchell Street, which connected Georgia's capitol on the east with Terminal Station on the west, was home to numerous railroad hotels. Here, many of the prostitutes Chief James L. Beavers had driven from Charles C. Jones's houses only six months earlier had resumed their trade. Though it can't be said with certainty that any of these women had been receiving gentleman callers in the less than romantic confines of the factory basement, such a prospect was not unimaginable. As even Leo Frank, in his only public comment on the matter, told the *Georgian:* "In a plant this size, where 170 people are employed and the force is continually shifting, it is quite probable that some of them were low characters." Then, in a crack that could not have played well at 175 Decatur Street, the superintendent added: "Under our present conditions of morals in Atlanta with the segregated district abolished, these low characters have undoubtedly grown worse. That our janitor was bribed to allow them into the building is not an unbelievable suggestion."

All this, however, was preamble. The development that convinced many Atlantans that something untoward had been going on at the factory and, more critically, intimated that Leo Frank was not only involved but had manifested a prurient interest in Mary Phagan, occurred at Wednesday afternoon's opening session of the coroner's inquest. Initially, the 15-year-old newsboy George Epps—one of the last witnesses to testify on this day—had not sparked much curiosity. The jury, which was meeting in the police commission's third-floor headquarters boardroom, had already heard from the expected headliners. Sergeants Dobbs and Brown and Officer Anderson had described the scene that had confronted them in the plant basement Sunday morning. Newt Lee had reiterated his tale, in the process relating that he'd spent the two hours Frank had banished him from the premises Saturday afternoon at a patent-medicine show whose main attraction—a fire-eating Negro—drew throngs of credulous blacks to a corner beneath a downtown viaduct. The revelation had both leavened the mood and reinforced the view that Lee was too simple a soul to have gotten mixed up in a murder plot.

After taking his place at a long cluttered table at the head of which sat Coroner Paul Donehoo, six jurors and Fulton County Physician J. W. Hurt and at the foot of which a battery of reporters and stenographers had dug in, Epps—a towheaded whippersnapper who struck the *Constitution*'s man as "bright [and] quick witted"—grabbed the room's attention by declaring that on the day of Mary Phagan's death, he had ridden to town with her on the English Avenue trolley. During the trip, Epps said, the two had made a date to watch the Confederate Memorial Day parade and then attend a movie, the one hitch being that Mary first had to visit the National Pencil Company and pick up her wages, a prospect, Epps emphasized, that had frightened her:

> She began talking about Mr. Frank. When she would leave the factory on some afternoons, she said, Frank would rush out in front of her and try to flirt with her as she passed. She told me that he had often winked at her and tried to pay her attention. He would look hard and straight at her, she said, and then would smile. It happened often, she said. She told me she wanted me to come down to the factory when she got off as often as I could to escort her home and kinder protect her.

Epps had little else to say (before stepping down, he described how he'd waited in vain for Mary on April 26 at their prearranged meeting place, a downtown drugstore), but little else was required. Here was a statement that would resonate with just about any mother or father who'd stood by helplessly as poverty had forced their daughters to forsake the stable, sexually constraining world of home for the fluid, sexually liberating—and menacing—world of employment. As one contemporary observer later noted: "No girl ever . . . go[es] to work in a factory but that her parents feel an inward fear that one of her bosses will take advantage of his position to mistreat her, especially if she repels his advances. This fear is readily converted into passion." Epps, in other words, had touched the nerve where the deracinated dirt farmer's pride in the past converged with his anxiety about the future, whetting his suspicion that child labor served all too often to gratify not only lust for profit but lust for flesh.

Thursday morning, the *Constitution* splashed the charge atop its front page. Boomed the headline:

FRANK TRIED TO FLIRT WITH MURDERED GIRL
SAYS HER BOY CHUM

And the worst seemed still ahead. By noon Thursday, some 150 factory employees—many of them young girls adorned in their Sunday finery and palpitating with excitement—were waiting in the halls outside the police commission boardroom. Mary's coworkers had been subpoenaed to testify at the inquest's second session. But as the hours ticked by and the session did not start, it became clear that at least for now, the anticipated revelations would not be forthcoming. No one was surprised by the delay—no one, that is, who knew and admired Fulton County's coroner.

At 35, Paul Donehoo was a careful man—he had to be. Left blind by a childhood bout of meningitis, Donehoo had managed through imagination and perseverance to achieve not only self-sufficiency but success. As a boy, he'd learned to make his way unassisted around Atlanta by training his ears to "hear solids," to distinguish between a wall and a door, empty streets and traffic. Later, he'd earned his law degree by convincing a fellow attorney-in-embryo to read cases aloud to him at night. As for the Georgia code and key legal precedents, he'd committed such matters to memory, turning his mind into a virtual law library. Though he'd served as coroner for just four years in 1913, he'd already won praise for his thoroughness. In fact, some people believed his disability actually aided him in his work. As the *Journal* reported: "Not being able to see with his eyes, he is not easily diverted from the point at issue and refuses to allow the witness to wander." Since in Fulton County the coroner—as opposed to the medical examiner—was responsible solely for conducting inquests, such grit was no small asset.

While Donehoo initially appeared to have been as swayed by Epps's story as were others, by Thursday he'd reconsidered, and after consulting with Chiefs Beavers and Lanford, he decided to suspend hearings into the Phagan murder until the atmosphere cooled. In explaining the move, Donehoo remarked: "I would not be holding this jury if I were satisfied or were reasonably certain as to the facts in our possession. A case like this, so deeply wrapt in mystery, cannot be solved in a day. And why should the public demand such great haste? It requires weeks and sometimes months before some of these mysterious cases can be cleared. It is only in the magazines that solutions are forthcoming in a day."

In the wake of George Epps's testimony, two contradictory images of Leo Frank would begin to evolve. One flickered to life in the consciousness of Atlanta's working class, the cracker majority who identified with Mary Phagan. The other unfurled in the interior world shared by the city's German Jews, the privileged enclave that saw Frank as one of its own. In the first,

Frank was cast as a defiler of young girls. In the other, he appeared as an exemplary man and loyal husband. Over time, these notions would solidify into the irreconcilable points of view that would obtain during the long ordeal ahead.

That many Atlantans had now begun to see Frank as a sexual predator is nowhere made clearer than in the files of the Pinkerton Detective Agency. Starting Thursday, May 1—the day after Epps leveled his charge—at least two and occasionally as many as seven Pinkerton agents would be in the field. The operatives did not devote their efforts solely to exploring the allegations of impropriety swirling around Frank. The typed reports they submitted daily to factory lawyers and to headquarters address every facet of the investigation. Still, the dossiers suggest that the Pinkertons—and, by extension, the Atlanta police, for the files prepared by the Pinkerton assistant superintendent Harry Scott invariably begin: "John Black and I then made an investigation"—devoted a large proportion of their energies to running down reports of Frank's purported sexual misconduct. For reasons that had to do with the fact that these dispatches contained material damaging to both Frank and the state, they were never made public and were indeed accessible to only a select few in each respective camp, not just at the time but down through the years.

The names of the Pinkerton investigators who conducted the probe are referred to in the files merely by initials. But the agents who played the greatest roles are identifiable, and they must be mentioned, for their predispositions may have colored their findings. H.S. was, of course, Harry Scott. Meanwhile, L.P.W. was L. P. Whitfield. At 31, with dark hair parted in the middle and plastered down on the sides, eyes swimming behind thick-lensed glasses and dewlaps folding into his collar, Whitfield came across as something of a Milquetoast. A native of the Civil War battlefield town of Kennesaw a few miles north of the Phagans' Marietta homeplace and a devout Baptist, he devoted his free time to his church choir. But harmless as he seemed, Whitfield possessed a strong will and a sharp mind. More important, he was Scott's rival.

Typical of the kind of thing the Pinkertons looked into was a lead that had materialized Tuesday or Wednesday when a trolley car conductor assigned to the same car that had transported Mary Phagan to town April 26 fished from beneath a seat a puzzling note addressed to the police and purporting to relate Frank's history of sexual advances toward the victim. L. P. Whitfield was the agent assigned to follow this thread, and eventually it led him to the Bellwood home of Helen Ferguson, the pencil factory worker who'd informed Fannie and J. W. Coleman of their daughter's murder. In Whitfield's account of the Ferguson interview can be heard the terrified yet titillated voice of Atlanta's working girls:

> At 6:00 P.M., I met Helen Ferguson and secured a statement from her, Miss Ferguson stated that city detectives had allowed her to read a letter which was addressed to police headquarters, which letter stated that Mary Phagan told that Leo M. Frank had put his arm around her, and asked Mary if she wanted to take a joy ride of Heaven, and that Mary Phagan had asked Frank, "How?" to which Frank replied that he would show her some day. This letter was signed "A 13-year old chum of Mary." Helen Ferguson stated that Grace Hicks wrote this letter and that Grace resides at #100 McDonough Road, Atlanta, Ga., as she knew Grace Hicks' handwriting.

Grace Hicks, of course, had identified the body at the funeral home Sunday morning.

But it wasn't just overwrought teenagers who were making such charges. One of the most compelling leads the Pinkertons looked into was provided by three men—O. S. Clark, H. B. Sibley and T. R. Malone; respectively a parcel check clerk, a gateman and a security guard at the Terminal train station. Their story involved an alleged lover's spat they'd witnessed on the eve of the murder between a man who looked like Leo Frank and was ticketed on Southern Railways to Washington, D.C., and a girl who resembled Mary Phagan. In his report, a Pinkerton agent known only as F.C.P. quoted Clark as telling him:

> At 11:00 A.M., I was on duty at the parcel check room at the Terminal Station, Atlanta, Ga., when I noticed a man about 5 ft. 10 in. in height, weight about 135 to 140 lbs., age 25 to 26 years, wearing a dark brown suit of clothes, black derby hat, brown hair, smooth shaven, slender face with sharp features, hazel eyes, wearing no vest, come to my window with a medium sized tan hand satchel to be checked. I checked same, and at the same time, I saw a girl, about 15 years of age, 5 ft. 4 in. tall, [w]eighing about 110 to 115 lbs., blonde, wearing a gray or lilac colored suit, rather well developed, with a full face and wearing a large hat, skirts that struck her legs just above her shoe tops, or where shoe tops would be, come from over near the negro waiting room, and meet the man. I noted that this girl was crying and talking to the man quite a good deal. Just before dismissing them from my mind, I looked on the tag which was on the satchel, I saw a name and an address, I have forgotten the name, but the address was the National Pencil Company, Atlanta.

From there, T. R. Malone picked up the story, informing F.C.P.:

> Going back to Friday, April 25th, 1913—at 11:00 A.M. when the man and
> the girl left the gates and started towards the parcel check room . . . a
> stranger to me, but a man whom Mr. Sibley called Mr. Hill, and myself
> talked about the couple. Someone remarked, "I wonder if they are man
> and wife." Mr. Hill spoke up and said, "No, her name is Mary—(paused)
> Mary,—something—Campbell, I think she used to live near Marietta, Ga.
> Her mother married again about one year ago. They live down here
> now." . . . I understand Mary Phagan's mother's name is Coleman. I believe
> Mr. Hill meant to say Coleman.

Like so many others, Clark and Malone, upon hearing of Mary Phagan's
murder, had raced to Bloomfield's, and each swore that the body laid out
there belonged to the girl they'd seen arguing with the man who fit Frank's
description. Unlike the "joy ride of heaven" tale, this story could not be
kept under wraps, receiving prominent play in all three papers. The *Journal,*
in fact, gave it a double-deck banner:

WITNESSES POSITIVE MURDERED GIRL WAS SAME WHO
CREATED SCENE AT THE TERMINAL STATION ON FRIDAY.

Even as the Pinkertons were trying to get to the bottom of the Terminal
Station sighting, they were also looking into charges that prior to the mur-
der, Frank had seduced and impregnated several of his female workers.
Initially, most of the tips revolved around an erstwhile employee named
Lena Bernhardt. To no avail, Harry Scott and John Black quizzed plant per-
sonnel about the young woman. Finally, they called at the girl's residence.
Reported Scott:

> Detective Black and myself then went to the home of Miss Lena Barn-
> hardt [*sic*], where we saw her mother, and questioned her closely, after
> which she stated that Mr. Frank was not the father of the child, but that
> a Mr. Cosby, who was at one time a chauffeur for J. Carroll Payne [an
> Atlanta lawyer], was responsible for same: That the matter had been aired
> in the courts and settled.

Thus the connection between Bernhardt and Frank was dispelled, but as
Whitfield's file for the same day—the day the hearings were scheduled to
reconvene—makes plain, this was not the end of the accusations involving
Frank's alleged peccadilloes:

The National Pencil factory was closed today, as a majority of the employees were subpoenaed to appear before the coroner's inquest, and I had Mr. Mendenhall [a tipster] to accompany me to Police Headquarters, where the inquest was being held, and Mr. Mendenhall designated two men to me, who he stated had informed him that Frank had been familiar with several of the girl employees and that they were afraid to testify against Mr. Frank, etc., I learned that these men's names are Ely Burdett and James Gresham. Mr. Mendenhall further stated that other men employees of the pencil factory had told him similar stories, but he did not see any of these men at the inquest.

Sounding a similar note, Paul Whitaker, a former factory employee and friend of Mary Phagan's, subsequently told F.C.P.:

I have . . . seen Mr. Frank . . . at times when talking to some of the women employees, it seemed to me that he rubbed up against them a little too much. I noticed this often, but never said anything about it.

One of the most ubiquitous reports connecting Leo Frank to Mary Phagan maintained that on the day of the murder, the victim had been accompanied to the factory by another girl. While little Mary had gone inside to pick up her wages, this companion had waited outside until a man, presumably Frank, came to the door and told her Mary had work to do and would not be down for a while. F.C.P. was the Pinkerton operative assigned to check out the story, and his labors eventually led him to the home of its source, a certain Mrs. Holmes. Afterward, F.C.P. filed a report that though addressing only this one woman suggests how worked up the general populace had become:

I went to Mrs. Holmes' house at 2:30 P.M., but she was not in. She resides in South Decatur [an Atlanta suburb] near Whiteford Ave., and I remained there until she returned, at which time she informed me that she was a "dreamer" and that she did not know these things to be true, except that they "just came to her in her sleep." I observed that this old woman, who lives alone, is in a way an intelligent woman . . . She reads all the news about the Phagan murder case, and I think, she drew these conclusions and thinks of them so much that she does not know whether she read them or whether some one told her . . . that is, she is well read to the extent that she is crazy.

Other allegations against Frank would also prove to be feverish figments of the sort produced by overexposure to Hearst journalism. Yet as the more credible leads the Pinkertons were pursuing suggest, not all the charges could be so easily dismissed. Just because most were apparitions did not rule out the possibility that some were not.

If Atlanta's good country people were suffering from what might well have been diagnosed as a collective sexual hysteria, then its German-Jewish elite were afflicted by the opposite side of the same malady, a collective sexual denial. To his coreligionists, Leo Frank was a collage of respectable emblems—Cornell grad, engineer, married man, president of the B'Nai Brith. That he could have been seized by those priapic impulses to which no male is immune, that he could have been tempted by any of the hundred-odd adolescent girls who gazed up at him each day from their workstations—well, such a prospect was not to be considered. Or, if considered, it could not be articulated. Which is why when eminent local Jews began speaking out for Frank, their remarks were by necessity platitudinous. Hence the comments of B'Nai Brith lodge member Milton Klein—carried in all three newspapers on Friday, May 2—in response to George Epps's inquest testimony:

> Leo Frank, the superintendent and general manager of one of Atlanta's largest and most promising industries, spends two hours in his office on a holiday after generously relieving the watchman during these hours. His habits are regular and industrious and his life, while in Atlanta, is perfectly blameless in every respect. The terrible crime committed in his plant calls forth the closest scrutiny of Mr. Frank's relations with his 200 workmen and women. Only the highest words of praise and confidence in his character are heard on all sides.
>
> I have worked with Mr. Frank for years in various charitable organizations and have ever found him the most polished of gentlemen, with the kindest of heart and the broadest of sympathy. To such an extent it is recognized among his fellow lodge men that we have honored him with the office of president, which is the highest rank in our organization. He is a liberal supporter of many worthy enterprises. But his greatest work has been among his own employees at the factory. The first to report in the morning and the last to leave at night, every day and holidays, he has labored to build up a factory that in spirit and efficiency is second to none south of the Mason and Dixon's line.
>
> After the magnificent work he has done in his adopted home, shall we without consideration, emphasize every bit of gossip which unjustly and groundlessly connects him with this awful tragedy? No one seeks more fervently to discover the real perpetrator of this atrocious crime than Mr. Frank.

Leo Frank's image among Atlanta's German Jews, in short, arose not from their worst fears but from their best wishes—wishes, it must be added, born not of a week's worth of headlines and innuendo but of five years' worth of close association. Yet wishes still.

From August 6, 1908—the day Frank had arrived in Atlanta and checked in to the Kimball House, a sprawling Victorian dowager at Peachtree and Decatur streets that for half a century was the city's landmark hotel—he had unfailingly impressed friends and business associates as considerate and responsible, albeit somewhat rigid.

Away from the factory in those first months, Frank had listened to classical music on his Victrola (he loved Strauss waltzes), read copiously (as a boy, he'd named his toy sailboats for the characters in James Fenimore Cooper's *Leatherstocking Tales*) and taught himself to play chess. His approach to the game, as it was to so much else, was systematic. On the first page of a three-by-five pad, he neatly inscribed the title: "Chess Notebook No. 1." On the second, he appended his signature. On the third, in a handsome draftsman's hand, he drew stylized pictures of all the chess pieces, adding a key that described their powers. Then, on page after meticulous page, he inked in chessboards on which he worked out such basic gambits as Scholar's Mate, the Ginoco Piano and Philador's Defense. Beneath the diagrams, he jotted down observations for future use. "Good against Rui Lopez attack," declared a typical entry.

Orderly and inward, a stranger in the South, Frank had carapaced himself behind a wall of work and intellect. This wall, however, was not without windows. Much as he might try to present himself as an exemplar of dispassionate reason, the factory superintendent was prone to fits of anxiety. Particularly upsetting to Frank were his clashes with Sig Montag. While Frank was in charge of operations, Mister Sig controlled the purse strings, and he frequently called Frank into his office at Montag Paper Company to upbraid him for some financial shortcoming. Inevitably, the superintendent left these sessions shaking and fumbling for a cigarette.

More than anyone, Lucille Selig had first perceived that Frank's brainy hauteur masked a fragile and uncertain young man. Which may explain why, when later asked what had initially attracted her to her future husband, she mischievously responded: "I liked to make him blush."

Lucille had enjoyed numerous opportunities to bring the blood to Frank's cheeks. Upon checking out of his temporary residence at the Kimball House, Leo had rented a room from Lucille's widowed aunt Sophie at 93 East Georgia Avenue just down the street from Emil and Josephine Selig's house at number 68. Within a week of moving in, he had been introduced to Lucille, and by early autumn of 1908, he was accompanying her to the theater and functions hosted by the city's German-Jewish elite.

Lucille was twenty in 1908, and she was a series of contradictions. Raven-haired, sloe-eyed, olive-complected, she possessed a pretty face made prettier still because of her wit and intelligence. As the *Georgian* would subsequently declare: "She inclines to that perfect brunette type so often encountered in the women of her race. As a girl, which can not have been so very long ago, she must have been surprisingly lovely." Yet Lucille's natural beauty was marred by the fact that she was overweight. Had it still been the nineties, the age of the Rubenesque ideal, her plummy amplitude might have been regarded as an asset, but by the time Frank came into her life, the era of the hobble skirt and the Gibson Girl had dawned, and radiant though Lucille was, neither vivacity nor fashion could hide her zaftig form.

Similarly, while Lucille was well connected—on her mother's side, the clan boasted the Temple's cofounder, on her father's, a line of increasingly prosperous businessmen—she herself had never been completely secure. It was Lucille's uncle Simon who owned West Disinfecting. Her father was merely a salesman in the family firm. As a consequence, after graduating in 1906 from Girl's High School, where she'd acquired secretarial skills, Lucille had herself become one of Atlanta's working girls, first taking a stenographic position at the Jewish-owned Atlanta Paper Mills Company, then switching to a job in the same capacity in the regional offices of Swift Meats.

Lucille was at once a perceptive young woman and a carefree girl who seemed caught between a desire to be taken seriously and a fantasy that she could enter into that life of beaus and balls that in the South was the province of her sex but was for her—because of her Jewishness, her weight, her self-awareness—unattainable.

Romantic but practical, fun-loving but high-minded, blithe but tinged with sadness, Lucille was all these things, and all were apparent in the shopping lists she regularly jotted down. These lists—among them one dated January 23, 1909, a period when her fondness for Frank was deepening—provide an index to Lucille's dreams:

Gibbs:	$10.00	lining:	$2.80		
shields:	.25	4 silk:	.40		
cotton:	.05	bone:	.45	lace:	$5.00
Walshe:	$1.00	Wilson:	$1.50		
Russell:	$1.00	Orpheum:	.75		
Ma:	$5.00	suit:	$17.25		
carfare and foolishness:	$5.00				
Lycett:	$1.00	presents:	$5.00		
Lena Jahoot:	$1.30	belting:	.50	tie:	.29

The prudent miss who did her own sewing, the debutante manqué who splurged for Gibson blouses and new outfits, the dutiful daughter, the earnest face in the crowd at the theater, the lighthearted spirit who craved gaiety and laughter—such was the collection of hopes and aspirations that was Lucille Selig. Such was the child who fancied she could see through the Yankee intellectual delivered to her doorstep.

For Lucille, Frank's arrival in Atlanta was a godsend—in part because so few Jews of marrying age resided in Dixie, a circumstance that during the years surrounding the century's turn gave impetus to an annual round of soirees in Atlanta and New Orleans whose purpose was to marry off the region's sons and daughters of Israel. But even if Lucille had been besieged by suitors, there can be little doubt that she'd still have fallen for Frank. As she would later recollect: "If there are such things as cases of 'love at first sight,' Leo Frank's love for me and my love for Leo Frank is a case in indisputable point." On Valentine's Day 1909, Lucille gave Frank her heart—cut from red construction paper, his name emblazoned on it.

On June 9, 1909, just ten months after his arrival in Atlanta, Leo proposed and Lucille accepted. The next morning, Lucille departed by train to spend a few days in Athens, Georgia, with her uncles, Simon and Bud Michael. The Michael brothers were eccentric twins whose success as merchants had enabled them to build adjoining Greek-revival mansions on one of the college town's most fashionable streets, Prince Avenue. For Lucille, visits with these cultured in-laws meant dances, teas and card parties attended by professors and students. It was as close to genuine Southern bellehood as a Jewish girl from Atlanta could get. And it was here, in the midst of the University of Georgia's graduation festivities, that Lucille received her first love letters from her betrothed. Stilted in person, Frank was stilted in prose as well. Yet in a series of increasingly warm missives, he revealed himself also to be gentle, awkwardly gallant, dutiful, a mild gossip and social. Here is what Lucille—and, by extension, Atlanta's German-Jewish community—would come to believe was Leo Frank's true voice.

On June 10—the very day Lucille left town—Frank stole some time at work to write:

> Tho' I have not heard so, I take it for granted that you arrived safely in Athens, and have by this time begun what I hope will be an enjoyable sojourn. Enjoy yourself to the fullest. You would not believe it, but between the last sentence and the next one, 20 minutes have elapsed. Mr. Sig came in to talk to me—nuff said!
>
> Last night, I brought home some work from the factory and put in two hours work . . .

After I got thru . . . I dropped over to your house to see the party. I am just as much delighted (?) with poker as ever . . . [The Seligs loved poker, whereas Frank preferred bridge.] We had a splendid day at the factory yesterday. If we do as well to-day we will better last week's results.

If you can spare a few minutes from the busy social hours of the Athenian day, I should be glad to be the recipient of an epistle.

With best wishes to your folks in Athens and much love to you, I am, dearest, fondly your beau . . .

On June 12, Frank wrote again, describing a Friday-night service he'd attended at the Temple and teasing Lucille about a date he'd made in her absence with Mister Sig's daughter:

Your postal card was duly received and I was very glad to learn that you had begun your trip to Athens so auspiciously.

Only a few minutes ago your mother phoned me that she had received a long letter from you and invited my perusal of same. I will drop in on my way to supper to-night.

Last Thursday night, I paid a visit to the [Jacob] Haas's, who invited me for tomorrow supper. I accepted. Last night, I attended service at the Temple and I enjoyed it very much. Dr. Marks [sic] was not there. A young man who is studying to be a rabbi conducted the service and delivered the lecture. The latter was a perfect jewel and was enjoyed by all. The Dr. had better look to his laurels. After service, I went home with Mrs. Straus and visited her daughter, Fae.

Tonight, I am to take Harriet Montag to the Lyric. Are you jealous? . . .

By June 14, five days after Lucille's departure, Frank's formal reserve had begun to dissolve. Yet even as he waxed emotional, he still could not resist correcting a lapse in his wife-to-be's prose style. Though in love, he remained himself:

Your two letters of the 11th and 13th respectively brought gladness and joy to our midst and balm to our hearts. That we don't write longer letters is because matter fails to write about.

I can't say that the evening of Saturday last, spent with Harriet was one of unmitigated pleasure. I tried my best, and the celestial denizens of heaven could do no more . . .

I don't expect that I will be very active socially this week. There is a carnival for the benefit of the Educational Alliance [a Jewish charity] on the Hebrew Orphan's Home lawn, to which you would have gone if you would have been here.

At the Lyric is the "Milk White Flag," and at the Casino "Dr. Barry" with E. May Spooner in the leading role, as the histrionic attractions!

Athens is not doing much for you intellectually! You are a past master in the use of slang. The latter is always the evidence of a paucity of vocabulary . . .

Your kindly words for me are much appreciated and are treasured up on the scrolls of memory.

I am not much on the sentimental letter writing. Read between the lines and see if you can feel the warmth of the writer's feeling for you . . .

Yours for eternal happiness . . .

Finally on June 16, two days before Lucille was to return home, Frank made his feelings evident:

Was carried "transcendentally" to the seventh heaven of happiness and joy by the receipt of your letter of the 14th. Glad to learn that the good times keep up. I presume that the dance last Monday night was the best ever! If you wore the "pannelled effect" I'll wager you broke a few hearts. Mine is broken by "absent treatment." Everybody remarks how thin I'm getting. Are you affected that way?

On Monday night I met your mother and Mr. and Mrs. Marcus at Ponce de Leon [an Atlanta amusement park]. We did not have such an ecstatic time.

Last night I attended the lawn fete for the Settlement. I escorted Aunt Betty. After we got there she shifted for herself. I saw her home. They certainly took the starch ($) out of me. I dropped $3.75 and have really nothing to show for it.

Please let me know the time when your train is scheduled to arrive in Atlanta so I can greet the Goddess Athena . . .

Leo Frank and Lucille Selig were married on November 30, 1910, at the Seligs' Georgia Avenue home, Dr. David Marx officiating and only family and a few close friends in attendance. The house, in the announcement's phrase, "was artistic with quantities of smilax and vases of pink carnations in all the rooms." A Cornell classmate served as Frank's best man. Lucille, who entered on the arm of her father, wore a white charmeuse satin gown trimmed in princess lace and pearl garniture. Orange blossoms were twined through her tulle veil, and she carried white roses and lilies of the valley.

During the nearly two and a half years of their marriage, the couple had by every visible criteria been content. Yes, there were occasional disagreements about such innocuous differences as taste in music—Lucille was drawn to ragtime, while Leo preferred symphonies. And yes, there had been a disappointment. Both husband and wife said they wanted a child, but thus far they'd failed to bring one into the world. (Seven decades later, Katie Butler, a former factory employee in her 80s, would tell her physician that she and Lucille were both pregnant during the early winter of 1913 but that Lucille had suffered a miscarriage. If Mrs. Butler's memory was reliable, her claim—while not clearing Frank of philandering charges—certainly suggests that he and Lucille maintained sexual relations.) Such matters aside, however, the Franks were evidently happy. "I suppose there are many husbands in the world as good as Leo," Lucille would later say, "and it may be therefore that I am foolishly fond of him. But he is my husband, and I have the right to love him very much indeed, and I do. If I make too much of him, perhaps it is because he has made too much of me."

On the afternoon of May 5, following a four-day cooling-off period, Paul Donehoo reconvened the inquest. From the outset, it was clear that Leo Frank's character had become the central issue. He would be the session's only witness. Wary as the coroner was about rushing to judgment, he wanted to elicit a version of the facts before the factory superintendent had an opportunity to consider the effect those facts might have upon the prosecution.

The Leo Frank who now faced Donehoo, the jurors and a horde of reporters bore no resemblance to the agitated man detectives had encountered the morning Mary Phagan's body was discovered. Collected and articulate, dressed in a dark suit, he came across as the picture of responsibility and civility. He seemed everything that his friends and family believed him to be and nothing that his detractors suggested that he was.

Donehoo started his examination with several inquiries into Frank's early work experiences and the circumstances that had brought him to Atlanta; then he shifted to the events of April 26. The superintendent provided a seemingly thorough accounting of himself. Some of the details were new, most were not. In Frank's telling, his activities on the day of the murder appeared beyond reproach. He related how he'd arrived at work at 8:30, met with his department heads, then walked to Montag Brothers at 10:00 to pick up the mail, which was delivered to that address. He told of returning to his office at 11:00, dictating several letters to the stenographer Hattie Hall, greeting some casual visitors (among them Emma Clark and Corinthia Hall, both factory employees) and sorting through invoices. Then, he recalled how Hattie Hall and the 14-year-old office boy Alonzo Mann had departed around noon, leaving him alone until Mary Phagan appeared at the door. In his recounting of this meeting, Frank made the session's first bit of news:

> About 12:10 or 12:15 this little girl who was killed came up and got her envelope. I didn't see or hear anyone with her. I didn't hear her speak to anyone who might have been outside. I was in my inside office working at the orders when she came up. I don't remember exactly what she said. I looked up, and when she told me she wanted her envelope, I handed it to her. Knowing that employees would be coming in for their pay envelopes, I had them all in the cash basket beside me, to save walking to the safe each time. The girl left. She got to the outer door and asked if the metal had come. I told her no.

That Mary Phagan had inquired about the metal and Frank had answered negatively had not heretofore been publicized.

Donehoo, however, did not linger here. (In all likelihood, the coroner already knew about the exchange, as Frank had mentioned it to Harry Scott during their initial interview, telling the Pinkerton man, according to his report, the same thing: "She asked about the metal, and I told her it hadn't arrived.") Thus the superintendent resumed his narrative of the day's events, reeling off the well-known story about directing Mrs. Arthur White to leave the factory, locking in her husband and another workman upstairs and departing himself. The only fresh details seemed trivial. As he was walking into the house for lunch, Lucille and her mother were rushing out to the opera's matinee. After eating a bite with his father-in-law, he lay down in the parlor and smoked a cigarette. Eventually, he said, he strolled back toward town, speaking to some relatives on the street before catching a trolley. With roads blocked for the Memorial Day parade, the car stopped on the edge of the business district, and he completed the trip on foot, waving to a couple of employees in the crowd.

Now came the rest of the familiar narrative: the return to work, the arrival of Lee, the encounter with Gantt. Frank reviewed it all again, although he did offer a new perspective here, placing a fact the detectives regarded with suspicion into a context that made it seem benign. The reason he'd never phoned Lee after hours before was that the night watchman had just started working at the factory two weeks earlier, having transferred from a company-owned slat mill on the outskirts of town. Frank said he'd called Newt's predecessor frequently.

Low-key and direct, Frank's testimony suggested that for him, April 26—save for the disruptions occasioned by the opera and the Memorial Day parade—had been just like any other Saturday: busy, ordered and book-ended by scenes of domestic tranquility.

Yet unremarkable as Frank's recitation had been, it would not end on a dull note. In response to a question from Donehoo asking if he had any last thoughts about the day, Frank dropped a bombshell, a piece of information that if true provided him with an alibi covering the sole gap in his April 26 timetable, the 55-minute-span between the hour Mary Phagan left his office and the hour he departed for lunch. As the *Constitution* reported it:

> Frank . . . startled his audience with the declaration that he was visited by Lemmie Quinn, a pencil plant foreman, less than 10 minutes after the girl of the tragedy had left the building Saturday.

According to Frank, Quinn remained only a couple of minutes, but the duration of his stay was irrelevant. What mattered was that he was there at the very time the investigators were beginning to theorize little Mary came to her terrible end.

Even the unflappable Donehoo was jarred by the manner in which Frank threw out this fact as if he only just recalled it. How could you forget such a thing? the coroner demanded. To this reasonable query, Frank replied that Quinn's visit had simply slipped his mind until the Monday after the crime when Quinn himself had reminded him. Donehoo did not raise the next logical point—why had Frank waited a week to divulge the information? Instead, as was his wont, he moved methodically on.

After four hours of examination, Frank stepped down. In Donehoo, he'd found the perfect interlocutor, a man whose attention to detail enabled Frank, the archetypal engineer, to present a plausible blueprint of his April 26 activities. More important, the coroner, for reasons that were never explained, did not inquire into the charges leveled by George Epps. Finally, even the revelation of Quinn's visit seemed to be a victory for Frank. This because Quinn, when contacted by reporters, confirmed Frank's story. No wonder that the newspapers' verdicts were unanimously approving. Boomed the headline atop the next day's *Georgian:*

FACTORY SUPERINTENDENT'S STATEMENTS ON WITNESS STAND
CONSIDERED DISTINCTLY FAVORABLE TO HIM

And the *Constitution,* which had played up Epps's charges, now gave equal time to Quinn, running out the front-page caption:

LEO FRANK INNOCENT, NEW WITNESS TELLS DETECTIVES

The vision endorsed by the German-Jewish community seemed in the ascendant. Frank had spoken, and as would shortly become clear, he intended to speak no more. From this day forth, he would essentially disappear into his cell in the Fulton County jail, the lockup to which he'd been transferred. A forbidding institution usually referred to, in homage to the seven-story stone turret that guarded its main entrance, as the Tower, the facility would become Frank's new home. Here, he would exhibit such reticence (no interviews, no responses to any further developments) that the press would christen him with the evocative moniker by which he would afterward be widely known—the Silent Man in the Tower.

The debate regarding Leo Frank's character was far from over. When the Phagan inquest reconvened three days hence, it would be at the top of the agenda. Only now, the story would not be so pretty. During the interim, the detectives had located several young men and women—all either former factory employees or relatives of former employees—who claimed to have seen a different side of Frank, and late on the afternoon of May 8, they filed into the police commission boardroom and one by one sat down at the head of the table.

First up was an ex-worker named Tom Blackstock:

"Do you know Leo M. Frank?" Donehoo began.
"Yes."
"How long have you known him?"
"About six weeks."
"Did you observe his conduct toward female employees in the pencil factory?"
"Yes, I've often seen him picking on different girls," Blackstock responded, describing how Frank would "rub up against" workers while pretending to instruct them in their tasks.

Tom Blackstock, however, could do no more than say he'd observed such behavior. Following him were two girls who could say they had experienced it firsthand.

Nellie Pettis was a poutingly pretty 14-year-old whose sister-in-law was a former factory employee:

"Do you know Leo Frank?" Donehoo again began.
"I've seen him once or twice."
"When and where did you see him?"
"In his office at the factory whenever I went to draw my sister-in-law's pay."

"What did he say to you that might have been improper on any of these visits?"

"He didn't say exactly—he made gestures. I went to get sister's pay about four weeks ago, and when I went into the office of Mr. Frank, I asked for her. He told me I couldn't see her unless I 'saw him' first. I told him I didn't want to 'see him.' He pulled a box from his desk. It had a lot of money in it. He looked at it significantly and then looked at me. When he looked at me, he winked. And as he winked he said: 'How about it?' I instantly told him I was a nice girl."

At this point, the coroner sharply interjected: "Didn't you say anything else?"

"Yes I did," Nellie Pettis replied. "I told him to go to hell!"

With that, the Pettis girl stepped down, only to be followed by another Nellie, 16-year-old Nellie Wood. Unlike her predecessor, the Wood girl was garishly, almost slatternly, made up. But no matter how crumpled the petals, she was still a flower of Southern womanhood, and her story helped to complete the emerging picture:

"Do you know Leo Frank?" Donehoo inquired.

"I worked for him for two days."

"Did you observe any misconduct on his part?"

"Well, his actions didn't suit me. He'd come around and put his hands on me when such conduct was uncalled for."

"Is that all he did?"

"No. He asked me one day to come into his office saying that he wanted to talk to me. He tried to close the door, but I wouldn't let him. He got too familiar by getting so close to me. He also put his hands on me."

"Where did he put his hands?"

"He barely touched my breast. He was subtle with his approaches and tried to pretend that he was joking, but I was too wary for such as that."

"Did he try further familiarities?"

"Yes."

"What did you tell him when you left his employ?"

"I just quit, telling him that it didn't suit me."

In a chorus of young voices, then, Frank's briefly rising star was eclipsed. Declared the headline atop the next morning's *Constitution:*

Sensational Statements Made at Inquest by
Two Women, One of Whom Had Been an Employee,

Who Declared that Frank Had Been Guilty
of Improper Conduct Toward His Feminine
Employees and Had Made Proposals to Them
in the Factory.

The opposing images of Frank couldn't have been more polarizing—and, in a court of law, less relevant. Unless his lawyers took the almost inconceivable step of making his character the basis of the defense, his behavior prior to April 26, 1913—good or bad—would be inadmissible. Which was why, while it may have been easy to damn or praise Frank, it was not going to be easy to prosecute him.

SIX

Skulduggery

Shortly after dawn on Monday, May 5, the stillness of Marietta's municipal cemetery was broken by the sound of picks and shovels hitting home as gravediggers began disinterring Mary Phagan's body. At last, an autopsy was to be conducted. Six days after the funeral and nine after the murder, Dr. Henry Fauntleroy Harris, secretary of the Georgia Board of Health, had come up by car from Atlanta to establish the exact cause of the girl's death and end speculation regarding what, if any, other horrors she'd endured.

Also present were Fulton County Physician J. W. Hurt, who'd made the initial cursory examination of the remains, and Coroner Donehoo, but both deferred to the 46-year-old Harris, in title and reputation Atlanta's foremost medical figure. An Alabama native and 1890 graduate of Philadelphia's highly regarded Jefferson Medical College, Harris had been on the cusp of a great deal of pioneering work, ranging from efforts to eradicate that bane of the South's rural population, pellagra, to cancer-cure experiments. A member of the American Association of Pathologists and Bacteriologists, the doctor, prior to moving to Atlanta, had served as an associate professor of pathology at Jefferson Medical.

With the body lying on a blanket on the ground, Harris worked at a deliberate pace, probing wounds, trepanning the skull, taking tissue samples and removing the stomach. He had no fear of being observed, for the press had not been informed of the postmortem, and few people in Marietta knew anything about it. At noon, the procedure complete, the corpse was returned to its casket and to the earth.

Despite the secrecy, the news that Mary Phagan's body had been disinterred couldn't be kept quiet. An inevitability, as the examination had taken so long that Donehoo was tardy for the inquest's Monday afternoon session—the session at which Leo Frank testified. The late editions played up the story. Proclaimed the *Georgian:* PHAGAN GIRL'S BODY EXHUMED. But such headlines notwithstanding, little information regarding the autopsy was released.

That details regarding the Phagan postmortem were hard to come by was a tribute to the individual who had ordered the examination—Hugh Manson Dorsey, solicitor general of Fulton County. For a couple of days now, the impression had been growing that Dorsey intended to wrest control of the probe from what he regarded as a bungling, leak-prone police force. As early as May 1, in fact, he had told the *Georgian:*

> The investigation has been hesitating. All leads given to the police have not been brought out. No effort has been made to establish if the shirt said to have been found in the ash barrel back of Lee's home was Lee's. The handwriting tests on the notes have not been exhausted—in fact, hardly touched upon. The marks on the girl's body might lead to an extensive [examination] that has never been made.

Had Dorsey been less politic, he could have continued his litany, adding to it the police's failure to keep the murder notes out of Harold Ross's hands, to secure the crime scene (countless gawkers traipsed through the plant the Sunday the body was located) or even to harvest such basic clues as the bloody fingerprints on the factory's basement door, which had remained in situ until the Tuesday following the killing when a private citizen had taken it upon himself to chisel them off, then deliver them to the station house. Yet the prosecutor knew he'd ultimately have to work in concert with Decatur Street, thus shortly after leveling his complaints, he'd summoned Chiefs Beavers and Lanford to the Thrower Building, the temporary home of Fulton County government. (The granite courthouse that to this day houses Atlanta's judicial system was in 1913 only partially completed.) By session's end, Lanford, at least, had been placated. "He seemed pleased with our progress," the detective chief had told reporters. "He denied the circulated report that he was disappointed in the lack of evidence we had gathered." Though Beavers had emerged stony-faced from the gathering, there can be no doubt that Dorsey's gambit had succeeded, for Detectives John Starnes and Pat Campbell were soon assigned to his staff, and Harry Scott began briefing him regularly as well. As the mystery entered its second week, the *Journal* proclaimed: "Dorsey is probably the only man who is in touch with every phase of the investigation."

In short, the Monday, May 5, autopsy of Mary Phagan marked the emergence of Hugh Dorsey as the central figure in the probe, a debut Dorsey made official later that day when, in the midst of the inquest's afternoon session, he negotiated his way through the packed police commission boardroom and took a seat directly behind Donehoo, to whom he promptly began whispering suggestions.

While no statute prohibited Dorsey from inserting himself into this early phase of the investigation, it was almost unheard of in Georgia for a prose-cutor to assume an active role in a case until it reached the grand jury. Over the next days, the press would vigorously debate the appropriateness of the solicitor general's actions. Replying to grumbles that he'd exceeded his authority, Dorsey made no apologies. "The burden of convicting the perpe-trator of this horrible crime, whoever he may be, will fall directly upon my shoulders and I don't propose for that reason, if not for many others, to let it [the inquiry] drag along," he told reporters. Then, lest anyone doubt his resolve, he not only ordered Dr. Claude Smith, the city chemist, to examine the shirt found at Newt Lee's house and the blood spots discovered on the factory floor, but he orchestrated another dramatic raising of the dead.

Around 2 P.M. on Thursday, May 7, Mary Phagan's remains were disin-terred for the second time in less than a week. The object of this latest autopsy would be both forensic and medical. Testifying to its dual purpose was the fact that Dr. Harris was joined at the grave site by an unidentified fingerprint technician.

As before, a blanket on the ground served as the operating table, and also as before, Harris removed at least one organ. Moreover, he apparently snipped a few locks of hair from the body's head. This last action, the *Jour-nal* acidly noted, was necessitated by the fact that some hair taken by Dr. Hurt during his preliminary exam and "which was in possession of the police has been lost." It was the work of the fingerprint technician, however, that attracted the most curiosity. Reported the *Constitution:* "A chart was made of the cuts and bruises on the face and body and photographic plates were made of the fingerprints on the throat." Added the *Georgian:* "The fingerprints on the body were to be photographed and compared with the fingerprints of persons under suspicion."

Most of what the press wrote about the second postmortem consisted of conjecture, for this procedure was shrouded in more secrecy than the first. Did the examination show that Mary Phagan had been raped, that her body had been mutilated? These questions—in references to "the crime that was taken for granted by all to have preceded the actual killing" and "wounds about the chest and shoulders"—darted in and out of the newspaper ac-counts, but confirmations were impossible to obtain. Harris, complying with Dorsey's instructions, refused comment, but even if the doctor had been so inclined, he would not have been ready to make a statement until he fin-ished his lab work—a task projected to take several weeks. Furthermore, when reporters contacted Newport Lanford, they learned that the detective chief hadn't been informed of the additional autopsy. Dorsey was securing his position in the classic manner—by managing the collection and flow of information.

To most Atlantans it was clear why Hugh Dorsey had taken command of the Phagan case—he needed a courtroom victory. During the nearly three years since he had been appointed the Fulton County solicitor general, Dorsey had shown an alarming propensity for losing high-profile trials. Just two weeks earlier, the city had watched gape-jawed as a jury acquitted one Callie Scott Applebaum of murder. Mrs. Applebaum—a lovely, albeit lethal, vamp—had been discovered in a locked hotel room with a discharged revolver, a tale involving a temporary blackout and a husband shot in the head. Yet counsel for the mysteriously widowed defendant had argued persuasively that Jerry Applebaum had died by his own hand. The verdict had been rendered on April 25 and thus dominated the front pages on the day of Mary Phagan's murder.

The Applebaum decision was only Hugh Dorsey's latest defeat. In the spring of 1912, he had failed to convict Daisy Grace, an Atlanta society figure, of the attempted murder of her husband, Eugene. The Grace proceedings—still fresh in Atlantans' minds—offered some worrisome parallels to the Phagan case. For starters, the *Atlanta Georgian,* just purchased by Hearst, had used the trial to give the city a first taste of yellow journalism. For another, the investigation had been marred by inept police work. Finally, the lawyer who'd successfully defended Mrs. Grace was Luther Rosser.

No prosecutor, of course, wins every battle, but Dorsey had a way of losing that made Atlantans shake their heads. A case in point had occurred in December 1910 when he was bested in what had at first seemed an open-and-shut affair. The defendant, a black man named Charles Tanner, had been charged with stealing a suit of clothes from a pawnbroker. What made conviction appear certain was that Tanner was, in one reporter's phrase, "an unusual negro." To wit: He had twelve fingers, six on each hand, and as a consequence, his accuser had identified him "beyond a shadow of a doubt." But at the trial, the defense had tripped the solicitor up by calling Tanner's cousin Jonas to the stand. The *Journal* described the scene and its consequences:

> When the latter negro was commanded to hold up his hands, he was found to have six fingers on each hand like his cousin. The resemblance between the two was marked, and in the face of this freak evidence the case was dismissed.

The Tanner debacle was not so much an example of Dorsey's bumbling as it was an incident that suggests that under his aegis the Fulton County solicitor's office lacked gravitas. (TWELVE FINGERS NOT SUFFICIENT IDEN-

TIFICATION, declared the *Journal*'s headline.) It would have been impossible to conceive of the episode having occurred during the lengthy reign of Dorsey's predecessor.

For thirty years, Charles Dougherty Hill had towered over the Atlanta courts. A figure of unquestioned probity and rare humility, "Old Man Charlie" — as Hill had been respectfully known — had possessed an innate sense of fairness and a keen respect for the power that had been vested in him. When pondering a defendant's fate, he would keep in mind the words of the Scottish poet Robert Burns: "Who made the heart, 'tis He alone decidedly can try us."

For all Hill's strengths, he had not been unflawed. His weakness for distilled Kentucky sunshine had been pronounced and had produced its share of embarrassments. But he had possessed a nobility of spirit and a gift for expressing that nobility in words. So stirring a speaker had he been that on days when he was scheduled to give a closing argument, other lawyers posted runners at the courthouse, instructing them to phone as soon as he rose from his seat. It had been on such an occasion that Old Man Charlie had uttered his eloquently brief last remarks.

While trying an inconsequential case on the afternoon of October 18, 1910, Hill had suffered what would prove to be a fatal stroke. After collapsing, he'd found himself surrounded by concerned faces, one of which belonged to a Negro protégé, a lawyer named Henry Lincoln Johnson. Link, as Johnson was known, had once practiced in Atlanta, but due to connections with the Republican Party, he'd received a patronage job with the federal government and had moved to Washington, D.C. Yet on this occasion, business had brought him back to Atlanta, and like any lawyer in town with some time to spare, he'd dropped by the courthouse to hear Old Man Charlie. When Hill had realized that Link's was among the visages peering down at him, he'd murmured from somewhere deep inside: "Old friends come home in the evening."

Three days later, 67-year-old Charles Dougherty Hill was dead, and within less than two weeks Hugh Dorsey had been tapped to take his place.

Though Dorsey had been elected to office in his own right in 1912, his hold on the job was tenuous. Among reporters, the consensus was that the Phagan prosecution represented nothing less than a last chance for him.

Hugh Dorsey was not, however, a man to be underestimated. The son of a distinguished jurist (Judge Rufus T. Dorsey, a post-Reconstruction state legislator), a graduate of the University of Georgia, matriculant to the University of Virginia Law School (he'd failed to receive a degree, returning home after one year) and partner in his father's well-connected Atlanta firm — Dorsey, Brewster, Heyman and Howell — he possessed most of the requisite bona fides.

Dorsey was born in the small town of Fayetteville some thirty miles south of Atlanta, and he enjoyed nothing so much as acting the rube, peppering his conversation with folksy witticisms and rural pieties. Yet he was reared in the city, and his friends included his Jewish law partner, Arthur Heyman; his Jewish college roommate, Henry Alexander; and even Luther Rosser, whose son, Luther Jr., had recently married Dorsey's youngest sister, Sarah. The fledgling solicitor was equally at home addressing a jury of poor dirt farmers or exchanging bons mots with the capital's elite, and in a state where a successful lawyer had to do both, this was a considerable asset.

In the end, though, it was Dorsey's personality that made him a potentially formidable figure. His demeanor, while not quite supercilious, was cool and mockingly predatory. There was something sharp, watchful, raptor-like about him, and it showed in his face. Cowlick plastered upon a high, eggish forehead, eyes circled by the liver-stained rings that were a family characteristic, lips frequently twisted into an appraising smile, Dorsey bore a striking resemblance to a shrewd young owl. As unimpressive as his record was, he conveyed the distinct impression that he wasn't worried, that he was just awaiting the right moment to swoop down. With the discovery of Mary Phagan's body in the National Pencil Company basement, that moment had come.

It quickly became apparent that it would not be easy for Hugh Dorsey to maintain control of the Phagan case. The difficulties facing him began to reveal themselves in the aftermath of what was ostensibly a triumph. On Thursday, May 8, the coroner's jury, following just ten minutes of deliberation, recommended that Leo Frank and Newt Lee be held for further questioning. Yet in the days ahead, attention would focus less on this decision than on the admissions made by two of the inquest's final witnesses, John Black and Harry Scott.

"Have you discovered any positive information as to who committed this murder?" Paul Donehoo had asked Black.

"No, sir, I have not," the police department's star investigator had replied.

To the same query, the Pinkerton agent had also answered in the negative. While such admissions did not reflect directly on Dorsey, they did suggest that barring some startling revelation turned up by the autopsies, he had little to work with, sparking doubts concerning not only what sort of case he would take into court but whether he could even secure indictments.

These doubts were given graphic incarnation in the Sunday, May 11, *Constitution.* Beneath a front-page cartoon depicting the city as an angry matriarch clutching a scroll labeled "Phagan Case" and glowering at a closed door labeled "Detective Dept.," the newspaper pointedly asked: "I wonder if they're all asleep in there?" With this cartoon, the *Constitution*—which had been editorializing against Decatur Street since the 1910 detective department scandal—staked out what would become a consistent antipolice position.

Meanwhile, misgivings concerning the status of the case also began cropping up in an altogether unexpected venue—the *Georgian*. In the sheet's May 11 editions, the political editor James B. Nevin dismissed the evidence upon which the coroner's jury had rendered its verdict as "horrible false details conjured up in some disordered brain hereabout . . . misinformation, near-facts, pure falsehoods, and prejudice. Who then DID murder Mary Phagan? The question is almost as far from an answer today, I think, as it was when Mary Phagan's body was dragged to light."

Nevin wasn't the *Georgian*'s sole voice of protest. On this same mid-May Sunday, the paper unveiled a new columnist—"The Old Police Reporter"—assigned full-time to the Phagan affair. The identity of the pseudonymous scribe would remain a mystery, but in a supportive, albeit fatalistic, passage in his inaugural effort, he revealed a predisposition in Frank's favor:

> I cannot help but sympathize with Frank in being held as he is on the very slight evidence presented against him. At the moment, it would seem as though he were a victim of circumstance and that he would have to take the consequences that follow being the superintendent of the factory and the last person to have seen Mary Phagan alive. And consequences, as George Eliot said, are unpitying.

Though the *Georgian*'s slowly emerging pro-Frank stance may have owed something to its editors' doubts regarding the superintendent's guilt, it owed more to the Atlanta Jewish community's disatisfaction with the paper's initial coverage and the stir that the vocal expression of the disatisfaction created higher up in the Hearst organization.

The *Georgian*'s first-day performance had been but an appetizer. The courses that followed achieved the journalistic equivalent of a gluttonous orgy as Foster Coates ordered extra after extra. Indeed, the *Georgian* had wantonly heaped one intemperance atop another. The LEE'S GUILT PROVED! headline had so agitated Atlantans that Mayor Woodward and Chief Beavers, fearing a lynching, put aside their differences long enough to issue a joint statement decrying the sheet's "sensational and misleading" reports. The paper had then insulted the city's Greek community by hypothesizing that since little Mary had been strangled and "the garrote" was favored among Mediterranean killers, suspicion should focus on the staff of the Busy Bee, a Greek-owned diner frequented by pencil factory workers. Yet the *Georgian*'s worst offense, the one that mobilized Atlanta's Jews, had come in the edition announcing Frank's arrest. It was there that Coates committed the cardinal sin of declaring an unconvicted suspect guilty. Above a photograph of Frank, the editor ran out a front-page banner flatly stating:

POLICE HAVE THE STRANGLER

As Herbert Asbury would later recall:

> Foster Coates made a blunder when Frank was accused of the crime and taken to Police Headquarters. He put an extra on the street, of course—and wrote a banner line for it which said without qualification that the strangler had been arrested! The type was even larger than we used when we tried to convince the citizenry that there was news when there was none. The line . . . had far-reaching consequences.

The next morning, groups of Atlanta's Jews had begun arriving at the *Georgian*'s newsroom. The complainants weren't the sort to be taken lightly. One party alone included Dorsey's partner, Arthur Heyman, and the insurance brokers Isaac and Arthur Haas, kin to the factory lawyer Herbert Haas and descendants of a founding Atlanta family. According to Asbury, these pillars of Southern Jewry "said the *Georgian* had called Frank guilty before his trial and that it showed the existence of an organized conspiracy to railroad him to the gallows . . . they raised the cry of persecution and demanded that the editor denounce the police and insist on Frank's immediate release, declaring that he was being persecuted because he was a Jew."

Whether the accusation of anti-Semitism had been justified at this moment is a matter of debate. Nonetheless, the following day, downtown merchants—many of them Jewish—began circulating a petition contending that the *Georgian*'s extras had "aroused the community to a dangerous degree" and asking Coates to use restraint. Here again, a fine point must be raised—were the merchants' motivations as pure as they maintained? As Asbury would subsequently assert:

> After the discovery of the girl's body the storekeepers and other businessmen rubbed their hands and chuckled a jovial Rotarian chuckle at the spectacle of crowds standing about staring at the headlines and the pictures; they thought so much excitement would bring people into town and

that business would be good . . . But business was not good; it was worse than it had been for many years. People did come into Atlanta, but both visitors and townspeople were so busy reading about the murder and enjoying their thrills over the pictures and the diagrams that they did not have time to buy anything.

So after a little while the merchants began to complain; they asked Coates, in person and through the advertising department, to let the excitement subside a bit so their customers could be lured back into their stores.

The merchants' pleas were heard—not just at the *Georgian* but throughout the city. The *Journal,* reeling from the Hearst sheet's performance, played the petition-drive story atop its front page beneath the headline: BUSINESS MEN PROTEST SENSATIONAL "EXTRAS."

All of which explains why on May 1, the same day the *Constitution* had headlined George Epps's allegations, the *Georgian* printed a banner proclaiming: THE SUPREMACY OF THE LAW! Beneath this line, Coates performed a seeming act of editorial contrition:

> It should not be necessary to say that THE LAW of the sovereign State of Georgia IS SUPREME, that all branches of the judiciary have their proper functions and perform their duties in a legal, time-honored way.
>
> These trite remarks are published that the public may understand that trials by newspapers, by experts, so-called have no judicial functions and are valueless.
>
> Therefore, let everybody, rich and poor, high and low, of whatever race and creed, look to THE LAW for judgement in a dignified way and not to newspapers or sensation mongers for legal advice that has no basis in any law book. It is time to recall Browning's beautiful words: "God's in his heaven, all's well with the world."

Coates was hardly repentant. Far from agreeing to temper his behavior, he had essentially absolved himself of responsibility. His line of thinking implied that words did not matter, that a newspaper could malign anyone so long as the courts sorted things out and the editor quoted poetry. As Asbury would later note: "Coates . . . was riding wild with the best story of his large experience and he refused to stop." In response, the city's Jewish business leaders put some steel into their objections. "The merchants began withdrawing their advertisements," Asbury wrote. "Some took them out immediately; others notified the paper that they would not renew their contracts. The *Journal* and the *Constitution* paid no attention to the demands of the Jews, and for a long time the *Georgian* ignored them also. But pressure was soon brought to bear in New York . . . little by little the editorial and news columns of the *Georgian* began to veer toward Frank."

Once the Jewish community's complaints reached New York, William Randolph Hearst would have been hard pressed to ignore them. Though Hearst liked to think of himself as someone who couldn't be bullied and while he had positioned the *Georgian*—with its anti-child-labor editorials—as the people's paper, he was always aware of his political and financial interests. And he was always willing, as he'd done repeatedly elsewhere, to alter a paper's stance to protect those interests. When it came to the *Georgian*'s coverage of the Phagan case, Hearst had a splendid opportunity to ascertain exactly where his interests resided, for shortly after Atlanta's Jews registered their protests, he and his wife visited the city, socializing with Governor-elect John Slaton and his wife, Sallie, and dining with various merchant princes, among them Walter Rich.

To most Atlantans, the *Georgian*'s evolving alliance with Frank was imperceptible. The headlines were still huge, the streamers still red, the extras still proliferating. But for Hugh Dorsey, the shift—when coupled with the damaging admissions made by Black and Scott and the skepticism with which the general populace regarded the police—presented a serious threat, one that would require him not only to build a stronger case but to undertake a shrewd campaign to manipulate public opinion.

The first important piece of new evidence Dorsey produced called into question a key part of Frank's self-professed murder-day itinerary—his statement that he had been at his desk for the 55 minutes between 12:15, when he said that Mary Phagan had left his office with her pay, and 1:10, the hour that he'd departed for lunch. The superintendent had, of course, bolstered this assertion at the inquest by testifying that Lemmie Quinn had stopped by for a visit shortly after little Mary took her leave. But on May 10, all three papers reported that Dorsey had secured an affidavit from a 14-year-old ex-factory employee named Monteen Stover, who said she'd dropped in at Frank's office at 12:05 on April 26 to pick up some outstanding pay and found it deserted. While Monteen's statement was not released, she revealed the salient details to the *Constitution:*

> I went to the pencil factory that Saturday to draw my pay. The front door and the door leading to the second floor were unlocked. The whole place was awfully quiet and kinder scary as I went up the steps.
>
> The minute I got to the office floor I looked at the clock to see if it was time to draw my pay . . .

It was five minutes after twelve. I was sure Mr. Frank would be in his office, so I stepped in. He wasn't in the outer office, so I stepped into the inner one. He wasn't there, either. I thought he might have been somewhere around the building, so I waited. When he didn't show up in a few minutes, I went to the door and peered further down the floor among the machinery. I couldn't see him there.

I stayed until the clock hand was pointing exactly to ten minutes after twelve. Then I went downstairs. The building was quiet and I couldn't hear a sound.

Shortly after acquiring Monteen Stover's affidavit, Dorsey moved to commandeer the front pages by announcing that he'd hired "the world's greatest detective" to solve the crime. And who was this Sherlock Holmes? To that quite legitimate inquiry, the solicitor offered only an enigmatic smile.

While several reporters expressed initial qualms regarding the so-called mystery sleuth's existence, most were soon regurgitating Dorsey's periodic, albeit vague, updates regarding his exploits. One day, the solicitor revealed that his man was "already compiling evidence," the next that he was leaving town on a secret assignment. Such releases went a long way toward creating the impression that the solicitor was not just in charge but in touch with an expert answerable only to him.

The tack, however, was risky. Beavers and Lanford had already endured one humiliation at Dorsey's hands, and they bridled at the prospect of another. Huffed Chief Lanford: "He [the solicitor] has some mighty good men connected with his office, and I see no need why he should employ any 'world-beater' detective to assist him." Lanford speculated that the state's "A-1 man" was none other than one of the police detectives—Starnes or Campbell. But to this theory, Dorsey demurred, putting the detective chief in an even more untenable position. By May 14, Lanford was sounding embattled. "The squad at headquarters are not inferior when it comes to efficiency. In fact, the city detectives have unearthed the larger portion of evidence now at hand." Several days later, Lanford warned that a breach had developed between his department and Dorsey.

Contradictory reports regarding the investigation now began to appear. At the urging of a handwriting expert hired by the mystery sleuth, Dorsey publicly dismissed any lingering suspicion that Newt Lee had composed the murder notes. But Lanford disagreed with this assessment, stating: "I have not been able to satisfy myself that the negro is not connected with it in some way. He knows more than he has told." By mid-May, the *Constitution,* which was politically allied with the solicitor and a reliable barometer of his thinking, was reporting that "Dorsey believes the crime was committed in the basement, and that she [Mary] was conscious when carried there." (The solicitor was persuaded to this opinion by a woman who told him that at 4:30 on the afternoon of the murder, she'd heard screams emanating from the factory cellar.) Meanwhile, Lanford and Beavers held firm to their original theory "that the victim was rendered unconscious by being struck upon the back of the skull when her head hit the planing machine on the second floor." Not that headquarters wasn't working up its own surprises. Before many days passed, Lanford was titillating reporters with tales of an unidentified telephone operator who on the night of April 26 allegedly overheard "a secret conversation between two attachés of the factory" regarding the crime. When apprised of this development, Dorsey confessed ignorance, but he regained momentum by intimating that "startling new arrests" were imminent. The extent to which the solicitor was perpetrating a stunt here can't be known, but no one was apprehended, and from Lanford's perspective Dorsey appeared to be playing to the gallery. It was the detective chief's turn to throw up his hands. The investigation had degenerated into a turf war.

By late May, the newspapers were using the phrase "multi-cornered" to suggest the polarized configuration. In one corner stood Dorsey and his mystery detective. (As it turned out, this shadowy figure actually existed. An ex-Pinkerton agent named Frank Pond, he served as the solicitor's eyes and ears for a month. Beyond the fact that he used numerous aliases during this period, little is known about what he contributed.) In another stood Chiefs Beavers and Lanford and the detectives working under them. In still another stood the Pinkertons, although their ties to Decatur Street led many to view them as a police auxiliary. And in a fourth stood a newcomer, a brilliant outsider whose appearance signaled a growing disgust—especially among Atlanta's elite—with the inhabitants of the other three.

Word that William J. Burns was en route to Atlanta inspired the kind of fanfare usually reserved for visiting heads of state. BURNS CALLED INTO PHAGAN MYSTERY; ON WAY FROM EUROPE, sang the *Georgian*'s May 12 banner.

William Burns was no stranger to headlines. Since 1911, when he solved one of the new century's greatest mysteries—the 1910 bombing of the *Los Angeles Times* building—he had been accorded endless hosannas. Burns had traced the *Times* bombing (which had occurred in the midst of a union dispute and left 20 employees dead) to the International Association of Bridge and Structural Iron Workers. His efforts contributed to the conviction of two union members. The *New York Times* christened him "the greatest detective certainly, and perhaps the only really great detective, the only detective of genius whom this country has produced."

Not one to practice false modesty, Burns would have found little to quarrel with in the *Times*'s assessment. Short and stout with florid jowls and flaming red hair and mustache, the investigator, according to his official biographer, "was far more suggestive of a successful salesman or even a theatrical personality than a highly skilled detective." Featured speaker of the Alkahest Lyceum and Chautauqua System, friend of Sir Arthur Conan Doyle and subject of a series of obsequious film biographies—one of which, *The Exposure of the Land Swindlers,* had drawn crowds to Atlanta's Alcazar Theater earlier in 1913—Burns had achieved a status rivaling that of the era's movie stars.

Since the Grand Panjandrum himself was abroad tracking a wealthy missing person, it fell to the director of his Chicago office, a detective named C. W. Tobie who'd helped crack the *Los Angeles Times* case, to set up the Atlanta operation. Shortly after arriving in town, Tobie received an eight-hour briefing from Dorsey. At the session's close, the solicitor, while not casting his lot with the Burns agency, came close: "I gladly welcome Mr. Burns. I welcome his investigator who is now on the job. I will give him and his staff complete co-operation." In return for such support, the Burns operative agreed to submit copies of his daily reports to the solicitor.

Predictably, news that William Burns was on the job—and that Dorsey was glad to have him—did not sit well with Chiefs Beavers and Lanford, who perceived the development as yet another insult and threat. If possible, Harry Scott was more upset, as the Pinkertons had recently lost one of their most lucrative clients—the 11,000-member American Bankers' Association—to the Burns Agency.

Consequently, Tobie, despite the glowing advance notices, began work in a climate of mistrust. Avoiding the press, the detective visited Marietta to familiarize himself with the dead girl's family and friends, then he traveled to an unidentified South Georgia town to search for a previously unremarked-upon boy rumored to have accompanied Mary to the factory on April 26.

By May 20, reporters had smoked Tobie out, and if the statements he gave are any indication, everything he'd learned tended to reinforce police findings. "The girl was lured into the rear of the second floor, on which were found the blood spots and hair strands," he told the *Constitution.* "Advances were made. She resisted, attempted to flee. A scuffle ensued. Blind with madness, she was struck. She fell backward. Her head struck the lathing machine. While still unconscious, the garrote was formed in the wrapping cord. The body was lowered to the basement. Hoping to direct suspicion to another source, the slayer penned the mysterious notes."

In less strained circumstances, Tobie's analysis almost certainly would have delighted both the police and the Pinkertons. Instead, those by now understandably defensive men seized on a comment the operative didn't even make, a remark—proferred by a powerful Atlantan instrumental in contracting the Burns Agency—suggesting that contrary to Tobie's own modest claims, he had in actuality inaugurated "a new phase [in the] investigation, one entirely overlooked before that will be productive of startling developments."

Both John Black and Harry Scott were quick to respond to the rebuke they perceived in the words "entirely overlooked." Declared the city detective: "We have overlooked nothing. We have run to earth countless thousands of rumors, and we have worked systematically." The Pinkerton man echoed his friend: "We have overlooked nothing."

Meanwhile, Tobie imported a new fingerprint expert—P. A. Flak, a Briton with offices in New York—to examine both Leo Frank and Newt Lee. But before long, the Burns agent hit a wall. With witnesses reluctant to answer questions and behaving as "if they were under instructions," he sensed that "some secret" force was "obstruct[ing] his efforts at every turn of the road."

Tobie's problems didn't stop there. Rumors that he had once abducted a baby soon began circulating around Atlanta. As it happened, Tobie had in fact whisked a child out of one parent's hands and into the other's during a custody case in Kansas, but "kidnapping" was too strong a word for it. Nonetheless, the operative soon found himself spending as much time denying accusations as he did investigating the Phagan murder.

Tobie, in short, had stumbled into a conflict that eclipsed the one between Hugh Dorsey and the police, a conflict that threatened to turn Leo Frank into a pawn in a battle between divergent factions at war over Atlanta's future.

The events that not only contaminated the investigation with the stench of local politics but exacerbated the religious and class tensions inherent in the affair cannot be understood without addressing the man who'd engaged the Burns Agency. Thomas B. Felder was one of the best-known lawyers in the South, an audacious figure both personally and professionally. Everything about the Colonel—as the 48-year-old Felder, in the best Southern tradition, was known—bespoke grandiosity. In appearance, he was a cane-carrying popinjay. In conversation, he was a self-promoter. And in society, he and his wife, Ann—president of the Atlanta Players Club—were on intimate terms with all the quality folk, among them Georgia's first lady of the theater and her husband, the governor-elect. With Sallie Slaton starring in the Players Club's spring production of *The Importance of Being Earnest,* the Felders and the Slatons were frequently linked in print, whether it was in an item reporting their presence at a postrehearsal supper party or one praising the women for loaning their respective silver tea services for use as stage props.

To his social and financial peers, it little mattered that Felder had played a pivotal part in one of the day's most outrageous legal escapades. As counsel to Charles W. Morse, Felder represented a man whose name had become synonymous with stock market scandal. Though often referred to as the "Ice King" for his role in a 1906 plot to corner New York's commodities market in ice, Morse was best known for his 1907 run on United Copper, a plunge setting off a collapse that bankrupted numerous trusts and threatened the market itself until J. Pierpont Morgan—in a history-making show of force—stopped it single-handedly. In 1910, Morse had been convicted of tampering with the books of the Bank of North America and sentenced to fifteen years at Atlanta's Federal Penitentary. Enter Felder. In 1912, after examinations by government doctors showed that Morse was dying of Bright's disease, Felder had applied to President William Howard Taft for an executive pardon, which Taft had granted.

Even at the time, the Morse pardon exuded a whiff of impropriety. Many were those who doubted whether Morse was truly suffering from a fatal illness. As 1912 became 1913 and the Ice King had yet to expire, the doubters had multiplied. Either the government had employed bad doctors—or Thomas Felder was an exceptional lawyer. Whichever, Morse recovered, and the news would eventually emerge that he'd faked the symptoms of Bright's disease by imbibing a cocktail consisting of various irritating soaps. Morse would remain among the living until 1942.

Thomas Felder was not judicial timber, although nearly everyone in his circle was aware of that long before the Morse pardon, for he had floated into Atlanta society on a veritable stream of alcohol. Just how many breweries, distilleries, distributors and bar owners the Colonel counted as clients is uncertain (40 was the number critics bandied about), but what it all added up to was an undeniable reality: Felder was the city's reigning liquor lawyer.

Yet Felder's alliances with Atlanta's racier sorts ultimately ran deeper, for he was closely associated with that fashionable rake who until just six months before the Phagan murder had purveyed not only hooch but harlots. The Colonel was counsel to Charles C. Jones, proprietor of the Rex and deposed prince of Mechanic Street—the man who'd been the primary target of Chief Beavers's campaign against the houses in the city's midst.

Felder's ties went all the way to the office of Atlanta's bibulous mayor.

Jimmy Woodward was also one of the Colonel's cohorts. And what had the mayor been up to in the months since the restricted district was shuttered? Most recently, he'd been canvasing members of the police commission to see if he could secure the votes necessary to topple the Beavers administration.

All of which explains why Beavers and Lanford were dismayed when, only a week after Mary Phagan's murder, Colonel Felder—who'd never expressed any interest in the plight of Atlanta's poor working girls and who, as an associate of Jones, could even be said to be an exploiter of the class and sex—announced that several of little Mary's Bellwood neighbors had employed him to investigate the crime. Skepticism mounted following Felder's May 13 visit to New York, where he engaged the Burns Agency, then increased further on May 16, when he unveiled a subscription drive to raise $5,000 that would subsidize the renowned detective. By the time Felder issued his first statement on the case—the one claiming that the authorities had "entirely overlooked" crucial clues—Beavers and Lanford were convinced that he was attempting to use the Phagan probe to promote his own nefarious agenda.

The debate over Felder's motives came to a head on May 17 when he released the names of those Atlantans who'd thus far contributed to his fund. Not that the Colonel was all that forthcoming. For one thing, he said that many of his backers—among them a dozen "business leaders" and "society ladies"—had requested anonymity. But of the supporters whom Felder was willing to identify, one was the aforementioned Charles C. Jones and the others were Jews, most notably the industrialist and Chamber of Commerce official William J. Lowenstein and the philanthropist Joseph Hirsch. For Beavers and Lanford, the connections seemed obvious. Here was proof that Felder and by extension Burns were allied with a group that included Frank, his religious and economic peers and the flesh peddlers and corrupt politicians who'd opposed the police department's war on vice.

Lanford's suspicions were, of course, only that. To discredit Felder, the detective chief needed evidence, and on May 17, he got some in the form of a notarized affidavit signed by Mary Phagan's stepfather, John W. Coleman:

> The affiant, while at the police station during the coroner's inquest . . . was approached by a man somewhat under the influence of liquor, [who] said to the affiant, "I am working for the law firm of T. B. Felder, and I would like to have you go to his office, as he wants to see you, and I advise you to employ him." Affiant said, "No, I won't go to his office." The piker then said, "Will you talk to Colonel Felder if I bring him here?" whereupon the affiant agreed . . . He came back in a few minutes with Felder. Colonel Felder then said, "I want you to employ me to prosecute this case. It will

not cost you a cent." The affiant told him he did not want to employ
him . . . and affiant did not employ him.

Had the statement concluded here, it might not have raised any eyebrows.
But in a distinctly Lanfordesque addenda, it continued:

> Affiant is thoroughly satisfied with the great work done by Chief of Police
> Beavers and Chief of Detectives Lanford and the able men working under
> them, as he believes, as thousands of others do in Atlanta, that they have
> the real murderer in jail . . . The affiant cannot reconcile himself to the
> conduct of Colonel Felder, who is posing as a prosecuting attorney and
> wanting five thousand dollars from the people of the City . . . The affiant
> does not believe [Felder is] anxious to prosecute the men under arrest.

Whatever the affidavit's provenance, Lanford now possessed a document that could scuttle Felder. After locking the statement in a safe, the
detective chief made his move.

On Sunday, May 18, Felder picked up the telephone at his home in the
North Atlanta suburb of Buckhead and heard a familiar voice. Arthur S.
Colyar, Jr., a self-described freelance writer and investigator who'd assisted
the Colonel in previous adventures, was calling to say that Lanford had
obtained the Coleman affidavit. Furthermore, Colyar implied that he knew
a disgruntled police employee who for a price would provide Felder with
the item before it could be used against him. His curiosity piqued, the
Colonel invited Colyar to confer with him the following afternoon.

At the appointed hour, Colyar, accompanied by none other than C. Gay
February—Lanford's secretary and the man who'd penned the fake affidavits at the heart of the 1910 police scandal—appeared at Felder's office to
broker a deal. The terms: For $1,000 and freedom from prosecution, Febru-
ary would turn over not just the Coleman statement but a graft list revealing that Beavers and Lanford, their crackdown on the restricted district
notwithstanding, were on the take from a new generation of madams in far-
flung locales. Now genuinely intrigued, Felder agreed to another session,
this one on neutral ground.

Around 3 P.M. on Wednesday, May 21, Thomas Felder entered the
Williams House, an aging but still popular hotel located on Forsyth Street a
few blocks north of the National Pencil Company. Awaiting him in Room
31 were Colyar, February and an innocuous-looking wooden chest. Nestled
imperceptibly beneath a slightly ajar drawer were two transmitters. Several
red wires hidden in the crevices of the chest snaked away from these cunningly positioned bugs, disappearing into the keyhole of a door that opened

into an adjoining room. Behind that door was a Dictograph with its operator, headphones clamped over his ears, standing by.

After voicing a few pleasantries, Felder broached the subject that had brought the men together.

> "Now what I say to you is strictly confidential," he began. "Day before yesterday, I saw Woodward."
>
> "You saw Woodward, Monday?" Colyar asked.
>
> "Yes. Woodward says now it is all right for you to get the papers, and we will pay you for them."

At this point, February entered the discussion.

> "Let me understand you. You want this Coleman affidavit and all other Phagan affidavits that I can get hold of?"
>
> "Yes," Felder answered. "Colyar told me that he was to have the evidence that would get those two chiefs out of commission."
>
> "Will $1,000 be paid if we can get the papers?" Colyar inquired.
>
> "Yes," Felder said.

As swimmingly as it all had gone, the conversation ended on a discordant note when Colyar proposed the East Lake Country Club, a golfing resort just beyond city limits, as the spot to consummate the transaction. Fearful of receiving stolen documents outside Atlanta, Felder blanched. He wanted to do the deed in town. Thus the talks broke off. Yet prior to departing, the Colonel agreed to summon several associates to continue negotiations.

Late Wednesday afternoon, the second shift began arriving at the Williams House. First came one of Felder's associates, E. O. Miles, but when Mayor Jimmy Woodward and Charles C. Jones materialized, the magnitude of Colyar's catch revealed itself.

> "Do you think Frank murdered that girl?" Colyar was soon asking Miles.
>
> "I never have believed it," Miles replied. "I think the whole case was handled badly. They had an extra on the street at 6:30. They should have never allowed all the persons they did on the premises. Just after the murder there were only a few scents and tracks, and the man who did the murder could have easily been tracked. They should have looked for footprints and fingerprints."

Colyar then posed the same question to Woodward.

"Phagan case?" the mayor grunted. "I think it has been mighty mussed up."

After getting these attacks on the record, Colyar maneuvered his prey onto even more dangerous grounds.

"Did you tell Tom Felder," he asked Woodward, "that you authorized Felder that if he got the proof for you, you would see that he got paid for it?"

"I told Felder," the mayor replied, "that on matters of this kind that I am satisfied that certain parties would be willing to pay the money."

Woodward, in essence, had endorsed the payoff, but Colyar wanted the mayor to state that he was willing to countenance theft.

"Only two men can get the evidence," Colyar said. "February and Chief Lanford."

"Get anything that looks like graft," Woodward answered. "I don't care who it hits, and especially Beavers."

With that, everything—even the spot where the transaction would be completed (Miles didn't object to East Lake)—was settled, and Woodward departed, followed soon thereafter by Miles and Jones, who'd been noticably reticent throughout the meeting.

Charles C. Jones may have been, as one reporter later put it, "too foxy" for the Dictograph, but Thomas Felder and the others weren't so nimble. Not that many folks could have outmaneuvered this prototypic electronic surveillance device. Nonetheless, Newport Lanford wasn't taking chances. In fact, he spent much of the next day securing notarized statements from everyone involved in the sting. The plan was to arrest Felder, stolen papers in hand, at the East Lake Country Club, then deluge the press with a blizzard of transcripts and depositions. With one flourish, the detective chief intended to vanquish not only the individuals who'd expressed doubts regarding the department's Phagan investigation but the cabal of sin mongerers and cosmopolites who opposed Decatur Street's overall war on wickedness.

There was, however, a central player in the drama whose motives Lanford had not examined. On paper, 46-year-old Arthur Colyar seemed reliable. The son of a former publisher of the *Nashville Banner* and grandson of a former governor of Tennessee, he'd said his only interest in the Felder case was journalistic (he claimed he wanted to write an exposé of municipal corruption), and the detective chief had believed him. This was a mistake.

Colyar was one of the subtlest knaves ever to hit Atlanta, and as with so many dishonest souls, he infused every mendacity with an element of truth. His interest in Felder actually was journalistic—just not in the way the police imagined. Sometime on Thursday, May 22, Colyar paid a call at the *Journal*'s newsroom. Toting a valise stuffed with copies of the Coleman affidavit, the Williams House transcript and other documents connected with the probe, Colyar was in the market to sell. And as it turned out, the *Journal*'s editors, desperate to scoop the *Georgian,* were in the market to buy.

On Friday, May 23—the day before Lanford intended to apprehend his quarry—Atlanta was once again bombarded with headlines. Roared the *Journal*'s front-page banner:

COL. THOMAS B. FELDER DICTOGRAPHED BY CITY DETECTIVES

Beneath this screamer, the paper ran out everything it had. Here were enough scintillating comments and juicy depositions to keep Atlantans enthralled for days. More significant, the material portrayed Felder as a slick grafter and intimated that sinister forces were trying to derail the Phagan investigation.

Though Chiefs Beavers and Lanford were initially incensed by Colyar's premature publications, they soon realized how utterly their enemies had been routed and pressed their advantage. Boomed the double-deck banner atop the May 25 *Journal:*

"FELDER IS THE MOUTHPIECE OF THE VICE GANG,"
DECLARES CHIEF JAS. L. BEAVERS

Herein, Beavers vowed he would battle the forces embodied by Felder "to the finish if I die in my tracks," asserting that "the issue is now between the decent people of the city and the gangsters who have controlled the city for years. This has outgrown the Phagan case and has assumed the proportions of the hottest fight in the political history of Atlanta."

And a fierce fight it was. Felder began his defense by distributing a 5,000-word broadside to all three newspapers. In this statement, the Colonel, claiming that the Williams House transcripts had been doctored, dismissed the entire episode as "but the symptom or manifestation of one of the most diabolical conspiracies ever hatched by a venal and corrupt 'system.' " Then the Colonel threw his haymaker, accusing his accusers of the very offense of which he stood accused. Namely, he charged Beavers and Lanford with undermining the prosecution of Leo Frank.

"I would have the people of this community know," the Colonel improbably proclaimed, "that from the day and hour of the arrest of Leo Frank, charged with the murder of little Mary Phagan, Newport Lanford and his coconspirators have left no stone unturned in their efforts to shield and protect the suspect. [They] have winked at forgery, suborned perjury, and employed every base agency their low and groveling criminal instincts could contrive and conjure."

As to what possible motive Beavers and Lanford might have had for deflecting suspicion from Frank, Felder was quoted as having told an associate: "This damned fellow Lanford knows that Frank killed [Mary Phagan], but he has sold out to the Jews for big money which he is getting and has got, and he is trying to discredit myself in his effort to protect this damned Jew."

The two chiefs didn't let Felder's allegations go uncontested. Regarding his claim that the Dictograph records had been doctored, Lanford simply released the name of the operator who'd transcribed the session — George Gentry, nephew of the president of Southern Bell Telephone. And as for the accusation that the police were in Frank's pocket, the detective chief tersely and credibly responded: "It is easy for anyone to see that there is no police plot to protect Frank." Then, in a sally worthy of Felder himself, Lanford added: "As for Tom Felder's charges of graft, all Atlanta knows they are untrue, unfounded and are but the explosions of a distorted brain — a brain deformed by years of treachery."

Even more damaging to Felder, the press seconded Lanford's dismissal of the suggestion that the police had sold out to Jewish money. Noted the *Constitution:* "Up until the time Mr. Felder had begun to 'bombard' the public with statements of his belief in Frank's guilt, it was generally believed he was in the suspect's employ."

For the embattled denizens of Decatur Street, Felder had turned out to be a blessing. Yet Beavers and Lanford were unable to capitalize any further on their good fortune, and this was because of the man who'd enticed Felder to take part in the Williams House sessions.

"Career of A. S. Colyar Reads Like Some Story in the Arabian Nights," declared the headline atop the May 24 *Constitution.* The paper's antipolice sentiments notwithstanding, the facts presented in its account were indicting. From youth, Colyar had exhibited a talent for deception. As a young man visiting Mexico under false pretenses, he'd been received "with great éclat" at ceremonies attended by the nation's president. What made the incident something more than a college-boy prank was that Colyar had then used his bogus credentials to bilk the American ambassador out of a sum variously reported as between $1,000 and $10,000. Subsequently, Colyar was admitted to the Middle Tennessee Insane Asylum. Soon thereafter, he fled his home state and had henceforth essentially run amuck, making a living by romancing rich women and hoodwinking church congregations. Though Colyar did once serve jail time, the *Constitution* reported that "probably no man in Tennessee has imposed so successfully upon the public and has escaped so lightly."

Within hours after news of his criminal past hit the streets, Colyar was under arrest on fraud charges stemming from an outstanding warrant, and Felder and Mayor Woodward were back in business. Through a friend, Felder accused the police of fraternizing with "a moral degenerate." Meanwhile, the mayor cackled: "Now isn't Colyar a fine specimen to be hired by the city detectives." Attempting to deflect such barbs, Chief Beavers maintained: "He [Colyar] may be a crook, but it is no uncommon thing for one crook to turn up another." Felder and Woodward, however, would have none of it. Indeed, the Colonel proposed that Beavers "be stripped naked and ridden through Atlanta on a cart with a sign reading 'Reform Chief' hung from his neck."

Where once the Phagan investigation had merely been in danger of becoming a jurisdictional squabble, it was now degenerating into a calumnious rhubarb pitting faction against faction, class against class, faith against faith.

The first casualty was the Burns Agency, which withdrew from the investigation on May 27. In announcing the decision, C. W. Tobie noted: "This is a helluva family row and no place for a stranger. I came down here to investigate a murder case, not to engage in petty politic[s]. All of this stuff seems to have been brewing for some time, and it has just now come to the surface." With that, Tobie returned to Chicago, and William Burns was denied the chance to look into Mary Phagan's murder while clues were still fresh.

For Thomas Felder, the repercussions were worse. As far as the Phagan case was concerned, the Colonel was finished. Though he would later succeed in getting a grand jury to investigate the Atlanta police, he had revealed himself to be not just a servant of Bacchus but a cad and a cur.

In the end, however, the Dictograph episode's only true victim was Frank. The superintendent would always be suspected of having employed Felder, and though the charge was never proven, it was never laid to rest. While it was likely true, as Luther Rosser would subsequently assert, that "Felder does not, nor has he at any time, directly or indirectly, represented Frank," Frank's counsel failed to address, much less explain, why such notable Jews as Lowenstein and Hirsch lent their names to Felder's cause. The most charitable explanation was that these men, fearful for one of their own, were duped. Even so, what many Atlantans took away from the episode was the impression that the Jewish community was in business with the likes of Charles C. Jones. Thanks to Felder the anti-Semitism Atlanta's Jews had perhaps prematurely feared might enter the case found a place to hang its hat. This was not, however, the Colonel's most damaging bequest to Frank. Felder did his real damage at headquarters. As Rosser would later put it: "Once Felder charged Newport Lanford with favoring Frank, the detective settled in his mind the guilt of Frank and from that moment bent every energy of his department, not in finding the murderer, but in trying to prove to the public that Felder was wrong in charging him with trying to shield Frank."

The Dictograph scandal was not without survivors. No matter how badly Beavers, Lanford and Woodward had acquitted themselves, they had done nothing out of character and were thus seen no differently than in the past. But there was only one real winner in the affair—Hugh Dorsey. Exhibiting uncanny dexterity, Dorsey had perched himself not just above the fray but in a position that allowed him to keep an eye on both Felder and Decatur Street. Following his initial daylong briefing of C. W. Tobie, he'd met regularly with Felder regarding the Burns Agency's involvement, and if Chiefs Beavers and Lanford had been sent packing, he would have been ready to embrace a new police regime. Simultaneously, however, he had advised Lanford on the legality of Dictographing Felder and had assured the chief that it was "perfectly legitimate." Dorsey had played both sides, and he'd done it with verve. When it had briefly looked as if Lanford might be unable to locate a Dictograph, the solicitor, knowing full well the chief's intentions, had contacted Felder and devilishly sought to borrow his. As it turned out, the Colonel was unable to supply the gadget and was thus saved from being hoisted by his own petard.

Adroit, brazen, poker-faced—Hugh Dorsey was all these things, but native cunning could carry him only so far. Weathering the Dictograph storm was one matter, but presenting a case to the grand jury was another. Considering the skeptical response accorded the coroner's jury's finding, Leo Frank's indictment was hardly a foregone conclusion.

While the Felder affair had raged, Dorsey had devoted most of his efforts to refining his case. Postponing other trials and twice delaying the grand jury sessions themselves, the solicitor—aided by Starnes, Campbell, the mystery detective Frank Pond and an assistant named Newton Garner—had interviewed scores of witnesses. Not surprisingly, much of the intelligence filtering into Dorsey from both the Pinkertons and the police focused on the charges of sexual impropriety against Frank.

Whatever the ultimate utility of the intelligence, Dorsey now knew that some of the specific accusations—among them the "joy ride of heaven" anecdote and the item suggesting that Frank and a girl who looked like Mary Phagan had created a scene at Terminal Station the day before the murder—were false, products, in the first case, of an overheated mind; in the second, according to the Pinkerton files, of an instance of mistaken identity. Dorsey also had reason to question the story that had convinced many Atlantans that Frank had lusted after little Mary—the story George Epps had told to the inquest. In the wake of Epps's testimony, Pinkerton agent L. P. Whitfield had visited the victim's mother at her Bellwood home. What she said, had it been made public, could well have recast the investigation:

> Mrs. Coleman also stated that she . . . never heard Mary speak of any boy friends and that the statement that George Epps made . . . that Mary was a chum of Epps and that he had an engagement with Mary at a local drug store was to her mind incorrect, as she had heard Mary say that she detested Epps and Mrs. Coleman is sure that Epps did not have any engagement with Mary on Saturday afternoon as stated. Mrs. Coleman further stated that she has never heard Mary say anything about Superintendent Frank only as an official of the Pencil Company.

Owing to the identity of the Pinkerton agent involved, Dorsey may well have discounted Mrs. Coleman's remarks. As the case had progressed, Whitfield, unlike his rival Scott, had begun to believe that Frank was innocent. Nonetheless, Mrs. Coleman's statement—which was, of course, also in the hands of defense attorneys—was not going to go away.

Yet even as some of the allegations against Frank were coming under attack, other charges were flooding in. On May 11, the *Constitution* devoted a chunk of its front page to the story of Robert House, a private detective who alleged that on several occasions in 1912, he'd observed Frank and an unidentified girl enter a secluded grove near the Druid Hills subdivision. Eventually, House said, he'd followed the couple, adding that when Frank realized he and his consort had been spotted, he'd begged for consideration. "I don't want you to see the girl," House recalled Frank saying. "I admit that we came here for immoral purpose. Please don't make a case against us or arrest us. It would disgrace us both. We will leave instantly." According to House, he'd initially let the matter drop, informing the police of it only after the Phagan murder.

Hard upon the House revelations, Dorsey received a deposition signed by a madam named Nina Formby alleging that on the night of the murder, Frank—ostensibly a good customer—had called her looking for a room in which he could dispose of Mary Phagan's body. The Formby affidavit, dated

May 11 and taken in Newport Lanford's office by Detectives W. T. Chewning and J. N. Norris, was from the start a subject of dispute. Lanford insisted that the statement tied the crime to Frank. But in a May 14 interview, a "boarding and assignation house" proprietor named Etta Mills told a Pinkerton man that Mrs. Formby was untrustworthy. "I asked Miss Mills what she knew of the Famby [*sic*] woman," noted agent W. D. MacWorth, "and she stated that the Famby woman was fast and a hard drinker, therefore, irresponsible for her talk." When reports that her statement was being questioned hit the press, Mrs. Formby replied that Frank's supporters were trying to bribe her, telling the *Constitution* that on several occasions she'd been offered large sums to leave town until the Phagan trial ended.

After weighing the character evidence, Dorsey ultimately concluded that Frank had frequently used his position to force himself upon female employees and that such an attempt had led to Mary Phagan's murder. As he would later assert: "Extraordinary passion goaded on this man." Just as surely, however, Dorsey realized that unless the defense introduced the issue at trial, any references to Frank's past would be inadmissible.

Which was why even as he was trying to sort through the mass of sexually tinged evidence, Dorsey was preparing a circumstantial — and far more circumspect — case. At its core, his presentation to the grand jury would revolve around time: the time Mary Phagan left home, the time she reached the factory and, most critical, the time of death. Though Dr. Harris had yet to complete his lab work and Dorsey would therefore be unable to advance an exact hour to the grand jury, the preliminary examination had suggested that little Mary had died around 12:15 — about the time Frank said she'd departed his office, about the time Monteen Stover said his office was empty.

The Phagan grand jury convened at 11 A.M. on Friday, May 23, with twenty-one of the twenty-three jurors present. Journalists, of course, were barred by law from attending, but Dorsey took no chances. To make sure that neither prying eyes nor Dictographs penetrated the Thrower Building chamber in which the sessions were held, doors and windows were shut tight, crevices sealed with papers. Yet even if a reporter had managed to evade the defenses, he wouldn't have learned much, for Dorsey had decided to present only the bare amount of evidence needed to secure an indictment.

Despite these precautions, some of what went on during the two days of hearings leaked, for the *Journal* reconstructed a rough outline of Dorsey's presentation. Relying on the testimony of R. P. Barrett, the machinist who discovered the bloodstains and hair on the factory's second floor, the solicitor abandoned his flirtation with the basement as the murder site, opening his case by arguing that the crime occurred in the metal room. Dorsey then called Dr. Hurt to establish the time of death. Hurt was followed by Monteen Stover. Next came B. B. Haslett, one of the detectives who'd assisted in the investigation, and James M. Gantt, the dismissed bookkeeper. Both testified to Frank's anxiety—the former on the day of his arrest, the latter on the day of the killing.

Advancing a motive, however, was not so easy. As had recently been made public, Dr. Hurt had reached the startling conclusion that Mary Phagan had not been raped. With Dr. Harris still on the sidelines, Dorsey was forced to lean on the testimony of two nonexperts: Sergeant L. S. Dobbs, one of the responding officers, and undertaker Will Gheesling.

The thrust of Dorsey's case was straightforward: Frank, after raping Mary Phagan, murdered her and then attempted to do away with the remains. According to the *Journal*, the most telling aspect of the solicitor's presentation lay not in his theory but in the fact that he evidently did not adduce any physical evidence. Regarding the results of the tests he'd ordered on Lee's shirt and the red spots found near Barrett's workstation, Dorsey was silent. More remarkably, he didn't address what many saw as the crime's most significant clues—the murder notes.

If the grand jurors were disturbed by this lack of detail, they gave little indication of it, evidently taking on faith Dorsey's assurances that at the appropriate moment, he would reveal all. Once the solicitor left the body to its deliberations, its members needed but five minutes to return an indictment against Frank. As for Lee, whose case had also been under consideration, the jurors deferred action. He would be held as a material witness should the state need him later.

Thus Hugh Dorsey had cleared the first hurdle, and what made the victory impressive was the fact that like most such bodies, the grand jury was comprised of businessmen who might have been expected to sympathize with Leo Frank. The group's foreman, L. H. Beck, was president of Atlanta's largest hardware concern. More significantly, four Jews—George A. Gershon, A. L. Guthman, Sol Benjamin and future Chamber of Commerce president Victor Hugo Kriegshaber—sat on the panel. While it's not known how these men voted (only twelve yeas were required to indict), all except Kriegshaber (who was out of town) had been on hand. This is a notable fact, suggesting that initially, Dorsey may well have convinced three of Frank's coreligionists that his case against the superintendent was sound.

Not surprisingly, Dorsey failed to convince many other Atlanta Jews. Even less surprisingly, he failed to convince the *Georgian*. "State Faces Big Task in Trial of Frank," proclaimed the headline atop its piece on the grand jury's findings. Focusing on the state's lack of physical evidence, the Hearst sheet predicted that Luther Rosser was going to have a field day in court:

It is regarded as likely that the defense will claim first of all that the State has failed to establish Frank's connection with the crime. The defense will represent that the most the State has done is to establish that he had the opportunity to commit the murder. Frank never was seen with the girl, either on the day of the strangling or before. It is not known that he ever spoke to her except in connection with her work. None of Frank's clothing has been found with blood stains upon it. No finger prints upon the girl's body or clothes were identified as his. None of his personal belongings were found near the girl's body. Absolutely nothing was discovered in the search of the detectives that fastened the crime on him.

The *Georgian* also pointed out that there were others in the factory at the time of the slaying, "this fact opening the way to the argument that it need not have been Frank who did it." Finally, the paper addressed one of the more recent sexual allegations, arguing that even if verified, it was irrelevant:

> Should the State be able to prove beyond a doubt that it was Frank whom the park guard discovered, the defense will still be able to say that this fact no more connects Frank with the murder than it does hundreds of other persons.

Though the *Georgian* was the only paper to question the grand jury's decision, it is notable that at this critical moment, no one unconnected with the investigation praised it. No one, in short, proclaimed the case closed. In fact, the *Constitution*—whatever its allegiances to Dorsey—didn't even report Frank's indictment on its front page, playing it, instead, inside.

SEVEN

A Clean Nigger

T hat any Negro would lead Hugh Dorsey, the investigators and most Atlantans out of the wilderness of uncertainty and acrimony and onto the high plain of clarity and accord was strange enough, but that a shiftless, no-count Negro would emerge at this juncture in the case and like some Delphic oracle issue pronouncements that would ultimately be embraced over the word of a white man suggests nothing less than a miracle.

James Conley had been arrested back on May 1 after E. F. Holloway, the pencil company's day watchman, spotted the Negro sweeper standing at a second-floor factory water cooler washing red stains out of an old blue work shirt. His startled reaction—he evidently dropped the garment into a recess in the floor—suggested he had something to hide, but once he was in custody, he told a straight tale, swearing that he'd just been trying to rinse away some rust marks because he had nothing else to wear to the coroner's inquest. Typical, thought the detectives, who agreed to release Conley as soon as a chemical analysis of the stains was completed.

During the early days of his incarceration, Jim, as Conley was generally known, had done nothing to attract his captors' attention. Squat and chunky with a powerful torso and coarsely handsome features framed by a broad forehead and prominent jaw and dominated by a strong nose and slabbed lips, he'd seemed unworthy of curiosity. Only later, noting his creamy ginger-root complexion, mustache and almond-shaped eyes, would a reporter observe: "Jim Conley isn't a cornfield negro. He's more of the present-day type of city darkey."

Jim's initial statement to John Black and Harry Scott—a statement the detectives didn't even bother to take until fifteen days after his arrest—had merely confirmed what first impressions suggested. In a long recitation of his murder-day itinerary, he'd told the investigators:

On Saturday, April 26, 1913, I arose between 9 A.M. and 9:30 A.M. and ate my breakfast. At 10:30 I left the house ... and went to Peters Street and visited a number of saloons ... I purchased a half pint of rye whiskey from a negro who was walking along Peters Street about 11:00 A.M., I paying 40 cents for this whiskey. I visited the Butt-In saloon and went back to the pool tables and saw three colored men shooting dice, and I joined them and won 90 cents from them. I then purchased some beer, paying 15 cents. I then walked up the street and visited Earley's beer saloon, purchased two beers and wine, paying ten cents for same. This was all the money I spent on Peters Street, and I arrived home at 2:30 P.M. and I found L. Jones [Lorena Jones, Conley's common-law wife] there and she asked me if I had any money. I replied yes, and gave her $3.50 (one dollar in greenback, and the rest silver money). I drew $3.75 from the pencil factory on Friday . . . At 3:30 or 4:00 P.M. Saturday, April 26th, I purchased 15 cents worth of beer and then returned to the house . . . I remained at home Saturday night.

Yet even if the police had discovered a discrepancy in Conley's account, he still would have been free from suspicion, for he swore he could not do what the Phagan girl's killer or accomplice, one of whom surely authored the murder notes, could do: write. No, he was just shuffling Jim, dark and dim. As another reporter noted: "He talks slowly and deliberately with a kind of African drawl and some of his vocabulary is so peculiarly 'niggerish' that it is hard to distinguish, at times, what he means."

Little is known about the 29-year-old Conley's youth beyond the fact that he was born in Atlanta and that his parents worked at the busy Capital City Laundry on Mitchell Street. But if his job history can be taken as a guide, his life had been filled with hardship and trouble. During his teens, he sawed wood at a lumberyard. At twenty-one, he hired on at a South Forsyth Street stable. After a year grooming horses, he graduated to handling them, laboring first for Orr's Stationery Company as a delivery boy, then for a physician as a buggy driver. In 1911, Jim went to work at the National Pencil Company. Initially, he was assigned to the respected and visible position of elevator operator, but not long before the Phagan murder he was busted down to sweeper and was evidently in danger of sinking lower. By all accounts, he had a drinking problem, and according to E. F. Holloway, it had grown intolerable. "About a week before the crime was committed," the day watchman told the *Georgian,* "the forelady of the trimming and finishing department, Miss Eulah May Flowers, went to the top floor of the building to look over the stock of boxes. When Conley was not sweeping, he was supposed to fill the box-bin with boxes. When Miss Flowers moved toward the bin to look in she stumbled over a form. She screamed and fell back. It was Conley. He was dead drunk."

Neither this position—prone—nor this condition—liquored up—was new to Conley. He had been arrested so many times for drunk and disorderly conduct that he'd adopted the alias of Willie Conley in the hope that he could stay one step ahead of the law. Most of his crimes had resulted in mere fines, but on several occasions, the offenses (among them a rock-throwing incident and an armed robbery attempt) had been more serious, and he had served two sentences on the chain gang. Three months before the Phagan killing, Jim had fired a shot at Lorena Jones, whom he did not hold in high esteem. (In his initial statement, he told the police: "This woman is not my wife . . . I have [only] been having intercourse with Lorine.") Though Jim's aim proved faulty, he did graze another Negro woman standing nearby. The incident earned him a stay in jail.

Here again, though, none of this prompted questions by the detectives probing the Phagan murder. To them, ignorance, inebriation and a predisposition to violent outbursts were common black vices. That Conley might in reality have been a complex character, that he might have emerged from a society that had inculcated him with a heritage as various and an intelligence as keen as any white man's, was not considered.

Like the more populous and infinitely more powerful white city it stretched across, in writer W.E.B. Du Bois's phrase, "like a great dumbbell . . . with one great center in the east and a smaller one in the west," black Atlanta was deeply divided along lines of class and wealth. Similarly, the colored masses not only outnumbered the erudite few, they made the bigger noise.

Vine City—black Atlanta's western hub and Jim Conley's home—lay just beyond the spires of downtown's Terminal Station. This pie-shaped section of eroded red-clay hills and gullies was wedged between a railroad right-of-way and the all-black Atlanta University complex, which included not just AU but Clark, Spelman and Morehouse Colleges. The neighborhood had accommodated a majority of the new arrivals who since 1890 had doubled the capital's Negro population. Here, in shotgun shanties lining unpaved, refuse-choked streets, unskilled men, women and children lured from the depressed agricultural counties to the south by, as one put it, "the smell of money" inhaled instead the acrid aromas of raw sewage and disappointment. Here, human suffering was quantifiable: the average life span was thirty-five years.

Vine City's primary export to white Atlanta, at least as measured by the press, consisted of gambling, guzzling and gunplay. The neighborhood was the site of countless "Negro Monte Carlos," gathering spots, in the *Journal's* estimation, for the "colored man who could no more keep out of a crap game than he could resist a slice of red watermelon on the hottest day of July." Then there were the section's many "blind tigers," sources of refreshment and, like the illicit casinos, objects of frequent police raids. In these parts, things were lively, and when they were not, they were often deadly. The April 2, 1913, *Constitution* carried a typical dispatch out of Vine City:

> After an evening's festival and entertainment, a score of negro merry-makers at 45 Rock Street were thrown into excitement when shooting broke out among several of the celebrators and one of them, George Benson, dropped down dead at the hour of midnight. From midnight till dawn of yesterday morning police and detectives were busy searching the neighborhood arresting all they could find who were known to have been at the ill-fated carousal.

Sooner or later, many Vine City residents appeared before Judge Nash Broyles, the longtime magistrate of Atlanta's Recorder's Court. "Jedge Briles," as he was known to blacks, meted out justice to a disproportionately high number of Negroes (of 14,045 cases tried in 1900, 9,500 involved blacks). For reporters, the judge's courtroom was a prime source of material, and for novices, a visit constituted a rite of passage. Shortly after Harold Ross arrived in Atlanta, the *Journal* dispatched him there. Writing in his characteristic first-person-plural voice, he recorded what he saw:

> Being of that vast class of society which calls itself respectable, we have never been in police court before and are, therefore, shocked by what confronts us. Negroes—scores of them—banked up on tiers of benches on one side of a railing which divides the room in half, a dozen policemen lolling in chairs near the judge's rostrum—all of this is disconcerting. It is not even a pleasing sight. But we are out to see the police court! So we will subdue for the nonce our first and decidedly respectable inclination to leave and take seats among the policemen.

Most reporters who spent time in Judge Broyles's court found the assignment more congenial than Ross's account suggests he did, cranking out sketches that reinforced white Atlantans' views. A *Constitution* account of some byplay that ensued one afternoon in 1910 during a debate between Broyles and a Negro defendant regarding the identification of a certain powdery white substance is emblematic:

> "Shucks, jedge, I'll just show you dat ain't no cocaine." Two long, black fingers trembling with eagerness shot across the bar of justice and dipped into the little black box which Recorder Broyles held in his hand and an instant later, Ben Green, a denizen of Darktown, was smacking his lips in absolute disregard of fines or jail sentences. Ben had had his "dose."

Predictably, the citizens of Vine City were not amused by Nash Broyles. Over the years he had sentenced thousands of them to the Atlanta Stockade. The prison—which even now dominates a high bluff on the city's eastern fringes—took its cue architecturally from the Tower, right down to the crenellated ramparts. But where the Tower merely looked medieval, the Stockade was a genuine throwback. A 1909 investigation by the *Georgian* determined that cell blocks were infested by rats. Inmates wore riveted shackles, and troublemakers were strapped into the "bucking machine," a device of the warden's own invention. Among the blacks tortured in this apparatus was a thirteen-year-old girl who later died. As Judge Broyles freely admitted, he would never consign white children to the stockade, for "to do so would mean their complete ruin."

That Atlanta's Negroes did not demand better treatment—that they did not rise up in protest—was due to the vigilant efforts of the twin hobgoblins the city's whites had contrived to keep them in their place: Jim Crow and Judge Lynch.

Atlanta was the capital not only of the New South but of the Jim Crow South. In 1905, the Georgia general assembly, responding to the influx of blacks pouring into the city, had enacted one of the region's first Jim Crow ordinances, the Separate Park Law. Soon thereafter, restaurants, bars, train cars, barbershops, elevators, the Grant Park Zoo, haberdasheries, even the Carnegie Library were segregated by race.

Atlanta's Negroes were also held in check by an ominous extralegal authority. Between 1882 and 1930, Georgia recorded 508 lynchings (only Mississippi eclipsed this number). "In almost every other state," one historian later noted, "the practice hit a peak between 1880 and 1900 and remained steady or declined thereafter; however Georgians lynched more blacks between 1900 and 1920 than they had in the previous twenty years." Most such atrocities took place in rural communities, but not always.

On a Saturday afternoon in late September 1906, Atlanta's 3 afternoon newspapers—the *Journal,* the *Georgian* and the *Evening News* (soon to merge with the *Georgian*)—had reported the rape of a white woman by a "black fiend." With the state having just endured a gubernatorial campaign that turned on the issue of disfranchising Negroes, the stories were incendiary. Still, a disaster might have been averted had it not been for the *News.* In the space of just a few hours, the paper issued several extras, each bannered by irresponsible and fallacious headlines: TWO ASSAULTS, THIRD ASSAULT, FOURTH ASSAULT. By sundown, some 5,000 angry whites had gathered on Decatur Street. From the top of a car, Mayor Jimmy Woodward had begged for calm, but the crowd ignored him. By 11:00, the mob had increased to 11,000, and its members were well armed—one hardware store sold $16,000 worth of guns and ammunition that evening. It was at this point that shots rang out. The two black barbers on duty at Herndon's Barber Shop offered no resistance, but they were murdered anyway, their bodies dumped at the foot of the Marietta Street monument to the bard of the New South, Henry Grady. Thereafter, chaos reigned. As one contingent of rioters bludgeoned a crippled black shoeshine boy in the middle of Peachtree Street, another stormed a hotel, killing three Negro passersby. A third group breached a trolley station and began pulling black passengers from their seats. All the while, the police refused to intercede, and Governor Joseph M. Terrell initially turned down a request to declare martial law.

By the time the militia was summoned, the worst was over. When Sunday dawned, 20 Negroes lay dead.

Sunday night, when the reassembled white mob marched again—this time on Darktown, the east side counterpart to Vine City—the torch-carrying vanguard was met by a hail of bullets, and its members retreated. As the evening wore on, several other assaults were similarly repulsed. Atlanta's Negroes, armed with guns shipped south in caskets earlier in the summer by a Chicago undertaker, had made their stand. While fighting would resume on Monday, black leaders cited the defense of Darktown as the turning point in the conflict. The irony here was not lost on these leaders. In the words of William Crogman, future president of Clark College: "The whites kill . . . good men. But the lawless element, the element we have condemned fights back, and it is to these people that we owe our lives."

When the rioting ceased, 25 Negroes were dead, and 150 had been wounded. (Just one white was listed as killed, although years later a black mortician asserted that the police, striving to minimize casualties, ordered him to bury several whites in Negro cemeteries under cover of darkness). Moreover, a terrifying message had been delivered. A letter to the *Georgian*'s editor put it succinctly: "Let's continue to kill all negroes who commit the unmentionable crime and make eunichs of all new male issues before they are eight days old." Though such surgical solutions were not in this instance implemented, the effect of such talk was profound. In the wake of the 1906 clash, "good darkeys" bowed and shuffled a bit more obsequiously, while "bad niggers" juked and jived a bit more cartoonishly. Either way, they kept out of white folks' line of fire by sinking into minstrel show Negroism. (For those who protested, retribution was swift. Jesse Max Barber, editor of Atlanta's *Voice of the Negro,* fled to Chicago after the authorities threatened to sentence him to the chain gang unless he retracted a letter to the *New York World* accusing Atlanta's newspapers of instigating the riot.) The extent to which such behavior was an act varied from individual to individual, but one thing is certain: Only a damn black fool would not have acted like a damn black fool had he found himself in Jim Conley's shoes.

Despite the fact that Jim Crow and Judge Lynch were so firmly ensconced, an altogether different black Atlanta—one of financial and cultural attainment—was arising a few blocks north of Darktown as well as around the west-side Negro colleges. This community was spurred by catalysts from both without and within Dixie.

The catalyst from without was the very embodiment of America's Robber Baron might: John D. Rockefeller. Since 1882, when he donated $250 to the struggling all-black Atlanta Female Baptist Seminary, Rockefeller, a devout Baptist, had functioned as the great white angel to the city's education-minded Negro aspirants. In 1884, when the Standard Oil magnate and his wife, the former Laura Spelman, visited Atlanta to check on the seminary's progress, the trustees changed the school's name to Spelman College. In the wake of this emotional event, Rockefeller began buying land on Atlanta's west side, providing the real estate not only for Spelman's expansion but for two new colleges for Negro men—Clark and Morehouse. In 1886, Rockefeller Hall, Spelman's first brick building, was completed, and over the years it had been joined by other impressive structures. By 1913, graduates noted for their Christian zeal and Victorian manners were marching forth yearly from these institutions.

The catalysts from within were, in their way, also Rockefelleresque—visionary black capitalists who saw in the vacuum the Jim Crow South had created fertile ground for businesses that could provide goods and services to the neglected Negro market. On April 1, 1913, several hundred well-dressed Negroes had gathered on Auburn Avenue, Atlanta's Great Black Way, to dedicate the most visible manifestation of this homegrown Negro achievement: the $110,000, five-story Odd Fellows Building, the city's first office structure paid for and built by blacks and as such a symbol of the race's strivings.

Like several of Atlanta's other notable Negro enterprises—most especially Standard Life Insurance and Atlanta Mutual Life—the Odd Fellows offered something blacks could not obtain elsewhere: loans at fair rates. By 1916, the society boasted assets of $1 million.

In most cases, the fiscal well-being of fledgling black concerns like the Odd Fellows was precarious. In the 1920s, the Odd Fellows, owing to a feud among members, collapsed into receivership, while Standard Life fell into the hands of outsiders. Still, that such operations had opened their doors at all signaled a new day for Georgia blacks, and in the case of Atlanta Mutual

Life, which was a genuine and enduring success, the benefits were not just monetary.

Atlanta Mutual was the brainchild of Alonzo F. Herndon, who dominated not only the black community's finances but its politics (he helped found the NAACP). And he owed it all to his skills in the tonsorial arts. Simply put, Herndon gave a stylish haircut.

Born a slave, Herndon had opened his eponymously named barbershop shortly after arriving in Atlanta in 1882. Due to his deft touch with a blade and his elegant bearing, Herndon's business prospered from the start, attracting an all-white clientele that included lawyers and politicians from every part of Georgia. Eventually, Herndon moved uptown to Peachtree Street, in 1913 expanding and redecorating his shop. Now Dixie's Beau Brummels entered this manly sanctum through sixteen-foot mahogany-and-beveled-glass doors (copies of a pair Herndon had admired during a vacation to Paris) that opened into a room tiled floor to ceiling in white marble and lit by bronze electric chandeliers. Lining the walls, twenty-three chairs attended by liveried Negro barbers beckoned.

By keeping the South's white bosses talcumed and trimmed, Herndon became a millionaire, and in 1905, he founded Atlanta Mutual. Within six years, the business had grown from a one-room outfit into a behemoth boasting 70,000 policyholders and 84 branch offices.

Herndon's enduring legacy to black Atlanta can be seen in the institutions he endowed, institutions that not only provided a setting for Negro society but cast spiritual and educational light into the firmament. At the center of his elite black universe stood the First Congregational Church, a stone chapel that to this day presides over Courtland Street in East Atlanta. The building was erected in 1908 and featured a library, a small gym and cooking facilities that were the envy of both black and white Christians throughout the city. The men and women who filled the sanctuary on Sundays included lawyers, educators and doctors who gave their prayers to God and their votes to the Republican Party. Testifying to the congregation's ties to the party of emancipation is the fact that President Theodore Roosevelt attended the dedication services.

In the end, what made the First Congregational Church a force in black Atlanta was its pastor. The Reverend Henry Hugh Proctor stood six feet six inches tall, and out of doors he always wore a black Stetson and a long black double-breasted jacket with a two-button flyaway tail. "When you saw him walking down the street," recalled his friend and parishioner Kathleen Adams, "you knew he was a godly man. Small children pictured God as looking like him." But Proctor was not godly just in bearing. Son of a Tennessee slave, he was a graduate of Nashville's Fisk University and had studied at Yale's Divinity School. (He did not finish his doctorate, but he completed a thesis entitled "The Theology of Slave Songs.")

Despite Proctor's academic affinity for Negro spirituals, his pulpit stylings bore no resemblance to those soulfully gyrating, amen-riddled perorations that left congregations in so many of Atlanta's black houses of worship slain in the spirit. Declared Kathleen Adams: "Reverend Proctor was a teacher in his pulpit. His language was superb and dignified. The only man I ever heard who matched him was W.E.B. Du Bois. Church was used as a schoolroom."

Henry Hugh Proctor's friends included the great Negro leaders of the era. When visiting Atlanta, Booker T. Washington usually stayed with him. At the same time, Proctor was on good terms with the renowned educator's avowed foe, Atlanta University's W.E.B. Du Bois, whose book *The Souls of Black Folk* took Washington to task for capitulating to the white man's view that black colleges should provide industrial as opposed to liberal arts educations.

That Proctor could maintain a relationship with a radical such as Du Bois (the author, sociologist and NAACP cofounder resigned from Atlanta University's faculty in 1910 after his militant opinions led to a clash with the administration) bespoke great diplomatic skills, for he was himself a conciliator when it came to whites. Proctor's sermons were often homilies taken from the lives of such men as Rockefeller and Roosevelt. Meanwhile, he regularly solicited funds from the likes of Coca-Cola's Asa G. Candler. Then there was the fact that his Negro critics accused him, so to speak, of harboring Caucasians in the woodpile.

The charge against Proctor and his parishioners was based on skin pigmentation, but in a broader sense, it went to the heart of the divide that separated Atlanta's uptown blacks from their poor country cousins. Benjamin Davis, publisher of the city's most combative Negro newspaper, the *Atlanta Independent,* frequently articulated the complaint. In his editorials, Davis accused Proctor and his flock of "having exclusive mulattoes in their society and for their associates." He believed that the Congregationalists practiced their own form of segregation.

Davis was particularly vexed by the sponsors of a 1914 black medical convention who asked that "only light-skinned Atlanta negroes" attend their soiree. He also resented the fact that the Owls, Atlanta University's most exclusive fraternity, selected members "on color and financial status." As John Dittmer notes in *Black Georgia in the Progressive Era, 1900–1920:* "Mulattoes as a group had economic and educational advantages dating back to slavery, when they made up a disproportionately large percentage of house servants and free blacks. As sons and daughters of slaveholders they often received special training and privileges . . . Subsequent economic success enabled them to educate their own children, who in turn became doctors, teachers, and business leaders." Recipients of this good fortune displayed prejudice toward the rural blacks who by 1900 had begun streaming into the city. Kathleen Adams spoke for her crowd when she snapped: "I remember when Martin Luther King [Sr.] came to town in the back of a wagon." (When the father of the civil rights leader arrived around 1919, he actually drove a Model T, but by his own confession, he was a "country bumpkin.")

Yet the hauteur of this light-skinned aristocracy notwithstanding, Benjamin Davis's reasoning collapsed in the face of one inarguable fact: Neither Jim Crow nor Judge Lynch bothered making the distinctions that so troubled him. Furthermore, men like Herndon and Proctor, while clearly sophisticates, earnestly attempted to raise up the very Negroes whom Davis believed they scorned, and their principal vehicle was education. As Proctor liked to say: "Our church is the mother of Atlanta University."

First Congregational provided Atlanta University's endowment. To be sure, AU and neighboring Morehouse, Clark and Spelman exposed their students to a life beyond the ken of the Vine City children who lived within sight of the AU clock tower. (Freshmen grappled with Cicero's *De Senectute* and *De Amicitia* and Xenophon's *Anabasis,* while seniors took Du Bois's Afro-American history class.) But the colleges' alumni and by extension the Negro gentry did not ignore their unlettered brothers and sisters. Many graduates of Atlanta University went into Vine City and, in classrooms that public school superintendent William Slaton, the governor-elect's brother, termed "a disgrace to civilization and unfit for cattle," taught youngsters to read and write. Forty-five percent of the city's Negro teachers were AU products, and most of the others came from Morehouse and Spelman.

It was in this way that Atlanta's black aristocracy ministered to the multitude. Here was how even the unlikeliest of Vine City characters could have acquired the tools that enabled initiates to decipher and form written words and enter the larger world.

While it never would have occurred to Detectives Black and Scott to ask, Jim Conley was one of these initiates. Indeed, he'd been directly touched by the institutions John D. Rockefeller, Alonzo Herndon and Henry Hugh Proctor built. In the late 1890s, Jim had attended Mitchell Street Elementary, Atlanta's best Negro public school. There, he'd been tutored by Alice Carey (Spelman, 1893) and Ara Cooke (Atlanta University, 1896). Mrs. Carey was Mitchell Street's principal, Miss Cooke a teacher, and though they had Jim as a pupil for only two years, by the time he left, he could read and write.

Just how long Conley thought he could fool John Black and Harry Scott with his impersonation of a mumbling, subliterate Rastus is unknown. Most likely, he believed the detectives would never catch on. Yet on Friday, May 16, the police began to perceive their prisoner if not for who he was, then at least for who he wasn't.

This revised portrait of Conley might never have emerged had not two Pinkerton operatives paid a call at the Southwest Atlanta home of Mrs. Arthur White. Why it had taken the detectives so long to renew their interest in Mrs. White—who'd figured previously in the investigation due to the fact that on April 26 she'd dropped by the factory to see her husband, one of the mechanics who'd been working on the fourth floor—is uncertain. In their initial meeting, Leo Frank had told Harry Scott that Mrs. White had mentioned seeing a strange black man lurking in the lobby during her visit. At the time, no one followed up, but upon hearing Mrs. White repeat the story ("To the best of her recollection," the Pinkertons reported, "he was a black negro and dressed in dark blue clothing and hat"), the agents thought of Conley. After finishing with Mrs. White, they rushed to headquarters. There, in a conference with John Black, they inquired into the status of the man who at this juncture had been sitting uncharged in the police lockup for two weeks.

What inspired the detectives' next move has always been disputed. Subsequently, Frank would claim that he was "the man who found out or paved the way to find out that Jim Conley could write," asserting that upon learning of the authorities' interest in Conley, he sent a messenger bearing this intelligence to the Pinkertons. Perhaps so, but in the report the agents submitted to both defense counsel and the police, they failed to mention Frank's contribution. They wrote that following their meeting with John Black, they had gone to the National Pencil Company and questioned E. F. Holloway and assistant superintendents Herbert Schiff and N. V. Darley as to Conley's ability to write. It was there, they reported, that "Mr. Holloway stated that Conley could read and write for he had often seen the negro with pencil and pad taking stock in the various bins." It was also there that the operatives learned that Frank had been paying the jewelry firm of Patrick & Thompson a dollar a week from Conley's salary, which suggested a previously unknown intimacy between boss and employee.

Acting on the suggestion of either Schiff or Frank, who later contended that he instructed his emissary to tell the investigators to "look into a drawer in the [office] safe where they would find the card of a jeweler from whom Conley bought a watch on the installment," the Pinkerton agents visited Patrick & Thompson. There, an employee gave them a contract bearing Conley's signature. Additionally, the employee told the men they would find similar documents at Saul & Abelson and Jones & Phillips Jewelers.

At this point, the agents began to realize the consequence of their discovery, and after securing the other contracts, they returned to the Pinkerton offices and made a comparison of Conley's signatures with photographic copies of the notes found beside Mary Phagan's body. According to their report, the results were conclusive: "The handwriting appears to be identical, all characteristics being similar."

On the strength of this finding, the Pinkerton agents descended into Vine City to interview Lorena Jones. The men met Conley's common-law wife at her 172 Rhodes Street home. She divulged two important clues. First she said that Conley, contrary to his original claim, owned four shirts, a revelation that gave the lie to his reason for washing the blue one. Then she alluded to a disturbing incident that occurred a few hours after little Mary's murder and suggested that at the time her husband was eerily animated. As the investigators reported it:

> About 3:00 P.M. on Saturday, April 26th 1913 she left James Conley sitting in front of the fire place in her home while she went to a nearby store to get some snuff; that when she returned to her home she did not see Conley and she stepped to a washstand . . . and Conley jumped up from behind the washstand and she said that she screamed and Conley said he hid from her just to scare her.

By Saturday morning, word of the Pinkerton agents' breakthroughs had reached nearly everyone connected with the case. But what the detectives perceived and what Conley revealed still differed. (Indeed, this was the weekend Conley made the statement maintaining that he'd spent April 26 innocently.) As Harry Scott reported: "We were unsuccessful in having Conley make any damaging admissions in this case." Moreover, when the detectives brought Mrs. Arthur White to Decatur Street to view a lineup that included Jim and twelve other blacks, the results were inconclusive. First she picked out "a negro wearing a green derby hat," then Conley. Regardless of the headway the investigators made on Friday, Jim remained elusive. On Sunday, the police decided to submit him to the specialty of the station house, the third degree.

On what was otherwise a dull and drowsy afternoon, Harry Scott and John Black removed Conley from his cell, placed him in a six-by-eight-foot cubicle, beamed a light in his face and actually tossed the key out the open transom into the hallway where the *Constitution*'s ubiquitous Britt Craig was stationed. From this vantage, Craig managed to hear what occurred in the tiny room, and his account gave Atlantans the most detailed picture of how the detectives started to drag a story from Conley:

> "Well, Jim," Black began, "we've got the deadwood on you. Better cough up and tell us something."
>
> "Honest, white folks, I swear 'fore God and high heaven I don't know a thing," Conley replied.
>
> "Listen," Scott asked as he made a show of pulling a piece of paper from his pocket, "can you write?"
>
> "Naw, sir, I can't. I never could."
>
> "Will you swear it?"
>
> "I shore will."
>
> "Do you know the penalty for perjury?"
>
> "Naw, sir—what is it?"
>
> "Twenty in the gang—maybe more."
>
> "What's perjury?"
>
> "Swearing a lie."
>
> "But I ain't goin' to swear no lie."
>
> "You will if you swear you can't write," Scott replied, unfolding a watch contract bearing Jim's signature and handing it to the prisoner.

According to Craig, Conley was momentarily dumbfounded, but after seeing that the officers indeed had the deadwood on him, he conceded: "White folks, I'm a liar."

Following this admission, Scott and Black asked Conley to jot down his ABCs, which he did. Then one of them ordered: "Write, 'that long tall black negro did this by himself.' " Upon hearing the words, Jim winced, but slowly, deliberately, he again began scribbling. When he was finished, his inquisitors collected his work, observing that he favored some of the same idiosyncratic spellings that graced the murder notes. With no further ado, the detectives accused Conley of writing the messages found by little Mary's body.

> "I didn't do it," Jim swore. " 'Fore God, I didn't."
>
> This protestation inspired Scott to mutter: "You'll be hung just as sure as you're a foot high and black."
>
> "But I ain't guilty," Jim again protested. "I don't know a thing about them notes or that killing—honest, white folks."
>
> To which Black added as if for good measure: "There ain't a jury in the world—even a nigger jury—that'd believe you didn't kill this girl. They'd hang you or lynch you—likely lynching."

On that note, the detectives put a halt to the grilling, but instead of returning Conley to his old quarters, they took him to a basement level isolation cell described in the press as dark and desolate. There, Jim would ponder the events of the past few hours.

How long Conley remained in solitude is unknown, but on Saturday morning, May 24 — a week after being submitted to the third degree and just hours before the grand jury indicted Leo Frank — he summoned John Black and uttered the words that would eventually enthrall all Atlanta: "Boss, I wrote those notes."

Within minutes, Conley found himself standing in Newport Lanford's office. There, in the presence of Harry Scott, C. Gay February, Lanford and Black, the Negro enlarged upon his startling admission. Realizing the import of Jim's testimony, the officers soon escorted him to the Thrower Building. Hugh Dorsey had earlier been informed that Conley could write, but he had put little stock in the news. His reaction to this latest revelation was apparently not much more enthusiastic. (The solicitor did tell the grand jurors of Jim's contention, but he would later assert that the body returned its indictment on the strength of the case as he'd presented it.) However, he was intrigued enough that he sat in with the group from headquarters as February — who'd figured so prominently in both the 1910 detective department scandal and the Felder episode — took Conley's statement:

> On Friday evening before the holiday, about four minutes to one o'clock, Mr. Frank came up the aisle on the fourth floor . . . where I was working and asked me to come to his office . . . When I went down . . . he asked me could I write and I told him yes I could write a little bit, and he gave me a scratch pad and . . . told me to put on there "dear mother, a long, tall, black negro did this by himself," and he told me to write it two or three times on there. I wrote it on a white scratch pad, single ruled. He went to his desk and pulled out another scratch pad, a brownish looking scratch pad, and looked at my writing and wrote on that himself . . . he asked me if I wanted a cigarette, and I told him yes . . . and he pulled out a box of cigarettes . . . and in that box he had $2.50, two paper dollars and two quarters, and I taken one of the cigarettes and handed him the box and told him he had some money in the box, and he said that was all right I was welcome to that for I was a good working negro around there, and then he asked me . . . if I knew the night watchman and I told him no sir, I didn't know him, and he asked me if I ever saw him in the basement and I told him no sir, I never did see him down there, but he could ask the fireman and

maybe he could tell him more about that than I could, and then Mr. Frank was laughing and jollying and going on in the office, and I asked him not to take out any money for that watch man I owed, for I didn't have any to spare, and he told me he wouldn't, but he would see to me getting some money a little bit later. He told me he had some wealthy people in Brooklyn and then he held his head up and looking out of the corner of his eyes said "Why should I hang?" . . . When I asked him not to take out any money for the watch, he said you ought not to buy any watch, for that big fat wife of mine wants me to buy her an automobile but he wouldn't do it; I never did see his wife. On Tuesday morning . . . before Mr. Frank got in jail, he came up the aisle where I was sweeping and held his head over to me and whispered . . . be a good boy and that was all he said to me.

Here at last was an answer to the conundrum that had stumped the police since Sergeant L. S. Dobbs discovered the murder notes on the factory's basement floor, yet it was an answer wrapped in riddles. Consequently, neither Lanford nor Dorsey expressed much faith in it. To the contrary, their initial reaction was one of incredulity, even fear, each contending that Conley's rambling tale was untrue and a threat to the chain in which they'd ensnared the guilty man. The detective chief quickly branded Jim's disclosure "false in every detail." Meanwhile, the solicitor spent Saturday afternoon quizzing Conley, initiating a catechism that would continue off and on for two days. As one investigator later declared: "Never has a witness been put through such a severe cross-examination." But to no avail. Jim "stoutly maintained" his story.

On Monday, after Black and Scott administered another dictation test and Conley again spelled key phrases and words (among them "night watchman" as "night witch") just as they were spelled in the genuine items, the official skepticism began to diminish. "Conley wrote the notes," one detective announced. "It doesn't take an expert to realize that beyond a shadow of a doubt his hand penned the words on the two bits of paper."

Yet despite the growing consensus that Jim wrote the notes, officers still doubted the rest of his story. For starters, there was the matter of timing. Observed one reporter: "Conley's delay in making his confession until Frank's indictment seemed likely is a link against him." Then there was the fact that no one at Decatur Street believed that Frank would have asked Jim "Why should I hang?" when to do so would have been to confess in advance that he was going to commit a capital crime. This objection pointed to the most glaring implausibility of all—Conley's claim that the notes were composed a day before the murder. Everything about the evidence suggested that the act had been spontaneous. As the *Georgian* remarked: "No theory that has placed the responsibility of the crime upon Frank has held that he planned it deliberately a day before it was committed. The unanimous theory of those who have believed Frank guilty is that he did it on the necessity of the moment to prevent the girl from revealing the attack which is supposed to have proceeded the killing. If Conley's story is true, it means that the murder was premeditated." Which is why detectives, while conceding that Jim wrote the notes, were convinced he was lying about the rest of it.

The squad at headquarters was not alone in expressing such qualms. As a whole, the press remained similarly unpersuaded. At the *Journal* and the *Constitution,* writers essentially ignored Jim's affidavit. At the *Georgian,* meanwhile, the smart money—influenced not a little by the sheet's biases— was betting that Jim himself would be indicted for the murder. Argued the Hearst forces: "Careful study of the negro's story has revealed absurdities in its structure which bring the deed to Conley's door."

Disturbed by the inconsistencies in Conley's exceedingly peculiar tale and aware that he could as easily ruin the state's case as strengthen it, the detectives now chose a new tack. Over the next three days, Harry Scott persistently accused Jim of murdering Mary Phagan and vowed to see him hang for it. Meanwhile, John Black commiserated with Conley, bringing him drinks, pies, sandwiches and consolation.

Not surprisingly, the *Georgian* accused the officers of manipulating Conley to deliver testimony damaging to Frank: "The police questions were, of course, all put with the idea of gaining information against Frank. The police refused to admit that suspicion was turning or should turn to Conley, who has told one falsehood after another since his arrest. They tried resolutely to construe every one of his statements as against Frank and would not admit that the continued contradictions of the negro made his value as a witness next to nothing." Simultaneously, however, the *Journal* contended that the investigators "questioned [Jim] as if they are convinced he committed the murder."

Whatever the detectives' motives, their actions left Conley scared and disoriented. Observed the *Constitution:* "Conley grew weak, lost appetite, slept very little." On Tuesday, May 28, the Negro was removed from his cell and again taken to Newport Lanford's office. There, he confronted two sights calculated to heighten his distress. One was the person of E. F. Holloway, the man who'd spotted him washing his shirt on May 1. Holloway was there to state that he had also seen Jim somewhere else—at the pencil factory on April 26. But it wasn't Holloway's presence that undid the Negro. Rather, it was a copy of that afternoon's *Georgian.* Boomed the page-one banner: SUSPICION TURNED TO CONLEY; ACCUSED BY FACTORY

FOREMAN. In the story that inspired this screamer, Holloway proclaimed that he was "thoroughly convinced that [Conley] strangled Mary Phagan when about half drunk." After reading the article, Jim requested a private audience with John Black. The next day, C. Gay February notarized what would be referred to as Conley's second affidavit:

I make this statement, my second statement, in regard to the murder of Mary Phagan at the National Pencil Factory. In my first statement I made the statement that I went to the pencil factory on Friday, April 25, 1913, and went to Frank's office at four minutes to one, which is a mistake. I made this statement in regard to Friday in order that I might not be accused of knowing anything of this murder, for I thought that if I put myself there on Saturday, they might accuse me of having a hand in it, and I now make my second and last statement regarding the matter freely and voluntarily, after thinking over the situation, and I have made up my mind to tell the whole truth . . . without the promise of any reward or from force or fear of punishment in any way.

I got up Saturday morning, April 26th, between 9 and half past 9. I was at home, 172 Rhodes Street. There is a clock on the Atlanta University and I looked at that clock after I put on my clothes; I went to the door and poured some water out of the wash pan . . . Then I washed my face and I eat some steak and some liver and bread and drank a cup of tea, and then I sat down in a chair a little while, about ten minutes, I guess, and then I told my wife to give me back the three dollars and I would get some paper money to keep her from losing it, to pay her rent with, and she gave it to me, and I told her I was going to Peters Street, and I went to Peters Street. [Here, Conley repeated the description of his visits to the Butt-In Saloon and other haunts.] Then I started to the Capital City Laundry and on my way there I met Mr. Frank, at the corner of Forsyth and Nelson Streets going to Montags, and he told me to wait a few minutes, and he asked me where I was going, and I told him I was going to . . . see my mother, and he didn't say nothing, only he said to wait a minute until he come back . . . and I stood there until he come back, he was gone about 20 minutes, I guess. He come back and told me to come to the factory, that he wanted to see me, and I went to the factory with him, walking behind him . . . Just to the right of the steps as you go in, he put a box for me to sit on. There was some great big boxes back further. He told me to sit down there until I heard him whistle. He just took his foot and pushed a box over there for me to sit on. Then he told me not to let Mr. Darley see me. [Here, Conley provided an account of the people—among them Mrs. White, E. F. Holloway, a young factory girl named Mattie Smith, and N. V. Darley—who came in and out of the plant that morning.] After . . . about 15 or 20 minutes . . . there . . .

wasn't any passing at all, and I sat there on the box with my head against the trash barrel. I stretched my feet out and put my hat in my lap . . . and the next thing that attracted my attention, Mr. Frank whistled for me twice, just like this (indicating), and when he whistled I went on up the stairs and the double doors on the stairway were closed and I opened them and they shut themselves, and Mr. Frank was standing at the top of the steps and he said, "You heard me, did you?" and I said, "Yes, sir," and Mr. Frank grabbed me by my arm and he was squeezing my arm so tight his hand was trembling. He had his glasses on, and he had me just like he was walking down the street with a lady, and like he didn't want me to look behind me at all, and I thought it was because he had me so tight that made him tremble, and he carried me through the first office and into his private office, and then he come back in there, and he didn't say nothing, he grabbed up a box of sulphur matches, and he went back in the outer office, the door was open between his office and the outer office, and then he saw two ladies coming and he said to me, "Gee, here comes Miss Emma Clark and Miss Corinthia Hall" and he came back in there to me, he was walking fast and seemed to be excited, and he said to me, "Come right in here, Jim," and he motioned to the wardrobe and I was a little slow about it and Mr. Frank grabbed me and gave me a shove and put me in the wardrobe and he shut the doors and told me to stay there until after they had gone, and I just heard Miss Emma say, "Good morning, Mr. Frank are you alone?" and Mr. Frank said "Yes." . . . I stayed in the wardrobe a pretty good while, for the whiskey I had drank got me to sweating . . . After a while, Mr. Frank . . . let me out . . . and I said, "I got too hot in there," and he said, "Yes, I see you are sweating." . . . Then Mr. Frank asked me to sit down in a chair . . . and he said, "Jim, can you write?" [Here, Conley recounted how Frank, after dictating the murder notes to him, gave him a box of cigarettes.] . . . Then I asked Mr. Frank if that was all he wanted with me right now, and he said yes . . . and I went to the beer saloon across the street and opened the cigarette box and it had two paper dollars in there and two silver quarters, and I laughed and said, "Good luck has done struck me," and I bought a ten-cent double header and then went back to Peters Street . . . and I walks up there to the moving picture show and looked at the pictures and they didn't seem to be any good . . . and I struck out for home, and when I got home it was about half past two o'clock, and I took the bucket and went to Joe Carr's at Mangum and Magnolia Street, and got fifteen cents worth of beer in it and came back home and sent the little girl to get a dime's worth of stove wood and a nickle's worth of pan sausage, and I eat half the pan sausage up raw, and I give my old lady $3.50, and the other little change I kept it, and I laid down across the bed and there is where I stayed until about half past eight that night, and I got up and set in front of the fire a little while and got to swimming at the head and I didn't leave home no more until Sunday. [Here, Conley detailed how he'd spent the following day, asserting that he'd not learned that the girl he called "Mary Puckett" had been murdered until he returned to work on Monday.] . . . On Thursday . . . I got my subpoena . . . Then I went down to wash my shirt so I could have a clean one to wear to court . . . I got a little rust on it . . . They brought me down here and found there was no blood on the shirt, and give me my shirt back, and that's all I know.

Conley's second affidavit, as opposed to his first, created a sensation. Both the *Journal* and the *Constitution* splashed the Negro's tale across their front pages. The investigators who had labored so long on the case also endorsed the statement. Harry Scott insisted that it "had practically cleared the mystery and was the most important bit of evidence in the hands of the state." At headquarters, the reviews were just as glowing. "The negro Conley is regarded by detectives as their most material witness," reported the *Constitution*. "He is the missing link, they think, which connects the chain of circumstantial evidence which they have gathered."

Yet for all this, dissenters still could be found. Indeed, there was a nest of them at the National Pencil Company. Just hours after Conley's second statement was secured, the *Journal* interviewed Schiff, Darley and Holloway. With Schiff speaking for all three, the men proposed that the new affidavit's principal revelation—the news that Jim was at the scene of the crime on April 26—cast suspicion not on Frank but on the Negro:

Now the theory of the crime we entertain is simply this: Conley came in following Miss Smith and expected to rob her as she came down with her money. When Mr. Darley happened to come down with her, Conley gave up his attempt but continued to wait. Later, he saw little Mary Phagan come in and waited until she came down. Then he grabbed her and tried to get her purse. A scuffle by the elevator ensued and the negro knocked the girl down the elevator shaft. He quickly followed her, going down by the trapdoor. He found her cut and bruised and unconscious. Then he tied the cord around her neck and choked her to death. He wrote the notes himself and then pulled the staple off the rear basement door and left the place.

In sum, the men hypothesized that the murderer was not, as Hugh Dorsey contended, motivated by lust but by a pathetic desire to steal the $1.20 in wages Mary Phagan had collected the day of the crime. To buttress their point, they asked a simple question: What happened to little Mary's purse and the two half dollars and change she had received only seconds before her death?

The misgivings cited by the pencil company employees found a sympathetic ear at the *Georgian.* Remaining true to its pro-Frank stance, the paper observed: "Three responsible officials of the plant have outlined plausible theories as to how the negro could have committed the crime. They have compiled a most laudable explanation of how he killed the Phagan girl. With each cross-examination of the negro by the police in their attempts to secure more evidence against Frank, Conley has only ensnared himself."

John Black and Harry Scott, however, did not share such a belief. Reported the *Journal:* "Little if any credence is placed by the detectives in the theory of the officials and employees of the National Pencil Company that Mary Phagan was killed by James Conley and that his motive was robbery." While the investigators were puzzled by the disappearance of the victim's bag and pay, they were sure they'd turn up. Still, the doubts tempered the euphoria at headquarters. Moreover, the police developed some misgivings of their own. Most vexing was the fact that nowhere in the second affidavit did Jim ever indicate that when he wrote the notes, he knew a crime had been committed. By his account, Frank had simply dictated them out of the blue. In hopes of getting to the bottom of it all, the detectives decided to stage a confrontation between the accuser and the accused.

Around 8:00 P.M. on Wednesday, May 28, a delegation consisting of Chiefs Beavers and Lanford, Harry Scott and Jim Conley marched the few blocks from 175 Decatur Street to the Fulton County Tower. At the door, the men spoke to Sheriff Wheeler Mangum, who in turn conveyed their proposal to his star prisoner, whose friend Milton Klein happened to be visiting. For Frank, the invitation presented a terrible quandary. If he was guilty, the last thing he would have wanted was to sit down with Conley in the authorities' presence. Yet there were perfectly innocent reasons why he would have been wary, chief among them his memories of the disastrous jailhouse session Scott and Detective John Black had brokered between Newt Lee and him.

Legally, as Chief Beavers had been instructed before he embarked on this mission, Frank was not required to see anyone outside his lawyer's presence—at the time an impossibility, as two days earlier, Luther Rosser had taken the train to rugged Rabun County where he was representing the Georgia Railway and Electric Company in its ongoing court fight to open the Tallulah Gorge power plant. Yet after Frank, using Klein as a go-between, declined to meet with Conley, the police cited the decision as evidence of the superintendent's involvement in Mary Phagan's murder.

"Detectives who pin faith to the negro's story and believe Frank guilty," reported the *Constitution*, "speculate upon the prisoner's unwillingness to face the sweeper. If he is not guilty, they say, he likely wouldn't object to facing the negro. They say that it is damaging to his plea of innocence to refuse the negro an audience." Eventually, Conley himself seconded this opinion, telling the *Journal:* "I wish they would let me face Mr. Frank and tell him just what I have told the detectives. One of us would go down, and it wouldn't be me."

While such insinuations further blackened Leo Frank's reputation, the detectives still faced the dilemma that had inspired their attempt to bring Conley and the superintendent together in the first place. The inconsistencies permeating Jim's depositions had not gone away. Accordingly, the officers decided to sweat the Negro yet again.

The Thursday afternoon interrogation of Conley lasted four hours and was, by all accounts, the most ruthless grilling he endured. Beginning about 2:45 in Newport Lanford's office, various officers—among them Lanford, Beavers, Harry Scott and Pat Campbell—peppered the Negro with a dizzying barrage of questions, making him vividly aware of the treacherous ground on which he was treading. Unlike during previous sessions, there were few outbursts, and perhaps because reporters had been barred, a tense calm prevailed. Attesting to the importance of the examination was the fact that Newt Garner—Hugh Dorsey's assistant—shuttled in and out of the room every few minutes importing lines of inquiry while exporting answers. At times, Garner literally ran between headquarters and the solicitor's office. The activity finally came to a halt at dusk when C. Gay February—present now at the creation of all of Jim's affidavits—was called to notarize yet another. An hour later, the Negro, his fingers twitching nervously, sweat streaming off his brow, was escorted back to his cell, and a triumphant group of lawmen emerged to meet the press. At last, declared Chief Beavers, the Phagan murder had been solved, and shortly thereafter, the police released what would come to be known as Conley's third affidavit:

On Saturday, April 26, 1913, when I come back to the pencil factory with Mr. Frank I waited for him downstairs like he told me, and when he whistled for me I went upstairs and he asked me if I wanted to make some money right quick and I told him "Yes, sir," and he told me that he had picked up a girl back there and had let her fall and that her head hit against something, he didn't know what it was, and for me to move her, and I hollered and told him the girl was dead, and he told me to pick her up and bring her to the elevator and I told him I didn't have nothing to pick her up with and he told me to go and look by the cotton box there and get a piece of cloth, and I got a big wide piece of cloth and come back there to the men's toilet where she was, and I tied her up, and I taken her and brought her up there to a little dressing room, carrying her on my right shoulder, and she got too heavy for me and she slipped off my shoulder and fell on the floor right there at the dressing room and I hollered for Mr. Frank to come there and help me, that she was too heavy for me, and Mr. Frank come down there and told me to pick her up, damn fool, and he run down there to me and he was excited, and he picked her up by the feet, her head and feet were sticking out of the cloth and then we brought her on to the elevator, Mr. Frank carrying her by the feet and me by the shoulders, and we brought her to the elevator and then Mr. Frank says, "Wait, let me get the key," and he went into the office and got the key and come back and unlocked the elevator door and started the elevator down. Mr. Frank turned it on himself and we went on down to the basement and Mr. Frank helped me take it off the elevator and he told me to take it back there to the sawdust pile, and I picked it up and put it on my shoulder again, and Mr. Frank, he went up the ladder and watched the trap door to see if any-body was coming, and I taken her back there and taken the cloth from around her and taken her hat and shoe which I had picked up upstairs right where her body was lying and brought them down and untied the cloth and brought them back and throwed them on the trashpile in front of the fur-nace, and Mr. Frank was standing at the trap door at the head of the ladder. He didn't tell me where to put the things. I laid her body down with her head towards the elevator, lying on her stomach and the left side of her face was on the ground and the right side of her face was up, and both arms were laying down with her body, by the side of her body. Mr. Frank joined me back on the first floor. I stepped on the elevator and he stepped on the elevator when it got to where he was, and he said, "Gee, that was a tire-some job," and I told him his job was not as tiresome as mine was, because I had to tote it all the way from where she was laying to the dressing room, and in the basement from the elevator to where I left her. Then Mr. Frank hops off the elevator before it gets even with the second floor and he makes a stumble and he hits the floor and catches with both hands, and he went on around to the sink to wash his hands, and I went and cut off the motor, and I stood and waited for Mr. Frank to come from around there washing his hands, and then we went on into the office, and Mr. Frank he couldn't hardly keep still, he was all the time moving about from one office to the other, then he come back into the stenographer's office and come back and he told me, "Here comes Emma Clark and Corinthia Hall." [Here, Conley recounted his soujourn in the wardrobe.] Then . . . Mr. Frank . . . asked me to write a few lines on that paper, a white scratch pad he had there, and he told me what to put on there, and I asked him what he was going to do with it and he told me to just go ahead and write, and then after I got through writing Mr. Frank looked at it and said it was all right and Mr. Frank looked up at the top of the house and said, "Why should I hang, I have wealthy people in Brooklyn," and I asked him what about me, and he told me that was all right about me, for me to keep my mouth shut and he would make everything all right, and then I asked him where was the money he said he was going to give me and Mr. Frank said, "Here is two hundred dollars," and he handed me a big roll of greenback money and I didn't count it; I stood there a little while looking at it in my hand, and I told Mr. Frank not to take another dollar for that watch man I owed and he said he wouldn't—and the rest is just like I told it before. The reason I have not told this before is I thought Mr. Frank would get out and help me out, but it seems that he is not going to get out and I have decided to tell the whole truth about this matter.

With that, the statement ended, although scrawled on its last page was a handwritten addendum penned after the text was typed to explain what happened to the heretofore never mentioned $200:

> While I was looking at the money in my hands, Mr. Frank said: "Let me have that and I will make it all right with you Monday if I live and nothing happens," and he took the money back and I asked him if that was the way he done and he said he would give it back Monday.

If the reaction to Conley's first affidavit was disbelief and the reaction to his second was grudging acceptance, the response to his third was unchecked enthusiasm. Friday morning, Atlantans awakened to a double-deck banner atop the *Constitution:*

CONLEY SAYS HE HELPED FRANK CARRY BODY
OF MARY PHAGAN TO PENCIL FACTORY CELLAR

With this one revelation, dozens of clues gathered during the month since little Mary's death—fragments that had heretofore refused to coalesce—suddenly adhered to the powerful pull of the Negro's story. Finally, the hair on the second-story factory lathe, the blood on the floor and the murder notes fit together. "The negro's affidavit," reported the *Journal,* "is regarded by the detectives as the most important link in their chain of evidence against the factory official." Echoed the *Georgian:* "Chief Lanford and Scott announced Thursday that they considered the negro's final affidavit proof conclusive of the suspected superintendent's guilt and were thereby ready to place the case on trial." At last, the city was persuaded that Conley had told all, and the odd thing was, it was his initial dissembling that gave his ultimate assertions the sharp glint of credibility. As whites saw it, Negroes were by nature mendacious. Falsehoods and fabrications clung to them like dirt to a boy. Only by submitting them to the rough scrubbing of interrogation could the guises and guiles that were their protective coloration be washed away. As Jim himself, when asked what had convinced him to open up, would tell writers: "Finally, the thing got to workin' in my head so much that I just couldn't hold it any longer. I couldn't sleep and it worried me mightily. I just decided it was time for me to come out with it and I did. I . . . told the truth, and I feel like a clean nigger." The next day, the police would trot out their gleaming black beauty for a triumphant spin around the block.

Shortly after noon on Friday, May 30, Chief Beavers's limousine eased to a halt in front of the National Pencil Company. The sight of the vehicle, its curtains drawn, sent a buzz through the employees milling about on their lunch break. The buzz intensified when the car's occupants—Beavers, Newport Lanford and a handcuffed Conley—emerged onto the sidewalk, where they were soon joined by Detective Campbell, Harry Scott, Herbert Schiff, E. F. Holloway and a trailing phalanx of reporters. Once the group entered the factory, the police ordered lingering workers to leave, then barred the door. Though all of Atlanta would learn about it in the newspapers, only a select few would be physically present for Conley's apotheosis.

After Jim was uncuffed, he walked partway up the stairs leading to the office floor.

"Where did you first see Frank when he whistled to you twice?" someone asked.

"Right here," Conley replied, pointing to the top of the steps. "He asked me if I wanted to make some money right quick and I told him I did. Then he said he had picked up a girl back there who had hit her head against something and he wanted me to bring her body to the elevator."

With all eyes now on him, Conley led his auditors to the rear of the metal department. There, he pointed out a spot near a men's toilet where he maintained he'd discovered Mary Phagan's body lying doubled up, adding—in his first reference to the cause of death—that the cord apparently used to strangle the girl had been knotted around her neck, extending at right angles on both sides.

"When I got back here, I got scared and hollered to Mr. Frank and said that the girl was dead," Jim explained. "He was standing in that doorway right there. He told me to get a sack and put her body in that." As if on cue, Conley began to play out the scene, walking to a box in the middle of the room and extracting a piece of bagging, which he held up for all to see, commenting: "This is jus' like I got that day except that this has got a little more cotton in it and the other one was slit."

The task of bundling the body in the bagging was hard, Jim recalled, but loading it onto the elevator was harder still. "He [Frank] picked up her feet, and I carried her shoulders. Just when we got by the window Frank was so nervous that he dropped the girl and her feet dragged on the floor."

Conley ushered the group to the lift, speaking along the way of how he'd waited with the grim cargo while Frank ran to his office to fetch the key that unlocked the fuse box. Upon the superintendent's return, Jim said, they'd promptly done what he and the party did now—descend to the basement. There, Conley resumed his narrative.

"I took her body out of the elevator. Mr. Frank helped me. He told me to take the body up to the trash pile in front of the furnace. I put the girl on my shoulders again and walked up there with her and dropped her right there." Jim indicated the spot a few feet to the left of the furnace where Newt Lee had found "the package." Then he rushed on: "I pulled the bagging out from under her and threw it there on the pile of trash in front of the furnace. Mr. Frank, he waited there at the trapdoor to see if anyone was coming. Before that I went back upstairs and got her hat and shoes and brought them down in the basement."

At this point, Chief Beavers interjected: "Show us the way you left the girl's body." Once again acting out the part, Jim dropped to the cinder-covered ground. Lying on his left side, he pressed his face into the dirt, crooked his right arm under him and splayed his left inertly behind him. His feet pointed to the rear of the building.

Seeing Jim sprawled out that way, Harry Scott whispered to the reporters: "You can't help but believe him." No one disagreed.

And there was more. After dusting himself off, Conley directed the group's attention to the trapdoor at the front of the factory. "Frank climbed up this ladder," he said, "and I ran the elevator back up. He met me on the first floor and got in the elevator with me and rode with me up to the second floor."

That stated, Jim once again began to perform. Just as he said he'd done on April 26, he switched on the lift, paused in the lobby, then continued to the office floor. Stopping the car six inches below the lip, he surprised the men who'd ridden up with him by tripping and falling to his knees as he stepped out—just as he said Leo Frank had done.

After walking to a sink and washing off—again, just as he said Frank had done—Conley led his audience into the superintendent's office, took a seat behind the desk and, sticking to the story he'd advanced in his final affidavit, started to soliloquize: "Mr. Frank sat down in his swivel chair and turned and twisted for a moment, turning first white and then red and sort of gasping as he talked. We heard footsteps outside, and Mr. Frank hurried me into this wardrobe."

Here, Jim paused long enough to hop in and out of the piece of furniture before plowing ahead: "He told me to come out of the wardrobe. For a minute or two he clasped his hands and swayed about in his chair as if he was sick. Then he turned to me and told me to write on a pencil pad which was lying on the desk beside me. He dictated and I wrote: 'That long, tall black negro did this by himself.' "

His hands a flurry of activity, Jim indicated the surface upon which he said he had penned the murder notes, an inkstand he said Frank had used as a paperweight to hold down the first one and the drawer from which he said the superintendent had removed a new, different-colored pad.

"He handed me this pad and then told me to write another note," he said. "He dictated this note also and as far as I can [remember] it went like this." Whereupon Conley began to write, producing a rough facsimile of the second missive:

Dear mother a long tall black negro did this boy himslef he told me if I wood lay down he wood love me play like the night witch did this boy himslef.

After recounting once again how Frank had allegedly asked, "Why should I hang when I have got rich folks in Brooklyn?," Jim concluded his monologue by racing through the story regarding the $2.50 he'd found in the cigarette box and the $200 his boss had proffered only to retract.

Sensing that the show had ended, Newport Lanford asked Jim a last question, one designed to undercut any charges that he had been coerced: "Have you been abused or threatened by the officers into making this confession?"

"No sir," Conley replied. "The officers have treated me kindly . . . I am telling this because I want to tell it."

Not that the reporters needed any such reassurances. To a man, they rushed back to their newsrooms and banged out accounts of the production they had witnessed that accorded it an unassailable legitimacy. Roared the *Journal*'s double-deck banner:

CONLEY TAKEN TO FACTORY, SHOWS WHERE GIRL WAS FOUND—
HOW THEY PUT BODY IN BASEMENT

Meanwhile, the *Georgian,* though subtly suggesting that Conley might have been parroting a story concocted by the police, also applauded:

> Conley appeared perfectly composed . . . his earnest and apparently truthful bearing gave his dramatic story, told in a matter of fact way, a convincing power that evidently had its effect on every one who was listening to his recital . . . [He] did not hesitate for a moment during the entire time he was showing his part in the crime, and his frankness of speech and clocklike work impressed the officers that he was at last telling the exact truth.

With Chief Beavers declaring there was no need for further questioning and Hugh Dorsey announcing that the state would hold Jim as a material witness, the drama was over. Accordingly, Conley was remanded to the Tower. There he was expected to remain until it came time for him to testify.

EIGHT

A Tramp Alumnus

Not since Uncle Remus had a black man's story so enthralled Atlanta. On street corners throughout the city, newsboys hawking Friday's afternoon editions cried, CONLEY LAYS BARE PHAGAN CRIME, and outside the Tower, congregations of the curious gathered just to be near the remarkable Negro. At some point early in the evening, an unlikely couple wended their way through these onlookers. Lorena Jones, Jim Conley's common-law wife, was bringing a young white lawyer named William Smith to meet her husband.

On the surface, there was nothing peculiar about the visit. Despite the fact that Conley's account of little Mary's murder had won widespread acceptance, he still needed legal counsel. The violent slaying of a virginal Georgia girl was not the sort of outrage a shiftless black man generally succeeded in attributing to a college-educated white man in a Southern courtroom.

Yet the true sponsors of this get-together were not especially concerned with Conley's fate. Several days earlier, an *Atlanta Georgian* editor had approached William Smith and offered to pay his fee if he could secure the state's star witness as a client. Despite the potential for divided loyalties, such third-party arrangements were not at the time unusual, and the lawyer had agreed to the proposal. Shortly thereafter, he and Lorena, who was also in cahoots with the Hearst forces (Conley's wife had served as one of the newspaper's emissaries to Smith), were standing in Jim's cell.

The pair found Conley in good spirits. Indeed, he was downright giddy with relief. In the hours since concluding his tour of the factory, he had been holding forth to an endless stream of gawkers and reporters, dazzling them with fact and philosophy. Rather bitterly, he'd described his alleged partner-in-crime's stinginess: "Mr. Frank, he ain't paid me nuthin' yet, like he promised to do, and the only thing I got out of it was that two dollars he gave me in the cigarette box." But then, lest he sound motivated by anything other than noble purposes, he'd added: "I done told the truth 'fore God and high Heaven. If He was to tell me this very minute that He was going to hit me with a streak of lightning if I didn't tell the straight of it, I couldn't say a thing on earth 'cept what's in that affidavit." The larger Jim's audience, the more garrulous he seemed to grow.

While William Smith was as captivated by Conley's declarations as the next man, his overwhelming reaction was one of alarm. From his perspective, the Negro's indiscriminate jawings not only jeopardized whatever schemes were afoot in the *Georgian* newsroom; worse, they opened him up to people who cared even less about his well-being than Hearst's vultures. As far as the lawyer could determine, the crowd auditing Jim's remarks included jailhouse sharpies willing to twist his words for a quick profit, and friends of Leo Frank hoping to entrap him into making incriminating statements.

Little wonder, then, that Smith, "after receiving from Conley ratification of my employment," spent the rest of this initial session urging his new client to keep his mouth shut. "Practically my entire communication at that time," the lawyer would subsequently recollect, "was relative to a policy of silence I advised he should adopt."

Conley, however, was in no mood to take such suggestions to heart. The very next morning, he conducted what amounted to a jailhouse levee for the *Journal*'s Harold Ross and Harllee Branch, offering up another round of beguiling clues and reflections—this time from a cozy perch on his bunk. "The girl must have been dead for about 15 minutes when I saw her for when I lifted her body to push the crocus bagging under it I took hold of her forearm and it was cold," he told the reporters. "Her hat, one slipper, a piece of ribbon and her parasol lay several feet away. I never did see any purse." Then, striking a comfortably resigned note, Conley added: "When the judge calls me up before him I am going to ask him not to ask me any questions, but to simply sentence me. If it's to hang, I'll stick to my story, and if it's life imprisonment, there'll be no change." Mesmerized by his sudden notoriety, Jim quite simply could not stop talking.

On Saturday afternoon, William Smith, Hugh Dorsey and Newport Lanford met in the solicitor's office to discuss what had become a mutual problem. Like Conley's lawyer, the authorities were disturbed by Jim's volubility, but for a different reason. To them, his pronouncements posed a threat to the case against Leo Frank. Considering the number of times the Negro had already contradicted himself, there was ample possibility that he might offer up an entirely new tale. And even if he didn't change tunes, he was almost certain to reveal information the prosecution hoped to save for the trial.

After several hours of deliberation, the men emerged with a solution to their dilemma. Conley would be transferred from his laxly guarded quarters in the Tower back to the constantly monitored headquarters lockup.

There, access would be restricted, in Smith's words, "to only such officials as were approved by me." Dorsey, who was familiar with the *Georgian*'s stake in all this, felt comfortable with the arrangement. Smith was a friend, and a friend who happened to represent both the prosecution's principal witness and the Hearst newspaper deserved consideration.

Despite its patent irregularity—the county jail, after all, was the legal and proper lodging place for state prisoners—the decision to remove Conley to the station house elicited few protests. In part, the lack of response was due to ignorance in the newsrooms of the *Journal* and *Constitution* as to the *Georgian*'s role in the matter. Then there was the not inconsequential reality that on the day the transfer was made, Luther Rosser was still out of town representing the Georgia Railway and Electric Company in its fight to open the Tallulah Gorge generating project.

During the next week, however, one man began to despair over the part he had played in these machinations—William Smith. Conley's lawyer did not regret the fact that he had helped place Jim out of harm's way. As he'd subsequently tell the press: "I did this in a sincere effort to protect Conley from the perjury of his fellows and in an effort to have him given a square deal." Rather, he rued forming the alliance that brought him into the affair in the first place, belatedly realizing that the *Georgian*'s emerging pro-Frank stance could only mean that its editors wished Conley no good. In unpublished autobiographical notes written years later, the lawyer, while not elucidating all the dynamics, would acknowledge that he'd misjudged Hearst's intentions: "In a very short time, I became convinced that the major interest of the newspaper was to obtain all possible information about the murder or any facts in relation thereto. I became equally convinced that premature publicity of any possible defensive matter might be injurious to Conley's interests."

Why Smith ever allowed himself to swallow the notion that the *Georgian*'s purposes could have been otherwise was a subject he never sufficiently addressed, but ambition played its part. Like nearly every lawyer in Atlanta, he wanted to insinuate himself into the Phagan case, and the newspaper granted him entree. Yet it really wasn't that simple, for Smith was not by nature an opportunist. He was, in fact, an idealist of the sort who had difficulty attributing to others motives less high-minded than his own.

William Smith had been guilty of both self-interest and self-deception, but once he confronted his mistakes, he quickly extricated himself from the moral quicksand. Sometime during the first week of June, he appeared in the *Georgian*'s Alabama Street newsroom. There, in a meeting with the paper's editors, he stated that it would be impossible for him to furnish them with any information about Conley's defense. The financial ramifications of this sudden about-face were apparently significant. "I sacrificed the compensation I was to receive from interests worth millions," the lawyer subsequently told a reporter. Yet he did not regret the decision, for it freed him to pursue a higher calling.

Almost from the instant he met Jim Conley, Smith had felt duty-bound to stand by the "penniless and friendless" black man. For one thing, Leo Frank had already made the grounds of the impending legal battle clear. "No white man killed Mary Phagan," the factory superintendent had reportedly told a prison attaché upon hearing of Conley's affidavits. "It's a negro crime, through and through." The Negro to whom Frank was referring was, of course, poor Jim, and as Smith later phrased it, the accused was going to use every bit of his "great influence and unlimited financial means" to bring the point home to a jury.

Yet Smith's resolve was galvanized by more than outrage at Frank's wherewithal. The simple but profound fact of the matter was that he believed Conley was telling the truth. As the lawyer would subsequently write, he "shared the view of the prosecuting attorney, which was that Mr. Frank was guilty of the crime as the sole principal."

Accordingly, Smith aligned himself with Hugh Dorsey. Later, he would remember: "My justification for this course was based upon my own belief that in aiding the State to secure [Frank's] conviction, I was directly serving the interests of Conley, my own client." William Smith had decided that the surest way of saving Jim Conley's neck was to assist in breaking Leo Frank's.

Few Atlanta lawyers were better suited to the task at hand than 33-year-old William Manning Smith. During his eleven years as a member of the city's bar, he had developed a reputation as a fierce defender who frequently represented underdogs. Initially, circumstances had forced him into this role. "I had a very difficult time in the early part of my career," he subsequently wrote. Smith had scraped for the legal profession's crumbs—court-appointed assignments representing the destitute, which in Georgia's capital usually meant Negroes. Over time, he had prospered, and his clientele's pigmentation had lightened. By 1913, most of his clients were white. Nevertheless, the fact remained that to many, Smith—though he would have abjured the phrase—was a "nigger lawyer."

In Atlanta's legal hierarchy, nigger lawyers ranked above contempt but beneath respect. They had more in common with the geegaw peddlers and insurance salesmen who trod darktown's dusty paths than with the advocates who jousted in the high halls of justice. Not that they didn't fulfill a necessary function. With fewer than ten black lawyers practicing in the state of Georgia, these white attorneys handled nearly all legal transactions among Negroes and most legal business between the races. Yet there was little prestige in the work. How could there have been when much of it was performed in such noisy infernos as Recorder's Court?

Through the years, Smith had spent a good deal of time in Judge Nash Broyles's courtroom. There, he had defended a plethora of Negro ne'er-do-wells whose backgrounds were similar to Jim Conley's. Yet his involvement with Atlanta's blacks did not stop in the lower realms of legal purgatory, was not confined to those arenas where the best one could achieve for a client was a reduced sentence in the stockade. While Smith frequently represented Negroes, what distinguished him from the others—and what would redound so favorably to Jim Conley—was that he was dedicated to the race on some deeper level and was willing to champion its members in the state's higher courts, in the legislature, and even on the stump.

In 1911, representing an elderly Negro woman known in court documents only as Rich, Smith took an almost unimaginable step—he sued the Georgia Railway and Electric Company for damages to cover injuries his client received during a streetcar scuffle between a white conductor and a young black man who refused to pay his fare. At the trial, several witnesses testified that the Rich woman was severely bruised when the conductor beat and then pushed the unruly passenger down on top of her. Though the rail line's counsel disputed these accounts, a jury found that the conductor had failed to "exercise that extreme care and caution which a prudent man would exercise" and awarded the plaintiff a small financial compensation.

Out of penuriousness or, more likely, in an effort to keep the thousands of black Atlantans who regularly rode the trolley cars—since the 1906 race riot, a locus of increasing tension—in their place, Georgia Railway and Electric refused to settle, appealing the verdict to the state's Supreme Court. On June 29, 1911, that body issued an extraordinary decision:

> We are not unaware of the trying situation in which street-car conductors in many of our Southern cities are often placed by the insolent and designedly offensive conduct of that lower element of the negro race which makes it a point to take advantage of their position as passengers to use to street-car employees, while on duty, wanton and insulting language which they would not dare to use under other circumstances . . . We know . . . that a bad negro is just about the meanest and most vicious animal ever created . . . but as judges, we must lay down rules of law which are applicable to all races alike, and it will not do to say . . . that a railway con-

ductor can be allowed to imperil the safety of his passengers by his acts of violence, provoked, even though most naturally . . . The evidence fully authorized the verdict.

Georgia Railway and Electric Co. v. *Rich* was not the first case in which William Smith had put himself on the line for a Negro. In 1910, he was appointed by the court to represent a black man named Roger Merritt who had been convicted and sentenced to death for raping a white woman. A worse predicament was almost inconceivable, as the victim had identified the defendant as her assailant. Yet the presiding judge believed the victim was lying and had ordered the case retried, instructing Smith to "handle the matter with great care" or "it would mean death for Merritt," which "he did not deserve." In the ensuing trial—where the white woman again pointed out the black man as her assailant—Smith prevailed. As he later put it, he convinced "the jury that there was a reasonable doubt of Roger Merritt's guilt."

For Smith, however, Merritt's acquittal was only half the battle. Though his client was free, the lawyer had requested the court to return the Negro to the county jail as a place of refuge against the inevitable lynch mob. Then, Smith had sought advice from an old and considering the times unlikely associate: the Reverend Henry Hugh Proctor, the pastor of Atlanta's First Congregational Church and spiritual leader of the city's black elite.

In all likelihood Smith and Proctor met during the 1906 race riot, where each participated in peacekeeping efforts. (The lawyer, a captain with the state militia, saw duty when the guard was summoned to restore order, while the minister joined a biracial committee to mediate grievances.) By 1908, the two were working together to defeat a bill before the Georgia legislature that would have decreased the already negligible sum the state allotted its Negro schools. And by the early teens—when Proctor appointed Smith to the previously all-black standing committee that served as his congregation's advisory board—they were friends.

In the matter of Roger Merritt, these improbable allies decided to pursue the only course that offered their recently exonerated charge a fighting chance against Judge Lynch. After raising the necessary funds, Proctor left the plan's implementation to Smith. Working in the dead of night, the lawyer, accompanied by the Fulton County sheriff and several deputies, escorted Merritt to Terminal Station, arranged rail passage to an out-of-state city where the black man could establish a new life, then stood guard until the train pulled away.

William Smith's commitment to Georgia's Negroes arose from more than a simple willingness—acquired early on when he was struggling—to take cases others refused. He believed that the Southern white man owed his black brethren a great debt. Smith was, in fact, a zealot on the subject, proselytizing not only to the saved but to the unreconstructed, as the keynote address he delivered at the 1912 Confederate Memorial Day observances in Augusta, Georgia, illustrates.

Speaking from a podium overlooking Augusta's Magnolia Cemetery—the final resting place of thousands of men who had perished defending slavery—the lawyer who in just a few short months would be preparing Jim Conley to testify against Leo Frank had the temerity to suggest that his generation's "chief duty to our honored dead" was to elevate the Negro. With that, Smith had proclaimed:

> Out of this war grew the most serious problem that any defeated people [have ever been] called upon to face. In my judgement, the ten million negroes made through Lincoln's proclamation free, independent, American citizens are here to stay. The rightful solution to this problem staggers the wisdom of our civic students. That it must be solved, no right thinking Southerner would question. These ten million negroes forcibly exiled from their native homes ignorant and practically helpless are now, under providence, wards of the Southland. That we could deal with them other than honorably is not to be considered. I have faith in the broadminded, sane, and conservative spirit of our people in the handling of this problem and believe that [it] will be solved by Southern white men with as heroic a devotion to principle as that of their fathers who fought in the cause from which the present negro problem had its birth.

Though Smith stopped short of defining his solution to the racial dilemma, he was undoubtedly endorsing a position that was far ahead of its time and place.

Smith's obsession with the black man's dilemma was no passing fancy. As early as 1898, when he was a mere college sophomore, he'd discoursed on the issue at Atlanta's Intercollegiate Oratorical Contest, for years one of the signal events in the lives of Georgia's stripling statesmen. Attended by thousands of vocal partisans and accorded reams of newspaper coverage, the annual competition drew entrants from the state's principal colleges—the University of Georgia; Georgia Tech; Mercer University in Macon; and North Georgia College, a military school nestled in the mountain town of Dahlonega. To the victor went the John Temple Graves medal—a gold coin engraved with the state seal and named for the *Georgian*'s founder, the contest's patron—and a tacit invitation to enter politics.

Considering the stakes, it's hardly surprising that the debaters usually elucidated some position upon which everyone in the state already agreed. Nevertheless, William Smith—clad in the dress grays of his alma mater,

North Georgia—stepped onto the stage of the ornate DeGive's Opera House, took in the vast throng of lusty-lunged fraternity lads, pretty girls wearing the school colors of their favorites and sundry political horseflesh appraisers and began to address "The Negro Problem."

The text of young Smith's declamation is long lost. (In later years, the lawyer summarized the speech as a "plea to the college men and women of Georgia for a fair and just deal for the 'Brother in Black.' ") Also lost is any account of how the address compared to that given by the eventual winner, a Mercer student who confined his thoughts to "The South's Contribution to the American Republic." There is, however, a surviving review. It comes from the office of future Howard University president Wilbur P. Thurkield, at the time chancellor of Atlanta's Gammon Theological Seminary, an institution for the training of Negro ministers. Wrote the educator: Smith's discourse "was not tarnished by those vilifying flings which orators both young and old are wont to make."

At the turn of the century, rare was the Southern Cicero who could resist racism's crowd-pleasing appeal. Over in South Carolina, Senator "Pitchfork" Ben Tillman got 'em going by vowing that Negroes were "akin to the monkey." Meanwhile, in Mississippi, Senator James Vardaman played to the house by asserting: "Educate the negro, and you spoil a good field hand and make an insolent cook." It was no different in Georgia. Yet William Smith, even at the impressionable age of eighteen, even on an occasion crucial to his dreams, refused to join the chorus. Worse, he purposely sang off-key ("Brother in black?" "A fair and just deal?"). By the time, fifteen years later, when he took on Jim Conley as his client, Smith had grown even more impassioned regarding the Negro cause. This, despite the fact that in every other discernible way, he was as typical a Southerner as ever mixed grits with gravy.

To anyone who'd met William Smith on the streets of Atlanta in 1913, sounded him out on his work, political connections and career aspirations, then visited with him, his wife and his children, the conclusion would have quickly dawned that here was the Southern beau ideal in midcareer.

For openers, Smith comported himself as an officer and a gentleman, and even when clad in a business suit, he exuded a martial air. He strode through life chest out, stomach in, hat cocked over his brow. Though slender and of only medium height, he seemed imposing beyond his size. Possessed of bright blue eyes and a cannonading voice, he commanded attention. Yet for all that, one could not say that Smith was a bellicose sort, for in the best Sir Walter Scott style, he tempered his pugnacity with gallantry, graciousness and grandiloquence. The man could ladle on the language, perfuming conversations with bits of Tennyson, inquiring after your daddy, praising anything Dixiefied from cotton bolls to watermelons.

Then there was the fact that while Smith may well have started out at the bottom of the legal profession, he'd eventually become a partner in the firm of Chambers, Daley and Smith, where he was expected to do much more than defend Negroes pro bono publico. The idealistic lawyer spent much of his time litigating prosaic criminal and civil cases. In 1907, he'd lost a nasty battle to remove the executor of a contested will. Also in 1907, he'd prevailed in a fight over a $75 real estate commission. In 1909, he'd successfully petitioned Georgia's Supreme Court to overturn a decision that had allowed a sheriff to seize a team of mules from an indebted party, auction the animals, then use the proceeds to pay the claimant. And in 1910—proving that, like most lawyers, he wasn't above exploiting a technicality in defense of a client—he'd managed to get complaints against a check forger thrown out of court by arguing that the defendant had been indicted under the general, as opposed to the specific, statute covering the offense.

Chambers, Daley and Smith was concerned with more than just litigation. The senior partner—mustachioed, orotund Aldine Chambers, an Atlanta city councilman—was building a machine designed to elevate himself to the city's mayoralty, and he spent most of his energies backing candidates who might one day help him. Meanwhile, Walter Daley would eventually be elected president of the Atlanta school board. A readiness to work the hustings was a job requirement at the firm, which suited the junior partner just fine.

William Smith aspired to office himself, in particular the one that until 1910 had been occupied by Charles Hill. Like many other Atlantans, Smith had revered the late solicitor general, and he had sought to emulate him. As he would later write:

> It was then my ambition to eventually become the Solicitor General or prosecuting attorney. This position was then filled and had been filled for many years, by Mr. Charles D. Hill. Solicitor General Hill was a remarkable advocate, an intensely human man, having all the virtues of a great soul and yet not free from many of the foibles of life. Mr. Hill knew, from his own experience, the weaknesses of man and woman. He was a great prosecutor, not only because he was a great lawyer, but because he was a great soul. I hoped that when Mr. Hill yielded the Solicitor Generalship, that I might fall heir to it and that I might have the privilege of trying to be as great a prosecutor as Mr. Hill had been, not only in his deeds, but in his broad and kindly dealing with his fellow men who were in trouble.

Whatever Aldine Chambers made of Smith's desires and the lofty sentiments that animated them, he did not discourage the young lawyer. To a foxy old pol like Chambers, a well-intentioned, golden-tongued scrapper was exactly the sort one wanted on the stump promoting one's own affairs and those of one's cronies.

By 1913, Smith had played key roles in two of the era's fiercest campaigns. The first was Atlanta's 1908 mayoral race. Initially, this contest had promised little out of the ordinary. In the fall Democratic primary, the right bibulous Jimmy Woodward had once again captured a majority. But between the casting of the Democrats' votes and the usually pro forma general election, Woodward had gone on another bender. The morning after, he had admitted his transgression (although he claimed he'd imbibed for medicinal purposes only) and begged forgiveness. The electorate, however, would not be kind. At a meeting of 25 leading Atlantans, the millionaire banker Robert F. Maddox was drafted to run against Woodward. Which was where Smith came marching in.

William Smith's military bearing was no affectation. Not only was he a graduate of North Georgia (where he'd been cadet major) and an officer in the state militia, but he was also president of a battalion of civic-minded, Sousaesque sorts who'd dubbed themselves the Young Men's Marching Club. As the name suggests, these gumptious gents liked to march, usually on such occasions as Independence Day, but in the aftermath of Woodward's spree, Smith vowed that he and his troops were going to march Maddox into city hall.

On the evening of November 28, 1908—four days before the general election—William Smith's torchlight parade in support of Maddox snaked its way through the streets of downtown Atlanta. Estimates as to the number of participants varied (the young lawyer ordered 10,000 torches for the occasion), but whatever the total, the procession was so long it took twenty minutes to pass any given point on the route. The *Journal* called it "one of the biggest public demonstrations, political or otherwise" in many years, adding descriptively:

> From an eminence the procession looked like a long river of molten metal flowing through the streets. Incidental to its main purpose—that of enthusiastic endorsement of Mr. Maddox for mayor—the procession was one of the prettiest night displays that the city has ever seen.

At the head of that molten river was Smith, and on December 2, when Maddox defeated Woodward by 4,000 votes, the up-and-coming lawyer received considerable credit.

An auspicious political baptism—and one that boded well for Aldine Chambers, who was reelected to the city council in the Maddox landslide. In 1910, however, Smith had plunged into deeper waters: the Georgia gubernatorial race pitting *Journal* founder Hoke Smith against incumbent Joseph Brown. The enmity between Smith and Brown was long-standing. (In 1908, Brown had defeated the then incumbent Smith in a campaign fought on the slogan "Hoke and Hunger, Brown and Bread.") And what gave their ill will an added toxicity was that surrogates broadcast it across Georgia. Joe Brown was many things, but one thing he was not was a speaker. Hence he dispatched an army of articulate seconds to stand up for him throughout the state. Though Hoke Smith thrived before audiences, he could not be everywhere at once and employed a competing speakers' bureau, one of whose number in 1910 was an Atlanta lawyer who happened to share the same surname.

Young William was no relation to old Hoke, but he stumped up and down Georgia for his man. And out there in the little crossroads towns at the forums and barbecues where the war was waged, he often found himself in verbal battle with one of Joe Brown's soldiers who, like himself, was an ambitious Atlanta lawyer: Hugh Dorsey.

The campaign-trail sparrings between Smith and Dorsey hardly rivaled the Lincoln-Douglas debates; nevertheless, they would change both mens' lives. Most immediately, they made Dorsey's career and scuttled Smith's dreams, for as it so happened, Joe Brown whipped Hoke Smith by some 60,000 votes, and a few months later, when Charles Hill died, a grateful Brown rewarded his surrogate by appointing him solicitor general of Fulton County. (Whether Smith ever possessed a chance of attaining this office is, considering his impolitic views on race, doubtful, although in 1909, he'd assisted Hill in the successful prosecution of a particularly loathsome murderer and had been written up in the newspapers as a qualified candidate.) Smith and Dorsey's 1910 clashes also produced a less predictable result— the combatants formed a backstage friendship that would influence the course of events three years later.

Away from the campaign trail, Smith was an avid joiner who knew most of the secret handshakes and attended many of the rituals of Atlanta's fraternal organizations. Worshipful master of the city's Masonic Lodge #96, chancellor commander of the Knights of Pythias and royal vizier of the Knights of Khorassan, the young lawyer was forming associations with men from every walk of life.

Then there was Smith's relationship with his wife and children. The lawyer had met Mary Lou Baker in 1903 on a double date arranged by a mutual friend, an outing that had actually paired Mary Lou with the friend and Smith with the friend's sister. By evening's end, it was obvious where true affections resided. Within days Smith was pursuing Mary Lou, within weeks they were engaged. The couple wed on December 20, 1905, in the palm-frond-strewn sanctuary of Atlanta's Park Avenue Methodist Church, and soon thereafter boarded a train headed north. Richmond, Washington, New York—it was a whirlwind honeymoon, but one moment stood out. At the Statue of Liberty, Smith insisted upon kissing his bride on every last landing of the seemingly endless metal stairway spiraling to the top of the monument.

Like most Southern men, Smith idealized women. In a flight of college-days poetry, he'd rhapsodized about "beautiful Southern queens, dreams of loveliness more graceful than any storied nymph." Yet Atlanta-reared Mary Lou Baker was no typical belle. While lovely in form—brunette hair that glinted red at the tips, high cheekbones, green eyes—she came from rugged North Georgia mountain stock and was characteristically strong-willed and independent. Someday she hoped to teach English.

By 1913, the Smiths had two children—six-year-old Mary Lou (after her mother) and three-year-old Frank—and they lived on Lucile Avenue in Atlanta's smart West End section. Their bungalow took a bow to tradition on its front porch, where chairs and a wooden swing bespoke lazy summer evenings. Inside, however, the emphasis was decidedly modern: indoor plumbing, an up-to-date kitchen and a spacious sleeping porch where the entire brood—in keeping with the rage for fresh air that was sweeping the nation—could inhale the night breezes. But lest a visitor think he'd entered the sanctum of some cosmopolite, the backyard would disabuse him of the error, for this well-worn expanse was the exclusive province of two goats, Billy and Dan. On Sunday afternoons, Smith hitched carts to the animals, summoned trusty Caesar—a massive Saint Bernard–collie mix—and organized excursions for his daughter and son that left no doubt as to his red-clay origins.

On the surface, then, William Smith was the archetypal Southern male. Yet on a deeper level—where his concern for racial justice arose—there were profound differences, and one of the earliest, most dramatic manifestations of these differences occured far from his native Georgia.

On a summer day in 1901, the streets of Quebec, Canada, were lined with crowds awaiting the arrival of the duke and duchess of Cornwall—the future King George V and Queen Mary of England. Guarding the parade route was a batallion of red-coated troops, one of whom was a very young Smith.

Smith's temporary position as a private in Her Majesty's 85th Regiment had been arranged through the wire-pulling of friends, and it was the highlight of an adventure that had begun four months earlier. Originally, he and his University of Georgia Law School roommate were going to spend two years bicycling around the world, but after graduation the roommate changed his mind. Smith, however, was not deterred. With $65 in his wallet and a dirk and pistol in his pocket, he'd climbed atop his machine and pedaled away from Athens alone. Existing, as he'd subsequently write, on "half rations of an inferior grade, sleeping in jails, box cars, unfinished buildings, church door steps, barns, woods and equine hotels," he'd inched northward, reaching Washington, then New York City—where for ten days he lived under a flight of stairs at Broadway and Fourteenth Street—and finally Quebec.

A crimson uniform, however, was not for Smith. ("If any Southern boy has inherited a prejudice against the 'stars and stripes,' " he'd later recall, "he should visit some alien land, and be thrilled through at the sight of his country's flag.") After performing a few more ceremonial duties connected with the royal visit, he resumed his peregrinations. From Montreal, he shipped as a deckhand on the steamboat *Hamilton* to Toronto. Then he bicycled to Niagara Falls. Following an unintentionally long stop at the International Bridge (several days earlier, President William McKinley had been shot in nearby Buffalo at the Pan-American Exposition, and although his assassin had been arrested, border crossings were prohibited for a time), Smith proceeded to Buffalo. There, he took a "cheap trip" through the exposition. Then he departed for points west, working his way across the Great Lakes to Chicago on the *E. P. Wilbur,* a four-stick freighter.

With winter clamping down, Smith turned south, but he was in no hurry to reach home. Earning money by shoveling coal or unloading freight, the lawyer hoboed through Illinois, Indiana, Kentucky and Mississippi, eventually arriving in New Orleans. There, he labored briefly on the docks, but after hearing that hefty sums could be made "cutting cane on a sugar plantation," he left for the Delta. The work, however, was brutal, so it was on to Dallas and Mexico.

Sometime during January or February 1902, Smith returned to Atlanta riding the blinds on a fast passenger train. All told, he had been away seven months. He was jobless and nearly broke (he'd spent his grubstake, lost his pistol, and his bicycle and dirk had been stolen), but he considered the expedition a great success. As he'd later put it, he'd "seen something of America before settling down," worked side by side with "Chinese, dagoes and negroes," and "learned a great deal about his fellow Americans in all levels and walks of life," especially those "so unfortunate as to have hardly more than food, clothes, and shelter." Yet what makes the trip crucial to any understanding of Smith and vital to a comprehension of the bond he felt with the black race has little to do with experiences gained or sympathies broadened. Instead, one must ask why Smith embarked on the journey at all, why he truly was—as the editors of the University of Georgia student magazine titled the account he wrote of his exploits—"A Tramp Alumnus."

Smith was only 22 when he lit out for the territories, but already he bore the markings of, if not a future governor, then at least a man destined for a more auspicious start in life than a law practice dedicated to defending poor Negroes.

It was at the state university in Athens—where he had enrolled upon graduating from North Georgia—that Smith had made the sort of noises that suggested he was a comer. First, he'd joined a fraternity, Sigma Nu, that, while not as tied to the capitol as such rookeries as Sigma Alpha Epsilon and Kappa Alpha, included in its 1902 pledge class the lank-locked boy from Sugar Creek, Georgia, who would dominate state politics for the next fifty years: Eugene Talmadge. Of greater significance, though, was the fact that Smith, building on what he'd accomplished at North Georgia, had quickly risen to the top of the school's preeminent debating society.

To be a champion rhetorician at the University of Georgia at the turn of the century was to hold nearly as exalted a position on campus as did the quarterback of the Bulldog football eleven. Week after week, the student newspaper, *The Red and Black,* featured the exploits of the college's verbal warriors, whether in competition among themselves or with teams from other schools, on its front page. The principal clubs—Phi Kappa and Demosthenian—faced each other from opposite sides of the campus's main quadrangle in seeming equipoise, but while each had its merits, Demosthenian had by far the more storied pedigree. In its federalist-period temple during the years before seccession, such legendary figures as Robert Toombs, the firebrand who in 1861 had announced Georgia's intention to leave the Union by shouting from the United States Senate floor, "Georgia is on the war path! We are as ready to fight now as we ever shall be," had honed their rhetorical skills. By the time Smith joined in 1900, Demosthenian's members were no longer arguing the need to expand slave territory and were instead hashing out such contemporary issues as "Resolved that the Interference with Strikes by Judicial Injunction Is a Menace to the Liberties of the Working Class." Still, Demosthenian was a shrine to the Old Order, and as the society's "senior orator," Smith was not only its star speaker but the carrier of the flame.

Just how utterly William Smith had surmounted this fabled Southern institution—and how secure his future must have seemed—had been made abundantly clear on February 19, 1901, when he'd taken his place in the pulpit of the university chapel and facing a packed house that included not only the entire faculty and student body but the girls of the Lucy Cobb Institute, delivered one of the school year's most anticipated orations: Demosthenian's centennial anniversary address. Stylishly outfitted for the occasion in tux and tails, young Smith had for once told an audience what it wanted to hear. True, he'd managed to challenge his fellow Demosthenians to honor the past by confronting the problems of the present, declaring: "The Northern states with their better educational facilities have outstripped us in the race for prosperity. Should treasures be poured into our coffers, we could aid in the work of educating the sons and daughters of our State." But first and foremost, he'd paid homage to tradition. Robert E. Lee, Toombs, the valiant Demosthenians who'd died for the lost cause—all received bouquets. Furthermore, Smith had indulged in a little atypical race baiting. Touching on the scientific wonders that the twentieth century, Demosthenian's second century, would witness, he'd predicted that rocket travel to other planets would produce a happy result: "Negroes will be banished as far as possible to Neptune [and] the Caucasian will stay upon this orb, and the 'Stars and Stripes' will wave over all." In summation, Smith had borrowed from Thomas More, likening each of his fellow Demosthenians to a "vase in which roses have once been distilled. You may shatter the vase, if you will, but the scent of the roses will cling round it still." That scent, of course, was the scent of an all-encompassing heritage, of Southern history.

For a shining moment, then, William Smith had stood atop the edifice of the Old South, and by his lights, he should have found a starting place for himself in the ranks of the state's legal aristocracy. Perhaps an advantageous judicial clerkship would have been in order, or maybe a position with a venerable Atlanta or Augusta firm. But in the end, Smith—son of Dixie though he was—was never going to be embraced by the bar's elite, for while he may have bestrode the symbol of the ancien régime, he had not emerged from its dusty reality, nor could he have, for quite literally, he had no family.

By the time William Smith had entered law school, he was alone in the world. His father, William Sr.—a salesman for an Augusta, Georgia, brick manufacturer—had died in 1889. A few years later, in 1896, Smith's mother, Dora, followed her husband to the grave. This left just Bill—then sixteen— and his older sister, also named Dora, then eighteen. Drawing on a small inheritance, the two had moved to mountainous Dahlonega, where they'd settled in a rambling boardinghouse owned by a colorful local, one Aunt Barney. The dream was that brother and sister would attend North Georgia, and in the spring of 1897, they'd begun classes. But this attempt to create a semblance of normality was soon dashed, for it was also in 1897 that

Dora contracted chorea, a debilitating nervous disorder. On August 24, following a nasty fall, she died in her brother's arms.

How William Smith endured these losses can only be imagined, for while he'd later write perceptively about other painful subjects, he never touched on this period. Possibly, his childhood had prepared him for such trials, for his father may have been the sort of profligate who leaves a son no choice but to grow up fast. At the elder Smith's funeral in 1889, the Reverend Lansing Burrows, pastor of Augusta's First Baptist Church, had intriguingly remarked: "Of late the cares and pressures of business had dulled his youthful experience of grace [but] God visited him about four years ago and he returned to his place beneath the throne." If Smith Sr. fell from grace in the usual way, if he was an improvident tippler, then one can speculate that Smith Jr., who eschewed drink, had been fending for himself a long time. Another clue to the young man's resolve might be found in the ringingly titled address he gave in Atlanta in 1900 when he again represented North Georgia at the Southern Oratorical Contest: "The Triumph of Individualism." But however Smith managed it, this much is certain: He not only survived, he flourished. Yet as he ascended to the pinnacle of college-boy success, he found that his deprivations had transformed him into what for the era was a rarity below the Mason-Dixon Line: a young man unbound.

In 1900, the white South—as it still would be on the day Mary Phagan was found murdered—was rigidly divided into two classes, both based on family. You could be a patrician, or you could be a cracker. What you could not be was neither, for while there was some transmigration between these spheres, so powerful were their respective social, cultural and financial gravitational fields that few people fell between them, and even those who did eventually allied with one or the other. The appearance, then, of an independent being hurtling into adulthood without parents, connections or money, was seen if not as a threat to the established order then at the least as the equivalent of an unnamed and hence worrisome comet arcing through the heavens. Thus when William Smith, even though he'd left the university trailing clouds of glory, returned from his wanderings, he discovered that the doors to the state's legal establishment were closed to him. As he would later write:

Upon arriving at Atlanta, I made application to a number of prominent law firms. Failing in securing an opening in any law office as I was practically a stranger I decided to open my own law office and did so. No matter how difficult the way, I determined to go forward.

And so William Smith hung out his shingle and started looking for clients, and while he never put it in so many words, as he surveyed the bumptious turn-of-the-century capital of the New South, he saw thousands of Negro freedmen—at the time, only 39 years removed from bondage. The gulf between this young lawyer—this white freedman—and these blacks was vast, yet not so vast that gazing across it, each could not perceive a kindred spirit. It was in that instant of recognition that the path to Jim Conley's jail cell began.

NINE

Skirmishes

J ust days after Jim Conley signed his final affidavit, a series of shrieks and protestations loud enough to penetrate a closed door exploded from Hugh Dorsey's office. The source of these cries was Minola McKnight, the 20-year-old black woman who cooked for the Franks and the Seligs. Only a few minutes earlier, Minola had been taken into custody at the 68 East Georgia Avenue home the families shared and brought to the Thrower Building. Though at first blush this frightened creature did not seem the sort who could have shed light on the Phagan case, the solicitor had reason to believe that she possessed a critical piece of information—the time Leo Frank arrived home for lunch on April 26.

To Dorsey, the precise minute Frank sat down at the table the afternoon of the murder had suddenly become a matter of utmost importance. During the past week, the solicitor had determined that if, as Conley insisted, Frank began dictating the murder notes at 1:00 P.M., he could not possibly have finished the task, rushed upstairs to confer with the laborers Arthur White and Harry Denham regarding the status of their work, escorted Mrs. White out of the factory and then made a ten-minute trolley trip across town—all before 1:20, the hour that not only he but his parents-in-law swore he reached home. There was, however, an ostensibly far more objective authority yet to be consulted—the dutiful black soul who'd prepared and served Frank's meal.

The interrogation of Minola McKnight was, by all accounts, an ugly spectacle. According to the *Georgian,* Dorsey submitted the woman to "the severest sort of grilling." In this, he was assisted by Detectives Starnes and Campbell. Yet these intimidating white men bothered Minola less than a supposedly sympathetic black man who also participated in the session. That man was her husband, Albert. It was Albert who'd informed his superiors at work—who in turn called Dorsey—that his wife had told him Frank didn't arrive home until after 1:30 on April 26, and it was now Albert who was most unrelenting in the effort to persuade Minola to confirm this version of events.

But Albert's exertions were to no avail. Despite his entreaties and admonitions, Minola not only refused to verify her husband's account, she accused him of lying to the authorities. The two had recently quarreled, she maintained, and Albert had fabricated his tale in an attempt to get back at her. From this rock, Minola would not budge. Following several fruitless hours, Dorsey ordered her arrest on the charge of suspicion. While the prospect of going to jail further upset the cook, it didn't change her mind. As she was being booked, she repeatedly shouted to the boys at headquarters: "I don't know a thing about it." And long into the evening, she kept up a defiant chatter out her cell window, proclaiming her innocence and Frank's, too.

A night behind bars apparently failed to soften Minola's resolve, but the next afternoon, something did. The process began when Campbell and Starnes reappeared and led the prisoner from her cell to a room adjacent to the detectives' third-floor bullpen. There, Albert McKnight was again waiting, this time in the company of a lawyer named George Gordon, and two white businessmen—Ernest H. Pickett and Roy L. Craven—each of whom had a decided interest in this matter. Noted the *Constitution:*

> Both men are employees of the Beck & Gregg hardware concern, the head of which, L. H. Beck, is foreman of the grand jury which indicted Leo Frank. Significance is attached to this connection of the jury's foreman. The veil of mystery is lifted [further] by the fact that Albert McKnight, husband of the imprisoned servant, is also a porter at the Beck & Gregg establishment.

In other words, Albert worked for Pickett and Craven, who in turn worked for a man without whose cooperation Dorsey could not have secured an indictment against Frank. It was all very cozy, so much so that after Attorney Gordon obligingly retired to a hallway, the detectives surrendered Minola to the Beck & Gregg contingent's care, not returning until a couple hours later, at which point, following a brief conversation with the woman, Starnes produced pen and paper, then summoned a familiar figure— departmental secretary C. Gay February. Shortly thereafter, Minola gave her statement, whereupon she was freed.

Had Hugh Dorsey succeeded in plugging the leaks that had plagued the state since day one, the contents of the piece of paper to which Minola's name was now affixed might not have been revealed until the trial. In fact, soon after the affidavit was obtained, the solicitor told the *Constitution:* "I will not talk regarding the McKnight woman. Too much publicity at this stage will do inestimable injury." The higher-ups at 175 Decatur Street did not, however, share Dorsey's reticence. Quite to the contrary, Newport

Lanford was so eager to publicize the coup that he instructed a typist to pound out carbons of Minola's statement for all three newspapers, and within hours extras were rolling off the presses. Boomed the *Georgian:*

COOK'S SENSATIONAL AFFIDAVIT

The most sensational aspect of Minola McKnight's statement concerned not the time Frank had appeared for lunch on April 26 but the time he'd departed. Minola still clung to the family line that the superintendent had arrived home at 1:20, but in a devastating revision, she'd added that he'd rushed off ten minutes later without touching his food, a direct contradiction of Frank's testimony at the inquest, where he'd sworn that he'd spent half an hour at the house conversing with Lucille and his mother-in-law before they left for the opera, dining with his father-in-law, then, once lunch was finished and the older man had strolled into the backyard, stretching out on the living room sofa for a cigarette and a nap. According to Minola, however, the superintendent had done none of these things, had in fact quickly made himself scarce. As to why he'd been in such a hurry, the cook didn't say, but the clear implication was that he and Jim Conley had unfinished business back at the factory.

For all of this, Minola's affidavit would not have prompted the *Constitution* to term it "fully as startling as the recent confession of James Conley," had it not been for her other revelations, which involved what purportedly transpired in the house at 68 East Georgia Avenue the weekend of the murder and in the days that followed.

On the subject of Frank's behavior the night of Saturday, April 26, Minola painted a picture tending to confirm the detectives' theory—born of Lucille's comment the next morning to John Black regarding the depletion of the house liquor cabinet—that the superintendent had been drunk:

> Sunday, Miss Lucille said to Mr. Selig that Mr. Frank didn't sleep so good Saturday night. She said he . . . wouldn't let her sleep with him, and she said she slept on the floor on the rug by the bed because he was drinking. Miss Lucille said Sunday that Mr. Frank told her Saturday night that he was in trouble, that he didn't know the reason why he would murder, and he told his wife to get his pistol and let him kill himself. I heard Miss Lucille say that to Mrs. Selig. It got away with Mrs. Selig mighty bad. She didn't know what to think.

Then there was the vexing matter of the many days that had passed between Frank's arrest and Lucille's return visit to the Tower, a matter that Minola said dismayed her, too:

I don't know why Mrs. Frank didn't come to see her husband, but it was a pretty good while before she come to see him, maybe two weeks. She . . . said: "Minola, I don't know what I am going to do."

Finally, Minola alleged that her employers, upon hearing that Hugh Dorsey planned to question her, tried to buy her silence:

> When I left home to go to the Solicitor General's office they told me to mind how I talked. Up to the time of the murder I was getting $3.50 a week. But last week she paid me $4, and one week she paid me $6.50 . . . One week Mrs. Selig give me $5, but it wasn't for my work.
>
> They just said, "Here is $5, Minola," but of course I understood what they meant even if they didn't tell me anything . . . I understood it was a tip for me to keep quiet. They would tell me to mind how I talked, and Miss Lucille would give me a hat.

While Dorsey would have preferred the publication of Minola Mc-Knight's affidavit to have been delayed, now that it was in print, he attempted to seize the tactical advantage. In one stroke, he declared, he had not only buttressed Conley's story but torn the roof off the Franks' home, revealing that Leo's anxiety the morning Mary Phagan's body was discovered was but the half of it. Moreover, he had teased out another simmering issue—Lucille's failure to visit her husband behind bars—and introduced a new one: the family's purported attempt to bribe a witness. By all rights, the solicitor should have again been able to proclaim victory. Yet he could not.

Even as the McKnight statement was being splashed across Atlanta's front pages, the overwhelming reaction was that Dorsey had overplayed his hand. The *Georgian,* its decision to showcase the story notwithstanding, scoffed at the affidavit, cautioning in a subhead:

> Incoherent Statement by Employee of
> Frank Household That Must Not
> Be Taken as Legal Evidence Until
> Heard and Corroborated in Court.

And the Hearst sheet wasn't alone in its skepticism. Noted the *Journal:* "The affidavit is nearly all hearsay evidence, and therefore inadmissible in court." Even more worrisome, added others, was the role Albert McKnight and his superiors at Beck & Gregg had played in the drama. Most damaging, though, was the fact that fewer than twenty-four hours after the statement appeared, its author repudiated it.

Following her release from headquarters, Minola had returned to the

tiny shack she and her husband shared several blocks from the Franks'
house. It was there that a *Georgian* reporter spoke to her:

> "Did you sign any affidavit in the office of Chief Lanford?" was the first
> question asked of the McKnight woman.
> "No, sir, I never had a pen or pencil in my hand," she replied.
> "Have you read what this affidavit says as it was published in the
> papers?"
> "It was read to me; I can't read."
> "Is there anything in there that you said?"
> "No, sir; it's most all a pack of lies."
> "Where did they get all that stuff, then?"
> "I don't know sir; I don't know."

When Hearst's man pressed Minola as to why her counsel had allowed the
investigators to put words in her mouth, she bristled: "I ain't got no lawyer,
'cept God. He's my lawyer. You jus' put that in the paper. You jus' tell them
that I ain't got no lawyer, 'cept God."

Minola's affidavit could not, of course, be made to go away simply
because she now disavowed it. Furthermore, the authenticity of her recantation was undermined by the fact that it appeared in a paper whose propensity to embellish the truth was well known and whose prodefense leanings
were continually growing more apparent. Nonetheless, Minola's renunciation—which was picked up prominently by the *Journal* and even grudg-
ingly acknowledged by the *Constitution*—called into question both the
methods detectives had used in obtaining her statement and those they'd
used in obtaining others, particularly Conley's. For the first time since seizing control of the investigation, Dorsey found himself overexposed and
vulnerable.

The same day Dorsey ordered Minola McKnight's arrest, Luther Rosser
refused comment to a *Journal* reporter trying to divine the defense's pretrial strategy. "Luther Z. Rosser maintains his sphinxlike attitude and
declines to discuss the theory of the defense," the paper observed. Such
taciturnity by Frank's counsel—"Luther Z. Rosser maintains his usual
silence," echoed the next morning's *Constitution*—had become commonplace in the month since the inquest concluded. Not only had Rosser said
nothing to contest the rumors of sexual misconduct swirling around Frank,
but he'd made no effort to rebut Conley's affidavits. In part, he may simply
have wanted to avoid repeating the mistake he'd made earlier when by
speaking out he antagonized the police. Then again, he may have been dis-

tracted by other business. After all, the week Conley unburdened himself, he'd been away in Rabun County helping the Georgia Railway and Electric Company push its Tallulah Gorge power project through the courts. In the aftermath of the McKnight debacle, however, Rosser found his voice. It belonged to his client's wife.

Lucille Frank's open letter to the citizens of Atlanta ran in all three papers the day after the McKnight affidavit appeared. By turns aggrieved, exasperated and exhortatory, the letter made it plain that Rosser—who was doubtlessly speaking through Lucille—was ready to take the offensive:

> The action of the Solicitor General in arresting and imprisoning our family cook because she would not voluntarily make a false statement against my innocent husband brings a limit to patience. The wrong is not chargeable to a detective acting under the necessity of shielding his own reputation against attacks in the newspapers, but of an intelligent, trained lawyer whose sworn duty is as much to protect the innocent as to punish the guilty. My information is that this Solicitor has admitted that no crime is charged against this cook and that he had no legal right to have her . . . imprisoned.
>
> That the Solicitor, sworn to maintain the law, should thus falsely arrest one against whom he has no charge and whom he does not even suspect and torture her, contrary to the laws, to force her to give evidence tending to swear away the life of an innocent man, is beyond belief.
>
> Where will this end? My husband and my family and myself are the innocent sufferers now, but who will be the next to suffer? I suppose the witnesses tortured will be confined to the class who are not able to employ lawyers to relieve them from the torture in time to prevent their being forced to give false affidavits, but the lives sworn away may come from any class . . .
>
> It is not surprising that my cook should sign an affidavit to relieve herself from torture that has been applied to her for four hours . . . It would be surprising if she would not, under such circumstances, give an affidavit.
>
> This torturing process can be used to produce testimony to be published in the newspapers to prejudice the case of anyone the Solicitor sees fit to accuse . . . It is hard to believe that practices of this nature will be countenanced anywhere in the world outside of Russia.

Lucille's arraignment of Dorsey concluded, her tone softened. After denying the charges advanced in Minola's affidavit ("My husband was home for lunch and in the evening at the hours he has stated on the day of the murder . . . Neither on Saturday nor Saturday night, nor on Sunday, nor at any other time, did my husband by word or act . . . demean himself otherwise than as an innocent man"), she described the hardships she'd suffered since Leo's arrest:

> I have been compelled to endure without fault, either on the part of my husband or myself, more than it falls to the lot of most women to bear. Slanders have been circulated in the community to the effect that my husband and myself were not happily married, and every conceivable rumor has been put afloat that would do him and me harm.

Then, in closing, Lucille did something she'd heretofore not done. She publicly proclaimed her faith in Leo:

> I know my husband is innocent. No man could make the good husband to a woman that he has been to me and be a criminal . . . Being a woman, I do not understand the tricks and arts of detectives and prosecuting officers, but I do know Leo Frank, and his friends know him, and I know, and his friends know, that he is utterly incapable of committing the crime that these detectives and this Solicitor are seeking to fasten upon him.

The most effective thing about Lucille's letter was that it left Dorsey almost no room to operate. If he fired back, he ran the risk of appearing to badger a long-suffering woman. If he said nothing, he implicitly endorsed her allegations.

Once again, though, Dorsey proved himself to be nimble. Speaking off-the-cuff shortly after Lucille's communication was made public, he brushed aside the notion that his investigators were pressuring witnesses. "Minola McKnight was not 'sweated' while she was in my office, nor was she 'sweated' anywhere else," he told the *Journal.* "Merely she was confronted with her husband." Then, in a formal response released the next day to all the papers, the solicitor danced away from the substance of Lucille's charges entirely. Coolly, pointedly, he sought to present himself as a disinterested public servant simply carrying out the at times disagreeable tasks dictated by his office:

> I have read the statement in the Atlanta newspapers over the signature of Mrs. Leo M. Frank, and I have only to say, without in anywise taking issue with her premises, as I might, that the wife of a man accused of crime would probably be the last person to learn all of the facts establishing his guilt, and certainly would be the last person to admit his culpability . . . A bill of indictment has been found by the Grand Jury, composed of impartial and respected citizens of this community, and as Solicitor General of this circuit, charged with the duty of aiding in the enforcement of our

laws . . . I welcome all evidence from any source that will aid an impartial jury, under the charge of the court, in determining the guilt or innocence of the accused. Perhaps the most unpleasant feature incident to the position of prosecuting attorney arises from the fact that punishment of the guilty inevitably brings suffering to relations who are innocent of participation in the crime, but who must share the humiliation flowing from its exposure.

This, however, is an evil attendant upon crime, and the courts and their officers cannot allow their sympathies for the innocent to retard the vigorous prosecution of those indicted for the commission of crime, for were it otherwise, sentiment, and not justice, would dominate the administration of our laws.

Dorsey wasn't finished. The McKnight episode had also presented him with a splendid opportunity to thrust a dagger through the heart of a particularly loose-lipped demon—Newport Lanford. The moment Minola's affidavit had appeared in print, the solicitor had written the detective chief "urging him to take steps to prevent [more] 'leakage.' "Then, following the publication of Lucille's letter, he went further, calling on the grand jury to investigate 175 Decatur Street. In order to stave off such a probe, Lanford quickly caved in, commanding his men, himself presumably included, to stop discussing the case with reporters. The *Constitution,* whose disdain for the police hierarchy was only heightened by its pro-prosecution stance, applauded, editorializing:

If the Phagan tragedy shall produce no other result than the recent "shut-up" order of the detective department it will not be entirely lacking in compensation.

Yet for all Dorsey's deftness, there can be no doubt that the McKnight episode had hurt the state's case, doing for the defense what the defense had seemed incapable of doing for itself—creating a platform from which Rosser could both cast aspersions on Dorsey's methods while beginning the task of reversing a month's worth of bad publicity about Frank. As the *Georgian*'s Old Police Reporter put it: "To be strictly truthful, I must say that the man in the street believes Leo M. Frank guilty of the murder of Mary Phagan but the statement in defense of her husband given out by Mrs. Leo Frank had a steadying effect and has cleared the atmosphere considerably." Hoping to capitalize on the change of climate, Rosser jumped right back into the papers with a second open letter from Lucille to the citizens of Atlanta. This time, the obvious intention was to nail the solicitor with his own words:

I think fairness to Mr. Frank requires that the public should clearly understand Mr. Dorsey's position as stated by him in his reply to my statement that he proposes to use testimony which comes from witnesses as the result of torture.

His real position, as gleaned from his card, can be stated in the following sentence which he employed:

"I have only to say without in anywise taking issue with her premises as I might . . . that I welcome all evidence from any source that will aid an impartial jury, under the charge of the court, in determining the guilt or innocence of the accused."

That is to say, he thinks it unnecessary to waste time in disputing the fact that the detectives are procuring testimony from witnesses by torture. He considers this point immaterial. He believes he is thoroughly justified in using tortured testimony if it is turned over to him, for he says: "I welcome all evidence from any source."

The *Journal* and the *Constitution* stated that he had my cook arrested and carried to his office and quizzed to such an extent as to drive her into hysterics, and that after this he sent her screaming to the police station . . . After she left his office she was taken to the detectives' torture chamber, and, according to the *Atlanta Constitution,* she there had the third degree applied to her to the point of exhaustion, after which, she made an affidavit, which the detectives . . . gave out to the papers.

The solicitor had no charge against this cook and did not suspect her of any crime. Yet Mr. Dorsey waves this aside as trivial . . . because he says: "I welcome all evidence from any source," clearly implying that he will take it from the torture chamber if it is offered to him.

When Mr. Dorsey introduces this third degree evidence to the jury, can it be supposed that he will at the same time tell the jury that it comes direct from the torture chamber?

Lucille's new statement made it even harder for Dorsey to elude the charge that he was strong-arming witnesses, and it transformed his evasive rhetoric into an issue in its own right. All of which may explain why the solicitor let the salvo pass and failed to respond to an interview Lucille subsequently gave to the *Georgian*'s Old Police Reporter in which she reaffirmed her belief in Leo's innocence, praised his character ("He has always been the most kind, the most generous, the most thoughtful, the most considerate, and the most affectionate of men") and pointed proudly to his many charitable affiliations. While Lucille did confess that her husband was "no saint," the sole failings she could recall were that he smoked cigarettes and drank beer—although never to the point of intoxication. Otherwise, she said, "He ever has been just the plain, more or less studious and serious minded, Leo, gentle and thoughtful, sincere and true. He is my husband, and I love him very much."

Lucille Frank's avowed belief in Leo's moral integrity could not, of course, explain away the numerous salacious stories to the contrary or expunge the charge against him. Furthermore, as the superintendent's wife admitted in her second letter, her comments carried no legal weight: "Mr. Dorsey and the detectives know that I cannot go on the witness stand and deny the affidavits they have published in the newspapers. Under the law a wife will not be permitted to testify either for or against her husband. The law puts this absolute seal upon my lips." Still, she had what for now amounted to the last word.

During the early days of June 1913, Luther Rosser basked in the glow of accomplishment and acclaim. Quite aside from his successful campaign to give Dorsey a taste of his own medicine, the lawyer had finally vanquished the hillbilly John Muirs who'd opposed the opening of the Georgia Railway and Electric Company's Tallulah Gorge power station. Now the plant's turbines could generate electricity, industries across the state could expand and, not incidentally, wealthy Atlantans could build vacation homes overlooking the crystalline lakes that backed up behind the project's dam. God, in short, was in Rosser's heaven, and if things developed as he intended, the man who posed the most serious threat to Leo Frank would be indicted for the murder of Mary Phagan before he could ever utter a word in court.

Rosser launched his attack on Jim Conley just two days after Lucille Frank's last letter appeared in print by issuing yet another statement to the newspapers. This time, though, he spoke for himself, and as was his style, he made no attempts at diplomacy. The state's star witness was "a very ordinary, ignorant, brutal negro not unacquainted with the stockade [who] began to talk, and negro-like, to talk so as to protect himself." Newport Lanford, meanwhile, was if not "insane" then "temporarily out of his head." Had the detective chief and his officers "kept open minds seeking only the murderer and not seeking to vindicate their opinions, the negro would have by this time told the truth." Then there was the process whereby the police had secured Conley's affidavits, a process for which the defense counsel reserved his deepest scorn:

> Conley made one statement. It did not meet the announced opinions of Lanford. He made another. This second was not up to the mark; it did not sufficiently show Frank's guilt. Another was made, which was supposed to

be nearer the mark. Whereupon there was great rejoicing. Forgetting all others, this last statement—reached through great tribulations—was proclaimed the truth, and that there would be no other statement . . .

But what a statement! So full of contradictions, so evidently made for self-protection and wherein was so easily apparent the guiding hand of detectives.

Rosser's intent was not so much to brutalize Conley or ridicule Lanford as to persuade the judge who would preside at Frank's trial—68-year-old Leonard Roan, a well-respected jurist who in the 1890s had been Rosser's law partner—to order the Negro's transfer from the station house back to the Fulton County Tower. As long as the state's star witness remained in police custody and thus in the hands of officers with a vested interest in securing Frank's conviction, the lawyer argued, the truth would never emerge:

> This negro is not to give any other or further statement if the detective department can prevent, unless made under their supervision and direction. He must, at all times, be under the influence and control of Lanford. He must have Lanford's sucking bottle at all times to his lips, sucking Lanford's views and theories of this case.

Roan's response to Rosser's sortie was swift and sure. Early the next day, he informed Dorsey that he was inclined to return Conley to the Tower. On this point, the judge asserted, the law was explicit: The Negro was a material witness, and material witnesses belonged in the county facility, where Sheriff Wheeler Mangum was charged with shielding them from anyone—detectives included—bent upon influencing their testimony.

The defense was, of course, elated by the news, for Rosser believed that once Conley was freed from what the *Georgian* termed "police petting," he'd revert to form and talk to the press, becoming not only his own worst enemy but the prosecution's, too, for inevitably, he would slip and reveal what actually happened on April 26, which, by the lawyer's reckoning, was this: That Saturday morning, desperate for cash and "made passionately insane by liquor," Jim had been lurking in the pencil factory lobby. When he spotted Mary Phagan, mesh purse in hand, descending the stairs from Frank's office, temptation overcame him. He struck the girl, dropped her body into the basement through the elevator shaft, then clambered down the scuttle hole ladder. Upon discovering that the child wasn't dead, Conley gagged her with strips of cloth ripped from her underskirt, tied her around the neck with a length of twine fished from the floor and dragged her to the rear of the cellar. There, he strangled her. As to the issue of rape, Rosser considered it either inconvenient—its mention could rekindle the charges of impropriety swirling around Frank—or irrelevant, as he'd concluded Jim had been motivated less by sex than by greed. That is, the lawyer believed that Conley's reason for attacking little Mary had been to rob her. Otherwise, why had her purse, an item whose $1.20 in contents could hardly have interested Frank, disappeared? Finally, there were the murder notes, in Rosser's view the unalloyed product of the Negro mind. Only a Negro could have concocted a scheme to pin the crime on some other Negro, and only a Negro could have imagined that anyone would swallow the notes' logic. It was all clear, and Rosser was certain that once Conley was no longer being force-fed his lines by Newport Lanford, the grand jury would see. This, at least, was how things were supposed to work.

Shortly after Roan expressed his inclination to transfer Conley to the Tower, Hugh Dorsey—joined by William Smith—appeared in Judge Roan's chambers and filed a petition meant to derail the defense lawyer's plans. Yet exactly what the solicitor had in mind was hard to comprehend, for his petition was peculiar. He argued neither against Conley's return to the county facility nor for his continued incarceration at headquarters. Instead, he asserted that Jim was not a material witness and should be released from custody altogether.

Rather than grant or deny Dorsey's strange request, Roan set a hearing on the matter for two days hence.

During the brief interim, the logic behind Dorsey's move became apparent. He still regarded Conley as a material witness, yet he realized that if the Negro retained that status, Roan had no legal alternative but to remand him to the Tower. To avoid such an outcome, the solicitor intended to engineer Conley's release, then rearrest him as a suspect—though he suspected him of nothing—and hold him at headquarters indefinitely. And the beauty of it was, Rosser couldn't do a thing about it. Should Frank's lawyer fight the petition on its merits, he would find himself arguing that the Negro should be held to testify against his client. If he contested the final plan, he would be forced to maintain that the Negro was not a suspect.

Dorsey's petition had checkmated the mighty Rosser. Still, both sides had to go through the charade of Roan's hearing and accordingly, a small army of lawyers and reporters convened in his chambers at 10:00 A.M. on Friday, June 13. Though the solicitor's position didn't need bolstering, William Smith nevertheless produced an affidavit from Conley in which the Negro asserted that threats had been made against him during his brief stay in the Tower. Smith also tendered a statement of his own maintaining that the county lockup was often protected by only a single guard and was therefore accessible to anyone intent on harming his client. Meanwhile, Rosser submitted a statement to Roan as well, but the defense lawyer appeared resigned to the inevitable. In fact, he termed his communication a "protest," acknowledging that he was running up the white flag even as he denounced Dorsey's petition as a "farce meant to continue the present illegal confinement," accused the state of "winking" at justice, archly congratulated Smith for his "wise" decision to abandon Conley to the prosecution's whims, then raked Newport Lanford over the by now familiar coals:

> That the detectives should wish to keep Conley in custody and entertain him at the city's expense is not at all surprising. They have already extracted from him extravagant, unthinkable confessions, three or four in number. To these statements they have given the widest publicity, and to the credibility of the last one they have staked their reputations and hope of place. . . .
>
> Can any fair-minded man believe that Lanford is a fair man to be the custodian of this ignorant negro? What chance would he have to retract any lie he may have told, or if in a repentant mood he should wish to tell the truth? This negro in the city prison, in the power of Lanford, apart from all questions of truth, would be just as dangerous as Lanford would wish him to be. No one knows that better than Lanford, and no one would feel it as acutely as will this negro.

For six indignant pages, Rosser carried on this way, yet in the end, his observations had no bearing on Roan's thinking. Neither, for that matter, did Smith's. In fact, without reading either man's submission, the judge asked the lawyers if any of them considered Jim Conley to be a material witness. Though Dorsey considered him to be exactly that, he said nothing. As for Rosser, he, too, kept his opinion to himself. With everyone in such seeming accord, the judge promptly granted the solicitor's petition. It all took under ten minutes.

Accordingly, at 11 A.M., Friday, June 13—less than an hour after Roan made his decision—Newport Lanford appeared at the door of Conley's station house cell and announced: "Well, Jim, I am going to release you."

Though Conley received the news with a bewildered look, he silently accompanied the detective chief to the desk sergeant's office. After opening the docket book to the Negro's name, Sergeant A. J. Holcombe entered the following notation:

> Released, June 13, 1913, by order of Judge L. S. Roan, of the superior court, Stone Mountain Circuit.

This formality observed, Lanford took Conley by the arm and walked him through a door opening into an enclosed auto passageway, then up an alley to Decatur Street. There, as a small crowd watched, the detective chief relaxed his grip. Jim was a free man. Yet before the Negro could so much as move, Detective J. F. McGill—who "by some peculiar chance," as the *Journal* dryly put it, was stationed on the sidewalk looking for "suspicious personages"—rearrested him, whisking him back into headquarters, where Holcombe was, of course, waiting with his docket book. Once the new charge—"suspicion"—was noted, Lanford returned Conley to his cell, which was fine by Jim. "I didn't want to get out anyhow," he told his captor—and that, likely as not, was the truth.

With Conley off-limits, Dorsey was ready for court. He ordered his assistants to organize the guts of his case—the Negro's affidavits, a chart detailing the principals' movements on April 26, depositions regarding Frank's alleged peccadilloes, chunks of inquest testimony and Dr. Harris's autopsy report (which the state had finally received but whose contents would not be revealed until trial). He also hired Frank Hooper—an ex-prosecutor from Americus, Georgia, who boasted an impressive conviction record—to serve as his associate. Things, finally, were falling into place, so much so that despite the date now set for the proceedings to begin—June 30—being practically upon him, Dorsey decided to take a vacation. After securing a promise that the grand jury would resist any defense effort to use his absence to engineer Conley's indictment, he began packing. Yet even with this contingency covered, the solicitor needed to confer with one last individual before leaving town.

Saturday, June 14. In just a few minutes, the afternoon train for New York would pull out of Atlanta. Up and down the covered sidings that extended back from the great Moorish fortress of Terminal Station, passengers hurried to their cars. In the distance, a smoke-wreathed locomotive groaned. Yet standing off to the side, seemingly oblivious to the blur of activity and the fast-approaching hour of departure, Hugh Dorsey huddled in conversation with William Smith. The two had a critical piece of business to discuss. As a matter of course, any lawyer whose client is held more than a few days on such nebulous grounds as suspicion will initiate habeas corpus proceedings. But Smith, in return for the solicitor's pledge—contingent on Frank's conviction—to go easy on Conley, agreed to take no such action. The Negro would remain in jail. Only after consummating this deal—which amounted to an insurance policy on the state's star witness—did Dorsey climb aboard.

In the wake of Hugh Dorsey's hornswoggling of Luther Rosser, the aware-ness dawned among such Frank supporters as Sig Montag and Herbert Haas that the solicitor was a more formidable enemy than had at first been imagined. Though this realization didn't prompt second thoughts about Rosser—who, after all, was known less for his sleight of hand than for his ability to argue a case—it did suggest that it wouldn't hurt to bring in some new legal blood.

If the mighty Rosser was the gladiator Atlanta's wealthy employed to smite their foes, Reuben R. Arnold was the envoy they dispatched to cement business relationships, diffuse conflict and, generally speaking, lend an air of civility to the transactions through which discreet people adjudi-cate their differences and secure their fortunes. Grandson of a two-term Whig congressman from the Tennessee mountain town of Greeneville and son of a Confederate colonel who, following the Civil War, migrated to Atlanta and prospered at business and at the bar, Arnold grew up in a world of privilege at Deerland, the elegant home his father built on Peachtree Street just north of town. After attending the University of Georgia, he returned to Atlanta to practice law.

By the summer of 1913, the 45-year-old Arnold had made his name and his fortune as the principal in a firm whose most lucrative client was the *Atlanta Journal.* The lawyer's relationship with the newspaper had its roots in his long-standing association with its founder, Georgia's junior United States senator, Hoke Smith. Arnold was one of the politician's most trusted lieutenants. In fact, the men were so close that in 1910, when Smith took sick the day before he was scheduled to announce his candidacy against Joseph M. Brown for the state's governorship, Arnold delivered the cam-paign kickoff address.

That Hoke Smith tapped Arnold to make such a speech was no surprise, as the lawyer often served as a mouthpiece for his friends and his class. Dur-ing the first months of 1913 alone, he'd debated an Anti-Saloon League offi-cial bent on seeing Georgia's 1908 prohibition law enforced not just at cheap near-beer saloons but at such august watering holes as the Piedmont Driving Club; published a statement attacking a provision in the tax laws that gave tenant farmers (most of them Negro) power to take deductions that landlords (most of them white) opposed; and—sharing the dais with Rabbi David Marx—gave the keynote address at the Atlanta Chamber of Commerce's annual banquet.

What made Arnold an effective presence on either the stump or the after-dinner podium wasn't so much his speaking ability—although, like most Southern lawyers of his generation, he could turn a phrase—but the fact that in words and being he articulated the values his social and financial peers held most dear: property, prosperity, propriety. One of those men for whom the word "solid" was invented, Arnold stood six feet tall with broad shoulders and a thick middle and gazed out at an audience through a reassuringly bland face animated by soft blue eyes and topped by short blond hair parted on the side and combed over the ear. He was impressive but not threatening, handsome but not affected.

All of this, however, is not to say that Arnold was the sort of counsel who served chiefly as window dressing. He was a good book lawyer, the type who off the top of his head could dictate, say, the documents necessary to place a struggling company into receivership. He was also a superb litigator, more dangerous in court than one might at first imagine. As the *Constitution* put it:

> The sting of Reuben Arnold is as sharp as an adder. He's mighty polite about it—injects the poison skillfully, without mussing up the patient's clothing or causing him any unnecessary loss of blood, but the poison works just as surely. He is also some goat getter—a sort of polite purloiner of goats, is Reuben.

Moreover, Arnold possessed an expertise in medical evidence that could prove of value in a trial where the interpretation of autopsy reports might determine guilt or innocence.

Still, Mister Rube, as he was deferentially known, was better suited to winning over a jury than pummeling a witness, more skilled at building up a misunderstood client than attacking the state. He was the perfect complement to Luther Rosser.

Word that Reuben Arnold was affiliating with Leo Frank's defense hit the front pages while Dorsey was out of town. "I hazard not a thing in saying that there is no reason to believe Mr. Frank guilty of this horrible murder," the lawyer declared in his first public comment on the case. Then, underscoring the assumption at the heart of the defense's thinking, he added: "I do not believe that any white man committed the crime." Yet for all the credibility Arnold lent his new client, the fact remained that the non-white man to whom he was alluding was safely ensconced at the station house, his allegations unshaken, his presence overshadowing everything that lay ahead. Whatever it took, the defense had to do something to cripple Jim Conley's effectiveness before court convened.

On the swelteringly hot afternoon of June 24—six days prior to the date the trial was scheduled to start—Luther Rosser and Reuben Arnold ap-

peared in Judge Leonard Roan's chambers. In mid-July, Frank's lawyers explained, they were both due in court in the distant hamlet of Swains-
boro in connection with the J. W. McNaughton murder case. (In 1911,
McNaughton, a physician, had been convicted of poisoning his mistress's
husband with arsenic.) Citing the likelihood of a scheduling conflict, the
men sought a postponement. Nonsense, replied Hugh Dorsey, just back
from vacation and on hand to oppose the request. The Frank proceedings
would be history by mid-July. The defense was stalling. Whatever the
virtues of either side's positions, Roan paid them little heed. If the trial
began on June 30, he interjected, it would by necessity be held in the judicial system's cramped and airless temporary home, the Thrower Building.
However, if it could be delayed a month, there was another option. A courtroom in the old Atlanta City Hall—a brick and marble confection at the
corner of Pryor and Hunter streets just across from the nearly completed
Fulton County Courthouse—would be available. While itself dowdy and
undersized, the alternate venue boasted numerous windows—during a
southern summer, no small attribute. There was also, the judge confided,
something else: "Gentlemen, some months ago I promised my wife that I
would take her to the seashore on the week of July 4 and spend some days
there with her."

Such was the aversion toward the prospect of conducting a lengthy trial
in the stultifying Thrower Building and such was the respect for Roan—
who, complaining of fatigue, had added that he could use a break as well—
that the matter ended here. Dorsey dropped his objections and joined
Rosser and Arnold in an enthusiastic discussion of the judge's trip. The
press responded just as congenially, with the *Journal* splashing a photograph of an implacable-looking Mrs. Roan atop its front page beneath the
headline: SHE REALLY POSTPONED THE FRANK TRIAL. Yet the bonhomie
and bon voyages aside, all concerned knew that Roan's decision to delay
the proceedings by a month—court would now convene on July 28—constituted a break for Frank, giving the defense one last opportunity to neutralize the state's star witness.

Unlike the first attack on Jim Conley, which had been predicated on the
notion that the Negro, if left to his own devices, would implicate himself,
the attack Rosser and Arnold now unleashed was carefully calculated and
aggressive. Henceforth, they would operate less like lawyers than investigators, building their case much as the police would against a suspect.
The goal, even at this late hour, remained Conley's indictment for Mary
Phagan's murder. Barring that result, the attorneys hoped to amass such a
body of evidence that come July 28, they could turn the tables on the prosecution, in effect establishing Frank's innocence by proving the Negro's
guilt.

The opening shot in the assault on Conley was fired in the July 9 editions of the *Georgian* under the front-page banner:

NEW PHAGAN EVIDENCE FOUND

The development that occasioned this headline was the discovery of a piece of pay envelope bearing Mary Phagan's employee number in the factory lobby near where Frank's accuser admitted he was sitting on the day of the killing. The clue, the Hearst sheet argued, pointed "more strongly than ever to robbery as the original motive for the attack upon the girl," focusing "suspicion more directly upon Conley." What the *Georgian* failed to mention, however, was that this piece of evidence was neither new nor universally agreed upon as reliable.

Both the prosecution and the defense had known of the existence of the pay envelope scrap for two months. It was part of a cache of equally intriguing finds located on the afternoon of May 15 in the factory lobby by Pinkerton operatives L. P. Whitfield and W. D. MacWorth—the same detectives who had secured, respectively, the statement from Mrs. Coleman tending to discredit George Epps and the statement from Etta Mills tending to discredit Nina Formby. According to the report submitted by MacWorth, this is what the men discovered:

At the trap door I found what I took to be blood stains and also several pieces of cord used to tie bundles of pencils, and which was entwined in the pipes of a radiator adjoining the trap door. I also picked up a roll of paper and on examining it, found it to be the end of an envelope. I could see the number #186 stamped in the left-hand corner and a name written in lead pencil. I gave the paper to L.P.W. to take to the daylight, and he returned, saying that the name on the envelope was M. Phagan. Below the name could be seen the tops of figures, the plainest of which is the last, an aught.

And there was more. As Whitfield noted in his file, the two also located one last object:

We then secured an electric light and searched the floor around the trap door for blood stains, and we found several places that appeared to be spotted with blood. We also found a club with blood on it.

While the implications of the Pinkerton agents' finds were clear, their provenance was not. Yes, the club—a stout rolling-pin-like implement used by draymen to scoot heavy boxes across the floor—could have been wielded in the attack upon little Mary, inflicting the wound above her left ear. And yes, the tangle of cords—one of which showed indications of having been freshly cut by a knife—could have provided the length employed to strangle her. And yes, the piece of pay envelope (the "aught" visible beneath the name corresponded to the zero that would have concluded the line denoting the victim's wage: $1.20) could have been the victim's. But as Lanford and Dorsey had been asking since the discoveries were made, why hadn't any of the numerous detectives who'd scoured the factory during the nearly three weeks that passed between the murder and the day MacWorth and Whitfield struck gold noticed these clues? Furthermore, how was it that two agents who seemed to sympathize with Frank had made the finds? From the start, the police believed the items were plants.

Yet in the days following the *Georgian*'s exclusive, only the subtlest hints—the *Constitution* and *Journal* failed to run the story, while simultaneously rumors began circulating that a rogue faction of Pinkerton detectives had allied with the defense—indicated there were doubts as to the finds' authenticity. Around town, the word was that new evidence implicating Conley had surfaced. Which was just as Frank's lawyers wanted it.

Hard upon the revelation that the dead girl's pay envelope had been recovered came the news—again courtesy of the *Georgian*—that an eyewitness to Mary Phagan's murder had been located. This was Will Green, a 39-year-old Negro carnival worker from St. Louis, whose story, at least as the paper reported it, did everything but name Jim Conley as the killer:

> I was in Atlanta for a few days. I was shooting craps on the first floor [of the pencil factory] with this negro that Saturday. This fellow was half drunk and was losing money to me. He got mad and cursed his luck.
>
> Before long a little girl went upstairs. This negro said he was going to take her money away from her when she came down. I thought he was fooling at first, but when she came down he started for her. I yelled at him not to do it, but he kept right on. Then I skipped out, for I didn't want to get mixed up in any trouble. I stayed around town until the next Monday, and then I read all about how a little girl had been killed . . . and I knew that she was the one I had seen come downstairs at the factory.
>
> I got out of town right away and went back to St. Louis.

Will Green's narrative was also not without flaws. As with the clues located in the factory lobby, the carnival worker's existence had been known to the police since May, when an informant had wired headquarters from St. Louis. At the time, the detectives—who'd yet to question Conley and thus had no reason to believe he had been at the plant on April 26—had reacted coolly. Later, in the wake of Conley's affidavits, the defense had recognized

Green's import. By then, though, the carnival worker had vanished. During June, a posse comprised of Pinkerton operatives and Hearst stringers pursued Green down the Mississippi from St. Louis to Cairo, Illinois, then into Kentucky, Tennessee and finally Birmingham, where, according to the *Georgian*'s July 13 exclusive, the man had been cornered. But the paper had glossed over the inconvenient fact that Green was not actually in custody, that he'd merely been traced to the Alabama city. Moreover, its account had failed to mention the equally salient point that Green's allegations were hearsay. The Negro had supposedly passed them on to a friend who'd in turn telegraphed the police. In the brain-numbing glare of the headlines, however, the holes in the *Georgian*'s tale seemed minor. Most Atlantans believed that the carnival worker would be in court on July 28 to testify against Conley. Which, again, was exactly how Frank's lawyers wanted it.

With fresh evidence in hand and an eyewitness allegedly en route, all the defense needed to complete its case against Conley was a confession, and by mid-July it was claiming to be in possession of exactly that. William H. Mincey, a 43-year-old country schoolteacher who worked weekends for the American Life Insurance Company, had declared that on the afternoon of the murder, a drunken Jim Conley had told him he'd killed a girl earlier in the day. Intense and thin with deep-socketed eyes and a theatrical mustache, Mincey had made a favorable impression on Luther Rosser, and his sworn affidavit seemed to represent a genuine breakthrough. "We place the utmost reliance in it," Frank's counsel proclaimed. "It forms one of the strongest foundations for our belief in the guilt of Jim Conley."

Attesting to the significance of Mincey's statement was the fact that even the *Constitution* and *Journal* gave it ample coverage, yet as with all news auguring well for Frank, it was the *Georgian* that played the story hardest, portioning out chunks of it in a series of increasingly frenzied extras that culminated with the July 14 publication of a first-person account authored by Mincey himself. Screamed the front-page double-deck banner:

MINCEY'S OWN STORY
Tells How Conley Confessed Killing Girl

As Mincey recounted it, he had watched the Confederate Memorial Day parade on April 26 and then, hoping to drum up business, walked to Vine City, the territory he'd been assigned by American Life. Entering the neighborhood on Mitchell Street, he said he'd made calls at homes on Electric Avenue and Rhodes Street before heading up a dirt path that gave onto Carter Street. Like most "policy men" — as insurance agents were known to blacks — Mincey believed he had a gift for recognizing customers. Yet in the

Negro "with his head leaning down on his chest" sitting in front of a house off Carter Street, Mincey believed he'd found someone who behaved less like a prospect than a suspect:

> I stopped and got into a conversation with the negro about insurance. He told me his name was Jim Conley. I saw at once there was something wrong with him. He was nervous and excited, and tried to put me off and get rid of me by telling me to come to 172 Rhodes Street next week and he would take insurance. But as the negro had excited my curiosity by his incoherent, scattering way of talking and his nervous and excited manner, I remained standing there firing questions at him.
>
> He told me he was in trouble. I asked him if they had had him in jail or the stockade. He said no, but he was expecting to be in jail, and that right away. I asked him what for.
>
> He said, "Murder, I killed a girl today."
>
> I said: "Oh, I see! You are Jack the Ripper."
>
> The thought that occurred to me was that he meant he had killed some negro woman, and the only thing that seemed peculiar to me was that he said "girl" instead of "woman."
>
> I said: "Why did you kill her?"
>
> He began to get angry and I saw he was drunk.
>
> He said: "Now, that is for me to know and you to find out."
>
> I did not attach much to what he was saying, thinking it was the babbling of a drunken negro; but his restless, quick glancing around and his keeping his eyes on me, and the wild, unnatural glare in his eyes caused me to want to press him further to find out really what he had been doing.
>
> I said: "Let me write your insurance this afternoon," and started down to where he was.
>
> He said: "Don't you come down here," speaking this in an angry, threatening manner. This caused me to press him the more.
>
> I said: "No, I will take your application now," and continued.
>
> He said: "I tell you not to come down here."
>
> When he saw I was coming on anyway, he jumped up, and as he went round the corner of the house he said: "I have killed one today and I don't want to kill another."
>
> I said: "Well, one a day is enough; that is 365 a year," turned and walked off.

Gripping as this account was, it, too, was problematic, undermined by Mincey's spotty chronicle of his early attempts to alert the authorities to Conley's confession. On the Tuesday after the murder, he claimed he'd visited the factory only to find that no one would listen to him, and had left "thoroughly disgusted." Following the Negro's arrest, he maintained he'd stopped by headquarters, where an officer whose name he couldn't remember had allowed him to question Jim, who denied meeting him. Finally, he contended he'd mailed an anonymous letter to Dorsey informing him of what Conley said and urging him to take action. Only when nothing happened, he added, had he contacted Rosser.

In sum, Mincey appeared to be both self-dramatizing and self-pitying, an insight that didn't escape the state's lawyers. In response to the tale, Frank Hooper declared: "I sincerely doubt if [the] Mincey affidavit will ever be heard from as a seriously considered piece of evidence in the Phagan case. The statement was undoubtedly made and sworn to, but the prosecution will be able to disprove it if its signer is called as a witness."

Still, William H. Mincey had struck a nerve, and the prosecution couldn't hide it. Not only did his affidavit force Dorsey to reinterrogate his star witness (CONLEY IN SWEATBOX AGAIN, raved the *Georgian* in a circus-type banner), but it led to another outing for Jim, this time to Vine City. There, Detectives Starnes and Campbell led the prisoner around the neighborhood to see if anyone could recall seeing him in a tête-à-tête with Mincey on the day of the crime. (No one could, although the factory's day watchman, E. F. Holloway, would soon confirm that Mincey had visited the plant on the Tuesday after the murder.) Meanwhile, Dorsey's staff was said to be tracking down acquaintances of Mincey for an assault on his credibility.

All in all, Luther Rosser and Reuben Arnold had pulled off an impressive feat. Leaving aside the myriad questions concerning methodology and veracity, they had built a case against Jim Conley grounded in physical evidence, supported by an eyewitness account and topped by a confession. At the least, the lawyers insisted, their new evidence warranted a hearing, but the prospect of receiving one was slim. In the history of Fulton County, not only had no grand jury indicted a suspect against a solicitor's wishes, no grand jury had met to consider such action against a solicitor's wishes. And there was no doubt as to the wishes of this particular solicitor, who'd made it plain from the outset that he'd fight any move aimed at undermining Conley's effectiveness in court.

Yet despite Hugh Dorsey's opposition, if ever there was a moment in which opposing counsel might persuade a grand jury to act against a solicitor's will, that moment was now. In early July, the term of the panel that had indicted Frank had expired, and a new panel—whose twenty members had not heard the prosecution's case—had taken its place. This group could prove sympathetic to the argument that the evidence connecting the Negro to the crime was stronger than the evidence on which Frank was indicted.

Which was why even as Mincey's affidavit was dominating the papers, Rosser and Arnold were lobbying the just-seated jurors to confound precedent and take up the case against Conley.

Predictably, the *Georgian* spearheaded the campaign. By this date, Hearst's sheet had largely abandoned objectivity, completing the process that had started in mid-May when it began flirting with a pro-Frank stance. As Herbert Asbury would recall in the *American Mercury:*

> Although evidence was constantly piling up against [Frank], toward the end we worked as hard trying to prove his innocence and build up sentiment for him and against the Negro, Jim Conley, who had confessed to helping Frank hide the body, as we did to find legitimate news of the case. The *Constitution* and the *Journal* turned more or less against Frank, though never violently so, largely because the *Georgian* had taken the opposite position.

Every Sunday, the Old Police Reporter—the *Georgian*'s pseudonymous man on the Phagan beat—weighed in either to attack the state's case or build up the defense's. On July 6, he analyzed the evidence with an eye toward highlighting all facts pointing toward Conley as the murderer. According to his calculations, there were eighteen such facts. A week later, he analyzed the same evidence looking for facts damning to Frank. Here, however, he could come up with only three, each of which he dismissed as sheer coincidence, whereupon he seized the opportunity to readdress the facts against Conley, proclaiming:

> If it can be shown to the Grand Jury that Conley did say to Mincey, "I have killed one girl today, and do not wish to kill another," and that he was in a half-drunken stupor when he said it, that, in connection with the other evidence against Conley unquestionably would seem to make it the present Grand Jury's positive DUTY to indict Conley, without further ado!

In his next column, the Old Police Reporter argued that past history notwithstanding, the grand jury was not answerable to the solicitor—was, in truth, answerable only to itself:

> It would be unusual for the Grand Jury to indict Conley with an indictment already standing against Frank for the same offense. It would not be an unheard-of thing, however.
>
> Grand Juries are laws unto themselves. They may indict whom they please and when they please.

Indeed, the law and their oaths make it imperative that a Grand Jury indict ALL persons they believe deserving of an indictment, regardless of whether that indictment affects pending cases advantageously or disadvantageously.

Relentless as the *Georgian*'s propagandizing was, the defense did not rely solely upon the paper in its efforts to influence the grand jury. Rosser and Arnold knew where to apply pressure, and they did, sponsoring a letter-writing campaign in which correspondents—many hiding behind the cloak of anonymity—beseeched the grand jurors to take up the case against Conley.

On July 18, W. D. Beatie—the realtor who'd been appointed foreman of the newly empaneled grand jury—arrived at Dorsey's office and, in a move that shocked the Atlanta bar, asked the solicitor to call the body into session to consider the new evidence suggesting that Jim Conley had murdered Mary Phagan. When Dorsey refused Beatie's request, the foreman, as the *Constitution* gravely recounted, "went over the head of the state's legal representative in Fulton County" and ordered the jury to convene on Monday, July 21, a week before Frank's trial was scheduled to begin. For the solicitor, the defeat was the worst sort of affront, threatening his case while flouting his authority. Afterward, all he could manage was a terse statement:

> The meeting's only purpose will be to exploit the evidence and embarrass the State, and I hope the Grand Jury when it meets will decide to leave the matter alone.
>
> The indictment of Conley at this time will be a useless procedure that will not stop the trial of Frank.
>
> Conley is in jail and is going to stay there for some time. He is where the authorities can put their hands on him, and he can be indicted much more properly after the Frank case has been disposed of than before, and by the delay there is no danger of a miscarriage of justice.

Just two days would pass between Beatie's announcement and the convening of the grand jury, making the fight for the jurors' loyalties as brief as it was intense.

Sallying forth for the prosecution was William Smith. In a statement published in the *Constitution* and *Journal,* Conley's lawyer, after alluding to "an unseen force" that had bullied the jury into taking up the case, attempted to reassure Atlantans as to his client's honesty while simultaneously hinting darkly that it was the silent man in the Tower who'd been less than forthcoming:

Jim Conley has been dealing fairly with the state of Georgia. His story has been an open book to the sworn, trusted prosecuting officers of this state. He is not skulking coward-like behind the protection of iron bars, nor have his lips been sealed with tomb-like silence, until he can spring suddenly in a court a well-prepared statement, which the state has no opportunity to investigate and disprove. Conley allows himself to be grilled, cross-examined and unceasingly questioned by the representatives of the state. He is talking and talking now. Conley says to the state of Georgia, here is my story, investigate it, sift it, and prove it a lie, if you can.

What more could the grand jury ask? Conley is giving the state a square deal; Conley is remaining a voluntary prisoner, and no honest citizen doubts that he will be held to account for his part in this terrible tragedy.

Smith's duty to Conley discharged, he then praised Dorsey, painting a picture of an independent prosecutor at war against the entrenched interests of capital and privilege:

If the grand jurors do not want to please Frank and his friends, if they do not want to help clear Frank, they had better leave this alone, for the present. The good people of this county elected Hugh Dorsey as the solicitor general. Under the law, this makes him the legal adviser of the grand jury. There is not a businessman on the grand jury that does not follow in his own affairs the advice of the lawyer . . . to whom he goes for counsel. Let the grand jury do with the public business what they would do with their own matters . . .

Does the grand jury think their legal judgement or their personal integrity above that of our solicitor general, or do they doubt the professional or private character of Hugh Dorsey? The people of this county know that Dorsey is straight; that in this case he is fighting brains, money and influence. I know that he is standing by what he thinks right, and with constant threats thrown at him that they will defeat him at the next election and with every handicap thrown in his way in the discharge of his duty in prosecuting a white man who has wealth and influence.

While Dorsey let Smith do his lobbying, Rosser and Arnold did their own. In a joint statement published Sunday in all three papers, Frank's lawyers again asserted that the solicitor possessed no authority to dictate the grand jury's actions:

The Grand Jury is an independent body; it is under the control of no one. A Solicitor General is the adviser of that body as to legal principles merely, but he has no right to exercise any sort of control in determining who shall or shall not be indicted.

To permit a Solicitor General to use the position intrusted to him by the people to decide for himself who shall not be indicted is a danger too great to be contemplated.

With that, Rosser and Arnold accused Dorsey of prosecuting their client merely for the "gratification of his professional pride," charged him with withholding evidence and suggested that he had manipulated the previous jury in such a way as to deny it access to Conley's affidavits prior to Frank's indictment. Finally, after dismissing Smith's remarks ("It is appropriate that he should bolster up the Solicitor, as he depends mightily upon the Solicitor to protect his negro."), the lawyers warned the jurors that if they did not indict Conley, the "community would resent the rank favoritism shown this confessed criminal."

The atmosphere inside the Thrower Building conference room the Monday morning the jurors convened to take up the case against Jim Conley was explosive. As one reporter put it, not since the days immediately after Mary Phagan's body was found had there been as much electricity in the air. With eighteen jurors—just enough for a quorum—present, Foreman Beatie shut the doors and Dorsey took the floor. The solicitor began by citing legal precedents. Turning to the appropriate authority, he read:

> The Solicitor General is to determine whether or not to commence a particular prosecution, or to continue a particular prosecution or to dis-continue one already begun. The Solicitor General draws the bill of indict-ment and examines the witnesses, not with a view to the interest of any client, but alone to subserve public justice.
>
> The whole prosecution from the time the case is laid before him is under his direction, supervision, and control.

Dorsey did not, however, stop here, proceeding to address the substance of his case against Frank and the reasons why he believed Conley's indictment would threaten it. After an hour on his feet, he sat down. Minutes later, the jury voted not to indict Conley. Considering the fact that the panel once again contained several Jews—among them Oscar Elsas, president of the Fulton Bag and Cotton Mill, which, not insignificantly, was a client of Rosser's firm—this was a stunning victory for the solicitor. When he emerged shortly after noon, he could not resist chiding the defense for the manner in which it had tried to go over his head:

I am requested by the Grand Jury to say that no action will be taken at this time on the James Conley matter, and that that body will not pay any attention whatever to anonymous communications.

Thus this final pretrial skirmish ended in triumph for the state. Not surprisingly, the defense attempted to downplay the defeat. Declared Reuben Arnold: "It made absolutely no difference to us. It was purely a technical point that would have been in our favor." But such soft-pedaling could not hide the magnitude of the loss.

During the remaining few days before court convened, the inevitable parrying and thrusting continued, shifting the advantage to the defense here, the prosecution there. Boding well for Frank was Chief Lanford's announcement that one of the state's most anticipated witnesses—Nina Formby, the madam who'd charged that Frank had phoned her on April 26 seeking a room—would not testify. According to the newspapers, the police no longer placed any credence in the woman's story. Meantime, the prosecution received a boost when Reuben Arnold made the mistake of asking the judge assembling the panels from which the Frank jurors would be drawn to select those panels not from the vast pool of petit jurors to which all registered voters belonged but from the smaller pool of grand jurors comprised of Atlanta's most inflential citizens. The judge not only rejected the request, but Dorsey seized upon it, branding the defense both elitist and desperate.

Such exchanges, however, were now the exception. The season of contentious preparation had ended. All was in readiness, and all eyes focused on the cells where the antagonists awaited.

At the Tower, Leo Frank, as he'd done almost from the first days of his incarceration, surrounded himself with friends and business associates. The afternoon before court convened, Frank's wife, his mother (who'd just arrived from New York), his friend Julian Boehm and a dozen other well-wishers gathered. Lucille brought hors d'oeuvres and fresh Georgia peaches and the mood was confident, reassuring. Had it not been for the surroundings, it would have been hard to imagine that the guest of honor would the next morning go on trial for his life.

Meanwhile, several blocks to the west at the headquarters lockup, Jim Conley was readying himself in quite a different way. Since late June, Conley had been participating in a series of late-night tutorials that would come to be known as the "midnight seances." These sessions were divided into separate sections—one focusing on the content of the Negro's upcoming testimony, the other on the delivery. The faculty charged with ironing out the substance of Jim's stories included Detectives Black, Starnes and Scott, Chief Lanford and Dorsey.

When it came to public speaking, however, Conley had but one instructor: William Smith. Over many long evenings, the lawyer edified his pupil on the rules of discourse, stressing the importance of enunciation, timing and maintaining eye contact with an audience. Then Smith, a fair mimic, gave the Negro a taste of Luther Rosser's corrosive manner, preparing him for the inevitable courtroom encounter. On the eve of the trial, Smith was breathing the heritage and fire of the South's oratorical tradition into this unlikeliest of Negro students. Not that the lawyer would have phrased it so grandly. Years later, describing what he'd hoped to accomplish, he bluntly stated: "to render Conley impervious to cross-examination."

TEN

Prosecution

A nd so July 28 came—hot, with high clouds and the temperature rising. Outside the redbrick pile of the old Atlanta City Hall this Monday morning, the crowd was so thick that the intersection of Pryor and Hunter was nearly impassable. Trolley cars could make the turn only with a squealing of brakes and clanging of bells. Yet for all its number, the throng was orderly and quiet, its members content simply to gaze at the windows behind which the great battle would now transpire.

Inside, the mood, depending on one's location, fluctuated wildly. In a vestibule just off the second-floor courtroom, Leo Frank paced back and forth, flicking a rolled-up newspaper at the furniture. To avoid the crush of curiosity seekers, Frank had been whisked into the building at 7:30. Since arriving, he'd made a brief statement predicting his acquittal to a reporter, then devoured the breakfast his brother-in-law Charles Ursenbach had brought him. Around 9:15, his wife and mother appeared. At the sight of the women, Frank smiled and raised his hands, and there followed a series of embraces. After Lucille took her husband in her arms, kissing him and fondling his hair, his mother grabbed his chin and shook it as if to say he couldn't lose. The gesture elicited a confident laugh from Frank, yet nothing appeared to truly ease his mind. Noted the *Journal:* "Hardly once during this morning did Frank sit down."

Up on the third floor in the rooms—one for whites, the other for Negroes—set aside for witnesses, there was also little sitting, but not due to any anxiety on the part of those assembled. To most of the 120-some people whose testimony would determine Frank's fate, this was a holiday. With what amounted to the entire workforce of the National Pencil Company subpoenaed, the halls were packed with blushing girls in summer dresses. Young male employees lounged in the doorways, smoking cigarettes. Though some of those summoned evinced a sober mien, giddiness prevailed. Observed the *Journal:* "The men and girls [were] laughing and chatting as if they were at a pleasure party. There is none of the morbid curiosity of the street crowd here."

In the courtroom itself, a refreshed-looking Judge Leonard Roan sat in his high-backed leather chair behind the bench exchanging pleasantries with the opposing counsel. At the defense table, Luther Rosser and Reuben Arnold, both in white linen suits, were the picture of patrician Southern lawyers even if Rosser, true to form, had forsaken neckwear. Hugh Dorsey, however, was not so elegantly turned out. From his blue cotton suit to his black brogans, the solicitor was every inch the people's advocate. What these sartorial differences suggested, sheer numbers reinforced. Swirling around Rosser and Arnold was an army of legal talent the likes of which the Atlanta courts had rarely seen. All told, the defense employed eight attorneys—among them Herbert Haas, of counsel to the pencil factory; Rosser's partner Stiles Hopkins, son of the president of Emory College; Rosser's son, Luther Jr.; and Oscar Simmons and Paul Goss, engaged solely to assist in picking a jury and carrying notebooks crammed with information to help them do so. Against this silk-stockinged legion stood Dorsey, his associate Frank Hooper, Assistant Solicitor Ed Stephens, William Smith—who was present not only in his capacity as Jim Conley's lawyer but as Dorsey's jury consultant—and office clerk Newt Garner, who lugged the guts of the state's case in two beat-up valises. Also sitting at the prosecution table, looking uncomfortable in his Sunday best, was a final interested party, Mary Phagan's stepfather, John W. Coleman.

The room in which the trial would take place had formerly been used for city council meetings. Hanging from the pressed tin ceiling, the clustered globes of a dozen electric chandeliers cast a soft glow throughout. Bisecting the hall laterally, a row of fluted columns formed a boundary between the gallery and the field of battle. These reminders of civic grandeur were not, however, what initially caught the eye. Perched at intervals along the room's horseshoe-shaped rail were six ozonators, precursors of the air conditioner. The machines reoxygenated the chamber and, in combination with the electric fans that were bolted everywhere to the walls, were expected to blunt the crushing heat. Confidence in the devices was such that exterior windows were shut. The *Georgian* predicted that the courtroom "probably will be the coolest and best ventilated place in Atlanta."

Yet despite its antiquated charm and innovative preparations, the old city hall facility was sorely lacking in one regard: size. Inside the tiny arena, the principals found themselves sitting in ladder-back chairs jammed practically on top of one another. The teams of opposing lawyers were barely an arm's length apart. The court reporters squatted on the lip of the podium supporting the judge's bench, their notebooks balanced on their knees, their feet braced against the witness stand. The press was consigned to a cramped table in a corner piled high with copy paper and contiguous to the jury box. Meanwhile, the 250-seat spectator section—today filled chiefly by prospective jurors—tightly embraced the room on three sides, creating a fishbowl effect.

At precisely 9:58 A.M., following an hour given over to the impaneling of the veniremen, Dorsey announced the case of the State versus Leo M. Frank for the murder of Mary Phagan, whereupon the swearing of witnesses — a procedure that in Georgia in 1913 was conducted at the opening of a trial — commenced. After the solicitor called his list, bailiffs escorted the men and women upon whose testimony the prosecution would rely to the bench, and the familiar do-you-solemnlies reverberated through the chamber. What occurred next, however, was unexpected.

Approaching the bench, Rosser and Arnold stunned the courtroom by asking Judge Roan for a special dispensation to swear their witnesses at a later hour. The defense list, they maintained, was as yet fragmentary, and to complete it this morning would occasion a long delay. Immediately, Dorsey was on his feet, protesting that it would be unfair to the state if opposing counsel was so indulged. Judge Roan agreed with the solicitor, rejecting the request but granting Frank's lawyers unlimited time to prepare, which, as it turned out, was no time at all.

Within an embarrassingly brief five minutes, Rosser and Arnold had fleshed out their list, and as Stiles Hopkins began to call the names, it instantly became clear why they had been loath to show their hand: They were contemplating the risky tack of introducing Frank's character as a part of their case. There was no other way to explain the scores of Atlanta Jews who had been summoned. Nor was there any other way to account for a delegation of Cornell faculty members and graduates from Ithaca and elsewhere in the North. Plainly, this list of well over one hundred names was more than just a list — it was a theory of the defense, one that carried with it the prospect that in rebuttal, the state could introduce witnesses to testify to Frank's bad reputation.

Hence before a word of testimony was uttered, the defense had suffered a tactical setback, although the damage was mitigated by the fact that the prosecution did not emerge from the process unscathed. Aside from Jim Conley, whom Dorsey had pointedly not called because he wanted to keep him at headquarters until the last instant, Albert and Minola McKnight were the state's most sensational witnesses. Their story of what allegedly transpired in the Selig home on April 26 destroyed Frank's alibi. Yet as nearly everyone in the courtroom noticed, when the clerk invoked Albert's name, no one answered. Bailiffs were quickly dispatched to search for the wayward Negro, but if his wife's disposition was any indication, his absence may have been a blessing to the prosecution. After Minola was sworn, she again disavowed her notorious affidavit.

Emotions in the little courtroom were still mildly atingle from these developments when Leo Frank, his wife and his mother made their entries. For Frank, this was his first public appearance since the coroner's inquest two and a half months earlier. Before he reached the defense table, he was surrounded by friends. The outpouring of affection was so intense that for several minutes the proceedings ground to a halt, giving the reporters at the press table the chance to scribble madly. To one of the *Georgian*'s men, the factory superintendent was the image of poise:

> If there was any fear in the heart of the young prisoner, it did not show in his calm features. He seemed perfectly assured and self-possessed.

Yet to a *Constitution* writer, he seemed overwhelmed:

> Frank looked quickly about him as he came into the crowded room. He appeared, as a person frequently is, unable to take in all at once the scene. As he made out the straining faces and searching eyes, it seemed to dawn upon him that he was the man for whom the crowd had gathered and at whom all eyes were turned. His expression seemed to indicate that he was telling himself, "It's my appearance that has brought this stir and what can these people be thinking about me?"

Whatever the disagreement regarding Frank's state of mind, there was accord regarding his attire, which the *Georgian* termed "natty." For this momentous day, he had chosen a light gray mohair suit set off by charcoal pin stripes and a "fancy" black-and-white tie. The look was dignified but hardly reserved. Lucille, too, was sober yet stylish. Black hat trimmed in black chiffon and netted by a pulled-back veil, black suit smartly tailored, beribboned black-and-white watch fob peeking out from a white silk waist, she was the definition of understated refinement. The couple made a striking impression. No one else in the chamber was so well dressed.

Once the Franks took their seats in a tight semicircle of chairs that linked the defense table to their right with the judge's bench to their left and looked directly across the packed courtroom at the jury box, order was restored, and the voir dire began.

One panel at a time, the veniremen filed into the box, and to each group, Hugh Dorsey posed the same carefully worded questions to determine whether any preconception as to guilt or innocence existed. Many of the potential jurors admitted outright to a prejudice, disqualifying themselves. Others, however, were not so forthcoming.

When a master plumber named A. F. Bellingrath confidently swore that he possessed an open mind regarding Frank, Reuben Arnold, who spoke for the defense throughout this process, consulted the notebooks prepared by Simmons and Goss. Then he was on his feet.

"Haven't you formed an opinion from reading the newspapers and haven't you expressed your opinion to the effect that Frank is guilty?" Arnold asked. "Didn't you express such an opinion in the presence of Mr. Brent?"

Confronted with this incident, Bellingrath allowed that he had said it "looked that way," and Judge Roan announced: "I think he should be set aside for his own sake."

Yet for every venireman shown to be leaning against Frank, there seemed to be another partial to him, as Dorsey demonstrated during his questioning of a shoe salesman named W. W. Hemmett.

"Haven't you recently expressed an opinion that Frank is innocent and Conley is guilty?" the solicitor asked Hemmett.

"No, I never have," Hemmett answered, whereupon Dorsey referred to notes furnished by William Smith, then reminded the prospective juror of a "certain talk he had with acquaintances," forcing him to admit that he had indeed said he would need to hear some pretty good evidence before he'd convict Frank. With no further ado, Roan rejected the man.

Thus were dozens of potential jurors found wanting. During these volleys, the Franks could not have responded more differently. Throughout the morning, Lucille seldom removed her gaze from the solicitor's face. Anger appeared to blaze from her eyes and seeming scorn curled her lips. Conversely, Leo was utterly engrossed in the process. When a new panel was brought in, he looked intently into the face of each man, beginning at the upper row and shifting his gaze from one to another until he had scrutinized them all. Like the engineer that he was, Frank was calculating angles and dynamics, attempting to identify in bone structure or expression the torque of latent hostility.

For both the prosecution and the defense, there was, of course, a final recourse should a venireman whom either side found objectionable survive the initial questioning. Each camp was allotted twenty preemptory strikes, and it was with an eye toward advising his counsel when to exercise the prerogative that Frank studied physiognomies. As the *Georgian* observed:

> Not infrequently, when the Solicitor had closed his examination and had said, "Juror, look on prisoner; prisoner, look on juror," Frank would turn to Attorney Arnold and an instant later the announcement would be made, "Struck by the defense." Frank evidently was playing a large part in the striking of jurors.

In contrast, Dorsey based his decisions on more objective criteria—striking, for instance, all veniremen opposed to capital punishment. Additionally, the solicitor chose not to strike any of the Negroes on the panels.

Hence when Earl Davis and E. E. Hawkins took their spots in the jury box—a place that blacks occasionally ended up in because, though barred from the all-important Democratic primary, they were allowed to vote in the usually meaningless general election and were thus eligible for jury duty—Dorsey accorded them his blessing, forcing the defense to expend two of its strikes or else find itself in the unenviable position of having to persuade an integrated jury that Jim Conley was a liar.

Of the twelve veniremen who composed the first panel, all were dismissed. The fourth, sixth and seventh panels also failed to yield a single juror. Yet the slow start notwithstanding, the process would not be unduly long. According to one observer, a majority of the candidates had "weighed the gravity of the situation" and were "prompt and intelligent" in answering their inter-rogators' queries. At 11:20, the first juror—Atticus H. Henslee, a traveling salesman with the Franklin Buggy Company of Barnesville, Georgia—was selected, and from that point forth, the group fell into place. By 1:25, when court recessed for lunch, the task was finished. In addition to Henslee, the body that would sit in judgment of Frank included F.V.L. Smith, an electrical manufacturing rep; Monroe S. Woodward, a salesman at King's Hardware; Deder Townsend, a bank teller; J. F. Higdon, a contractor; Marcellus Johen-ning, a shop foreman; F. L. Wisbey, a cashier; Fred Winburn, a railroad freight agent; J. T. Ozburn, an optician; W. S. Metcalf, a circulation clerk at the *Geor-gian;* W. M. Jeffries, a realtor; and Charles Bosshardt, a pressman at the Foote & Davies printing firm. Eleven of the men were married—one for just a few weeks—and five were fathers. For their trouble, each would earn $2 a day. All would be sequestered at the Kimball House for the duration.

Predictably, the boys at the press table knocked themselves out trying to size up the jurors. Commented a *Constitution* reporter:

> Of the many juries called upon to serve in famous cases in Fulton County, none has classed higher in intellectual fitness or physical appear-ance than the men who make up the Frank jury. For the most part the jury is composed of young men this side of 40—men who have the appearance of having succeeded in life and who give promise of still greater success.

Considering the jurors' occupations, this analysis seems inflated. Yet even the defense's fiercest champion, the *Georgian's* James B. Nevin, gave the group high marks:

> The jury apparently is much above the average—it was plain enough all along that the defense was seeking a jury of high intelligence, and a city jury, moreover.

When court reconvened Monday afternoon, Hugh Dorsey called Mrs. Fannie Coleman. In her black hat and veil, the victim's mother could not have made a more piteous first witness:

> "When did you last see Mary Phagan alive?" the solicitor began.
> "On the morning of April 26, at my home."
> "When did she get up, and when did she have breakfast?"
> "She got up about 11:00 and had breakfast right afterwards."
> "What did she eat?"
> "She ate some cabbage and some bread."
> "What time did she leave home?"
> "About a quarter to 12:00."

Despite its restraint, Dorsey's catechism was leading to an operatic pass, for as he was conducting it, his clerk was standing in front of the witness stand, laying out the items that in a matter of speaking would reincarnate the victim and evoke her horrible demise.

The clothes Mary Phagan had been wearing when Newt Lee found her body in the National Pencil Company basement made a heartrending display: bloodstained dress, torn hose, scuffed pumps, battered straw hat. At the sight, Mrs. Coleman broke down and sank back in her chair, her face hidden by a large palm-leaf fan. After the officer in charge of courtroom security fetched the poor woman a glass of water, she collected herself, but not for long. The grim tableau was too much to bear, and not just for her. Observed the *Journal:* "Many spectators in court were affected. Mrs. Frank, mother of the accused, put her own hand before her face and bowed her head." Evidently, however, Leo Frank's response was not so empathetic. As the *Constitution* acidly noted:

> During [Mrs. Coleman's] mental suffering, Frank carefully kept his eyes away from her, although he sat facing her and the jury. He seemed either unwilling or unable to view the mother's grief.

For the state, the case could not have opened more perfectly. Understanding that a mother's tears spoke louder than words, Dorsey promptly ended his examination, thereby appearing the soul of consideration but in reality putting the defense in a bad spot. At this juncture, the last words Frank's lawyers wanted to hear were: "The witness is with you."

When Luther Rosser approached the stand, Mrs. Coleman was still crying. The lawyer started his cross-examination in as kindly a way as possible. He

inquired softly if "Miss Mary's hat" appeared as it had on the morning of
April 26. No, Mrs. Coleman replied. On that Saturday, it had been adorned
with a ribbon and red flowers. Then he asked if Mrs. Coleman had actually
observed her daughter board the streetcar to town. Again, she replied no. The
stop was at a little store two blocks from their home. Gingerly, Rosser had
succeeded in touching on a vital defense assertion—that the victim had been
robbed of items Frank simply would not have taken—while also casting
doubt on the state's murder-day timetable, which to work as Dorsey intended
had to begin at 11:45. Yet for all the lawyer's care, he'd reached his limit:

> "Do you know a boy named Epps?" he asked, referring to young
> George, the newsie who'd told the coroner's inquest that Mary confided to
> him that Frank had made lascivious remarks to her.
> "Yes."
> "Was he a friend of Miss Mary's?"
> "Yes, to a certain extent, he was."
> "Did you not talk to a certain gentleman on May 3 . . ."

Before Rosser could complete the question, Dorsey was on his feet, objecting. The solicitor knew that on May 3, Mrs. Coleman had told Pinkerton
detective L. P. Whitfield that her daughter "detested" Epps. Since Dorsey
intended to call the boy, he had no intention of letting his opponent continue
in this vein, although for the court's consumption, he argued that Rosser's
line of inquiry was immaterial unless he was trying to impeach Mrs. Coleman.
In response, the defense lawyer denied that he was trying to impeach anyone
and twice attempted to rephrase the question, but each time, Judge Roan sustained Dorsey's objection, leaving Rosser no choice but to quit the field.

From the instant the state's second witness, the aforementioned George
Epps, bounded to the stand, the pall that just moments before had hung
over the courtroom lifted. Not only was the fifteen-year-old barefoot, but
his shiny noggin looked, in one reporter's words, "as though a barber had
passed a razor across it that very day."

Epps's testimony was not as Tom Sawyerish as his appearance. At least
not initially. Under Hugh Dorsey's examination, he gave a straightforward
account of his April 26 activities, swearing that he'd been on the English
Avenue car when Mary Phagan boarded that morning at 11:50 and that the
two had ridden to town together. At 12:07, he claimed, they'd disembarked
at the corner of Marietta and Forsyth streets. After promising to meet him
at 3:00 to watch the Confederate Memorial Day parade, Mary, the boy said,
had walked south on Forsyth to the pencil factory to pick up her wages.

In essence, this was the narrative Epps had told the coroner's jury. However, he wouldn't be allowed to address the subject that had shocked the inquest, for when Dorsey posed his next question, the one everyone was awaiting, Rosser fiercely objected, prompting the solicitor to withdraw it and sit down. Consequently, Dorsey's final query—"What did she say to you on the car in reference to L. M. Frank?"—hung in the air unanswered, floating on the periphery of the jurors' consciousness, either a bomb that hadn't exploded or a bubble that should have been pricked.

Yet the substance of Epps's testimony was ultimately of less import to the state than his ability to provide a needed comic interlude, one that came during the defense's cross-examination and at Rosser's expense, for true to his looks, young George was a hayseed jester capable of turning an overbearing lawyer's queries into unintended straight lines:

"How did you know what time it was when Mary Phagan joined you going downtown that morning?" Rosser began.

"I looked at a clock just before I took the car," Epps replied.

"You didn't say anything about a clock when you testified before the coroner's jury."

"Nope, but I looked at one just the same."

"How did you know what time it was when Miss Mary left you?"

"I estimated it from the time she got on the car, and I told it by the sun. I can tell time by the sun." This, with evident pride.

"You can tell the time to within seven minutes by the sun, then?"

"Yes, sir, I can," came back a childish treble.

"Did Mary get off the car with you?"

"Yes, sir."

"You went to sell your papers then?"

"Yes, sir. I thought I could sell them by 3:00 and meet her as she had agreed with me to do."

"Had you sold out by 4:00?"

"No, sir, I finished sellin' out at the ball grounds."

"What time was it when you finished selling your papers?" Rosser was plainly baiting a trap.

"I don't know, sir," Epps replied.

Sensing his quarry's obliviousness, Rosser pounced: "Couldn't you tell by the sun?"

"No sir, the sun had went down by that time," Epps retorted brightly, not only escaping, but winning over the courtroom.

Observed the *Constitution:* "The positive way in which little Epps replied, and the stress upon the 'had went' caused a general ripple of laughter." This mirthful wave had yet to diminish when, a second later, Epps, having tweaked the nose of Atlanta's legal Goliath, was excused.

Shortly after Monday's final witness, Newt Lee, took the stand, the proceedings were interrupted by an explosion of flash powder from the south side of the gallery, behind the press table, where half a dozen photographers were set up. The cameramen had been patiently waiting for the right shot, and now that it had come—Dorsey on his feet, hands in pockets, facing old Newt; Frank, arms folded across his lap, gazing impassively upon the jurors; reporters nibbling pencils; spectators leaning in—they opened their lenses. The resulting images would be stripped across the next day's front pages. These pictures, however, did more than freeze a moment. Their taking marked the end of the trial's first-day fanfare and the onset of genuine hostilities. Prior to this disruption, Dorsey had been merely setting the stage. Yes, Fannie Coleman and George Epps had caused a stir, but aside from enabling the solicitor to establish the contents of Mary's last meal and the approximate time she'd left for town, they'd failed to contribute anything substantive. From this point forth, the state's deponents would be capable of delivering testimony that if not refuted could spell doom for Leo Frank.

While little of what Newt Lee had to say was actually new, he would make a forceful witness. In part, his tale simply continued to fascinate. Of equal importance, however, was his attitude. At once humble yet reveling in the fact that as he sat on the stand in his store-bought suit, "dem big lawyers," as the *Georgian* phrased it, "was pay[ing] him respecks," the Negro cut an engaging figure, one Hugh Dorsey knew exactly how to exploit.

After quickly establishing Lee's presence at the factory at 4:00 on the afternoon of the crime and the fact that on the previous day, Frank had specifically instructed him to arrive at that hour, the solicitor went to work:

> "When you appeared at the factory to report on afternoons what did you generally do upon going up to the second floor where Mr. Frank's office is situated?"
>
> "Say, 'Howdy, Mr. Frank.' He usually called, 'Hello, Newt,' and if he wants anything he calls me into his office."
>
> "What did he do when you went to the second floor on Saturday, the 26th?"
>
> "He came to the door, rubbing his hands and saying he was sorry I had come so early. I told him I needed sleep and was sorry, too. He said go out in town and have a good time because I needed it."
>
> "Could you have slept in the factory?"
>
> "Yes sir. In the packing room."

Having completed one station of the cross, Dorsey directed Lee to the others. Regarding a topic he intended to make a major issue—the alleged skips in Lee's April 26 time slip—the solicitor's questions revealed that he suspected Frank of setting the Negro up from the outset:

> "What did Frank say when you came back?"
>
> "I went to the door and told him I was back, and he says, 'What time is it?' And I says, 'It lacks two minutes of 6:00.' He says, 'Don't punch yet, there is a few worked today and I want to change the slip.' "
>
> "What did he do then?"
>
> "Put in a slip for the time clock. It took him twice as long this time than it did the other times I saw him fix it. He fumbled putting it in while I held the lever for him and I think he made some remark about he was not used to putting it in."

From here, Dorsey danced Lee through the rest of the familiar narrative. Once again, Newt related how Frank had "jumped back frightened" upon meeting James M. Gantt on the sidewalk. Once again, he delivered the parable of the shoes, which began with Frank informing Gantt that his two pairs had been swept out and ended with Gantt, upon entering the plant, easily finding them. And once again, he told of Frank phoning at 7:00 to ask if things were all right, reasserting that the superintendent had never called before.

At this juncture, Dorsey was ready to elicit Lee's account of the discovery of the body, but before introducing the topic, he wanted to make certain that the Negro and, more important, the jurors could visualize the crime scene, which was why he unveiled a diagram of the pencil factory drawn for him by the *Georgian*'s Bert Green, hanging it on a wall to the judge's right where all concerned could see.

An elaborate poster-sized production, the illustration was a showstopper. And no wonder. During the celebrated Harry Thaw trial in 1907, Green, a *New York Journal* alumnus, had dazzled Manhattan with his depictions of murder victim Stanford White's apartment. For Dorsey, Green had created something just as provocative. The work's centerpiece was a cutaway rendering of the pencil factory picturing everything from Frank's office at the front of the structure to Mary Phagan's workstation at the rear to the now infamous elevator shaft, lobby scuttle hole and basement toilet from which Lee said he'd spied the body. Overlaying this architectural skeleton were three dotted lines in different colors, one charting dimensions, the other two—as a key at bottom left explained in no uncertain terms—representing paths "the accused" had traversed while committing the crime. Located at critical junctures along these black, red and green route markings were scarlet pinpoints and Maltese crosses that, as the key also helpfully explained, denoted such areas of interest as where blood had been discovered or "where Girl was murdered on Office Floor." As a final touch, several close-up photographs of details like the sliding basement door and a previously unmentioned lock on a metal-room door had been attached to the sketch's borders, lending both gloss and credibility to the whole.

The "Diagram of Phagan Murder—Venable Building" (as Green had labeled it) gave the state a potent piece of graphic firepower, and Dorsey wasted no time guiding Lee through it. The Negro indicated various sections of the building he'd entered while making his rounds the Saturday night of the murder and reiterated that the gas jet in the basement had been burning no brighter than a "lightning bug." Proud of his analogy, Lee elaborated: "Has you ever seed one whut's been hit with a stick? Hit jest do shine. Well, dat was dat light. Hit just was shinin', and dat's all." Then, he pointed out where he'd found the victim.

The factory tour complete, Dorsey steered Lee back to the topic of Frank. First, he brought up the matter of Newt's predawn effort to call his boss, eliciting the news that the telephone had rung eight minutes without anyone picking up. Next, he introduced Lee's Sunday-morning encounter with Frank, touching once more upon the time clock and securing testimony contradicting the superintendent's subsequent assessment that Newt's slip had been incorrectly punched:

> "When did you see Frank?"
>
> "I saw Mr. Frank Sunday morning at about 7:00 or 8:00. He was coming in the office."
>
> "How did he look at you?"
>
> "He looked down on the floor and never spoke to me. He dropped his head down this way."
>
> "Was any examination made of the time clock?"
>
> "Boots Rogers, Chief Lanford, Darley, Mr. Frank and I were there when they opened the clock. Mr. Frank opened the clock and said the punches were all right."
>
> "What did he mean by all right?" To this, Rosser objected, but Roan overruled him, allowing Lee to answer.
>
> "Meant that I hadn't missed any punches."

Finally, Dorsey asked Lee about his much debated late-night meeting with Frank at the police lockup on April 29, giving the Negro the chance to repeat his version of the encounter, which ended, of course, with Frank, exasperated by Lee's denials of involvement, cautioning: "If you keep that up, we will both go to hell." The solicitor could not have scripted a better exit line.

Luther Rosser's attempt to undo the damage Lee had done to Frank would not be entirely ineffective. During the first hours of a cross-examination that would spill over into the next day, the lawyer managed to extract a good deal of helpful testimony. As in the course of Dorsey's examination, much of what Lee had to say—his acknowledgment, for instance, that Frank, having just fired Gantt, had an innocent reason to be flustered by the man's appearance at the factory on April 26—merely restated information he'd revealed at the inquest. But Rosser also succeeded in eliciting several new tidbits that boded well for his client. On the afternoon of the murder, Newt told the lawyer, anyone could have entered or exited "that great big old rambling" building without Frank knowing. Then there was Lee's admission that Frank, unlike someone with something to hide, had not instructed him to avoid the basement during his rounds. In fact, the Negro confided that had he gone into the cellar every half hour as Frank expected rather than only occasionally, he'd have found the body sooner. And then there was Lee's insistence that he saw nothing out of place in the metal room during his passes through it that night.

Yet such successes notwithstanding, Rosser's approach to Lee seemed unproductively disputatious. He contested, for instance, the wording of his assertion that on the afternoon of the murder Frank had told him to go out and have "a good time," suggesting that what Frank had actually said was to go out and have "fun." Similarly, he took issue with his vivid lightning bug analogy, and during a particularly nasty string of questions—each beginning "How many times" and all implying that Newt had related his story so often he'd become confused—he came close to flat-out badgering the witness. In fact, when Lee at last cried, "I don't know, sir; there were so many blim-blamming at me so much that I couldn't keep count," he appeared to be accusing the lawyer of the same behavior. This, however, was just the start.

Rosser's Tuesday morning cross-examination of Lee would take only two hours, but in that brief span he would have at the Negro with a vengeance. The interrogation, a *Georgian* reporter would later note, "reminded me much of a big mastiff worrying and teasing a huge brown rat grimly bent eventually upon the rat's utter annihilation." Yet for all Rosser's forcefulness, this second round of questioning would reveal more about the lawyer than Lee, begetting doubts regarding not just his approach to Negro witnesses but the defense's theory of the crime.

Everything about Rosser's treatment of Lee was intended to intimidate him. Rosser began by asking about the events leading up to the discovery of Mary Phagan's body, honing in on the disparity between the Negro's claim that the girl was lying on her back and the responding officers' contention that she was stomach down. This was hardly a topic dear to Lee's heart, for it reintroduced one of the circumstances that had originally cast suspicion on him, but he met it head-on, explaining that by "back" he'd meant "side." Newt and the police had apparently seen the same thing. Not having broached this matter to obtain information favorable to Lee, Rosser changed the subject.

"You said yesterday that Mr. Frank jumped back when he met Mr. Gantt?"

"Yes sir."

Here, Rosser picked up a copy of the inquest transcript from the defense table and read aloud from Lee's testimony. The Negro had not mentioned Frank "jumping back."

"Well, they got that wrong," Newt exclaimed when the recitation ended, sending a buzz through the courtroom but providing Rosser with an opening he couldn't resist.

"That was a bad stenographer down there, wasn't he?"

At this, Hugh Dorsey objected. Rosser, however, was in no mood to be corrected by his younger counterpart, snapping: "Of course, this gentleman on account of his age is entitled to lecture me."

Judge Roan, seeking to appease both parties, ruled that as long as Rosser did not ask Lee to express opinions, he could question him about any inconsistencies between his remarks to the coroner's jury and his trial testimony. Yet before Rosser could get going again, Dorsey's associate Frank Hooper set the pot back to boiling by requesting that Frank's lawyer specify the session of the inquest to which he was referring. The body had convened three times to discuss the Phagan murder.

"I am always glad to accommodate these men whenever I can," Rosser responded airily.

To which Hooper retorted: "You have got to accommodate me."

Whereupon Rosser exploded, "No, I haven't. The man never was born whom I have got to accommodate."

Despite Rosser's outburst, Judge Roan ordered him to comply with the state's request—not that this changed anything.

Resuming his threatening stance before Lee, Rosser took up another discrepancy between the witness's direct testimony and his statements at the inquest. "You said yesterday," he began, "that when Frank put on the clock tape that Saturday it took twice as long as it did the other times you saw him do it. Why didn't you tell the coroner it took twice as long as it did before?"

"I did tell them it took longer."

"Then all this record here is wrong?" Rosser asked incredulously, holding up his copy of the transcript.

"I can't help about those records," Newt shot back, sending yet another quiver through the gallery.

If Luther Rosser had never met a white man he would accommodate, he'd surely never met a Negro he was going to let best him, and he wasted no time putting this one in his place, firing off a round of questions implying—no matter how irrelevantly—that Lee, prior to his arrest, had been shacked up with the woman who cooked for him. Though Newt denied the charge, his response was beside the point. The insinuation had been made.

Satisfied that he had gotten to Lee, Rosser took up the topic that had increased early suspicions against him.

"Were you down in the basement when the police found some notes?"

"They said something about a book."

"They read you something about the night watch doing it?"

Before Newt could answer, Dorsey objected. His grounds were procedural. The murder notes had yet to be introduced into evidence and were thus off-limits. Ridiculous, Rosser replied, and began to state his reasoning, whereupon Dorsey asked the judge to withdraw the jury. Roan so ordered, paving the way for a series of arguments by Frank's lawyers that not only presented their rationale and explained Rosser's treatment of Lee but suggested they were blindly rolling the dice.

After Dorsey produced the murder notes, Reuben Arnold introduced the defense's intentions:

> The defense expects to show that the two notes found in the basement of the National Pencil Company were very obscure notes and the police were trying to read them in the presence of Lee.
>
> They read this one: "He said he wood love me laid down played like the night witch did it but that long tall negro did buy his self."
>
> In an instant, Lee said, "That night witch means me." It showed familiarity with the notes. Isn't it strange that a negro so ignorant and dull that Mr. Rosser had to ask him a question ten times over could in a flash interpret this illegible scrawl?

More explicitly, Luther Rosser added:

> We've got to commence somewhere and at some time to show the negro is a criminal and we might as well begin here as anywhere else.

In other words, the defense hoped to establish that Lee was involved in Mary Phagan's murder, specifically, that he was somehow connected to the murder notes. Though Rosser did not elaborate further, the *Georgian* reported that Frank's lawyers were laying "the groundwork for their theory that Jim Conley was the murderer of Mary Phagan and that Lee assisted in writing the notes."

Not surprisingly, Hugh Dorsey scoffed at the defense's logic, but after pondering it all, Roan ruled that Rosser could continue, and the jury was returned.

Considering the build-up, what now occurred was not only anticlimactic but revealed that the defense hadn't thought its gambit through.

"When he said 'the night witch,' didn't you say, 'Boss, that's me?'" Rosser resumed.

"No, sir," Newt answered. "I said, 'Boss, it looks like they are trying to lay it on me.'"

This was the explanation Lee had advanced all along, and he enunciated it now with such certitude that after a couple of meaningless follow-ups, Rosser sat down, turning the witness back over to Dorsey. During the solicitor's redirect examination, he quickly established that Newt had not met Jim Conley until a month after the murder, when both were in jail, thus undermining the defense's contention that the men were accomplices. That settled, Dorsey approached Bert Green's diagram of the pencil factory. He intended to lead Lee through it one more time.

Before Dorsey could get started, however, Reuben Arnold was on his feet. "I object to that picture," he protested. "It is nothing but Mr. Dorsey's theory of the case. He's got all kinds of marks here." Why it had taken the defense so long to speak up about the diagram is unclear, but the protest fell on deaf ears. Roan ruled that since Dorsey was alluding to the work for reference purposes only, he could proceed, which he did with a flourish, using the umbrella Mary Phagan had been carrying April 26—the umbrella that had been discovered in the factory elevator shaft the next morning—as a pointer.

Rosser, as well, got a final shot at Lee, but it seemed unduly harsh. Returning to a tack that had already failed once, he tried to show that the Negro had been quizzed so continuously that he'd become bewildered: "The policemen and detectives talked to you all the time, didn't they? They fired a pistol beside you, didn't they? My friend John Black and those fellows talked to you day and night, didn't they? They cussed you and they praised you, didn't they?"

To all this, Lee allowed that the police had questioned him a good deal, but then, seizing a final chance to correct Rosser, he added: "Sir, they didn't praise me none." Shortly thereafter, he was excused.

As Lee descended, the gallery, noted one writer, "smiled an applause as gracious as bowing prima donna or stentorian tragedian ever received." Outside the courtroom, the Negro was asked if there was anything he wanted. Throat parched from the ordeal, he responded, "A chew of 'bacca, any kind," prompting an outpouring of quids and plugs.

The consensus among the newspapers was that Lee's testimony—particularly his account of Frank's nervousness on Saturday afternoon and the unexpected call later that night—had greatly aided the state. The bulk of the analysis, however, was devoted less to the substance of Newt's words than to the resiliency he had shown in the face of Rosser's blasts. Observed the *Constitution:*

> Seasoned courthouse officials and old reporters marveled at the way the negro held out against the crossfire of questions, all aimed at confusing him.

Added the *Journal:*

> The negro appeared to hold his own remarkably well under the rigid cross-examination by Mr. Rosser. He argued with the attorney without hesitancy and took open issue with the inquest record whenever the attorney contended that it conflicted in minor ways with his testimony in court.

Yet it was the *Georgian's* James B. Nevin who contributed the sharpest critique, commenting not just on Lee's grace under pressure but on the miscalculations at the core of Rosser's approach. Regarding the lawyer's attempts to tie the Negro to Mary Phagan's murder, Nevin wrote:

> As for the examination of Newt Lee by Mr. Rosser, it impressed me often as a mere shooting in the dark, hoping to hit something.

Regarding the ferocity with which Rosser had gone after Lee, Nevin was even more dismayed:

> Time and again, Lee rallied and came back at his tormenter with telling effect—it is likely altogether that more than once the jury's sympathy went out to Lee in large measure while Rosser was grilling him—and to the darkey's occasional sallies and adroit sidesteps, the spectators in the courtroom frequently responded readily with approving titters and guffaws.

Nevin's most pointed remarks, however, were premonitory, casting an ominous light on Rosser's impending engagement with a "far more important sable figure," Jim Conley:

Will Conley be as nimble-witted as Lee was?

Will he be able to withstand the onslaughts of Rosser and Arnold even approximately as well as Newt stood them?

If he does——

At this juncture in the proceedings, Conley, of course, was still in the future. For Hugh Dorsey, the immediate task was to continue erecting the scaffolding of evidence that his star witness's testimony would cap, thus no sooner had Lee stepped down than he called Sergeant L. S. Dobbs. From Dobbs, the solicitor secured the familiar yet harrowing account of what the responding officers found in the factory basement. "The girl was lying on her face, the left side on the ground, the right side up. Her face was punctured, full of holes, and was swollen and black. The cord was around her neck, sunk into the flesh. Her tongue was protruding." After the sergeant identified the murder notes (which he had located), the cord and the strips of fabric that had in turn been looped over it, Dorsey asked him to demonstrate how the noose had been fashioned. On cue, Dobbs took the cord and tied it around the solicitor's outstretched arm.

In his examination of Detective John Starnes, Dorsey elicited a recitation of his guarded Sunday phone conversation with Frank, a comparison (over Arnold's objection) of Frank's nervousness with Lee's calm that morning and a description of the red stains discovered on Monday in the metal department. All of this was also well known, but what followed was not. First, Dorsey asked Starnes to detail an experiment he'd conducted with the plant clock that revealed that someone intent upon fabricating a time slip implicating Lee could have done so in minutes. Next, Dorsey ascertained that cord of the sort used in the crime had often been left dangling from a nail near little Mary's knurling machine. Finally, he established that a previously unremarked-upon door opening into the second-floor chamber where he contended Frank committed the murder was usually kept bolted (hence the photograph of the lock tacked to Green's diagram), isolating the spot from the rest of the building.

Though the defense did not stand idly by as the state advanced its points, Luther Rosser initially seemed at a loss on how to proceed. He started his cross-examination of Dobbs, for instance, by taking a last stab at pinning the crime on Lee. Considering Dobbs had supervised the test that indicated the night watchman's lantern was so smudged he could not have made out the body as he claimed and must have known more than he'd let on, the line of questioning was not inexplicable. It was, however, ill-advised.

Once Rosser spit Lee from his craw, however, he began to counterattack effectively along several fronts, serving notice that he intended not only to tear apart the prosecution's case but to attach enough contradictory additions to transform anything left standing into an evidentiary scaffolding of his own—one from which he planned to hang Jim Conley. For starters, Rosser got Dobbs to mention the trail running the length of the basement over which Mary Phagan's body had apparently been dragged. This was hardly news. Everyone acknowledged that the body had been dragged—everyone, that is, except Conley, who in his last affidavit had sworn he'd carried it on his shoulder. While Rosser failed to persuade Dobbs to take the next step and agree to the proposition that the trail began beneath the scuttle hole ladder (a proposition that had the sergeant confirmed it would have undermined the state's thesis that the body had been transported in the elevator), he didn't let this setback slow him down, moving quickly to introduce a number of other details Dorsey had ignored. First, he obtained the admission that the basement contained enough pads and pencils for the murder notes to have been written there. Then he secured the fact that the basement door had been crowbarred—again, a well-known particular, but for the state a vexing one, as Frank would have had no reason to take such action. Finally, he induced Dobbs to confess that he had casually examined Mary's underpants and consequently couldn't recall whether they had been slit with a knife or torn by hand. Why Rosser raised the distinction, he didn't say, intimating that all would be explained in time.

With Starnes, Rosser took essentially the same tack, beginning by trying to determine if there were further facts concerning the crime scene that the state had slighted. For openers, he focused on the basement door, specifically the metal staple that had been pulled from it. Had Starnes noticed that the staple was bent? Yes, the detective replied—which was exactly the answer Rosser wanted, suggesting, as it did, that whoever escaped out the back had used a considerable degree of force. Rosser then attacked the most damaging elements of Starnes's direct testimony. He started by assailing the detective's recollections of his Sunday-morning phone conversation with Frank, peppering him with questions designed to elicit discrepancies between his trial account and the version he'd given at the inquest. As he'd done when Rosser used the strategy against Lee, Dorsey frequently objected, but Judge Roan allowed the examination to continue, and while the differences it produced were inconsequential, Starnes eventually confessed: "I cannot give the words of the conversation between myself and Mr. Frank." This admission secured, Rosser tore into the rest of Starnes's story. Could the detective swear that the red spots discovered on the metal-department floor were blood? "I don't know that the splotches that I saw there were blood," Starnes conceded. Weren't cords like those located near Mary's workstation also to be found in the basement? Not exactly, Starnes responded. Those cords had been "cut up in pieces" shorter than the length used in the crime. Then how about elsewhere in the plant? Yes, Starnes acknowledged, "there generally were pieces of cord in all parts of the building." Finally, Rosser asked the detective to critique the responding officers' performance, earning the concession that they had overlooked such clues as Mary's hat.

Rosser had at last begun to exhibit his vaunted prowess, yet as Dorsey briskly demonstrated when the witnesses were turned back over to him for redirect examination, the prosecution was not going to surrender any ground.

During his second pass at Dobbs, Dorsey did his best to derail the idea that the body had found its way to the basement other than via the elevator. "A man couldn't get down that ladder with another person," Dobbs testified. Then Dorsey mocked the notion that the basement door would have required any great strength to jimmy, eliciting the statement that the staple, far from being bent, was straight and smooth as if from frequent removals.

During his second go at Starnes, Dorsey attempted to bolster the point that no matter the exact words, Frank's demeanor on the morning the body was discovered had been suspicious. This he did by glossing over the phone call and focusing on some of Frank's later behavior at the factory, specifically his effort to joke with his coworker Darley regarding the fact that he wasn't wearing his typical brown suit but was instead clad in blue. ("Did anyone else joke that morning?" the solicitor inquired. "No," Starnes replied.) Then, in an attempt to combat the doubt generated by Starnes's inability to say whether the red spots discovered in the metal room were in fact blood, Dorsey produced several chunks of stained wooden floor, which the detective identified as the pieces chipped up the Monday after the murder. Having thereby established the evidence's tangibility, if not its chemical composition, Dorsey hurried on, ending his exam by using Starnes to introduce what would be a recurring theme—the alleged preferential treatment accorded Frank since his arrest. Dorsey was subtle here, merely asking the detective to recall how Frank, prior to his transfer to the Tower, escaped confinement in the headquarters lockup by securing a private room adjacent to Chief Lanford's office.

With the conclusion of Starnes's testimony late Tuesday, the pattern that would prevail for the next several days had been set. The battle would seethe back and forth as one side, then the other, fought to get across its theory of the crime. As in most circumstantial evidence cases, these theories rested on numerous, conflicting details, none more prone to dispute than those concerning the murder scene itself. Which was why the significance of a skirmish that took place once Starnes stepped down was immediately recognizable.

Afternoon shadows had begun to fall when Judge Roan asked opposing counsel if they had any business to conduct before he called the day's session to an end. Yes, Dorsey replied, he wanted to enter some material into evidence. The murder notes, the length of cord, Mary's clothing—all were acceptable to the defense. A final item, however, was not. After examining Bert Green's factory diagram, Luther Rosser exclaimed: "Oh, no, this will never go into the evidence. If my brother wants to insist on it, why I ask that the jury be excused while we argue it."

Once the jurors departed, Rosser resumed: "Your honor, this thing is not admissible." Then, turning to Dorsey, he added: "I didn't think you or my friend Hooper would try to put such a thing as this over me—seriously." Yet beneath his jocularity, Rosser was in deadly earnest. Here was a work that depicted Frank meeting Mary Phagan in his office, accompanying her to the metal room, then carrying her body to the basement in the elevator. Here, in other words, was a work that presented some of the case's most debatable points as if they were proven facts, and on the heels of Rosser's protest, an outwardly chastened Dorsey conceded: "I realized that the plat was inadmissible." Accordingly, Roan ordered the solicitor to remove "anything argumentative" from the illustration, bringing the session to its close.

Yet when court reconvened Wednesday morning, the issue had not been resolved. All printed matter had been excised from the diagram, but the Maltese crosses and the colored lines remained. Leaping to his feet, Reuben Arnold objected: "You don't have to label a horse to see it is a horse." In response, Dorsey acknowledged that the markings represented theories. But he then produced several precedents dug up for him by William Smith, who since the trial's first day had been posted in the solicitor's law library. "As issues arose," Smith later recalled, "I would make a rapid examination of the authorities and send Mr. Dorsey a brief summary." In this instance, Smith's research showed that Georgia judges had previously accepted similar works into evidence, and Roan ruled that "State's Exhibit A" could be admitted without further alteration. Consequently, the illustration would hang in the jurors' view until the state rested and abide in their minds for who knew how long.

The trial's atmosphere would now grow more heated in every sense of the word—for, as by this juncture was apparent, the much heralded ozonators were a bust. On Tuesday, the temperature inside the courtroom had reached 91 degrees. Consequently, Wednesday found spectators falling back on an older but more reliable technology, the handheld fan, and reporters removed their suit jackets. To the request that attorneys be allowed to do likewise, Judge Roan humorously demurred. "Lawyers must wear coats," he said. "If I let them go in shirtsleeves, they'd feel so comfortable this trial might never end." Roan did, however, order the windows opened. The cooling effect of this action, if any, was offset by making the proceedings accessible to the multitudes, transforming a row of contractor's sheds lining the construction site across Hunter Street where Atlanta's new courthouse was rising into a spillover gallery. For the duration, a veritable knothole gang would colonize the sheds' rooftops, intensifying the sensation for those within that the eyes of the city weighed palpably upon them.

Stultifying though the courtroom was, Hugh Dorsey pressed resolutely ahead, beginning his examination of Wednesday's initial witness, Boots Rogers, by inquiring into the scene that had greeted him and Detective John Black in the parlor of the Franks' Georgia Avenue home the Sunday the body was discovered. Here, the solicitor was presenting some of the case's most ambiguous material, but he marched his witness through it as if nothing was in doubt, not just securing the expected account of Frank's anxiety but playing up new nuances, among them the possibility that the superintendent had been hungover. This Dorsey did merely by asking: "Was anything said about whisky?" "Yes," Rogers replied, first recalling Black's suggestion that Frank, far from needing the much discussed cup of coffee, actually needed a drink, then Lucille's response that her ailing father had downed the contents of the house's only bottle that very night. In the wake of Minola McKnight's affidavit, such recollections could only have sparked the most obvious inference.

Dorsey next elicited Rogers's version of the morning's subsequent doings. First, there was the stop at the morgue: "Mr. Gheesling caught the face of the dead girl and turned it over towards me. I looked then to see if anybody followed me and I saw Mr. Frank step from outside of the door into what I thought was a closet." Then the visit to the factory.

Of the many details regarding Frank's behavior that Sunday, none were potentially more damaging than those pertaining to the hour he spent with Rogers, Black and Assistant Superintendent N. V. Darley at the plant, and under Dorsey's questioning, the witness ticked them off—the several requests for a cup of coffee, the comments regarding the connection between insurance regulations and the unlocked fuse box, and the difficulty starting the elevator. After securing an account of the tour of the basement, the solicitor directed Rogers to the most damaging detail of all—Newt Lee's time slip:

> "What did you do then?"
>
> "Mr. Frank says, 'I had better put in a new slip, hadn't I, Darley?' Darley told him yes, to put in a slip. Frank took his keys out, unlocked the door of the clock and lifted out the slip, looked at it and made the remark that the slip was punched correctly."
>
> "Where was Newt Lee?"

"Lee was right behind me, handcuffed."

"Where was Darley?"

"He was right there."

"What happened next?"

"Mr. Frank went to his office, brought out a new slip. He took out the old slip and wrote on it 'Removed 8:26.' "

"What did he do with it?"

"He folded it once and went into his office."

"Did you see that slip?"

"Yes, I glanced at it. The first punch was 6:01 and the second at 6:32. There did not appear to be any skip in it."

Thus once again, Frank's ultimate assertion regarding Lee's punches was contradicted. After obtaining a last mention of the superintendent's anxiety that morning, Dorsey turned the witness over to the defense.

Luther Rosser began his cross-examination by immediately establishing that Rogers had never seen Frank before the Sunday the body was discovered and couldn't know "whether his nervousness was natural to him or not." Then, after a few other questions designed to put a generally less sinister spin on Frank's actions that morning, the lawyer reintroduced the matter that Dorsey had so insinuatingly broached:

"Was anything said about a little drink doing you all good?" he asked.

"Yes. Black said something about a drink. Mrs. Frank called to Mrs. Selig and she said there was no whisky in the house; that Mr. Selig had an acute attack of indigestion the night before and used it all."

This was the reply Rosser had been seeking. "He had an attack of acute indigestion and drank up all the liquor," he repeated. "Well, I have those attacks occasionally myself." Coming from the mighty Rosser, such self-deprecation, no matter how calculated, was disarming, and the courtroom dissolved into laughter in which, to everyone's surprise, Leo Frank joined. FRANK LAUGHS FOR FIRST TIME DURING TRIAL WHEN HOME INCIDENT IS TOLD, boomed the *Georgian*'s headline. And no wonder. Not only had Frank never previously laughed during the proceedings, save for the flicker of interest during the jury selection process, he hadn't exhibited any emotion at all. Observed the *Georgian*'s Fuzzy Woodruff: "Arms akimbo, glasses firmly set, changing position seldom, Leo M. Frank sits through his trial with his thoughts in Kamchatka, Terra del Fuego, or the Antipodes, so far as the spectators in the courtroom can judge . . . To those who believe Frank guilty, his personality is not one to arouse pity." Yet now, Frank removed the mask just long enough to reveal that he had a sense of humor.

From here, Rosser's interrogation of Rogers degenerated. Though he exacted the concession that there was a chance Frank had seen Mary Phagan's body at the morgue, and secured the fact that the factory elevator was "noisy," he expended most of his energy battling Dorsey for literal dominance of the courtroom. The fight started when Rosser positioned himself in such a manner that the solicitor could no longer see the witness. To Dorsey's request that he move, he replied: "Get a stick, Hugh, and keep me punched out of the way." With that, Rosser barreled ahead, but in his elation at this successful bit of school-yard bullying, the lawyer ignored two vital points. First, he did nothing to counter Rogers's testimony regarding Lee's time slip. Second, he paid no heed to a statement the witness made near the end of his cross-examination concerning a most enigmatic clue:

> In the elevator shaft there was some excrement. When we went down on the elevator, the elevator mashed it. You could smell it all around. It looked like the ordinary healthy man's excrement . . . that was before the elevator came down. When the elevator came down afterwards it smashed it and then we smelled it.

However upset Leo Frank may have been the Sunday Mary Phagan's remains were discovered, and however compelling the evidence located in the factory metal room was, Hugh Dorsey knew that to win a conviction, he would have to move beyond these concerns to the matter of motive. He had to prove that Frank had been acquainted with and attracted to little Mary. Which was why once Boots Rogers left the stand, Dorsey called Grace Hicks.

Sixteen-year-old Grace, a cherub-cheeked girl in a white dress adorned at the neck and elbows by blue ribbon, had, of course, identified Mary Phagan's body, and Dorsey opened his examination by gently returning her to that horrific moment. Yet after posing just a couple of questions regarding the topic, he dropped it. For the task at hand, the witness's recollections of Mary dead were less important than those of her alive:

> "Was she pretty?"
> "Yes. She was fair-skinned, had light hair, blue eyes, and was well developed for her age."
> "Where did you work?"
> "In the metal room."
> "How often was Mary at the factory?"

"Nearly every day."

"Where was Mary's workplace?"

"Right next to the dressing room."

Here, Dorsey briefly abandoned this line of inquiry to introduce the fact that the Monday following the murder, Grace had seen the red spots on the metal-department floor near the dressing room. Then he resumed:

"A person going from the office back to the rear of the second floor would have had to pass the dressing room, the place near where Mary Phagan worked, wouldn't they?"

"Yes."

"Did Frank pass there every day?"

"Almost every day. He would come back two or three times a day to see how the work was going on."

"When was Mary at the factory last to work?"

"The Monday before April 26."

"Why didn't she work that week?"

"The metal hadn't come."

"Where was the metal kept?"

"In a little closet under the stairway."

"When was the regular payday?"

"Saturday at 12."

"Was anyone paid off Saturday, April 26?"

"Most of them were paid off the Friday night before, as Saturday was a holiday."

As to why Mary Phagan hadn't been among those who'd received their wages on Friday, Dorsey didn't ask, preferring to conclude on this allusive note.

No matter how much Grace Hicks's testimony appeared to have advanced the state's case, by putting the girl on the stand Dorsey had provided the defense with an opportunity, and once Rosser took the floor, he wasted no time initiating what would prove to be a devastating cross-examination:

"You worked at the factory a year?"

"I worked there five years. Mary worked there a year."

"In those five years, how many times did you speak to Mr. Frank?"

"Three times."

"How many times did you see him speak to Mary Phagan?"

"I never saw Mr. Frank speak to Mary Phagan or Mary Phagan speak to Mr. Frank."

"Did he speak to the girls when he came through the metal room?"

"No. He just went through and looked around."

"What did he say when he spoke to you?"

"He was showing a man around and I was laying on my arm mighty near asleep and he says: 'You can run this machine asleep, can't you?' And I said, 'Yes, sir.' The other times he spoke to me on the street."

Had Rosser gone no further, he already would have exposed Dorsey's attempt to use Grace to suggest a link between Frank and Mary Phagan for the flimsy enterprise that it was. But the big man was just limbering up. In Grace, he had at his disposal a state's witness who could do more damage to the state than to the defense—and he intended to see that she did. First, there were those worrisome red stains on the metal room floor. While Rosser did not ask about them per se, he did ask about the floor, eliciting the admission that not only was it "awful dirty" and not only did the "white stuff" used in the department get all over it but that the polishing room, where paint was stored, happened to be nearby. Conceded Grace: "I have seen drops of paint on the floor. I have seen it leading from the door straight across from the dressing room out to the cooler where the women come out to get water. The floor all over the factory is dirty and greasy. And after two or three days, you can hardly tell what is on the floor."

The prosecution's blood evidence further undermined, Rosser then used Grace to strike a preemptive blow at that other avidly awaited exhibit of scientific proof—the strands of hair discovered on a metal-department lathe the Monday following the murder. Dorsey, of course, was reputedly ready to argue that the hair had come from Mary Phagan's head, but after what this witness would testify, such a theory was going to be more difficult to advance.

"Miss Grace," Rosser began, "there is a place up there where you comb your hair, isn't there?"

"Yes."

"Where is it?"

"Sometimes, we sit over at the machine and comb our hair and sometimes when I want to curl my hair with a poker or anything I go over there to the table right by the window and light the gas and curl my hair."

"How far from the machine where you sit and comb your hair is the lathe where the strands of hair were found?"

"About fifteen feet."

"Was there another girl who sat near Mary who had hair like hers?"

"Yes, Magnolia Kennedy sat on one side of her and I sat on the other. Magnolia's hair was sandy, too."

During his redirect, Dorsey salvaged what he could, but regardless of the fact that Grace told him she'd never seen any red paint in the metal room, and despite her admission that she still worked at the factory—which implied that she was beholden to Frank—the damage was done. Headlines told the tale. Cried the *Georgian:*

GIRL'S STORY HELPS FRANK

Echoed the *Journal,* albeit more soberly:

Defense to Claim Strands of Hair Found
Were Not Mary Phagan's

Only the *Constitution* abstained. By the time the morning sheet's Thursday editions went to press, Grace's story would be subsumed by far more dramatic news.

The state's next witness, Detective John Black, was highly anticipated. From the beginning, he'd been involved in every aspect of the investigation, and Dorsey intended to use him both to firm up the foundation of his case and to contribute a few new pieces.

Unlike the other officers summoned the morning Mary Phagan's body was discovered, Black testified, he'd already been acquainted with Leo Frank. Prior to that Sunday, he averred, he'd twice met the superintendent when visiting the pencil factory on routine police business. On neither occasion, he added at Dorsey's behest, had Frank betrayed a particularly excitable nature.

Black's psychologizing prompted an objection from the defense, and Judge Roan admonished the solicitor to stick to the facts. But this reproof notwithstanding, Dorsey had enhanced the detective's credibility on a vital issue, paving the way for the assault that now followed:

"When you saw Frank the morning of April 27 did he seem nervous?"

"Yes."

"Why?"

"Because he had some considerable trouble putting on a collar. It seemed that he couldn't tie his necktie."

"What did he say about going to the factory?"

"He kept on insisting on getting a cup of coffee, and I finally told him that I had been up until one o'clock the night before and had then been aroused at four o'clock in the morning and hadn't had any coffee or break-fast, either. I told him we'd better go to the factory and get that over with."

Which, of course, was Dorsey's destination, too. After a nod to the events at the morgue (Black, too, maintained that Frank couldn't have seen the victim's face), he introduced the subject of the factory tour, dwelling on the incident to which he'd so consistently returned:

"Did you see him go to the clock?"

"Yes. He looked at it, made an examination, and said it had been punched correctly up until 2:30 A.M."

"Did Frank state at any time that the clock was inaccurate?"

"He said on Tuesday that the clock had been passed three times."

"Did Frank produce a time slip at that time?"

"Yes, a slip which he gave to Chief Lanford on Monday."

"What became of the slip he had Sunday?"

"He carried it into his office on Sunday morning."

"Who was present Sunday morning when he stated the slip had been punched regularly?"

"Detective Starnes, Chief Lanford, Newt Lee, Boots Rogers and myself."

"When did you first hear Frank state the slip was incorrect?"

"I cannot swear. It was Tuesday or Monday, one or the other."

"Who was being held at that time under suspicion of the crime?"

"Newt Lee."

"Frank was not then under arrest?"

"No."

The solicitor's intimation couldn't have been more pointed.

Dorsey was not finished with Black. As the detective's testimony regarding Lee's time slip brought home, what made him so valuable to the state was his ability to discuss the developments that over an interval of days had increased suspicion of Frank, and it was with the intention of putting more such material before the jury that the solicitor now inquired if Frank had engaged counsel prior to being taken into custody. Despite the de rigueur defense objection, Judge Roan sustained Dorsey, and the detective replied: "When Mr. Frank was down at the police station on Monday morning, Mr. Rosser and Mr. Haas were there. About 8 or 8:30 Monday morning Mr. Rosser came to police headquarters." This circumstance thus pegged to a period twenty-four hours before Frank's arrest, the solicitor delved into the role the lawyers had initially played:

"Did you hear Haas make a statement in Frank's presence?"
"Yes. Haas demanded of Chief Lanford that the officers accompany Mr. Frank out to his residence and search his residence."
"What were Haas's grounds for making such a demand?"
"He stated that he was Mr. Frank's attorney and demanded to show that there was nothing left undone."
"What time was that?"
"About 11:30."

That Dorsey was contemplating suggesting a link between the visit to Frank's home and the subsequent visit to Lee's shack (where the police found the infamous bloody shirt), there can be no doubt, but significantly, he did not at this juncture go further. Instead, he broached several other matters, among them the arrest of James M. Gantt, eliciting the statement that the ex-bookkeeper was not apprehended until Frank fingered him. Finally, he asked if Frank's bearing had altered from day to day. Replied Black: "After his release Monday, he seemed very jovial. On Tuesday he was sullen." Something amiss thereby implied, the solicitor sat down.

Whatever good Black seemed to have done the state's case, within thirty seconds Luther Rosser was ripping away the integument of expertise and probity in which the man cloaked himself and exposing the sinew of incompetence and deceit that many believed constituted the inner fiber of the entire Atlanta Police Department:

"You didn't release Mr. Frank," Rosser began innocently enough, "until the word was given from the chief of detectives, did you?"
"I suppose not."
"Do you mean anything by the word release?"
"I spoke before I thought when I uttered it."
"Wasn't his detainment equivalent to arrest?"
"I can't say so."
"Then you retract a thing you said under oath?"
"Yes, I retract the word release."

Just that easily, Rosser had suggested why Frank had retained counsel on Monday. Moreover, he'd bewildered Black. This, though, was merely the overture:

"Wasn't it 10:00 before I got to the station?" Rosser now asked, know-
ing full well he had indeed arrived at that hour.
"No . . . you got there between 8:30 and 8:00."
"Will you swear it?"
"I won't swear it . . . I don't know."

And just that easily, Rosser had suggested that Black's memory was unreliable. This, though, was still merely the overture:

"Who was present when you talked to Frank on the time previous to
Sunday?" Rosser now inquired, referring to Black's professed earlier con-
versations with the superintendent.
"I don't remember."
"As a matter of fact, you can't swear truthfully that you spoke to him at
all, can you?"
"Not positively."

With that, the dam burst. What time had Detective Starnes phoned Frank
on Sunday morning? Black didn't know. What time had he arrived at the
Franks' home? Black didn't know. What kind of tie had Frank experienced
such difficulty with? Black didn't know. Then:

"Hurry and scurry is an enemy to memory, isn't it?"
"Yes."

Black was collapsing. "The detective's features flushed crimson," noted
the *Georgian*. "He mopped his face which was running with perspiration.
Then he held his handkerchief up by two of its corners to dry in the breeze
from an electric fan." Still, Rosser had at him, particularly regarding the evidence relating to the crime scene. First, he took up the purported bloodstains:

"You went through the factory with Frank?"
"Yes."
"Who else went?"
"I don't know—several people."
"And none of you saw the splotch said to be blood?"
"No, sir."
"How many of you went over the building?"
"I don't know exactly."
"Perhaps thirty people?"
"I don't know."

"This large horde made up of officers and curiosity seekers went over the factory and nobody saw these alleged blood spots?"

"No, sir."

"How long was the factory open on Sunday morning—till about 12:00, was it not?"

"I don't know."

"How many times did you go to the factory that morning?"

"Twice."

"Detective Starnes went over the factory with you, did he not?"

"Yes."

"Campbell and Beavers, too?"

"I don't know about Beavers, but Chief Lanford did."

"And no blood spots were discovered that day?"

"Not so far as I know."

Then Rosser addressed, at long last, the matter of Lee's time slip:

"You saw Frank at the clock?"

"Yes."

"He opened the clock and took out a slip?"

"Yes."

"When did Frank turn over this slip that he took out of the clock?"

"I don't know."

"Didn't you tell Mr. Dorsey a few minutes ago that he turned over the slip on Monday morning?"

"I don't remember."

"Look here, Black. Is your memory so bad you can't remember what you told Dorsey twenty or thirty minutes ago? And yet you attempt here to state the words of conversations that occurred more than three months ago?"

There was no answer.

Having tarnished Black's credibility concerning the matters to which he had testified, Rosser would now tackle the matters to which he had not testified. The hope here was to steal a march on Dorsey, who by earlier letting Black off the hook regarding his search of Frank's home and all that followed had unwittingly opened himself to attack.

Rosser sprang his offensive by asking Black if he'd been at headquarters Monday when Frank disrobed. Not surprisingly, Dorsey objected to this, but Judge Roan, noting that the solicitor had flirted with the subject during his direct examination, allowed the question, and simple as that, Rosser had co-opted a key portion of the state's case. Now Frank's counsel would determine how the murky series of occurrences that had ended in the discovery of the bloody shirt at Lee's would be presented to the jury, and he started by asking Black if the station house striptease had inspired the trip to Frank's home. Yes, the detective replied, adding: "We went out there and examined the clothes he'd worn the week before and the laundry, too. Mr. Frank went with us and showed us the dirty linen." Rosser then grilled Black about a later outing:

"You also went to Lee's house?"
"Yes."
"What did you find?"
"A bloody shirt."
"Where is it?"
"Mr. Dorsey has it."

At this, Rosser asked the solicitor to produce the shirt, which he was obliged to do, handing it to his adversary, who then displayed it to the witness:

"Is that the shirt, Mr. Black?"
"Yes, sir."
"What time did you find it?"
"Tuesday morning, about 9:00."

The Hugh Dorsey who now undertook Black's redirect examination was not the same man who'd heretofore so coolly withstood Rosser's taunts. Visibly agitated, he tried to introduce a line of inquiry that would suggest Frank had inspired the search of Lee's home, but when Rosser sharply objected, he looked to Roan for help, exclaiming:

Our contention is that this shirt was a plant and Frank's request was a ruse to get the police to search his house and then Newt Lee's house and thus throw suspicion on the negro.

As soon as these words left Dorsey's mouth, the *Georgian*'s James B. Nevin glanced at Rosser and, as he put it, "saw what I expected to see — a momentary flicker of a smile about the lips and eyes."

Dorsey, however, was oblivious, and when Roan ruled that he could continue, he secured a couple of statements that seemed to confirm his claim that Frank had engineered the expedition to Lee's. To wit: Black swore that Frank had not only informed him that he believed the night watchman had failed to divulge everything he knew about the murder but that the missed punches showed he would have had "an hour to have gone out to his house and back."

On the surface, Black's testimony appeared to buttress Dorsey's thesis, but the reason for Rosser's smile—and the likely reason the solicitor had avoided getting into this subject at the start—became plain once Dorsey asked the detective when Frank had said such things. Black's answer couldn't have been more disastrous: "I don't remember whether that was before or after I went out to Lee's house and found the shirt."

Realizing what had just occurred, Dorsey blanched. Under his questioning, his witness had undermined the surmise atop which a part of his evidentiary construct stood, suggesting that the links between anything Frank had said or done and the search of Lee's house were tenuous at best. And while the solicitor would attempt to recover, eventually exacting Black's assurance that Frank's remarks regarding the missed punches had preceded the trip to Lee's, such an admission was of little help. Dorsey had suffered a self-inflicted wound, and all he could do was cede the floor.

For the first time since the trial began, Luther Rosser held the advantage, and he used it. "Don't you know, Black," he began his last assault, "that as a matter of fact, that shirt was found before Frank ever said anything to you about the misses in that time tape?"

The detective opened his mouth, but no answer came forth.

"Don't you know it?" Rosser persisted.

Still no answer.

Whereupon Rosser extracted his pocket watch and held it before the witness. After an excruciating minute or so, the judge attempted to intervene, but Rosser urged: "Give him time to answer, your honor."

A few seconds later, Black confided: "I don't remember." Then he balefully added: "I don't like to admit it, but I am so crossed up and worried that I don't know where I am at."

At this, Rosser snorted, "Come down."

Once again, headlines told the tale. Declared the *Georgian:*

Collapse of Testimony of Black Great Aid to Defense

Seconded the *Journal:*

Detective John Black "Goes to Pieces"

But it was Dorsey's supporters at the *Constitution* who played the story hardest. Beneath the page-one banner DEFENSE RIDDLES JOHN BLACK'S TESTIMONY, the morning paper reported:

When Wednesday's session of the Leo M. Frank trial had come to a close, the friends of the accused were filled with high hopes for his acquittal. They were nothing short of jubilant . . .

The feeling was based on the fact that the testimony of John Black . . . who had worked up a large share of the evidence against Frank, fell to the ground . . .

Time and again, Black contradicted himself . . .

Solicitor Dorsey had stated that he expected to show that Black had gone to Lee's house only after Frank had informed him that several punches were missing from the time slip taken from the register clock . . . that after Frank's house had been searched for incriminating evidence at the suggestion of Herbert Haas, that Frank sought to have Lee's house searched and that the bloody shirt was really a "plant."

Black's answers failed to bear out the contention of the solicitor.

The verdict was unanimous. As the *Georgian*'s James B. Nevin observed:

There is a feeling, growing more fixed every day, I think, that the State, if it hopes to win, must set up something more than it has yet made public!

If the State has some big cards up its sleeve, if it is prepared to surprise the defense . . . then the case yet is in its infancy and the real charge against Frank still is to be made out.

If the State has no unrevealed evidence and is NOT prepared to strike the defense heavy and unanticipated blows, it is but the simple and honest truth to say here and now that the feeling, vague and elusive enough, but unmistakably there, [is] that acquittal eventually will come to Frank . . .

The Black debacle, according to still another reporter, "was enough to stun any man," but Hugh Dorsey righted himself immediately. He started the process in the waning minutes of Wednesday's session by calling James M. Gantt, the dismissed pencil company bookkeeper. Predictably, Dorsey asked Gantt to reiterate his account of Frank's nervous reaction to their encounter outside the factory the afternoon of the murder. Then he guided his witness to new territory:

"Did you know Mary Phagan?"
"Yes, I knew her when she was a little girl."
"Did Leo M. Frank know Mary Phagan?"
"Yes."
"How do you know that?"
"One day she had been in the office talking to me about a mistake in her

time. When she left, Mr. Frank turned to me and said, 'You seem to know Mary pretty well.' "

Gantt's assertion, of course, contradicted Frank's denials that he'd been acquainted with the girl, and Dorsey followed up with a series of inquiries suggesting that Frank had manufactured the bookkeeper's $2 payroll shortage to get rid of someone he regarded as an impediment to his lecherous designs. During cross-examination, Luther Rosser sought to discredit Gantt by compelling him to admit he'd told the inquest he had never seen Frank with little Mary and was unaware he knew her. Yet such concessions, damaging though they were, did not negate Gantt's story. Dorsey had deftly reintroduced the idea that Frank had been eyeing his victim all along, checking the defense's momentum.

Thursday morning, Dorsey began building some momentum of his own. Pinkerton agent Harry Scott, though serving at Frank's behest, had helped John Black collect much of the prosecution evidence, and after taking the stand, he dropped a bombshell, reversing himself regarding a crucial comment Frank made during their initial conversation. Heretofore, in both his first report and at the inquest, Scott had maintained Frank stated that after paying Mary Phagan on April 26, he'd answered her parting query as to whether a metal shipment had arrived with an unequivocal "no." Now the detective proclaimed: "He replied that he didn't know."

This shocker, implying that Frank had responded ambiguously to little Mary in an effort to lure her to the metal room, contributed mightily to the state's theory of the crime. Yet as Dorsey realized, the defense could chalk up anything Scott said to his being in league with the authorities; thus before he went further, he endeavored to persuade the jury that the Pinkerton agent's true allegiances were more complex. The solicitor did so by posing some seemingly straightforward inquiries regarding Frank's mood during the pair's inaugural meeting and a bid he supposedly made to direct suspicion at Gantt. When Scott, in turn, professed ignorance of such matters, an outwardly exasperated Dorsey looked to Judge Roan: "Your honor, I have been misinformed as to what the witness would testify. I have been misled." Toward that end, the solicitor requested the opportunity to "refresh" Scott's memory.

Immediately, Rosser sensed something wrong. "Questions like these grate on my ears like the false notes from a piano," he roared, adding that unless the solicitor intended to impeach Scott, he was on shaky ground. To this, Dorsey responded that impeachment was the furthest thing from his mind, insisting that he merely wanted to hold Scott to his word. Then he brazenly stated his case: "Your honor, if there ever was a time when a witness should be led, it is now with this detective who was hired by the pencil factory and has been working with the attorneys for the defense. When I talked with him and he told me things and now he testifies differently, I have a right to lead him."

After consulting precedents, Roan ruled that while Dorsey could not lead the witness, he could reacquaint him with specific points of his story. The upshot: Scott was soon recalling that at the meeting in question, Frank took deep breaths and his eyes were "large and piercing." Moreover, he added that Frank laid "special stress" on Gantt's attentions to Mary Phagan.

And so by dint of pettifoggery, Dorsey managed to have it both ways with Scott, distancing him from the police and tying him to Frank even as he exacted more damaging testimony. Nonetheless, the solicitor still wasn't satisfied. In a final attempt to insulate Scott, he asked: "Was anything said by one of the attorneys for Frank about you suppressing evidence?"

Here again, Rosser objected, but while Roan sustained him, he allowed Dorsey to rephrase the question, and soon Scott was revealing: "The first week in May, Superintendent Pierce [Scott's boss] and I went to Mr. Herbert Haas's office . . . and had a conference with him as to the Pinkerton Agency's position in the matter. Mr. Haas stated that he would rather we would submit our reports to him before we turned [them] over to the police. We told him we would withdraw before we would adopt any practice of that sort."

With that, Dorsey managed to have it a third way with Scott, making it appear that whatever his connections to 175 Decatur Street, they were rooted in the interest of justice; and on that note, he returned the agent to the subject of the investigation itself, eliciting his account of Frank's station house encounter with Newt Lee: "Frank hung his head the entire time the negro was talking to him, and finally in about thirty seconds, he said, 'Well, they have got me too.' Mr. Frank was extremely nervous at that time. He was very squirmy in his chair, crossing one leg after the other and didn't know where to put his hands."

Dorsey could not have staged a stronger comeback, and after securing Scott's profession that in the early days of the probe he'd conducted a "thorough search" of the factory lobby and "found no pay envelope or bludgeon" and, more vitally, his assertion that a week after the murder, Frank told him he'd been at his office desk "every minute" between 12:00 and 12:30 the afternoon of April 26, he returned to his chair.

Luther Rosser opened his cross-examination of Scott with a flurry, establishing that while Herbert Haas may have requested advance copies of the agent's reports, he'd also indicated "he wanted the murderer caught regardless of who it was."

Yet from this point forth, Rosser would struggle, for as the *Georgian* noted: "Scott refused to be cowed." The Pinkerton agent easily evaded Rosser's thrusts. Why hadn't he reported Frank's attempt to incriminate Gantt? "Because the day I made this report Gantt was released from police headquarters and was regarded as no longer a suspect." Why hadn't he told the inquest of Frank's anxious station house interview with Lee? "You should remember, Mr. Rosser, that I was answering only questions that were asked me by the coroner, and that he didn't draw out and cross question me."

Similarly, Scott was unflappable in the face of Rosser's stabs at portraying him as a police toady:

> "Your agency works with the police, does it not?"
> "Yes, on criminal investigations."
> "You always hook up with the police and go down the road with them, don't you?"
> "We work in harmony with the police."

The only time Rosser again laid a glove on Scott came after he reminded the detective that another factory official—Assistant Superintendent Darley—had accompanied Frank to their all-important first get-together. Confronted with this fact, Scott was forced to confess that he didn't know which man had brought Gantt's name into play. "I am not sure whether I got the statement about Mary Phagan being familiar with Gantt from Mr. Darley or Mr. Frank," he admitted.

That, however, was that. Though Rosser had Scott dead to rights when it came to his last and most significant line of questioning, he couldn't make anything stick:

> "Mr. Scott, you say now that Mr. Frank told you when the little girl asked him if the metal had come, Mr. Frank replied, 'I don't know'?"
> "Yes."
> "Didn't you swear before the coroner that he said, 'No'?"
> "Yes. I have said about half and half all the time."
> "Didn't you say in a report to me that he said, 'No'?"
> "Yes."
> "Did you mean I don't know? Don't you know that the meanings of the words are quite different?"
> "It was just a grammatical error. I now swear positively he said, 'I don't know.'"

In the face of such resolve, there was nothing Rosser could do but sit down. As the *Journal* flatly concluded: "Scott proved a difficult witness for Mr. Rosser."

The 14-year-old girl who replaced Harry Scott on the stand made a fetching picture. Blond hair piled beneath a broad-brimmed hat, cheeks flushed but expression composed, tan cotton dress cut well above the ankles, Monteen Stover was yet another pretty factory girl. She was also one of the state's most important witnesses. If the story she swore to just a week after the murder stood up, she could not only establish the prosecution's time line but undermine Frank's claim that he'd been in his office "every minute" between 12:00 and 12:30 the afternoon of April 26. Dorsey promptly steered her to the issue at hand:

"Did you go to the factory on the Saturday Mary Phagan was killed?"
"Yes, sir."
"What time?"
"12:05 o'clock."
"How long did you stay?"
"Five minutes."
"What did you go for?"
"To get my pay."
"What floor did you go to?"
"The second."
"To where?"
"To Mr. Frank's office."
"Did you see Mr. Frank?"
"No."
"Did you look at the clock when you went in?"
"Yes. I walked up to it. It was 12:05."

The implications here couldn't have been blunter, and after securing the seemingly meaningless fact that the girl wore tennis shoes on April 26 and the recollection that the double doors opening into the metal room had been ominously shut that day, Dorsey turned her over to the defense.

Rosser did what he could with Monteen. Perhaps, he suggested, she'd failed to enter the inner chamber where Frank usually worked, stopping instead in the anteroom. No, she replied, "I went through the first office into the second." All right then, Rosser rejoined, what did the furniture look like? The desks? The wardrobe? The girl couldn't recall, but as opposed to what her interrogator was trying to imply, this inability was not owing to heedlessness on her part. As she explained: "I was looking for a person and didn't notice any of these objects." Monteen was not going to be contradicted, and while Rosser did exact the concession that the metal-department doors were often shut on off days, he again had little choice but to retire.

Following the Stover girl was the 18-year-old factory machinist R. P. Barrett. One of those young men who seem both dull and cunning, Barrett had lived a hard life and, in turn, had been hardened. From Dorsey's vantage, however, Barrett was the salt of the earth, for he had discovered the evidence upon which the state's theory of where the murder took place rested. The red stain on the metal room floor, the white stuff smeared atop it—the solicitor swiftly secured the particulars. Then, rather than ask Barrett to relate in words how he'd located the accompanying hair samples, Dorsey handed him pencil and pad and asked him to draw what he'd seen. The resulting sketch depicted the strands the machinist said had been twined around his lathe handle, and on its strength, the solicitor took a crack at connecting those strands to Mary Phagan:

> "Did anyone else see the hair?"
> "Yes," Barrett responded.
> "Was Magnolia Kennedy there?"
> "Yes."
> "Did she identify the hair?"

Before Barrett could reply, Rosser exploded: "It would be only hearsay. Only the God of the universe could identify the hair." Roan sustained the objection, thus the jurors wouldn't hear Magnolia's widely reported assertion that the hair had come from little Mary's head. Not that Dorsey allowed the setback to slow him down. Betraying no dissatisfaction, he obtained Barrett's assurance that neither the red stain—which the machinist insisted was blood—nor the hair had been present at quitting time the Friday before the murder. Then he introduced a new and potentially devastating piece of evidence—a scrap of pay envelope that Barrett claimed he'd spotted beneath Mary Phagan's machine several days after the killing. Printed atop the scrap was a partially visible "p" or "g." As Dorsey had known it would, "State's Exhibit U" rocked the courtroom, providing him with the perfect ending point.

Once again, Rosser gamely rose to his feet, and while he failed to get Barrett to back down regarding the red stain ("I could tell it was blood") or the hair, he did persuade him to concede that the envelope scrap could have belonged to anyone. "There is no number or amount on the envelope, no name on it, just a little loop, a part of a letter." Having exacted that admission, Rosser then asked the machinist if he'd aided Dorsey in his investigation. When Barrett all too eagerly answered yes, Rosser returned to the defense table. He'd done what he could—which wasn't much. According to the *Georgian,* "Barrett made probably the best witness the state called during the forenoon."

The striking young woman who unexpectedly took a seat among the spectators at the start of Thursday's afternoon session may have been, as she claimed, another of the Atlantans for whom the trial's allure was irresistible. But this explanation strained credulity. The last time Callie Scott Applebaum had been in a courtroom, she had herself been on trial for murder. What's more, her highly publicized acquittal had inspired widespread misgivings regarding the prosecutorial skills of Hugh Dorsey. No, Mrs. Applebaum, fashionably turned out and professing faith in Frank's innocence, was in the gallery as part of a defense ploy to rattle the solicitor.

That Frank's counsel had resorted to such a tactic was the first indication that Dorsey had begun to worry them, but the solicitor resfused to be shaken. Picking up where he'd left off Thursday morning, he spent the day's remaining hours presenting witnesses who could bolster his contention that the crime had occurred in the factory metal room. Mel Stanford, a plant janitor, corroborated Barrett's testimony that neither the red stains nor the hair discovered the Monday following the murder had been present the preceding Friday. Dr. Claude Smith, chemist for the city of Atlanta, resolved any doubts as to the composition of the stains, declaring that microscopic examination had shown them indeed to be blood. (Smith also reinforced the state's theory that the shirt found at Newt Lee's house had been a plant, echoing the view that the garment had been purposely wiped over a bloody surface.) And Mrs. George Jefferson, a polishing-department employee, affirmed Detective Starnes's assertion that twine of the sort used to choke Mary Phagan was stored in the metal room.

The defense had at each of these witnesses, but the only one Luther Rosser managed to shake was Dr. Smith. During a pointed cross-examination, the chemist confessed that the tests he'd performed on the wood chipped up from the metal room floor had yielded but four or five corpuscles of blood of indeterminate origin. Reported the *Journal:* "He admitted that the blood might have been from a mouse."

Smith's revelation regarding the state's blood evidence would not, however, constitute the only defense triumph during Thursday's waning hours. As his last witness of the afternoon, Dorsey summoned E. F. Holloway, the factory's day watchman. In an affidavit taken during the investigation, Holloway had told Detectives Starnes and Campbell that prior to leaving work the evening before the murder, he had locked the second-floor electric switch box. The assertion gave the lie to Frank's claim that the box, due to an insurance company edict, was kept unlocked, and the solicitor expected Holloway to repeat it. Such testimony would pave the way for the prosecution's argument that Frank had unlocked the box the day of the crime so that he and Conley could turn on the elevator and transport Mary Phagan's body to the basement. Yet when Dorsey posed the question, Holloway unexpectedly offered a different story, declaring that while he had locked the box late Friday, he had unlocked it Saturday morning for Denham and White, the two workmen laboring on the building's top floor, to plug in a saw.

These setbacks notwithstanding, there can be no doubt that Dorsey had regained the upper hand. Noted the *Georgian:* "The state fared better Thursday than any other day during the trial."

Thursday night, thundershowers drenched Atlanta, cooling and clearing the air. But the relief lasted only a moment. August had come, and Friday morning the city awakened to what now seemed its constants—the heat and the trial. By 8:40, the sweltering building at the corner of Hunter and Pryor streets was already filled to capacity, as were the coveted perches atop the adjacent construction sheds.

The day's session opened with Hugh Dorsey testing his luck. Leo Frank's closest business associate, N. V. Darley, was a reluctant witness. Nonetheless, the solicitor called the assistant factory superintendent. Dorsey was gambling that he could wrest the sort of admissions from Darley that the man's loyalties would make all the more devastating.

First, the solicitor wanted corroboration of earlier claims by various witnesses as to Frank's anxiety on the morning Mary Phagan's body was discovered. "Was he done up?" he asked. To this and several similar inquiries, Darley tendered equivocal responses, making it plain he would rather not say anything that might incriminate his boss. But Dorsey hammered away, eventually eliciting the statement: "I could perceive that his whole body was trembling."

Next, the solicitor wanted support for the prosecution's contention that the mysterious club located in the National Pencil Company lobby in mid-May was as much a plant as the bloody shirt found earlier at Newt Lee's house. After obtaining Darley's acknowledgment that the factory had been well cleaned in the murder's immediate aftermath, Dorsey turned to the prosecution table, retrieved the club and hurled it to the floor in front of the witness stand.

"Was any club of this sort turned up during the cleaning?" he demanded.

"No," Darley replied.

"And was not this a thorough cleaning?"

"It was."

With that, the solicitor sat down.

From the moment the affable Reuben Arnold rose to his feet to conduct his first cross-examination of the trial, it was clear that the defense intended to make the prosecution pay for having put someone so sympathetic to Frank on the stand. Mister Rube began by asking Darley if he realized that both the state's blood and hair evidence had been discovered by "Christopher Columbus Barrett." Understandably, Dorsey objected to this sarcastic question, but after Arnold explained that he hoped to show Barrett had been less interested in the truth than in the reward money, Judge Roan allowed it, and Darley replied: "It is my understanding that Barrett has been doing most of the discovering done in the building. He has lost quite some time since the murder, and buys quite some extras and reads them." Having thereby cast doubt on Barrett's motives, Frank's co-counsel proceeded to use Darley to attack Barrett's findings themselves. For openers, there were the spots on the metal room floor. Such spots, the witness stated, were actually common due to the fact that female workers experiencing the onset of their menstrual cycles had to walk through the area to reach the nearest women's restroom, as did injured workers seeking first aid. Then there were the strands of hair found on Barrett's lathe handle. Declared Darley: "I don't think there were over 6 or 8. It was pretty hard to tell the color." Finally, there was the scrap of paper purportedly torn from Mary Phagan's pay envelope. As Darley described it, the shop was often littered with such scraps. This because, upon receiving their wages from the nearby payroll window, employees eagerly ripped open the envelopes, scattering pieces everywhere.

The assault upon Barrett's discoveries thus completed, Arnold directed Darley's attention to several other claims the prosecution had adduced as proof that the crime had been committed in the metal room. According to Detective John Starnes and Mrs. George Jefferson, twine of the sort that had been used to choke Mary Phagan and paper of the sort upon which the murder notes were written could be found chiefly on the plant's second floor. Yet as assistant superintendent, Darley was better qualified than anyone to speak to these subjects, and he did, telling the lawyer: "I have seen these cords that we tie up slats and pencils with in every part of the factory. I have raised sand about finding them in the basement." Then, after being handed one of the murder notes: "Yes, I have seen all kinds of papers down in the basement. The paper that note is written on is a blank order pad. That kind of little pad is used all over the factory. The foreladies make their memorandum on that kind of tablet. They are all over the building."

Had he simply quit, Arnold already would have succeeded in marring the foundation of Dorsey's case, but Darley's thorough knowledge of plant operations made him the ideal witness to introduce the defense's contention that Frank's workload on April 26 had been so heavy that he could never have completed it had he just committed a murder. Hence, Arnold asked for an account of the tasks Frank normally undertook on Saturday afternoons, receiving in reply a description of the computations involved in preparing the weekly production and sales report. "A skillful, clear-headed man," Darley informed Mister Rube, would need three hours, and as of 9:40 on the morning of the slaying, Frank had not started. Yet upon arriving at the factory early the next day along with the investigating officers, Darley said he found the report finished.

By this juncture, Hugh Dorsey realized what was happening, and in a pained voice asked, "Are you through with him, Mr. Arnold?" But his opposing number wasn't about to let up, replying, "Oh, no, no. We haven't got a good start with him yet." Darley was just the man to launch the argument that the factory elevator was so creaky that if, as Conley had sworn in his affidavits and was expected to testify, it had been used to take Mary Phagan's remains to the basement, the two workmen laboring upstairs at the time would have heard it. He was also just the man to debunk the claim that the metal shop provided a secure place to conduct a tryst or commit a crime. "There is no lock on the metal room doors," he testified, meaning that the department's main entry—as opposed to the secondary one depicted on the prosecution diagram—could not be secured. Finally, Darley could credibly advance the thesis that Frank's behavior on the morning Mary's body was located, far from being suspicious, was typical. Recalling a day several years before when Frank arrived at work after having seen a child run over by a streetcar, he told Arnold: "He came in about 2:30 and he couldn't work any more on his books until a quarter after four. He trembled just as much on that occasion as he did on the Sunday after Mary Phagan was killed."

Mercifully for the state, Judge Roan chose this moment to recess for lunch, bringing an end to the rout. Upon commencing Friday's afternoon session, Arnold at last handed Darley back to Dorsey for redirect, but try as he might, the solicitor could not undo the damage. For all of that, however, Dorsey did not seem upset about the way things had gone. The witness had, after all, been a calculated risk. Yet apart from this awareness, the solicitor had another reason not to agonize. Like a shrewd cardplayer, he'd divested himself of most of his weak suits and would finish out the game dealing trumps.

As soon as Dr. Henry Fauntleroy Harris, medical bag in hand, approached the witness stand, the crowd inside the packed courtroom tensed. During the months since Harris supervised the exhumations of Mary Phagan's body, speculation as to what light science would shine on the crime had only increased. Save for Jim Conley, no witness was more avidly awaited.

Thin and pale, skin tautly drawn over high cheekbones, rimless spectacles camped atop a sharp nose, Harris appeared at once vulnerable and severe. Which he was. For the past week, he had been suffering from the flu, and it was with difficulty that he had risen from bed. Yet now that he was before the jury, he did his best to affect the unassailable posture common to his profession, at the solicitor's request crisply enumerating his degrees and honors.

From the outset, Harris did all that Dorsey asked and more, delivering testimony that not only completed the state's circumstantial case against Frank but provided solid medical rationales for several points Conley was expected to make later. Regarding Mary Phagan's badly bruised right eye, the doctor contended that his examination had shown that the blow causing the injury had been inflicted before death by a "soft instrument," most likely a fist. Regarding the jagged wound behind the girl's left ear, he said it, too, had been suffered while she was alive, most likely when she had fallen backward into a sharp object. The surrounding tissue had been "shoved upward slightly," a circumstance that would not have obtained had she been clubbed. Though Harris believed the traumas were sufficient to have knocked the child out, he didn't think they killed her. "Strangulation," he declared, "was beyond a doubt the cause."

Having thus secured support for his theory of where and how the murder had been committed, Dorsey directed Harris to the question of when. After obtaining the doctor's acknowledgment that he had examined the dead girl's stomach and removed 160 cubic centimeters of cabbage and biscuit, the solicitor asked how far the material had progressed toward digestion. "Very slightly," replied Harris, reaching into his bag and extracting a vial that held several pieces of nearly intact cabbage floating in a preservative medium. "This," he said, "is some of what I removed from the stomach."

As Harris displayed the vial to the jury, Dorsey asked how long the cabbage had been in Mary Phagan's system before death. "I am confident," answered the doctor, "that it could not have been there for more than half an hour." While the weight of this assertion—which recalled both Mrs. Coleman's testimony that her daughter had eaten just past 11 A.M. on April

26 and Monteen Stover's claim that Frank was not in his office at 12:05 —
hung in the air, Harris removed two other vials from his bag. Both were
filled with a pasty, unrecognizable substance. Displaying them to the jury,
the doctor announced that they contained cabbage taken from the stom-
achs of "normal persons" after an hour of digestion. The demonstration
provided the backdrop for Harris's definitive utterance as to the time of
death: "She was either killed or received the blow upon the head thirty or
forty-five minutes after her last meal."

Compelling as all this was, it was Dorsey's succeeding area of inquiry
that electrified the courtroom. The question:

Dr. Harris, did you ever examine the vital organs of Mary Phagan's body?

The answer:

I made an examination of the privates of Mary Phagan. I found no sper-
matozoa. On the walls of the vagina there was evidence of violence of
some kind. The epithelium was pulled loose, completely detached in
places, blood vessels were dilated immediately beneath the surface and
there was a great deal of hemorrhage in the surrounding tissues. The dila-
tion of the blood vessels indicated to me that the injury had been made in
the vagina some little time before death. Perhaps ten to fifteen minutes. It
had occurred before death by reason of the fact that these blood vessels
were dilated. Inflammation had set in and it takes an appreciable length of
time for the process of inflammatory change to begin. There was evidence
of violence in the neighborhood of the hymen.

Though Harris did not spell it out, his testimony clearly conveyed the
state's position — Mary Phagan had suffered some sort of sexual violation
that, while leaving no seminal fluid, constituted rape.

There was, at this juncture, more that Dorsey wanted to explore, but before
he could proceed, Harris, complaining that he was "utterly exhausted,"
abruptly asked to be excused. After receiving the doctor's assurances that he
would return as soon as he was able, Judge Roan assented. At first blush, Harris's departure seemed another setback for the state. But as the solicitor well
knew, the doctor's leavetaking, which denied the defense the chance to get a
timely crack at him, was a gift. As he told the *Constitution:* "It is perfectly plain
sailing from now on. We have a mass of evidence and it is only a question of
knitting it together."

Dorsey's confidence was borne out by Friday's remaining witnesses.
From Mrs. Arthur White, he secured the information that she had seen an
unidentified Negro lurking in the factory lobby on the day of the murder

not, as had been initially reported, at noon but around 1 P.M., a time consistent with the claim Conley had made in his first affidavit that this was the hour Frank had summoned him upstairs to write the murder notes. From Albert McKnight, whom the bailiffs had finally tracked down, he elicited the anticipated assertion that not only had Frank not eaten lunch on the afternoon of the crime but that he'd returned to work after spending just ten minutes at home. Though Luther Rosser eventually obliged McKnight to recount a few of the dismaying details relative to the procurement of his wife's infamous affidavit, the defense was able to do little else with either of these witnesses.

Determined to build on Friday's victories, Dorsey kicked off Saturday's half-session by calling Helen Ferguson. Hair neatly plaited into braids that fell down the back of a white dress adorned by a bow at the neck, this 16-year-old factory worker was familiar to all who had followed the investigation. On the morning Mary Phagan's body was discovered, she had informed Fannie and John W. Coleman that their daughter had been killed. Now she had been summoned to deliver one of the state's most damaging bits of information, and the solicitor wasted no time eliciting it.

> "Did you see Frank on April 25, the Friday before the murder?" Dorsey began.
> "Yes," Ferguson replied.
> "At what time?"
> "At about 7 o'clock in the evening."
> "What was said?"
> "I asked Mr. Frank for Mary Phagan's money."
> "Well, what did he say?"
> "He told me that I couldn't get it; that Mary would be there Saturday and she could get it then all right."
> "Had you ever got Mary Phagan's money for her before that?"
> "Yes, on two occasions."

Though Helen would subsequently tell Luther Rosser that both times she had picked up Mary's wages she had received them from someone other than Frank, and while she would admit that on April 25 she had forgotten her friend's payroll number, possibly explaining Frank's refusal, neither acknowledgment softened the blow. As she reiterated to the defense lawyer when he asked her to repeat Frank's response to her request: "He said that she'd be there Saturday."

Hugh Dorsey next called Dr. J. W. Hurt, the Fulton County medical examiner. Though the solicitor fully expected Dr. Harris, once recovered, to put the finishing touches on the medical portion of his case, he wanted to reinforce the main points while they were still vivid in the jurors' minds. Which was what he did, obtaining Hurt's endorsement of Harris's findings that the wound to the back of Mary Phagan's head had been made by a "blunt-edged instrument" striking "from down upward," that her right eye had been blackened by someone's fist and that she had died of strangulation.

Yet much as Hurt helped the state, he would also harm it. As the newspapers had already reported, he and Dr. Harris were in dispute regarding a key matter, and rather than let the defense raise it, Dorsey attempted to defuse the issue by doing so himself, concluding his examination by asking the doctor if little Mary had been raped. Replied Hurt:

> I discovered no violence to the parts. There was blood on the parts. I didn't know whether it was fresh blood or menstrual blood. The vagina was a little larger than the normal size of a girl that age. It is my opinion that this enlargement of the vagina could have been produced by penetration immediately preceding death.

Frank's lawyers, of course, would have preferred to secure Hurt's uncertain answer to this vital question themselves, but despite the prosecution's effort to pull the sting, they were not about to leave it alone. Indeed, Reuben Arnold, whose hiring had been in part predicated on his medical knowledge, sharply cross-examined the doctor on the issue. Ever so delicately, Mister Rube posed a series of questions designed to suggest that little Mary, contrary to widely held and deeply felt convictions, had not been a virgin. Eventually, the doctor confided: "Her hymen was not intact, and I was not able to say when it was ruptured. I saw no indication of injury to the hymen."

Arnold wrapped up by directing Hurt's attention to one other critical topic—the wound on the back of Mary Phagan's head. As the doctor now acknowledged, the wound had not necessarily been inflicted by a fall against Barrett's lathe. It could as easily have been suffered during a tumble down the factory elevator shaft.

During his redirect examination of Hurt, Hugh Dorsey had every intention of putting the pieces back together again, but he was almost denied the chance, for it was at this pass, following a brief recess, that the trial of Leo Frank nearly ended. As spectators were settling down and lawyers were huddling, Judge Roan emerged from his chambers carrying the *Georgian*'s latest extra. Blared the red banner: STATE ADDS LINKS TO CHAIN. When Reuben Arnold noticed jurors not only reading the headline but craning their necks to make out the underlying story, which detailed the prosecution's late-Friday triumphs, he and Rosser approached the bench. Roan, upon being informed of what had occurred, ordered the twelve-man panel from the room.

The debate over whether a mistrial should be declared raged until Frank's lawyers, revealing that they expected to prevail in the present proceedings, announced they would be satisfied if Roan simply instructed the jury, as Rosser put it, "to disregard this headline." Though Dorsey countered that no admonition was necessary, maintaining that the panel had been previously exposed to newspaper coverage damaging to the state, the judge seized upon the defense's proposal. After recalling the jurors, he advised:

> Gentlemen, it has been said by some that you have been able to see some writings or headlines in the newspapers that might influence you. If you have seen anything in the newspapers or heard anything, I beg of you now to free your mind of it, regardless of whether it be helpful to the state or to the defense.

The crisis thereby averted, Hurt returned to the stand and Dorsey went back to work, quickly extracting statements that negated some of what Arnold had accomplished during his cross-examination. Yet for all intents and purposes, the argument sparked by Judge Roan's indiscretion had brought the day's abbreviated session to a conclusion. The first week was over.

Late Saturday, as Hugh Dorsey plotted strategy in his Thrower Building office and Leo Frank rested in his cell, police officers escorted Jim Conley into a secluded courtyard behind the station house where, as the *Constitution*'s Britt Craig put it, they "turned a liberal hose" on him until he was as "shiny as the brass trimmings on a 1914 model auto." Then, courtesy of William Smith, the Negro was treated to a haircut and a shave. Finally, he was outfitted with a new suit of clothes and a pair of dress shoes.

Conley's turn on the stand was at hand, and if anything, it was regarded as more critical to the trial's outcome than ever. To be sure, the prosecution had by this juncture presented a mass of circumstantial evidence against Frank. Even the *Georgian*'s James B. Nevin, in a summary of events to date, conceded as much:

> The State HAS definitely shown that Leo Frank might have murdered Mary Phagan and that he DID have the opportunity to accomplish it.

Having shown that the OPPORTUNITY was there, and that the murder likely was consummated during the time limits of that opportunity, the elements of the case need but be knitted properly together to make dark the outlook for Frank.

Yet the defense had badly roughed up several of Dorsey's witnesses. Moreover, Frank had not been connected to Mary Phagan in anything other than a cursory fashion. The issues at the heart of the matter remained unresolved. Looking ahead to when court reconvened, the *Georgian* declared:

The questions to be thrashed out are these:

Did Leo Frank, between 12 o'clock and the time he left the pencil factory, after paying Mary Phagan her pittance of wages, lure or follow her into the back of the second floor, there assault her and kill her? Did he then secure the services of Jim Conley to conceal the body?

Or did Jim Conley, half drunk, loitering in the dark hallway below, seeing little Mary Phagan coming down the steps with her mesh bag in her hands, brooding over his lack of funds wherewith to get more whisky, find in this setup an opportunity to secure a little money—the violent killing of the girl following?

About Conley—ever and always about Conley—the Frank case revolves, and will revolve until it ends.

Would-be spectators began arriving at the old city hall at 6:30 Monday morning, and by 9:00 the line stretched single file down Hunter Street to the state capitol a quarter mile to the east. The scene, noted the *Journal,* was reminiscent of that before a World Series baseball game. Shortly after the 250 available seats had been allotted, Hugh Dorsey cried, "Bring in Jim Conley." The request sparked a smattering of applause, but deputies quickly restored order, and following a brief delay, Chiefs Lanford and Beavers led the Negro into the courtroom, William Smith bringing up the rear. As Conley passed the defense table, he gazed evenly at Frank, who returned the gaze in kind. Once the witness was seated and sworn, Dorsey went right to work.

"Do you know Leo Frank?" the solicitor asked.

"Yes, I know him. There he is," Conley replied, indicating the bespectacled figure who sat between his wife and mother ten feet away. At this, Frank turned to Lucille and whispered a few reassuring words.

"Did you have any conversation with Mr. Frank on Friday, April 25?" Dorsey continued.

"Yes, sir," Conley answered. "About three o'clock, Mr. Frank come to the fourth floor where I was working and said he wanted me to come to the pencil factory on Saturday morning at 8:30."

"Had you ever been back there before on Saturdays?"

"Yes, sir. Several times."

"How often?"

Immediately, Rosser objected. The subject, he said, was immaterial. Roan concurred, and the solicitor returned to the Saturday in question.

"Who got there first? You or Mr. Frank?"

"We met at the door and I followed him in."

"What conversation did you have?"

"Mr. Frank said that I was a little early. I told him it was the time he'd said for me to come. He said I was a little too early for what he wanted me to do. I asked him what he wanted. He said he wanted me to watch for him like I had on other Saturdays."

"What had you been doing on other Saturdays?" Dorsey asked.

Again, Rosser objected, but this time Roan overruled him and Conley responded, "I had watched for him while he was upstairs talking to young ladies."

Lest anyone miss the point, Dorsey demanded a description of the job's responsibilities.

"I would sit down at the first floor and watch the door for him," Conley replied.

"How often had you done this?"

"Several times."

"Was Frank up there alone on those Saturdays?"

"No, sometimes there'd be two young ladies and another young man. A lady for him and one for Mr. Frank."

"Was Mr. Frank ever alone there?"

"Yes, sir. Last Thanksgiving day."

"Who came then?"

"A tall, heavy-built woman."

Having thus managed not only to introduce the first strong whiff of sexual impropriety but to suggest a pattern of relevant past dealings between Frank and his accuser, Dorsey steered the examination back to the Saturday of the murder. According to Conley, upon being told that he'd arrived ahead of schedule, he asked the superintendent for permission to visit his mother at the Capital City Laundry. The understanding, he said, was that later that morning, he and Frank, who also had some outside business, would meet on a prearranged street corner opposite the Montag Paper

Company. This, he added, they did, whereupon the two returned to work, the superintendent walking so briskly that he nearly bowled over a man carrying a baby.

"Now, when you got to the factory," Dorsey asked, "what happened?"

Here, Conley pivoted toward the jury and exhibiting the polish he'd acquired under Smith's tutelage (Jim spoke "with the voice of a young teacher of elocution," noted the *Journal*) unburdened himself of his story's most critical details. "We went in," he began, "and Mr. Frank told me about the lock on the front door. 'If you turn the knob this way, nobody can get in,' he said. Then, Mr. Frank told me to come over and said, 'Set on this box.' He said there'd be a young lady up here pretty soon and 'We want to chat awhile.' Mr. Frank said, 'When I stomp, that's her, and you go shut the door. And when I whistle, you can go and unlock the door and come up and say you want to borrow some money and that will give her a chance to get out.'"

Conley's positioning the morning of the crime thereby established, Dorsey asked him to name the people who'd subsequently entered and exited the building, and he did, mentioning Assistant Superintendent Darley, the factory employee Mattie Smith, a "peg-legged" Negro drayman, an unidentified woman who worked on the plant's fourth floor, watchman Holloway and Lemmie Quinn. Then he said: "The next person I saw was Miss Mary Perkins. She came in and went upstairs."

"Who is Miss Mary Perkins?" Dorsey inquired.

"That's the lady that's dead," Conley answered, revealing for the first time that he'd seen the victim alive the day of her murder. "I heard her footsteps going toward the front of the office, and then I heard steps going toward the metal room. The next thing I heard was her screaming."

"Then what did you hear?" asked the solicitor.

"I didn't hear anymore."

As Conley related these assertions, Frank continued to exhibit little emotion, but neither of the women at his side could conceal their feelings. Lucille bowed her head as if she'd absorbed a blow, while his mother gazed up, in the *Georgian*'s phrase, "with an expression of pathetic pleading at the negro witness."

There would, however, be no relief. For starters, Conley informed the court that the next person he saw pass through the lobby was Monteen Stover. When asked how she was dressed, he confirmed what the girl had herself testified, replying, "She was wearing tennis shoes and a raincoat." Conley then told of Monteen's departure, which was followed, he said, by the sound of "tiptoes coming from the metal department" and, after a brief pause, "tiptoes running back" toward the same place. Once the noise ceased, Conley added, he had fallen asleep, not awakening until "I heard Mr. Frank stomping over my head."

"Then what happened?" asked Dorsey.

"I heard Mr. Frank whistle."

"Well, what did you do when you heard Mr. Frank whistle?"

"I unlocked the door just like he said and went upstairs. Mr. Frank was standing at the head of the stairs shivering. He was rubbing his hands together and acting funny."

"Show the jury how he was acting."

Evincing the same skill for charades with which he'd captivated reporters during his tour of the pencil factory two months earlier, Conley bounced to his feet, knees knocking, arms shaking. Then he sat back down, and Dorsey resumed.

"What did Frank have?"

"He had a little cord in his hands—a long wide piece of cord."

"Did you look at his eyes?"

"Yes, sir."

"How did they look?"

"His eyes was large. They looked funny and wild."

"Did Frank say anything to you?"

"Yes, sir, he asked me if I saw a little girl pass along up there. I told him yes, I saw two but one went out; but that I didn't see the other come out."

"Well, then what did Frank say?" Dorsey asked. The question was no different than those that had preceded it, but it elicited an answer unlike any thus far:

> He says, "Well, that one you say didn't come back down, she came into my office a while ago and wanted to know something about her work and I went back there to see if the little girl's work had come, and I wanted to be with the little girl, and she refused me, and I struck her and I guess I struck her too hard and she fell and hit her head against something, and I don't know how bad she got hurt. Of course, you know I ain't built like other men." The reason he said that was, I had seen him in a position I haven't seen any other man that has got children. I have seen him in the office two or three times before Thanksgiving and a lady was in his office, and she was sitting down in a chair and she had her clothes up to here, and he was down on his knees, and she had her hands on Mr. Frank. I have seen him another time there in the packing room with a young lady lying on the table, she was on the edge of the table when I saw her.

With that, Conley had gone further than he had in any of his affidavits, flatly asserting what had previously been merely intimated—namely, that Frank had pursued Mary Phagan sexually, killing her when she resisted his advances. Even more damning, however, were his allegations regarding the factory superintendent's sexual preferences. To accuse Frank of attempted rape and murder was bad enough, but to imply that due to some unspecified physical abnormality he had tried to perform what most Atlantans would have considered an act of perversion and what Georgia law regarded as the capital offense of oral sodomy was devastating. Spectators and jurors, noted the *Georgian*, "strained forward in their seats," while reporters silently speculated as to why the defense did not object to the new and by every legal standard inadmissible charge. "Apparently," concluded the *Constitution*, "they were willing for him to go the limit, depending on breaking him down later and discrediting the whole story."

Dorsey now initiated a line of questioning designed to elicit the well-known but essential guts of Conley's story. The sight of little Mary lying dead outside the factory metal room, the bundling up of the body, the toting of the awkward load the length of the building, the help ultimately lent by Frank—to all of these things did the Negro attest. So, too, did he reaffirm other critical elements of his tale, among them those concerning the transportation of the remains to the basement, the return trip to the second floor (complete with a description of Frank's fall when exiting the elevator) and the sweaty minutes he claimed to have spent closeted in the office wardrobe during the unexpected visit by Emma Clark and Corinthia Hall.

The final matters to which Dorsey directed Conley's attention involved Frank's alleged attempt to cover up the crime. Much of this material—particularly as it related to the composition of the murder notes—was also familiar, but the Negro did illuminate several murky points. Regarding the origination of the scheme, he asserted: "Mr. Frank says, 'I can tell you the best way for us to get out of this. You write what I tell you.' " As to why he cooperated, he declared: "I was willing to do anything to help Mr. Frank, him being a white man and my superintendent, too." Yet a desire to accommodate his boss was not Conley's sole motivation. Profit was also a factor, and he took this occasion to provide a fuller account of the cash offer Frank purportedly made only to withdraw later. The $200 payment, the Negro claimed, was contingent not just on his penning the notes but on his performing one more task—burning the body. The prospect, however, terrified him. "I was scared and I told Mr. Frank to come down with me and watch," he testified. "Mr. Frank said he couldn't go down there, and then Mr. Frank said to hand him that money. 'Is that the way you are going to do me?' I asked Mr. Frank and he said, 'You just keep your mouth shut.' " According to Conley, it was shortly after shushing him that Frank looked to the ceiling and exclaimed: "Why should I hang? I have wealthy people in Brooklyn." And it was shortly after making this statement, the Negro added, that the superintendent once again beseeched him to help dispose of the remains. " 'Can you come back this evening and do it?' " he said Frank asked, promising: " 'I will fix the money.' " Conley confessed that he agreed to the request the second time around, but he said that upon leaving the factory, he went to a saloon and drank a doubleheader, then stumbled home and fell asleep. As to how the murder notes ended up beside the body, he maintained ignorance. He said he next saw his boss three days later at work. "He walked up and said, 'Now remember, keep your mouth shut,' and I said, 'All right,' and he said, 'If you'd come back on Saturday and done what I told you to do with it down there, there wouldn't have been no trouble.' "

On that line, Dorsey might have ended, yet in order to ensure that the jurors could visualize Conley's story, he instructed the Negro to indicate various important spots on Bert Green's factory diagram. Then, sending the first signal that he would call witnesses to support Conley's claims regarding Frank's sexual misconduct, he asked the Negro to name the woman who'd been in the superintendent's office on Thanksgiving 1912. Conley responded that he could not remember, but when the solicitor followed up by asking him to identify the man who'd joined Frank for several of his other purported trysts, the Negro replied: "Mr. Dalton." Shortly thereafter, Dorsey returned to his seat.

Just how well Luther Rosser and Reuben Arnold comprehended the enormity of the job confronting them was evidenced by the fact that rather than launch directly into Jim Conley's cross-examination, they requested a recess and retired to an anteroom to discuss strategy. As everyone who had heard his narrative understood, Conley would not be easily broken down. "The negro forgot nothing, omitted nothing that he had told before," observed the *Georgian*. "He never was confused." Yet this is not to say that his latest version of events was regarded as unassailable. Several of the very factors that had made the account gripping raised doubts as to its veracity. "Jim's story was so completely at the tip of his tongue—even the minutest things— that his testimony had a recitative air," reported the *Journal,* echoing a misgiving that had met earlier tellings. Then there were the many details that had not appeared in what had heretofore been viewed as Conley's definitive utterance—his last affidavit. Finally, however, there was the overarching issue of race. "Jim Conley has upset traditions of the South," declared the *Georgian*'s Fuzzy Woodruff. "A white man is on trial. His life hangs on the words of a negro. And the South listens to the negro's words. But the South has not thus suddenly forgotten the fact that negro evidence is as slight as tissue paper. The South has not forgotten that when a white man's word is brought against a negro's word, there is no question as to the winner." All of which explains why when Frank's lawyers returned, Hugh Dorsey could be seen shifting nervously in his chair.

Luther Rosser began by gently querying Conley regarding his personal and job history. After obtaining a few unremarkable particulars, the lawyer shifted to the topic of the Negro's education. When Jim claimed to be not much of a reader ("I can't read the newspapers good," he said), the big man merely grinned.

"You can make out some words in the newspaper, can't you?"

"Yes, sir, little words like 'dis' and 'dat.' "

"You can spell 'dis' and 'dat,' can't you?"

"Yes, sir."

"Can you spell 'cat'?"

"Yes, sir, I can spell that word."

"Well, how do you spell it, with a 'c' or a 'k'?"

"With a 'k.' "

"Why, sure you do." Rosser beamed, ignoring the gallery's titters. "Jim, you and I understand each other thoroughly, don't we?"

"Yes, sir, we sho' does, sir," Conley replied, although his expression suggested differently. But what was lost on him was not lost on others. Noted the *Constitution:*

> Wise lawyers in the courtroom saw what was coming. They realized that Mr. Rosser was reaching out for Jim like a small boy does for a dog he wants to get his hands on when the dog is rather shy and refuses to let himself be approached.
>
> Like the boy who stoops down and chirps at the dog and shows friendship on his face, the shrewd lawyer [was] conspiring to get his hands on the witness.

The defense had decided to flatter and encourage Conley, hoping that his natural gregariousness—the trait that had always worried Dorsey and Smith—would, over time, lead him to incriminate himself.

Patiently, then, the ordinarily impatient Rosser wooed Conley, and in short order, he achieved some impressive results, ascertaining several facts the state had hoped would not surface. For one, the Negro admitted that despite earning a steady salary, he was often in debt. For another, he revealed that to escape the creditors who routinely gathered around the pencil factory on payday, he frequently departed through the basement door. The wobbly circumstances of Conley's financial life were, of course, vital to the defense's theory of the crime. So, too, was the news that he used the plant's rear exit to make getaways.

Yet promising as this approach initially seemed, the defense was taking a risk. While the Negro might implicate himself, he almost certainly would further implicate Frank. Though Rosser was aware of the danger, he hadn't anticipated how quickly he would encounter it. Following a few more questions regarding various aspects of Conley's employment, the lawyer raised the topic of the extracurricular duties Jim claimed to have performed for Frank, asking: "When was the first time you watched for him?"

"July," Conley matter-of-factly replied.

"Was a lady with him?"

"Yes, Miss Daisy Hopkins."

"What time was it they came that first time?"

"About 3:00 or 3:30 in the afternoon."

"What were you doing?"

"I was sweeping when they came in but Mr. Frank called me to his office and asked me if I wanted to make some money, and then he told me to watch the door for him. I went down and watched, and pretty soon the other lady came with Mr. Dalton. They came upstairs to Mr. Frank's office, stayed there ten or fifteen minutes. They came back down and went into the basement. I don't know how long they stayed [but] Mr. Dalton went out laughing and the lady went up the steps. Then the ladies came down and left, and then Mr. Frank came down. He gave me a quarter and I left."

Hugh Dorsey hardly could have scripted an exchange more injurious to Frank. In a matter of seconds, Conley—by providing the name of one of the superintendent's alleged strumpets—had significantly bolstered the state's case. But Rosser stuck to his course, hoping that the Negro would eventually trip and fall. In the same amiable tone, he continued to quiz Conley regarding his further experiences as Frank's lookout. The results, however, didn't change. On a subsequent Saturday, Jim said, Frank and Daisy had met alone in the office. His tip was 50 cents. Then there was Thanksgiving, which marked the visit of the aforementioned heavy-built woman. Conley couldn't recall her name, but he did provide a vivid description:

> The lady had on a blue skirt with white dots on it and white slippers and white stockings and had a gray tailor-made coat with pieces of velvet on the edges.

He also recalled the amount of his tip—$1.25—and with abundant pride, he recited the compliment he claimed Frank paid him in this elegant creature's presence:

> After the lady came down, she said to Mr. Frank, "Is that the nigger?" And Mr. Frank said, "Yes," and she said, "Well, does he talk much?" And he says, "No, he is the best nigger I have ever seen."

And so the remainder of this Monday morning went, right up to 12:35 when court recessed for lunch. During the break, Leo Frank informed friends that his accuser's story was "the vilest and most amazing pack of lies ever conceived in the perverted brain of a wicked human being," and he expressed every confidence that Rosser would soon demonstrate as much. Others, though, were not so sure. Observed the *Georgian*'s James B. Nevin:

> The crossing of Conley, upon which this case unquestionably will turn, will be either Rosser's victory or Rosser's defeat.

Moments before the proceedings reconvened Monday afternoon, Judge Leonard Roan startled the gallery by ordering all women from the courtroom, the sole exceptions being Frank's wife and mother. "I am doing this," Roan said, "on account of the character of the evidence"—meaning, of course, that he believed Conley's testimony was unfit for female ears. Understandably, the 175 spectators at whom the edict was directed reacted angrily. Flashes of resentment darkened the faces of grandmothers, middle-aged housewives, chorus girls, even, according to the *Constitution*'s Britt Craig, "a painted-cheek girl with hollow eyes who bore the unmistakable stain of crimson." But despite the smoldering looks, no one voiced a protest. Soon enough, the seats that had been occupied by members of the fairer sex were filled by men, and the trial got back under way.

From the instant Luther Rosser, having learned that Conley spent his lunch hour with William Smith and Detectives Starnes and Campbell, snorted that the group probably devoted more time to rehearsing stories than eating, it was plain he was through making nice. Gone were the helpful nods and pleasant smiles. Moreover, rather than merely ask the Negro for additional instances when he had served as Frank's lookout, the lawyer tried to pin him down to exact dates, hoping to catch him in a lie. Yet here again, Conley defied expectations; his powers of recall, so acute prior to the break, abruptly vanished. Questioned as to how he'd occupied himself the Saturday before first watching for Frank, he said he didn't recollect. Questioned as to the Saturday afterward, he said the same thing. And so on and so forth until finally, following seven similarly fruitless forays, Rosser barked: "You don't remember any of these dates, Jim?"

"No, sir," Conley replied, only too happy to agree with his inquisitor.

Worrisome as Conley's sudden forgetfulness was to the defense, his apparently inexhaustible glibness engendered even greater concern, for far from wilting under Rosser's newfound aggressiveness, he seemed to bloom. Pressed about his past, he unabashedly confirmed that he'd been frequently incarcerated and was a heavy drinker. Grilled as to when he'd initially spoken with Frank other than on business, he calmly related a history of "joking" and "jollying" around the factory, asserting that the superintendent would often "goose" him. Then there was more regarding Daisy Hopkins.

"Do you know where she lives?" demanded Rosser.

"No, sir."

"Is she married?"

"I don't know."

"What's the color of her hair?"

"Don't remember."

"What's the color of her complexion?"

"What's 'complexion'?"

"You're dark complected—I'm white complected."

"Oh, she was white complected."

"What kind of ears did she have?"

"Ears like folks."

"I didn't expect her to have ears like a rabbit," Rosser snapped, putting an end to this absurd volley but also betraying a first sign of frustration. Shortly thereafter, the defense, anxious to regroup, sought another recess.

As Luther Rosser reapproached the witness stand, he held before him a sheaf of typewritten documents. Jim Conley's four affidavits—starting with the one of May 18, in which he falsely claimed not to have visited the National Pencil Factory on the day of Mary Phagan's murder—composed the text from which the defense would work for the rest of the afternoon. The intention was to confront the Negro with the statements' many fabrications.

"At police headquarters," Rosser began, glancing over the first of the documents, "you told Black and Scott that you got up at 9:30 on the morning of the 26th, didn't you?"

"Yes, sir," replied Conley.

"That wasn't so, was it?"

"No."

"You lied, didn't you?"

"Yes, sir."

"You told them you left home that morning about 10:00. That wasn't true, was it?"

"No, sir."

"The truth is, you lied all the way 'round?"

"I told some stories, I'll admit."

"Didn't you tell Black and Scott that you bought half a pint of whisky on Peters Street at 10:00?"

"No, sir. I told Mr. Black about 10:30."

"Well, that was not so, was it?"

"No, sir."

"Didn't you tell them that after you bought some liquor at 11:00 you went to some other saloon?"

"I don't remember saying anything about 11:00, but I told them I went to Earley's Saloon."

"Well, didn't you tell them you went to the Butt-In Saloon after that?"

"Yes."

"Then you told some things that were not true, did you?"

"Yes, sir."

"Did you look them straight in the face and lie?"

"No, sir. I hung my head."

There was just one more thing Rosser wanted to know about that initial statement: "Didn't you tell Black and Scott some things that were true and some that were not?"

Yes, Conley replied mildly, he'd done exactly that. Then, throwing a punch his adversary did not expect, he added: "I didn't want to give Mr. Frank away [so] I held back some of the truth, but I wanted to tell some and let him see what I was going to do and see if he wasn't going to stick to his promise as he had said."

Rosser tried not to flinch. "Oh, well," he said lightly, "we'll get to that later on." But he was plainly stunned. He had allowed Conley to articulate the state's rationale for the mendacities that marred both the first affidavit and all the others. Now there was little choice but to slug it out. Which was what he attempted to do, pummeling Conley with a series of derisive queries about his May 18 session with the detectives. "Did you look 'em in the eye?" he snarled. "Did you hang your head?" Then, finally: "Jim, what are some of your other lying habits?" To all of this, the Negro could do no more than state: "Sometimes, I played with my fingers."

The damage thus papered over, Rosser turned to Hugh Dorsey and boasted: "You've had your day. Now, I'm going to have mine." Then he turned back to Conley, asking: "Tell me why it was you sent for Black on May 24?" What Rosser was hoping to hear was the Negro's account of the genesis of his second statement, the one in which he revealed how he'd taken down the murder notes. But again, Conley caught the lawyer unawares, replying: "Well, I wanted to tell something. I hadn't heard from Mr. F____."

This time, Rosser was quicker to cover up, cutting Conley off before he could finish, and immediately, Dorsey was on his feet. "The witness has a right to explain his answers," he objected. "He said he had heard nothing from Frank and he was waiting for some word." Judge Roan, however, overruled this solicitor, and a shaken Rosser returned to his original topic of interest.

The details attendant to the creation of Conley's May 24 affidavit were crucial to Leo Frank's cause. This document had enabled the police to link the superintendent to the murder notes. In a sense, the prosecution's entire case flowed from it. Yet here, too, the defense was handed a setback, for no sooner did Rosser get started than the Negro once more lapsed into deep forgetfulness. Following another litany of "I don't remembers," his nemesis wearily remarked, "Jim, you've got a poor memory." And that, essentially, brought Monday's proceedings to a close, although before court adjourned for the evening, the defense did accomplish something it had long advocated, convincing Judge Roan to transfer Conley back to the Tower. Considering all that had transpired during the months since the Negro was placed in police custody, the move seemed too late to make any difference, although not everyone thought so. "This man, as your honor knows, has been through a most severe ordeal," protested William Smith, fearful of what might befall his client at the county facility. In response, Sheriff Wheeler Mangum, who happened to be present, promised Roan that Conley would be well treated. But Smith was not so sure. "Isn't it true," he asked, "that Mr. Frank has additional food served to him?" With that, Rosser had endured enough. "You send him something extra if you want him to have it," he bellowed. "That's what I want to do," answered Smith. Which was why as darkness fell on this hot August evening, Conley found himself not only sitting down to a steak supper courtesy his lawyer but in receipt of an exceedingly personal gift from him—a crisp new pair of undershorts to replace the ones he'd sweated through on the stand.

Tuesday morning began much as Monday had ended. Confronted by Rosser with his May 28 declaration that on the day of the crime he'd eaten a leisurely breakfast at home—an assertion his direct testimony contradicted—Conley readily conceded that the initial story was untrue. Asked to recollect an incident he'd sworn to in another of his statements, he cited his weak memory. Pushed to account for his exceeding forgetfulness during the cross-exam thus far, he explained: "When I told a lie I knew it wouldn't fit and I'd have to change it, so I didn't remember much about it." Within an hour, Conley had admitted to a multitude of falsehoods and a dozen times claimed lapses in recall—none of which tarnished his major allegations.

Though Rosser's anger was increasingly evident ("Don't you know a nigger never had sausage on the table without eating it?" he snapped during the exchanges regarding the witness's murder-day repast), so, too, was a new strategy. Where on Monday, the defense's lead counsel had addressed Conley's affidavits one at a time, he would now shift abruptly among not just all four of them but also the trial record in an attempt to grind Jim up in his own widely divergent and still-evolving narratives. "I'm going to see if he can tell the same lie twice," the lawyer remarked in response to Hugh Dorsey's unsuccessful objection to the tactic.

At first, Rosser's change of approach seemed effective. The sequence of events that had brought Conley and Leo Frank together on April 26, the amount of time he'd subsequently waited for Frank outside the Montag Paper Company, Frank's description of the task at hand—about each of these matters Jim gave (or acknowledged having given) conflicting accounts. Yet despite such minor stumbles, the Negro refused to be either entangled or flustered. Sometimes defiant, sometimes mocking, occasionally even bored, Conley seemed to have taken Rosser's measure. And on those occasions when the lawyer appeared to have found an opening, the Negro shut him down by employing what would eventually be regarded as a signature phrase:

> "Jim, all these lies—I won't call them lies; I'll call them stories—did you notice them before you went to jail or afterwards?"
>
> "I disremember."
>
> "Jim, to whom did you make your first change in your confession?"
>
> "I disremember."
>
> "You disremember a whole lot, don't you?"

To which Conley said nothing, although shortly thereafter, during a sifting of one of his other utterances, he gave the same answer: "I disremember."

By 11:00, it was plain that Rosser was not only never going to undo his quarry in this way but that if he stuck with the strategy any longer he'd lose the sole audience that counted. Reported the *Georgian:* "During Mr. Rosser's questioning, a number of the members of the jury were inattentive." Thus it was that as noon approached, Rosser resumed a more conventional line of attack, zeroing in on several improbable points in Conley's direct testimony concerning the actions he and Frank had purportedly undertaken at the factory during the minutes just before and just after Mary Phagan's murder:

> "You said yesterday that Frank showed you that day how to unlock the door, didn't you?"
>
> "Yes, sir."
>
> "Well, hadn't he showed you before?"

"Yes, on Thanksgiving day."

"Well, why did he do it again?"

"I don't know."

Similarly:

"You say he told you he was going to stamp on the floor and when you heard him whistle to unlock the door and come upstairs?"

"Yes, sir, he told me that after he told me to sit down on the box."

"He had told you about these signals before, hadn't he?"

"Yes, sir, on Thanksgiving."

"Why did he repeat it?"

"I don't know, sir."

Yet once more, the forward momentum of Frank's counsel was short-lived, for on the larger issues, Conley would not be shaken. Indeed, his answers to Rosser's succeeding questions were essentially verbatim to those he'd given Dorsey. How did Frank look in the crime's immediate aftermath? "He had a cord and was trembling." What did he say? "He asked me if I saw that little girl come up here a while ago, and I told him yes, sir. I saw two of them come up and I saw only one go out. He said, 'Uh, huh. That little girl that didn't go out came up to the office. She went back to the metal room to see about some work. I went back there with her. I wanted to be with her and she refused me.' " Just that quickly, Conley had reiterated some of his most damaging assertions. Worse, he had lost none of his brashness. After directing the Negro to his rendition of the disposal of little Mary's body, Rosser asked:

"You got some burlap, didn't you?"

"Yes, sir."

"How big a piece?"

"Well it was longer than me."

"How wide was it—about two feet?"

"I don't know, sir."

"Well, what do you call two feet?"

"This is what I call two feet," cried Jim, putting the toe of his right shoe against the heel of his left and lifting them high off the floor.

The sight of Conley thrusting his feet in his interrogator's face prompted laughter throughout the gallery. Once order was restored, court adjourned

for lunch, concluding the morning on what for the defense was an igno-
minious note symbolizing the futility of its entire enterprise. Observed the
Journal:

> When a recess was ordered, Jim Conley had been [under] cross-
> examination for eight hours. Beyond showing to the jury that the negro
> had lied in the several affidavits given by him to the police and that by
> his own admission he had drunk a mixture of wine and beer on the morn-
> ing that Mary Phagan was murdered, Luther Z. Rosser had made little
> progress. Questions hurled at [the witness] with a view to trapping him
> were without effect.

Shortly after court reconvened Tuesday afternoon, Judge Roan, acting at
the defense's request, ordered the jury out, allowing Reuben Arnold to
introduce an audacious motion that indicated he and Luther Rosser now
despaired of breaking down the most inflammatory parts of Jim Conley's
story. "We move first," declared Mister Rube after citing grounds of irrele-
vancy, "to exclude the testimony of Conley relative to watching for the
defendant, and we withdraw our cross-examination on the subject."

"We also desire to withdraw from the record," Arnold added after glancing at a section of transcript and citing the same grounds, "that part of Conley's statement in which he tells of Frank having told him that 'he was not
built like other men.' " The lawyer then began to quote the pertinent passages, but after uttering just a few words, he noticed that Lucille Frank,
dreading what was to come, had started to cry, and he stopped. "Your
honor," he said, indicating Frank's wife and mother with his hand, "I would
prefer not to read this in the presence of these two ladies, and I therefore
pass it to your honor that you may read it in silence."

For the next few moments, the courtroom was inordinately quiet. Yet
once the judge looked up, the battle was loudly and contentiously joined,
for as each side understood, the trial's outcome could very well hinge on
who prevailed here.

From the state's perspective, Conley's account of having stood guard for
Frank and his description of what he'd witnessed while doing so was anything but irrelevant, and right off the bat, Hugh Dorsey emphasized the
point:

> The value of this evidence certainly is apparent to your honor. This evi-
> dence in all manner will be amply corroborated. This evidence goes to
> show who killed little Mary Phagan. Our case if this evidence is expunged
> will have been done inestimable damage.

That said, the solicitor turned to the legal issue at hand. Yes, he conceded, as "an original proposition," the testimony in question probably was inadmissible. But, he added pointedly, by failing to make "a timely plea," by, in fact, cross-examining Conley on the self-same testimony, the defense had forfeited the right to seek its removal. "Is it just," an indignant Dorsey asked in conclusion, "to let these men give this negro a gruelling examination and, after they have thrashed it out, to let them expunge his statement? Has it come to this?"

Such was the force of Dorsey's argument that Reuben Arnold immediately attempted to turn it right back around:

> There is no use in getting wrought up over this matter. I could, if I wanted to, tear up a little turf myself. The person who is hurt is the defendant. He is done grievous injury by this vile evidence.

Then Arnold called attention to the underlying weakness in the solicitor's logic:

> The state admits that it is illegal evidence. The only ground that they want it retained on is that we didn't make timely objection. In a criminal case, you can never try a man but for one crime. That is the old, Anglo-Saxon way. I am coming under a general rule when I say this ought to be ruled out.

And so the question was framed, but any prospect of a speedy resolution was quickly dispelled. "I will reserve my decision until I thoroughly consider" both positions, Judge Roan announced from the bench, whereupon the jury was returned.

Though the gallery and a raptly attentive city knew that at least insofar as it concerned Conley's allegations of sexual misconduct and perversion, Leo Frank's lawyers had thrown themselves upon the mercy of the court (DEFENSE MOVES TO STRIKE MOST DAMAGING TESTIMONY, screamed the *Journal*'s banner), the twelve men who would decide the case remained unawares. Hence Luther Rosser pressed ahead at what the *Georgian* termed "his hopeless task." The transportation of Mary Phagan's body to the factory basement, the dispersal of her belongings in the trash, the return trip to the superintendent's second-floor office, the surprise appearance of Emma Clark and Corinthia Hall, the writing of the murder notes—Rosser challenged Conley's testimony on all of these matters. And each time, the

Negro withstood the onslaught, darting away here, delivering consistent responses there.

Following so closely on the stumbles and rebuffs of the morning, this latest series of failures proved almost more than Rosser could bear, and as the afternoon wore on, he grew downright confrontational. Indeed, he often seemed motivated less by a desire to elicit information helpful to Frank than by a consuming need to unnerve Conley. During a sequence of questions regarding the Negro's assertion that in the course of his grisly labors, he'd dropped little Mary's body on the metal room floor, Rosser cracked: "You are twenty-seven years old. Do you mean to tell me you can't carry 110 pounds?" Returning to the subject of the cloth in which Conley claimed to have wrapped the child's lifeless form, the lawyer, in an attempt to pin down the sort of fabric from which it was made, snorted: "I suppose you don't know whether cloth is woven or knitted or just grows." Then there was the much commented upon topic of Jim's recently refurbished wardrobe. Whatever others may have thought of the makeover, Rosser viewed it as another indication of fraudulence, grumbling: "They put some new clothes on you so the jury could see you like a dressed-up nigger." The only thing the lawyer got out of Conley by way of these jibes was the admission that it was he who'd defecated at the base of the elevator on the day of the murder. "As to how that dung came to be in the shaft," the negro recalled, he had gone down the ladder at the suggestion of the previously mentioned peg-legged drayman, stopping "right by the side of the elevator, somewhere about the edge of it." Yet what, if anything, Frank's lead counsel made of this intelligence is uncertain, for as with the earlier testimony concerning the unsavory substance, he did not follow up.

Rosser concluded his work Tuesday by laying the groundwork for the appearance of the defense's most anticipated witness—W. H. Mincey. Taking pains to get Conley on the record regarding the smallest details in the insurance agent's much publicized affidavit alleging a suspicious April 26 run-in with the Negro, the lawyer inquired:

"Did you meet a man named Mincey [who] said you promised to take some insurance with him?"

"No, sir."

"Didn't you tell him that you could not take any insurance—that you were in trouble?"

"No, sir."

"Didn't you say that you had killed a girl and that you didn't want to kill any more people?"

"No, sir."

"Didn't he say that one a day would be 365 a year?"

"No, sir."

For Rosser, Conley's denials—contradicting, as they did, the key points in Mincey's story—provided reason for optimism. So, too, did the fact that while making them, Jim evinced his first signs of anxiety. Reported the *Georgian:* "He moved uneasily in his seat. He refused to meet the eyes of his inquisitor. He fidgeted with his hands." Now more than ever, in short, the defense was justified in believing that in the insurance agent, it had at its disposal a powerful antidote to the state's Negro.

Tuesday ended, then, with a triumph for Rosser and Arnold, although the day's earlier innings belonged decisively to Dorsey. There was, however, no clear victor here, nor could there be until Judge Roan rendered his decision regarding the admissibility of the sexually charged portions of Conley's testimony. Observed the *Constitution:*

> Would Judge Roan rule for the state or the defense? This was the question which was asked by everyone of his neighbor. Would the state be allowed to still further press the advantage it had made, or would it have to close deprived of this evidence? The air was full of doubt and uncertainty.

By nine Wednesday morning, a throng more than double the courtroom's capacity had congregated in front of the old city hall, filling the sidewalks and spilling into the streets. Once again, however, Atlanta would have to wait. Shortly after gaveling the session to order, Judge Roan announced that he was still studying the defense motion, deferring his decision until following the noon recess.

Thus, during the next few hours, the trial would proceed in a climate of unbearable anticipation, but proceed it did, for a key piece of business remained unfinished.

By way of wrapping up his cross-exam of Jim Conley, Luther Rosser devoted a substantial chunk of time simply to reading the Negro's affidavits aloud, ending each installment with the question "This is what you swore, isn't it, Jim?" Repeatedly, Conley would answer, "Yes, sir," whereupon the lawyer would pause, allowing the jury to ponder the glaring discrepancies among the various statements. Then, following a few inquiries into Jim's behavior around the pencil factory in the days after Mary Phagan's murder, inquiries plainly designed to set the stage for several more defense witnesses, Rosser at last returned to his seat.

Not that Conley's interminable turn upon the stand was done. In fact, as soon as his tormentor sat down, Hugh Dorsey was on his feet, initiating a brief but critical redirect examination. Its purpose: to present a solution to one of the case's most vexing mysteries, a puzzle that from the start had stumped investigators and lawyers alike.

"Did you ever see Mary Phagan's pocketbook or mesh bag?" the solicitor began.

"Yes, it was on the desk in Mr. Frank's office when I went there to write the notes."

"Describe it."

"It was a wire-ish looking pocketbook like the ladies carry, light-colored and had little chains on it for the ladies to hold to."

"What did Frank do with it?"

"He put it in the safe."

Having thereby elicited testimony that if true not only further implicated Frank in the murder but destroyed the defense's theory that Conley had stolen the purse, Dorsey had gotten everything he had wanted from his Negro and turned him back over to Rosser.

"Why didn't you tell all of this when you were telling the whole truth to the detectives?" Frank's counsel demanded incredulously.

"I don't think they asked me."

"When did you first tell any detective about it?"

"I don't remember."

Upon hearing this exceedingly tired retort, Rosser's face darkened with rage. But he said nothing, and following a couple of innocuous final queries, the state's star witness was excused.

The time was 11:10, and all told, Conley had testified for more than 15 hours, over 13 of them under cross-examination. Still, his ordeal was not done, for no sooner had he been escorted from the courtroom than he found himself surrounded by reporters. "Jim," advised William Smith, who by this point had reached his client's side, "don't you say a word to anybody, do you hear?" The newspapermen, however, made such a noise that the lawyer—on the condition that he got to do the questioning—relented.

"How did you like it, Jim?" Smith asked.

"I liked it fine."

"What do you think of Rosser?"

"He shore goes after you, don't he."

"What did you want most, Jim, while Rosser was grilling you?"

"Outside of wonderin' when he was goin' to quit," Conley replied with a wide smile, "I guess I wanted to smoke most."

With that, Smith produced a cigarette, and Jim fired up, exhaling slowly. Shortly thereafter, the lawyer, realizing that his client was exhausted, dismissed the press, leaving Conley alone with a stack of newspapers in which, contrary to his countless assertions that he could not make sense of the printed word, he quickly immersed himself. Meanwhile, several deacons from the Reverend Henry Hugh Proctor's First Congregational Church— which, as it had done with other poor black clients of Smith's, had agreed to pay for representation for Conley—arrived on the scene and handed the lawyer an envelope containing his fee in full—$40.

Court reconvened at two Wednesday afternoon outside the jury's presence. Over lunch, Judge Roan had studied several conflicting legal precedents, among them one provided by Hugh Dorsey in which a Georgia court had overruled a defendant's belated objection to prejudicial testimony, allowing it to stand. The magistrate in that action: Leonard Roan. Yet poorly as this fact augured for Leo Frank, it was balanced by the report that entering into his deliberations, the judge had confided that he considered the allegations in question to be, at heart, immaterial.

Which was why, when Roan looked down from the bench and announced, "I have serious doubts as to the admissibility of this testimony as an original proposition," the defense had good reason to believe the ruling was favorable. But in his next breath, the judge dashed any such hopes. "I am going to allow this testimony to remain," he declared. "It may be extracted from the record, but it is an impossibility to withdraw it from the jury's mind."

Before Roan could say another word, the packed courtroom exploded in what one reporter described as "a riot of applause." Some spectators hooted, others pounded their feet on the floor, still others shouted the news out the windows. The demonstration was so spontaneous and intense that the judge initially appeared too astonished to react. After a few seconds, Reuben Arnold leaped from his seat, roaring, "I will ask for a mistrial if this continues." But upon realizing that with the jury withdrawn, such a motion was groundless, the lawyer amended his request, sputtering, "I shall ask that the court be cleared." Soon enough, however, Roan recovered his wits, and by sternly admonishing the gallery while directing deputies to remove the most vociferous offenders, he restored order. Yet there could be no mistaking the significance of what had transpired. Not only had the decision done severe damage to the defense (ROAN'S RULING HEAVY BLOW, boomed the *Georgian*), but the throng's boisterous response indicated that Atlanta's sympathies had turned overwhelmingly against Leo Frank.

With Jim Conley's testimony fully on the record, Hugh Dorsey, intent upon completing a crucial examination that had been cut short the previous week, resummoned Dr. Henry F. Harris, and for the remainder of the afternoon, the still-ailing physician, ensconced in an upholstered armchair brought in for his comfort, further detailed the microscopic observations he'd made during Mary Phagan's autopsy. Considering the pulse-quickening quality of Conley's turn upon the stand, Harris's cool assertions regarding the time of the child's murder (a lack of hydrochloric acid in the stomach offered added proof that death had occurred within 45 minutes of eating) came across as a touch academic. Yet in a sense, this was just the note the state wanted to strike. The *Georgian*'s Fuzzy Woodruff observed that Jim Conley's story was "a ragtime composition, with the weirdest syncopations, and then came Dr. Harris right on his heels and gave evidence full of soundness and learnedness. To the spectators, it seemed that they had just heard 'Alexander's Ragtime Band' played and then a Bach fugue for an encore."

And what made the move all the more effective was the fact that during his cross-examination of Harris, Reuben Arnold struggled. Yes, the physician admitted, "the science of digestion is rather a modern thing." And true, he added, "every individual is almost a law unto himself." But save for these broad concessions, Harris stuck to his position. Noted the *Constitution*: "Arnold failed to develop anything of material benefit to the defense."

Thursday morning, Hugh Dorsey produced the white witness whose job it was to verify Jim Conley's assertion that Leo Frank regularly entertained prostitutes in his pencil factory offices.

About 35 years old, brown-haired, with heavy eyebrows, a thin moustache and tightly compressed lips, C. Brutus Dalton, a carpenter for the Western and Atlantic Railroad, gave every appearance of being a hard case—considering the purpose of his testimony, just what the solicitor wanted.

"Do you know Leo M. Frank?" Dorsey began.
"Yes."
"Do you know Daisy Hopkins?"
"Yes."
"Do you know Jim Conley?"
"Yes."
"Did you ever go to Frank's office with Miss Daisy Hopkins?"
"Yes."
"Was Frank there?"
"Yes."
"Did you ever go down in the basement?"
"Yes."
"Where in the basement?"

To this, Dalton took a pointer and turning to Bert Green's diagram indicated the plywood enclosure where following Mary Phagan's murder the police had discovered a cot and numerous female footprints.

"Did you ever see Conley on those visits?"

"Yes."

"Who was with Frank?"

"Why, sometimes two and sometimes one young woman."

With that, Dorsey turned the witness over to the defense.

From Luther Rosser's perspective, Dalton presented a now familiar problem—a vague and disreputable witness whose very vagueness and disreputability ended up validating his allegations. Nonetheless, the lawyer did what he could with him, rapidly ascertaining that not only was he unsure of the dates he'd visited Frank's office but that he could not say with certainty whether the women he'd seen there—far from being fallen creatures—were not such employees as the plant stenographer. A couple of aspects of Dalton's story thus blunted, Rosser turned his attention to a topic that Dorsey had purposely ignored. To call the witness a career criminal would have been harsh but not overly so. As he now admitted, he had been arrested numerous times for offenses ranging from stealing corn and cotton from farmers to burglarizing a machine shop, along the way serving a sentence on the chain gang. Rosser's point: Dalton wasn't the type with whom Frank ordinarily consorted.

The last word, however, belonged to Dorsey, who during his redirect examination obtained several damning particulars. For one, Dalton backed up Conley's account of how the office trysts worked, asserting that the Negro had stood guard in the lobby and generally received a quarter tip for his services. For another, he revealed that Frank kept "Coca-Cola, lemon and lime and beer" on the premises. Finally, as to the possibility that the women present on the Saturdays in question might have been there in an official capacity, he simply stated: "I never saw the ladies in his office doing any writing."

Once Dalton left the stand, Dorsey, indicating that his work was almost done, undertook the task of placing various exhibits—among them the bottles containing cabbage extracted from Mary Phagan's stomach—in evidence. Then he asked Rosser and Arnold to produce the National Pencil Company's financial records, including the factory cash and bank books. Upon receiving the lawyers' assent, the state rested, leaving the defense in an awful spot. Reported the *Georgian:*

Every single thing that Solicitor General Hugh Dorsey declared in advance that he would get before the jury is there now.

One by one the prosecutor has forged the links in the chain that he maintains fixes the guilt of the Phagan murder on Leo Frank and Leo Frank alone.

And the strongest of these links was, of course, Jim Conley's testimony, which in the end dazzled even the *Georgian*'s James B. Nevin, who conceded that its many minor mendacities aside, the Negro's account could in the main be true, concluding:

If the story Conley tells IS a lie, then it is the most inhumanly devilish, the most cunningly clever, and the most amazingly sustained lie ever told in Georgia!

ELEVEN

Defense

L eo Frank's lawyers, declared the *Georgian,* now faced a single task: "THE UNDOING OF CONLEY. Without Conley, the State is rendered helpless." In the same breath, however, the same paper argued that "the biggest element in the case is the time element," asserting that if the defense could establish that Mary Phagan met her death at some point later than 12:05 on April 26, the narrative Hugh Dorsey had so seamlessly woven would unravel. Others, though, believed that the damage inflicted by the prosecution was such that Luther Rosser and Reuben Arnold had no choice but to pursue a more dangerous tack. "Not one in a hundred defendants place their character in issue when on trial for murder," noted the *Constitution,* "but a condition has arisen in the Frank case which may cause his attorneys to think it wise to take this step. It came when James Conley testified to misconduct on the part of the defendant which would brand him as an outcast among men." The alternatives were various and risky. All of which may explain why when Dr. Leroy Childs, the first man up for Frank, walked into the courtroom just before noon on Thursday, Arnold told reporters: "Further than this witness, I do not know what line we will pursue at the present."

A 1906 graduate of the University of Michigan medical school, Childs had been in surgical practice in Atlanta for five years. His appearance on the stand indicated that the defense would initially attack the state's time line. Hoping that the young surgeon could counter Dr. Henry F. Harris's critical findings regarding the hour of Mary Phagan's demise, Arnold directed his attention to the foodstuff upon which the calculations were based, inquiring: "Is cabbage considered a hard food to digest?"

"It is generally considered the hardest," replied Childs, citing the vegetable's high cellulose content.

Whereupon Arnold produced the vial containing the cabbage removed from little Mary's stomach, which Harris maintained had been ingested no more than 45 minutes before the girl died. "Look at this cabbage," the lawyer instructed. "Was it well masticated?"

"Not very well."

"Where does cabbage begin to be digested?"

"In the mouth, when ptyalin in the saliva acts on it."

"Does it keep up in the stomach?"

"No, the acids of the stomach neutralize the ptyalin."

"Then where is cabbage really digested?"

"In the small intestines."

"When it goes out of the stomach, it is really undigested, is it not?"

"Yes. It may pass out of the body entirely in the undigested form."

"Are there a great many things that retard digestion?"

"Yes, the psychic causes—fright, anger and sudden mental excitement."

Here, Arnold once again held up the vial containing the cabbage in question. Then, in a query constructed so as to remind the jury of the lengthy period that had elapsed between the date of Mary Phagan's murder and the date her remains were autopsied, he demanded: "Take a human body that has been interred nine days. Take out the stomach and in the contents find cabbage and certain remnants of wheat bread. Could you hazard an opinion or guess that the person had taken it into his stomach one-half or three-quarters of an hour before death?"

"I certainly could not," answered Childs.

"How long would you say it was possible for cabbage like this to stay in the stomach?"

"I have seen cabbage less digested than that which had been in the stomach for twelve hours."

From the defense's perspective, Childs's observations could not have been more helpful, and after eliciting a couple of other tidbits (among them that the bruise to little Mary's eye could have been caused by a lick to the back of her head and that the inflammation in her vagina could have been produced by a digital examination made by Dr. J. W. Hurt during his preliminary postmortem), Arnold turned the surgeon over to Dorsey for what proved to be an ineffectual cross-examination. Childs held to his position that the time of Mary Phagan's death could not be pinpointed with anywhere near the precision claimed by the state. Reported the *Georgian:* "Childs's testimony if believed by the jury served utterly to demolish the most sensational declaration by Dr. Harris."

Having delivered a strong first blow to the prosecution's murder-day chronology, Frank's lawyers called a familiar and problematic figure. During his initial turn upon the stand, Harry Scott had given the defense fits, but it would now use him to launch its assault on Jim Conley. After establishing that the Pinkerton agent had been at headquarters in mid-May when Mrs. Arthur White tentatively picked Conley out of a lineup as the Negro she'd seen lurking in the pencil factory lobby on April 26, Luther Rosser inquired: "Was there any effort on Jim's part to change his features as if he desired to escape identification?" Though Dorsey successfully objected to the wording of this question, once Frank's counsel rephrased it, Scott replied: "He was chewing his lips and twirling a cigarette in his fingers. He didn't seem to know how to hold on to it. He could not keep his feet still." The implications could not have been clearer. Conley had been more nervous at the prospect of being placed at the scene of the crime than had been previously made known.

Rosser's primary interest, however, was in four subsequent headquarters gatherings in which Scott had played a role. These, of course, were the sessions that produced Conley's conflicting affidavits. The lawyer's hope was to cast doubt on the entire process, accomplishing what he had so plainly failed to achieve during his cross-examination of the Negro.

"Didn't Conley verbally deny to you on May 18 that he had any connection with the murder?" Rosser began after glancing at Jim's statement of the same date.

"Yes."

"Give us a picture of what you and [John] Black did to him."

"We talked pretty rough to him."

"You gave him the third degree, didn't you?"

"I wouldn't say that we use the third degree."

"Didn't one of you wheedle him and the other sympathize with him?"

"I'll admit that we used a bit of profanity."

"How long was the grilling you gave him that Sunday?"

"Two hours."

A sense of the detectives' techniques thereby conveyed, Rosser began to question Scott on the topic of how Conley's narrative had evolved. After reaffirming that in his affidavit of May 24, Jim, while confessing to a part in the affair, had asserted that Frank dictated the murder notes the Friday before the crime, the lawyer asked: "On May 27, how long did you sit with him?"

"Five or six hours."

"You impressed upon him the fact that his May 24 statement was not plausible and that his story of writing the notes on Friday would show premeditation, didn't you?"

"Yes."

"You saw him again on May 28?"

"Yes."

"You stayed with him all day that time, explaining that his statement was absolutely unbelievable?"

"Yes."

"On this day, he made another statement?"

"Yes."

"This time, he changed his dates from Friday to Saturday?"

"Yes."

"He said it was his last statement, didn't he, and that he had made up his mind to tell the truth?"

"Yes."

Scott was not relating much that was new here, but Rosser was bringing attention to the investigators' participation in the shaping of Conley's story. For the first time, the jury was hearing a straight version of how it had all worked, one unencumbered by the evasions and memory lapses that had marked the Negro's telling of the tale. Accordingly, Rosser steered the Pinkerton agent to the subject of the May 29 affidavit, the one that Jim had sworn was the affidavit to end all affidavits.

"In that statement, he said nothing about watching for Frank, did he?"

"No."

"Did you try to get him to tell about the mesh bag of Mary Phagan?"

"Yes. He denied having seen it."

"Did he tell you anything about Frank putting it in his safe?"

"He told me nothing about it."

"Did he tell you he'd seen Mary Phagan that day?"

"No."

"Did he tell you he heard someone tiptoe to Frank's office?"

"No."

"Did he tell you he heard somebody stamp, and that then he went to sleep and the next thing he heard was the whistling?"

"No, sir."

"Did he tell you about Frank showing him how to lock the door?"

"No, sir."

Each of these responses ran counter to an allegation Conley had ultimately leveled from the stand. After touching on several other instances in which the Negro had evidently held back on the detectives, Rosser returned to his seat, and Dorsey initiated what proved to be another unavailing cross-examination. True, the solicitor secured Scott's endorsement of Conley's final version of what had transpired on April 26. But he could not reverse the overall impression, meaning that when the Pinkerton agent stepped down and court recessed for the day, the defense had succeeded in introducing a note of skepticism regarding the manner in which the all-important affidavits had been obtained. Observed the *Constitution:* "Scott's statement created a telling effect, and it is said to have caused the wavering of opinion [concerning] the negro's story."

On Friday, Frank's lawyers brought to the stand the woman whom Conley claimed had been one of the superintendent's paramours. Daisy Hopkins was an angular country gal clad in a yellow straw hat and a striped cotton dress that, according to the *Georgian,* "looked a bit too short." While taking the oath, she initially raised her left hand, and throughout her testimony, she chewed gum. But lack of refinement notwithstanding, this rag and bone and hank of hair was, as Reuben Arnold quickly established, married. Moreover, from October 1911 through June 1912, she had worked in the second-floor packing room of the National Pencil Factory, and during that time, she told the lawyer, Frank never spoke to her and she "never did speak to him." That said, Arnold asked: "Did you ever go into Frank's office and drink beer and cold drinks with other women?"

"No. I never went into his office, and I don't drink."

"Do you know C. B. Dalton?"

"I know him when I see him."

"Did you ever go to the pencil factory with Dalton?"

"No. I never did."

"Did you introduce him to Mr. Frank?"

"No, I did not."

"Did you ever go into the factory basement with Dalton?"

"No. I don't even know where the basement is. I never have been in it."

Considering the havoc Conley's assertions regarding Daisy and Frank had wrought, her blanket denial of any untoward involvement with either the superintendent or Dalton gave every promise of constituting a signal victory for the defense. Yet no sooner had Dorsey started his cross-examination than this victory was all but snatched away. Right off the bat, the solicitor, by inquiring into whether the woman recalled the place where she had exchanged vows or even knew her husband's initials, insinuated that she may have been wed in name only. Then the solicitor expressed interest in a certain medical condition for which "Miss Hopkins"—as he insisted upon calling her—had been seeking treatment. Dorsey was implying that Daisy suffered from venereal disease, an implication her hesitant and vague reply of "stomach trouble" merely reinforced. Finally, the solicitor asked point-blank: "Have you ever been in jail, Miss Hopkins?"

"No, sir," she answered after a long pause.

"Why, Miss Hopkins, didn't this man get you out of jail?" Dorsey rejoined, indicating his assistant, Newt Garner.

"No, sir, but he was along."

"Well, you were in jail now. And who got you out?"

Here, Daisy pointed to William Smith, who, as it happened, had represented her.

"What were you in jail for, Miss Hopkins?"

"Somebody told a tale on me," Daisy responded.

"Weren't you there for reasons of immorality?"

"They accused me," the woman at last admitted, "of fornication."

Though Arnold succeeded in subsequently establishing that Daisy had never been convicted and was released after paying a fine, the fact that her trustworthiness and character were so plainly questionable rendered her, in the end, of dubious value, and she stepped down having, in all likelihood, marginally reinforced Conley's story.

In the wake of Daisy Hopkins's disappointing turn upon the stand, the defense called W. M. Matthews, the motorman on the English Avenue trolley that brought Mary Phagan to town on April 26, and Arnold again set about attacking the state's time line, eliciting the potentially pivotal assertion that little Mary did not get off the car until 12:10—a full five minutes after the prosecution contended that she was dead. Frank's lawyer then directed Matthews to a topic of nearly equal import, obtaining his assurance that the girl's self-professed beau George Epps, far from sitting beside her on the ride, wasn't on board. With that, Arnold turned the motorman over to his counterpart.

Dorsey took issue with just about everything Matthews had said, scoffing at his ability to remember four months after the fact the precise hour Mary Phagan had exited the trolley and forcing him to concede that if asked to describe Epps, he would be hard-pressed to provide any distinguishing characteristics. Yet these triumphs notwithstanding, the solicitor's efforts to undermine the motorman's testimony ultimately failed. For one thing, Matthews evinced no doubts regarding the details of his April 26 run, even recollecting a conversation he'd had with little Mary. For another, once the motorman stepped down, Arnold summoned W. T. Hollis—on the day of the murder, the conductor on the English Avenue car—who corroborated his coworker on every significant point, including the one about the Epps boy not being on the trip. All of which, of course, augured well for the defense, not only raising the hoped-for doubts regarding the state's chronology but shining a harsh light on the claims of two of its most important witnesses. Reported the *Georgian*:

If the testimony of the street car employees is accurate, it completely upsets Jim Conley's story that he saw Mary Phagan enter the factory before Monteen Stover came in. By the Stover girl's own testimony she entered the factory at 12:05 o'clock and left at 12:10 o'clock. Thus, she had gone by the time the Phagan girl arrived.

It also serves to destroy the significance of the Stover girl's testimony that Frank was absent from his office when she arrived there. As Mary Phagan had not yet arrived, according to the testimony of the street car men, it could hardly be regarded as a suspicious circumstance that Frank was not in his office, if it develops that he really was not.

Heretofore, through a myriad of witnesses but primarily through the factory diagram produced by the *Georgian*'s Bert Green, Hugh Dorsey had determined what the jury knew about the layout of the crime scene. The plant basement, metal department and office—in the eyes of the twelve men who would determine Frank's fate, these spaces existed only as the solicitor had pictured them. Now, however, the defense would challenge the prosecution's portrait. It started by calling a practitioner of that most exacting profession, civil engineering.

Within minutes of taking the stand, Albert Kauffman was unscrolling blueprints of the National Pencil Factory on the jury-box rail and, at Reuben Arnold's direction, pointing out potentially significant elements of the plant's design that the state had failed to mention. To begin with, at the rear of a long hallway leading back from the first-floor elevator lobby, a previously unremarked-upon five-foot-wide chute opened into the basement only a few yards from where Mary Phagan's remains were found. Chiefly used for sliding heavy boxes to the lower level, this chute, declared the engineer in a phrase that made the implications obvious, "was big enough for one or two human bodies or even a pony." Then there were the swinging doors through which employees entered and exited the metal department. As Kauffman's schematics plainly revealed, the doors were glassed in at the tops—yet another impediment to the room's utility as a trysting place. Similarly, the plans showed that Frank's office was hardly the spot for afternoon beer parties with women of ill repute—the windows lacked curtains or shades. Last but not least, there was the matter of the office safe. "The safe is four and one-half feet high," the engineer asserted, adding that "a person five feet and two inches tall could not see over [it]." Simply put, even if the superintendent was seated at his desk on April 26, Monteen Stover could well have missed him if the safe's door was open.

In his examination of his next witness, a photographer named John Quincy Adams, Arnold again treated the jury to a visual display, this time in the form of eight-by-ten glossies of the factory. First came a shot of Frank's inner office, the view of the desk blocked by the open safe door. Then one of the metal-department floor that brought home the close proximity of the women's restroom to the spot where bloodstains were discovered. Finally, an image of the gears and pulleys at the top of the elevator shaft, stilled here but in the jurors' minds, or so the defense hoped, a clangorous rebuke to Jim Conley's claim that he and Frank had managed to transport little Mary's body in the lift without anyone having heard.

Though the state did not concede the testimony of Kauffman or Adams, Frank Hooper—who henceforth would alternate with Dorsey in the conducting of cross-examinations—was able to do little with either witness. True, he got Kauffman to admit that the famous factory scuttle hole was, at two feet by two feet three inches, too small for someone to have carried Mary Phagan's body through. And yes, he induced Adams to allow that during the several months that elapsed between April 26 and the day he took his photographs of the plant, someone could have rearranged the office furniture so that the open safe door obscured Frank's desk. But as court recessed for lunch, the consensus was that at the least, Arnold had succeeded in challenging the prosecution's depiction of the crime scene, and at the most, had laid the groundwork for a new theory of what had transpired. Proclaimed the *Constitution*'s page-one headline:

> Defense Will Seek to Show That Mary Phagan's Body Was Tossed Down a Chute in Rear of Pencil Factory And Not Taken Down by Elevator as the State Insists.

Shortly after the proceedings reconvened Friday afternoon, Frank's lawyers unveiled the exhibit that they believed would settle the matter of the crime scene's appearance and configuration for all time—a six-and-one-quarter-foot-long scale model of the National Pencil Factory constructed out of pasteboard by an expert pattern maker. Like Bert Green's diagram, the model provided an exposed view of the plant's inner workings. Also, it was intricately detailed, featuring everything from dollhouse-sized furniture in the superintendent's office to a miniature boiler and trash pile in the basement. Yet unlike Green's diagram, the model was free from such editorial embellishments as Maltese crosses, dotted lines and written keys. From the defense's vantage, here was a three-dimensional representation based solely on the facts, and once it was situated on the courtroom floor in front of the jury box, Reuben Arnold summoned assistant plant superintendent N. V. Darley to elucidate the ways in which those facts undermined the prosecution's theories.

Darley had done Leo Frank a world of good when testifying for the state, and he came through for his boss once again. Arnold began by directing his attention to a previously undiscussed section of the factory building—a self-contained first-floor enclosure running from the rear of the elevator shaft to the back wall. For several years, this space had comprised the work-room of the Clark Woodenware Company, a manufacturer of cartons and boxes, but since January, when the concern moved to quarters across town, it had been vacant. Though the empty chamber's connection to the Phagan murder initially seemed obscure, Mister Rube immediately zeroed in on the relevant detail—a presumably sealed entrance just behind the spot where Jim Conley claimed to have been sitting on the morning of April 26.

"Has this door been kept locked, Mr. Darley?"

"We kept it locked after the Clark Woodenware Company moved out, [but] two or three days after the murder we found it broken open."

Arnold then asked whether the former Clark Woodenware location pro-vided any access to the basement. Yes, it did, responded Darley, indicating an opening that represented a never before mentioned second scuttle hole. Here was yet another conduit through which little Mary's body could have been dropped into the cellar. When several of the jurors stood to get a bet-ter look, it became plain they were at least contemplating the possibility that one of the prosecution's central hypotheses might be in error.

During his cross-examination of Darley, Hugh Dorsey labored to quell such doubts. But despite his eliciting the admission that for all the assistant superintendent knew, it could have been the investigating officers who broke into the long-shuttered Clark Woodenware space, the main point remained unchallenged. For now, at least, the defense's version of reality was ascendant, and though more remained to be said on the topic, once Darley stepped down, the factory model was removed from the courtroom.

Arnold used Friday's concluding witness, the National Pencil Company day watchman E. F. Holloway, to resume the assault upon Jim Conley, obtaining in rapid succession statements that undercut a number of the Negro's most deleterious charges. After asserting that he had not missed work since June 1912, Holloway declared that he had never seen the fac-tory's front door locked on a Saturday. "I always kept the door," he said. "I never turned it over to Conley or anyone else." Holloway also scoffed at the Negro's claim that Daisy Hopkins visited the plant on weekends. "I have never known Mr. Frank to have any woman on Saturday excepting his wife," he testified. "She came there on Saturdays and went home with him about once a month." And besides, he added in response to a related ques-tion, so many factory employees—among them salesmen bringing in orders and laborers servicing machinery—dropped by unannounced on weekends that even had Frank been thus inclined, the office would have been the last place to indulge in "immoralities." Then there was Conley's story alleging wild goings-on in the plant on Thanksgiving Day 1912. Holloway utterly dismissed this tale. Not only had he been there until noon on the holiday, and not only had he not seen the white-shoed, white-stockinged creature the Negro had sworn was the guest of honor, but the likelihood that a female would have been out in such a summery getup was slight — Atlanta had been hit by a snowstorm that afternoon. Finally, Arnold asked Holloway if he'd ever witnessed any of the horseplay between Frank and Conley to which the Negro had attested. Replied the day watchman: "I never saw Mr. Frank goose, pinch or joke with Conley."

Holloway's testimony constituted the most potent attack yet on the state's Negro, but by the time Dorsey finished with him, his motives — if not his veracity — would be in serious dispute. Though Holloway's pro-Frank sympathies had been apparent since late May when, along with several other pencil company employees, he'd proclaimed his belief in Jim Conley's guilt, the solicitor suspected that the day watchman, far from simply taking sides, had tried to tamper with the prosecution's case. Specifically, he believed that Holloway had attempted to persuade Newt Lee's predecessor as night watchman to announce that the superintendent had been in the habit of telephoning him at work after hours, a declaration that would, of course, have made the much discussed call to the factory the evening of Mary Phagan's murder seem less sinister. Hence the solicitor began by grilling Holloway as to this point, and while the day watchman denied any impropriety, he was, according to every account, badly rattled. This, however, was just the prelude. Dorsey followed up by accusing Holloway — who had, after all, spotted Conley washing the infamous red stains from his shirt — of being actuated by nothing more than a desire for the reward money. Here again, the day watchman repudiated the charge, but when the solicitor asked him whether he'd told the police that Jim was "his nigger," thereby implying that if Conley was convicted he should be the financial beneficiary, he conceded that he'd made such a statement. Bluntly put, Holloway was anything but a disinterested party, and regardless of the good he'd done the cause at the outset, he departed the stand, in the *Georgian*'s estimation, having "partly spoiled" what was otherwise a "very favorable day for the defense."

Saturday's half-session opened with the return of the barefooted newsboy, George Epps. Initially, the subject of Reuben Arnold's examination — an interview George and his sister Vera had given to the *Georgian*'s John Minar on the Sunday little Mary's body was discovered — appeared not to promise much. But after establishing that the boy recalled meeting with the reporter, the lawyer promptly led him onto thin ice, demanding: "Did he ask you and your sister when was the last time you saw Mary Phagan, and did your sister say Thursday?"

Confronted by this direct challenge to his story of having seen the victim on Saturday, April 26, Epps hastily replied, "I wasn't there then," adding that just before Minar initiated the exchange at issue, he'd momentarily ducked out.

"Weren't you there when he asked that question?" Arnold pressed.

"No. I was not."

While Frank's counsel believed he had caught George in a crucial lie, he would leave it to his next witness to bring the point home.

Like most of the *Georgian*'s journalistic mercenaries, John Minar was a veteran of numerous Hearst newspaper battles, and Arnold used him to maximum effect by posing essentially the same question he'd posed to Epps. The reporter's response was that George had very definitely been with his sister as he'd asked them when they last saw little Mary. Vera, he confirmed, had answered Thursday.

"When did George Epps say he saw her?"

"The boy said he saw her occasionally going to work in the mornings."

"Did he claim or breathe a thing about seeing her after Thursday?"

"He did not."

During his cross-examination of Minar, Frank Hooper endeavored to cast aspersions on the reporter's reliability by emphasizing the *Georgian*'s pro-defense editorial stance, at one point inquiring: "Haven't you had directions to get everything possible that is favorable to the defendant?" Yet this line of attack accomplished little, for as Minar coolly reminded Dorsey's assistant, at the time of the Epps interview, Newt Lee was the primary suspect. Whereupon Hooper returned to his seat, having done nothing to blunt the burgeoning impression that young George's account of riding into town with Mary Phagan on the day of the murder was a fabrication.

Not only was Herbert Schiff, the National Pencil Company's other assistant superintendent and Saturday's final witness, well versed in details relevant to factory operations, he possessed a winning and convincing personality. Arnold hoped to accomplish a great deal with him. After establishing that Schiff had missed just two Saturdays at the office since June 1, 1912, and that he generally worked alongside his superior, the lawyer asked: "Did you ever see Jim Conley on Saturday afternoons?"

"No."

"Did you and Frank ever have women up there?"

"No."

"Did Mrs. Frank ever come to the factory on Saturday afternoons?"

"Quite often."

"Did you know this man Dalton?"

"Never saw him."

"Do you know Daisy Hopkins?"

"Yes."

"Did you ever see her come back on Saturday afternoon alone or with anybody else?"

"I did not."

Nearly a year of Saturdays thus innocently accounted for, Arnold directed Schiff's attention to the holiday on which Conley maintained Frank had indulged in his most outrageous debauch. After obtaining confirmation of E. F. Holloway's assertion that Thanksgiving 1912 had indeed been "cold and snowing," Arnold startled the courtroom by eliciting the fact that Jim actually had been in the building that day. "I ordered Conley to come back to clean up the box room," Schiff recalled. Far from hurting Frank, however, this news ultimately helped him, for as the assistant superintendent added, the Negro had finished his labors at 10:30 and left before noon—before, in short, the elegant, white-shoed woman purportedly arrived.

"When did Frank leave?" the lawyer followed up.

"About twelve. We left together. I saw Frank to his car for home."

By Schiff's account, then, neither Conley nor Frank was at the plant at the time of the alleged frolics. But lest there be suspicion that the superintendent might have returned later, Arnold inquired: "Do you remember anything Frank had to do that day?"

"Yes," Schiff replied. "He went to a B'Nai Brith affair."

Coming so quickly on the heels of his refutation of Conley's charges regarding Frank's Saturday activities, Schiff's debunking of his account of the Thanksgiving romp suggested an inevitable line of inquiry.

"Do you know Jim Conley's general character for truth and veracity?" Arnold demanded.

"Yes."

"What is it?"

"Bad."

"Would you, knowing his character, believe him on oath?"

"I would not."

With that, Arnold was momentarily finished with the subject of Conley and pointed Schiff to his other principal area of interest—the amount and kind of office work Leo Frank had completed on the Saturday of Mary Phagan's death. Though the defense had, of course, touched on this topic during the trial's opening week, no one save the accused himself could speak more authoritatively than Schiff to the computations the factory's weekly financial sheet entailed. Which was exactly what the lawyer asked him to do. After glancing over the April 26 sheet, Schiff began a painstaking account:

Under the heading "Material Costs," the first figure 2719 and ½ represents the number of gross that we manufactured for that week. To get that figure

> Mr. Frank had to enter all his packing reports for Thursday containing two
> or three pages, each of them containing 12 to 15 or 18 items. He had to cal-
> culate and have a separate report as to each kind of pencil and then add
> them up. We manufacture over a hundred kinds of pencils. That week we
> dealt with about 35 different kinds. To do this you have to add, multiply,
> classify and separate each pencil into a different class.

And these equations, Schiff added, covered only finished pencils. The different raw materials—slats, rubber, lead—had to be similarly broken down.
Same with packing supplies—boxes, wrappers and the like. Initially, the
assistant superintendent's atomization of all this may have struck the jurors
as overly detailed, but as he proceeded, speaking of deliveries processed
and orders fulfilled, a potentially exonerating vision of Frank's activities on
the day of the crime came to life. In it, the factory boss, far from resembling
the sexual deviant depicted by the state, emerged as a paragon of modern
management, a dispassionate, attentive executive busily balancing columns
of numbers and presiding over engines of production. After carefully citing
a few last figures, Schiff, confirming an earlier witness, proclaimed: "I think
it would take about three hours to go through the calculations and complete the sheet." At which point Arnold produced a bundle of previous
reports written by Frank. After the assistant superintendent pronounced
the one compiled the afternoon of little Mary's demise to be identical to the
others in all relevant aspects, the sheets were placed in evidence: proof, or
so the defense hoped, that the Saturday of the killing had been no different
for Frank than scores of Saturdays before.

Arnold concluded by eliciting several pieces of information that while
not earthshaking in and of themselves added up to a forceful volley. First,
Schiff testified that it was he—not Frank—who'd manned the payroll window the Friday prior to the murder, which cast terrific doubt on Helen Ferguson's claim that Frank had rebuffed her request for Mary Phagan's pay
that evening. Schiff also confirmed that just as his superior had told Black
and Starnes the morning little Mary's body was found, the pencil company's insurance agent had ordered that the factory's electrical switch box
be kept unlocked. Moreover, he suggested yet another way in which the
girl's remains could have been transported to the basement, telling the
lawyer that the elevator's metal doors could be pried open by hand, meaning that someone could be pushed through the opening without activitating
the motor. Finally, Schiff declared that when he came to work the Monday
following the crime, the office safe was open, and there was no mesh purse
inside. On that note, Arnold sat down.

Hugh Dorsey began his cross-examination not by attacking the substance of Schiff's testimony but by trying to paint him as a shameless pro-

Frank loyalist. The solicitor sought to convey this impression through a series of questions designed to suggest that in the days immediately follow-ing Mary Phagan's murder, the assistant superintendent had maligned the dead girl's character by telling various officials she was pregnant and about to lose her job. Reuben Arnold, however, would not countenance such a line of inquiry and neither, it turned out, would Judge Roan, who sustained each of the defense's many objections. Dorsey then changed tacks, honing in on the amount of time Schiff contended was necessary to complete the factory's financial sheet. Here again the solicitor came up short. Yes, he got the assistant superintendent to concede that he'd never actually clocked Frank doing the job. But that was it. In fact, when Dorsey presented the April 26 report to Schiff and asked how he could be certain Frank had not prepared it in advance, he was informed that as of quitting time the previ-ous evening, work on the sheet had not started. Of course, Dorsey wasn't about to let such a rebuff stop him, but with the lunch hour now at hand, he did not protest Roan's decision to adjourn for the week. As the newspapers agreed, the prosecution was spinning its wheels. Reported the *Constitution:* "Saturday was by far the best day the defense in the Frank trial has had." And most observers expected better days ahead. Noted the *Georgian* in its Sunday editions:

> As all interest centered in the dramatic story of Jim Conley while the case of the prosecution in the Frank trial was being presented, so the pub-lic now is awaiting with the keenest expectancy the tale that W. H. Mincey, pedagogue and insurance solicitor, will relate when he is called this week by the attorneys for Leo M. Frank.
>
> Conley swore as glibly as though he were telling of an inconsequential incident in one of his crap games that Frank had confessed to him the killing of Mary Phagan.
>
> Mincey will tell a similar story, except that Conley will be named as the man confessing the crime.

The trial's third week started exactly as its second had ended—with Hugh Dorsey trying to break down Herbert Schiff. During the course of Monday's first two hours, the solicitor thoroughly sifted the assistant super-intendent, eventually obtaining several seemingly significant admissions. To begin with, Schiff acknowledged that Leo Frank could have finished the fac-tory's financial sheet the Saturday morning of the murder. Then, in response to a question implying that Jim Conley received special treatment at the plant, he conceded that the Negro's untrustworthy reputation notwith-standing, his superiors never considered firing him. Finally, he allowed that had Mary Phagan's body been dropped into the basement through the

Clark Woodenware space's scuttle hole, it would have landed in a location where Newt Lee would have spotted it far earlier than he did.

By the time Reuben Arnold completed his redirect examination, however, most of the damage had been repaired. Regarding the financial sheet's preparation, Schiff declared that during the five years he'd worked at the National Pencil Company, Frank had without exception written up the document on Saturday afternoons. As for not dismissing Conley, Schiff offered a rationale that few who heard it would have rejected, asserting that trustworthy Negroes were simply hard to find. Considering that Dorsey had made a concerted effort to discredit Schiff, the survival of his testimony's main points represented a great triumph for the defense. But it would not be without a cost, for from this moment forth, the solicitor would conduct himself far more fiercely.

No sooner had Arnold finished examining his next witness—Dr. George Bachman, a French-born physiology professor at the Atlanta College of Physicians and Surgeons who continued the assault on Dr. Harris's autopsy findings—than Dorsey gave an initial indication of just how rough he now intended to play.

"Are you an expert chemist?" the solicitor began.

"I am so far as the body is concerned."

"What is amidulin?"

"I never heard of the word."

"Well, if you have never heard of amidulin, did you ever hear of erythrodextrin?"

"Write it out."

And on it went, with Dorsey firing fifty other medical tongue twisters at Bachman, only a few of which the professor could decipher and several of which occasioned outbursts of laughter from a gallery that delighted in watching an erudite furriner be made to appear ignorant. Though some of the terms had to do with digestion and were therefore relevant to the issue at hand, the solicitor's goal was to divert attention from the substance of the professor's testimony.

Whatever pause Hugh Dorsey's treatment of Bachman may have given Frank's lawyers, they began Monday's afternoon session by calling yet another physician, Dr. Thomas Hancock, chief of medicine for the Georgia Railway and Power Company. A graduate of Columbia University who had been in practice for 22 years, Hancock projected the sort of certitude that made him just the man to speak to an ugly allegation. Hence, Reuben Arnold opened his examination by inquiring: "Have you made a physical examination of Leo M. Frank?"

"Yes."

"Is he normal?"

"I have examined the private parts of Leo M. Frank and found nothing abnormal. As far as my examination disclosed he is a normal man sexually."

Having thereby gone a long way toward debunking Conley's claim that Frank "was not built like other men," Arnold directed Hancock's attention to the substance of Dr. Harris's testimony, swiftly securing one more learned dissent before turning the witness over to his counterpart.

Dorsey's cross of Hancock was even more worrisome than his examination of Bachman, for with his very first question, he introduced an issue that would not only negate any good the venerable physician had done Frank but would further tarnish the accused's character.

"You don't mean to say," the solicitor commenced, "that homosexuality is confined to defected patients?"

"In my experience, I have not touched on that line," Hancock responded in a puzzled tone.

"Didn't you say that you had examined Frank?"

"Yes, but I judged merely from his outward appearance."

"You know but little, then, of homosexuality?"

To this, Hancock could do no more than shrug. Whereupon Dorsey sat down, having brazenly sailed another line of objectionable questioning past the defense.

Realizing, albeit belatedly, that the state's insinuations regarding Leo Frank's sexual orientation could not be left unchallenged, Arnold began the examination of his next witness, Dr. Willis Westmoreland, a socially well-connected Atlanta physician, by demanding: "Did you at our request on yesterday examine Leo M. Frank?"

"I did."

"Did he appear to be a normal male human being?"

"From the examination of the private parts of Leo M. Frank he appears to be a perfectly normal man."

Having thus elicited at least a reaffirmation of Hancock's findings on this point, Arnold steered Westmoreland to the topic of Dr. Harris's autopsy report, securing not only one more denunciation of the health board secretary's work but getting into the record a vital yet heretofore unpublicized fact: Harris had discarded Mary Phagan's stomach following his post-mortem, destroying any opportunity for an independent analysis. The usual custom, declared Westmoreland, was to save at least a portion of such organs.

Though Westmoreland's testimony seemed irrefutable, Dorsey was not deterred. Right out of the chute, the solicitor honed in on the fallacy of judging a book by its cover, inquiring: "Aren't sexual inverts normal so far as physical structure is concerned?"

"Yes."

Plainly, Dorsey was not going to let the issue of Frank's purported deviancy drop. Yet he briefly put it aside, concluding his questioning by grilling Westmoreland regarding his relationship with Harris. As it turned out, the witness, while serving as president of the Georgia Board of Health, had instigated an investigation into Harris's response to a malaria outbreak in the central part of the state. When the probe exonerated Harris, Westmoreland had resigned from the board. The solicitor's point could not have been clearer: Westmoreland's criticism of Harris's handling of the Phagan autopsy grew out of a professional grudge.

During his redirect examination of Westmoreland, Arnold did what he could to ameliorate the damage, obtaining the physician's assertion that he bore Harris no ill will. Their dispute had been purely scientific. That said, the lawyer took a shot at discrediting an insinuation rooted in Conley's testimony, asking whether trauma of the sort evident in Mary Phagan's sexual organs could have been inflicted by cunnilingus. Replied Westmoreland: "The human tongue could not produce any signs of violence in the vagina."

As Monday's final witness, Arnold summoned a renowned accountant to reiterate the most significant portion of Herbert Schiff's testimony. Joel Hunter's Atlanta-based business attracted clients from across the country, and by his calculations, Leo Frank could not have completed the 150 distinct computations involved in the preparation of the pencil factory's weekly financial sheet in under 172 minutes. Not surprisingly, Dorsey vigorously challenged Hunter's assessment, demanding to know whether the superintendent's familiarity with plant operations might have enabled him to balance the numbers more quickly. But to the solicitor's chagrin, the accountant replied that Frank's superior knowledge probably caused him to take longer, as at the bottom of every column, he had to stop and consider what the results meant in terms of the performance of various departments and the status of outstanding orders. Hunter's assertions lent further legitimacy to Frank's version of his activities on the afternoon of the murder. Which was why, despite the session's many reversals, the *Constitution* termed it "the best the defense has thus far had."

Tuesday morning opened with yet another accountant on the stand. According to C. E. Pollard of the American Audit Company, the pencil factory's weekly financial sheet was even more complicated than Joel Hunter allowed, involving 209 computations and requiring 191 minutes to prepare.

While Pollard did contradict Hunter on one key point, conceding during Frank Hooper's cross that "a man can do his own books more quickly than a third party," in the end, his testimony more than confirmed the defense's contention regarding the task's time-consuming nature. Now Reuben Arnold needed to verify that Leo Frank did not start the job on April 26 until after returning to his office from lunch. Which was why he called the stenographer for the Montag Brothers Paper Company as the day's second witness.

Unlike most of the women summoned thus far during the trial, Hattie Hall was a brisk and efficient professional, and no sooner had she taken her seat than she was telling Arnold that Frank had practically begged her to come in on April 26, informing her "that he had work that would take him until 6 o'clock." Though Hugh Dorsey objected to the stenographer's recounting of the superintendent's comment, Judge Roan overruled him, enabling Hall to go on at greater length. As she told it, her first conversation with Frank that Saturday had occurred early in the morning by phone when she'd advised him that her duties at Montag Brothers—her primary responsibility—were such that she wouldn't be able to get away. Yet by 10 A.M., when Frank appeared at the paper factory to pick up the mail and again asked for help, she had made enough progress to answer affirmatively, and sometime between 10:30 and 11:00, she made the five-minute walk to Forsyth Street. Upon reaching Frank's office, Hall said she'd immediately pitched in, filling out a number of order acknowledgments and taking dictation on several letters, which she then typed and handed to Frank for his signature. Altogether, she added, the tasks had required about an hour. Having thus traced Hall's activities on the day of the murder until nearly noon, Mister Rube handed her the critical document.

"Was Frank doing any work on this financial sheet when you were there that morning?" he inquired.

"No, sir. Throughout the time I was there, he did no work on the financial sheet."

This was the response Arnold had been seeking, and on its strength he sat down.

During his cross-examination, Dorsey tried to induce Hall to admit that she really wasn't sure what Leo Frank had been doing in his office between 11 and noon on April 26, but she held her ground, asserting: "When I was in there he was at work on a pile of letters." Similarly, when the solicitor attempted to get the stenographer to concede that Frank had spent previous Saturday mornings preparing the financial sheet, she again resisted, maintaining that on the occasions with which she was familiar, the superintendent had never done so. Then there was the matter of a $4.50-per-week pay hike Hall received on August 1. The obvious implication here was that

Rudolph and Rae Frank, circa 1895
(William Breman Jewish Heritage Museum, Atlanta)

Leo Frank, age nine (WBJHMA)

Leo Frank (right) with a friend in his Cornell dorm room, circa 1905
(WBJHMA)

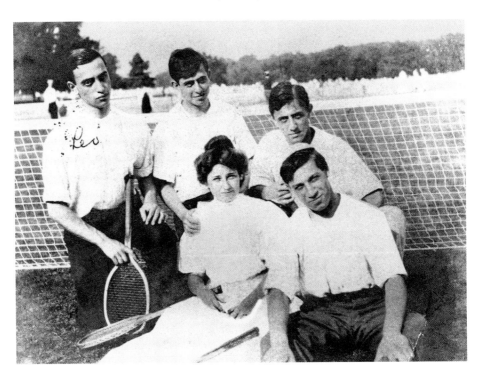

Leo Frank on Cornell's tennis courts, circa 1905
(WBJHMA)

Lucille Selig, circa 1909
(WBJHMA)

Lucille Selig and Leo Frank, circa 1909
(WBJHMA)

Mary Phagan, circa 1913
(Joe McTyre Collection, Alpharetta, Georgia)

National Pencil Company, circa 1913
(Atlanta History Center)

Mam that negro hire down here did this i went to make water and he push me doun that hole a long tall negro black that hoo it wase long sleam tall negro i write while i play with ... he said he wood love me land down an play like the negro witch did it but that long tall black negro did buy his slef

The murder notes
(American Jewish Archives,
Cincinnati Campus, Hebrew Union College/Jewish Institute of Religion)

Evidence!

In the photograph are shown the dress, the shoes, the hat, a stocking and the hair ribbons worn by Mary Phagan when she was murdered; also twine noose with which she was strangled.

A photograph of the clothes Mary Phagan was wearing
when she was murdered and the rope with which she was strangled,
which ran in the *Atlanta Georgian* on April 30, 1913

An editorial cartoon in
the *Atlanta Constitution* that attacks the Atlanta police, May 11, 1913

Atlanta police headquarters, circa 1913
(Atlanta History Center)

POLICE HAVE THE STRANGLER

USTRIA WILL MOVE ALONE ON MONTENEGRO

Final Announcement of Decision to Force Evacuation of Scutari Is Made.

Fire Probe Delayed Again for Witness

Martin in England, His Family's Theory

Your Name There?

DETAILS OF BIG PONY CONTEST ANNOUNCED

There Is Every Reason for Starting Now if You Wish To Be One of the Winners.

VOLS SCORE IN FIRST; BRADY OPPOSES BECK

Teams Battle For Final Game, Guilty Registers on Perry's Timely Double.

By Percy H. Whiting.

THE GAME

RACES

Officials of County Schools Open Meet

Foe of Steel Trust Is Now a Bankrupt

NEW TORPEDO BUOY WILL SAVE NAVY MUCH MONEY

Late this afternoon, Chief of Detectives Lanford made this important statement to a Georgian reporter: "We have the strangler. In my opinion the crime lies between two men, the negro watchman, Newt Lee and Frank. We have eliminated John Gantt and Arthur Mullinax."

LEON M. FRANK, manager of the National Pencil Company, who has been taken in custody by the police and locked up in a cell in connection with the slaying of little Mary Phagan.

Leo M. Frank.

FRANK AND NEGRO ARE GIVEN "THIRD DEGREE"

Attorney Barred, Then Admitted

Frank To Be Kept Under Guard

The Atlanta Georgian, April 29, 1913

Hugh Dorsey
(*Atlanta Journal-Constitution*)

Luther Rosser, uncharacteristically wearing a tie, 1913
(WBJHMA)

Jim Conley, 1913
(*Watson's Magazine*)

Reuben Arnold, 1913
(Courtesy Thomas Arnold)

William Smith,
"A Tramp Alumnus," circa 1900
(Courtesy Walter Smith)

Leo and Lucille Frank at the trial
(Joe McTyre Collection, Alpharetta, Georgia)

Hugh Dorsey examining Newt Lee on the opening day of the trial
(William Pullen Library, Georgia State University)

Leo Frank portrait for Collier's, 1914
(WBJHMA)

Tom Watson at the time of the Frank case
(Southern Historical Collection,
The Library of the University of North Carolina at Chapel Hill)

Governor John Slaton, 1915
(Joe McTyre Collection, Alpharetta, Georgia)

Downtown Atlanta, looking North on Peachtree Street, 1914
(Atlanta History Center)

Herbert Clay at the wheel with Marietta belles, circa 1910
(Marietta Museum of History)

Sig Montag had given the raise to influence its recipient's testimony. Once more, however, Hall demurred, responding that the increase had long been scheduled and was, in truth, a condition of her employment. Whereupon Dorsey returned to his seat.

For Arnold, Hall was the perfect witness—competent, steady and informed—and during his redirect, he used her to even more telling effect. First, in answer to a question regarding whether Frank had telephoned any-one while she was in his office on April 26, the stenographer stated that he had called a salesman named Harry Gottheimer and suggested that he drop by after lunch. Then Rube asked whether the superintendent said anything to Hall before she departed for the day. "He asked me," she replied, "to stay all afternoon and help him, that he was busy." Neither of these actions was consistent with the thinking of a man planning a midday tryst. And that, of course, was the point.

After his success with Hall, Arnold shifted his focus from the Saturday of the murder to the Saturdays that preceded it, summoning a series of witnesses whose sole function was to discredit the testimony of C. Brutus Dalton. Each of these individuals, all of whom were from Dalton's home county east of Atlanta, was, in the *Constitution*'s phrase, "a sturdy farmer or fairly well-to-do citizen," and none of them had a good thing to say about the man the state had put up to substantiate Jim Conley's charges regarding Leo Frank's past liaisons. To a one, they said they would not believe Dalton on oath. Confronted by such unanimity on the subject, Hugh Dorsey de-clined to conduct a single cross-examination.

Next up for the defense was the National Pencil Company's 14-year-old office boy. Arnold's hope was that Alonzo Mann, who though he'd worked only half a day on April 26 typically remained on the premises until 4 P.M., could further undermine Dalton's and Conley's allegations regarding Frank's Saturday afternoon assignations. But while the youngster stated that he'd never seen Dalton around the place, much less witnessed Frank bring-ing women in for drinks, and while Dorsey, during a brief cross-examination, failed to shake these assertions, his testimony was marred by the fact that he seemed unduly nervous. Noted the *Journal:* "He was frightened by his expe-rience in court, and the stenographer had difficulty in hearing his answers."

Following on the heels of the halting and shy Alonzo Mann came a confi-dent and effusive factory inspection department employee who, as he approached the stand, stopped at the defense table and made a sweeping bow to a beaming Leo Frank. As it turned out, Wade Campbell's testimony would give the accused even more reason to smile. As the brother of Mrs. Arthur White, he was in a position to recount his sister's original assertion as to what she'd witnessed at the plant during her critical midday visit on April 26. "She told me," he informed Arnold, "that she had seen a negro sitting at the elevator shaft at 12:00 on Saturday." During the state's presentation of its testimony, Mrs. White had, of course, maintained that the hour was 1 P.M.

For the prosecution, Campbell presented a familiar problem, and Dorsey confronted it in a familiar way, emphasizing the witness's sympathies for Frank. Hence, Campbell was soon revealing that he had formerly been roommates with one of Frank's principal partisans, assistant plant superintendent N. V. Darley. Yet notwithstanding this admission, Campbell did not waver during the solicitor's repeated attempts to get him to say that his sister had told him she'd seen a Negro sitting near the factory elevator shaft not at 12:00 but at 1:00. Again and again, Campbell repeated that the time she'd stated was noon, leaving Dorsey with little choice but to sit down, whereupon Judge Roan gaveled the morning session to a close.

Of all the testimony the prosecution had presented to bolster its allegation that Leo Frank had intentionally lured Mary Phagan to his office on April 26, none had been more persuasive than that of Helen Ferguson, and it was in the hope of countering her claim that the defense began Tuesday afternoon's session by putting up yet another factory girl:

> Getting right to the point, Reuben Arnold asked Magnolia Kennedy, "Were you there when Helen Ferguson drew her pay Friday night?"
> "Yes. I was behind her, and had my hand on her shoulder."
> "Was Mr. Frank there?"
> "No."
> "Who was there?"
> "Mr. Schiff."
> "Did she ask Mr. Schiff for Mary's money?"
> "No."
> "Would she have had any business going to Frank for Mary's money when Schiff paid off?"
> "She wouldn't have any."

Having thus scored what the *Journal* termed "a direct contradiction of Helen Ferguson's testimony," Arnold was done.

Hugh Dorsey responded to the Kennedy girl's injurious revelations by changing the subject, using the witness to introduce a damaging assertion that the defense had thus far managed to keep out of the record:

> "Were you at the pencil factory on Monday, April 28?" he inquired.
> "Yes, sir."
> "Did you discover any hair around the metal room anywhere?"

"Mr. Barrett discovered some on the lathe."

"You identified it, didn't you?"

"Yes. It looked like Mary's hair."

With that, the solicitor directed Magnolia's attention to the substance of what she'd told Arnold, obtaining not only her admission that she had not been with Helen Ferguson every hour of Friday, April 25, but her concession that workers who missed their pay sometimes collected it from Frank. Considering how the Kennedy girl's testimony started, Dorsey had reason to feel pleased that this was how it ended.

In the wake of Magnolia's appearance, the defense called the pencil factory's former office boy. A self-assured 15-year-old, Philip Chambers was the antithesis of Alonzo Mann, and after establishing that he had always remained in the building on Saturday afternoons until 4:30, Arnold sought his point-by-point rebuttal of Dalton and Conley's allegations regarding Frank's weekend activities. The boy's responses:

"Mr. Frank never did have any women in there."

"I never saw any drinking there."

"I have never seen Dalton come in there."

"I have never seen anybody watching the door on any Saturday that I was there."

"I have never seen Mr. Frank familiar with any of the women in the factory."

"I have never seen him talk to Mary Phagan at all."

For Dorsey, Chambers's myriad refutations constituted a genuine threat, yet rather than attack any of the particulars, the solicitor again reversed fields, returning to the volatile topic that had obsessed him the previous day:

"You and Mr. Frank were pretty friendly, weren't you?" he began.

"Just like a boss should be."

"Did you ever complain to J. M. Gantt that Frank had made improper advances to you?"

"No, sir."

"You didn't tell Gantt that Frank had threatened to discharge you if you did not comply with his wishes?"

"No."

As Dorsey started to pose yet another question on the subject, Reuben Arnold at last objected, moving to rule out everything that had just been said. Not surprisingly, the solicitor countered, arguing that he had a right to show the relationship between the witness and the accused. At this, an incensed Arnold rose to his feet and facing the bench declared:

> It's the most unfair thing I've ever heard of in a court proceeding. It's the vilest slander that can be cast upon a man. If courts were run this way it could be brought against any member of the community—you, me or the jury. No man can get a fair showing against such vile insinuations. If this comes up again, I will be tempted to move for a new trial.

Judge Roan's decision to strike the entire exchange from the record could not have been more cut-and-dried, but whether in so doing he removed it from the jurors' minds was hard to say. Either way, with this avenue of inquiry closed, Dorsey returned to his seat, allowing Chambers to depart.

Minola McKnight's repudiation of her infamous affidavit regarding Leo Frank's comings and goings on April 26 and the atmosphere in the family's household during the succeeding days had, of course, been given the widest circulation. Nonetheless, the Negro cook's story focused such a damning light on the methods employed in the case by the Atlanta police—not to mention undermining the state's time line—that Arnold chose this moment midway through the afternoon to put her on the stand. The decision was inspired, for within minutes Minola was indignantly describing her mistreatment at the hands of the detectives, recounting how they had thrown her in what with inadvertent aptness she called "the control wagon" and driven her to headquarters, where they "worried and threatened" her until she made a false statement. The truth, she reaffirmed, was that Frank, just as he maintained, had returned home for lunch on the day of the crime at 1:20 P.M., eaten his meal, then left at 2:00. As for her charges of subsequent worrisome activity at 68 Georgia Avenue, she once more disavowed them, too.

During his cross-examination of Minola, Dorsey—as he'd done when news of her renunciation broke—invoked the name of Albert McKnight, demanding to know whether this figure had not simply "confronted" her with "what you had told him about things you had seen and heard around the house." Yet as she'd done before, the woman denounced her husband, his coworkers at Beck & Gregg Hardware and the detectives. These men, she reasserted, had tried to get her "to tell a lie," keeping her "locked up" until she did. So insistent and unwavering was Minola in this contention that the solicitor had little choice but to cede the floor.

No sooner had Dorsey sat down than Arnold summoned a pair of witnesses whose purpose was to resume the assault on Jim Conley. Corinthia Hall and the young woman who followed her, Emma Clark, were the factory foreladies who, according to Conley, had appeared at the plant office on the afternoon of April 26 in the immediate aftermath of Mary Phagan's murder, necessitating his hasty banishment to a sweaty wardrobe. But as they both told it, while they did visit the building that day, they arrived at 11:35 A.M. and left about 11:45, which meant, of course, that they'd come and gone well before the crime occurred, well before Leo Frank, even if he were the killer, would have needed to hide an accomplice. The women's stories were replete with so many convincing specifics (each recalled seeing Hattie Hall, who went home at noon, at work at the super-intendent's desk) that in the space of just a few minutes they had negated one of Conley's most vivid claims, in the process raising doubts as to the credibility of his entire account. Which explains why Hugh Dorsey, resort-ing to a favorite strategy, let their testimony enter the record essentially intact, asking Hall just a couple of unavailing questions, then waiving his right to cross-examine Clark. From the solicitor's vantage, the less said about any of this, the better.

Arnold called Lucille's parents as Tuesday's final witnesses, and first Emil, then Josephine, Selig testified that Leo Frank had exhibited no anxi-ety either at lunch on April 26 or at a poker party later that evening. In fact, they maintained, he'd been cheerful and lighthearted; both recalled that during the card game, he'd delighted the table by reading aloud a humorous item from *Metropolitan* magazine concerning the misadventures of a base-ball umpire. Finally, the Seligs swore that they could not remember the telephone—which Arnold took pains to emphasize was downstairs in the dining room—ringing early the next morning, contending that once they and their daughter and son-in-law were upstairs with bedroom doors shut, the device was difficult to hear.

Lucille's parents hardly seemed targets for a productive cross-examination, but Dorsey, perceiving a point of vulnerability, promptly elicited damaging admissions from them regarding their understated reac-tions to the news of Mary Phagan's death.

"Do you mean to tell this jury," the solicitor demanded of each, "that a girl had been found murdered in the basement of the factory of which your son-in-law is the superintendent and yet you paid no attention to anything said about it?"

"Yes," the Seligs in turn replied, conceding that on the Sunday the body was discovered, the crime went undiscussed in their house.

For Dorsey, there could have been no better stopping point, but before Mrs. Selig could step down Arnold, realizing that he had to do something, leaped to his feet.

"The facts in this case were harrowing, and you didn't want to know about them, and you were ill, besides?"

"Yes."

"You had an operation the next day, did you not?"

"Yes, I was ill."

In the end, however, what had been said had been said, and the day concluded with the impression having registered that Leo Frank's well-known Atlanta family had responded callously to an unknown child laborer's death.

Though Wednesday began with Reuben Arnold summoning still another respected physician to take issue with Dr. Harris's findings, then putting up one more batch of small-town elders to cast aspersions on C. Brutus Dalton's veracity, by midmorning the proceedings had reached a critical turning point, for it was at this juncture that the defense called its first character witness.

A 15-year acquaintance and Pratt Institute classmate of Leo Frank, Alfred J. Lane, had journeyed to Atlanta from New York, where he worked as a merchant, to deliver but one piece of testimony, and he did it, noted the *Journal,* "with emphasis," proclaiming the defendant's character to be excellent.

Immediately following Lane to the stand came several other equally enthusiastic New Yorkers, among them another of Frank's classmates from Pratt and one from Cornell. Like their predecessor, these old friends all spoke highly of the accused factory superintendent, but ultimately, the content of their testimony was of less import than the fact of their appearance, which signaled that the long-anticipated battle over that most subjective determination, a man's good name, had begun.

Not that there weren't several remaining rounds that the defense intended to fire at the substance of the state's case. Once the last of this initial group of character witnesses stepped down, Arnold briefly resumed his attack by calling a time and motion expert to discredit Jim Conley's claim that he and Frank had dragged Mary Phagan's body from the factory metal room to the elevator, transported it to the basement, then concocted the murder notes in under half an hour. As Dr. William Owens told it, studies he'd conducted at the plant using stand-ins for the alleged participants and a 107-pound bag of sand for the victim proved that the task would have required at least 36 minutes. Which meant that had the two begun, as Conley maintained, at 12:56 P.M., it would have taken them until at least 1:32 — nearly a quarter of an hour after the superintendent arrived home for lunch. Though Frank Hooper, in his cross-examination, succeeded in getting Owens to concede that because he'd been fiddling with a stopwatch during his experiment, the actual events could have unfolded more rapidly, the main point remained intact—timewise, the Negro's account did not add up.

Hard upon Owens's appearance, Arnold summoned yet another former factory office boy. Sixteen-year-old Frank Payne's task was to complete the demolition of one of Conley's most colorful allegations, and he promptly obliged, informing Mister Rube that on Thanksgiving 1912, he'd worked alongside Jim at the plant and that the two had finished their tasks and departed by 10:30 A.M. In short, the Negro was simply not on the premises during the hours he claimed Frank was alone in the office with the white-shoed woman. True, in his cross-examination, Dorsey forced Payne to admit that he had not actually seen Conley leave the building that holiday morning, but in the end, this concession was of minor note. The boy's testimony had achieved its purpose.

Then came Lemmie Quinn, who was on the stand when court adjourned for lunch Wednesday and back when it reconvened, rehashing the story of his surprise appearance at the factory on the afternoon of April 26. After eliciting Quinn's account of finding Frank working at his desk around 12:20, thereby casting more doubt on the state's murder-day chronology, Arnold turned his attention to the motivation of one of the case's most debated figures, inquiring: "Did Mr. Barrett ever make any statement to you as to the reward if Mr. Frank should be arrested?"

"Yes, he mentioned it several times."

"What sums, if any, did he mention to you?"

"He mentioned $2,700 and $4,500."

"How many times did he mention the reward to you?"

"I don't remember. It was so numerous that I can't recall them."

Dorsey went after Quinn with a vengeance, but while he managed to get him to repeat the well-known yet still vexing fact that Frank had initially not remembered his April 26 visit, and though he secured the further admission that Quinn had not mentioned the visit to the police until a week after the slaying, he could not shake him regarding the essential point. He steadfastly maintained that he'd dropped by the factory and found the superintendent immersed in work near the hour the prosecution contended little Mary met her death.

This renewal of the defense's onslaught on the state's case notwithstanding, one needed to look no further than the afternoon's principal witness to realize how utterly the focus had shifted—and how perilous the new course would be. John Ashley Jones was an Atlanta representative of the New York Life Insurance Company. Eighteen months before Mary Phagan's murder, he had ordered a report on Frank preparatory to writing a policy.

The results, he told Arnold, had proven the factory superintendent to be "first class physically as well as morally." Responding to the lawyer's final question, the agent swore that Frank's character was good.

If there were any doubts as to how Hugh Dorsey planned to combat such testimony, his cross-examination of Jones laid them to rest. "Mr. Jones," the solicitor began, "don't you know of Frank's relations with the girls down there at the factory?"

"I have never heard any talk of Mr. Frank's practices with the girls there," replied the insurance agent.

"Then you didn't hear that he took girls in his lap down there at the factory?"

Before Jones could answer, Arnold was on his feet. "That is outrageous," he shouted. "I shall move for a mistrial if such a question is asked again. It is unjust and prejudicial that the gossip of crack-brained extremists should be allowed to come before this jury."

Countered Dorsey: "I'm not four-flushing. I'll bring witnesses here to prove all I have charged."

Following a moment's consideration, Judge Roan—bound by the fact that the defense had introduced the issue of character—rejected Arnold's objection. Whereupon the solicitor resumed his questioning of Jones, demanding: "You never heard that Frank went to Druid Hills with a little girl, did you?"

"No."

"Didn't you hear about twelve months ago of Frank kissing girls and playing with the nipples of their breasts?"

At this, Rae Frank rose from her seat at the defense table and shaking a trembling finger at Dorsey shrieked: "No, nor you either." The suddenness and intensity of the outburst brought the trial to a halt as spectators, oblivious to the judge's rapping, rushed to the rail. Meanwhile, the elder Mrs. Frank, defying the family members attempting to restrain her, kept up her tirade. Later, it would be widely reported that she cast aspersions on the solicitor's faith, dismissing him as either a "Gentile dog" or a "Christian dog." But the confusion was such that her exact words were lost. All that can be said for certain is that once order was restored and the woman was led from the courtroom, she could be heard to sob, "My God, my God."

Rae Frank's indignant eruption served merely to goad Dorsey on. In fact, no sooner had she been packed into a taxi and sent to her in-laws' Georgia Avenue home than the solicitor picked up where he'd left off, asking Jones: "Did you ever hear L. T. Coursey or Miss Myrtice Cato say Frank would walk into the dressing room without offering any explanation for his intrusion?"

"No," came the reply.

"You didn't hear how he stood and looked at poor little Gordie Jackson?"

"No."

"You didn't hear what he tried to do to Lula McDonald and Rachel Prater?"

"No."

"You didn't hear what he said to Mrs. Pearl Darlson when he stood talking to her and her daughter with money in his hand, and you didn't hear how she hit him with a monkey wrench?"

"No."

Following several similarly insinuating queries, Dorsey sat down, and shortly thereafter, court adjourned for the day. Subsequently, Arnold termed the solicitor's behavior vile and slanderous. Dorsey, on the other hand, viewed himself as the aggrieved party, telling reporters: "They have abused me." Either way, something poisonous had entered the air. Boomed the banner atop the next morning's *Constitution:*

MOTHER OF FRANK DENOUNCES SOLICITOR IN COURT

The first hour of Thursday's session found each side seeking relief from Judge Roan for what both perceived as the excesses of the previous afternoon. Before the jury was seated, Hugh Dorsey requested that Rae and Lucille Frank be excluded from the proceedings for the duration, while Reuben Arnold asked that the testimony of John Ashley Jones be stricken from the record. "I appreciate the feelings of the wife and mother of the defendant," stated the solicitor, "but there is going to be much more testimony that will be very objectionable to them. I must ask your honor's protection." Responded Frank's counsel: "The solicitor's examination of Mr. Jones yesterday was wholly unwarranted and much more reprehensible than the act of this man's mother. He tried to get before the jury in an illegal way acts he could not get before it in a legal way. The jury system is very lame if this sort of evidence is admitted." As it turned out, however, Roan disappointed all comers, ruling that the two Mrs. Franks could remain while overruling the objection to Jones's testimony. At which point the twelve men who would determine the defendant's fate filed in, and the examination of witnesses resumed.

With a cooling-off period in order before the topic of Leo Frank's character was reintroduced, the defense chose this moment to buttress the superintendent's account of his activities during the early afternoon of April 26. Attesting to the fact that Frank left the factory by 1:10—which contradicted Conley's allegations—was a stenographer for an Atlanta medical supplies firm. As young Helen Kerns told it, she was shopping at Kress's that Saturday and had just looked at a clock in front of a nearby jewelry store when she noticed the superintendent, with whom she'd once interviewed for a job, standing at the corner of Alabama and Whitehall awaiting a trolley. Lending credence to this testimony was that of the Franks' across-the-street neighbor. According to Mrs. Albert Levy, she was sitting on her porch at 1:20 when she saw Leo get off the car and walk into his home. The state did its best to discredit these witnesses, but to no avail.

Frank's version of his preprandial peregrinations on April 26 thus corroborated, the defense sought to better establish his movements a bit later on. From Lucille's Athens kin, Jerome and Mrs. M. G. Michael, and from Hennie Wolfsheimer—all of whom were standing outside Mrs. Wolfsheimer's house a few doors from the Franks' that Saturday afternoon—Arnold confirmed that following lunch Leo boarded a 2:00 trolley back to town, a fact that gave the lie to Albert McKnight's claim of an earlier departure. Reinforcing this point, Rebecca Carson, forelady of the pencil company's sorting department, swore that she saw Frank near Rich's Department Store around 2:25 and then at Jacob's Pharamacy ten minutes later. Here again, the state failed to shake any of these witnesses. Moreover, Carson provided the defense with an ancillary victory by relating a story about some suspicious behavior on Jim Conley's part the Monday after Mary Phagan's murder. As she told it, several factory employees were discussing the crime and their whereabouts at the time it occurred. When Conley's turn to speak came, she said he announced: "I was so drunk I don't know where I was or what I did." Later in the same conversation, she added, Conley quit the room when someone offered that the killer was most likely the Negro whom Mrs. Arthur White had spotted at the bottom of the plant stairwell on the day of the tragedy.

Momentum having shifted back to the defense, Arnold secured tributes to Frank's good character from a Brooklyn lawyer who'd known him since boyhood and from his Cornell roommate. Though Frank Hooper mocked the Cornell alum's assertion that his old school chum "associated with the finest class of students," he failed to damage his or his predecessor's positive assessments.

Pleased as Frank's lawyers were to have successfully revived their risky new strategy, there were still a few more pieces of direct evidence they wanted to get before the jury. Which was why Mister Rube chose to conclude the morning's session by summoning the man to whom Frank reported at work.

As principal stockholder in the National Pencil Company and president of a thriving paper manufacturer, Sigmund Montag was the imperious embodiment of Atlanta's Jewish elite. The story Arnold elicited from him initially seemed to cast many of Frank's actions in the immediate aftermath of the murder in a more sympathetic light. Montag testified that on the morning Mary Phagan's body was discovered, he was at least as nervous as Frank. "I was very much agitated and trembled," he allowed. Next, he addressed the circumstances surrounding how the factory superintendent acquired legal representation before being charged. As Montag told it, he was solely responsible. When he heard on the Monday following the crime that Frank—whom he characterized as being of "very limited acquaintance"—had been taken to headquarters, he called Herbert Haas. "Mr. Haas answered that he didn't like to leave home that morning, that his wife was expecting a new arrival, so I sent my automobile after him. He then telephoned for Mr. Rosser." Finally, Montag took on the issue of the Pinkerton Detective Agency's role in the probe, insisting that in hiring the firm, the pencil company was only trying to solve the crime.

From the instant Hugh Dorsey began his cross-examination of Montag, it was plain that he meant to hang him with his own words.

"You say that Frank had a limited acquaintance here?" the solicitor started off.

"Yes."

"Isn't he president of the B'nai Brith?"

"I think so."

"How many members has that organization?"

"Between 400 and 500, I should say."

Montag's rationale for engaging Frank's legal counsel made to appear implausible, Dorsey turned to the subject of the Pinkerton Agency.

"You were so much interested in this case that you hired the Pinkertons. And yet you didn't tell the police about their discoveries?"

At this, Luther Rosser broke the silence he'd maintained during the past few days. But Judge Roan overruled his objection, and Dorsey pressed ahead, soon enough eliciting the answer that the defense's lead counsel had seen coming.

"You got the report on the finding of that stick, didn't you?"

"I did."

"And of the finding of that envelope?"

"I did."

"What did you do with these findings?"

"I gave the reports to Mr. Rosser."

With that, Dorsey started in on the matter of Frank's anxiety the morning the body was found. But before the solicitor could finish propounding his first question, Montag cut him off. "Mr. Dorsey, don't twist anything I say."

"He will anyhow," cracked Reuben Arnold in an aside audible through-out the courtroom.

At which point Dorsey and Arnold charged each other like ballplayers at the start of a brawl. "For a minute or two," reported the *Journal*, "a physical encounter seemed imminent." Eventually, though, the men were separated.

Rosser conducted the defense's redirect examination of Montag, but aside from securing the fact that there would have been no reason for him to forward the Pinkerton reports to headquarters, the police having received their own copies, he could do little to make things better. After he returned to his seat, court recessed for lunch.

Save for factory worker Harry Denham, who affirmed the defense's con-tention that the plant elevator had not been run on April 26, the witnesses who trooped to the stand Thursday afternoon did so for only one reason—to attest to Frank's good character. The procession began with another con-tingent of Cornell men. First came John Todd, a classmate who was now a purchasing agent at the Crucible Steel Company in Pittsburgh. Then C. D. Albert, a professor of machine design. Then C. E. Vanderhoef, foreman of the university's foundry. "The loyalty with which Frank's instructors flocked to his aid" was moving, noted the *Constitution*, adding, "The sordid sur-roundings lost some of their grimness as witness and prisoner gripped hands silently or spoke the few simple words of greeting."

Following these proponents, none of whom Dorsey seriously challenged, came a second, much larger group comprised almost entirely of Atlanta Jews. Leading off was Rabbi David Marx, followed by the new Chamber of Commerce president, Victor Hugo Kriegshaber. Thereafter came lawyer Max Goldstein, Hebrew Orphans Home superintendent R. E. Sonn, Termi-nal Station employee Albert Levy and Federation of Jewish Charities sec-retary Alex Dittler. Here again, most of the testimonials went into the record uncontested. But in a couple of instances, they did not.

With Arthur Heyman, Hugh Dorsey found himself in the unusual posi-tion of being given a chance to cross-examine the senior partner in his own law firm, and he did so with surprising relish, forcing Heyman to concede that his glowing assertions regarding Frank's character were based on fewer than seven or eight meetings.

Dorsey saved his toughest cross-examination, however, for Thursday's final witness. Milton Klein was one of Frank's closest friends, and after establishing that he'd seen the superintendent at the Tower nearly every evening since his arrest, the solicitor inquired: "Were you there when Con-ley sought to confront Frank?"

After Judge Roan sustained Luther Rosser's objection, Dorsey rephrased the question: "Tell us, Mr. Klein, did Conley come down there?"

"Yes," replied the witness, and with that, the devastating story that the defense had until now managed to keep out of the record was suddenly fair game.

"Did Frank see Conley?" Dorsey began.

"No."

"Did the detectives bring Conley to the front of Frank's cell?"

"Yes. I went to the front and acted as his spokesman."

"Then Frank didn't come out at all? He stayed in the back end of his cell all the time."

"I said he did not come out."

During Rosser's redirect exam, he elicited the key fact that he had been out of town at the time in question and had instructed his client to speak to no one until his return. Nonetheless, Dorsey's point remained intact—given the chance, Frank had refused to face his Negro accuser.

On Friday morning, Hugh Dorsey made headlines by announcing that a 16-year-old Georgia girl named Dewey Hewell had been returned to the city from the Home of the Good Shepherd (an institution for unwed mothers) in Cincinnati, Ohio, and was being held at headquarters. Though neither the solicitor nor Chief James Beavers would reveal the girl's connection to the proceedings, the meaning of her appearance was unmistakable. As the *Constitution* reported: "Dewey Hewell has been brought back to give testimony against Frank."

The morning's other news-generating revelation was that W. H. Mincey, the insurance salesman who claimed that Jim Conley had confessed Mary Phagan's murder to him, would not testify. Exactly why Frank's lawyers decided not to call the much anticipated figure was never sufficiently explained. Later, Luther Rosser claimed: "The only use we would have had for Mincey was to contradict Conley, and as Conley got on the stand [and] contradicted himself enough [we did not need] other witnesses to do it." Yet considering the buildup, such a rationale was unbelievable. More likely, Rosser and Arnold had arrived at the conclusion Dorsey had reached early on—neither Mincey nor his story could withstand scrutiny.

Against this deeply disheartening backdrop, the defense pressed ahead, opening the day's session by summoning another group of Atlanta Jews to attest to Frank's good character. By the lunch recess, the jury had heard platitudes from 40 of the factory superintendent's coreligionists, only two of whom Dorsey cross-examined.

In a move plainly intended to enliven a day in danger of degenerating into a monotonous cataloging of Leo Frank's virtues, Friday afternoon saw the defense briefly resume its attack on Jim Conley. The initial shots were fired by the pencil factory's Negro drayman. As peg-legged Truman McCrary, to whom Conley had referred during his turn on the stand, told Reuben Arnold, he'd worked at the plant every Saturday during the past three years and had "never found the front door locked on a Saturday afternoon, never seen Jim Conley there watching, never seen him guarding the door."

Following McCrary to the stand was another factory Negro. Arthur Pride was a handyman, and like his predecessor, he said he rarely missed a Saturday and had never seen "Jim Conley sitting and watching the door." Moreover, he had some generally disparaging words for the state's star witness, asserting: "Jim Conley's character for truth and veracity is bad. I would not believe him on oath."

The state aggressively questioned McCrary and Pride, yet both men held firm. Indeed, in his examination of the latter, Frank Hooper inadvertently bolstered the defense's position when, after eliciting Pride's contention that he did not associate with Conley, he asked: "Jim's not a high-class negro like you, is he?"

To which Pride convincingly replied: "I ain't a high-class nigger, but I am a different grade from him."

With that, the defense called another batch of character witnesses—all of them factory girls. No group of women was in a better position to help Leo Frank, and Reuben Arnold went enthusiastically to work, securing from the first to take the stand—polishing department forelady Mary Pirk—not only an endorsement of the plant superintendent's moral fiber but a denunciation of Jim Conley's. In fact, Pirk harbored such negative feelings toward Conley that on the Monday after Mary Phagan's murder, she told Arnold, she'd accused him of the crime. "He took his broom and walked right out of the office and I have never seen him since," she recalled.

The moment Hugh Dorsey opened his cross-examination, any thought that he would show Pirk the deference he'd shown the Cornell grads and Temple members vanished:

"You say you never heard Frank talked about generally?" the solicitor started off.

"He was a perfect gentleman to me," the witness replied.

"Well, what did the other girls say about him?"

"I don't remember anything."

"You mean you never heard him accused of any act of immorality?"

"No."

"You mean you've never heard of him watching the girls in the dressing room?"

"No."

"Did you know Mary Phagan?"

"Yes."

"Did you ever see Frank talking to her?"

"No."

"You never heard of the time, two weeks before her death, that he had her in a corner and she was begging him and trying to get away from him?"

"No."

Before Dorsey could again open his mouth, an exasperated Luther Rosser began to object, but Judge Roan silenced him. "There is no use repeating objections that have already been ruled on."

Up next for the defense was a young female factory machine operator. Like her coworker, Iora Small vouched for Frank's character. She also denigrated Conley, telling Arnold that in the murder's aftermath the Negro not only read all the extras but carried himself suspiciously. "He had on an old Norfolk coat with a belt around it and it buttoned just as tight around his neck as it could be," she said. "Before that he had gone around there all open and loose."

On cue, Dorsey went after Small, yet instead of trying to use her to insinuate untoward behavior on Frank's part, he took a different tack, inquiring into her attitude toward Negroes. Her response: "I don't know of any nigger on earth I'd believe."

"Then you wouldn't believe Newt Lee or Pride or anybody else whose skin is black? They're all on the same plane?"

"Yes."

Small's point of view was inherently racist, and as he'd done before, Dorsey took advantage of the opportunity to use this fact against the defense.

Still, Arnold stuck with the plan, calling one more factory machine operator to utter one more tribute to Leo Frank and strike one more blow at Jim Conley. As 17-year-old Julia Fuss told it, not only was the superintendent an exemplary human being but on the Wednesday of his arrest, none other than Conley had conceded as much. "I talked with Jim," she testified, "and he told me he believed Mr. Frank was just as innocent as the angels from heaven."

Here again, to no one's surprise, Dorsey fired right back.

"You never heard of any familiarity of Frank's with any of the girls . . . or boys?"

"No."

The specter of Frank's purported homosexuality once more raised, Dorsey honed in on Conley's alleged postmurder remark exonerating the superintendent, implying that the comment was inspired by the Negro's desire to protect his accomplice. Soon thereafter, the solicitor returned to his seat, but despite having done some damage, he'd failed to diminish the defense's accomplishment — three of Mary Phagan's female coworkers had testified on Frank's behalf.

With late afternoon shadows beginning to fall, Luther Rosser, who since Arnold's clash with Dorsey had been increasingly handling examinations, called as the session's last witness the woman whose outburst just 48 hours before had brought the trial to a halt. Now, however, Rae Frank was, in the *Constitution*'s words, "perfectly composed," which was no wonder, for her task was to introduce a piece of evidence that seemed destined to help her son. The item was a letter Leo had written to his uncle Moses on the afternoon of April 26, but no sooner had Mrs. Frank started to read it aloud than Frank Hooper cut her off, terming the document immaterial and inadmissible. The defense countered by declaring that since Frank had composed the letter during the period in which the state charged he was committing or covering up the crime, it could not be more relevant, and Judge Roan concurred. Thus court concluded with the defendant's mother, after identifying the missive as one she had first read in Moses Frank's New York hotel room on April 28, intoning:

> Dear Uncle,
>
> I trust that this finds you and dear Tante well after arriving safely in New York. I hope that you found all the dear ones well in Brooklyn . . . Lucille and I are well.
>
> It is too short a time since you left for anything startling to have developed down here. The opera has Atlanta in its grip, but that ends today . . .
>
> Today was "Yondef" here, and the thin gray line of veterans, smaller each year, braved the rather chilly weather to do honor to their fallen comrades.
>
> Enclosed you will find last week's report. The shipments still keep up well . . .
>
> The next letter from me, you should get on board ship. After that I will write to the address you gave me in Frankfurt . . .
>
> Your affectionate nephew,
> Leo M. Frank.

Saturday began with Hugh Dorsey's cross-examination of Rae Frank, and from the start, it was clear that he meant to make the defendant's mother regret having dressed him down on Wednesday.

"Do you have any rich relatives in Brooklyn?" the solicitor began.

"No."

"What is the value of your estate?"

"I have no estate."

"What do you live on?"

"We have a little money out at interest."

"How much is that?"

"About $20,000," the increasingly beleaguered-looking woman replied. Though such a sum did not make Rudolph and Rae Frank wealthy, it was, as Dorsey knew, more than anyone on the jury had invested. Which was why he pushed ahead in the same vein, elicting another fact that indicated affluence: The family owned a house in Brooklyn valued at $10,000. A sense of the Franks' assets implied, the solicitor inquired into the source of those assets.

"In what business is your husband?" he asked.

"He is not in business at present."

"Ah, he's a capitalist, is he?" Dorsey pointedly rejoined.

To which Rae Frank sadly shook her head. Whereupon the solicitor took up the subject of Moses Frank's fortune, eventually forcing the witness to admit: "He is supposed to be very wealthy."

Though Luther Rosser, in his redirect, did his best to put all of this information in a different light, allowing Mrs. Frank to explain that her 67-year-old husband had earned every penny through hard work and was now so "broken down" that he'd been unable to come south for his son's trial, the damage was done. As the *Georgian*'s Old Police Reporter put it: "The examination of Rae Frank as to the extent of her wealth injected some vague suspicion into the minds of the jury," echoing Jim Conley's claim that in the wake of the crime, Leo Frank had said, "Why should I hang, I have wealthy people in Brooklyn?"

The remainder of the day's abbreviated session saw another procession of factory girls—all of them in summer dresses and wide-brimmed straw hats—take the stand to attest to Leo Frank's good character. For the most part, these young things limited their remarks to a few words, but Sarah Barnes could not contain herself. "I know Mr. Frank and I don't know anything in the world against him," she cried. "I love my superintendent. I'd be willing to die for him."

Once again, Hugh Dorsey refused to let such encomiums enter the record uncontested. During some of his cross-examinations, he posed the now expected query as to "acts of immorality" on Frank's part. During others, he raised the possibility that various girls had been coached. Yet all came to naught for the solictor until the very end, which was when it most mattered.

Eighteen-year-old Irene Jackson, the daughter of an Atlanta policeman, was Saturday's final character witness, and like her predecessors, she'd been called to praise Frank, but even during Arnold's questioning, she'd responded ambivalently, managing merely an "I suppose" when asked if the superintendent's behavior at work was good. Once Dorsey got hold of her, she related a series of incidents that, if true, went a long way toward confirming the state's thesis.

As the Jackson girl told it, she and a coworker named Emily Mayfield had been sitting in the factory's second-floor women's dressing room one day when Frank pushed open the door:

"Were you dressed?" the solicitor asked.
"Yes."
"And Miss Mayfield?"
"She was undressing."
"Miss Mayfield was partly undressed?"
"Yes, she had off her top."
"What did Frank do?"
"He smiled or made some kind of face."
"Did he ever go there any but the one time when you were in there?"
"Yes. He opened the door and looked in one day when my sister was lying down in there."
"When your sister was lying down?"
"Yes. She had her feet resting on a stool. I was there."
"What did Frank do?"
"He just walked in and walked out."
"Did you ever hear that he often went and looked in at the girls dressing?"
"Yes," the witness replied, detailing a third occurrence—this one involving yet another worker with her top off—to which she'd been privy.

During his redirect examination of the Jackson girl, a scrambling Arnold established that the dressing room in question had long been a place where workers gathered to gossip and flirt through open windows with passing boys and was subject to spot checks by both foreladies and Frank. Still, such a reality could not explain away what sounded like unwarranted intrusions on the superintendent's part. Noted the *Constitution:* "Miss Jackson['s] testimony that on three separate occasions Leo Frank had opened the door to the women's dressing room and gazed upon her and others in various stages of dishabille fell like a thunderbolt in the camp of the defense."

And so the third week of what was now the longest and by general consensus most bitterly fought trial in Georgia's history came to a close. Thus far, 203 witnesses (34 for the state, 169 for the defense) had testified, and the transcript—which ran to 3,000 legal-sheet pages—exceeded 875,000 words. Exactly where, after all of this, the case stood was hard to say. In the best of the weekend's many assessments, the *Georgian*'s Old Police Reporter asserted that "the defense unquestionably has given the state serious concern in the way it has brought forward the time element and that in separate and distinct directions." The Hearst paper's pseudonymous scribe also believed that Frank's character witnesses, particularly the factory girls, had achieved their purpose. But even granting that Rosser and Arnold had established in the jurors' minds that Mary Phagan reached the pencil plant on April 26 ten minutes later and Frank departed half an hour earlier than the state maintained and that they had likewise shored up their client's reputation, the Old Police Reporter believed that the defense faced an uphill climb. First, he noted, "It is unique in the annals of judicial procedure in Georgia, as it is contrary to the entire theory of the law, that Leo Frank should be combatting at one and the same time" both the charge of murder and the allegation of perversion. The combination, the writer feared, could prove fatal, and, sounding a theme others would echo, he felt the dilemma was "the fault" of Frank's own counsel. Then there was the undeniable power of Conley's testimony as a whole. Declared Hearst's man:

> Many people are arguing to themselves that the negro, no matter how hard he tried or how generously he was coached, still never could have framed up a story like the one he told unless there was some foundation in fact.
>
> And if there remains the impression of even a little foundation in fact the defense is damaged beyond repair.
>
> It gets back to where it started and where it will end—it is Conley pitted against Frank.

Which was why it was small surprise that over the weekend, Rosser and Arnold announced that they would put Leo Frank himself on the stand. Under Georgia law, the defendant in a capital case was permitted to make an unsworn statement free from cross-examination. Though such a statement consequently lacked the weight of testimony under oath, the jury could choose to accept it in whole or in part. For Frank, the risk, of course, was that the jury could also choose to reject such a statement—or, worse, hold it against him.

By 7 A.M. Monday, hundreds of Atlantans were lined up outside the old city hall in hopes of obtaining one of the seats within. Those lucky enough to gain admission would, however, have to wait for Frank's appearance on the stand, as the defense devoted the morning to putting a few more pieces of testimony before the jury. In an effort to reinforce the view that no sexual activity had been occurring at the factory, Reuben Arnold called Godfrey Weinkauf, manager of the concern's lead mill, who stated that during the year prior to Mary Phagan's murder, he'd visited Frank in his office every other Saturday afternoon and had never seen any women there. Of more urgent import, Emily Mayfield, one of the workers the superintendent purportedly ogled in the plant dressing room, took the stand to assert that the incident never happened and to denounce the story's source, Irene Jackson, as a liar. Finally, though, the session was given over to a valedictory covey of character witnesses, the majority of them again female employees. For the most part, Hugh Dorsey refused to challenge these girls. Thus the endorsements of Lillie Mae Goodman, Lizzie Barnes, Grace Atherton, Ida Holmes, Zellie Spivey and Minnie Smith entered the record intact. Yet as the solicitor's cross-examination of one of the last of them demonstrated, he had merely been biding his time.

"You say you have never heard anything bad about Frank?" Dorsey asked Lula Wardlaw.

"No."

"You're sure you never heard from Hermes Stanton and H. M. Baker, in charge of the Hapeville trolley, that Frank had a little girl on the car the Saturday before the murder?"

"No."

"You never heard that Frank had his arm around the girl and tried to get her off the car and into the woods?"

"No."

With that, Dorsey, having ruined what the defense had hoped would be a seamless prelude to Frank's big moment, was done. Shortly thereafter, court adjourned for lunch.

Aside from appearing somewhat pale, Leo Frank exhibited no signs of anxiety upon taking the stand at 2:15 Monday afternoon. During the recess, he'd read over his statement—the bulk of which he'd dictated to Lucille weeks earlier—while having his throat sprayed by a physician who'd been treating him for a mild cold. Thus sure of what he intended to say and in good voice, the superintendent simply started in.

To begin, Frank, who sat with his hands clasped before him and a folder of notes on his lap, provided a summary of his personal and professional background: his birth in Texas and his Brooklyn boyhood, his education and his apprenticeships, his "sojourn abroad" learning the pencil business and his move to Georgia. Only when discussing his wife did he even obliquely address the state's charges. "I married in Atlanta, an Atlanta girl," he said. "My married life has been exceptionally happy—indeed, it has been the happiest days of my life." Here, Lucille smiled up at her husband from her seat directly behind the defense table. Yet he did not continue in this relevant and intimate vein, giving instead a description of his responsibilities at work. "My duties," Frank asserted, "were as follows: I had charge of the technical and mechanical end of the factory, looking after the operations and seeing that our product was turned out in quality equal to the standard set by our competitors. I looked after the installation of new machinery and the purchase of new machinery. I looked after the purchase of the raw materials which are used in the manufacture of pencils, kept up with the market of those materials, where the prices fluctuated, so that purchases could be made to the best possible advantage."

Rational and authoritative, Frank's intention, according to the *Georgian,* was to convince the jury of his high position, then "picture his every movement" during the weekend of the murder, thereby demonstrating "the physical impossibility of his having committed the crime and disposed of the body as Conley describes." This demonstration would constitute the heart of his statement.

Frank opened with an account of his activities on Friday, April 25—a day that, by his telling, was devoted almost entirely to the preparation of the factory's payroll. The calculations involved in determining the amounts owed, a trip to Montag's to execute the necessary checks, a stop at the Atlanta National Bank to cash the checks, an afternoon spent filling some 200 numbered envelopes with bills and coins and placing them in slots for distribution at the familiar elevator-lobby window—the superintendent mentioned each phase of the process. Save for an indirect refutation of Helen Ferguson's claim regarding her attempt to collect Mary Phagan's wages ("No one came into my office who asked me for a pay envelope or for the pay envelope of another"), he avoided any reference to the allegations against him.

Friday dispensed with, Frank shifted to the case's most critical day, and he did so by stepping down from the stand and placing a sheaf of invoices that he contended had occupied him on the morning of Saturday, April 26, on the jury-box rail. Then, with what the *Journal* described as the earnestness one can imagine him employing to address a buyer over his desk at the factory, he gave an explanation of the documents' significance. "Of all the mathematical work in the office of the pencil factory," he said, "the work I now have before me is the most important. It is very important that the prices be correct, that the amount of goods shipped agrees with the amount which is on the invoice, and that the terms are correct. I know of nothing else that exasperates a customer more than to receive invoices that are incorrect."

Frank's presentation, dispassionate and cool, was the antithesis of Jim Conley's testimony. But rather than continue in this same formal yet accessible manner, the superintendent plunged into the fine points of the dozen or so invoices. Evidently, he believed he needed to establish that the work was so involved that it had required him, just as several witnesses had sworn, to defer the all-important financial sheet until the afternoon. Yet from the outset, there was something unnerving about the resulting assembly line of details. "The first order here is from Hilton, Hart & Kern Company, Detroit," he began. Then, mechanically spitting out figures, he added: "The customer ordered 100 gross of No. 2 of a certain pencil, 125 gross of No. 3 and 50 gross of No. 4. We shipped 100 gross of No. 2, 111 and ¼ gross of No. 3 and 49 gross of No. 4. The amount of shipment of No. 3 is short of the amount the customer ordered. Therefore, there is a suspense shipment card, as you will notice." Mercifully for the jurors, Frank glossed over the specifics pertaining to the next few invoices, synopsizing one from S. H. Kress by saying, "These five and ten syndicates have a great deal of red tape." But such restraint was atypical, for within minutes he was embarked on a lengthy discourse on F. W. Woolworth's freight policies, which were complicated, he stressed, by an 86-cent credit that the chain received for every 100 pounds of merchandise ordered.

And so for the next hour Frank's statement would proceed. After delivering his initial explication of the invoices as they related to shipping, he went back through them from a different perspective. "Starting here with order 7187 and continuing through 7197," he said, "there is a series of initials, and these initials stand for the salesman who is credited with the order. In other words, if a man at the end of the year wants to get certain commissions on orders that come in, we have to very carefully look over those orders and see to whom or to which salesman or to which commission house or to which distributing agent that order is credited. So therefore, it takes a good deal of judgment and knowledge to know just to which salesman to credit. Sometimes, I have to go through a world of papers to find just to whom a certain order is to be credited."

Frank's zeal for the arcana of the invoicing chores he claimed to have performed on the morning of April 26 was made to appear all the more excessive by what seemed to be a corresponding unwillingness to discuss the prelunch period's most germane particulars. Yes, he gave what felt like a full accounting of his trip to and from Montag's to fetch the mail. (The superintendent did not, however, respond to Conley's charges regarding the outing. As he saw it, his version of events, due to its inherent logic, would carry the day.) And yes, he provided what by every indication was a believable description of the 11:45 appearance in his office of Corinthia Hall and Emma Clark, recalling the department in which the girls worked and the reason they'd dropped by—one of them had left a coat upstairs. But when it came to the main event—an event he got to only after a tortuous detour through the letters he'd dictated to stenographer Hattie Hall just before noon—he had little to say. In fact, his initial comments on the subject that the jurors and, by extension, all of Atlanta wanted to hear him address required just a third of a page of transcript:

> To the best of my knowledge, it must have been from ten to fifteen minutes after Miss Hall left my office, when this little girl, whom I afterwards found to be Mary Phagan, entered my office and asked for her pay envelope. I asked for her number and she told me; I went to the cash box and took her envelope out and handed it to her, identifying the envelope by the number. She left my office and apparently had gotten as far as the door from my office leading to the outer office, when she evidently stopped and asked me if the metal had arrived, and I told her no. She continued on her way out, and I heard the sound of her footsteps and she went away. It was a few moments after she asked me this question that I had an impression of a female voice saying something; I don't know which way it came from; just passed away and I had that impression. This little girl had evidently worked in the metal department by her question and had been laid off owing to the fact that some metal that had been ordered had not arrived at the factory; hence, her question. I only recognized this little girl from having seen her around the plant and did not know her name, simply identifying her envelope from her having called her number to me.

That in the wake of months of rampant and scurrilous speculation Leo Frank would devote a mere 236 words to the encounter at the center of the mystery struck many as passing strange. Surely, he had more to say on the matter. And, in truth, he did. Yet as the hundreds sitting in the courtroom and the thousands across Atlanta snapping up extras would to their further dismay discover, the superintendent first intended to give a thorough elucidation of the work he insisted he'd done on the financial sheet on the afternoon of April 26.

In an effort to establish the sheet's significance, Frank introduced this portion of his statement by unveiling a box containing the 140 varieties of pencils manufactured at the Forsyth Street factory. Laid out like candies, the bright wooden wands with their crisply stamped brand names and brass caps presented a vast array of colors and types, underscoring the need for a complex accounting system. The jury, however, barely caught a glimpse of the display, as Hugh Dorsey promptly objected that the sampler had not been entered into evidence. Judge Roan concurred, and the exhibit was removed. The data — as the superintendent consistently referred to it — would have to speak for itself.

"Now, one of the most intricate operations," Frank began, holding up the financial sheet for his audience's perusal, was the "working out" of the numbers used to establish the cost of raw material. "Wood slats," he apprised the room, "are figured at 22 cents per gross. Then, we figure rubbers according to the character of the pencil manufactured: 6 and ½ cents cheapest, 9 cents medium, 14 cents high-grade. Then come the tips. Then the lead, which is taken from this sheet, multiplying 15 cents for the better lead and 10 cents for the cheaper lead. Then, 5 cents a gross has been figured out after months of careful keeping track of what we use [for] such materials as shellac, alcohol, lacquer, aniline, waxent and oils." To no one's surprise, the superintendent claimed that following lunch on April 26, he'd performed all of these computations.

This was just the start. Owing either to obliviousness or, as many who heard him later concurred, to an unwillingness to face reality, Frank would set forth nearly every category of data charted on the financial sheet. Regarding an entry headed "Repacking," he explained: "One of the tricks of the trade, when we have a slow mover, some pencil that doesn't move very fast, is to take something fancy and put them in with these slow movers. That is a trick all manufacturers use in packing assortment boxes. We send into the shipping room and get some pencils which have already been packed and bring them in and repack them in the display box. Therefore, it is very necessary in figuring out the financial sheet to notice in detail the amount of goods packed and just how many of those had already been figured on some past report. We don't want to record it twice, or else our totals will be incorrect. Therefore, showing the amount of goods which were repacked is necessary." At this juncture, the superintendent paused to indicate the line on the document where the proper notation had been made. Then he added: "That was figured by me on Saturday afternoon, April 26. It shows right here. That is my writing right down there: '18 gross 35-X pencils, 10 gross 930-X.' "

Quite apart from issues of motivation, Frank's arrogance here was astounding. In fact, in the midst of one especially long-winded remark, he gazed at the paper in his hands and declared: "This sheet, the financial,

I may say is the child of my own brain, because I got it up. The first one that ever was made, I made out." Whereupon he ran through various other data—"Investments," "Values," "Fixed Charges"—that the document allowed him to keep abreast of, boasting that he always knew where the factory stood regarding everything from the price of labor to net and gross profits.

By 4:35, when Judge Roan ordered a brief recess, Frank had been ratcheting on for the better part of two and a half hours. And while he may have convinced some of those listening that the work he'd done on the financial sheet the afternoon of the murder demanded intense concentration, it's doubtful he persuaded anyone to the related conclusion that he was guiltless. Indeed, the more probable reactions were suspicion and disbelief. Here was a man who for all his reliance on the precise language of management seemed to be manifesting a kind of hysteria.

Had Frank ended his statement at this juncture, there can be little doubt that it would have been judged an unmitigated disaster. Yet finally, he took up the genuine issues at hand. And he did so in surprisingly human—and humanizing—terms.

After the recess, Frank addressed the actions he'd undertaken in the immediate aftermath of Mary Phagan's murder that had made him a suspect in the crime. Regarding his much discussed anxiety on the morning the body was discovered, he confided:

> Gentlemen, I was nervous. I was completely unstrung. Imagine yourself called from sound slumber in the early hours of the morning, whisked through the chill morning air without breakfast, to go into that undertaking establishment and have the light suddenly flashed on a scene like that. To see that little girl on the dawn of womanhood so cruelly murdered— it was a scene that would have melted stone. Is it any wonder I was nervous?"

At long last, Frank was attempting to win the understanding of the twelve men who would decide his fate. Which was why, as he continued his account of the events that culminated in his arrest, he sought to portray himself as a victim of both misunderstanding and sloppy and corrupt police work. As an example of the former, there were the rumors that arose from the fact that his wife did not visit him during his first days in jail. After terming such rumors "dastardly," the superintendent attempted to correct the record, proclaiming:

The date I was taken into custody, my wife was there. But I thought I would save her the humiliation of seeing me in those surroundings. I expected any day to be turned loose and returned once more to her side at home. Gentlemen, we had to restrain her. She was willing to be locked up with me.

Then there was the detectives' behavior, particularly during the headquarters encounter designed to force a confession from Lee. After the effort failed, Frank asserted, John Black and Harry Scott "grilled the negro and put words into his mouth that twisted not alone [my] English but distorted my meaning. I decided then and there that if that was the line of conduct they were going to pursue, I would wash my hands of them." It was in keeping with this choice, the superintendent added, that he refused to meet with Jim Conley, explaining:

> I did not speak to Conley not because I did not want to . . . but because I didn't want to have things twisted. I knew that there was not a word that I could utter that they would not deform and distort and use against me.

Slowly, surely, Frank had come alive, and he finished in impressive fashion:

> Gentlemen, I know nothing whatever of the death of little Mary Phagan. I had no part in causing her death nor do I know how she came to her death after she took her money and left my office. I never even saw Conley in the factory or anywhere else on that date, April 26, 1913 . . .
>
> The statement of the negro Conley is a tissue of lies from first to last. I know nothing whatever of the cause of the death of Mary Phagan and Conley's statement as to his coming up and helping me dispose of the body, or that I had anything to do with her or to do with him that day is a monstrous lie . . .
>
> The story as to women coming into the factory with me for immoral purposes is a base lie and the few occasions that he claims to have seen me in indecent positions with women is a lie so vile that I have no language with which to fitly denounce it . . .
>
> Gentlemen, some newspaper men have called me "the silent man in the tower," and I have kept my silence and my counsel advisedly, until the proper time and place. The time is now; the place is here; and I have told you the truth, the whole truth.

Coming at the conclusion of a discourse that had consisted largely of tedious tabulations and rote recitations, Frank's forceful peroration moved nearly all who heard it. "Very few in the courtroom had much to say until they had managed to subdue that troublesome lump in their throats," observed the *Georgian*. Not surprisingly, those most affected were members of the superintendent's family, particularly Lucille, who burst into tears, prompting Leo to descend to her side and take her in his arms. Meantime, a stout county deputy dabbed his eyes while juror Marcellus Johenning gave vent to several deep sobs. "That boy put it all over you and me," Luther Rosser was heard to mutter huskily to Reuben Arnold as the two made their way to the door.

The next morning, however, the assessments were decidedly more sober, for no matter how engaging Frank had been at the end, the fact remained that taken as a whole, his statement was problematic. Commented the *Georgian*'s James B. Nevin: "There will be those who see evidence of monstrous coldness and unfeeling design." Most telling of all was the news that Rosser and Arnold had not read the superintendent's remarks in advance. Like many parts of the lawyers' presentation, this last one had been made with an apparent lack of regard for either their client's vulnerability or their own.

TWELVE

Verdict

A ll that remained before Leo Frank's fate was consigned to the jury
were the final evidentiary maneuvers and rhetorical flourishes. First
among these was the state's presentation of its case in rebuttal, and
if there were any doubts regarding what its main element would be, they
were dispelled shortly after Tuesday's session opened when Hugh Dorsey
suggested that Lucille and Rae Frank leave the courtroom, as what was to
come "would be embarrassing for ladies to listen to."

Dorsey launched his attack on Frank's character with an examination of
Daisy Hopkins. But the factory superintendent's alleged consort thwarted
the solicitor, continuing to maintain that she possessed no knowledge of any
trysting place in the plant basement. Moreover, when Dorsey attempted
to quiz her regarding what the *Journal* termed "unprintable" acts she'd
purportedly boasted of performing with Frank, Judge Roan upheld the
defense's objection, declaring: "You cannot bring any new criminal charge
against this defendant."

Still, Dorsey pressed forward, summoning four witnesses who denigrated
the trustworthiness of Hopkins. He followed these with ten witnesses who
lauded the credibility of C. Brutus Dalton, who'd not only connected Frank
to incidents of sexual impropriety but corroborated Jim Conley on the subject. Then the solicitor, in the *Journal*'s phrase, "sprang a sensation," calling
a former factory employee who swore that regardless of his many denials,
the superintendent knew Mary Phagan:

"Did you ever see Mr. Frank talking to Mary Phagan?" Dorsey asked
16-year-old Willie Turner.
"Yes, on the second floor."
"How long was that before the murder?"
"About the middle of March."
"What was said?"
"I heard her say that she had to work."
"What did he say?"
"He said he was the superintendent of the factory."

"How was she acting?"

"She backed off from him, and he walked toward her."

After that, the defense objected. "They want to bring out another charge," roared Reuben Arnold.

But the prosecution held firm. Responding to Arnold's allegation, Frank Hooper insisted: "It is not true, and it is not the point at issue." Whereupon the gallery burst into applause. A vigorous rapping from Judge Roan immediately restored order, yet the outburst provided one more indication of the deteriorating atmosphere. Worse, following a moment's consideration, Roan allowed Turner's observations to remain in the record, and though Luther Rosser, in his cross, got the boy to admit that he could not give a description of Mary Phagan, the point seemed settled—Frank had been acquainted with the girl.

The state devoted the bulk of Tuesday's remaining hours to countering other facets of the defense's case.

From Roy Craven and E. H. Pickett, Albert McKnight's supervisors at Beck & Gregg Hardware, Dorsey elicited testimony reaffirming the veracity of Minola McKnight's pretrial statement alleging suspicious behavior on Frank's part in the aftermath of the murder. Swore Craven:

I was present when Minola made her affidavit. I told her that Albert had said that [she] overheard Mrs. Frank tell Mrs. Selig that [on the night of the crime] Mr. Frank came home drinking and made Mrs. Frank get out of bed and sleep on a rug by the side of the bed . . . he had murdered somebody. Minola [confirmed] that this was what happened.

Added Pickett:

Minola . . . said she was instructed not to talk and her wages had been raised by the Seligs.

Dorsey next introduced several streetcar employees to attest that the English Avenue trolley that had carried Mary Phagan downtown on April 26 often ran ahead of schedule. The assertions potentially placed the victim at the factory earlier than had been thought, lending further credence to the prosecution's murder-day time line. One of the streetcar men, a conductor named George Kendley, claimed that he'd actually seen little Mary walking toward the plant before 12:05 on the afternoon of the tragedy, which would have put her in the superintendent's officer prior to Monteen Stover's arrival.

During Tuesday's final hours, Dorsey took a second shot at presenting specific allegations of impropriety against Frank by summoning Nellie Wood—the slatternly former factory worker who'd testified at the inquest that the superintendent once fondled her breasts. But Judge Roan upheld the defense's objection, telling the solicitor: "The law shuts you out." Boomed the headline atop the next morning's *Constitution*: STATE IS HARD HIT BY JUDGE'S RULING BARRING EVIDENCE ATTACKING FRANK.

From the moment the proceedings reconvened at 9 A.M. Wednesday, Dorsey could do no wrong. First Roan, over the objections of Rosser and Arnold, ruled that the solicitor could call witnesses to take issue with the defense's assault on the state's medical evidence. Minutes later, Dr. Clarence Johnson and Dr. George Niles seconded Dr. Henry F. Harris's findings regarding the time of Mary Phagan's death, and Dr. John Funke echoed Harris's determination that she'd suffered some unspecified form of sexual violence.

Dorsey then struck a blow at the defense's claim that the factory's metal room floor was frequently stained by the blood of injured workers, calling a former plant machinist named J. E. Duffy, who testified that when he was cut in an accident there, his wound was promptly bandaged.

With that, Dorsey reintroduced the topic around which his case in rebuttal revolved, summoning a young former factory employee named Myrtice Cato:

"Are you acquainted with the general character of Leo M. Frank prior to and including April 26, 1913?" he asked.

"Yes."

"Was that character good or bad?"

"Bad."

"How long had you worked there?"

"Three and a half years."

With that, Dorsey turned the witness over to the defense. But Rosser, knowing that if he challenged Myrtice, the solicitor would be permitted to delve into the particulars upon which her allegation was based, simply told the girl: "Come down."

Dorsey's next witness was another former factory worker, and she, too, responded in the affirmative when asked if Frank's general character was bad. But where with her predecessor, the solicitor had been content to leave it at this, with Maggie Griffin he would attempt to go further. Indicating that he knew he was testing the limits, Dorsey informed his witness, "Now I am going to ask you a question, and I don't want you to answer it until the judge tells you whether you can or not." Then he inquired: "Are you acquainted with the general character of Leo M. Frank as to his relations with women?"

Following the expected objection, Judge Roan sent the jury out, and the opposing sides faced off. As Rosser saw it, the court had already found against such testimony. "This, however, is different," replied Dorsey. Though he vowed to abide by Roan's ruling as far as specific incidents were concerned, he contended that the defense, by examining several girls regarding Frank's overall conduct with them, had itself broached the broader subject. Furthermore, he asserted that one of the female witnesses put up by the the defense had once disappeared into a plant dressing room with the superintendent. That witness: Rebecca Carson. According to the solicitor, the law granted him the right to use Griffin to rebut Carson's attestations. For Roan, Dorsey's logic was persuasive, although the judge ordered him to refrain from posing queries about Carson until she could be recalled. With that, the jury returned, and the solicitor picked up where he'd left off:

> "Do you know the general character of Leo M. Frank as to his attitude toward women?" Dorsey again asked Griffin.
> "Yes, I do."
> "What is it?"
> "Bad."

Owing to the fact that Carson could not be immediately located, the solicitor at this point turned Griffin over to Rosser, who once more refused to cross-examine.

The bill for placing Frank's character in evidence had come due, and Dorsey intended to see that it was paid in full. The morning's remaining hours would see a steady parade of former factory employees take the stand to level essentially unchallenged blows to the superintendent's reputation as it pertained to female workers. To each of these women and girls, the solicitor posed the same question: "Do you know Mr. Frank's character for lasciviousness?" And from each he received the same answer:

> "Bad," declared Mrs. C. D. Donnegan.
> "Bad," declared Mrs. H. H. Johnson.
> "Bad," declared Marie Karst.
> "Bad," declared Nellie Pettis, echoing her testimony at the coroner's inquest.
> "Bad," "bad," "bad," "bad," added Mary Davis, Mary Wallace, Estelle Winkle and Carrie Smith.

Throughout this ordeal, Frank's lawyers sat on their hands.

And Dorsey wasn't done. He called two former factory employees to corroborate Willie Turner's testimony that Frank had been acquainted with Mary Phagan. First came young Ruth Robinson, who swore that she'd once seen the superintendent stop at little Mary's workplace and show her how to insert an eraser into a nearly completed pencil. Then came Dewey Hewell, the 16-year-old whose return to Atlanta the week before from a Cincinnati home for unwed mothers had sparked headlines. After establishing that the girl had been employed at the pencil plant during the months preceding the murder, the solicitor inquired:

> "During the time you worked there did you know Leo M. Frank?"
> "Yes, sir."
> "Did you know Mary Phagan?"
> "Yes."
> "Did you ever see Frank talking to Mary Phagan?"
> "Yes."
> "How often?"
> "Sometimes two or three times a day."
> "What did you see him do?"
> "I saw him put his hand on her shoulder."
> "Did he call her by any name, and if so, what?"
> "Yes, sir. He called her Mary."
> "Where did he stand when he spoke to her?"
> "He would stand close to her."

Though Rosser at least examined Robinson and Hewell, he did so tentatively, doing no more than ascertaining that little Mary was always in the company of a group of employees when the two saw Frank talking with her.

By the time the defense finished with Robinson and Hewell, Rebecca Carson had made her way to court. Dorsey had only one question for her: "Did you ever go into the dressing room on the fourth floor with Leo M. Frank?"

"No," she answered emphatically.

After Carson stepped down, Dorsey surprised Rosser and Arnold by calling Myrtice Cato as his initial rebuttal witness. "Did you ever see Miss Rebecca Carson go into the private dressing room on the fourth floor with Leo M. Frank?" he asked.

"Yes," replied Myrtice.

"How often did you see them go in there together?"

"I never saw it but twice," the girl conceded. Then she added: "That ain't all I know."

"Wait a minute," shouted Rosser, his face pinkening. Yet just that quickly, the lawyer caught himself, and in a milder tone, he briefly sifted Myrtice, establishing that on both of the purported occasions, plenty of other employees, once more, were standing nearby. Not that this was how the girl's appearance ended. During his redirect examination, Dorsey asked Myrtice how she happened to have observed Frank and Carson enter the dressing room. "I was looking up the aisle," she said, then again boasted: "And that ain't all I saw, either."

Dorsey followed Myrtice with the witness the defense had been expecting—Maggie Griffin. Like her coworker, Maggie maintained that she'd seen Frank and Carson disappear into the fourth-floor factory dressing room. "Yes, sir," she said. "Three or four times." Worse, she contended that they had "stayed in there fifteen to thirty minutes." To this, Rosser successfully objected, but as to the larger issue, he again had to settle for the concession that on the occasions under discussion, "other women were about."

How Dorsey could do still more damage to Frank on the character issue was at this juncture difficult to imagine, but he had one last blow to inflict, and he used the morning's final witness to inflict it. Mamie Kitchens was yet another pretty factory girl, and after nailing down that she'd worked on the plant's fourth floor for two years and was still an employee there, the solicitor secured the fact that she had not only not been called by the defense to attest to Frank's rectitude but that several other females in her department had been similarly ignored. Having thereby implied that the superintendent was fearful of what some members of his current workforce would say if placed on the stand, Dorsey threw his haymaker, asking: "Were you ever in the dressing room on the fourth floor with Miss Irene Jackson when this defendant, Leo M. Frank, came in?"

"Yes," answered Kitchens. "I was in the dressing room with Miss Irene Jackson when she was undressed. Mr. Frank opened the door, stuck his head inside. He did not knock. He just stood there and laughed. Miss Jackson said, 'Well, we are dressing, blame it,' and then he shut the door."

Though Rosser managed in his cross-examination of Kitchens to establish that the incident to which she'd referred had occurred during business hours, such an admission could not soften the impact of either this girl's testimony or that of those who'd come before. Boomed the front-page banner atop the *Georgian*'s midday edition:

WOMEN ARRAIGN FRANK'S MORALS

While Hugh Dorsey would have been hard-pressed to find a better stopping point, a few other elements of the defense's case still worried him; he devoted Wednesday afternoon to tying up loose ends. For starters, he sum-

moned two men who often rode the English Avenue streetcar and swore that
in the days immediately after the murder, W. M. Matthews and W. T. Hollis
had both said that on her last trip, Mary Phagan had sat next to George Epps.
During cross-examinations, Rosser established that one of these witnesses
was the son of a police officer involved in the investigation. Still, the charges
hurt. Dorsey then recalled Boots Rogers and Sergeant L. S. Dobbs, each of
whom maintained that on the morning the body was discovered, they had
checked alternate entrances into the factory basement and found them
"cobwebby and dusty." Having thereby partially undermined the notion that
the victim's remains could have reached the plant's lower level via a route
that contradicted the state's theory, the solicitor summoned several individuals who took issue with Frank's declaration that the much vaunted financial
sheet required three hours to fill out. With that, he was done.

There wasn't much the defense could hope to accomplish during its surre-
buttal. Yes, Rosser and Arnold put up a pawnbroker to attest that one of the
men who'd sworn that Mary Phagan's trolley often reached town ahead of
time had hocked his watch several months before the murder and would
have been hard-pressed to make such a judgment. Yes, they called several
witnesses who asserted that George Kendley, who claimed he'd spotted little Mary walking into the factory before 12:05 on the day of the crime, was
an avid anti-Semite who'd been publicly voicing his views. Declared J. M.
Asher: "Kendley was talking real loud and discussing the Frank case and he
suddenly said: 'The damn Jew, they ought to hang him.'" Echoed T. Y.
Brent: "Kendley said Frank wasn't anything but an old Jew," and if the court
didn't get him, he knew men who would. And yes, over Dorsey's objection,
Frank was permitted to retake the stand to make an addendum to his
unsworn statement. Proclaimed the superintendent:

> In reply to the statement of the boy [Willie Turner] that he saw me talk-
> ing to Mary Phagan when she backed away from me, that is absolutely
> false, that never occurred. In reply to the two girls, Robinson and Hewell,
> that they saw me talking to Mary Phagan and that I called her "Mary," I
> wish to say that they are mistaken. It is very possible that I have talked to
> the little girl in going through the factory and examining the work, but I
> never knew her name.
>
> In reference to the statements of the two women who say that they saw
> me going into the dressing room with Miss Rebecca Carson, I wish to state
> that that is utterly false. It is a slander on the young lady, and I wish to state
> that as far as my knowledge of Miss Rebecca Carson goes, she is a lady of
> unblemished character.

Save for these flurries, the defense was finished, and at 5:30, court adjourned for the day.

Closing arguments commenced at 9:05 Thursday morning, with the state, in the person of Frank Hooper, speaking first. That Dorsey let his co-counsel open was astute. Smooth and reassuring rather than confrontational and irreverent, elegantly attired as opposed to modestly dressed down, Hooper was well suited to lay out the case that the solicitor would then attempt to hammer home.

Starting with the issue of character, Hooper challenged the jurors to choose between the defense's witnesses and the state's. The girls who'd testified for Frank were for the most part currently employed at the factory and therefore, he asserted, susceptible to the superintendent's manipulations. In order to keep their jobs, they'd said what they'd been told to say. The girls who'd testified against Frank, however, were primarily former employees and hence free to speak the truth. That was why, Hooper added, the defense had declined to cross-examine them. Gesturing to Rosser and Arnold, he declared:

> They had the right to inquire of these witnesses on what grounds they based their opinion of the defendant's bad character. What did they do? They dismissed the witnesses without making any inquiries.

The disparity between the praises uttered by the defense's character witnesses and the reproofs voiced by the state's could not, of course, be explained as merely a function of the National Pencil Company's financial leverage. Too many men and women over whom the Forsyth Street operation held no sway had taken the stand on Frank's behalf. And even though nearly all of these citizens were Jewish, their uniformly high positions in Atlanta society lent considerable credence to their endorsements. If the prosecution was to convince the jury that the accused truly was morally reprehensible, it needed to negate these testimonials, too. Which was what Hooper now tried to do. Fixing his audience with a confident gaze, he began by acknowledging the inherent paradox, asserting:

> It may seem strange, gentlemen, that a man who associated with bankers, businessmen and who's the head of a big concern should have sought out a man like Dalton for company. But have you ever considered that when he was dealing with a certain side of his life, he sought companions congenial to those pursuits?

That said, the lawyer unveiled what for the state would be a defining metaphor:

> You doubtless have read *Dr. Jekyll and Mr. Hyde.* This defendant, like
> Dr. Jekyll when the shades of night come, throws aside his mask of
> respectability and is transformed into a Mr. Hyde. And then he does not
> seek the companions of Dr. Jekyll, but like Hyde goes to a lower stratum
> where he picks up Dalton and his kind and goes with them instead of with
> the men who have come here to give him a good character.

The state's stance on Frank's character articulated, Hooper addressed his next subject, Jim Conley. Here again, he depended largely upon a figure of speech. The Negro, he averred, was to the case what Stone Mountain—a massive granite outcropping just east of the city—was to Atlanta: intrinsic and unavoidable. "I don't blame the defense for pitching their fight on Conley," he said. "They had to break him." For three days, Luther Rosser had pitted his "wily, trained mind" against that of the "ignorant black man." The result: like Stone Mountain, Conley still stood. "And why didn't they break him?" Hooper asked rhetorically. Whereupon he paused, then said:

> It was because Conley, after all the lies he had told, eventually had
> arrived at the truth, and the truth is stronger than these lawyers.

From the state's vantage, both its star witness's testimony and the allegations concerning character were just part of a broader demonstration of guilt rooted in accounts of Frank's actions before the murder and in its aftermath. So now Hooper gave the jurors a selective recapitulation. First, of course, there was the engagement of Conley as a lookout and his positioning in the factory lobby on the morning of April 26. Then came Mary Phagan's arrival. "Without knowing the horrible death that awaited her," the lawyer said, "she went blithely to where sat this defendant to get her $1.20. Since that day, not a word has come from her lips."

At this, little Mary's mother, who at the session's outset had taken a seat at the prosecution table, began to weep.

With Mary Phagan dead, Hooper declared, Frank focused on the pressing matter of disposing the body and concealing the crime. Thus he summoned Conley to the second floor. Despite the superintendent's purported hand-wringing, the lawyer contended that his initial moves—the transporting of the remains to the basement, the trip to the fourth floor to assure himself that workers Denham and White remained in the dark and to escort Mrs. White from the building—were cool and calculating. So, too, were his subsequent actions. He sent Newt Lee away at 4 P.M. to give Conley a couple more hours to return to the factory and burn the body. He ordered the night watchman to help Gantt search for his shoes because the fired bookkeeper had been a friend of little Mary's and he didn't want him snooping around the place. He telephoned Lee from home that evening to make certain that his handiwork remained undetected. Frank's lone slip—the murder notes. Asserted Hooper:

> The idea that Jim would have written those notes himself is absurd. You know these negroes. You know their traits. Would one of them have done a thing like that? What object could Conley possibly have had in planting those notes by the body saying that a negro had committed the crime?

Come Sunday morning, of course, the state maintained that Frank's dread had returned. "Even before he was suspected, he showed unmistakable signs of nervousness," Hooper reminded the jurors. Yet he soon regained his sangfroid. Beginning Monday, "he made a concerted effort" to cast suspicion on Lee. By changing his mind as to whether the night watchman had correctly punched the time clock in the hours prior to the body's discovery, the superintendent in effect dispatched Detective Black to Lee's house "where somebody had planted a shirt." Here, Hooper held up the garment in question, allowing the twelve men who sat before him to examine how it "appeared to have been wadded up and wiped in blood." And if that wasn't proof enough of the garment's fraudulence, the lawyer, revealing that the prosecution was as willing to play to racial stereotypes as the defense, proclaimed: "The shirt had no odor of the negro."

By the state's lights, the shirt found at Lee's home was simply the first of many defense deceptions. Others included the bloody stick and piece of pay envelope located in the factory lobby several weeks after the murder. "There was also," Hooper recalled, "a fellow named Mincey. You remember that my brother Rosser examined Jim very closely about this man. That was done, you all understand, for the purpose of laying the foundation to impeach Jim. The point is: Where is Mincey now? It looked like this whole fight might turn on Mincey, but we haven't heard one word from him."

With that, Hooper—whose job had been merely to present an outline of the state's presentation—was essentially done, although he did have a last point to make: The jurors, far from being distinct from their fellow citizens, were Everymen. Declared the lawyer: "I have heard men say that they thought one thing, but when they were on a jury they had to decide another way, but it was never intended that such should be the case."

Reuben Arnold led off for the defense. Where Hooper's job had been to set a tone, his was that and more. Standing before the bench, he began by addressing his counterpart's final comment, remarking conversationally: "My friend Hooper said that a juror is not different from anyone else on the streets trying to get at the truth." Then he boomed:

> God grant that we can get away from the streets. What's the use of having juries if we don't. Juries should be set up on a hill, away from the multitude where prejudice and passion cannot reach them.

That after four weeks of crowds outside the courthouse and barely restrained galleries within, Arnold would start with a plea to the jurors to resist popular opinion was no surprise. What followed, however, was startling—the lawyer asserted that the hostility that had dogged Leo Frank from the outset arose from the fact of his Jewishness. The defense was opening its argument by claiming that religious prejudice against the factory superintendent had permeated the case. Referring to one of the state's concluding witnesses, streetcar conductor George Kendley, Arnold asserted:

> This man Kendley said they ought to hang Frank because he is a Jew. I'd rather be in Leo Frank's house than his. I'd rather be in Leo Frank's shoes than his.

Kendley's discriminatory feelings, Arnold noted, were rooted in the fact that "Frank comes from a race of people that have made money." Furthermore, he added, the streetcar conductor wasn't the only Atlantan who harbored such feelings:

> I tell everybody, all within the hearing of my voice, that if Frank hadn't been a Jew he never would have been prosecuted. I am asking my kind of people to give this man fair play. Before I'd do a Jew injustice, I'd want my throat cut from ear to ear.

And so the issue that had long been percolating beneath the surface had come into the light. Frank's prosecution, Arnold charged, was motivated by anti-Semitism. The lawyer did not, however, linger on the claim, devoting the remaining minutes before and the hour after the lunch recess to undoing the damage the state had done to the superintendent's reputation.

Much of what Arnold had to say regarding the allegations of moral turpitude against Frank was predictably indignant. He termed C. Brutus Dalton and his ilk "jail birds and convicts, the dregs of humanity," while dismissing the factory girls who'd denigrated the superintendent's character as "disgruntled former employees." As to the possibility that Frank might actually have seduced any of his workers, he fairly scoffed: "If he had started something with one of the girls, demoralization would have reigned in the whole place. He couldn't have gotten any work out of the other girls, and Montag would have fired him."

Yet Arnold pitched the bulk of his argument on a higher plane, one predicated on the assumption that the jurors, like himself, were worldly men. In view of the concerns regarding power, privilege and predation raised by the Phagan murder, this was a risky tack; in view of the many ugly allegations that were part of the record, the lawyer had scant choice but to pursue it.

The basic point Arnold hoped to convey was that a majority of the improper acts attributed to Frank were, in fact, not improper at all. First, there was what he called "the little dressing room incident," of which he asked the jurors:

> What did it amount to? Wasn't everything done openly and above board, and in broad daylight? There was no bath in the dressing room, no toilet, and the girls themselves admit that there had been flirting in that room. Gentlemen, isn't that exactly the way you'd expect the superintendent of a big factory to conduct himself?

Then there was the charge that Frank had placed his hands on Mary Phagan's shoulders:

> You can go out here to Piedmont Park any Sunday afternoon and see five hundred girls and boys with hardly anything on, and the boys are grabbing them by the arms and legs and are having a gay old time. And I don't mean to say by this that I think the world is going to the dogs. It's a sign that we are getting more broad-minded, that we are learning some sense about these matters. And let me tell you something, gentlemen of the jury, deliver me from one of these prudish fellows that never looks at a girl and never puts his hands on her and is always talking about his own virtue. He's the kind I wouldn't trust behind the door.

And then, finally, there was the allegation that the pencil plant itself was a den of iniquity, with Frank as its corrupting head. To this, the superintendent's co-counsel simply said: "The factory is no better and no worse than any other factory of about that size in the city of Atlanta."

Arnold's intention here was to relegate all the insinuating testimony against Frank to the realm of unsubstantiated gossip and to elevate the general level of discourse. But lest he fail in this effort, he struck a different tone in his concluding comments on the superintendent's character:

> Gentlemen, we are not claiming perfection for this defendant any more than we claim it for ourselves or than you claim it for yourselves; and no more than Mr. Dorsey and his associates should claim it for themselves. Let the man who is innocent cast the first stone. We are not trying this man on everything that may have been said about him. We are trying him for murder.

That said, Arnold launched a wide-ranging assault on the circumstantial evidence that formed the foundation of the state's case, vowing: "Before I get through I'm going to show you there never was such a frame-up against a man since God made the world."

The frame-up got started, Arnold declared, because the authorities at first believed that Frank was the sole person in the factory at the time of Mary Phagan's murder who'd had the opportunity to commit the crime. "Nobody knew that Jim Conley was down there by that elevator hole," he reminded the jury. Consequently, Detectives Black and Starnes had pursued only those clues that might implicate the superintendent, particularly the bloodstains and strands of hair located in the building's metal room. This, insisted the lawyer, was a tragic misstep, for the blood and hair were plants made by their reward-obsessed discoverer, R. P. Barrett. "Would Frank have tried to hide the blood by smearing it with haskoline and calling attention to it?" he inquired. Would a man as meticulous as the superintendent have left the hair in plain sight? "It's the clumsiest botch I ever saw." But the investigators, he ruefully added, had made up their minds and refused to entertain other possibilities.

While the plot's preliminary acts unfolded, asserted Arnold, no one in Atlanta followed more attentively than Conley. From the newspapers, talk around the factory and, after his own arrest, talk inside the Tower, the Negro posted himself on every development. "He had weeks and weeks to do it. He knew they were trying to make a case against Frank." Thus, Conley was ready when the police, after determining that he could not only write but had written the murder notes, accused him of involvement in little Mary's demise. "He lay in his cell and conjured up the story he has told, and it is monstrous." With that, the lawyer had introduced one of his central premises. Where the state contended that the Negro's account was what remained after the initial deceptions were stripped away, the defense—in its lone nod to Jim's intelligence—argued that it was the self-serving work of a splendid imagination.

In an effort to provide further proof of Conley's cunning, Arnold at this point brandished copies of the Negro's various affidavits, marveling aloud at the care with which he had "felt his way along," altering inconvenient details at the suggestion of the detectives. Yet even so, the lawyer argued, Conley's testimony contained a sufficient number of absurdities to render it implausible. For one, there was his assertion that prior to the murder, he'd often stood guard at the factory building's Forsyth Street entrance while Frank consorted with women upstairs. "That's ridiculous," declared Arnold, citing that during the period in question, the plant shared the door with another tenant, the Clark Woodenware Company. "Frank wouldn't have had any right to lock the place up and shut them out." Then there was his claim that on the afternoon of the crime, despite having just heard little Mary scream, he allowed Monteen Stover to ascend to the second floor unchallenged. Staring directly at the jurors, the lawyer exclaimed, "Gentlemen, it fatigues my indignation to suppose that such splendid citizens as yourselves would believe a lie like that." Then there were his statements regarding two other April 26 visitors, Emma Clark and Corinthia Hall. "Bear in mind," urged Arnold, "that these women, in testimony corroborated by other witnesses, say they came to the factory 30 minutes before Conley says they were there." And as for his allegation that Frank hid him in a wardrobe to avoid being seen by the women, the lawyer noted, "Even if Frank had killed the girl, he could have let Emma and Corinthia come in and see Conley without arousing their suspicion. He was the superintendent, and Conley worked there." Most preposterous of all was Jim's contention that after he'd taken down the murder notes, Frank remarked, "Why should I hang? I have wealthy people in Brooklyn." Glancing around the room, Arnold asked, "Do you reckon a white man ever would have made a statement like that? Do you reckon he would have broken down and yelped like a dog?" At this, jurors and spectators alike chortled.

Having thus in two hours exposed more flaws in Conley's story than Luther Rosser had in three days, Arnold accused the Negro of Mary Phagan's murder:

> Conley admits he was right there behind the elevator when that little girl came into the factory. And he was right there when she came down. It took but two steps to get her mesh bag. Probably his aim was robbery. Here was a drunken, crazed negro, hard up for money. The little girl probably held to it when he grabbed it. He struck her in the eye and she fell. It is but the work of one moment, gentlemen, to push her into that elevator shaft.
>
> Why go further than this black wretch there by the elevator shaft, fired with liquor, fired with lust and crazy for money? Why, negroes rob and rav-

ish every day in the most peculiar and shocking way. But Frank's race don't kill. They are not a violent race. Some of them may be immoral, but they go no further than that.

With that, Arnold briefly returned to the defense table, retrieving a six-foot-high chart that presented the defense's minute-by-minute account of the whereabouts of Frank and other principals in the case on the day of the crime.

Though the chart's crisply lettered entries cataloged everything from Minola McKnight's 7:30 A.M. arrival at the Franks' home to fix breakfast to the 10:25 P.M. departure of the family's poker party guests, Arnold was interested only in details pertaining to the period between noon and three in the afternoon. Which was why he began by pointing to the lines noting that Monteen Stover reached the pencil factory at 12:05, followed by Mary Phagan at 12:12. "No matter how much Mr. Dorsey tries to move up the streetcar schedule," the lawyer said, these times had been verified by the state's witnesses as well as the defense's, and they established that even if Frank was not in his office when Stover appeared, this did not support the claim that he was at that moment choking the life out of little Mary. She was not yet on the premises. That said, Arnold ran his hand down the chart, stopping at a notation reading "12:20—Lemmie Quinn." To the lawyer, this was another critical moment, and he lingered on it:

> The sworn evidence gives Frank only eight minutes between the time Mary Phagan came to the factory and the time Quinn came. Could Frank have attacked her in just eight minutes? And then been back at his desk, a normal man digging into his work, in eight minutes?

Having thus exposed two vulnerabilities in the prosecution's murder-day chronology, Arnold attempted to expose one more. According to his chart, Frank left the plant for lunch at 1:00. Also according to the chart, Helen Kerns saw Frank waiting for a trolley at Alabama and Whitehall streets at 1:10, while Mrs. Albert Levy saw him exit the same trolley at Georgia and Washington avenues at 1:20. After reminding his audience that Conley testified the superintendent had not departed the factory until 1:30, the lawyer asserted, "Gentlemen, these witnesses—one a pure, sweet little bud, the other, it's true, a Jew, but she was telling the truth—make it as clear as holy writ that Conley was lying, that he is a liar fit only for the lower regions." That said, Arnold again pointed to his chart, focusing on an entry recording Rebecca Carson's glimpse of Frank returning to town on a streetcar around 2:20. Methodically, he was endeavoring to illustrate that the state's version of the superintendent's activities on the afternoon of April 26 was not credible. What, then, remained? Nothing, he insisted, but "the twin P's—prejudice and perjury." Speaking with the zeal of one whose purpose was to conduct an exorcism, the lawyer pivoted away from the chart and addressing Dorsey directly roared:

> Away with your miserable lies about perversion, away with your mangy street gossip, away with your Jew-lynching witnesses, away with your third-degree testimony, away with your trumped-up evidence. If you are fair, you must stick to the facts.

With the clock now ticking down to 6:00 P.M. and evening encroaching, Arnold strode to the jury-box rail and made his concluding entreaty:

> Gentlemen, never has there been such malice displayed in the prosecution of any case. The crime was horrible. God grant its perpetrator may be punished, and I think that we can prove that Jim Conley is the man who should receive the punishment. Let us follow the law and not follow prejudice. Frank's alibi is complete, and Jim Conley has been proven a liar. The whole case is a fabrication, a frame-up pure and simple.
>
> Gentlemen, write a verdict of not guilty and your consciences will be clear.

Noticeably lighter than at the trial's start, features drawn and eyes dull, the Luther Rosser who rose Friday morning to speak the defense's last words bore little resemblance to his familiar antagonistic self. In a worn whisper that barely carried over the buzz of the electric fans, the exhausted lawyer opened by echoing Arnold's plea to the jurors to insulate themselves from the "hostile and overzealous" spirit of Atlanta's streets.

Rosser then took aim at the prosecution's case, beginning with the character evidence. His first target was the allegation that the National Pencil factory was a hotbed of immorality. Since the plant's founding in 1908, he stated, it had employed countless souls, yet after weeks of "microscopic examination" the police had been able to locate only a few who would swear against it, foremost among them C. Brutus Dalton. The very thought of this witness angered the big man, and he hoarsely rasped:

> Did you take a look at him when he went on the stand? God Almighty, when he writes on a human's face, doesn't always write beautifully, but he never fails to write legibly. If you were to meet Dalton in the dark, wouldn't you instinctively put your hand on your pocketbook?

Dalton, Rosser added, was exactly the sort who would go "down that scuttle hole into the basement, into the inner sanctum of filth." Not that the lawyer believed that Dalton or, for that matter, anyone else had actually used the factory as a trysting place. For one thing, Rosser asserted pointedly, had the plant been the site of such activities, Chief Beavers's "vice squad" would have exposed that during its recent campaign against prostitution. For another, had even a whiff of wrongdoing reached the ears of the citizens whose children composed the bulk of the company's workforce, they would have protested so vociferously that the business "would have been wrecked on the rocks of bankruptcy."

Rosser next challenged Frank Hooper's contention that the upstanding Atlantans who'd attested to Frank's rectitude were in no position to know his true nature. Gesturing to the superintendent, the lawyer declared:

> Maybe there are such things as Dr. Jekylls and Mr. Hydes. My friend Hooper may know more about that than I do. But do you judge men by the exceptions? No, you judge them by the majority rule. When the good and decent men and women of his neighborhood come to the stand and say his character is good, you believe them.

Finally, Rosser proclaimed that the many insinuations notwithstanding, Dorsey had failed to prove any history of undue familiarity between Frank and Mary Phagan. Regarding Ruth Robinson's claim that she'd heard the superintendent call little Mary by name, the lawyer asserted that it meant nothing. As to Willie Turner's profession that he'd observed the girl backing away from Frank in fright, he sadly shook his head, remarking, "I'm sorry for that boy. Think of the claws with which these detectives dragged his statement out of him. Picture the way they treated Minola McKnight, then think of him." Which left only Dewey Hewell's charge that on several occasions, she'd seen the superintendent place his hands on Mary's shoulders. To this, the lawyer ticked off the names of the witnesses—among them the state's Grace Hicks—who had sworn that the superintendent had not been acquainted with the victim.

With that, Rosser attacked the state's circumstantial evidence case, beginning with the charge that Frank had lured Mary Phagan to his office on Saturday, April 26. The facts, he contended, just didn't support such a conclusion. "How did Frank know Mary wasn't going to come on Monday or Tuesday?" demanded the lawyer. "And how did he know no one else would be in his office when she got there? He's a smart man, but he's not a seer."

The allegations of premeditation on Frank's part thereby covered, Rosser assailed the charges of suspicious behavior in the murder's aftermath. Referring to the superintendent's failure to answer the telephone when the police initially tried to notify him of the crime, he declared, "Gentlemen, when Frank didn't hear the telephone ringing that morning, it was a sign of peace of mind and good conscience." Regarding Frank's reaction to the sight of Mary Phagan's body at the morgue, Rosser asked, "Is there anyone within the sound of my voice who would not have been nervous if they had seen that little girl cut off in the beginning of her young life lying there disfigured—a beautiful flower smeared in the mud, crushed in the cinders?" The lawyer was most forceful, however, on a matter of which he had firsthand knowledge—his hiring by Frank the Monday following the murder. "Let's examine what happened," he urged. "When they took him to the station house, he was under arrest—John Black's testimony proved as much." The superintendent, unaware of the police force's checkered past, "failed to recognize his dilemma," yet others understood, and it was through their efforts that Rosser was engaged. Facing the jurors, the lawyer asserted:

> Sig Montag, who has been here a long time, knew this old police crowd. He knew what danger there was to Frank. So he called up Herbert Haas. Haas didn't want to go. His wife was expecting. That's why Haas called [me]. And I went down there. They weren't happy to see me. But I had a right to be there, and Frank had a right to have me there. Dorsey tells you this is an indication of guilt on Frank's part. Gentlemen, when the solicitor reaches the age in years that I have, he'll regret it.

Spent though he obviously was, as Friday's midday recess approached, Rosser, cognizant that the defense's hour upon the stage was nearly done, summoned the extra ration of strength necessary to launch a vigorous assault on the remaining elements of the state's case. Pacing before the jury, sweat pouring down his neck and into his shirt until the thin alpaca sport jacket he'd chosen for this pivotal occasion stuck in patches to his shoulders, he started by disputing Dorsey's claim that Frank had hired the Pinkerton Detective Agency to shield himself. Not only was this not so, but in truth, by engaging the outfit, the superintendent had brought the wolf to his door. Declared the lawyer:

> Gentlemen, take a look at this spectacle if you can.
> Here is a Jewish boy from the North. He is unacquainted with the South. He came here alone and without friends, and he stood alone. This murder happened at his place of business. He told the Pinkertons to find the man, trusting to them entirely, no matter where what they found might strike. He is defenseless and helpless. He knows his innocence and is willing to find the murderer.
> Yet they try to place the murder on him. God, all merciful and all powerful, look upon a scene like this.

Rosser then took issue with Dorsey's charge that in an effort to implicate Newt Lee as the killer, Frank had altered the night watchman's time slip from the evening of the crime and had planted the bloody shirt at his home. Regarding the time slip, the lawyer declared that the superintendent was not the only factory official who'd initially stated Lee had punched it correctly; N. V. Darley had been likewise mistaken. As for the shirt, while he didn't say so outright, Rosser intimated that it had been John Black—not Frank—who'd soaked the garment in crimson and secreted it in the barrel the night watchman used as a bureau. He'd done so, he implied, because he was the one who'd hoped to pin the murder on Lee; failing that, he'd decided to use the shirt against the superintendent. In the end, though, Frank's lead counsel not surprisingly reserved his harshest salvos for the state's star witness.

Despite its many parts, Rosser's concluding attack on Jim Conley, which would carry over into the early afternoon, was meant to convey one transcendent point. To wit: Everything about the Negro that had mesmerized the jurors, whether it was his appearance or, most important, his testimony, was a fabulous, self-protecting invention polished to a high gloss by Dorsey and his minions. "Who is Conley?" Rosser asked by way of introducing his thesis. "Who did he used to be? And was he like his old self when you saw him?" After letting these questions hang briefly in the air, the lawyer bluntly answered:

> Conley is a plain, beastly, drunken, filthy, lying nigger with a spreading nose through which probably tons of cocaine have been sniffed. But you weren't allowed to see him as he is.

That said, Rosser turned a furious gaze upon the occupants of the prosecution's table. "Think of what they did," he began, whereupon without calling William Smith by name, he enumerated the various personal services Conley's lawyer had provided his client before the state placed him on the stand. Proclaimed the big man:

> They got a dirty, black negro and in order to give impetus to his testimony they had a barber cut his hair and shave him, and they gave him a bath. They took his rags from his back, and he came in here like a slicked onion. They tried to make him look like a respectable negro.

Conley's account of the crime, argued Rosser, had been similarly buffed. While he, like Arnold, believed that Jim's initial statement had been the fruit of his own fertile mind ("Every Southern man knows that negroes can make up gruesome stories"), he maintained that "the finest faculty in the

South" had assisted in the creation of what followed. Again indicating the prosecution team, the lawyer proclaimed:

> There's Professor Starnes, who holds the chair in theology. And Professor Black, he of the third degree. And there, in charge of them all, is Dean Lanford. Dean, I greet you.

As Rosser, warming to his satire, enthusiastically told it, the detectives charged with refining Conley's tale at first "put him in high school." There, they worked out the worst rough spots. "Here's the way they would do it," he asserted. "Professor Scott would say, 'Now stand up, James and recite. Why James, that couldn't be right. It couldn't have been done on Friday.' 'That's right, boss. It was Saturday.' 'That's better James. Now repeat.' And so they went on." After several weeks of instruction, the lawyer added, Conley graduated to the university, where he met "Professor Dorsey" and took courses in such subjects as sexual perversion. It was thanks to the advanced tutoring that the account Jim ultimately gave on the stand contained so many new details.

What the jury made of Rosser's spirited tribute to Conley's station house alma mater cannot be known, but amused or not, the lampoon raised a troubling question: If Jim's testimony was so obviously a fabrication, why hadn't Frank's lead counsel exposed it as such during his cross-examination? Facing the men who constituted his only real audience, the lawyer confronted the matter head-on:

> My friend Hooper said that I didn't break the negro down. And its true, he stuck to his story word for word—like an actor. You know, you can take an actor and let him memorize his lines, and if you wake him in the middle of the night, he can pick right up in his speech. But if you ask him about something else, he's lost. That's the way it was with Conley. Every time he got away from the main story, he either admitted that he had lied or he said, "I disremember." Gentlemen, there is no better sign that a man has memorized his story and that he is lying than those words. You can look through the record of his testimony and find page after page where he said, "I disremember." In the law books, those words stand as the badge and sign of perjury, and they brand Conley as what he is—a trained parrot.

With that, Rosser was essentially finished. He spoke a few disparaging words about the state's medical evidence; he reiterated some inconsistencies in Dorsey's murder-day time line. But in the end, as one of his final comments to the jury made plain, he framed the decision as a racial one. Declared the lawyer:

If you, as white men, should believe Jim Conley, it will be a shame on this great city and on this great state and will be until the end of time.

Whether Hugh Dorsey's decision to begin his closing argument by portraying the state as the victim of a brutalizing defense team resulted from genuinely bruised feelings or shrewd calculation, he could not have chosen a better gambit. No sooner had Rosser returned to his seat than the solicitor asserted that he and Frank Hooper had not only been outnumbered by Frank's counsel but that they had been maligned and mistreated by them as well. Speaking from behind the prosecution table, he declared:

> The gentlemen have abused me. They have abused the detectives. They have heaped calumny on us to such an extent that that good lady, the mother of this defendant, was so wrought up that she arose and in this presence denounced me as a dog.

And so there it was: the embattled state's attorney versus the blue-stockinged barristers. The humble people of Atlanta versus the wealthy outsiders.

The gauntlet thus thrown down, Dorsey promptly countered the defense's eleventh-hour allegation that the prosecution had been motivated by discriminatory leanings. " 'Prejudice and perjury,' says Mr. Arnold," remarked the solicitor, repeating his counterpart's charge. Then, looking up at the jurors, he incredulously inquired:

> Gentlemen, do you think that I, or that these detectives, are actuated by prejudice? Would we as sworn officers of the law have sought to hang Leo Frank on account of his race and religion and passed up Jim Conley, a negro? Prejudice?

These questions all but obliterated the defense's accusation. And if they did not, there was something else. According to the solicitor's narrow but indisputably accurate reading of the record, it was Frank's lawyers who injected the issue of religious bias into the proceedings. "Not a word emanated from this side," he asserted. "We didn't feel it. We would despise ourselves if we had. But ah, I have never seen any two men manifest more delight or exaltation than Messrs. Rosser and Arnold when they seized upon George Kendley," the witness who'd purportedly stated that the superintendent should hang because of his Jewishness. Though he stopped short of saying so, the solicitor couldn't have made his point clearer—the cry of anti-Semitism was a desperate ploy to salvage a losing case.

With that, Dorsey paid homage to a pantheon of Jewish statesmen and business leaders. "I honor the race that has produced a Disraeli, the greatest Prime Minister that England has ever produced," he began, then doffed his hat to Confederate secretary of state Judah P. Benjamin and a number of local sons of David, among them the lawyer Henry Alexander, his University of Georgia roommate. Yet lest anyone think he was endorsing the defense's claim that Jews did not commit violent crimes, the solicitor then introduced a rogue's gallery of Hebrew malefactors—Abe Hummel, Herman Rosenthal, Abe Reuf—all culled from recent front pages. "This great people," he insisted, "rise to heights sublime, but they sink to the depths of degredation, too, and they are amenable to the same laws as you or I and the black race."

Dorsey then addressed what he contended was the only material that should have any relevance—the evidence proving that Frank had murdered Mary Phagan. And he started with what he termed "this character proposition." First, he reiterated his co-counsel's claim that the Atlanta Jews who'd attested to the superintendent's outstanding moral fiber had never seen his dark side. "Dr. Marx, Dr. Sonn, all these other people who, as Mr. Hooper said, run with the Dr. Jekyll of the Hebrew Orphans' Home, don't know the Mr. Hyde of the factory." That said, he vouched for the credibility of the former employees who'd testified to Frank's lasciviousness, declaring that Rosser and Arnold's dismissal of them as liars was, in fact, evidence of their truthfulness, then averring that even if he and the detectives were as corrupt as the defense maintained, they could not have compelled the girls to swear falsely. "Do you think that we could go and get nineteen or twenty of them and through prejudice or passion get them to come up here and say that the man's character is bad and it not be the truth?" In the end, however, the solicitor directed his sharpest comments at his opposing numbers for their failure to cross-examine these young women. After lifting a thick legal tome from the table in front of him, he looked up at his audience, then demanded:

Now gentlemen, put yourself in Frank's place. If you are a man of good character, and twenty people come in here and state that you are of bad character, is it possible, I'll ask you in the name of common sense, that you would permit your counsel to sit mute? You wouldn't do it, would you? If a man says that I am a person of bad character and it's a lie, I want to nail the lie, to show that he knows nothing about it. This book says it's allowable to cross-examine a witness, to see and find out what he knows, who told him these things. Yet these able counsel did not do so, and I'm here to tell you that this thing of itself is pregnant, pregnant, pregnant with significance.

Predictably, there was much more that Dorsey wanted to say regarding the issue of Frank's character, but with late afternoon now approaching, he had time to address just one last point—the superintendent's alleged penchant for bursting in unannounced on unclothed female employees. Resorting, as was his style, to yet another rhetorical question, he turned to Frank, then back to the jury, and inquired:

> What business did this man have going into those dressing rooms? You tell me that to go up there, shove open the door and walk in was part of his duty when he had foreladies to do it? You tell me he did this to stop the girls from flirting?

After citing the many witnesses—among them the defense's own Irene Jackson—who'd attested to the superintendent's intrusions, the solicitor gathered his notes and Judge Roan brought down the gavel.

Not that the day's events were over. Rather than disperse as they'd done following previous sessions, the trial's 250 spectators, at the request of William Smith, lingered on the sidewalks in front of the courthouse. Supper, shows, dates—all could wait. And did, until 6 P.M., when Hugh Dorsey appeared on the steps. At which point, the multitude—on Smith's cue—burst into applause.

In anticipation of Saturday's court session, a crowd began forming in front of the old city hall at 5:45, and by 9:00, when the doors swung open, it numbered more than 1,000. Within minutes, the allotted seats were taken. Though one reporter maintained that "absolute decorum" prevailed, another sensed an "unspoken fear of trouble" in the air. Either way, observers concurred that the attendees were almost to a soul sympathetic to the state. They had come to hear the case for conviction put over.

Picking up where he'd left off Friday, Hugh Dorsey rounded out his remarks on the character issue by declaring that even if Leo Frank had been a pillar of rectitude prior to Mary Phagan's murder, it "would amount to nothing." The solicitor then cited a number of mostly Jewish personages who despite high status had committed terrible misdeeds. Think of the Old Testament's David, he urged, "a great character until he put Uriah in the forefront of battle in order that Uriah might be killed and David take his wife." Or consider Judas Iscariot, "a good character and one of the Twelve," until he "took the thirty pieces of silver and betrayed our Lord, Jesus Christ." And don't forget Benedict Arnold, a hero of the Revolution who deceived the nation and whose name became "a synonym for infamy." That Dorsey, his protestations of the day before notwithstanding, was attempting to stir anti-Semitic sentiments there can be no doubt. And these weren't the only juices he hoped to stimulate. Looking over at Frank, he mentioned an altogether different sort of fallen angel:

> Oscar Wilde was an Irish knight, a literary man, brilliant, the author of works that will go down through the ages. But the Marquis of Queensberry discovered there was something wrong between Oscar and his son. Oscar Wilde was convicted, and in his old age went tottering to the grave, a confessed pervert.

Having thus thrown several questionable punches, Dorsey moved on to the topic of Frank's alibi. Approaching the chart the defense had used to illustrate its version of how April 26 unfolded, he pointed to the entry stating that the superintendent had left the factory for lunch at 1:00 P.M. Then, after instructing a bailiff to turn the display toward the wall, the solicitor read a copy of the statement Frank had made for Newport Lanford on the Monday following the crime in which he asserted that he had left the factory at 1:10. Considering the significance Arnold had attached to the earlier departure time, the ten-minute discrepancy was extremely damaging, and Dorsey knew it, exclaiming:

> Up goes your alibi, punctured by your own statement when you didn't know the importance of the time element in the case.

Not only did Frank's initial telling contradict his lawyer's, it also contradicted that of his principal corroborating witness, Helen Kerns, who'd testified that she'd seen the superintendent standing at Alabama and Broad streets at 1:10 that April Saturday. Moreover, as Dorsey revealed, the Kerns girl's father worked for the Montag Paper Company, and though he didn't say so outright, he implied that Sig Montag had coerced little Helen into swearing falsely.

With that, Dorsey asked the bailiff to turn the defense's chart back around, enabling him to discuss another entry, the one indicating Lemmie Quinn's appearance in the factory office at 12:20 on April 26. "This is a fraud," he boomed, reminding the jurors that at first, "Frank had a mighty hard time remembering Quinn was there," not mentioning the fact until after he'd conferred with counsel. The reason for the superintendent's reticence, he added, could be found in Conley's testimony that Quinn had come and gone before Mary Phagan arrived, making his visit irrelevant. Concluded the solicitor: Frank's lawyers had altered the true sequence of events, and loyal Lemmie had acquiesced.

Having thereby blown two large holes in Frank's account of his murder-

day itinerary, Dorsey lambasted the defense for accusing the state of sub-
orning perjury. To the contrary, he proclaimed, it was Frank's witnesses
who'd lied on the stand, and Kerns and Quinn weren't the only ones. Take
the female worker who after vouching for the superintendent's good character had announced that she would stake her life on his innocence. Such a
profession practically guaranteed that the girl had dissembled, asserted the
solicitor, adding:

> I know enough about human nature to know that this willingness to die,
> this anxiety to put her neck in a noose that ought to go around Leo Frank
> was born of something more than just platonic friendship. Whenever you
> see a woman willing to lie down and die for a man not related to her, who
> occupies the relation towards her of an employer, you may know that there
> must be a passion beyond that which ought to obtain between a married
> man and a single woman.

The morning now half gone, Dorsey walked to the edge of the jury box
and unleashed a new and entirely unexpected attack. His weapon—the letter Frank had written to his uncle Moses on April 26, a document that had
gone into the record, over the state's objection, as proof that the superintendent had spent the afternoon of the murder innocently.

"Listen to this," Dorsey began, then read the letter aloud, focusing initially on the line "It's too short a time since you left for anything startling to
have developed down here." After pausing to let the words sink in, the
solicitor looked up at the jurors and exclaimed:

> Too short! Too short! Startling! Tell me honest men, fair men, coura-
> geous men, true Georgians seeking to do your duty, that that phrase
> penned by that man to his uncle on Saturday afternoon didn't come from
> a conscience that was its own accuser. Too short a time—the line shows
> that the dastardly deed was done in an incredibly short time. Nothing
> startling—I tell you that letter shows on its face that something startling
> had happened, and that there was something new in the factory.

Having exposed what he saw as an unconscious expression of guilt on
Frank's part, Dorsey honed in on the passage where the superintendent
described "the thin gray line of veterans" who'd braved Confederate Memorial Day's chilly weather. Here, analysis gave way to vituperation:

> I tell you that rich uncle didn't care a flip of his finger about the thin gray
> line of veterans. All he cared about was how much money had been gotten
> in by the pencil factory.

Though Moses Frank, a Confederate veteran himself, likely had relished news of the Memorial Day observances, Dorsey was again trying to kindle damaging associations. He was also laying the foundation for an outrageous interpretive leap, one whereby the letter, whose recipient was at the time in New York, would lend credence to Conley's claim that in the crime's aftermath, the superintendent had looked to the ceiling and exclaimed: "Why should I hang? I have wealthy people in Brooklyn." Roared the solicitor:

> Didn't have wealthy people in Brooklyn, eh? This uncle of his was mighty near Brooklyn. His people lived in Brooklyn, and that's one thing sure and certain, and old Jim never would have known it except Leo M. Frank had told him, and they had $20,000 in cool cash out at interest.

Ugly as Dorsey's concluding insinuations had been, they did not signal a full-blown descent into demagoguery. He now exhibited what appeared to be genuine humility in the face of a grave responsibility, telling the jury, "I have a difficult task, and I wish I didn't have to do it." Moreover, his treatment of the next item on his agenda would be calm and based on a seemingly superior understanding of the evidence.

Dorsey opened his discussion of the murder notes—a topic Frank's lawyers had inexplicably given short shrift—by echoing Frank Hooper's assertion that such communiqués were simply not typical of Negroes. But more than just dispel the theory that Conley had composed the notes, the solicitor intended to prove that they were the original expressions of the superintendent. He believed that they actually revealed Frank as their author and hence the killer.

"This letter I hold in my hands," Dorsey began, referring to the note scrawled on the yellow National Pencil Company order blank, "says, 'the negro did it.'" After letting that simple phrase reverberate for a moment, the solicitor grabbed several pages of trial transcript containing portions of Conley's testimony, then declared: "Old Jim here, every time he opened his mouth, says, 'I done it.'" As illustration, Dorsey then read a few examples: "'I locked the door like he done told me.' 'He done just like this.' 'I told Mr. Frank the girl was done dead.'" The conclusion was clear—had Conley composed the note in question, he would have written "the negro done it" instead of the grammatically correct "the negro did it." As the solicitor bluntly asserted: "It's the difference between ignorance and education."

Dorsey then moved on to the second murder note (the one jotted on a piece of lined white paper), paying particular attention to the phrase: "that negro did by his slef." Frank had inserted this line, the solicitor averred, to ward off any suspicion that two men—he and Jim—had been involved in the crime; Conley would not have needed to draw such a distinction. Flipping back to the first note, Dorsey cited another phrase he regarded as a dead giveaway. Looking at the superintendent, he said:

> You make this poor girl say, "I went to make water." You tell me Conley would have written that when there was no place for her there by the scuttle hole? Where did she go to make water? Right back there in the same direction she would have gone to see about the metal.

Here, Dorsey sought to acquaint the jury with two related points. First, he flatly announced that pads that contained company order blanks could be found only where Conley swore the notes were written—the factory office. Then he insisted that by not speaking up regarding the Negro's ability to write when detectives had initially shown him the notes, Frank had been attempting to shield himself and his accomplice. These charges provided the solicitor with a perfect jumping-off place for his last words on the topic:

> I tell you, gentlemen, that a smarter man than Starnes, a smarter man than Campbell, a smarter man than Black—in the person of Leo M. Frank—felt compelled to write these letters, which he thought would exculpate him, but which instead incriminate and damn him. This man here, by these notes purporting to have been written by little Mary Phagan, by the verbiage and the language and the context, in trying to fix the crime on another, as sure as you are sitting in the jury box, has indelibly fastened it on himself.

Dorsey next began hammering home one of his argument's central themes, namely, that Frank's April 26 encounter with Mary Phagan was the result of weeks, if not months, of plotting. Gesturing to the accused, the solicitor asserted, "This man had been expecting for some time to cause this little girl to yield to his blandishments and deflower her." As evidence, Dorsey cited the testimony of "country boy" Willie Turner, who "as far back as March" had witnessed Frank trying to "force his attentions" on Mary. Then there was the testimony of Dewey Hewell, "from the Home of the Good Shepherd," who'd seen the superintendent "place his hands" on the poor thing's shoulders. And finally there was James M. Gantt, who swore that the superintendent had asked about the girl and whose firing removed an obstacle to the plan.

The opportunity Frank had long coveted, Dorsey insisted, at last presented itself on Friday, April 25, when Helen Ferguson asked for Mary Phagan's pay envelope. The superintendent rejected the request knowing that his action would result in the appearance of the object of his desire the next day. It was at this point, the solicitor added, that Frank sought out Conley and engaged him to perform the service he'd frequently performed in the past.

"Ah, gentlemen, then Saturday comes, Saturday comes," Dorsey thrillingly intoned. Following a sketch of Frank's alleged activities during the morning hours, the solicitor asserted that Mary Phagan reached the factory at 12:05 and that the superintendent escorted her to the rear of the second floor "to see whether the metal had come." That said, Dorsey turned toward the accused and with the full force of his being leveled his initial accusation:

> You assaulted her, and she resisted. She wouldn't yield. You struck her and you ravished her and she was unconscious.

At this, the victim's mother screamed, then buried her head in the arms of little Mary's sister Ollie, who was today also seated at the prosecution table. For the solicitor, there could have been no better backdrop, and he vigorously pressed ahead, demanding of Frank's lawyers:

> You tell me she wasn't ravished? I ask you to look at the blood—you tell me that little child wasn't ravished? I ask you to look at the drawers, that were torn. I ask you to look at the blood on the drawers. I ask you to look at the thing that held up the stockings. Oh, no, there was no spermatazoan and there was no semen, that's true. But as sure as you are born, that man is not like other men. He saw this girl. He coveted her. Others without her stamina and her character had yielded to his lust. But she denied him, and when she did, not being like other men, he struck her. He gagged her.

By now Rae and Lucille Frank were also sobbing, but Dorsey did not halt, turning back to the superintendent and leveling his ultimate accusation:

> You gagged her, and then quickly you tipped up to the front, where you knew there was a cord, and you got the cord and in order to save your reputation which you had among the members of the B'nai Brith, in order to save, not your character because you never had it, but in order to save the reputation with the Haases and the Montags and the members of Dr. Marx's church and your kinfolks in Brooklyn, rich and poor, and in Athens, then it was that you got the cord and fixed the little girl whom you'd assaulted, who wouldn't yield to your proposals, to save your reputation, because dead people tell no tales.

Having thus not only charged Frank with Mary Phagan's murder but found a new way to make his Jewishness appear to be a factor, Dorsey capped this portion of his address with a last thunderbolt. In a line that managed to serve as an apologia for one of his least savory witnesses and invoke the specter of extralegal violence, he asserted that in killing little Mary, the superintendent was motivated by a final consideration—the knowledge that had he let her live, "ten thousand men like Kendley would have sprung up in this town and would have stormed the jail." Such things "oughtn't to be," said the solicitor, but his qualification did not negate the remark.

As he'd done before, Dorsey now throttled back, quietly attending to some outstanding business. First, he contested the defense's claim that the blood and hair located on the factory's second floor the Monday after the murder had been planted. Not so, he asserted, reminding his audience that at the time R. P. Barrett made the finds, no reward had been posted. Next, he reiterated the contention that the only dubious items entered into evidence had been planted by the defense, ticking off a list that started with the crimson-soaked shirt planted at Newt Lee's house and included the twine and club located in the factory lobby in mid-May when Rosser "realized something had to be forthcoming to bolster up the charge that Conley did it."

And so it would continue until 1:30, when Dorsey—to the surprise of a gallery that fully expected him to finish his presentation by day's end—pulled a handkerchief from his pocket, wiped the sweat from his face and simply stopped. "I am mighty tired, your honor," he said by way of explanation. "I hardly feel that I can go on."

At that, Reuben Arnold rose and joined Dorsey at the bench, where following a ten-minute conference, Judge Roan turned to the jurors and announced: "Gentlemen, the solicitor has more to say but cannot go further as he's exhausted. As much as I hate to do it, I think I have to adjourn until 9:00 Monday."

The next morning, Atlanta's papers repeated the court's rationale for extending the trial another week. "Only the limitations of human endurance, taxed to its utmost, kept the Frank case from going to the jury Saturday afternoon," declared the *Constitution*. But in fact, the truth was more complicated, reflecting an awareness by all involved of the increasingly volatile atmosphere in the city. As the *Augusta Chronicle*, one of the many out-of-town sheets that had staffed the proceedings as the denouement approached, reported:

> The real reason the trial of Leo Frank was abruptly adjourned Saturday was a fear of the same element which brought about the great Atlanta riot [of 1906]—the lower element, the people of the back streets and the alleys, the near-beer saloons and the pool rooms. The Saturday night crowd in

Atlanta, beer drinking, blind-tiger frequenting, is not an assemblage loving law and order. A verdict that displeased these sansculottes of Marietta Street might well result in trouble.

According to the *Chronicle,* Judge Roan and the lawyers from both sides, in consultation with Governor John Slaton (who was said to have placed the state militia on call), had agreed not to let the case go to the jury over the weekend.

Thus Sunday passed with Atlanta in limbo, and nowhere was the suspense felt more intensely than in Leo Frank's cell at the Tower. Throughout the day, friends poured in, and to all the prisoner expressed confidence regarding the outcome. To himself, however, Frank couldn't have been sure. The state's evidence was persuasive, and Dorsey's speech had impressed even his detractors. With uncharacteristic admiration, the *Georgian* termed it "a white hot philippic, the greatest ever heard in a criminal court in the South."

That a vocal majority of Atlantans was openly pulling for Leo Frank's conviction could not have been plainer. The enormous crowd gathered in front of the old city hall Monday morning applauded Hugh Dorsey as he entered the building. Anxious to make certain that this critical last session was not itself marred by such demonstrations, Judge Roan wasted no time warning the men and women lucky enough to gain admission to be careful, lest their behavior "invalidate all the work that has been done in the past four weeks." With that, a hush fell over the gallery, and the solicitor rose to his feet.

Dorsey began his concluding push by offering a discourse on circumstantial evidence. Though he conceded that "this circumstance or that circumstance" might not be strong enough to convict Frank, he insisted that when taken together, the pieces that had been placed before the jury constituted "such a cable and such a strand that it was not only impossible to conceive of a reasonable doubt but of any doubt at all." The solicitor then reiterated the most damning particulars.

There was Lucille's failure to visit Leo during his first days of incarceration. Though Reuben Arnold objected to Dorsey's "unfair and outrageous" attempt to imply that the superintendent's wife had stayed away because she questioned her husband's innocence, Roan—after reminding the defense lawyer that Frank had himself mentioned the matter in his statement—ruled that the subject was fair game. Thus the solicitor said: "I tell you, gentlemen, that there never lived a woman, conscious of the rectitude of her husband, who wouldn't have gone to him through snapshooters, reporters and everything else. And you know it."

There was Frank's refusal to meet with Conley in late May when Chiefs Beavers and Lanford brought the Negro to his cell. Proclaimed Dorsey:

> Gentlemen of the jury—and if you have got enough sense to get out of a shower of rain you know it's true—never in the history of the Anglo-Saxon race, never in the history of the African race in America, did an ignorant, filthy negro accuse a white man of a crime and that man decline to face him.

Then there was the jailhouse get-together that did take place—the one between Frank and Newt Lee. Dorsey simply did not buy the superintendent's account of the session, and turning to him, he inquired:

> Did you make an earnest, honest conscientious effort, as an innocent employer would have with his employee, to get at the truth? No. According to Lee, you hung your head and quizzed him not, but predicted that both Lee and you would go to hell if Lee continued to tell the story, which he tells even to this day.

Having raised several of the circumstances that in the wake of Frank's arrest had whetted investigators' suspicions, Dorsey next focused on what he regarded as a group of earlier incriminating actions. Many of these—the superintendent's abrupt shift of Lee's April 26 starting time from four to six P.M, his refusal to let the night watchman spend the intervening hours in the factory, his attempt later that afternoon to keep James M. Gantt from entering the building to search for his shoes, his seven P.M. phone call from home to check on Lee—were familiar. Others, however, had not been previously adduced. For instance, Dorsey read much into the fact that Lucille rather than Leo answered the door when the police came to their house following the discovery of Mary Phagan's body, seeing it as a sign of Frank's evasiveness. Similarly, he felt that the superintendent's insistence on having N. V. Darley on hand for the subsequent tour of the plant indicated that he'd needed someone "to sustain his nerves." Finally, there was Frank's late-Sunday visit to the morgue; in the solicitor's view, it sprang from an atavistic impulse. "Like a dog to his vomit, a sow to his wallow, Frank went to view the remains of this poor innocent little girl."

At midmorning, Dorsey changed course. His remarks on the medical evidence were brief but pointed. First, he praised the humble Southern food that had served as the source of the state's findings as to the hour of Mary Phagan's demise:

I tell you, gentlemen, that there is no better, no more wholesome meal than cabbage, and when the stomach is normal and all right, there is nothing that is more easily digested. And I tell you that cabbage, cornbread, and buttermilk is good enough for any man.

Then he saluted Dr. Roy Harris on the same grounds, terming him "a Georgia son who holds the highest honor that can be given to a man in his profession in the state." That said, Dorsey blasted the defense's outside experts, dismissing Dr. Leroy Childs as "the man from Michigan" and Dr. George Bachman as "the man from Alsace-Lorraine." All of it was prefatory to the main point:

This cabbage proposition fastens and fixes and nails down with the accuracy which only a scientific fact can do, that Mary Phagan met her death between the time she entered the office of the superintendent and the time Mrs. White came up the stairs at 12:35 to see her husband.

By this juncture, Dorsey had been speaking for the better part of three days. He had attacked the conduct of Frank's lawyers even as he had defended his own. He had revisited familiar pieces of evidence, interpreted enigmatic clues and illuminated previously ignored ones. He had both denounced Frank's character and emphasized his Jewishness and wealth. Through it all, however, he had barely mentioned the figure around whom everything revolved and about whom his audience longed to hear more. Which was why when he brought up his star witness, he did so in the confident tone of a general who'd held his crack troops in reserve until the end:

So far, not a word about Conley. Not a word. Leave Conley out, you've got a course of conduct that shows that Frank is guilty. Now, let's discuss Conley.

Yet rather than plunge into Conley's story, Dorsey began by praising the white man who'd corroborated its most salacious elements. C. Brutus Dalton, asserted the solicitor, enjoyed "the confidence of the people among whom he lives," and his testimony as to the chores the Negro had previously performed for Frank was absolutely credible.

Next, Dorsey rebutted Luther Rosser's claim that William Smith had gotten Conley shaved and showered and outfitted in a new wardrobe in a cynical attempt to keep the jurors from seeing him as the disreputable Negro he truly was. Not so, maintained the solicitor. Smith had been motivated by no other force than "the charity in his heart," and for this he deserved "not condemnation but thanks."

Dorsey appeared ready to launch his peroration, but once more he digressed, offering a rationale for Conley's transfer from the laxly guarded Tower to the police lockup. Though the topic was germane, the solicitor was obviously stalling.

From this point on, however, there would be no more pauses. As the clock ticked toward noon, Dorsey elucidated the evidence and testimony that as he phrased it again and again sustained Jim Conley:

> The defense's failure to cross-examine our character witnesses sustains Jim Conley.
>
> Frank's relations with Miss Rebecca Carson, who is shown to have gone in the ladies' dressing room with him, sustains Jim Conley.
>
> Your own witness, Miss Jackson, who says that this libertine and rake came in when these girls were in there reclining and lounging after they had finished their work and tells of the sardonic grin that lit his countenance, sustains Jim Conley.
>
> Monteen Stover, as to the easy-walking shoes she wore when she went up into Frank's room, sustains Jim Conley.
>
> Monteen Stover, when she tells you that she found nobody in that office, sustains Jim Conley.
>
> The testimony of Boots Rogers, that the elevator box was unlocked, sustains Jim Conley.

His litany completed, Dorsey turned to the jury and in the voice of a man who'd long been awaiting this moment vowed:

> Gentlemen, every act of that defendant proclaims him guilty. Gentlemen, every word of that defendant proclaims him responsible for the death of this little factory girl. Gentlemen, every circumstance in this case proves him guilty of this crime. Extraordinary? Yes, but nevertheless true, just as true as Mary Phagan is dead. She died a noble death, not a blot on her name. She died because she wouldn't yield her virtue to the demands of her superintendent.
>
> Your honor, I have done my duty. And I predict, may it please your honor, that under the law that you give in charge and under the honest opinion of the jury of the evidence produced, there can be but one verdict, and that is: We the jury find the defendant, Leo M. Frank, guilty!

Whereupon the bells of the nearby Church of the Immaculate Conception began to toll twelve, giving the solicitor—whose earlier diversions now made sense—the opportunity to repeat his last word between each succeeding chime: "Guilty! Guilty! Guilty!" Until finally the bells sounded no more.

No sooner had Dorsey returned to his seat than Reuben Arnold, after requesting that the jury be sent out, asked for a mistrial. The motion, which the lawyer had written hastily in pencil and which he now read aloud, was predicated on the many partisan outbursts that had occurred during the course of the proceedings. Starting with a mention of the applause that had greeted Judge Roan's decision of two weeks earlier to allow into evidence Conley's testimony accusing Frank of sexual perversion and ending with a reminder that this very morning the solicitor's arrival had been greeted with cheers, Arnold cited five incidents that he believed had "tended to coerce and intimidate" the jurors, who when they were not in court, he stressed, sat in a room just twenty feet away. "Your honor," declared the lawyer, "the behavior of the spectators throughout this trial has been disgraceful."

Predictably, Dorsey not only opposed Arnold's motion but disputed the facts upon which it was based, asserting that even if there had been displays of emotion, "it is ridiculous to say that they amounted to anything."

At this, Arnold, after recalling to the judge that he had himself witnessed the gallery's conduct, asked him to "take cognizance of these facts and certify to them."

"Of course I heard the cheers," replied Roan, "but whether the jury was influenced, I don't know."

Arnold sought permission to summon several of the deputy sheriffs who'd supervised the jurors over the past month, and presently R. V. DeVere and Charles Huber took the stand. The deputies' testimony, however, was inconclusive. Though DeVere stated that the jurors had heard the applause, he maintained that they did not know which side it favored. As for Huber, he said that he had not learned of Friday evening's demonstration until Saturday, a claim that even as it undermined the defense's point drew snickers from the audience that seemed to affirm it. "Why, your honor," Arnold complained. "You can't keep them quiet now."

In the end, however, Roan overruled the defense's motion, and the jury was returned. The judge's charge was in most ways pro forma. He reminded the twelve men that the law accorded Frank the presumption of innocence. He defined the concept of reasonable doubt. He spoke of the differences between direct and circumstantial evidence. Then he discussed character evidence, informing the jurors that good character was no bar to conviction but emphasizing that "an instance of misconduct shown by the state doesn't mean the defendant is guilty." As to Frank's statement, the judge reminded his audience that the superintendent had not been under oath when he made it. "It is with you as to how much of it you will believe or how little." This said, Roan told the jurors that if they found against Frank, they would have the option of recommending mercy. If they did not so recommend, he added, the court would have no choice but "to sentence the defendant to the extreme penalty." With that, the judge brought down his gavel, whereupon Lucille Frank leaned back in her chair, closed her eyes and clasped her throat as if about to faint. As for her husband, he appeared, as always, unaffected.

The jury began its deliberations at 1:35 P.M. in a chamber two floors above the courtroom. After a month in the fishbowl, the space was relatively isolated, although even here, the men were not free from scrutiny. As it so happened, the sixth story of the nearly completed courthouse offered a perfect vantage on the scene, and a gaggle of reporters had congregated there. Not that they could ascertain much from such a remove. True, they observed that the jurors' first act was to elect Fred Winburn, the railroad freight agent, foreman. And yes, they noticed that early on, the men passed around the bottles containing cabbage samples. But otherwise, they could do little but speculate as to various dispositions.

As the jury got down to work, considerable and significant activity was simultaneously under way in the Thrower Building office of Leonard Roan. There, at the judge's suggestion, representatives of the defense and the state were completing an agreement whereby the presence in the courtroom of both Frank and his lead lawyers would be waived for the reading of the verdict. Roan, conscious of the increasing hostility in Atlanta, believed that in the event of an acquittal, the superintendent and his counsel could well become the targets of violence.

Shortly after this arrangement was finalized—and just an hour and forty-five minutes after the jurors took up the case—the reporters looking on from across the street flashed the news. The panel, following only two ballots, had reached a verdict. Since it would take time for some of the principals to get back downtown, the jury remained out until 4:56 P.M. By then, a crowd of five thousand was packed around the court building. Though mounted policemen rode through the throng, there was no containing the restive and anticipatory air.

For all the commotion outside, the courtroom itself was silent. The space had been cleared of spectators. Thus only Dorsey and Frank Hooper at one table, Rosser's son, Luther Jr. and his partner, Stiles Hopkins, at the other, a few curious lawyers and a delegation of newsmen heard the key exchange.

"Gentlemen, have you reached a verdict?" asked the judge.

"We have, your honor," replied Winburn, at which point the foreman unfolded a sheet of paper and in a trembling voice declared: "We have found the defendant guilty."

No sooner had Winburn spoken than the reporters rushed en masse to an adjacent room and over multiple lines installed for just this purpose began phoning their offices. As they barked into mouthpieces, crowd members clustered at the windows picked up the news and in seconds, observed one journalist, "the cry of guilty took winged flight from lip to lip. It traveled like the rattle of musketry. Then came a combined shout that rose to the sky. Hats went into the air. Women wept and shouted by turns."

The demonstration shook the courtroom—so much so that an overwhelmed Dorsey ceded the task of polling the jury to Roan. "Is that your verdict?" the judge twelve times asked over the noise, and twelve times the reply came back, "Yes." There was no recommendation of mercy, though Roan, mindful of what was occurring outside, announced that he would delay sentencing. Thus it was done, and as John W. Coleman, little Mary's stepfather, shook hands with the jurors, the solicitor made his way toward the door.

Standing on the old city hall steps, Dorsey blinked with astonishment. For blocks in every direction, the streets pulsated with cheering souls, while overhead, windows were crowded with women and children. Reported the *Constitution:*

> The solicitor reached no farther than the sidewalk. While mounted men rode like Cossacks through the human swarm, three muscular men slung Mr. Dorsey on their shoulders and passed him over the heads of the crowd across the street.
>
> With hat raised and tears coursing down his cheeks, the victor in Georgia's most noted criminal battle was tumbled over a shrieking throng that wildly proclaimed its admiration. Few will live to see another such demonstration.

After being deposited at his office, Dorsey grabbed a fistful of belongings, then made his way to a waiting car. To shouted requests from reporters for comment, he would say only, "I feel sorry for his wife and mother." With that, the machine pulled slowly away, the solicitor shaking hands with wellwishers as policemen held open a path. Up Pryor Street into the central business district the vehicle crept, thousands still screaming their approbation and from the skyscrapers ahead a bright fluttering of handkerchiefs.

Across town at the Fulton County Tower, the mood was, of course, different. In fact, the news so shocked a group of Leo Frank's friends—among them Rabbi David Marx, a young lawyer named Samuel Boorstin and Dr.

Benjamin Wildauer, a politically connected dentist—that they called Dr. Howard Rosenberg, then waited in the lobby for the thirty minutes it took the Franks' physician to arrive before mounting the metal steps to the superintendent's cell. The entourage found Leo and Lucille sitting side by side. After Frank rose to greet the men, it fell to Rosenberg to deliver the grim tidings. To which Frank incredulously responded: "My God! Even the jury was influenced by mob law." Lucille, however, could not mask her heartbreak. Noted a reporter who took in the scene: "Mrs. Frank huddled closer to her boyish-looking husband. There was a wild stare in her eyes. She threw her arms about his neck and sobbed bitterly. He stroked her head and pleaded with her to be brave." Following a brief interlude, Rosenberg prevailed upon Lucille to let him drive her home, where her parents and Leo's mother were waiting. Though Lucille refused comment to the newsmen who met her outside, Wildauer soon appeared and issued what would be Frank's one official statement: "I am as innocent today as I was one year ago." Soon thereafter, the Seligs' Negro chauffeur arrived with the convicted man's supper, which he ate with relish. Then he retired.

Many Atlantans behaved as if they hoped the day would never end. Long into the night, people stood on corners discussing the verdict. Others called friends. (Southern Bell executives announced that the volume of phone usage in the city Monday broke records.) And everyone, it seemed, bought extras. All three papers published special editions, but predictably, it was the *Georgian* that outdid itself, printing 131,208 copies, more than triple its pre-Hearst circulation.

Tuesday dawned with Atlanta still besotted from Monday's events. Which was why Judge Roan informed just a few people regarding the time and place of Leo Frank's sentencing. As a consequence, when the superintendent walked into a Thrower Building courtroom at 10:20, the only individuals present were Rosser and Arnold, assistant solicitor Ed Stephens and a handful of reporters. So secretive were the proceedings that Lucille did not learn of them in time to be at her husband's side, meaning that when the judge asked Frank if he had anything to say before hearing his fate pronounced, he could seek solace solely from within. Not that the convicted man appeared at a loss. Looking Roan directly in the eyes, in a clear voice, he declared: "I say now, as I have always said, that I am innocent. Further than that, my case is in the hands of my lawyers."

With that, Roan remarked, "Mr. Frank, I have tried to see that you had a fair trial for the offense for which you were indicted. I have the consciousness of knowing that I have made every effort." Then, using words prescribed by law, the judge proclaimed:

It is ordered and adjudged by the court that on the tenth day of October, 1913, the defendant, Leo M. Frank, shall be executed by the sheriff of Fulton County. That said defendant on that day between 10 o'clock A.M. and 2 o'clock P.M. shall be hanged by the neck until he shall be dead, and may God have mercy on his soul.

In the wake of Frank's sentencing, Reuben Arnold submitted a motion to Roan announcing the defense's intention to seek a new trial, and October 4 was set as the hearing date. Soon thereafter, Frank's lawyers distributed a statement indicating how vehemently they intended to pursue the fight:

> The trial which has just occurred and which has resulted in Mr. Frank's conviction was a farce and not in any way a fair trial.
>
> The temper of the public mind was such that it invaded the courtroom and pervaded the streets and made itself manifest at every turn the jury made and it was just as impossible for this jury to escape the effects of the public feeling as if they had been turned loose and allowed to mingle with the people.
>
> It would have required a jury of stoics, a jury of Spartans, to have withstood this situation.

The defense's allegations would be difficult to prove. Even as Rosser and Arnold were asserting that the men who tried Frank had been influenced by public sentiment, the *Georgian* had an extra on the streets in which an unnamed juror maintained: "The jury heard none of the cheering for Dorsey outside the courtroom at any time. We heard the crowds in the courtroom laugh at times, and we laughed, too, but that had no effect." To the contrary, the anonymous panelist declared, the body based its decision solely on the facts. "Don't think that we had not considered the case fully," he said. "And don't think that there was a man amongst us that wanted to do what we did. Yet, day after day, the pressure grew heavier as the case was put before us. From a slight dread it became an oppression, then a nausea and at last a sickening sense that Frank was the guilty man and we were going to give the world that verdict."

And so the most furiously fought legal battle in Georgia history had ended where it began—in discord and dispute. There was, however, one place in Atlanta where unanimity and harmony reigned. Boomed the *Georgian*'s headline:

JIM CONLEY, THE EBONY CHEVALIER OF CRIME,
IS DARKTOWN'S OWN HERO

In the following text, the paper's James B. Nevin portrayed a Negro community in complete accord. After discussing the general reaction, the reporter gave the last word to a shoe-shine boy with "a smattering of education and an ingratiating manner." Observed this representative black man:

Well, boss, dem niggers down on Decatur Street, dey ain't talking of nothing but Jim Conley. He's the most talked about nigger anywhere, I guess. I hears him complimented on all sides. He done got de best of de smartest of 'um. Nobody can fool er nigger like Jim.

THIRTEEN

Appeals in and out of Court

On or near Labor Day, 1913, barely a week after Leo Frank's conviction, Rabbi David Marx walked into Atlanta's Terminal Station and boarded a train for New York. At forty-one, balding and graying at the temples, the leader of the city's Reform congregation betrayed no evidence of heartache or perturbation. Judging solely by appearances, he was, as always, the cool and aristocratic diplomat who seemed at home in every part of the capital of the New South. In truth, however, the rabbi was distraught. He was also furious, believing that the jury's verdict against Frank could be explained only by a sentiment that he'd heretofore maintained barely existed in Georgia: anti-Semitism.

Marx was not alone in such feelings. Secure and accepted as members of Atlanta's German-Jewish elite had traditionally believed themselves to be, in the days since the trial ended many of them had begun to manifest a deep sense of unease. The initial public display of this unease occurred the night of Frank's conviction when even as the bulk of the city's populace still celebrated, the rabbi's wife drove up to the Fulton County Tower to retrieve her husband and in a tearful voice was heard to tell him: "Oh, please take me away from Atlanta." In light of the fact that Eleanor Marx's father, Abraham Rosenfield, was one of the Temple's cofounders, her remark suggested a wound that went to the core of the Washington Street community. Two mornings hence, the *Macon Telegraph*, indicating again that only the out-of-town press was willing to call attention to the ill will the proceedings had unleashed, confirmed as much, reporting:

> The long case and its bitterness has hurt the city greatly in that it has opened a seemingly impassable chasm between the people of the Jewish race and the Gentiles. It has broken friendships of years, has divided the races, brought about bitterness deeply regretted by all factions. The friends who rallied to the defense of Leo Frank feel that racial prejudice has much to do with the verdict. They are convinced that Frank was not prosecuted but persecuted.

Marx was headed to New York to alert the leaders of American Jewry to Frank's plight, which he believed was commensurate to that of Alfred Dreyfus, the French military officer who, after being convicted of treason in 1894, was shown to have been the victim of an anti-Semitic plot and, following worldwide agitation, pardoned. As the rabbi, in an August 30 letter to a potential convert to the cause, had himself put it:

> I would like to enlist your assistance in what is without doubt an American "Dreyfus" case that has just developed in Atlanta . . . the evidence against Frank is purely prejudice and perjury. The feeling against the Damned Jew is so bitter that the jury was intimidated and feared for their lives, which undoubtedly would have been in danger had any other verdict been rendered.

Marx hoped to see a number of people in the city, but two stood out.

At fifty-five, Adolph S. Ochs, publisher of the *New York Times,* was not only the most powerful figure in American journalism, he was the profession's most powerful Jew. (Moreover, hc was a Southern Jew, reared in Knoxville, Tennessee, who'd founded the *Chattanooga Times,* of which he was still proprietor.) Yet even so, Ochs was loath to involve himself in Jewish issues. "Mr. Ochs is a non-Jewish Jew," noted his trusted editorial assistant Garet Garrett. "He will have nothing to do with any Jewish movement." The most marked instance of this reluctance had occurred during the Dreyfus affair, when the publisher resisted pleas to take the lead in championing the French officer's exoneration. More recently, he had rejected an invitation to join the American Jewish Committee, a group composed of some of the country's most influential Jews. Though Ochs was a sympathetic and, indeed, sentimental soul, his reasoning seemed inarguable. He was determined, in Garrett's words, never to let the *Times* become "a Jewish newspaper." Securing his interest in the matter of Leo Frank was hardly a fait accompli.

The other New Yorker at the top of Marx's list was Louis Marshall, president of the American Jewish Committee. At fifty-six, Marshall was widely regarded as attorney-at-large for the Jewish people. A partner in the firm of Guggenheimer, Untermeyer and Marshall and an expert in constitutional law, he had spent much of the past decade fighting anti-Semitism. In 1905, he'd led a successful battle to open New York's restricted Lake Placid Club to Jewish members. Soon thereafter, he'd conducted a victorious statewide campaign to outlaw discriminatory practices at hotels. And in 1911, he'd spearheaded a triumphant nationwide drive to force the United States to abrogate an international treaty that had been used by hostile Czarist authorities to keep American Jews from freely conducting business in Russia. What made this last accomplishment impressive was the fact that after President William Howard Taft resisted an initially quiet lobbying effort, Marshall, a Republican, enlisted the Democratic presidential aspirant Woodrow Wilson in a public campaign to force the issue. When the pertinent bill came before Congress, it passed by a 300-to-1 vote.

However, Marshall, too, was reluctant to involve himself or his organization in most of the reported incidents of anti-Semitism that crossed his desk. "We are always talking too much about Jews, Jews, Jews, and we are making a Jewish question of almost everything that occurs," he was wont to say. The thing to keep in mind, he often added, was "to avoid the appearance of crying wolf." Thus when asked to initiate action against, say, a production of William Shakespeare's *The Merchant of Venice* on the grounds that the character of Shylock was a prejudicial stereotype, he invariably said no. Only truly just causes—ones rooted in incidents where Jews' rights and freedoms as American citizens appeared to be threatened—received Marshall's attention. He was also quite capable of shying away from anything having to do with Leo Frank.

Since Ochs was at the time vacationing in Europe, Marx was shunted off to one of the *Times*'s assistant editors. After presenting an overview of the Frank case to this underling, the rabbi asked that the paper—which had printed only three brief pieces on the trial—look into the topic and prepare a comprehensive article. The editor agreed to make some inquiries, but following a call to his Atlanta stringer, he went no further. As Garet Garrett would write: "The correspondent . . . reported that there was a lot of anti-Jewish feeling against Frank, and that the worst thing for him that could happen would be for the Jews to rally to him, as Jews."

Marshall's response to Marx's appeal was more encouraging, although if it was a call for action the rabbi wanted, he went away disappointed here as well. The American Jewish Committee president believed that the Frank case met his criteria for involvement, agreeing with Marx that the factory superintendent had not received a fair trial and that anti-Semitism was a factor. By September 5, in fact, Marshall was alerting his highly positioned Jewish friends to what had happened in Atlanta. Frank's conviction, he wrote fellow committee member Dr. Joseph L. Magnes, was a "horrible judicial tragedy." To Irving Lehman, scion of the great merchant-banking family and himself a respected lawyer, he asserted, "The case is almost a second Dreyfus affair." Still, Marshall believed that an all-out campaign would be precipitous and likely damaging to the condemned man's hopes. On September 9, he informed Frank's friend Milton Klein, who had written to second Marx's plea for support, that he preferred to work indirectly:

> It would be unfortunate if anything were done . . . from the standpoint
> of the Jews. Whatever is done must be done as a matter of justice, and any
> action that is taken must emanate from non-Jewish sources.

Exhibiting a keen understanding of the resentment Southerners would
likely feel toward Northern intervention in general and Jewish intervention
in particular, Marshall proposed to work behind the scenes to change Atlantans' thinking. As he wrote Lehman:

> There is only one way of dealing with this matter and that is in a quiet,
> unobtrusive manner to bring influence to bear on the Southern press [to
> create] a wholesome public opinion which will free this unfortunate young
> man from the terrible judgement which rests against him.

It appears to have been no coincidence that in response to these cool
reactions, either Marx or others in Leo Frank's camp chose this moment
to solicit the assistance of a more confrontational Northern Jew. Simon
Wolf, a prominent Washington lawyer who was both president of the capital's chapter of the B'Nai Brith and director of Atlanta's Hebrew Orphans
Home, was not a reticent soul. In mid-September he circulated a letter to
the members of the Union of American Hebrew Congregations counseling
action on Frank's behalf. By the month's end, Jewish publications from
Minnesota to Alabama had taken up the cause. Proclaimed the September
26 issue of Cincinnati's *American Israelite:*

> Frank's religion precluded a fair trial . . . The man was convicted at the
> dictates of a mob, the jury and the judge fearing for their lives.

This development infuriated Louis Marshall. Writing on September 27 to
Adolph Kraus, president of the national B'Nai Brith, the lawyer expressed
his "great regret [at] such articles as that which appeared on the editorial
page of the Israelite . . . They can do no good. They can only accentuate the
mischief." Making the same argument he'd made to Marx, Marshall added
that the best course was to lobby Southern newspapers to mount a homegrown effort for Frank. That way, the anti-Semitism that had arisen in
Atlanta "may not only subside but may be absolutely counteracted and
destroyed."

As Rabbi Marx was making the rounds in New York, Leo Frank's lawyers
in Atlanta were gearing up for the next legal battle. The first order of business was to prepare an amended motion for a new trial, and Luther Rosser

set to work. From Labor Day on, the Grant Building offices of Rosser, Brandon, Slaton & Phillips were a hive of activity. Plainly, the condemned man's counsel would argue that the many demonstrations in support of Hugh Dorsey during the just completed proceedings had intimidated the jurors. They would also contend that Judge Leonard Roan had erred in allowing Jim Conley's sexually explicit testimony to remain in the record. Yet beyond this, little was known. Rosser refused requests for interviews. And Reuben Arnold, having left town for a long-planned vacation, was unavailable for comment.

With months, possibly years, of wrangling ahead (the defense had already announced that if the application for a new trial was denied, it would appeal to the Georgia Supreme Court), Leo Frank now knew that the Fulton County Tower would be his home for the foreseeable future. By early September, he had undertaken the task of redecorating his six-by-eight-foot cell, seeing to it that the floors were polished, the walls scrubbed and two chairs and a table installed. Boomed the *Constitution*'s headline: CELL NOW LIKE LIVING ROOM. Frank also established a physical-fitness regimen. Rising each morning at seven, he would go to a window and breathe deeply while overlooking the sprawl of warehouses that surrounded the jail. Following twenty minutes of exercise with Indian clubs and a set of dumbbells he'd received permission to keep on hand, he showered, donned a robe and sat down to the newspapers. At 8:50, his father-in-law arrived with breakfast, which usually consisted of cantaloupe, rolls and coffee. Presently, Herbert Schiff or Sig Montag dropped by to discuss business matters with Frank, who while no longer in charge of day-to-day operations continued to consult on major decisions. At 1:30, dinner was served, and at 4:00 Lucille appeared, usually staying through supper. Most evenings, friends visited. But on others, Frank sat up alone studying his case, preparing a file of the evidence that he believed established his innocence. Despite his realization that the process would be lengthy, he possessed every confidence that he would not only win a new trial but that he would be exonerated. Noted the *Georgian:* "There is no suggestion of the dejected or broken man condemned to be hanged."

The reason for Frank's optimism became apparent on October 1 when his lawyers, just four days before the hearing date set by Judge Roan, released the amended motion. The document cited 115 reasons why the factory superintendent should be granted a new trial. As the defense saw it, the court never should have admitted Bert Green's chart of the pencil plant, with its colored lines indicating the paths the state maintained Frank had traveled while committing the crime. Nor should it have countenanced Dr. Henry F. Harris's "opinions" as to the hour of Mary Phagan's death. Then there were the questionable allegations of lascivious conduct against the superintendent, not to mention numerous portions of Hugh Dorsey's argument (the references to Lucille's initial failure to visit her husband in prison, for instance). Yet the elements of the motion that generated the most attention had nothing to do with the legality of the evidence but rather with the pretrial dispositions of the individuals who had rendered the verdict. Roared the *Journal*'s page-one headline:

JURORS JOHENNING AND HENSLEE BOTH ATTACKED
They Are Alleged to Have Gone on the Jury Prejudiced.

The motion's charges against shop foreman Marcellus Johenning and buggy salesman Atticus Henslee were almost identically worded. Asserted the first:

Johenning had a fixed opinion that the defendant was guilty prior to, and at, the time he was taken on the jury and was not an impartial juror.

Echoed the other:

Henslee was prejudiced against the defendant when he was selected as a juror, had previously thereto formed and expressed a decided opinion as to the guilt of the defendant and in favor of the state.

To accuse two of the jurors of pretrial bias was a risky tack. In the weeks since the proceedings concluded, Atlanta had elevated the men who convicted Frank to an exalted status. (On a mid-September Saturday, a forty-car motorcade had transported the twelve to an outlying park where along with Dorsey, Judge Roan and the reporters who'd covered the trial, they were treated to a magnificent spread of fried channel catfish, barbecue and Brunswick stew.) Yet the defense had not made the allegations lightly, accompanying the amended motion with a sheaf of supporting affidavits. Advancing the charge of prejudice against Johenning were a coworker named H. C. Lovenhart and his wife and daughter. As the three recalled it, they'd been discussing the Phagan murder with the shop foreman in May when he'd said of Frank, "I know that he's guilty." Advancing the claim against the better traveled Henslee were men from across the state. According to Samuel Aron of Atlanta, two days after the grand jury returned its true bill against Frank, he'd overheard the buggy salesman exclaim to a group at the downtown Elk's Club: "I am glad they indicted the God damn Jew. They ought to take him out and lynch him, and if I get on that jury I'll hang that Jew, sure." Farther afield, Mack Farkas, a livery stable owner in the Southwest Georgia town of Albany who frequently did business with

Henslee, declared that during a meeting shortly before the proceedings began, the buggy salesman had proclaimed, "I believe Frank is guilty."

No sooner had Hugh Dorsey looked over the amended motion and its supporting affidavits than he sought a week's delay of the new trial hearing. To this, Judge Roan readily assented. Following several days of work, Dorsey announced that he'd barely gotten started and asked for another postponement. It, too, was granted, whereupon he packed his files into several valises and along with his assistant, Ed Stephens, boarded a train for the south Georgia town of Valdosta. There, some two hundred miles from the myriad distractions of the city, the solicitor said he would be able to devote himself fully to the task of drafting the arguments with which he hoped to refute the defense's 115 grounds when court convened on the now scheduled date of October 22.

While in Valdosta, Dorsey did more than just prepare for the upcoming hearing. Realizing that he could not let the sensational charges against Johenning and Henslee go unanswered, he spent much of his time on the telephone orchestrating a campaign to present the two jurors as the men most Atlantans believed them to be—fair and courageous citizens whose only interest had been in seeing justice done. Not surprisingly, the first individuals to so declare were Johenning and Henslee themselves. Yet it wasn't just the men under attack who spoke up. The jury foreman, Fred Winburn, was equally vociferous, declaring, "The charges that the jury was prejudiced are untrue. The jurors were all men of honor and integrity." Others among the twelve also raised their voices, none more bluntly than pressman Charles Bosshardt, who asserted: "I say the charges are bosh."

Dorsey's decision to enlist the jurors in defense of the trial's fairness was shrewd. But if he expected Frank's lawyers to retreat, he was mistaken. Three days after Winburn and Bosshardt vouched for Johenning and Henslee, Reuben Arnold, back in town and fresh from his lengthy rest, blasted the two, telling the *Georgian:*

> Henslee's prejudice and that of Johenning alone constitute a situation that is sufficient to form a basis for a new trial. It is unthinkable that a man should be sentenced to death when two of the men were violently biased against him before a word of evidence was heard.

Arnold also revealed that he and Rosser had collected even more affidavits bearing on the individual who was clearly their principal target—Henslee.

Meantime, the defense chose this moment to call attention to a number of other affidavits submitted with the amended motion. These documents all had to do with the climate in which the trial had taken place, some focusing on the already much discussed outbursts of cheering for Dorsey, the rest addressing the heretofore unreported charge that members of the courthouse crowd had spoken with the jurors during breaks in the proceedings, exposing them to influences that by law should have been outside their purview.

Making the claim that the many displays of pro-prosecution sentiment were witnessed by the jurors were thirteen men and women who said they'd been in attendance at the proceedings or nearby during the incidents in question. As John Shipp, Samuel Boorstin and the others told it, when Dorsey received the thunderous ovation from the enormous crowd that had been awaiting him at 6 p.m. on the trial's final Friday, the jurors were only fifty feet away. Boorstin, who had, of course, been with Frank the afternoon of his conviction, added that during the few minutes it took the demonstration to subside, he'd followed the twelve back to their quarters at the Kimball House, where he'd spotted juror F.V.L. Smith taking in the spectacle from an upstairs room. In a similar vein, both Martha Kay and Mrs. A. Shurman contended that from where they sat in the courtroom on the proceedings' last day, they'd watched as the twelve, already in their box, listened to the roar that met Dorsey's arrival.

Making the claim that on several occasions spectators had spoken directly to the jurors were four other Atlantans who said they were either in the courtroom or in the vicinity during the incidents mentioned. According to W. P. Neil, he was sitting adjacent to the jury box near the end of the trial when a man he could not identify "took hold of one of the jurors with one hand, grasped his arm with the other and made a statement to him." Similarly, two witnesses contended that they'd been driving down Pryor Street on the Saturday before the verdict when they'd spotted the twelve out for a constitutional, accompanied not just by an escort of deputies but by five or six hangers-on who engaged the putatively sequestered men in conversation. While these deponents could not attest to what was spoken during the encounters they had observed, this was not the case with Isaac Hazan. As he told it, at midday on the trial's last Friday, he'd watched a group of ten or fifteen toughs accost the jurors on their way to lunch, shouting "that unless they brought in a verdict of guilty, they would kill the whole damn bunch."

Hugh Dorsey's response to the defense's second salvo was of a piece with his response to the first. He remained in Valdosta, while his surrogates in Atlanta disseminated just enough information to keep Rosser and Arnold from stealing all the headlines. Atticus Henslee, for instance, revealed that he had, in fact, publicly expressed a belief in Frank's guilt—but after the verdict was in. At the same time, the solicitor's office announced that Detectives John Starnes and Pat Campbell were back on the job, collecting depositions supporting the integrity of Henslee and Johenning and investigating their detractors. Two hundred miles away or not, Dorsey was evincing his characteristic dexterity.

The hearing on the motion for a new trial convened in the state capitol library at 9 A.M. on a crisp October Wednesday. Physically, the setting could not have been more sedate. Facing walls lined by dusty volumes and warmed by a coal fire on a metal grate, the lawyers—Rosser, Arnold, Herbert Haas and his cousin and fellow attorney, Leonard Haas, for the defense; Dorsey, Stephens and Frank Hooper for the state—sat at opposite ends of a long table, with Judge Roan in the middle. Though a couple of dozen curiosity seekers milled about in an adjacent hall, only reporters and detectives were granted admission. No sooner had the session started than it became clear that the state intended to challenge the wording of each of the motion's 115 grounds. Before the larger issues could be debated, every bit of the language in which they were framed would have to be hashed out.

By midmorning, a rancorous and time-consuming pattern had emerged. Rosser would read a ground aloud, Dorsey would object to its construction, Rosser or Arnold would object to the objection, then Roan would consider the competing merits and make his ruling. Typical was the clash over ground seven, which as originally submitted stated that Frank deserved a new trial because the court had erred in allowing John Black to testify that the factory superintendent employed counsel the Monday following Mary Phagan's murder. The solicitor took issue with the phrase "employed counsel," maintaining that the detective had in actuality said "had counsel." A review of the transcript proved Dorsey correct, whereupon Rosser indicated his displeasure by pounding a newly acquired cane on the floor and snarling: "You'd hang this man on the dotting of an 'i' or the crossing of a 't.'" Replied the solicitor: "You're making a mountain out of a mole hill." Either way, the judge ordered that the ground be reworded.

The summer's hostilities had yet to subside. On this first day, Dorsey spent the hour before lunch and an hour after arguing that the five grounds asserting that the court erred in accepting Conley's sexually charged testimony into evidence had to be rephrased to include a crucial fact that Frank's lawyers had curiously omitted—namely, that the defense did not object to the material until after cross-examining the Negro. Roan concurred. Conversely, Rosser devoted considerable time to fending off the solicitor's attempt to water down a ground contending that the jurors had been intimidated by "the pronounced and continuous applause" that greeted the court's decision to overrule the objection to Conley's explicit testimony. Here, Roan not only found for the defense but voiced his opinion that the twelve must have heard the outburst. Through it all, the tenor of the debate remained ugly. At 6 P.M., when the combatants went home for the evening, the judge had checked off only 42 of the motion's 115 grounds on a list he kept at his fingertips, and the names Johenning and Henslee had not been uttered.

On Thursday, despite the urging of Judge Roan to make haste and cease scrapping, the pace was again slow and tempers short. The day began with Arnold reading grounds 43 through 47 of the motion, each of which dealt with witnesses who'd been used by the state to accuse Frank of acts of immorality. As the defense saw it, the allegations of Irene Jackson and Willie Turner and the examination of Lula Wardlaw were prejudicial, and the court had erred by allowing them into evidence. Dorsey took issue with this view. Because the defense had not objected to the material during the trial, he argued, it could not do so now. True, conceded Arnold, he and Rosser had said nothing at the time, but, he then added, only because their earlier objection to the solicitor's questioning of John Ashley Jones—the insurance agent whose grilling regarding the factory superintendent's alleged fondling of an employee's breasts sparked Rae Frank's attack on Dorsey—served as an omnibus objection to any later such exchanges. After briefly puzzling over the matter, the judge ruled in the defense's favor.

Yet splendidly as things had gone for Rosser and Arnold at the morning session, following lunch the results were more mixed. The lawyers kicked off the afternoon by returning to the topic of the demonstrations that had periodically rocked the courtroom during the trial. But before they could read a single ground, Dorsey, still smarting from Roan's declaration of the day before regarding the outburst that greeted the decision to overrule the defense's objection to Conley's explicit testimony, asserted that the judge had no right to express such sentiments. "I can give my opinion if I wish," replied Roan, apparently putting an end to the matter. However, as Rosser proceeded to read each succeeding ground—one addressing the Friday afternoon demonstration, another the Monday morning display, still another a third incident—the judge again and again ordered that the defense's phrase "which the jury heard" be changed to read "which perhaps the jury could have heard."

When the hearing resumed Friday at 9 A.M., just a few grounds remained to be covered, the first of them involving, at long last, Johenning and Henslee. To these, Dorsey offered no protest, preferring to wait until he could contest the actual substance of the charges. The solicitor was likewise silent regarding several subsequent points. By midmorning, all that was left was a ground concerning the events that had prompted Rosser and Arnold to forfeit their client's presence at the reading of the verdict. To this, Dorsey did take exception, declaring that the lawyers had agreed to the arrangement at the time of its proposal and therefore lacked the right to revisit it. Rosser countered that the ferocity of the crowds was so great that they'd been forced into the decision. Moreover, the lawyer added that the pandemonium greeting the guilty verdict had denied Frank his ultimate safeguard—a quiet polling of the jurors. As proof of how bad the climate was, Rosser cited Roan's decision on the trial's final Saturday to allow the solicitor to halt his argument. In the process, the lawyer not only confirmed the report that the action had been taken due to fear of violence, but shed light on a piece of information that explained why Atlanta's newspapers had said nothing—the editors of the *Constitution,* the *Journal* and the *Georgian* had themselves secretly urged the judge to bring down the gavel. Confronted by these facts, Dorsey shrugged his shoulders, and Roan ended the session by accepting the concluding ground as written.

In theory, the presentation of the two sides' supporting documents—the task that would consume most of Friday afternoon and the final step before the commencement of formal arguments—did not offer much promise of headline-making revelations. And as Rosser and Arnold alternated in reciting the defense's affidavits, all of which had been dissected in the press during the past month, the low expectations seemed more than warranted. Yet no sooner had Frank's lawyers wrapped up and Dorsey begun to speak than pulses quickened, for the solicitor started off by dropping a bombshell. According to the statement of jury foreman Fred Winburn, not only was the embattled Atticus H. Henslee not biased against Frank, he had been the panel's lone holdout against conviction. In a quietly confident voice meant to underscore the significance of the jury foreman's disclosure, Dorsey read:

> I did not know how A. H. Henslee stood on the issue until after the first ballot had been taken; then said Henslee made a talk and stated that he had cast a doubtful ballot; there was one ballot marked "doubtful"; he explained to the jury why he cast this doubtful ballot, and submitted some suggestions with reference to the evidence. Up to that time, so far as I know, said Henslee had not intimated or expressed any opinion whatsoever with reference to any feature of the case.

The import of Winburn's affidavit was instantly apparent, and Dorsey followed it with nearly verbatim pronouncements from the other jurors—

to a soul, they seconded their foreman's assertion that had it not been for Henslee, they would have convicted Frank on the initial ballot. The clincher, however, was an affidavit from the buggy salesman himself. In the same steady tone with which he'd put forward the previous statements, the solicitor read:

> As illustrating the attitude which I occupied in this case, I will say that when it came time to vote, I cast a doubtful ballot. I did this on the first ballot because of the unanimity of opinion that Frank was guilty, as expressed by those jurors who discussed it after the court's charge and prior to the ballot, and for the purpose of forcing a full and free discussion of the case before rendering a verdict, as we understood it might consign Frank to his death. When on the second and last ballot a unanimous verdict of "Guilty" was rendered, I—in common with each and every other man on the jury—wept.

In the matter of a few moments, Dorsey had called into question one of the defense's central premises. As the solicitor continued to read from Henslee's statement, he went even further. According to the buggy salesman, contrary to the allegations of Samuel Aron, he'd never said to a group at the Atlanta Elks Club: "I'm glad they indicted the God damned Jew." Nor would he have. "The club has among its members a large number of Jewish people, many of whom are my friends." Henslee's response to Mack Farkas's assertion was equally convincing. Not only did he deny having seen the Albany livery stable proprietor in the weeks before the proceedings, he said that when he did call following Frank's conviction, he refrained from discussing the case "because the said Mack Farkas and the said Leo M. Frank were of the same religion and [I] did not want to hurt his feelings."

Having thus done what he could to rehabilitate Henslee, Dorsey next tried to rehabilitate Marcellus Johenning. First, the solicitor read affidavits from Winburn, Townsend and the others, all of whom swore that at no time during the trial did their fellow juror "express himself in a way to indicate that he was in the least bit prejudiced against Leo M. Frank." Then came the predictable statement from Johenning himself, in which he not only denied having felt or expressed any prejudice against the factory superintendent but pointed out that the Lovenharts were "of the same race and religion of Leo M. Frank."

While Johenning's assertions lacked the dramatic certitude of Henslee's, they effectively played upon the widely held view that Atlanta's Jews had blindly taken up Frank's cause. On their strength, Dorsey switched gears, introducing a number of statements to refute Rosser and Arnold's claim that the trial's partisan crowds had terrorized the jury into its verdict. The solicitor began by reading affidavits from each of the twelve men at the heart of the debate. Typical was the statement of the hardware store salesman Monroe S. Woodward, who, Dorsey related, had deposed:

> I did not at any time, while a juror, hear any applause except such as occurred in open court, and which was heard by the judge and attorneys in the case; I did not know there had been any cheering of anybody connected with the case at any time or that there had been any cheering in any way growing out of or connected with the Frank case, until after the verdict was rendered, and I was told about said incidents. The jury left the courtroom before the judge, lawyers and audience were permitted to leave, and there was never any applause or cheering inside of the court or outside of the court within my knowledge while the case was being considered.

A general disavowal thereby issued, the solicitor tendered Woodward's dismissals of a number of the defense's specific claims regarding the spectators' impact on the jury. For starters, the salesman disputed the charge that a group of hangers-on had strolled alongside the twelve during their constitutional on the trial's final Saturday. Then he denied the allegation that someone in the gallery had shaken hands with and spoken to one of the jurors. Finally, he denied the contention that the hurrahs following the verdict had influenced the polling of the jury.

Once he'd finished with the affidavits of Woodward and the others, Dorsey introduced supporting statements from court officials. Echoing the view that the jurors were not compromised by any of the trial's commotions or by contact with crowd members were the deputy in charge of security during the proceedings, the bailiffs who'd guarded the panel and the clerk of the superior court. These men were also unanimous in their dismissal of several of the defense's related allegations, most significantly Isaac Hazan's charge that rowdies had threatened the jurors with violence if they did not vote to convict.

After Dorsey read a last batch of affidavits, each of them attacking the integrity of one of the defense's standard-bearers and all undoubtedly obtained by Detectives Starnes and Campbell, Reuben Arnold took the floor. The lawyer began his argument by speaking directly to Judge Roan:

> It takes thirteen jurors to murder a man in cold blood. So I feel I am not only justified but required, by the scope of your honor's authority and duty and the tremendous responsibility that rests upon you, to argue to the court the facts of this unusual case.

This was a bold statement. Instead of addressing the points put forth in the motion, Arnold intended to readdress the evidence, sidestepping the body that had found against his client. As he saw it, he had no choice. Declared the lawyer: A religious bias "that has reflected no credit for two thousand years on the race to which your honor and I belong" infiltrated the courtroom, affecting the panel's judgment. The result:

> Argument was lost upon that jury. There they sat, huddled like twelve sheep in the shambles. Talk to me about those jurors not having been influenced by such surroundings. They may not know they were. Nor did the rabbit that ran through the briar patch know which briar scratched and which did not.

That said, Arnold plunged into the task of convincing his audience of one. His first topic — Jim Conley. Asked the lawyer:

> Was ever a case heard of before where the only witness on whose testimony the conviction rested was a party to the crime both before it was committed, by watching, and after it was committed, by helping to conceal the body; was a criminal of the lowest type and as absolutely devoid of conscience as a man-eating tiger; one who lied in writing four different times, and who never confessed anything about the crime until the evidence was discovered on him that he had written the notes that accompanied the body; who admitted he lied many times in his affidavits; and where after he made his last affidavit, the story that he brought into court was so unlike it that you could hardly recognize any points of similarity?

Arnold then reiterated the defense's theories regarding the origination of Conley's tale. The Negro, he told Roan, had heard "the slanders uttered against Frank" during the days following Mary Phagan's murder. After Conley's connection to the notes was subsequently discovered, "he saw his own life trembling in the balance and was compelled to say someone else was the real author and he named Frank." His initial statement, however, was rife with improbabilities. "Left alone," Mister Rube asserted, "the negro spread out over the whole territory of asininity." Which was why the detectives lent a hand. "They took his story like you would take a rough piece of timber and fashioned it over with the power of machinery." And it wasn't just the investigators who were involved. Turning to face Dorsey, Arnold accused the solicitor of interjecting the "perversion evidence" into the trial "merely to prejudice the jury." Then, turning back to the judge, he brought Friday's session to a scalding close:

If Leo Frank is hanged, I'd rather be dead and rotting in my grave than
in Hugh Dorsey's place. His conscience will drive him crazy, distracted and
to God only knows what ends. And it will be no less than his just deserts.

Saturday, Arnold directed Roan's attention to weaknesses in the state's
circumstantial evidence. First, he dismissed the incriminating inferences
Dorsey had drawn from Frank's April 26 letter to his uncle, insisting that
such expressions as "it's too short a time since you left for anything startling
to have developed" were commonplace. Then he repeated the defense's
chronology of the murder day, reasserting that Mary Phagan did not reach
the pencil factory until 12:10 P.M. — five minutes after Monteen Stover
claimed to have entered the superintendent's office and discovered it empty.
"Your honor," the lawyer insisted, "the state's case falls to the ground here.
Jim Conley says Mary Phagan came in before Monteen Stover came in."
And there were other discrepancies. After reminding the judge that the
Negro maintained it was 12:56 when Frank asked him to move the body,
Arnold posed a tough question: If, as several experts swore, the job and the
subsequent note writing took over thirty minutes, then how could such witnesses as Helen Kerns and Mrs. Albert Levy have seen Frank standing on a
downtown corner at 1:10 and exiting a streetcar near his house at 1:20?
There was only one answer: Frank, as he'd stated, had departed the building
at 1:00, unaware that a crime had been committed. "Your honor," declared
the lawyer, "this is not a case of believing the defendant to be innocent; we
are demonstrating his innocence."

Arnold next raised the topic of Frank's character. After once again praising the "upright and honorable" men and women whom he and Rosser had
put on the stand to vouch for the superintendent, he attacked the former
factory employees Dorsey had called to rebut such praise. Dismissing Irene
Jackson and the others as members of "the discharged employee class," he
told Roan: "Class hatred was played on here." Which was why, he added,
several of the state's witnesses had tried to link the plant superintendent
sexually with forelady Rebecca Carson. "Those little girls had been discharged by Miss Carson and glad to say anything against her." Was it any
wonder, the lawyer then asked, that he and Rosser had not cross-examined
them? "These girls could have been loaded with five thousand slanders.
That was what was done with Jim Conley. Every question we asked on that
line would have been used before that gaping mob against us."

Arnold next fired several salvos at the state's evidence suggesting a history of improprieties on Frank's part. Regarding Conley's testimony that he
had served as a lookout over a period of several months while the superintendent conducted liaisons with girls in his office, the lawyer was incredu-

lous. "That 'watching' story is preposterous. What good could Conley have done? What white man could this negro have kept out anyhow? But to bolster up their theory, some reason had to be given why Conley and Frank were coming in contact in a transaction that would ordinarily admit no confidants." Then there was the individual the solicitor had put on the stand to lend credence to Conley's allegations. With evident loathing, Frank's co-counsel spat: "Dalton! In this case they seem to have seined the lowest strata of society for the ugliest, dirtiest reptiles that move about in the ooze of the bottom."

Thus far, Arnold had confined himself to matters that he and Rosser had covered at least in part during their closing arguments at the trial, but he now steered Roan to a subject that the duo had unaccountably avoided—the murder notes. "These notes," he said, "are negro notes from beginning to end. They are idiotic and ridiculous and inconceivable to the intelligent brain." The lawyer then ticked off several particulars that he believed laid the missives' authorship at Conley's feet. For openers, he asserted that a phrase in the note jotted on the pencil company order blank indicated that Mary Phagan, just as the defense had maintained, had been murdered in the factory lobby: "This note says, 'He pushed me down that hole.' There is no hole she could have been pushed down in the metal room, but there are two holes on the ground floor at the bottom of the steps. One is the elevator shaft, the other is the trap door down which the ladder leads. Conley, knowing that he pushed the girl down one of these holes, unconsciously brings this fact out in the note." Then there was the line in the other note declaring that "a long tall black negro did this by hisself." Though the solicitor had maintained that the phrase fingered Frank in attempting to hide that two men were involved in the crime, Arnold believed that in actuality it reflected Conley's attempt to lay the murder at the feet of a slender Negro who had heretofore been unmentioned in the case, a plant boiler operator—"the negro hire down here"—named William Nolle. Finally, there was the fact that the notes existed at all, which to Arnold's thinking was incompatible with Conley's statement that the original plan had been to burn the body. "Conley," the lawyer argued, "saw that he must come up with an explanation for the notes. So he says they were written so that if he never came back to burn the body they would explain the killing. Yet Frank had no reason to believe the negro would not come back. Was ever an explanation more preposterous?"

Arnold's dissection of the notes, while long overdue, was cogent and effective. But his comments on the topic with which he concluded Saturday's session—the defense's failure to place William H. Mincey on the stand—were less so. Though he explained the initial enthusiasm those in Frank's camp felt for the insurance salesman ("Mincey claimed that Conley made to him a certain statement") and justified Rosser's grilling of Conley regarding the salesman ("It was our duty"), as to why the much anticipated witness was never called, he could say only:

> Mincey's tale may have been true, but it did not impress us as evidence that was probable and reasonable, and rather than burden our case with anything doubtful, we decided against putting him up.

Monday morning, after having spoken for the better part of three days, Arnold ended his argument where he had begun it. Anti-Semitism, he again asserted, offered the sole plausible rationale for the zeal with which the police had pursued Frank and the hostility that had surrounded the trial. Dorsey, he once more proclaimed, had fed "the poison of prejudice to those jaybirds in the jury box," one of whom—and here the lawyer made his lone reference to anything contained in the motion actually before the court— was Atticus H. Henslee. All of it, he repeated, had blinded the twelve to the truth: "The murderer of Mary Phagan was Jim Conley, a perpetual law-breaker who has a law-breaking race back of him." Having so stated, Arnold turned to Roan and urgently implored:

> If your honor denies this motion, so far as the facts are concerned, this case is forever at rest. The Supreme Court has no jurisdiction over questions of fact where the witnesses are in conflict. It takes errors of law for that court to interfere. Your honor alone has the duty and responsibility of approving this verdict or setting it aside.

Not surprisingly, Frank partisans took great heart from Arnold's oratory, anticipating not only a favorable ruling but, for the resulting rehearing of the case, a change of venue to the presumably less hostile port city of Savannah. Speculated the *Constitution*'s front-page headline: NEXT TRIAL MAY BE HELD IN CHATHAM COUNTY. Yet even as such hopeful prospects were being bandied about, back in the capitol library the state's lawyers were launching into their speeches, and from the start it was plain that they regarded Arnold's argument as beside the point. The murder notes' provenance, Jim Conley's veracity—the jury had already ruled on these matters. As Hugh Dorsey and Frank Hooper saw it, the sole issues at stake were those that had been raised in the amended motion.

As at the trial, Hooper spoke first, his primary task once again to pave the way for Dorsey. Beginning shortly after Monday's lunch break, the solicitor's co-counsel cast doubt on what the state viewed as the motion's most vexing ground—the allegations of prejudice against Henslee. Terming the charges "improbable and ridiculous," Hooper denounced the individu-

als who'd given the defense supporting affidavits, accusing them at best of
being mistaken, at worst of lying.

Following Hooper's brief remarks, Dorsey rose to his feet, but with the
cool autumn dusk already descending, he had time only to convey a hint of
what was to come, proclaiming:

> If the verdict of guilty against Leo Frank is set aside upon such trivial
> grounds as the convicted man's lawyers recite in their motion, it will justify
> very largely the contempt in which people are beginning to hold their
> courts and the administration of their laws.

Tuesday morning, Dorsey embarked on his presentation in earnest, beginning, predictably enough, with the subject of Henslee. He dismissed the
accusations leveled against the juror, then declared that even if he had
made the comments attributed to him, they did not constitute evidence
of pretrial prejudice. Rather, Henslee had merely expressed his opinion,
which, insisted the solicitor, was his right.

Till this point, Dorsey had maintained a conversational tone, but as he
took up his next topic—Arnold's allegations regarding the purported anti-
Semitism that had permeated the proceedings—he grew indignant:

> The people were not aroused against Leo M. Frank because he is a Jew
> but because he is a criminal of the worst type. In the name of the Gentiles
> of Atlanta, I declare that when the counsel for the defense charges the jury
> with bias and charges Atlantans with intimidating the jury with a display of
> mob spirit, they are slandering the citizenship of the entire community.

That said, Dorsey conceded that "the people in the streets did holler for
me." By his lights, however, the outbursts were meaningless. "The counsel
for the defense has chosen to warp them."

In the wake of his comments on the trial's atmospherics, Dorsey commenced his principal response to Arnold's argument. For three days, he
said, Frank's co-counsel had "ranged far and wide." He was "eloquent
tongued" and "impressively trembling." But none of it was relevant. "As I
understand it," the solicitor reminded Roan, "the only matters on which
your honor is to pass are the question of bias on the part of the jurors, the
question of cheering and demonstrations, questions of law and the question
of Conley's evidence in respect to the defendant's moral conduct."

With that, Dorsey cited a number of precedents upholding the admissibility of Conley's controversial testimony. Then he turned to Roan and by
way of ending declared:

Your honor said at the close of the trial that you had endeavored to see that Frank was given a fair and impartial trial. Either that statement meant everything or nothing.

Late Tuesday, Luther Rosser inaugurated the hearing's concluding argument by reemphasizing his belief in Frank's innocence, telling Roan, "As God is in the heavens above, I believe that in yonder cell rests an innocent man."

Wednesday, Rosser came on even stronger, taking violent issue with Dorsey's claim that in condemning the throngs congregating in the streets during the trial, Arnold had defamed all of Georgia:

What does Mr. Dorsey mean by the charge that Mr. Arnold criticized the whole state? Does he mean that those who crowded around the courthouse crying for blood are the people he so obligingly serves? If they are the people, thank God I do not serve them. They were there deliberately to scream with delight because the blood of a human being was about to be shed.

Though characteristic of Rosser, such talk was more than bombast. Realizing Dorsey, by ducking Arnold's sorties against the state's evidence, had undercut that line of attack, Frank's lead counsel was mounting a last-ditch campaign to highlight the amended motion's most compelling particulars. Accordingly, Rosser reviewed the allegations of pretrial bias against Johenning. He then revisited the affidavits involving Henslee. Which left one last ground — the solicitor's decision to elicit Conley's testimony accusing Frank of perversion. Turning to Dorsey, Rosser charged:

You might as well have put the brand of Cain upon Frank's forehead as to have introduced that revolting and maliciously false testimony. You destroyed his life the instant you brought that in. There is no doubt about it. When Conley poured out his filthy tale, there was left in the mind of the jurors no room for any thought that Frank might be innocent of murder. It damned him instantly.

Turning back to Roan, the lawyer brought his oration to a close:

Dismiss from your mind, your honor, the anarchy that the solicitor general threatens if another trial is granted. I dispute, your honor, that a new trial would be a blow to the judiciary. It will instead preserve justice, for there will come a time when the people will wonder how such things could have taken place as occurred in the trial of this man.

By 9 A.M. Friday, Judge Roan's Thrower Building chambers were packed to overflowing. The familiar players—Dorsey, Hooper, Arnold and Rosser—sat up front, while an army of reporters, several members of the Selig family and as many of the curious as the space allowed stood along the walls. After spending Thursday in deliberation, Roan had reached his decision, and the suspense, noted the *Georgian,* "was greater than the time last August when the crowd was awaiting the verdict against Frank." Yet unlike that hot afternoon, on this last day of October the mood was sober. Observed Hearst's man: "Impressed by the portentousness of the occasion, the people in the room looked on in silence and a certain dread expectancy."

For an hour, the tension mounted as Roan reviewed the motion, assuring himself that its grounds had been reconciled and affixing his signature where required. Then, at 10:04, with a slight tremor in his voice, the judge began to speak:

> Gentlemen, I have thought about this case more than any other I have ever tried. I am not certain of this man's guilt. With all the thought I have put on this case, I am not thoroughly convinced that Frank is guilty or innocent.

In the end, though, Roan's misgivings were not at issue here, for the law—as Hooper and Dorsey had contended—was clear, and it was the law that would prevail. Thus the judge concluded:

> But I do not have to be convinced. The jury was convinced. There is no room to doubt that. I feel it is my duty to order that the motion for a new trial be overruled.

The immediate reaction by the members of Frank's legal team was one of bitter disappointment. Within a few seconds, however, Rosser had recovered sufficiently to confirm that the defense would appeal and to insist that the judge's stunning admission of uncertainty be included in the Bill of Exceptions that would carry the case to the Supreme Court of Georgia. To this, Dorsey furiously objected. Yet before the dispute could escalate, Roan ended it by simply directing that his remarks go into the record. Which meant that terrible as the defeat that Frank had suffered was, the high court, whose winter term was slated to begin in mid-December, would have to take into account the trial judge's pronouncement that he entertained doubts as to the condemned man's guilt.

The debate regarding Roan's extraordinary statement began almost instantaneously. Proclaimed the *Georgian:* "Judge Roan has put himself at the head of that group of men and women who only ask for fair play." Out in the state, however, the consensus was less favorable. "Judge Roan displayed very bad taste and less judgment," declared one rural weekly. Asserted another: "It was none of Roan's business to be convinced of Frank's guilt."

There were equally heated discussions in legal circles regarding whether Roan's remarks would influence the Supreme Court's thinking. Though no one from either side commented publicly, privately lawyers in the defense camp believed that the judge had guaranteed the appeal's success. In fact, even as Rabbi Marx and Leonard Haas were informing Frank of Roan's decision (the condemned man took the news stoically, although Lucille, who was with him at the Tower, once more burst into tears), Herbert Haas was writing Louis Marshall:

> Our Supreme Court has held more than once that it will reverse the judgment of the lower court declining a motion for a new trial where, in the bill of exceptions, it is certified that the presiding judge himself is in doubt as to the guilt of the defendant.

On the evening of Saturday, November 8, exactly a week and a day after Leo Frank's motion for a new trial was rejected, a group of the nation's most powerful and best-known Jewish leaders filed into the Trustees Room of New York's ornate Temple Emanu-El, the city's preeminent Reform synagogue. The occasion was the monthly meeting of the executive committee of the American Jewish Committee, Louis Marshall presiding. Among those present were the Hebraic scholar and writer Cyrus Adler, United Jewish Charities president Cyrus L. Sulzberger and Chicago judge Joseph L. Mack, one of two Jews on the board of Harvard University. But by far the most commanding figure was Jacob H. Schiff, managing partner of the merchant banking house of Kuhn, Loeb and Company and the sole American financier acknowledged by J. Pierpont Morgan as a peer.

The topic that would dominate the committee's discussion, as the recording secretary delicately put it, was "the case of Leo M. Frank, the young man who was recently convicted of murder in Atlanta." At issue was whether the group, in the wake of the factory superintendent's latest setback, should enter the fray, and the members—despite unanimity as to the merits of the matter—were split regarding tactics. Arguing in favor of open involvement was Schiff. Imperious in his frock coat and white tie and animated by an abiding concern with social justice for his coreligionists, the banker wanted to start a public fund. (Frank's defense had thus far cost $50,000—most of it coming from his uncle Moses, who'd recently expressed a reluctance to keep spending.) Taking the other view, not surprisingly, was

Marshall. "It would be most unfortunate if our organization were to be considered championing the causes of Jews who are convicted of crimes," he explained. Such a position was, of course, consistent with Marshall's initial stance, yet it sprang from more than adherence to principle. A backlash against Jewish support for Frank had begun to manifest itself—and not just in Georgia.

JEWS FIGHT TO SAVE LEO FRANK, declared the headline atop the lengthy recapitulation of the case that dominated the *New York Sun*'s October 12 editions. The murder of Mary Phagan, the factory superintendent's arrest, the trial—all were evenhandedly presented. But when the piece, the first major account to run in the Northern press, raised the question of whether Frank's Jewishness had played a role in the outcome, it expressed doubt, noting: "Atlanta is probably freer of the Juden-hetze spirit than any city in the South." This was fair comment. What followed, however, was worrisome:

> Prejudice did finally develop against Frank and also against the Jews. But Frank's friends were responsible for this anti-Semitic spirit.
>
> Some Jews were credited with saying that even if Frank did kill Mary Phagan she was nothing but a factory girl.
>
> Such remarks as these soon caused a decided anti-Semitic feeling and it continued to grow during the trial of Frank. The feeling was increased when Frank's mother, who came here from Brooklyn to attend her son's trial, denounced Mr. Dorsey in the courtroom as "You Christian dog."
>
> The anti-Semitic feeling was the natural result of the belief that the Jews had banded to free Frank, innocent or guilty. The supposed solidarity of the Jews for Frank, even if he was guilty, caused a Gentile solidarity against him.

The choice facing the American Jewish Committee's executive committee was a stark one. To campaign publicly for Frank's exoneration would be to risk further charges of Jewish interference. Conversely, to do nothing would be to leave the factory superintendent without assistance from an organization whose purpose was to combat the very anti-Semitism that appeared to have been involved here. In the end, however, there was a third way, and it is what prevailed. Though the group closed the session by "resolving to take no action with respect to the Frank case," from this night forth, its members would work, just as Marshall had hoped, behind the scenes. The goal: to build a nationwide coalition of influential Jews who, whatever the decision by the Supreme Court of Georgia, could raise money for and shape opinion during the protracted fight that was sure to follow.

From a financial standpoint, the most important Northern Jew to take up Frank's cause in the wake of the November meeting at Temple Emanu-El was Albert D. Lasker. The Chicago-based advertising magnate's Lord & Thomas agency (predecessor to Foot, Cone & Belding) handled accounts ranging from Anheuser-Busch to Goodyear tires. Exceptionally innovative (Lasker essentially invented the idea of orange juice, which prior to his groundbreaking campaign for Sunkist oranges was a novelty item), with a knack for writing catchy copy ("The Grains that ARE SHOT FROM GUNS," boomed Lasker's slogan for Quaker Oats), Lord & Thomas was an industry pacemaker. Its billings for 1912 totaled $6 million.

As sole owner of the agency, the 33-year-old Lasker had built a fortune that enabled him to commission an enormous mansion on the grounds of Chicago's suburban Lake Shore Country Club, a center of Jewish social life. Yet Lasker was a restless soul. He also possessed a strong sense of his Judaic heritage. Though Texas-reared (his father was a Confederate veteran), he identified with a German uncle who as a member of the Reichstag during the nineteenth century was a vocal early opponent of the prejudicial treatment of Jews. Noted the advertising baron's biographer: "He detested anti-Semitism."

In late autumn, Lasker offered to do what he could to assist Frank. Quietly, he contributed $1,000 and arranged for donations in equal amounts from his father and from his close friend and fellow Lake Shore member Julius Rosenwald, the chairman of Sears Roebuck & Company. In mid-December, Leo Frank wrote Lasker, offering not just his gratitude but boldly expressing his faith in the battle's ultimate outcome:

> I thank you and your father, as well as Mr. Rosenwald, for the help you have given my cause.
>
> My attorneys and I feel confident that the Supreme Court will order a new trial on the showing of errors committed by the court below, and that this victory will be but the inception of a long line of successes which ultimately will spell my complete and acknowledged vindication.

During this same period, Adolph Ochs, responding to the appeals of Marshall, Lasker and Rabbi Marx—who upon making a second trip to Manhattan got in to see the publisher—committed the *New York Times* to Frank's cause. As Garet Garrett put it: "When Mr. O. returned from Europe, the same Georgia people convinced him of Frank's innocence." Not that Ochs was prepared to order up headlines. For all involved, there were too many risks. However, if and when the calculus changed, he and his great newspaper stood ready.

Shortly after 9 A.M. on Monday, December 15, Reuben Arnold rose to his feet in the state capitol chambers of the Georgia Supreme Court and initiated yet another round of oral arguments. "Your honors would not believe that such inconsequential and irrelevant evidence could be used to damn a defendant," he told the six-judge panel, repeating the defense's assertion that the case against Leo Frank was an unconvincing hodgepodge. Hugh Dorsey, of course, took the opposite view, maintaining that the evidence was strong and that the trial had been fair. Declared the solicitor: "If there were errors, and I doubt there were, they were minor." Luther Rosser reemphasized the contention that Jim Conley's sexually explicit testimony was inadmissible. "The jury may have thought they were writing 'guilty of murder,' " he roared, "but your honors, what they wrote in reality was 'guilty of perversion.' " The lawyers went on like this for the better part of two days, but when all was said and done, they had shed little light on the issues under consideration. "There was nothing much gained by the superabundance of eloquence released before the high court," observed the *Georgian*'s James B. Nevin. "Neither side exactly festooned itself with glory." In part, such reviews stemmed from the fact that Arnold and the others were talked out. More to the point, however, was an awareness that the moment for rhetoric had passed. As Nevin noted: "The court will proceed to its findings upon the written record and not otherwise."

The stack of documents that Georgia's Supreme Court justices—Samuel C. Atkinson, Marcus Beck, Beverly Evans, Joseph Henry Lumpkin, M. Warner Hill, and the chief, William D. Fish—would review in reaching their decision included the defense's Bill of Exceptions, the state's Brief of Defendant in Error, and the Brief of Evidence, a 600-page digest of the trial testimony approved by both camps.

For the most part, the Bill of Exceptions was simply a leaner version (103 instead of 115 grounds) of the amended motion. Here again were the charges of bias against Henslee and Johenning and the allegations that the outbursts during the trial had influenced the jury. Here again was a critique of Dorsey's closing argument. And here again was the assault on Conley's controversial testimony. There was, however, a critical new element, and it not surprisingly involved Judge Roan's admission of uncertainty as to Frank's guilt. "The words of his judgment betray on his part a mind wholly inconsistent with the settled conviction which a trial judge ought to possess in denying a motion for a new trial," the document averred. "From timidity or from misapprehension as to the law," Roan had "failed to exercise that discretion which it is his solemn duty to exercise." What he had done, though, was to articulate his misgivings, and according to precedents in such cases, the higher court "has repeatedly reversed the court below."

The Brief of Defendant in Error opened by taking vigorous issue with Rosser and Arnold's thesis that Judge Roan's expression of doubt provided sufficient reason for granting Frank a new trial. "It is not the office or function of a Bill of Exceptions to carry the views of the judge," the document declared, citing precedents of its own. "We submit that it would be as dangerous to permit a judge to impeach the integrity of his official finding after the judgment is concluded as it would be to permit the jury, after having been discharged, to impeach its own verdict." There followed a flurry of similarly sharp responses to the charges of bias against Henslee and Johenning, the claims that the courtroom demonstrations had influenced the jury and the allegation that Dorsey's argument had frequently strayed out of bounds. Trenchantly worded as these assertions were, those upholding the admissibility of Conley's explicit testimony were more trenchant still. First, the brief held that the Negro's charges were vital to an understanding of Mary Phagan's murder, stating: "Our contention in this case is that Frank was prompted to assail this girl because of his lasciviousness." And it wasn't ordinary lasciviousness. In an effort to prove that perverse sex crimes were the province of "a man of intelligence" (as opposed to blacks), the brief quoted from a standard text on deviancy, Dr. Richard Von Krafft-Ebing's *Psychopathia Sexualis*. To wit: "It is shown by the history of Babylon and Nineveh and also by the mysteries of life in modern capitals that abnormality of the sexual functions proves to be frequent in civilized races."

Over Christmas and on through the first weeks of the new year, Georgia's Supreme Court justices studied the two sides' conflicting contentions. On January 7, Frank's lawyers submitted a Reply Brief for Plaintiff in Error that attempted to rebut much of what the state had asserted, particularly its claims regarding Roan's publicly stated misgivings and Conley's sexual allegations. Though Dorsey chose not to respond to this latest salvo, the judges reacted as well they might, postponing any ruling for a month.

During the cold, short days of Atlanta's cold, short winter, the Supreme Court deliberated and the opposing camps waited until finally, at 11 A.M. on February 17, the judges issued a 142-page decision denying Frank's appeal by a four-to-two vote. Writing for the majority, Justice Atkinson dismissed the charges of prejudice against Henslee and Johenning, contending that "unless it appears there has been abuse of discretion," the matter rested with the trial judge. Similarly, the court found that the various outbursts punctuating the proceedings did not impugn their fairness. "The general rule," Atkinson asserted, "is that the conduct of spectators will not be ground for a reversal of judgment, unless a ruling upon such conduct is invoked from the trial judge at the time it occurs." As for Conley's explicit testimony, the majority ruled that it was "material and relevant" in that it "tended to show a practice, plan or scheme on the part of the accused," adding pointedly:

> From the condition of the body it might have been inferred that the person who did the killing sought to have a sexual relation, natural or unnatural, with the deceased . . . Conley said that the accused said, "I ain't built like other men." It was relevant to explain the expression above quoted to show previous transactions of the accused, known to him and to witness, which indicated that his conduct in sexual matters differed from that of other men.

Which left Roan's statement of doubt. Wrote Atkinson: "This court will not interfere because of the trial judge's oral expression as to his opinion. His legal judgment expressed in overruling the motion will control."

The news that he had been dealt yet another setback reached Frank shortly before noon in what had become the usual way—Rabbi Marx carried it to his cell at the Tower.

In a statement relayed to the press by Marx early in the afternoon, Frank expressed shock that his appeal had been denied. He was joined in this reaction by Rosser and Arnold, who, though they took hope from the dissent by Chief Justice Fish and Marcus Beck (the two wrote that Conley's allegations of sexual impropriety were "calculated to prejudice the defendant in the minds of the jurors and thereby deprive him of a fair trial"), were uncertain how to proceed. Reported the *Constitution:* "No fixed plans have been made by Frank's attorneys for further attack."

Meantime, Jim Conley, who was in the Tower awaiting trial as an accessory after the fact to murder, told the press: "I knew how it would be, and Mr. Frank knew it, too." Yes sir, he added, "the 'Ole Marster' up in heaven was looking down."

FOURTEEN

Brightness Visible

A s Leo Frank sat in his cell in the Fulton County Tower during the first week of March 1914, he found himself often thinking of the Swiss Alps and something that had happened to him there while touring Europe the summer after graduating from Cornell. It was an August morning in 1906, and Frank had made the 6,995-foot hike up Mount Pilatus in pursuit of its view of Lake Lucerne and the surrounding countryside. Yet no sooner had he reached the top than a storm descended, cutting off visibility. For an anxious several hours, the earth itself appeared to have vanished. Eventually, however, skies cleared, revealing not just the lake and the checkerboard of fields and villages spreading out from it but a glimmering rainbow that "seemed to reach across the world." Recalling the day from the perspective of his present circumstances, Frank saw in its movement from darkness to light a metaphor for the movement beginning to take place in his case. "My trial, my accusation, my rebuffs have been the clouds," he told a visitor. "The developments of the past few weeks are the rainbow of hope. And I am confident that the sun is to shine."

That less than a month after his appeal had been rejected by the Georgia Supreme Court, Frank could envision anything other than the lengthening shadow of the gallows attests to the fact that the intervening days had indeed witnessed a series of astonishing occurrences—all of them favorable to the defense.

The turnaround had started on February 20, when the *Atlanta Journal* broke the news that the strands of hair discovered on a National Pencil factory lathe during the early phases of the Phagan murder investigation had not come from the victim's head. Even more startling, the paper also reported that Solicitor General Hugh Dorsey had been notified of this piece of intelligence prior to Frank's trial but had withheld it from opposing counsel. As Dr. Henry F. Harris, who had microscopically compared the hair found at the plant with samples taken during his autopsies of little Mary's body, told the *Journal*'s Harllee Branch: "When I informed the solicitor that the two specimens of hair were not the same he simply remarked that he would let the matter end there." These revelations prompted an instantaneous reaction from Luther Rosser and Reuben Arnold, who in a joint statement accused Dorsey of prosecutorial misconduct. "He knew the truth and in spite of his knowledge urged upon the jury that this hair was evidence of Frank's guilt," the lawyers charged, adding: "The solicitor, in his zeal, misconceived his duty." Clearly caught out, Dorsey had tried to limit the damage, contending that Harris was merely offering an "opinion." Moreover, he asserted that the doctor's assessment notwithstanding, "the state's case had lost none of its strength, since it was not on such trifles that it was based," the hair being just "another addition to the mass of cumulative evidence against the defendant."

Hard upon the *Journal*'s exposure of Harris's finding, Frank's lawyers—revealing that they had long been awaiting such an opportunity—released a barrage of headline-making retractions by individuals heretofore firmly aligned with the state. The first of the disavowals to hit the papers came from Albert McKnight, the husband of Leo and Lucille's Negro cook, Minola, who now swore that his trial testimony had been fabricated. In a notarized affidavit made for C. W. Burke, a private detective working for Rosser, McKnight declared that at the behest of his employers at Beck & Gregg Hardware—who like so many others had been angling for the rewards offered in the slaying's aftermath—he had concocted his tale regarding Frank's failure to eat lunch the day of the crime and subsequent hasty departure from home. The truth, he warranted, was that he "did not see Mr. Leo M. Frank at any time or place on Saturday, April 26, 1913." At last, McKnight had conceded what his wife had maintained both before and after being jailed by Dorsey, in the process casting renewed doubt on the prosecution's theories regarding Frank's activities the afternoon of the murder.

The defense also made public an affidavit by erstwhile madam Nina Formby renouncing her damaging May 1913 deposition to the Atlanta police alleging that Frank was not only a patron of her establishment but had called on the day of the killing seeking a room in which to deposit Mary Phagan's body. Quite to the contrary, Formby announced, "Leo M. Frank had never been to my house. There had been no telephone conversation between Mr. Leo M. Frank and me." She said she had been coerced into swearing falsely by Detectives W. T. Chewning and J. N. Norris. Though Formby was, of course, regarded as an untrustworthy character—which was why Dorsey had kept her off the stand in August—her about-face resurrected misgivings regarding the methods investigators had used in collecting other allegations. As Frank himself would soon ask reporters: "If they were at such pains to make out a slanderous charge to turn opinion against me, is it not reasonable to assume that they would go even further in framing up evidence for use in the trial?"

Rosser and Arnold next unveiled a sweeping recantation by the loquacious bratling who had introduced the issue of sex into the case. In a 3,500-

word affidavit, George Epps proclaimed: "I now state that at both the coroner's inquest and the trial of Leo Frank I swore falsely. I now state that I was persuaded to give the false testimony in both of the before-mentioned hearings by Detective John Black. He told me, 'You go ahead and tell it just like I tell it.' " Bluntly put, Epps was accusing headquarters' lead investigator of not only having directed him to commit perjury but of having invented the charge that little Mary, in response to Frank's advances, had sought his protection. And if that weren't enough, there was this: Following the inquest, Epps said he had tried to inform Dorsey that his story was untrue. Yet the solicitor, he maintained, cut him off, snapping: "Just stick to that." For nearly a year, the boy added, he'd been a good soldier, although he'd felt "sorry" and was "glad of the chance to explain it and relieve my mind." Splashed atop Atlanta's front pages (TESTIMONY DOCTORED BY BLACK, boomed the *Georgian*), Epps's unexpected change of tune knocked the wind out of Dorsey. After denying that his young witness ever gave him reason to think he was lying, the solicitor declined further comment.

With the publication of George Epps's retraction, the state had suffered another severe blow—the fourth in two weeks. Little wonder that Leo Frank's spirits were rising. Yet the apparent crumbling of evidence explained only part of it. The news from outside Atlanta during this brief period had given the condemned man even more reason to take heart.

The headline atop page three of the February 18 editions of the *New York Times* could not have been more judicious: SPLIT COURT DENIES NEW TRIAL TO FRANK. However, the four columns of underlying text, which opened with the story's subject professing his innocence and then provided a summary of the case thus far, sent an unmistakable signal. As Adolph S. Ochs's confidant Garet Garrett noted in his diary, the publisher had at last "committed the *Times* to a campaign of righteous publicity."

"Crusade" might have been a better word for it. In the following days, the *Times* gave front-page treatment to every significant development in the story. EVIDENCE FOR FRANK HIDDEN, SAY COUNSEL, declared the above-the-fold topper on February 21. RETRACTS EVIDENCE THAT DOOMED FRANK, pronounced another on February 23. WOMAN ADMITS SHE LIED ABOUT FRANK, proclaimed still another on February 26. And on and on until by March 6 (the date the condemned man's account of his experience on Mount Pilatus appeared), the paper had run 25 articles on the case (nine on page one), elevating what had been a drama little known beyond Georgia's borders into a topic of national import.

The *Times*'s initial coverage had also spelled out what the country should think about the Frank affair. Though the paper dutifully reported much of the state's evidence, its pieces by and large read as if they'd originated from within the defense camp. Which, in many instances, they had.

On several occasions during this period, Ochs essentially turned over his news columns to Frank's lawyers, printing lengthy interviews unmediated by any skepticism and unencumbered by a word from the other side.

On March 2, beneath the front-page headline FRANK CONVICTED BY PUBLIC CLAMOR, the *Times* provided Herbert Haas free rein to recapitulate the entire affair from Frank's point of view. The lawyer, who by this juncture had assumed control of the defense's fund-raising efforts and was in New York staying at the Knickerbocker Hotel, took full advantage of the moment. After lambasting the Atlanta police for the manner in which they had conducted the investigation and scoring Dorsey for the way in which he had run the prosecution, he dismissed his client's chief accuser. "Conley had been arrested seven times between 1904 and 1912 for disorderly conduct. Fifty or sixty employees of the factory testified that they would not believe him under oath." Then he declared: "Frank's friends are absolutely convinced of his innocence. That he is the victim of a vile conspiracy, and that he is a man of the highest integrity and character, and that his innocence will ultimately be proved to the world there is not the slightest doubt."

On March 4, the *Times* accorded Luther Rosser—who it so happened was also in New York, conferring, as he phrased it, "with certain persons who are interested in the Frank case"—the same privilege it had given Haas. And like his counterpart, Rosser lit into the police and Dorsey before roughing up their star witness. "As for Conley, it would have been impossible to pick out a negro lower in the social scale." Then the condemned man's lead counsel—responding to the question "Why was Frank convicted?"— articulated what for most Americans would become the defining issue:

> The Jewish population of Atlanta is not large. Frank came to Atlanta a stranger and engaged in a new enterprise. He knew hardly anybody who was not of his own religion, being closely occupied with his business, and this fact rather counted against him. I really believe if Frank had been the son of a reputable Gentile, he would never have been arrested.

The *New York Times*'s entry into the fray had, of course, galvanized the defense. Adolph Ochs was in the fight for the duration. But for all of that, it was another northern Jew's decision to take up the cause in earnest that had produced the greatest elation, convincing Leo Frank that exoneration would indeed be his.

Sometime around the first of March, the Chicago advertising magnate Albert D. Lasker had stepped off a train at Atlanta's Terminal Station. Owing to an innate abhorrence of personal notoriety and an awareness of the need, in this instance, for discretion, Lasker had insisted that no one except those connected with the defense be told he was coming. The newspapers never mentioned he was in town. His presence, however, made itself immediately felt when on March 4, the renowned private detective William Burns—the same Burns whose agency had briefly taken up the investigation nearly a year before—arrived at Terminal Station and to a mob of reporters and photographers declared: "I am in the Frank case to the finish." Predictably, Burns's announcement set off a frenzy in the press. Roared the *Georgian*'s front-page headline: DETECTIVE PROMISES DECISIVE PROBE. And just as predictably, Lasker kept his name out of print, circulating the story that the condemned man's friends Milton Klein and Dr. Benjamin Wildauer had hired Burns. But the truth was that Lasker had engaged the investigator and paid his $4,500 retainer, and for the next week, Lasker, according to an associate, would "work day and night directing detectives and securing affidavits" on Frank's behalf.

From the defense's perspective, Lasker's appearance in Atlanta was an answered prayer—and not just because he had agreed to provide the funding for Burns. He had also agreed to put the same promotional genius that had made Quaker oats and Budweiser beer household names to use in convincing the public of Frank's innocence. If ever there was a time such savvy might matter, it was now, for as was becoming clear, the defense was preparing to launch a war to overturn the condemned man's conviction. The primary legal weapon: an extraordinary motion for a new trial. Though there could be no doubting the intensity with which the state would contest the motion, Lasker expected victory. As an aide to the Sears, Roebuck chairman Julius Rosenwald—who had, of course, donated money to the effort months before—put it in an early-March update: "Mr. Lasker's secretary, Miss Langan, told me, in a guarded way, that Mr. Lasker was very hopeful of a satisfactory outcome."

These, then, were the events that had convinced Leo Frank that though his dilemma remained unchanged, everything was different. Never was the alteration in mood more apparent than on the morning of March 7, when the condemned man emerged from the Tower to attend what by every right should have been a sobering proceeding.

The setting was the Thrower Building courtroom of Judge Benjamin H. Hill. Here, Hugh Dorsey would ask the lower court, which was now in receipt of the mandate from the Supreme Court returning the case to its jurisdiction, to set a new execution date. Yet from the moment that Frank— tan mackintosh draped over his shoulders, derby in hand—strode into the crowded chamber, the defense's fresh-minted optimism filled the air. For one thing, Reuben Arnold, exhibiting the certainty he and Rosser shared regarding the extraordinary motion's prospects, announced that he would forgo the de rigueur but usually futile request for clemency. More telling was what occurred once the preliminary business was done and Hill inquired if any other issues remained to be addressed. At this, Arnold said simply that his client wished to make a statement, whereupon the judge nodded his assent.

Approaching the bench, Frank began by diplomatically asking Hill not to take his remarks personally. "I well know," he said, "that your honor has naught to do with the vicissitudes of my case." Then, with a confidence and verve that suggested he intended to use the forum to make what amounted to the opening argument in his battle for a new trial, the condemned man declared:

> Law, as we know it, your honor, is but the expression of man's legal experience. It is but relative. It tries to approximate justice, but being man-made is fallible. In the name of the law many grievous errors have been committed—errors that were colossal and irretrievable. I declare to your honor that the state of Georgia is about to make such an error.

From this philosophical start, Frank turned to the specifics of his own dilemma. Arms raised, voice gaining in strength, he asserted:

> Your honor, an astounding and outrageous state of affairs obtained previous to and during my trial. On the streets rumor and gossip carried vile, vicious and damning stories concerning me and my wife. These stories were absolutely false and did me great harm as they beclouded and obsessed the public mind and outraged it against me.
>
> From a public in this state of mind, the jury that tried me was chosen. Not alone were these stories circulated on the street, but to the shame of our community, be it said, these vile insinuations crept into my very trial.
>
> The virus of these damning insinuations entered the minds of the twelve men and stole away their judicial frame of mind and their moral courage. The issue at bar was lost. The poison of the unspeakable things took its place.

With that, Frank squared his shoulders and in a tone at once resolute and resigned proclaimed:

> If the state and the law will that my life be taken as a blood atonement for the poor little child who was ruthlessly killed by another, then it remains for me only to die with whatever fortitude my manhood may allow.

But I am innocent of this crime. And the future will prove it.
I am now ready for your honor's sentence.

The unexpected eloquence of Frank's statement so jolted those in the courtroom that initially Hill seemed at a loss on how to continue. But after a moment's hesitation, the judge picked up a document headed "State of Georgia versus Leo M. Frank, No. 9410" and began to read aloud:

It appears that the defendant, Leo M. Frank, was on August 26, 1913, convicted of murder and thereupon duly sentenced by the order of this court to the punishment of death.

It is here and now ordered and adjudged that the sheriff of Fulton County be, and he is hereby, commanded to do execution of such sentence aforesaid on the 17th day of April, 1914.

"That is my birthday," Frank whispered upon hearing the date he would turn thirty so designated. But otherwise, he seemed undismayed. This was an individual previously all but unknown to Atlantans. Never again would he be called "The Silent Man in the Tower."

From this moment on, Leo Frank would speak regularly to local reporters while flooding national newspapers with written statements. Regarding the zeal with which Dorsey had tried him, he told the *Georgian:* "It is a terrible thing to suggest that a public official would advance his prestige at the expense of an innocent man's neck. And yet you can see how it is. There is not much glory in convicting a negro of a sensational crime." Pointing to a detail that he believed exonerated him, he informed the *Constitution:* "If I had been guilty, nothing on earth would have induced me to have revealed the fact that I had seen and talked with Mary Phagan in my office a few seconds before the prosecution claims I killed her. Would the man who killed Mary Phagan have freely and voluntarily stated that he saw her and talked with her just a few moments before she was supposed to have been killed?" And as for Conley, he told the *Journal:* "I am obliged to leave it to the intelligence and fair-mindedness of the community whether his successive perjuries, his motive to lie, the most powerful motive that could actuate a human being, and the utter improbability of his story does not render it unworthy of belief."

Coordinating these sallies was Albert Lasker, who covered the costs of circularizing Frank's remarks outside Atlanta as well as endorsed the slogan that soon tied them together: "The Truth Is on the March." After trying the line out as a tag for his written pronouncements, the condemned man began slipping it into interviews, and soon enough, not only was he using it much as advertisers used the catchphrases Lasker created for them, so were partisans elsewhere. A rallying cry had been born. And what made the cry effective was that circumstances continued to go Frank's way.

Frank's lawyers chose this juncture to unleash another flurry of news-worthy affidavits. The first came from young Helen Ferguson. In a statement made for C. W. Burke, the factory worker asserted that on the Saturday prior to Mary Phagan's murder, Jim Conley had accosted her in the plant lobby—the spot where Rosser and Arnold maintained the crime had occurred. "He was drunk—seemingly as drunk as could be," she swore. "I saw a whisky bot-tle in his hip pocket. He was staggering. His eyes looked queer and he didn't seem to know what he was doing. Then he came over toward me menacingly and I drew back, and as he pushed nearer me, I jumped to the stairs and ran as fast as I could." Though the Ferguson girl stood by her trial testimony alleging that Frank had thwarted her effort to pick up little Mary's pay the afternoon before the killing, the press played her declaration as a defense victory. Proclaimed the *New York Times*'s page-one headline: SAYS CONLEY MOLESTED HER.

No sooner had the Ferguson triumph hit the newspapers than Frank's lawyers released a pair of affidavits that Leonard Haas maintained would form "the strongest connecting links" in the extraordinary motion. As Ethel Harris Miller and Maier Lefkoff—both familiar figures in Atlanta's Jewish community but neither previously involved in the case—told it, they were walking down Whitehall Street around 1:10 the afternoon of the murder when Mrs. Miller saw Frank. "I spoke to him," she swore, "and Mr. Frank bowed and spoke to me, tipping his hat." The claim bolstered the superin-tendent's alibi. Hence Haas's enthusiasm. "The statements of Mrs. Miller and Mr. Lefkoff prove that Frank was not at the factory at the time the Conley negro states positively that they were disposing of the body," he declared. To this assessment, Frank happily concurred, telling reporters that he remembered meeting Mrs. Miller that April day, then adding: "The truth continues on the march."

Just how determined the defense was to establish its version of the truth became clear during the second week of March when a glossy eight-page pamphlet entitled "Some Facts about the Murder Notes in the Phagan Case" started appearing in the mailboxes of Atlanta's registered voters. Penned by the lawyer, Henry A. Alexander, who had recently been added to the defense team by Albert Lasker, the pamphlet—which was illustrated with crisply printed photographs of the documents under consideration—constituted the opening salvo in a two-prong attack intended to prove that not only did the contents of the enigmatic notes point to Jim Conley as their author and therefore little Mary's slayer, so did the very paper upon which they were written.

The murder notes had until now received scant critical attention. Save for Hugh Dorsey's assertions during his closing argument at Frank's trial that the proper usage of the word "did" in the notes indicated that a white man had composed them, and Arnold's comments to the contrary during the appeal, their strange syntax and lexicon had gone unaddressed. Alexander's study began to change all that. The lawyer had grown up with Southern blacks and was a student of their expressions and folklore. He had read and reread the notes, eventually focusing on a distinctive locution that appeared near the top of the one jotted on lined white paper: "he said he wood love me land down play like the night witch did it." To Alexander's thinking, the term "night witch" had been misunderstood from the start, when just after Mary Phagan's body was discovered, the responding officers had read the notes aloud to Newt Lee, who according to the police had replied, "Boss, that's me." Out of that exchange, the lawyer believed, had arisen the erroneous conclusion that the communiqués had been intended to implicate the night watchman—a purpose later easy to impute to Frank—when in fact, as he saw it, they had been intended to point in an altogether different direction. Alexander argued that the notes did not refer to Lee at all; they referred instead exactly to the figure named—"the night witch," a wispy hoodoo haint. "It seems to the writer of this article," Alexander contends in his pamphlet's key passage, "that in this expression there is disclosed a piece of superstition characteristic of the negro, and totally foreign to a white man. The idea that the girl was killed by a night witch, or, as the note expresses it, that the 'long tall black negro' would 'play like the night witch did it' is inconceivable as the thought of a white man."

Alexander's provocative interpretation struck a chord with many Atlantans. (A local pastor later wrote: "We had an old Negro woman working for us as cook and I asked her one day, 'Rebecca, what do colored people mean by night witch?' She replied, 'When children cry out in their sleep at night it means the night witches are riding them, and if you don't go and wake them up, they will be found dead the next morning.'") Yet persuasive as the lawyer was on the matter, his reasoning was in the end theoretical. Which was why what came next was crucial, for it was not theoretical in the least.

NEW EVIDENCE TO SHOW NOTES WERE WRITTEN IN THE BASEMENT, boomed the front-page headline over the *Journal*'s account of the second phase of Alexander's work, which he presented to reporters in person. After scrutinizing his pamphlet's high-quality reproductions and instigating a subsequent probe of factory records, the lawyer announced he had determined that the yellow preprinted National Pencil Company order sheet upon which the longest of the notes was inscribed not only bore the tracings of a purchase order issued years before Mary Phagan's death but that the order had been made out by a mechanic who'd quit his job in 1912 and whose files had been carted to the cellar. Elaborating on the basis for these conclusions, Alexander cited several newly legible details. For one, in the space marked "Order No. __" appeared a smudgy "1018," which further investigation had revealed corresponded with the number for a purchase of machine steel made from the Cotton States Belting Company in September 1909. For another, across the bottom of the sheet could be seen the impress of a partial signature belonging to Henry F. Becker, the former employee who had tendered the order. Alexander also asserted that the sheet upon which this note was written contained another telltale clue, which had always been apparent but had gone unappreciated. To wit: The dateline in the upper right-hand corner read "190__," whereas the printed sheets in use at the time of the crime had been updated to read "191__." Taken together, the lawyer concluded, these physical facts gave the lie to that part of Conley's testimony in which he claimed that the paper upon which he'd jotted the notes came from a pad kept in Frank's desk. What, then, had occurred? "The simplest explanation and the one which seems correct from every logical viewpoint," declared Alexander, was that the pad—like everything belonging to Becker—"was taken to the basement," remaining there until April 26, 1913, when "it was found by the negro and used by him to write the note through which he hoped to throw the blame on another."

Alexander's contentions regarding the murder-note paper produced euphoria in the defense camp. And as was now his wont, Frank immediately made himself available to reporters, proclaiming: "They will have to change Conley's statement again if they are to get around this. They will have to get him to say that instead of reaching in my desk and getting out a pad, I went down into the basement and brought that old pad up that bore Becker's duplicates and had him write on that." Then, more soberly, the condemned man elaborated upon Alexander's conclusions, averring that "none of Becker's old duplicate pads was ever in my office." Yet in the end, Frank could not suppress his glee. "I hope Solicitor Dorsey rests as easily in his bed tonight and sleeps as soundly and as free from worry as I shall. I have never felt more confident of ultimate acquittal than I do right at this moment."

How the defense could at this stage have been any better positioned would have been hard to imagine, but even as Frank was rejoicing over Alexander's deductions, a meeting was under way across town at the *Atlanta Journal* whose outcome would provide a still greater boost. The session, which took place in the office of the paper's editor and publisher, James R. Gray, had been requested by Harllee Branch. The reporter had been on the Phagan story since long before breaking the news regarding Dr. Harris and the misrepresented hair evidence, not only covering the trial but in tandem with Harold Ross conducting the May 1913 interview with Conley that prompted Hugh Dorsey to quarantine his star witness. During this protracted involvement, Branch had reached several disturbing conclusions, foremost among them that the jury had convicted an innocent man. He had also decided that, like everyone who had written about the case, he had failed to exercise sufficient restraint and was hence partially culpable in the result. "I had a feeling of personal responsibility," Branch would recall half a century later. "We'd printed all this stuff." Which was what drove him to seek out his boss. "I thought it was my duty to go and call Mr. Gray's attention to this," he said. "I knew it was unusual for a newspaper to step in while a motion was pending, but I thought that we—somebody—should come out for what was right, fair and just and demand this man have a new trial. Mr. Gray listened to me patiently and interestedly, and then he said, 'Harllee, let me think over that tonight.' He indicated to me that he himself had misgivings, that we'd muffed the ball."

By the next day, Gray—whose paper was represented, of course, by Reuben Arnold—had made up his mind. "He told me," said Branch, "he'd thought it over, came to the conclusion I was correct, and regardless of the effect on the *Journal,* the *Journal* was going to come out for a new trial."

On March 10, beneath the headline "Frank Should Have a New Trial," the sheet that Covered Dixie Like the Dew lent its voice to the condemned man's cause. The *Journal's* position was essentially this: The murder of Mary Phagan—"a young girl just budding into womanhood"—had so unhinged Atlanta that for the better part of a year, its populace lost the ability to think clearly. "A degree of frenzy almost inconceivable" had led the city to demand a scapegoat, and when Conley—"an irresponsible drunken negro, a man who would not have been believed under other conditions"—offered up Frank, the public suspended disbelief. By the time judicial proceedings began, the "fury" was such that an unbiased administration of justice was impossible. Lest his readers doubt this claim, Gray recreated the scene:

> The atmosphere of the courtroom was charged with an electric current of indignation which flashed before the very eyes of the jury. The courtroom and streets were filled with an angry crowd ready to seize the defendant if the jury had found him not guilty. Cheers for the prosecuting counsel were irrepressible in the courtroom throughout the trial and on the streets demonstrations in condemnation of Frank were heard by the judge and jury.

Frank's execution, after conviction under such "indescribable conditions as these," would, the editor argued, "amount to judicial murder." As a consequence, there was only one right course of action:

> In the name of Justice and in the name of the good people of the State of Georgia, who believe in fair play, who stand for the enforcement of law and the punishment of crime, after legal conviction, let this man be fairly tried. If he is guilty, he will be convicted again.

The publication of the *Journal*'s editorial sparked a far greater reaction than Branch or Gray could have anticipated, emboldening people who might otherwise have remained on the sidelines to enter the fight. In the days immediately afterward, letters voicing support for Frank poured in by the scores. Predictably, most of them came from Atlanta patricians. F. J. Paxon, the proprietor of the city's second largest department store, Davison-Paxon, leaped to the ramparts. As did Forrest Adair, a real estate developer. As did Eugene Muse Mitchell, a well-to-do lawyer whose precocious 13-year-old daughter Margaret was already writing stories about gallant knights and beautiful ladies that anticipated her novel *Gone with the Wind*. Yet it wasn't just the rich who spoke out. The following Sunday, many members of Atlanta's clergy followed suit. The Reverend L. O. Bricker, pastor of the First Christian Church, declared: "Frank should have a new trial because under the awful tension of public feeling, it was next to impossible for a jury of our fellow human beings to have granted him a fair, fearless and impartial trial." The Reverend Julian S. Rodgers, a Baptist, sought to quiet any still-stirring anti-Semitic sentiments, admonishing his congregation:

> The fact that Frank is a Jew should not discredit him. His race is the miracle of the ages. It stands out conspicuously for patience, forbearance and obedience to law. If Leo Frank is a criminal, it is not because he is a Jew, but in spite of it.

The *Journal*'s editorial was, quite simply, a call to arms, and by the next week, other Georgia papers—among them the *Albany Herald,* the *Dalton Citizen* and the *Thomasville Times-Enterprise*—had demanded a new trial for Frank, too. From afar, the *New York Times* breathed a sigh of relief:

> Even among the people of the City of Atlanta, the feeling in regard to Frank, convicted of the murder of Mary Phagan, has undergone a marked change. The belief grows and daily spreads that Frank was not convicted on the evidence, that he is a victim of the clamor and rage of an excited public.

The light, as Frank himself again declared, truly did seem to be breaking.

The first indication that the skies might once again darken for Leo Frank came, as had so much in this saga, in the form of a newspaper headline. "The Frank Case: When and Where Shall Rich Criminals Be Tried?" thundered the banner stripped across the front page of the March 19 edition of the *Jeffersonian*. After nearly eleven months of silence, the weekly organ of the populist firebrand Thomas Watson had joined the battle, its entry an unintended consequence of the *Atlanta Journal*'s alliance with the condemned man. As Watson declared in his opening blast:

> For many years, I have not taken the *Atlanta Journal,* nor have I read it. Recognized by everybody as the organ of Senator [Hoke] Smith and edited with the most utter disregard for truth and liberality, I have not cared to pay any attention to it.
>
> Last week, however, there came to my address a blue-marked wrapper enclosing the *Journal;* and the leading editorial was blue-marked also. As I got a copy, it is reasonable to suppose that everybody got a copy, just as everybody gets copies of Senator Smith's senatorial utterances—the same being equivalent to oracles from the fountain-head of Wisdom.
>
> The marked editorial in Senator Smith's newspaper bears the modest headline, "*FRANK SHOULD HAVE A NEW TRIAL!*"
>
> The case is still pending; Judge Ben Hill knows that he will soon have to pass upon an extraordinary motion for a new trial; hence, Judge Ben Hill is peremptorily, abruptly and insolently told by Senator Smith what *he must do.*
>
> The effort on the part of Senator Smith's newspaper to *degrade our Supreme Court,* vilify Judge Roan, brand twelve jurors with eternal infamy, blast the future of a *thoroughly brave and efficient Solicitor General AND TO DICTATE IN ADVANCE TO JUDGE BEN HILL* moves me to enter a protest against what seems to me a new and lawless method of trying a criminal case.

Had the Sage confined himself to the merits of the *Journal*'s position, his remarks might have been viewed as simply the comments of a fiercely opposing sensibility. But as his many references to Hoke Smith suggest, he was acting out of a deep-seated personal animus that found its roots in an incident that had occurred nearly a decade before and had nothing to do with Frank's pending motion. In 1907, Watson had gone to then governor Smith and requested a pardon for one Arthur Glover, a longtime loyalist under sentence of death for the murder of a female factory worker outside an Augusta textile mill. Since his support of Smith in the 1906 election had essentially put him in office, Watson viewed executive clemency for Glover as the payment of a political debt. The state's evidence, however, was solid, and Smith allowed the execution to proceed. Ever since this "betrayal," C. Vann Woodward would observe in his biography, *Tom Watson: Agrarian Rebel,* Watson's "desire to bring disgrace upon Hoke Smith [had] become a blinding obsession." In 1908, it led him to back Marietta's Joseph Brown in his victorious gubernatorial campaign against Smith, and now it was again the primary motivating factor. If the *Journal* was for Frank, then the *Jeffersonian* would be against him, and as Watson proceeded to make clear, he would relish the fight. Indeed, the stark juxtaposition the Frank case presented between rich and poor, capital and labor, meddling Yankee and native Southerner seemed tailor-made for him. Regarding the just instigated high-profile campaign to save the condemned man, Watson pointedly asked, *"Who is paying for all this?"* Then, taking a potshot at the clergymen who had jumped on the bandwagon, he demanded:

> Does the *church* invade the province of the State when preachers of a certain sort prostitute their sacred office and attempt to try criminal cases in their *churches?*

Finally, he raised what he saw as the tacit assumption behind the effort to win Frank a new trial, inquiring:

> Does a Jew expect extraordinary favors and immunities *because* of his race?
>
> In this case, the defendant is taking that position. Anyone who has noticed the New York papers has noticed the persistent efforts *made from Atlanta* to arouse the Hebrews into believing that Frank is a victim of race prejudice.
>
> Is it wise for the Jews to risk the good name and the popularity of the whole race in the extraordinary, extra-judicial and utterly unprecedented methods that are being worked to save this decadent offshoot of a great people?

Few foes were more formidable than Tom Watson. Equally worrisome, however, was the reappearance of another adversary—Hugh Dorsey. Having recovered from the setbacks of late winter, the solicitor was aggressively preparing for the approaching confrontation in court. Day and night, such prosecution stalwarts as Chief of Detectives Newport Lanford and John Black, Pat Campbell and John Starnes came and went from Dorsey's office, and soon enough, the broad outlines of what the solicitor had in mind emerged. For starters, he made it plain that he meant to challenge at least some of the many retractors, releasing an affidavit in which George Epps's father swore that his son had told him Mary Phagan was terrified of Frank. Second, he let it be known that he planned to contest a point that most thought he'd conceded—Dr. Harris's finding that the hair discovered on the factory lathe did not come from Mary's head. The solicitor revealed this intention in what for him was a perfect venue—the trial of Jim Conley on the charge of being an accessory after the fact to murder. Dorsey did not relish prosecuting a man who'd done so much for him. As he declared up front: "Conley had nothing to do with [the crime]. He was just Frank's fool and ought not to be punished." Dorsey did relish, though, the chance the proceeding gave him to get into the record testimony he could cite during the upcoming hearing. Hence in accordance with an agreement made in advance with Conley's lawyer, William Smith, the solicitor called only one witness, Will Gheesling, the undertaker who'd prepared Mary Phagan's body for burial. In response to a series of questions that had no bearing on Conley's case, Gheesling stated that on the morning after the murder, he'd washed little Mary's blood-matted scalp with a pine-tar soap that could have so altered her hair's texture and color as to destroy any similarity between it and the strands located by R. P. Barrett. Having thereby armed himself with a sworn statement that called Harris's assertion into doubt, Dorsey detailed the evidence against Conley, concluding: "If the law didn't demand his conviction, I would say let him go." In response, Smith argued that since Conley had been recruited merely to stand guard, "the only way [he] was an accessory was in that he helped Frank in furthering his sexual desires"—which was hardly illegal. Nonetheless, after just twelve minutes of deliberation, the jury found the Negro guilty. Yet once the verdict was returned, Judge Ben Hill imposed the lenient sentence of one year on the chain gang. There was, in short, but a single loser here—Leo Frank.

To say that William Burns's involvement in the Frank case allayed the defense team's concerns regarding Tom Watson and Hugh Dorsey would be an overstatement. Yet the detective's reputation was such that his mere presence in Atlanta—a presence that due to unfinished business in the North did not become permanent until the third week of March—outshone everything the Sage and the solicitor said or did. Just the sight of Burns settling down to breakfast each morning in the fern-filled pink-and-white dining room of the grand Georgian Terrace Hotel suggested that a higher power was now at work. Surrounded by half a dozen reporters, attended by a traveling secretary and assorted subalterns, and invariably clad in a crisp houndstooth suit that set off his famous red hair and mustache, the detective exuded energy and confidence. This was America's greatest private investigator, and between bites of his soft-boiled eggs and toast, he would regale the table with war stories, pausing only to dictate telegrams to clients and operatives in far-flung climes. Then, with the entire retinue in tow, he would stroll down Peachtree Street to his agency's local office, declaiming not just on aspects of the Phagan murder but on his certainty that he would solve it. "I have no doubt concerning the ability of myself and that of my associates to clear up this affair," Burns exuded on one of the first of these outings. "I have been able to clear up far more baffling mysteries."

Brash, boastful, at times bedazzling, Burns was also aware that as far as the Frank case was concerned, none of it would get him very far unless he simultaneously conveyed the impression that he sought the cooperation of the Atlanta Police Department and possessed an open mind regarding the possibility of his client's guilt. Early on, he declared: "I know the people of this community were justly incensed over this atrocious murder in their midst. The officials charged with the duty of bringing to justice the person or persons responsible for the crime are to be commended for the rigorous manner in which they took up the investigation." As for his own investigation, he vowed that he would "strike to the heart of the truth no matter who it affects," adding that if in the course of his operation he found that Frank was the murderer, he would say so.

While it's unlikely that Newport Lanford and company put any more stock in Burns's professions of evenhandedness than Burns did, they responded in kind. Proclaimed Lanford: "I will throw open to Burns all information available to my department." As a consequence, the private investigator began work in an atmosphere that on the surface was conducive to progress. He devoted his first days in Atlanta to poring over the Brief of Evidence used during the appeal to the Georgia Supreme Court and meeting with Luther Rosser, Herbert and Leonard Haas, Detective C. W. Burke (who would hereafter report to him) and, most extensively, Leo Frank. Following this opening round of discussions, he visited the pencil factory, where, as the *Journal* put it, he examined the crime scene from the ground up, starting in the basement and finishing on the second floor, paying special attention to Frank's office and the metal room. Then he announced plans to interview everyone from John Starnes and Hugh Dorsey to Monteen Stover and Jim Conley.

By the middle of his initial week on the job, Burns had grown even more optimistic about his prospects for success. "This case," he told the *Georgian,* "is easier than I expected. The facts will speak for themselves when made public. I am confident that Mr. Dorsey is open to conviction if it should develop that a grievous mistake has been made." Having thereby tipped his hand, the detective immediately backtracked, insisting: "I have never expressed any conviction as to the innocence or guilt of Frank and do not intend to do so until the investigation is completed." But as to the larger issue, he remained resolute. "The trail certainly looks clear enough to me, and I believe Atlanta and the country at large will be satisfied that the truth has been found when the final report is made."

Just what Burns had uncovered that enabled him to speak with such assuredness, he would not say. He did, however, offer a tantalizing clue. Like Dorsey and Lanford, he had determined that Mary Phagan's murderer had been motivated by an unnatural lust. But unlike the authorities, he did not believe that Leo Frank was so inclined. "In my work," the detective told the *Journal,* "I have had occasion to come in contact with abnormal people of all kinds, and I know them and their characteristics well. Many perverts occupy high places in society and in business. It is not a difficult matter for me to locate one. Abnormality has its unfailing marks. Frank is a normal man. I am satisfied of this fact."

The implications here were lost on no one. Burns was convinced he could do what the defense had failed to do at the trial—prove Frank's innocence by establishing his morality. More than that, he was convinced he could prove the killer's identity by establishing his immorality. He was not, though, ready to reveal the basis for his thinking. Most particularly, he was unwilling to discuss whether he'd developed fresh information that bore on Jim Conley's sexual predilections. When a *Constitution* reporter endeavored to smoke him out by asking whether the crime was committed by someone of "savage instinct and nature"—by, in other words, a Negro—all the man received was a noncommittal smile.

With a combination of bravado and guile, then, Burns had commandeered the investigation's center stage. Atop front pages in Atlanta and New York, headlines proclaimed his imminent triumph. BURNS IS CERTAIN AFTER WEEK'S WORK HE WILL CLEAR PHAGAN MYSTERY, boomed the *Georgian.* BURNS SAYS HE CAN SOLVE THE FRANK CASE, echoed the *Times.* Meanwhile, other national papers also took note. Blared the *Chicago Tribune:* "Detective Burns Says He Soon Can Prove Who Was Slayer of Mary Phagan." There would be, however, no quick solution, for following only eight days on the ground, Burns departed for the North to pursue unspecified new leads. Until his return, he would be represented in Atlanta by two legendary operatives. A polished swell known for working incognito, Guy Biddinger had pulled off Burns's greatest coup, tracking down John and James McNamara, the Iron Workers Union leaders who confessed to the 1910 bombing of the *Los Angeles Times* building. Less flamboyant but no less effective, Dan Lehon had in 1911 helped Burns expose extensive graft at the Illinois Central Railroad, a case celebrated by the muckraking journalist Lincoln Steffens.

In Burns's absence, Frank's supporters pressed ahead on several other fronts. To begin with, they stepped up the campaign to sway public opinion to the condemned man's cause, with Albert Lasker and Adolph Ochs again taking the lead. Lasker induced a number of influential Americans to join in the call for a new trial. The most prominent individuals to sign on were Thomas A. Edison and Henry Ford, but the most inspired choice was the adman's fellow Chicagoan, social worker Jane Addams. In a letter written at Lasker's behest to a Georgia suffragette, Addams beseeched women to "protest against the execution of a man concerning whose guilt there is so much room for doubt." Coming from the nation's greatest champion of the poor, the letter was intended to counteract the impression that Frank was nothing more than the darling of his wealthy Jewish supporters. Not surprisingly, it dominated front pages across the country.

Meanwhile, on every day but two during March, the *New York Times* published at least one article on the case. Many of these efforts were straightforward. Yet for each newsbreak, there were myriad plugs for the defense—a testimonial from the principal at Leo's alma mater, the Pratt Institute, several of Frank's self-circulated pronouncements, the text of a sermon by a Philadelphia rabbi demanding a new trial. The defining piece was a 7,000-word feature that ran beneath the unequivocal banner: LEO M. FRANK, AN INNOCENT MAN, MAY SUFFER A DISGRACEFUL DEATH FOR ANOTHER'S CRIME. Herein, staff writer Edward Marshall reported the results of a fact-finding mission to Atlanta highlighted by a lengthy interview with Jim Conley. According to Marshall, the Negro exhibited no remorse for either Mary Phagan's murder or for the part he admittedly played in it, proving himself to be "heartless, brutal, greedy, literally a black monster, drunken, lowlived, utterly worthless." Conley's only apparent concern was the poor quality of prison food. Concluded Marshall:

> That Leo Frank, the highly educated, well-connected and hitherto respected managing expert in lead pencil manufacture, should be doomed to die is not more astonishing than that this black human animal, confessedly a participant in the horror, should be alive to tell his dreadful tale.
>
> I am convinced that Leo Frank is absolutely innocent of the murder of Mary Phagan. I am convinced that there has been a great miscarriage of justice.

The defense did not rely solely on Ochs and Lasker to keep the story in the news during Burns's absence, picking this moment to release a draft of the extraordinary motion. The 60-page document contained much that was familiar, including the allegations concerning the hair evidence, the retractions by McKnight, Epps, and the others and the findings regarding the paper upon which the second murder note had been scrawled. Yet what rendered the motion, in Reuben Arnold's estimate, "the strongest ever filed in Georgia" was its additional bounty of fresh renunciations and charges. In one affidavit, erstwhile factory employee J. E. Duffy, who testified at the trial that a cut he'd suffered at work had not dripped on the metal room floor where blood alleged to have come from Mary Phagan's head wound was found, swore that in truth he'd bled profusely there. In another, a previously unmentioned Negro woman named Mary Rich, who ran a lunch wagon that served the pencil company neighborhood, declared that around 2:20 on the afternoon of the murder, Jim Conley—who'd consistently maintained that he was home by this hour—had emerged from the plant basement's back door and bought a 20-cent meal from her, then reentered the building. In still another, Lula Simmons, a second new name, asserted that around 4:30 on the afternoon of the murder, she'd been walking by the factory and heard screams emanating from the basement, a charge suggesting not only that the crime occurred later in the day than the state contended but in the location the defense maintained. In the end, however, the items that created the biggest stir involved the issue that had dominated the case from the start and was clearly going to dominate the approaching court fight—Leo Frank's character. For openers came affidavits from Dewey Hewell, Nellie Pettis, Nellie Wood, Ruth Robinson, Marie Karst, Mamie Kitchens and Carrie Smith—all state's witnesses—announcing that they had either been coached into making false accusations of sexual impropriety against their former boss or had done so unwittingly. (According to the Karst girl, she had responded affirmatively to Hugh Dorsey's question "Is Frank's reputation for lasciviousness bad?" only because she did not know what "lasciviousness" meant.) In this same vein but even more damaging to the prosecution was a retraction by C. Brutus Dalton, the murky figure who had confirmed Conley's account of Frank's Saturday debauches, the white man who had made a black man's tale of low doings in high places credible to 12 white jurors. As Dalton now told it, his testimony regarding office parties at which he and Frank shared women and beer was a police-department-produced fabrication drawn from the tawdry details of his life. After Detectives Starnes and Campbell had learned that he'd used the plant basement for assignations and that he'd tipped Conley 25 cents to stand guard, they paid him a visit to ask if Frank had ever "joined in the immoral conduct." When he replied no, Dalton averred, "Campbell and Starnes laughed and treated his statement as a joke and insisted that [he] should admit that the defendant was a man of bad character." The lawmen were so adamant, Dalton added, that he'd believed he had little choice but to assent to their version, though he knew "absolutely nothing about or against the defendant."

The reverberations from the release of the extraordinary motion—the formal filing of which led to the setting of an April 23 court date, which automatically triggered a stay of execution—had yet to subside when on Sunday, April 5, William Burns returned to Atlanta, immediately closeting himself with the operatives Biddinger and Lehon. Long into the evening, the three remained in conference, picking up again the next morning. Though there was much to discuss, at the top of the agenda were 49 pages of just discovered correspondence that Burns believed might well guarantee the success of Frank's new trial bid. Written between Christmas and late February, the jailhouse letters of Jim Conley and a female inmate named Annie Maude Carter not only lent support to the thesis that the Negro was driven by exceptional lust but revealed what could be a potentially relevant sexual obsession. In reply to a note in which Annie Maude referred enticingly to her hips, Conley declared:

> baby you ought not never said anything to me about your hipped why my dick went clean across my cell and i read it all night your letter i could not sleep honey you was right when you said that you had up there what i wants you said you would hold from the bottom why baby i know you can do that i just know that and every time [i] read that my long dick got on a hard why i would like to hold it in one of your hipped this morning and let you take everything that i have got there with me because i love you so much and if i could put my sweet long dick in your hipped i think i could make mama call me papa one time

Responding to the news that Annie Maude intended to post bail, Conley—in an effort to forestall such an eventuality lest another man "get it before i do"—again touched on his fixation, proclaiming:

> i want you to keep your ass right there [in jail] because it is good and you told me this last night in your letter that two hours fucking on your big fat ass would stop all of this [talk] well that right but you know that papa cannot lay on your ass that long before you would be done made me come if ever there was a man that want to lay on your ass that me and make me love it and i will show you better than i can tell you what i can do for you.
>
> now baby if you don't get out on no bond or if you do get out on a bond you [save] that right hipped for me cause if you hold your fat ass on the

bottom and make papa go like a kitty cat then you have won a good man that's me . . . if you let papa put his long ugly dick up in your fat ass and play on your right and left hip just like a monkey playing on a trapeze then honey papa will be done played hell with you . . .

i see that your mother said that somebody was going to give something on your bond tell her that you don't want to get out on bonds, because we are going to do what i say cause i want to stick my long dick in your ass.

well honey this is alright now be a good girl and save your fat ass for me and i will take care of it . . . give your heart to god and your ass to me

From Burns's perspective, Conley's consistently articulated fleshly preference ("miss Annie Carter Conley," the Negro enthused elsewhere, "got a fat ass and a sweet pee hole i do believe and they will be mine soon i will just want that ass honey") marked him as an unmistakable deviant. Speaking in general of the letters the detective later asserted that they established "beyond a peradventure of a doubt that Conley is an abnormal man, just the vile degenerate that I have heretofore pictured him." Even more significant, the letters prompted Burns to seek permission to examine the physical evidence introduced at the Frank trial. His theory—one that might explain the conflicting medical testimony as to whether Mary Phagan had been raped, one that Luther Rosser had flirted with during his cross-examination of Sergeant L. S. Dobbs regarding the condition of the victim's underwear— was that the girl had been anally sodomized and that the physical evidence would confirm as much, making Conley the likely culprit.

Thus it was that late on the morning of April 8, Burns—accompanied by Lehon, C. W. Burke (who had acquired the Carter-Conley correspondence) and Henry Alexander—called at Hugh Dorsey's Thrower Building offices. Since the era of good feeling among the various parties remained intact, the solicitor graciously received his visitors, granting them access to the evidence. What the men saw while studying Mary Phagan's clothing, though failing to confirm that she had been sodomized, disturbed and astonished them. To begin with, her undershorts, far from being ripped, had, as Rosser had intimated, been carefully cut from her legs so that her pudendum and pubic region could, in effect, be displayed. Similarly, a knit undershirt she had been wearing had also been cut from her torso, one incision starting beneath her right armpit and traveling across her chest, another curving around her left breast so that it, too, could be exposed. The killer had at least fetishized the girl's body. After an hour's observation, Burns and his associates thanked Dorsey for his courtesy, emerging onto the street to meet the predictable gaggle of reporters. Considering the nature of what the detective had just seen, it's no wonder that he was uncharacteristically discreet. This was not the occasion to discuss unprintable sex acts—or to offer interpretations. (By Burns's lights, the sliced-up garments further pointed the finger at Conley, if for no other reason than the work would have required more time than the state's theory of the crime allowed.) Nonetheless, the detective hinted at his probe's direction, announcing:

> After examining the clothes worn by Mary Phagan when she was mur-
> dered, I am more fully convinced than ever that the crime was committed
> by a pervert.

Having satisfied himself that he had amassed sufficient proof against Jim Conley, Burns threw himself into the corollary effort to demonstrate Leo Frank's good character. Indeed, even as the detective had been poring over the physical evidence in Dorsey's office, the first of a battery of physicians working at his direction was arriving at the Fulton County Tower. In all, six "specialists on nervous diseases," as the *Journal* termed them, would examine the condemned man for signs of degeneracy, and not surprisingly, they wouldn't waste much time reaching the same conclusion. As the April 9 editions of the *New York Times* reported, the medical experts "unanimously agreed that Frank was normal physically and mentally."

For Burns, the release of the physicians' glowing diagnosis was only the initial step. He took the second the next day by announcing a headline-grabbing $1,000 reward for definite "reports concerning acts of perversion on the part of Leo M. Frank." Burns anticipated few, if any, responses. Which was why Newport Lanford's reaction caught him unawares. Declared the detective chief: "I am not so hard up that I am going after that $1,000, but if Mr. Burns will come down here, we can give him all the information on that point he desires." The scare, however, was short-lived, for when Burns, again accompanied by Lehon and Henry Alexander, appeared at headquarters, Lanford refused to open his files, maintaining that to do so prior to the approaching court date would be unfair to all sides. Moreover, he made the claim that the prosecution had never charged Frank with perversion in the first place. "The state of Georgia and the city detectives [do] not now and never did claim that Leo Frank is a pervert. The charges of perversion had no bearing on the case and were injected by the defense." Lanford's pronouncement, which flew brazenly in the face of the facts, gave Burns a splendid opportunity, and he seized it, assailing the detective chief in interviews with both the *Georgian* and the *Journal,* then wiring Adolph Ochs:

> Police department today withdrew charge of perversion against Leo M.
> Frank . . . Bearing in mind the numerous filthy charges of perversion
> which saturated the community prior to the Frank trial and aroused their

passions, the charges of perversion injected into the case by the State upon the trial ... and in the Supreme Court of Georgia, the statement made today by Chief Lanford is a severe indictment of the police department of this city and of the outrageous methods used in the prosecution of Frank.

The following morning, the *New York Times* reprinted Burn's telegram verbatim beneath the ringing topper:

ABSOLVE FRANK ON IMMORALITY CHARGE

With the extraordinary motion hearing practically at hand, Leo Frank's supporters believed that victory was in their grasp. True, there had been further rumblings from Tom Watson. The same day the story broke that Burns's physicians had accorded the condemned man a clean bill of moral health, the banner atop the *Jeffersonian* had inquired: "The Leo Frank Case. Does the State of Georgia Deserve this Nation-Wide Abuse?" As the Sage saw it, the primary abuser was the *New York Times,* and in the process of acquainting his readers with a few of the sheet's one-sided utterances, he presented his assessment of where its loyalties resided:

> Mr. Adolph Ochs, a most useful servant of the Wall Street interests, runs a Tory paper in New York, whose chief end in life seems to be to uphold all the atrocities of Special Privilege and all the monstrous demands of Big Money.

Then, though he could not have known of Albert Lasker's role, Watson called attention to the larger forces that he sensed behind the pro-Frank publicity campaign, observing:

> Moving heaven and earth to bring influence to bear, Miss Jane Addams of Chicago was reached. Her letter is on its travels throughout the whole newspaper world.

Meantime, William Smith had turned down Burns's long-standing request to interview Jim Conley, decreeing that at least in this instance, the "movie picture, stage-lecturing sleuth" would not be allowed to indulge his penchant for "bombast." Similarly, Monteen Stover had also rejected Burns's overtures, beating a retreat from Samuel Boorstin's office after being summoned there to speak to the condemned man's friend, instead to come face-to-face with the detective. Finally, and most significant, Hugh Dorsey had again served notice that he intended to put up a fight. To begin with, he had released an affidavit from Albert McKnight in which the Negro—who had recently been jailed—retracted his retraction, reaffirming his allegation regarding Frank's failure to eat lunch the afternoon of the Phagan murder and contending that he'd withdrawn it only because Detective C. W. Burke had promised that if he did so, he would secure him a job as a Pullman porter. Additionally, the solicitor had revealed that he was considering bringing perjury charges against all other recanting state's witnesses who failed to return to the fold. Yet despite such troubling auguries, those inside the defense camp evinced little concern. In their view, they possessed not merely the evidence to prevail but, thanks to another infusion of Northern capital, the cash.

The key contribution came on April 20 in the form of a $5,000 draft from Albert Lasker. By this date, the expenses associated with the battle to win Frank a new trial had far exceeded preliminary expectations. According to Herbert Haas's calculations, the final figure would top $30,000, bringing the total expenditure to date to $80,000. Some of the $30,000 would go to lawyers, some to medical experts, but most was for Burns. As Haas had confided in a mid-April letter to a supporter: "I asked Mr. Burns and his associates for a wild guess and they stated that this investigation might cost as much as . . . $20,000." Initially, the condemned man's allies had attempted to raise the extra funds from family members and friends, and while they'd succeeded in securing a $2,500 pledge from the Fulton Bag and Cotton Mill's Oscar Elsas—a client, of course, of Luther Rosser and Governor John Slaton—they had failed to receive even a reply from the individual who'd bankrolled their earlier efforts, Frank's uncle Moses. Hence on April 17, with his war chest down to just $250, Haas had thrown himself on Lasker's mercy. "I hate to be compelled to write you this," he began, then laid out the financial realities, concluding: "I do not know that we could have done further for Frank if you had not come to his assistance."

Lasker's positive response, though not meant to be regarded as a blank check ("Believe me, my dear Mr. Haas," he wrote from his office above Chicago's Wabash Avenue, "there is a limit to the money that can be raised . . . I cannot assume any moral responsibility to raise unlimited money"), was generous. It included not merely the enclosed payment but another $5,000 "whenever you want it" and the promise to raise $5,000 more from such midwestern friends as Julius Rosenwald. Furthermore, Lasker— who from the outset had resented that his fellow crusaders from New York, while talking a good game, had yet to open their wallets—assured Haas that he would go to work on them and would not stop until they had contributed at least $10,000. Which, good to his word, he did, that same day penning the cordial equivalent of a shakedown letter to Louis Wiley, the business manager of the *New York Times*. Getting right to the point, Lasker asserted: "Surely, New York ought to give at least $10,000, and much more. The expense ran away beyond what I imagined it would . . . However, if it had not been for the energy, influence and money expended, Frank, innocent though he is, would have been hung long ago . . . Will you please get the ball in motion and raise the maximum amount you can?"

In Louis Wiley, Lasker had picked the perfect emissary to New York's socially connected and socially conscious Jewish elite. An obsequious yet droll bachelor who happened to serve as Adolph Ochs's financial aide, Wiley was a popular regular at the city's select restaurants and at parties in its best homes. He would know exactly whom to contact. And he did. On April 22, Wiley mailed a copy of Lasker's letter along with an explanatory note—typed on the *Times* letterhead—to Jacob H. Schiff. Whether Wiley contemplated that in seeking contributions in his paper's name he was compromising its objectivity remains unknown. Likewise, it's impossible to say whether he was aware of the views advanced in the fall of 1913 by the American Jewish Committee's Louis Marshall cautioning against an overtly Jewish fund drive. Regardless, by the date Wiley wrote Schiff, the *Times* had clearly crossed the boundary between journalism and advocacy. Moreover, with court slated to convene in Atlanta at ten the next morning, time was of the essence.

The extraordinary motion hearing, which convened in the library of the state capitol, started slowly, the initial session being devoted almost entirely to the presentation of the lengthy and by this juncture widely familiar document. But the second day saw a series of sensational developments. The first was the reading of an affidavit by Annie Maude Carter in which she not only acknowledged the existence of her correspondence with Jim Conley but alleged that in return for her acceptance of his marriage proposal, he'd confessed to Mary Phagan's murder. As Annie Maude told it:

> During Christmas week I was talking with Conley in his cell and he said he would tell me the whole truth about it. I asked him why he waited so long and he said, "If I tell you, will you marry me?" and I told him, "Yes." He then told me that he really did the murder of Mary Phagan, but that it was so plainly shown on Mr. Frank that he let it go that way. He begged me never to say anything about this.
>
> He said he was sitting on a box in the factory when the girl came down; that he told her someone had called her; that she turned back and he then struck her with his fist, knocking her down; that he dropped her through the hole; that he then took her around by the furnace, starting to burn her, but his conscience wouldn't let him; that he put her down there to make people believe Newt Lee did it; that afterward he found a piece of blank paper,

tears it in two, picks up a pencil and puts the paper on the cellar door and writes the notes; that he first took the notes and put them in her bosom, then he took them out and laid them by her side; that he then took a thing they opened boxes with and pulled the staple out of the back door and went out.

He told me that he kept the money he found in the purse, but gave the purse to a negro child.

I have not told this before because I only got out of jail March 9, 1914, but I want to tell the whole truth about what he told me while in jail, and I am willing to take the witness stand and swear to this at any time.

No sooner had reaction to the Carter affidavit subsided than Frank's lawyers let fly another shocker—a sworn statement by the Reverend C. B. Ragsdale, pastor of Atlanta's Plum Street Baptist Church, who averred that on the Monday night following little Mary's murder, he'd overheard Jim Conley confess the crime to a third party in an alley behind Terminal Station. As Ragsdale told it:

One of the men said to the other, "I am in trouble and want you to help me out. I killed a girl at the National Pencil Factory," and the other man said, "Well, who all was there?" and the first speaker said, "Nobody there but Mr. Frank, and I am not certain whether he was there or not." That immediately upon ending the part of the conversation here testified to, these two parties started out of the alley [and] deponent discovered that they were darkies.

In a supporting affidavit, R. L. Barber, a Plum Street Church member who said he was with Ragsdale the night in question, confirmed the preacher's account, adding that he had advised him against speaking out at the time for fear of getting "mixed up in the situation."

For Hugh Dorsey, the cumulative impact of the Carter and Ragsdale affidavits—which over his objections were added to the extraordinary motion as amendments—was devastating. Because he hadn't heard any of the charges before, much less had a chance to prepare, he had little choice but to ask Judge Hill for a one-week postponement. Yet what, if anything, the solicitor could do during this period was an open question. The defense had completed its case with a flourish. Declared Leo Frank in a circular released to the press shortly after court recessed:

A fair trial is what I want, what I am entitled to, and what no fair-minded man will deny me, and I appeal to the fair-minded people whose silent influence stands back of the courts and whose servants the courts are to see that I am given a fair trial.

FIFTEEN

Darkness Falls

Sometime early on the morning of Friday, May 1, an open-air touring car carrying William Burns and Dan Lehon departed downtown Atlanta, headed for the little crossroads community of Cedartown, 45 miles to the northwest. The detectives were on their way to interview a potential witness, and they were in a hurry. During the week that had passed since the initial hearings on the extraordinary motion, the optimism that had so infused Leo Frank's camp had given way to a fretful anxiety. Just the night before, Herbert Haas, in a despairing letter to Albert Lasker, observed: "Sentiment is as keen against Frank today as it was during the trial." The next round of hearings was reconvening this same day, and not only did Burns and Lehon hope to unearth new information that would be useful to the defense, by so doing they hoped to vindicate their reputation, for as they were well aware, the gathering storm had been largely precipitated by charges of impropriety against themselves and their associates.

The initial allegations had been leveled by Tom Watson. Boomed the headline atop the *Jeffersonian*'s April 23 edition:

How Much Longer Will the People of Atlanta Endure the Lawless Doings of William J. Burns? What Right Has This Sham Detective to Tamper With the Witnesses That Told the Truth on LEO FRANK, THAT FOUL DEGENERATE WHO MURDERED LITTLE MARY PHAGAN?

Watson regarded Burns as the embodiment of the interloping forces that he believed were attempting to subvert Georgia justice—"the conspiracy of Big Money against the law, against the courts, and against the poor little victim of hellish passion." Moreover, he was appalled by his methods. "If Burns were an honest man," he contended, "legitimately seeking to uncover crime, no one could criticize him. But when he comes to Georgia and begins to work on witnesses who have already testified under oath, *and when he uses threats, IF NOT BRIBES,* to prevail on them to change their evidence, *he makes himself a criminal.*" Taking the detective's effort to obtain a retraction from Monteen Stover as an emblematic example, the Sage inquired:

What right did Burns have to try to persuade, or intimidate, that young woman into committing perjury?

What right did he have to get her into Samuel Boorstein's [*sic*] office?

What right did he have to thrust himself upon the girl while she was there?

Such behavior, declared Watson, could be read in but one way: "The Great Detective is working to suppress the evidence." And it could be responded to in but one way:

> This man Burns richly deserves a coat of tar and feathers, plus a ride on a fence-rail. He has been engineering a campaign of systematic lies tending to blacken this state and tending to provoke an outbreak of popular indignation
>
> With all the bravado of a shallow bluffer, and with all the insolence of irresponsibility, he has gone to the extreme limit of toleration.
>
> There may not be a way by which the law can reach him, but there *is* a way to reach him.

The *Jeffersonian*'s broadside would not have done lasting harm had not subsequent events seemed to confirm Watson's charges. On April 27, the Reverend C. B. Ragsdale retracted his statement that he had overheard Jim Conley confess to Mary Phagan's murder, asserting that an unnamed Burns agent had paid him to make the claim. In an affidavit produced for Hugh Dorsey, the preacher swore that his tale was cooked up during several meetings with R. L. Barber and the anonymous operative, then presented to Dan Lehon and, finally, to Burns and Luther Rosser. Ragsdale's professed motivation: "They were just handing money out." In a related statement, the preacher's sons offered further insight into their father's actions, explaining that due to ill health and financial need, he had been easily victimized by Frank's allies. The evening the news broke, Ragsdale resigned his pastorate, ashamedly telling a church committee that he had received $200 for the false testimony.

Though Burns had immediately denied Ragsdale's accusation, terming it "a cowardly lie by a cowardly liar," the defense chose to cut the preacher loose, and on April 28, Rosser and Reuben Arnold asked Judge Benjamin Hill to strike his affidavit from the extraordinary motion. That done, the lawyers went to work trying to limit the damage, denouncing Ragsdale ("We want nothing to do with him," snorted Arnold) while simultaneously maintaining that at first, neither he nor Barber had given them reason to think any misconduct had been involved. In a joint statement issued by Rosser, Arnold, and Herbert and Leonard Haas, the defense contended: "On Thursday, April 23, 1914, there appeared at the office of L. Z. Rosser two men who claimed to have important information in reference to the Frank trial. [We] believed that they were acting from pure motives to correct the wrong of their former silence." The intention was to make the incident look like an aberration. Arnold even attempted to dismiss it as a joke, declaring: "Since the state set the example for lying by placing Jim Conley on the stand, it seems that all of the liars in Georgia are trying to break into this case."

Watson, however, would not let the matter die. Roared the double-deck banner atop the *Jeffersonian*'s April 30 edition:

> The Frank Case; the Great Detective; and the Frantic
> Efforts of Big Money to Protect Crime

As Watson saw it, the Ragsdale incident confirmed his earlier pronouncements. After ridiculing the substance of the preacher's original story (how was it, he asked, that Ragsdale and Barber were standing in a dark alley at the moment Conley was there admitting to little Mary's murder?), he pointedly intoned:

> God deliver us from a preacher who says he knew all the time that Frank was innocent but did not have the honesty and courage to say so until William J. Burns came upon the scene. If William J. Burns and lots of shekels had not arrived, Ragsdale apparently would have gone on preaching, while an innocent man was being hanged.

Ragsdale thus condemned, Watson lit into several of Burns's other contributions to the extraordinary motion, most devastatingly the Annie Maude Carter letters. To support his argument that the missives were as inauthentic as the preacher's tale, Watson called attention to the specific sexual preference they attributed to Conley. Then, drawing upon a broadly shared assumption among Southern whites as to the Negro libido, he proclaimed:

> Now, let me tell you a fact which all men who were raised on a plantation with negroes will substantiate. *Negro men will commit bestiality, but they will never commit sodomy.*
> The negro is naturally lustful and will take a female, even a beast, if it costs his life, but he never *takes a woman UNNATURALLY.*

And this was merely a prelude. In a far-ranging disquisition that seemed intended to suggest that Leo Frank would have been more inclined to indulge in the sort of acts mentioned in the Carter letters than Conley, the Sage rakishly added:

Is it possible that the Great Detective does not know the vital difference between the crimes of lust in the barbarian and the same crimes in *the degenerates* of civilization?

The excited barbarian, like the brutish negro, may commit bestiality; *but it is the degenerate of wealth and culture who commits sodomy.*

It was so in the Bible; it was so in the decay of Grecian civilization; it was the crime of luxury and corruption in Rome; it was the crime of effete Orientalism; it was the crime of Prince Eulenburg's elegantly decadent "set" at the imperial court of Germany.

In other words, sodomy, committed by a man *on a woman,* is peculiarly the rotten spot of a highly developed civilization.

Though there were obviously those who might have quarreled with Watson's conclusions regarding the Annie Maude Carter letters—not to mention his theories on perversion—few among them were readers of the *Jeffersonian.* No, Watson's growing constituency (in Atlanta, speculators who bought out newsstand stocks of his paper at the five-cent cover price were easily reselling them at a quarter a copy) regarded his insights as gospel. Asserted one correspondent: "You not only expressed my sentiments, but you expressed the belief of ninety per cent of the people (Gentiles)." Echoed another: "Tom Watson is a lighthouse of strength ever ready with tongue and pen to give courage to the wavering masses—for he loves them."

As the touring car carrying Burns and Lehon raced north, passing out of Fulton County into Cobb, the controversy raged on in the May 1 newspapers. HORRIBLE MISTAKE IN CASE OF FRANK, STATES W. J. BURNS, declared the *Constitution*'s front page headline, beneath which the detective not only again denied Ragsdale's charges but took issue with the most serious of Watson's claims. "In the matter of Ragsdale," he asserted, "I must say that his statement that I or anyone in the employ of the Burns agency bribed or attempted to bribe him is utterly untrue. In mentioning my name as one of those present when the affidavit was 'drawn' from him, he is stating an absolute falsehood." That said, Burns restated the contention that the Sage had so mockingly disparaged. "I have absolutely cleared Leo Frank of the charge of perversion, which was wholly responsible for his conviction, and I have also demonstrated beyond a shadow of a doubt that Jim Conley is a pervert and was the murderer of little Mary Phagan." Finally, he issued a public plea for understanding:

I would like to say one thing to the people of Atlanta. In all of my experience I have never been so moved as I have been in the Frank case.

Putting back of this statement my thirty years in the study and detection of crime, I say to you more earnestly than I ever spoke before in my life that in driving Leo M. Frank to his death without giving him a fair trial, you are making the most horrible, the most awful mistake I ever heard of.

The likelihood that such a mistake could be averted would, of course, increase if the mission upon which the detectives were now embarked — which was to meet a source who could supposedly further corroborate the allegations of degeneracy against Conley — succeeded.

The route to Cedartown runs through Marietta, but just as the Cobb County Courthouse — a handsome redbrick edifice whose clock tower soared above the tree line — came into view, the car carrying Burns and Lehon blew a tire. Hoping to make quick work of it, the detectives left their chauffeur with the machine and walked into Mary Phagan's hometown in search of a garage.

Though Marietta appeared on the surface little more than a satellite of Atlanta, it was, in truth, a fiercely independent place. At once agricultural (in 1910, Cobb County boasted 2,684 farms) and industrial (a sophisticated machine shop that produced sleek steam engines, a textile mill that turned out 14,000 pairs of men's half-hose daily, two busy furniture manufacturers and a well-regarded marble monument fabricator were all located here), the town afforded its 5,000 inhabitants a great degree of financial autonomy. Marietta's wealth manifested itself in the many stylish shops that surrounded its bandstand-adorned central square and in the numerous well-preserved antebellum homes that lined its best streets. What set the town apart, however, was less a matter of economics than of attitude. Forty-nine years after Appomattox, Marietta was still defiantly unreconstructed. The town tolerated Yankees, but it wouldn't be unfair to say that its basic view of them had not changed since 1862 when a group of Union soldiers dressed in civilian clothing slipped into Marietta and hijacked a northbound Confederate train, the Texas. What followed was one of the Civil War's most dramatic incidents — the Great Locomotive Chase, a harrowing pursuit that ended at the Tennessee line when the Texas ran out of fuel. Eight of the Northerners were hanged as spies, a fact of which Mariettans remained inordinately proud.

Not that Burns and Lehon, as they approached the Brumby Garage on Church Street just off the Marietta square, would at this late date have had reason to feel they were entering enemy territory. True, during the weeks since they had launched their investigation, the town had started to make its sympathies known. The local chapter of the United Confederate Veterans had inaugurated a campaign to erect an elaborate monument at Mary Phagan's grave. The Cobb County Democratic Committee, concerned that

Frank's fate, pending the result of the extraordinary motion hearing, could end up in the hands of John Slaton, had passed a resolution asking the governor, who was, of course, Luther Rosser's partner, to "define his position," becoming the first group to call attention to the fact that should executive clemency be requested, Slaton would face a conflict of interests. Still, such expressions hardly constituted threats, and the detectives would almost certainly have been quickly back on their way to Cedartown had they not been recognized by a passerby who aside from being a devotee of Tom Watson was the namesake of the South's most revered historical figure.

No sooner had Robert E. Lee Howell satisfied himself that the familiar-looking redheaded stranger standing in front of the Brumby Garage was Burns than he stormed up to the detective and in a frighteningly matter-of-fact tone announced: "I have promised to beat you if you ever came to Marietta, and here goes." With that, Howell, a diminutive but dangerous character who was the black-sheep member of a renowned Georgia family (one cousin was the editor of the *Constitution,* another Hugh Dorsey's law partner), slapped Burns's cheeks. Then he let loose with a barrage of curses, drawing a crowd. Many in the number—which, thanks to the fact that Marietta was teeming with farmers in town for a county election, reached several hundred—had been reading the *Jeffersonian,* and the cry of "Lynch him" rent the air.

Burns and Lehon suddenly found themselves confronting genuine peril (a knife-wielding member of the mob had to be physically restrained), and after realizing as much, the two did the only sensible thing. They made a run for it, Burns bolting into an adjacent neighborhood, Lehon heading to the nearby courthouse, where he took refuge in the sheriff's office. Accounts as to what happened next vary. According to Burns, he "walked down the back streets for about an hour," hoping that tempers would cool. An anonymous Mariettan, however, recalled otherwise: "The great detective ran through several dark alleys as fast as his legs would carry him, and those that saw him in action do say that he certainly showed a wonderful burst of speed." Either way, Burns eventually wound up behind locked doors at the Whitlock House, a hotel on the southwestern outskirts of town.

It didn't take long for word to spread where Burns was hiding, and within minutes the crowd from the Brumby Garage had recongregated. Several of Marietta's more "level-headed citizens"—as the *Constitution* termed them—appeared on the scene and one by one begged the throng to disperse, but to no avail. Whereupon Newton Augustus Morris, judge of the Blue Ridge Circuit, of which Cobb County was part, stepped to the fore and proposed a deal. In return for the detective's departure from Marietta, he demanded assurance of his safe passage. To this there was a general assent, yet success was hardly a foregone conclusion, as Burns's chauffeur, after being threatened by Robert E. Lee Howell, had patched his tire and fled. Soon enough, however, a White Sixty belonging to Thomas M. Brumby, proprietor of the town's largest furniture manufacturer, pulled up to the Whitlock House, and amid a shower of eggs—one of which hit Judge Morris in the head—Burns was whisked out of Marietta. Shortly thereafter, Cobb County mule dealer J. F. "Coon" Shaw bundled Lehon into his Overland 30 and departed as well. A disaster had been averted, but a chilling message had been conveyed. As the *New York Times* subsequently reported:

> Bob Howell's hand, which slapped Burns in the face, struck fire out of all Georgia. In a dramatic way, it focused attention on a growing opinion that money and "outside influence" were being used to save a rich man from punishment for the murder of a working girl.

Alarming as what had transpired in Marietta was for the defense, what had been occurring at the same time in the state capitol library back in Atlanta was possibly worse. From the moment the extraordinary motion hearing resumed, almost nothing had gone Leo Frank's way. The setbacks began when Judge Benjamin Hill rejected an eleventh-hour attempt by the condemned man's lawyers to make Burns's findings regarding the condition of Mary Phagan's underwear part of the motion. "I do not care to go behind the record in this case," declared Hill, contending that the trial jury had received ample opportunity to examine the garments, then adding: "Burns is simply giving his opinion." Hard upon this ruling, the judge dealt the defense a second blow by stopping Leonard Haas from reading the Annie Maude Carter letters aloud. While Hill agreed to take the missives into consideration, he asserted that their language was too offensive to be aired publicly. He would read them privately in chambers.

With the defense's hopes of establishing the specific manner in which Mary Phagan had been sexually abused thus greatly diminished and any chance for Georgians to reach their own conclusions regarding Jim Conley's predilections likewise lessened, Hugh Dorsey had launched into his countershowing. Speaking in general of the case Frank's lawyers had presented, he proclaimed: "If nothing added to nothing makes something, then there is something to this extraordinary motion." Next he denounced the methods that had been used in putting the case together, reiterating the accusation that the Burns agency had bribed Ragsdale while pointing out that Burns operatives had collected many other statements the defense had placed before the court. The implications could not have been plainer, but rather than dwell on them, the solicitor stunned the room by announcing that before he was done, he would prove Burns guilty of another transgression. The investigator, he charged, had spirited Annie Maude Carter out of Atlanta, making it impossible for state's officers to question her.

Having thereby suggested an extensive pattern of abuse, Dorsey—speaking from behind a table stacked with affidavits that had been gathered for the state during the past weeks by Detectives Black and Starnes and lawyer William Smith—began a systematic assault on the extraordinary motion. The first target was the defense's claim that the hairs discovered by R. P. Barrett on the factory lathe did not match those taken by Dr. Henry F. Harris during his autopsy. After citing undertaker Will Gheesling's recent testimony that the soap he'd used in preparing the remains for burial could have altered Harris's sample in ways that compromised any comparison, the solicitor read statements from a number of factory employees who contended that the hair found on the lathe matched Mary Phagan's. He followed these endorsements with one from a far more authoritative source—the victim's stepfather, John W. Coleman. His position was this: Whatever Harris's findings, the people who knew little Mary were in the best position to judge, and they had done so.

The object of Dorsey's next sally was the retraction the defense had elicited from Albert McKnight. The affidavit the solicitor now read suggested that the husband of the Franks' Negro cook would never have recanted had not C. W. Burke threatened him. According to McKnight, the detective—after promising to help find him the job as a Pullman porter—stated that if he did not renounce his assertion regarding the superintendent's allegedly suspicious behavior on the day of the murder, "the Jews" would get him.

To this point, Dorsey had not broken much fresh ground, but from here on out he would attack previously unchallenged portions of the extraordinary motion. For openers, he took aim at Lula Simmons, the woman whose claim that she'd heard screams coming from the pencil factory basement at 4:30 on the afternoon of the crime had been put forth by the defense to contradict the state's theories as to both the time and place of the murder. Through affidavits from neighbors, police officers and even a son-in-law, the solicitor portrayed Mrs. Simmons as a duplicitous creature who'd once run a house of prostitution. He then read a statement from Mrs. Simmons herself in which she not only repudiated the assertions attributed to her by Frank's lawyers but alleged that they had been fabricated by a man named Burns or Burke.

Mrs. Simmons's account thus discredited, Dorsey moved to reaffirm the prosecution's position as to when and where the murder occurred, introducing affidavits from W. T. and I. V. Tucker, a father and son who swore that around 12:10 on the afternoon of the crime, they had been passing the pencil factory and had heard screams coming from its second floor. During

Frank's trial, they said, they'd remained quiet for fear of getting "mixed up in the case." But upon learning of Mrs. Simmons's statement, they'd decided to come forth.

Helpful as all of this was to Dorsey, his main goal was the destruction of the half-dozen retractions the defense had secured from factory girls who at the trial had sworn to Frank's moral turpitude. The solicitor started the process by reading a statement from Carrie Smith, who after declaring that the recantation attributed to her was a forgery, unfurled a tale regarding the efforts of a heretofore unmentioned man known as "Mr. Maddox" to manipulate her. As the girl told it, Maddox, posing as an author writing a book on the case, had promised to share his commission with her if she would sign an affidavit repudiating her testimony. When she rejected the proposal, she said that Maddox lured her to the law firm of Rosser, Brandon, Slaton & Phillips where in an office marked "Mr. Slaton" he made the same overture. Again, she said, she declined.

No sooner had Dorsey finished with Smith's story than he presented a statement from Marie Karst, the factory worker who the defense maintained had testified to Frank's poor character solely because she'd misunderstood the solicitor when he'd used the word "lasciviousness." Yet according to what she now swore, the girl—though she'd indeed been stumped by the fancy term—had comprehended Dorsey's meaning perfectly well. As the *Journal* put it: "She knew Frank's relations with women and knew his character was bad." Moreover, according to Karst, during the preparation of the extraordinary motion C. W. Burke had hired her to "interview all the girl witnesses" against the superintendent. Midway into the job, she said, Burke informed her, "Well, I've got Carrie Smith where I want her." While Karst didn't spell it out, the point was clear—Burke and the mysterious Mr. Maddox were one and the same. Burke fired her, she added, when she refused his request to "live with Monteen Stover and persuade her to change her testimony."

Dorsey followed Karst's affidavit with one from Nellie Pettis, who likewise renounced her retraction and reiterated the truth of her trial testimony. Frank, she said, had made "improper proposals" to her. As if this weren't enough, she also claimed that during the weeks prior to the extraordinary motion hearings, someone resembling Mr. Maddox had tried to maneuver her into the defense camp.

As at both the trial and the coroner's inquest, Dorsey next introduced another Nellie. Nellie Wood's statement echoed the Pettis girl's in that it contained a renunciation of the retraction submitted by the defense and a reaffirmation of the original charges of sexual misconduct against Frank. In the end, though, this Nellie did her namesake a couple better. First, in an accusation that seemed to confirm one of Conley's most damaging claims, she said that the superintendent had once informed her he was "not like other men." Then she alluded to a previously unmentioned Burns operative named Jimmy Wrenn who, as she told it, had promised big money in return for an affidavit favorable to Frank.

With afternoon shadows lengthening, Dorsey concluded Friday's session by returning to the topic with which he'd started—the hair evidence. According to a statement from the factory machinist R. P. Barrett, Jimmy Wrenn had also recently approached him with a proposition—a lucrative job in exchange for a retraction of his testimony regarding the strands he'd found twined around his lathe.

On that note, Judge Hill adjourned the proceedings for the day, and Luther Rosser, Reuben Arnold, and Herbert and Leonard Haas immediately went into conference with Burns and Lehon, who'd just returned from Marietta. With the papers' late editions brimming with bad news ("Defense Affidavits Forged, Says Dorsey," boomed the *Georgian*'s headline; ANGRY CROWD DRIVES BURNS FROM MARIETTA, reported the *Journal*'s), there was little reason for cheer, and what reason there was decreased even further when early in the evening a Fulton County deputy sheriff rapped on the door and served Burns and Lehon with subpoenas demanding their presence in court at the resumption of hearings on Monday. When asked by reporters why he had summoned the detectives, Dorsey responded: "Oh, I merely want to ask them a few questions."

Owing to the fact that William Burns was due in Oklahoma the next week to testify in a federal case, Saturday morning found the various parties gathered inside a hastily procured Thrower Building courtroom. The ordeal now awaiting the celebrated detective—while less dangerous than the one he'd faced in Marietta—was nonetheless laden with peril.

Hugh Dorsey began by inquiring into whether news stories reporting that Burns had easily determined that Leo Frank was, as he'd put it, sexually "normal" were accurate. Yes, the detective readily replied, happy to repeat such a finding. To which the solicitor rejoined: "Do you profess to be able by talking to a man for a short while to tell whether he is a pervert?"

"No," Burns conceded, "but I feel by talking to him I can form a definite conclusion."

"How do you tell that a man is not a pervert?" Dorsey pressed.

Though Burns may not have sensed danger here, Reuben Arnold did, but Judge Hill overruled his objection, whereupon the detective declared: "I am somewhat a student of human nature. As I work with criminal classes, I frequently come in contact with them."

"Do you consider your opinion in the matter as trustworthy and accurate?"

"I do."

Having thus encouraged Burns's natural tendency to boast, the solicitor struck. "Did you have any conversation with Jim Conley before you reached the conclusion that he is a pervert?"

"No," came the response.

"Then, in this case you substituted a less trustworthy method?"

Burns countered by alluding to his determinations regarding Mary Phagan's underwear and the Annie Maude Carter letters, getting in a few words concerning the evidence that the defense believed Judge Hill had slighted. Conley, he said, "satisfies his passions in an unnatural manner." Yet his responses to the solicitor's further queries relative to the topic of deviancy were vague and unconvincing.

A key plank of Frank's new trial bid thereby made to appear less weighty than it was, Dorsey directed Burns to the charge that he or his agents had bribed state's witnesses to change their testimony. The detective denied the allegation, but significantly, he did not dismiss the possibility that in some instances, money may have changed hands, saying only: "If any of my men did such a thing, he violated all the rules of the agency." On the heels of this qualified assurance, the solicitor quizzed Burns regarding the agents assigned to the case, eliciting the admission that Jimmy Wrenn—the individual mentioned in Friday's tales of wrongdoing—was on the payroll. In fact, the detective allowed that he'd engaged a small army of operatives, among them Boots Rogers, the driver who'd carried the responding officers to the pencil factory the morning Mary Phagan's body was discovered, and L. P. Whitfield and W. D. MacWorth, the Pinkerton investigators who'd broken with Harry Scott over his zeal to pin the murder on Frank. The news that the detective had recruited men formerly associated with the prosecution set reporters to scribbling. The biggest stir, however, was caused by a new name, Carlton Tedder, who was an assistant to William Smith. While Burns didn't explicitly say so, the implication was that he'd hired an informant in the state's camp.

Though the behavior to which Burns had thus far admitted did not constitute criminal wrongdoing, his testimony had undoubtedly put him in jeopardy. Indeed, the more the detective revealed of his behind-the-scenes activities, the more he risked. Which was why when Dorsey started probing specific areas of alleged misconduct, Burns attempted to lay the responsibility on others. Regarding his first knowledge of the Reverend C. B. Ragsdale, for instance, he asserted:

> Lehon came in and said the character of the preacher had been sustained.
> I told him I would have nothing to do with it and advised him to take the
> matter to the attorneys and let them investigate it and do what they wanted.

Similarly, when the solicitor inquired into the provenance of the Annie Maude Carter letters, Burns reiterated that they'd been discovered by C. W. Burke, then added that they'd initially been called to his attention by Herbert and Leonard Haas. The detective was distancing himself from the extraordinary motion's strongest components.

Considering the fanfare with which Burns had been brought into the affair and the volubility with which he'd heretofore touted his progress, his newfound reticence not only seemed out of character, but it opened him up to attack from an altogether different angle:

"Tell us one thing you have done in the—how long is it, sixty days—you have been at work on this case?" Dorsey inquired.

"Well," replied Burns, "I have read the Brief of Evidence very carefully. I went over the factory. I interviewed the witnesses there, and I came to your office and examined the garments of the dead girl."

"There were over 100 state's witnesses," the solicitor shot back. "How many of them have you examined?"

"I don't know."

"Didn't you read the record," Dorsey then demanded, by that meaning the several thousand pages of transcript.

"I read the Brief," Burns repeated, conceding that he'd made do with the shorter summary used during the appeal.

"Name some of the witnesses you have examined?"

"Schiff, Darley, Lemmie Quinn, Holloway, Frank himself—I don't remember the others."

All of the individuals Burns cited were, of course, from the defense's side of the aisle. As a consequence, the solicitor catechized the detective concerning some state's witnesses.

"Have you seen Newt Lee?"

"No."

"Have you talked with Starnes and Campbell?"

"No."

"Have you talked with Dr. Claude Smith, who examined the blood stains on the second floor?"

"No."

"Did you talk to Mel Stanford?"

"No."

"Did you talk to Barrett?"

"No."

The conclusion thus seemingly inescapable, Dorsey rounded out his examination by posing a question whose answer, he believed, would confirm the charge he'd made on Friday in his introductory statement. Gazing directly at Burns, he asked: "Did you order that Annie Maude Carter be sent out of town?"

"I suggested it," the detective admitted.

"Who sent her out of town?"

"Mr. Lehon."

"Where did he send her?"

Here, Burns turned to the bench for help, but Judge Hill instructed him to respond, so he did: "To New Orleans."

"After she made her affidavit in this case and became a witness, you mean to tell the court that you had her sent out of the jurisdiction?"

"Yes," Burns reiterated, adding that he'd done so in order to keep the state's officers from "bamboozling her." Which was what he believed had occurred to Carrie Smith, Marie Karst and all the others who'd repudiated their retractions. Yet even if these things had happened, by acknowledging the role he'd played in sending Carter away, the detective found himself close to being in contempt of court.

From Dorsey's perspective, there could be no better ending place.

To give Reuben Arnold credit, he made a valiant effort to salvage Burns's turn upon the stand, opening his examination by introducing the hostile atmosphere in which the detective—notwithstanding the authorities' pledges of cooperation—had been forced to work.

"Mr. Burns," Arnold began, "have you found it difficult on account of the attitude of the public to make an investigation in this case?"

"Extremely so."

"Have you in all your experience ever encountered more stubborn and unreasoning prejudice?"

"I most certainly have not."

"Have you found it difficult to hold a man's evidence after you have obtained it?"

"I have."

The defense's thesis sketched out, Arnold directed Burns to particular instances in which he felt he'd faced interference. Regarding Conley, the detective repeated the story of how William Smith had rejected his request to interview the Negro. Regarding Albert McKnight, he reiterated that the husband of the Franks' cook had withdrawn his retraction only after being jailed.

Arnold next directed Burns to the topic of Conley's trial testimony, the hope being that he could take a crack at some of its well-known inconsistencies. But no sooner had the lawyer posed his first query than Judge Hill cut him off, citing the same rationale he'd given on Friday to bar the detective's opinions concerning the condition of little Mary's underwear. The jury had already passed on the matter.

Another vital avenue of inquiry thus precluded, Arnold found himself at a loss; hence he concluded by endeavoring to blunt the accusations of misconduct that had been leveled at the detective.

"Mr. Burns," he asked, "did you ever attempt to get anything in this case except the truth?"

"No."

"Did you ever by the offer of bribes, intimidation or any other improper methods seek to obtain evidence from witnesses?"

"I assuredly did not."

With that, Arnold was done, and Judge Hill brought down his gavel.

As the combatants filed out of the Thrower Building, a smiling Hugh Dorsey announced that he couldn't wait to get at Dan Lehon on Monday. Members of the defense team, however, said nothing. Which was understandable, for after what had just transpired, their mood was even darker than it had been the day before.

Yet silent as Frank's lawyers were in public, in private, they bled. "I regret to advise that the situation here is desperate," Herbert Haas wrote Albert Lasker that afternoon. Describing the morning's hearing, he asserted:

> Judge Hill allowed the Solicitor to inquire into every phase of Mr. Burns' investigation and connection with the case . . . every confidential matter that came to mind. The objections of the defense were promptly overruled. Mr. Arnold then conducted a cross-examination of Mr. Burns and after asking several questions was abruptly stopped by Judge Hill, with the admonition that he would not permit any questions to reflect on the verdict of the jury . . . In other words, the court ruled that the State could have the widest latitude to hurt Frank, whether the testimony was relevant or irrelevant, but that the defense could show up nothing by Mr. Burns that would help Frank.

The court, however, was not solely to blame. Providing the first indication of internal dissension, Haas noted: "It is the belief of nearly all of our friends that Burns's connection with the case has done us irretrievable damage." The lawyer admitted that he had been unable to pin down anything improper that had been done but added that he had no idea how the detective turned up Ragsdale. He also believed that Burns's infatuation with the press had both offended Dorsey and raised undue expectations. "We tried to keep Burns from talking all the time but there was nothing to stop him. Of course, that cannot be helped now, but it is our intention to call [him] off the case upon the termination of the . . . hearings." Whether the lawyer stopped to consider that the recipient of his letter bore the responsibility for hiring Burns cannot be known. But even if he did, now was no time for niceties. Taking a look around him, Haas concluded: "All of us feel that the situation is hopeless."

Hugh Dorsey was not about to put on the brakes. The solicitor intended to decimate the extraordinary motion. When the hearings reconvened back at the state capitol library at 10 on Monday morning, he called Dan Lehon to the stand, but where he'd grilled Burns on all manner of topics, he was now interested in only one—money. Who was financing the investigation? Were the fees paid by check or in cash? How and when were operatives compensated? The questions came in a relentless rapid fire, and though Lehon avoided any mention of Albert Lasker—he consistently named Herbert Haas as the probe's source of funding—he was forced into several damaging admissions. For one, he revealed that just days before the defense secured C. B. Ragsdale's affidavit, he'd advanced $500 to the agent who had alerted him to the preacher's story. For another, he said it was standard practice to give the likes of Boots Rogers and L. P. Whitfield the occasional ten spot to cover operating costs. Of course, Lehon added, there were innocent justifications for these expenditures, but despite such an assurance, his testimony seemed to confirm the widely shared view that the defense had been purchasing evidence.

Once Lehon stepped down, Dorsey turned to a stack of affidavits on the table before him and resumed his item-by-item assault on the new trial bid's individual parts. The first statement the solicitor read was by Ruth Robinson, who not surprisingly retracted her retraction as to Leo Frank's poor character, branding the document, witnessed by Detective C. W. Burke, a forgery. With that, the last of the factory girls whose repudiations were put forth just ten days earlier had recanted.

Dorsey now moved in a different direction, reading a retraction by Mary Rich, the Negro lunch-wagon operator who'd declared in an affidavit for the defense that Jim Conley had emerged from the basement of the National Pencil factory around 2:20 on April 26, 1913, purchased a meal, then returned to the building. But as Rich now told it, she had not seen Conley on the afternoon of Mary Phagan's murder and never made a statement saying she had. This was not, however, because Frank's allies had failed to seek one. A month or so before the hearings, the woman charged, a group consisting of C. W. Burke, Rabbi David Marx and Lucille Frank had approached her and asked that she make an affidavit. "You will take the rope from around my husband's neck," Rich claimed Lucille had said. She added that she'd replied, "I can't tell a lie like that," and had thought no more of the encounter until the newspapers reported that a statement attributed to her was part of the extraordinary motion.

Dorsey next read a statement by Helen Ferguson, which, while not a retraction of her affidavit for the defense, provided yet another damaging account of the tactics that Burns's agents allegedly employed in securing such affidavits. As the girl now told it, Jimmy Wrenn, operating under the alias J. W. Howard, had approached her several months earlier and invited her to the movies. Following a couple of dates, he introduced her to a man he said was his father but who she later learned was C. W. Burke. He asked her to renounce her testimony concerning Frank's purported refusal to give her Mary Phagan's wages. Though she said she answered no, Wrenn and Burke apparently continued to court her. "They said Frank was an innocent man. Jimmy said, 'I'd hate to be the main one to put the rope around his neck.' " She maintained that she again stood her ground, although she confirmed she'd told the men that she was scared of Conley. The detectives' efforts came to a conclusion when Wrenn overplayed his hand. "Jimmy tried to kiss me, and I hit him in the mouth," the girl declared, adding: "That seemed to cool him down. I haven't seen him since."

Significant as the Rich and Ferguson statements were to Dorsey's overall attack, they were, in the end, random sorties before another big push, this one aimed at destroying a portion of the extraordinary motion that had seemed unassailable.

Dorsey opened his assault on Henry Alexander's finding that the murder notes had been written by Conley on paper found in the factory basement by reading a certified copy of an Atlanta city ordinance prohibiting the storage of combustible materials for longer than six hours in any area of a building deemed a fire zone.

Against this backdrop, Dorsey then presented a number of affidavits intended to prove that the out-of-date order pads belonging to former factory mechanic H. F. Becker that Alexander contended provided the sheet upon which the longer note was composed had never reached the basement, but had instead been stored in Frank's office. The initial statement to this effect came from Philip Chambers, the onetime office boy who during the trial was subjected to a grilling by the solicitor suggesting that he'd been the target of the superintendent's homosexual overtures. According to Chambers, he had been present when Becker's desk, following the mechanic's last day at work, was moved to Frank's office. At the same time, the boy asserted, Becker's supplies, including order pads and carbon sheets, were put in a nearby closet. "No trash, books or papers were ever left piled in the basement," Chambers swore.

As corroboration for Chambers's affidavit, Dorsey next read a statement by the early suspect—and longtime Frank nemesis—James M. Gantt. As the fired factory bookkeeper told it, not only had he, too, been present the day Becker's desk was moved, but he'd helped place the relevant order pads in the closet adjacent to the superintendent's office. He also swore that as of his own last day at work—April 4, 1913—the pads were exactly where he'd left them.

Once he had put on the record the affidavits asserting that the order pads had been kept where Conley said they were, Dorsey produced a statement declaring that such pads had not been kept where Alexander said they were. As Atlanta fire inspector H. W. Otis told it, he frequently checked the plant, paying special attention to the area around the furnace where Mary Phagan's body was discovered. Between January 1, 1913, and the day of the murder, he said he'd twice ordered this area cleaned and had heard Frank instruct employees to do so. He was "personally positive" that no pads or paper were in the basement at the time of the crime.

The concluding element in Dorsey's attack on Alexander's determinations was aimed at their most credible—or at least most scientific—underpinning: the photographic analysis suggesting that the preprinted sheet upon which the longer note was written was a carbon of an order placed by Becker in 1909. Alexander had, of course, based his conclusion on the fact that the high-quality reproduction of the note published in his much discussed pamphlet revealed the smudgy purchase number "1018." But according to the affidavit the solicitor now submitted from photographer H. M. DeVore, who at the state's request had also photographed the notes and had used plates that provided even sharper resolution, the actual number was "1818." By itself, this discrepancy did not necessarily invalidate Alexander's larger point, but DeVore followed it up with a devastating charge. According to the photographer, Alexander had told him that the print reproduced in his pamphlet had been retouched at the lab. Though DeVore did not explicitly say so, the intimation was clear—the lawyer had doctored the image to get the results he wanted.

Having struck a blow that managed both to damage one of the extraordinary motion's main underpinnings and to threaten a lifelong friendship (Dorsey and Alexander had, of course, been college roommates), the solicitor introduced a retraction from J. E. Duffy. Contrary to his affidavit for the defense, the former factory worker now swore that he had not bled profusely on the plant's second floor from a cut suffered shortly before the murder. Sounding an increasingly familiar theme, he said Detectives Burke and Wrenn had secured the false statement with promises of financial gain made during a night on the town in a chauffeur-driven limousine. After reading the portion of the affidavit detailing the trio's perigrinations, the solicitor glanced at Rosser and Arnold and in a shot at the slogan Frank had been appending to his recent utterances cracked: "That was truth on the run."

Hard upon Duffy's renunciation, Dorsey presented one from a more critical witness. According to the latest statement of C. Brutus Dalton, his testimony alleging that Frank was acquainted with the notorious Daisy Hopkins and had conducted trysts in the pencil factory office while Conley served as lookout was nothing but the truth. He, too, he contended, had been lured into the defense camp by the siren song of a fast buck—$100 in cash and a like amount in railway passes. Had this shadowy figure said no more, it would have been bad enough, but far from being just a reiteration of his original accusations, his affidavit contained worrisome new details:

> I have on several visits to Leo M. Frank's office seen Frank with girls in his office, and I have seen Frank play with them, hug them, kiss them and pinch them . . . I saw Frank on two or three occasions take a girl and go to the back of the room where the dressing room is. On one occasion, Frank had six bottles of beer and I carried three more bottles to his office . . . In regard to the cot in the basement, I know that Leo Frank knew about it, because I have heard him speak of it.

In the wake of Dalton's statement, Dorsey unveiled several affidavits bearing on the Reverend C. B. Ragsdale, which made explicit what had heretofore been only a vague charge—Dan Lehon was the individual who had bribed the preacher. The solicitor then launched a concerted campaign against yet another of the extraordinary motion's principal planks—the Annie Maude Carter letters.

Dorsey began by reading the affidavit of Fred Perkerson, a recently released county prisoner who during his time in the Tower had attained trusty status. During his last weeks behind bars, Perkerson swore, he had noticed a fellow convict named George Wrenn—brother of Jimmy Wrenn, the Burns associate implicated in so much wrongdoing—talking with Frank's lawyers. Following one such meeting, Perkerson charged, Wrenn approached him, urging that he use his trusty privileges to enter Conley's cell, then "come out and declare Conley had confessed to the murder." Predictably, the former prisoner added, Wrenn promised that there was money in it for him. Perkerson also alleged that he'd seen Wrenn go into Conley's cell in the company of Annie Maude Carter. And he said he'd once observed Wrenn hand Carter a note that she, in turn, gave to Conley.

Dorsey followed Perkerson's affidavit with a statement from another former prisoner, Frank Reese, who confirmed that George Wrenn had made it known inside the Tower that he was in the market for a confession from Conley. He also declared that Wrenn and Annie Maude Carter seemed to be in cahoots.

Dorsey's clincher was an affidavit from the man at the center of the Carter matter—Conley himself. The state's star witness denied that he'd confessed the crime to the woman. Then, though he admitted that the two had carried on a correspondence, he affirmed the statements of Perkerson and Reese charging that George Wrenn had used Annie Maude as a courier to deliver incriminating letters to him. Finally, he alleged that the guards at the Tower, in league with Frank's allies, had made him vulnerable to attempted frame-ups by leaving his cell door unlocked.

Though none of the affidavits Dorsey presented regarding Annie Maude Carter went so far as to say that Conley was not the author of the salacious missives the defense believed tied him to Mary Phagan's murder, they indicated that Frank's surrogates had used the woman to entrap him. Consequently, once Judge Hill gaveled Monday's session to a close, he ordered the defense to return Carter to Atlanta, adding that if the woman was not produced, her correspondence with Conley and her statement alleging that he'd confessed to her would be expunged from the new trial bid.

Hugh Dorsey opened Tuesday's session of the hearings by asking the court to hold Dan Lehon on $1,000 bond pending a grand jury investigation into the methods that had been used in assembling the extraordinary motion. The request, which Judge Hill granted, suggested that the solicitor not only expected to prevail in the present battle but was contemplating subsequent prosecutions.

Dorsey began his final push by unveiling an affidavit by the woman whom, it now became clear, William Burns had not gotten out of Atlanta fast enough. According to Annie Maude Carter's statement to the police, she had not received any vulgar letters from Conley, and she did not believe him to be a degenerate. She also declared that in her conversations with Conley, he had never admitted to murdering Mary Phagan, always maintaining that Leo Frank was guilty.

Having thus taken a last shot at one of the extraordinary motion's most sensational elements, Dorsey turned his guns on its only still-unchallenged stronghold, reading an affidavit by George Epps in which the boy reaffirmed his assertion that Mary Phagan had confided her fear of Frank to him on the day of the murder. He never would have retracted his story, he said, had not a group of unscrupulous defense operatives whisked him off to Birmingham, Alabama, where they threatened him into doing so.

With that, Dorsey, believing that he had not only destroyed the substance of the extraordinary motion but had shown Burns and his men to be bullying dissemblers, concluded his countershowing.

Despairing as Leo Frank's lawyers were, they came back at Dorsey with everything they had. No sooner had the solicitor sat down than Leonard Haas stood up and, reaching into his own stack of affidavits, initiated a forceful rebuttal.

Haas's first goal was to cast doubt on Dorsey's contention that Albert McKnight had returned to the state's embrace, and he began by reading affidavits—two from Burke and Lehon, two from reporters—confirming McKnight's retraction of his allegation against Frank. The lawyer then read a statement by steadfast Minola McKnight, who also upheld her husband's repudiation of his testimony, while adding that she'd been present when he met Burke and that no money had changed hands.

Haas next sought to undercut Dorsey's claim that the many factory girls who'd renounced charges of poor character against Frank had likewise come home. Here again, the lawyer presented affidavits from the pertinent investigators corroborating the girls' retractions and denying any wrongdoing. Moreover, he introduced statements from two notary publics who'd witnessed the retractions. Finally, he read the affidavit of a Cincinnati man who attested to having been present at the Home of the Good Shepherd when Burke took Dewey Hewell's statement. Declared John C. Conroy: "She broke down, wept and said she had not sworn to the truth at the Frank trial. Burke held out no inducement to the girl."

Having thus done what he could to negate Dorsey's assault on a couple of the extraordinary motion's centerpieces, Haas endeavored to shore up some of its peripheral realms, reading affidavits from Rabbi Marx, Burke and Jimmy Wrenn denying any impropriety in, respectively, the obtaining of Mary Rich's statement, the eliciting of C. B. Dalton's and J. E. Duffy's retractions, and the securing of Helen Ferguson's statement.

Critical as it was for the defense to repulse Dorsey on all fronts, the core elements of the new trial bid remained the primary concern, and Haas now turned to two more of them, beginning by presenting an affidavit from assistant factory superintendent Herbert Schiff supporting Henry Alexander's findings regarding the paper upon which the murder notes were written. Contrary to what Chambers and Gantt had told the solicitor, asserted Schiff, the contents of H. F. Becker's desk—including the all-important order pads—had been dumped in the basement. That said, Haas took up the matter of Annie Maude Carter, reading a statement from Rabbi Marx—

who, it turned out, had been present when defense lawyers secured the woman's affidavit—attesting to the fact that she had sworn Conley had told her he was guilty and vowing that she had not been coerced. Haas's final submission of the day also bore on Carter. According to a study prepared by James Innis, a Chicago handwriting expert engaged by Albert Lasker to compare Conley's letters to Carter with the murder notes, the same hand that penned the letters penned the notes. The determination countered the state's insinuation that the letters were forgeries.

As Wednesday's session of the hearings began, the greatly diminished pile of documents atop the defense table made it plain that Haas was nearly done. Still, several last points needed to be addressed, and the lawyer threw himself into the job. First, he read a statement by George Wrenn in which the convict denied taking part in any plot to coerce a confession from Jim Conley. Then he presented a number of affidavits intended to disprove the state's charge that George Epps was railroaded into denouncing his assertion that Mary Phagan had been scared of Frank. True, conceded C. W. Burke, he'd taken the newsboy to Birmingham, yet he'd done so at his request. "Epps told us he was afraid of John Black and wouldn't make a statement in Atlanta," stated Burke.

The case in rebuttal thereby complete, closing arguments commenced. Leading off for the defense was Luther Rosser, but this was not the obstreperous Rosser who rattled opponents and windows alike. Suffering from a severe cold, the big man spoke from his chair, his voice no more than a whisper. Still, there was fire in his words—and obvious disdain for the duplicitous tactics he believed Dorsey had used to combat the extraordinary motion. For openers, he suggested that the solicitor had threatened many of the witnesses who'd repudiated their retractions, declaring: "Anybody who in the least understands human nature knows full well the power of the state—knows that this power is sufficient to cause a witness who has changed his testimony to change it back." Rosser devoted most of his energies, however, to spotlighting the fact that he believed even without any others required the court to grant Frank a new trial. That fact: the solicitor's suppression of Dr. Henry F. Harris's finding that the strands of hair discovered on Barrett's lathe did not match those taken from Mary Phagan's head. Had the physician's determination been known during the original proceedings, the lawyer insisted, the state could not have bolstered Conley's claim that the murder occurred on the pencil factory's second floor.

And without such bolstering, there would have been no conviction. From Rosser's vantage, the injustice here was undeniable, and reaching deep into himself, he raspily concluded:

> Your honor, let this point be made before a jury. No judge who ever loved the right can approve the conduct of those in that hair incident. My brother Dorsey should have caused Dr. Harris to tell all he knew. I ask your honor to deal with it in your heart and conscience.

With that, Rosser ceded the floor to Reuben Arnold, but no sooner had Arnold started to speak than it became clear that the extraordinary motion was most likely already dead. The moment of revelation came in the midst of some extended comments by the lawyer on the topic of perjury and the number of state's witnesses—among them Conley, Dalton, McKnight, Duffy and Epps—alleged by the defense to have been guilty of the crime. Before Arnold could complete his point, Judge Hill cut him off, asserting that under Georgia law, perjured testimony could not serve as the basis for a new trial unless the accused perjurer had been tried and convicted. Hearing this, Hugh Dorsey leaped to his feet, announcing that he could cite a dozen precedents supporting the court. For those in Frank's camp, the implications were devastating—the mass of retractions in which they'd placed such faith were legally meaningless. Reeling, Arnold muttered, "You could not hunt the penitentiary through to find such a set of witnesses as my friend convicted Frank with." But here, too, Hill stopped him, contending: "Credibility of witnesses is a matter for the jury. I think you are shut off as to credibility of witnesses."

With Frank's prospects fading to black before his eyes, Arnold did the only thing he could do—he jettisoned those aspects of the extraordinary motion that he believed could no longer help him. Overboard went all of the retractions, not just those by McKnight, Dalton and Epps but those by Pettis, Karst and the other factory girls. Also overboard went the charge of perversion against Conley. The lawyer based this decision in part on Hill's earlier ruling disallowing Burns's findings as to the condition of Mary Phagan's underwear, but he seemed to be cognizant as well of Tom Watson's musings on black sexuality:

> Burns isn't familiar with the vernacular of our negro, and that is why he believes Conley is a pervert. I understand he bases his opinion on the vile language used in Conley's letters. Conley isn't a pervert. There isn't any perversion in this case. Frank isn't—no one connected with it is. Mary Phagan was killed to slake the bestial lust of a depraved mind. This perversion business is rot.

Speaking directly to Judge Hill, Arnold announced that he would now limit himself to "three physical facts"—the determinations made by Henry Alexander regarding the order blanks upon which the murder notes were written; the suppression of Dr. Harris's finding that the hair discovered on the factory lathe did not match little Mary's; and the Carter letters, which, while they might not indicate degeneracy, suggested that the forces animating Conley were sufficient to inspire murder. Asserted Arnold:

> Those notes show that Jim Conley is as lustful and bestial a creature as ever lived in the world. They show that his body and mind were saturated and absorbed with lust. His original motive may have been robbery, but he followed it up with lust.

His case thus deflated and disfigured, Arnold returned to his seat.

In the wake of all this, not a lawyer or reporter in the room believed Judge Hill would find in Frank's favor. And he did not. After informing Dorsey that no argument from the state was necessary, the judge calmly and without further reflection denied the extraordinary motion.

Publicly, Leo Frank and his supporters reacted to the news that the new trial bid had been rejected with a mixture of stoicism, outrage and resolve. From his cell in the Tower, Lucille at his side, the condemned man told the *Georgian:* "I had expected that action. I have nothing more to say but may later." Meantime, the *New York Times* condemned the decision, editorializing:

> The trial of Leo M. Frank in Atlanta for the murder of Mary Phagan was from the beginning about everything that a murder trial ought not to be. Judge Hill of the superior court denied the extraordinary motion for a new trial, yet it is impossible to feel that the first trial was fair.

As for Frank's lawyers, they promptly vowed to appeal. "We are busy at work on the bill of exceptions and will carry the motion before the Supreme Court," announced Reuben Arnold on Wednesday evening.

Behind the scenes, however, the defense team brooded, and discord erupted anew—particularly in New York. "I have been disgusted at the farcical methods to which Burns has resorted," the American Jewish Committee's Louis Marshall wrote the *New York Times*'s Louis Wiley. "Every one of his acts has been a burlesque upon modern detective ideas. It is deplorable that a case so meritorious as that of Frank should have been brought to this point of destruction by such ridiculous methods." Marshall had similarly harsh words for the condemned man's Atlanta counsel, asserting: "I know that the lawyers in the case have tried their best and have been devoted to their client, but they have not at all times acted with good judgement." Summing up the mood in Manhattan, Samuel Untermeyer, Marshall's partner, informed Wiley: "I am afraid the whole business has been terribly botched."

And things would only get worse. As he had intimated, Hugh Dorsey immediately initiated proceedings against Burns and his operatives. Other agencies followed suit. By late May the detective was besieged. To begin with, the Fulton County grand jury indicted Burns and Lehon for subornation of perjury in the Ragsdale affair. Shortly thereafter, the same body indicted C. W. Burke and Jimmy Wrenn for their part in obtaining Helen Ferguson's statement. Meanwhile, the Atlanta City Council revoked Burns's license, forcing the investigator to close his local office. Simultaneously, Lehon and L. P. Whitfield were convicted of several Frank-related infractions and fined. As for the allegations of contempt in connection with Annie Maude Carter's removal to New Orleans, Burns and Lehon caught a break. Upon the woman's return to Atlanta, Judge Hill ruled that the two had complied with his orders. Not that the agency's problems were over. Following an angry speech by Chief James L. Beavers at the convention of the International Association of Police Chiefs, the organization rescinded Burns's accreditation.

Burns's difficulties in the aftermath of the extraordinary motion's failure were so extensive that Tom Watson, though delighted by the spectacle, feared that Georgians might lose sight of the fact that the detective was merely a pawn of the interests that sought to free Frank. Hence beneath a front-page banner ("The Frank Case: What Does It Reveal Concerning Conditions in Georgia?"), the *Jeffersonian* proclaimed:

> Let us not be deceived by the evident intention to make Burns the scapegoat.
>
> It is not fair. That rascal tried to do what those who hired him brought him here to do.
>
> What else did Haas expect of him? What else did the Atlanta papers expect of him? What else did the firm of Rosser, Brandon, Slaton and Phillips expect of him?

Having thus refocused attention on the genuine culprits, the Sage, citing that the governor's law office had been a locus of the Burns agents' activities, added:

> There isn't a right-thinking man of us who does not feel troubled because of Governor Slaton's connection with the lawyers of the defense.

Like the Cobb County Democratic Committee before him, Watson was alarmed by the increasingly real prospect that Frank's fate could ultimately be decided by Luther Rosser's partner.

First, however, there would be another legal battle, one that while beginning in Atlanta would almost surely wend its way to the United States Supreme Court. The foundation for this challenge had been laid in mid-April when Albert Lasker engaged a new set of defense lawyers to file a motion in Fulton County Superior Court asking that Frank's conviction be set aside on the grounds that his absence from the courtroom when the jury returned its verdict had deprived him of his constitutional right to due process. In a lengthy document, John Tye and Henry Peeples elucidated the incidents both inside and outside the packed arena in which Frank was tried that led Rosser and Arnold to accede to Judge Leonard Roan's suggestion that their client should stay away at the critical hour. The decision, the motion added, was made without Frank's knowledge or permission: "He did not waive said right, nor did he authorize anyone to waive it for him, nor consent that he not be present."

Hugh Dorsey, of course, vowed to fight the Tye-Peeples Motion (as it would henceforth be called) and when on June 5, nearly a month after Frank's new trial bid was rejected, the hearing opened before Judge Ben Hill in the Thrower Building, fight it he did. Because the solicitor conceded the point that the factory superintendent was not present to hear the verdict, most of his argument took the form of a demurrer. For starters, he asserted that the Georgia Supreme Court had already ruled on the issue of the atmosphere in which the trial was conducted, finding that it was not a factor. As for the harm Frank had suffered due to his absence, Dorsey scoffed, declaring that Judge Roan's polling of the jurors had ensured the verdict's sanctity. Finally, he declared that at the time in question, Rosser and Arnold had pledged not to appeal on these grounds. "This motion," the solicitor concluded, "is nothing but a trifling with the court."

Whereupon Dorsey ceded the floor to John Tye, who with his sights already set on the land's highest tribunal, countered:

> Our motion is founded on a constitutional right guaranteed by the Constitution of the United States. It is not trifling with the courts. It is merely an attempt to restore the rights and privileges that are due every American citizen. The right is inviolable for an accused man to face the jury and hear them say whether they stick by their verdict.

After consulting precedents, Judge Hill sustained Dorsey's demurrer, handing the defense one more loss and making the world that Frank and his allies inhabited an increasingly dangerous place. Indeed, just nine days after

Hill rendered his decision, in an incident the *Constitution* understatedly termed "mysterious," loyal Minola McKnight was knifed across her face. Despite suffering a five-inch wound, the Negress refused to reveal her assailant's identity to the police. Whether the attack was a random cutting or was intended to send a message, no one knew. All that could be said for certain was that when it came to the subject on which she had so persistently spoken out during the past year, Minola was through talking.

SIXTEEN

A Change of Heart

In the aftermath of the Burns debacle and the defense's twin defeats at the hands of Judge Hill, the fighting briefly halted, as if all involved had agreed to a cease-fire. With decisions on the appeals of the extraordinary motion and Tye-Peeples rulings not expected until midautumn, the story not only disappeared from the front pages (between July 1 and September 30, 1914, the *New York Times* mentioned the case just twice), but Tom Watson, with nothing in the news to provoke him, fell silent. As for Leo Frank, he settled in to what seemed like a pleasant routine. To the familiar mix of early-morning exercise and evenings with Lucille, he added a regular bridge game played through the mail with *New York Times* bridge writer Florence Irwin, who aside from praising his skills published one of his hands in an August column. This was a season during which the condemned man's cell filled not with legal documents but with letters from vacationing friends telling of glass-bottom boat trips from Los Angeles to Santa Catalina Island and of a little hotel in Santa Barbara "fronting on the ocean, with lawns of green velvet hue and flower beds circling the driveways."

During these outwardly tranquil months, a horrific but unrelated event occurred. In mid-June, two popular Atlanta sisters—Eloise Nelms Dennis, a postal clerk, and Beatrice Nelms, a Realtor—disappeared after cashing a large check. Several weeks later, the women's mother received a note, postmarked from Texas and purporting to have been written by Eloise, confessing to Beatrice's murder. A nationwide search was initiated—to no avail. The two seemed simply to have vanished, a fact that caused their friends at home—among them Jim Conley's lawyer, William Smith, and his wife, Mary Lou—tremendous concern.

The Smiths were particularly close to the Nelms sisters (Eloise had been Mary Lou's childhood playmate), so much so that as fears for their safety mounted, Smith telegraphed an individual who regardless of his questionable conduct during the upheavals through which Atlanta had just passed possessed an indisputable record when it came to tracking missing persons—William Burns. Following several communications, the detective agreed to dispatch agents to hunt for the Nelmses. In return, he asked not for a fee but for an unusual favor. As Smith later put it: "He wanted my promise to work on the Frank matter."

That Burns could entertain even a notion that Smith, who had played such a large part in Frank's prosecution, might lend a hand in digging up information beneficial to the defense would have struck most who'd followed the case as absurd. Yet notwithstanding the obvious barriers—the chief one being the lawyer's legal obligations to Conley—and unbeknownst to all but a few, there were several factors that made the detective's overture more plausible than it initially appeared.

First, among the affidavits submitted by the defense in support of the extraordinary motion was one secured from Smith. In the document, the lawyer asserted that prior to Frank's trial, he had witnessed the conversation between Hugh Dorsey and Dr. Henry F. Harris in which the physician first stated that the hair he'd snipped from Mary Phagan's scalp during his autopsy did not match that found wrapped around R. P. Barrett's lathe. Though the revelation had not kept Smith from continuing to assist the state, it had troubled him. As he would afterward write: "For some reason not as yet ethically or professionally explained, the prosecuting attorney called Dr. Harris to testify to other medical matters but failed to cause him to tell the truth about the hair."

Second, while Smith had from the start believed Conley's account of little Mary's murder and these many months later believed it still, early on he had experienced a vague misgiving. There was, as he expressed it, "something held back by Conley and about which he wanted to talk to his woman"—the maligned and eventually abandoned Lorena Jones. "He would not let me know about it and would not let me carry the message to her." So disturbed was the lawyer by this intimation that in June 1913 he had approached Atlanta's second-ranking police official, Newport Lanford. Intrigued, the detective chief arranged to place an officer in a crawl space above Conley's cell and lower the lights, at which point Smith arrived with Lorena, then departed. The surveillance effort, however, failed when an evidently suspicious Conley struck several matches and discovered that he was being watched. Smith's role in the operation was never revealed to Conley, and the two were soon at work preparing for the trial. But the lawyer could not entirely dismiss from his mind the impulse that had driven him to initiate what he acknowledged was a highly irregular scheme. "I have always felt that there was something Conley wanted to tell that woman that he dared not tell me," he subsequently declared. "I have felt that possibly he wanted to tell her something that she might cover up, some trace of the crime."

Finally and most important, others besides Burns—among them a revered old friend and a respected new acquaintance—had also urged Smith to rethink his position.

Berry Benson, who following the untimely death of Smith's parents had acted as his surrogate father, had made the initial approach. A legendary Georgia character, the 71-year-old Augusta resident was not only the author of a vivid account of his military service during the Civil War *(Memoirs of a Confederate Scout and Sharpshooter),* but he had modeled for the city's Italian marble monument to its Confederate veterans. (Benson's figure stands even now on a pedestal in the middle of Augusta's central business district.) The old soldier was more than just an icon. During Reconstruction, he had taken up accounting and risen to the head of the Georgia-Carolina branch of the National Auditing and Accounting Company. The job perfectly fit the man, who enjoyed numbers and puzzles of all types and spent much of his spare time decoding cryptograms, among them *Le Chiffre Indéchiffrable* (the undecipherable cipher) used by French and German intelligence at the turn of the century. Benson believed he'd broken this formidable code and was in frequent contact with the United States War Department as to his work's value to the government. Though Washington ultimately decided to rely on its own experts, the rejection did not dampen Benson's enthusiasm for such conundrums. "The harder the problems," he was fond of saying, "the better I like them." It was this predisposition that had prompted Benson to delve into the mystery of Mary Phagan's murder, with an emphasis on the written communications that served as the case's own *Chiffre Indéchifferable*—the notes found beside the dead girl's body. After procuring to-scale enlargements of the notes, Benson had used a surveyor's compass to perform a rudimentary but previously unconducted task—he measured the handwriting on both and the amount of blank space in their respective top and bottom margins. What he found was startling. For one, the letters in the note on the pencil company order sheet were fully a fifth greater in size than those in the one on lined white paper. Moreover, the note on the order sheet started midway on the page and proceeded in a hurried rush downward, leaving barely enough room for the last word, whereas its companion was carefully positioned, giving the appearance of premeditation. The differences led Benson to deduce that the notes were not, as opposed to what Conley had testified, written simultaneously but separately "with some interval of time elapsed." Buttressing this theory was a small but to Benson critical difference in the notes' compositions. While the order-sheet note rather carelessly pointed the finger at "a long tall negro black," the follow-up effort called specific attention to the alleged perpetrator's skin color by using "black" as an adjective—"a long tall black negro." As Benson saw it, the coffee-colored Conley, having dashed off the initial note in the heated aftermath of the killing, had subsequently and coolly written the other for the sole purpose of directing the police to someone who bore no resemblance to himself. The factory superintendent would not have seen this need. On the strength of these assessments and several others ("If Frank had dictated those notes," the former sharpshooter wrote, "he never would have said 'play like' in the phrase 'play like the night witch did it.' It is too childish—too niggery. He would have said 'pretend' "), Benson produced an analysis that appeared in the *Augusta Chronicle* on the eve of the extraordinary motion hearing. His conclusion: "It is my opinion that there is not a white man, either north or south of the Mason & Dixon line, who could have dictated those notes. If Frank did not dictate the notes, then Conley was the murderer." In the wake of his piece's publication, Benson journeyed to Atlanta for several long discussions with the young lawyer he regarded as a son.

No sooner had Benson come calling than Smith received a visit from a recent arrival in Georgia. Colonel James Perry Fyffe, a 49-year-old veteran of the Spanish-American War who had subsequently worked in both law enforcement (from 1906 to 1907, he was police chief of the Panama Canal Zone) and journalism (in the intervening years, he was city editor of the *Chattanooga News*), had been hired by Adolph Ochs in the spring of 1914 to cover the Frank case from Atlanta for the *New York Times* and, in another indication of the paper's unremitting partisanship, assist William Burns in compiling evidence that might exonerate the condemned man. Toward that last and largely secret end, Fyffe had developed a couple of fresh leads. According to his findings, the Atlanta Police Department, on top of its other mistakes in investigating the Phagan slaying, had failed to seek a laboratory test to determine whether the stains Jim Conley had been spotted washing out of his shirt prior to his arrest were blood or, as Conley claimed, rust. Furthermore, the squad had not attempted to match the Negro's fingerprints with those lifted from the plant's basement door—the portal through which the defense theorized Conley exited after committing the crime. Stunned as Smith was to learn of these oversights, it was Fyffe's insights into another clue—the murder note written on the factory order blank—that most impressed him. As the lawyer's youngest son, Walter, would recall years later: "This Chattanooga newspaper man asked Dad to read the note's first line out loud, the line that goes 'mam that negro fire down here did this.' Then he said to Dad, 'Don't you see—the line says he did it down *here*. If the note was written, as the state contended, in the office, it would have said "down *there*." The note was written by Conley in the basement.' This had a powerful effect upon Dad."

Thus it was that in late June, Smith—though not as yet fully swayed by the opposition's thinking and still cognizant of his professional commitment to Conley—informed Burns that he would indeed revisit the Frank case. (This even after the Nelms probe ended with the discovery that both sisters had been murdered outside San Antonio.) And thus it was that the spacious Lucile Avenue home that the lawyer shared with Mary Lou, their two children and Caesar, their Saint Bernard–collie mix, would now become a center of feverish activity. Here, Smith—aided substantially by his wife—would take a second look at the Phagan murder and conduct an exhaustive study of the record, all the while keeping in mind a line from Charles Dickens's novel *Little Dorritt:* "Let us examine sacredly, to see if a wrong has been done."

At the beginning of July, Smith visited the National Pencil factory. His goal: to familiarize himself with the scene of the crime. Upon entering the structure, the lawyer, who was accompanied by Mary Lou and the children, took in the oft-discussed details. The elevator, the stairwell behind which Jim Conley maintained he'd stationed himself, the pervasive darkness—things were just as he'd imagined. Still, at the sight of the scuttle hole, the words of the note jotted on the order sheet—"i went to make water and he pushed me down that hole"—popped into Smith's mind, forcing him to concede that there was merit to the defense's contention that this was where Mary Phagan was attacked. From the lobby, the family ascended to the second floor. Following a tour of the metal room, they stopped in Frank's office. There, Smith positioned himself in the desk chair and tried to envision what it would have been like to sit in that place and dictate the notes. As his daughter would subsequently write: "My father bent over so that his left cheek touched the spot where the notes would have been written" and proceeded to count 43 windows in the buildings on the opposite side of Forsyth Street that offered clear sight lines into the space. The feeling of exposure gave the lawyer a keen appreciation for another of Rosser and Arnold's assertions: "My father could not believe that a murderer would bring his accomplice to so publicly visible a spot." Next, the Smiths took the car into the basement. After noting the abundance of coal dust and pencil grinds strewn atop the earthen floor, the lawyer acknowledged that there was something else Frank's supporters might have right. As he would later put it: "I can understand how Mary Phagan's face could have been soiled by a struggle while alive and fighting on the dirt floor of the basement, but I am unable to understand how it could have happened on the hard wooden surface upstairs." Finally, Smith and his family returned to the lobby. The lawyer was curious about one more matter, and in an effort to get an answer, he sent Mary Lou back to the metal room. Long afterward, their daughter would describe what transpired:

My mother screamed, as Conley said he had heard Mary scream that day. Not a sound of my mother's voice reached us, though we were intently straining to hear her, and anxious to know if Conley had told the truth.

Following his initial round of sleuthing, Smith set up shop in a small study just off his kitchen. The heart of the operation was a wooden table that held the beginnings of a Leo Frank archive—chunks of the trial transcript, the Brief of Evidence, facsimiles of the murder notes and the Annie Maude Carter letters, and year-old copies of the *Journal,* the *Constitution* and the *Georgian.* Here, sitting in a straight-back chair, the lawyer embarked on the next phase of his work.

Though Smith had been in court both when his client took the stand and, three days later, when he stepped down, he had missed much of the intervening time. (Hugh Dorsey had asked the lawyer to return to his office and continue the job of running down precedents with which to combat defense motions.) As a consequence, he needed to verse himself more thoroughly in what Conley had told the jury before he could move forward. From the first morning's testimony, Smith gleaned little save for renewed surprise at the charges of degeneracy—like most, he had not heard them until the trial. Yet when he got to Rosser's cross-examination, he encountered a series of statements—all of them involving Conley's reading abilities—that astonished him. The Negro had, of course, not only contended that he could barely comprehend the newspapers, but he'd replied to follow-up questions regarding the spelling of a number of simple words with a string of orthographic laughers—"dis" for this, "dat" for that, and "kat" for cat. Now Smith, as he would subsequently put it, was also "forced to smile." It was, however, a smile of incredulity, for during the months prior to the proceedings, he had observed Conley devour countless newspaper articles. Most tellingly, he recalled that the Negro had paid rapt attention to a *Georgian* piece reporting the gallery's approving response to the humble locutions Newt Lee had voiced while he was a witness, particularly his comparison of the gas jet in the plant basement to a lightning bug: "Has you ever seed one whut's been hit with a stick? Hit just do shine. Well, dat was dat light." The recollection caused Smith to consider a sobering possibility: Conley had "resolved to play as ignorant as Lee, and he had done so for a double purpose—to make a good impression as a 'dis and dat' negro, such as Lee was, and in order that he might not be charged that he had gotten his story from the papers."

Lest he jump to any conclusions, Smith sought independent corroboration of Conley's actual level of literacy. It did not take long for him to find it. For openers, there was the May 28, 1913, *Georgian*—the edition of Hearst's sheet the Negro had read in Newport Lanford's presence prior to making his second affidavit. Among the words contained in the lead article were such relatively complex ones as "promptness, terrible, experience, impudent, improvement and arrest." The piece gave the lie to the masquerade the Negro had staged in court. Smith did not, however, stop here. Of greater value than any item Conley had been observed to have read would be those that he admittedly had written. Which was why the lawyer turned to the murder notes. His purpose: to discover if Conley's spelling was as abjectly bad as he'd attested. From the opening line of the note jotted on the company order sheet—"mam *that* negro fire down here did *this*"—it became clear that the answer was no. All told, Conley spelled "this" and "that" correctly four times in the notes. And these weren't the only communications in which the Negro acquitted himself well on this count. Smith's search of the Annie Maude Carter letters produced the following examples:

> "if you do right i will try to give you *this* world"
> "well honey *this* is all right"
> "you told me *that* two hours fucking on your big fat ass would stop all *this* talk"
> "*that* made me love you *that* much more"

Also in the Carter letters, there was this: "if you hold your fat ass on the bottom and make papa go like a kitty *cat* then you have won a good man." In brief, while Conley had told Rosser that "cat" started with a "k," in the heat of his epistolary romance, he'd spelled it properly, too.

Sitting in his study on a midsummer night, Smith for the first time realized that Conley had misled everyone associated with the prosecution, himself included, as to the scope of his intelligence. "We thought he was densely ignorant," the lawyer would later write, "when in fact he is shrewdly cunning." Yet before making the next logical leap, Smith wanted to explore one final issue. During the trial, the state had maintained that the murder notes could not have been authored by Conley because they were plainly the product of "an educated mind." Dipping into Hugh Dorsey's closing argument, Smith found the salient line, that the solicitor had set up by dramatically indicating Frank:

> This man here, by these notes . . . by the verbiage and the language and the context, in trying to fix the crime on another . . . has indelibly fastened it upon himself.

Dorsey had, of course, grounded his assertion by citing the correct use of the verb "did" in the notes. ("Mam that negro fire down here *did* this," began one. Ended the other: "that long tall black negro *did* it by his slef.") Dorsey was adamant that Conley would in both instances have used "done." Waving the transcript of the Negro's testimony before the jury, he had, in fact, roared: "Did and done. It is the difference between education and ignorance. Old Jim Conley, in his statement, which I hold in my hand, every time he opened his mouth, he says 'I done it.' " Reading this claim against the backdrop of his newly heightened awareness of the Negro's language skills, Smith couldn't be so sure. Thus once again, he turned to his archive. And once again, he was stunned. As a scan of the trial record showed, Conley had consistently used "did" properly:

page 936:	"Alright, I will do just as you said and I *did* as he said."
page 1009:	"I can't remember whether I *did* or not."
page 1014:	"I don't know, sir, whether he *did* or not."
page 1044:	"I don't remember what I *did*."
	"I don't know what I *did*."
	"I don't know, sir, what I *did* the next Saturday."
	"The next Saturday I *did* some watching for him."
page 1141:	"I *did* some writing before then."
page 1153:	"I know that I *did* some writing before then."
page 1270:	"Before I went to sleep, which I *did*."

All told, Conley employed "did" some fifty times during his three days on the stand. Yet on the chance that the Negro, while speaking correctly, might not write so well, the lawyer again consulted his source of last resort—the Annie Maude Carter letters. The results were the same:

"i don't care if you *did* do it or if you *did* not"
"if i *did* not love you . . ."
"but i *did* not know that you . . ."

And so on until the veil was ripped from Smith's eyes and he found himself agreeing with Berry Benson that Conley had not only authored the notes but had murdered Mary Phagan. As the lawyer would subsequently recall: "I [was] swept into the truth."

In the aftermath of his epiphany, William Smith was obliged to confront the dilemma that had been there since Burns recruited him. Jim Conley was his client, the black man to whom he'd pledged "a square deal." While the

lawyer, having seen the error of his thinking, could live with the moral ramifications of his change of heart, legally he was not so sure. Hence he turned
to his law books, and what he found suggested that he had more leeway than
he had initially realized. For one, confidentiality considerations did not in
this instance apply. Because he had developed the information that pointed
the finger at Conley through his own investigation (as opposed to from a
private confession by Conley himself) Smith was, in his estimation, "a competent and compellable witness." Then there was the fact that Conley had
already been convicted as an accessory; according to Smith's reading of the
double jeopardy statute, the Negro was thus immune from prosecution for
"the same transaction." Doubtless, the lawyer shaped these interpretations
to his own purposes, but there can be no question that in the end, he
believed that he had exhausted his professional responsibilities to Conley.
No matter how unenviable his position, he was, by his lights, free to act.

Exactly what action Smith would or could take was, however, another
matter. While he was certain that he now knew the true circumstances
of Mary Phagan's murder, the lawyer well understood that a majority of
Georgians—foremost among them Hugh Dorsey—would not be easily persuaded to his point of view. If he was ever to convince the authorities that
Conley was guilty, he would have to develop a powerful and comprehensi-
ble proof of his underlying theory that the murder notes were the products
of the Negro's mind. Toward that end, Smith turned to his wife. As an aspir-
ing English teacher who enjoyed diagramming sentences and, like so many
southerners, was a student of black dialect, Mary Lou believed that Conley
possessed a unique verbal fingerprint. The trick would be to demonstrate
that fingerprint's presence in the notes discovered beside little Mary's body,
then establish its pervasiveness in Conley's other known spoken and written utterances. As she saw it, everything else would follow. On an early
August evening, the two began.

Sitting opposite each other at the wooden table in the study off their
kitchen, the Smiths dissected the murder notes by vocabulary and sentence
structure, thereby assembling an inventory of their author's lexicon and a
catalog of his stylistic preferences. All told, the notes contained 63 words,
but after discarding pronouns like "i" and "he" and articles like "a" and
"the," the Smiths were left with 40 nouns, verbs, adjectives and adverbs that
seemed potentially representative. Similarly, the couple picked out a dozen
grammatical quirks and distinctive phrasings that also appeared to bear
their maker's mark. Which meant that brief as the notes were, they offered
some 52 possible clues as to the identity of the individual who'd conceived
of them.

Hard upon this creation of what amounted to a master list of linguistic
characteristics, the Smiths penciled each of the list's components at the top

of a separate notecard, then attached the cards with clothespins to lines they'd strung at the end of the study for both organization and visibility. Then came the difficult part. The two intended to go through Conley's four affidavits, the pages of trial transcript containing his testimony, and the Annie Maude Carter letters. Their purpose: to locate and record each instance in which the Negro had employed the diction or constructions they'd pinpointed in the murder notes.

And so almost every night for the remainder of the summer found the Smiths methodically poring over the collected works of Jim Conley. By early September, they'd filled so many notecards that the lines hanging against the far wall sagged from the weight. Here, the couple believed, was evidence that should be sufficient to persuade anyone.

To begin with, the language used in the murder notes was wholly consistent with the language Conley had used both on the stand and in his personal communications. Take the word "long," which appeared three times in the notes ("a *long* tall negro black" and "a *long* sleam tall negro" in one; "a *long* tall black negro" in the other). In his testimony, Conley had frequently trotted out the adjective, referring, for instance, to the twine with which Frank had purportedly strangled Mary Phagan as "a good *long* wide piece of cord." In the Carter letters, meanwhile, he had advertised his prodigious manhood by boasting: "if i could put my sweet *long* dick in your hipped i think i could make mama call me papa." And: "if you let papa put his *long* ugly dick up in your fat ass . . . then papa will done played hell with you." Then there was the word "down," which was also employed three times in the notes ("that negro hire *down* here did this" and "he push me *down* that hole" in one; "he said he would love me land *down*" in the other). In his testimony, Conley had relied on the adverb so often that after collecting 52 citations (among them: "we come on and went on *down* the elevator" and "we carried her out and laid her *down*"), the Smiths stopped. Time and again, this is how it went. Just as the noun "negro" was a staple of the notes, so had it been a staple in Conley's testimony ("the next person that come on was the *negro* drayman"). Same thing with "tall" ("she was a *tall* heavy built lady") and "hole" (Frank "was looking down in the *hole*"). Additionally, just as the verb "play" served in the notes as a synonym for sexual intercourse ("i wright while he *play* with me"), so had it served in the Carter letters ("honey if you let papa put his long ugly dick up in your fat ass and *play* on your right and left hip then papa will done *played* hell with you").

The Smiths' findings regarding Conley's modes of expression were even more conclusive. Consider the phrase "make water," which appeared in the note jotted on the company order sheet. Black vernacular for the verb "to urinate," the locution had struck the couple as foreign to anything Leo Frank could have said. As Smith would later write: "It may be that living in the South all my life, I am unable to speak authoritatively, but I venture the assertion that the term 'make water' is found a thousand times more often in the language of Southern negroes than in [that] of white Cornell alumni." And indeed, a search of the plant superintendent's unsworn statement at the trial and his subsequent written pronouncements had turned up nothing. However, on page 1264 of the transcript, there materialized the following remark by Conley relative to his movements on the morning of Mary Phagan's murder: "I did get up twice and go to the elevator and *make water.*" On top of this, the predicate form with which the notes' author had prefaced this bit of slang (the line reads in full: "*i went to* make water") also turned out to be a favorite of Conley's. Again from the official record:

page 954:	"*I went to* bring her up on my shoulder."
page 954:	"*I* run my right arm through and *went to* put it up."
page 957:	"*I* lit one and *went to* smoking."
page 960:	"*I went* down over *to* the near beer saloon."

All told, the Smiths had enumerated twenty-nine similarities between the murder notes and Conley's known remarks and writings. Among the others: Like the notes, the Carter letters lacked all punctuation; like the notes, the Carter letters lacked any capitalization; like the notes—of whose 63 words, 95 percent were monosyllabic—the Carter letters consisted chiefly of short nouns and verbs. Moreover, a majority of the misspellings that occurred in the notes ("sleam" for slim, "wright" for write) also appeared in the Carter letters. Perhaps most indicative, the couple found that a verbal tic that ran through the notes—the use of compound adjectives ("long tall black")—also ran through the Negro's testimony ("good long wide" and "little bitta chunky") and the Carter letters ("sweet long" and "long ugly"). In short, the Smiths felt they had built an overwhelming case. Yes, they knew that those associated with the prosecution might respond that Frank had purposely worded the notes so they would reflect Conley's verbiage and style. But they had a counterargument ready. As Smith would later put it: "Any sane man must admit that under the stress and excitement of a murder, Frank could not possibly have dictated those notes in two and a half minutes (the time Conley says in which the notes were written) in Conley's language. Even Joel Chandler Harris could not have done it."

In mid-September, on the strength of the murder-note study, Smith initiated what he hoped would be a series of productive meetings with key members of the Atlanta Police Department. Over the course of a week, he conferred privately with Chiefs James Beavers and Newport Lanford and Detective John Starnes. Despite the lawyer's evidence, each session went poorly. Typical was the encounter with Starnes. As Smith would later recall:

> In a personal interview with [Starnes] I made the suggestion that the language of the "death notes" could not possibly be that of Frank's but was unquestionably of Conley's manufacture.
>
> The reply came that it was the remembrance of this official that Conley did not claim that Frank dictated the language of the "death notes," but that Frank merely furnished the ideas written into the notes—that the language of the notes was Conley's. This was news to me.

From Smith's perspective, the kindest interpretation to give to Starnes's response was that he had a poor memory. Upon returning home, the lawyer and Mary Lou repaired to the little room where they'd spent so much of the summer, and just as he'd anticipated, the record bore him out. In his affidavit of May 24, 1913, Conley had told the police:

> he [Frank] gave me a scratch pad and told me what to put on it, and told me to put on there "dear mother a long tall black negro did this by himself;" and he told me to write it two or three times.

For his next meeting, this one with a more critical figure, Smith adopted a different tack. The lawyer and Hugh Dorsey were, of course, old friends. Yet even so, Smith—after acquainting the solicitor with his theories—laid on the flattery and charm. Seventy-five years later, his son Walter would recall:

> Dad told me that he compared Dorsey to a great artist who'd painted a masterpiece. Then he said he asked him to stand back from his achievement and consider the fact that beautiful as it was, it was fatally flawed. In such a case, he said he told him, there was only one thing to do—destroy the painting. He said Dorsey replied, "It's too late."

The solicitor's version of this discussion is unavailable. What is certain, however, is that like the others, he also rejected his visitor's entreaties.

Such setbacks notwithstanding, Smith remained undeterred. In fact, the failures drove him to take a more aggressive stance. If the results of his language test did not convince the authorities, maybe some new physical evidence would, and he believed he knew where to get it. As it turned out, Colonel William Perry Fyffe, the former Chattanooga newsman hired by Adolph Ochs to look into the Frank case, had not only learned that the police had failed to compare Conley's fingerprints with those found on the factory's basement door, he'd actually acquired the relevant pieces of the door. In other words, it was not too late to attempt a match. Thus it was that shortly after his session with Dorsey, Smith made his way to the Bellwood Prison Camp, the county facility where Conley was serving his one-year sentence. The Negro, unaware of his lawyer's transformation, was happy to see him and gladly accepted the glass of water he offered. After a brief talk, Smith retrieved the glass—which now had Conley's prints on it—and departed. Unfortunately for the lawyer, however, the prints—which he forwarded to an expert supplied by Burns—were too faint to be of use. Therefore in late September, Smith returned to the Bellwood camp. This time he carried with him some fingerprint paper. His plan was to ask Conley to place his hands on a sheet so that he could measure them for a pair of work gloves. After all, he'd given the Negro clothes in the past. Why shouldn't he again? Yet as Conley had so often shown, he was no one's fool. Despite Smith's earnest appeals, he refused to place his hands on the paper. As Walter Smith would later tell it: "Conley was wary and wouldn't press his fingers down."

While Smith had tried to be discreet, by early October he had been making the rounds for a month. At headquarters or Dorsey's office or the prison camp, someone had leaked what he was saying. Little wonder, then, that on Friday, October 2, the phone rang at the lawyer's home. A *Constitution* reporter was on the line: Had Smith changed his mind as to Leo Frank's guilt? "No comment," the lawyer replied and hung up. A few minutes later, though, he called the paper back and read the following statement:

> I have never ceased to be a student of the Frank case. Practically all of my spare time has been devoted to a study of it. I have come to the conclusion—or at least this is my personal judgement—that Leo M. Frank is innocent and that if a proper cooperation of officials can be secured, I have absolute faith that the mystery of the death of Mary Phagan will be solved.

Which was why on Saturday morning the Frank case was back on the front pages. Roared the banner atop the *Constitution:*

> Frank Not Guilty, Believes Conley's Lawyer;
> Plans to Obtain Freedom of "Man in Tower"

Not surprisingly, the *Georgian* accorded the story even bigger play. Proclaimed the circus-type topper stripped beneath its masthead:

CONLEY IS GUILTY SAYS HIS LAWYER

The next day, the *New York Times*—after nearly four months of silence—followed suit, booming:

CONLEY, NOT FRANK,
CALLED SLAYER
Attorney Smith Now Convinced
His Negro Client Killed
Mary Phagan

The ink was barely dry on the initial accounts of his about-face before Smith tried to take control of the already out-of-control story by issuing a fuller explanation of his thinking. In a statement distributed to all three Atlanta papers, he began by decrying the news's premature publication:

> The unfortunate publicity given my personal opinions as to the Frank case is much to be regretted. It was never my purpose, unless absolutely necessary to save human life, to give public expression to my views. In an effort to inspire further search, I was compelled to speak in confidence to some in whom I had every right to rely. There has been a give-way somewhere along the line, possibly a willful betrayal in order to accomplish a thwarting of my purposes and a handicap to my endeavors.

That said, Smith dispensed with the aggrieved tone and laid his cards on the table. First, he disclosed the potentially damaging particulars—his dealings with William Burns and his meetings with William Perry Fyffe. Then, in hopes of fending off charges that he'd forsaken his client, he offered his interpretation of the double jeopardy statute, asserting that Jim Conley was now out of harm's way. The ethical conflicts thus addressed, the lawyer detailed much of what he'd learned in the past months, including that there'd been no scientific tests conducted on Conley's red-stained shirt and no comparisons made between the Negro's fingerprints and those found on the factory's basement door. He also discussed the experiments he and Mary Lou had conducted at the plant, among them the one that to his mind proved that a person standing in the entry-level lobby could not have heard screams coming from the upstairs metal room. Moreover, he articulated an insight that had just occurred to him regarding one of the trial's less savory witnesses. "Reading the official record recently, I was amazed to learn that Conley charged Frank with immorality with Daisy Hopkins," he declared, adding:

> I know Daisy Hopkins, have represented her, have watched and studied Frank, and I know the types of the two people, their manner of living, their

levels in society, their personal appearances, and I know, as much as I can know anything in life without actually having been present, that Conley's statements as to this are untrue.

The sole topic on which Smith was not utterly forthcoming was the one at the core of his work—his determination regarding the authorship of the murder notes. Though he flatly announced that "upon a comparative study of the notes with the evidence of Conley and Frank and with the Annie Maude Carter notes, I conclude that the language of these notes is Conley's," he did not provide any of the supporting documentation that he and his wife had assembled. Whatever his past dealings with the authorities, the lawyer wanted to give them another opportunity to consider the material. "With the loyal and enthusiastic support of Chief Beavers, Chief Lanford and the men of the police department," he diplomatically predicted, the truth about the notes "will be made public" and "the responsibility for this murder will be placed where it belongs."

The response to the disclosure of Smith's dramatic change of heart split predictably enough right down the middle. Members of the defense camp were elated by the development. Speaking to reporters from his cell at the Tower, Leo Frank exclaimed: "It is unnecessary for me to say that I am gratified by the news. I could not believe it at first, for I knew that Mr. Smith had assisted in obtaining my conviction and I supposed him to be still of the same mind. But he has been close to Conley, and probably is the only man in a position to know what part of the negro's story was a fabrication." Meanwhile, Luther Rosser and Herbert Haas did what they could to bolster their new comrade's credibility, vowing that they'd exerted no influence on him: "We believe that these are his honest opinions and that he is giving them publicity from a sense of justice and conscience." As for the *New York Times,* it could already foresee a happy ending, asserting editorially:

> Attorney Smith's announcement that he now is ready to join hands with the Frank defense and assist this group of celebrated lawyers in working for the freedom of their client heralds the addition to the Frank support of the one man who probably can do more than any other in finally clearing away the last threads of mystery surrounding the murder of Mary Phagan.

Those aligned against Frank all but dismissed this latest turn of events. Replying to Smith's request that the authorities reconsider his findings regarding the murder notes, Chief Beavers allowed that as far as he was concerned, no new evidence had been produced. Hugh Dorsey was likewise unmoved, declaring:

The state stands right where it did a year ago last August when Leo Frank was convicted. Nothing has happened which would lead us to alter our theory in the slightest.

Not surprisingly, Jim Conley was dismayed. Talking to reporters from the yard of the Bellwood Prison Camp, he asserted: "Only a few days ago, Mr. Smith was out to see me. He always told me he believed I was telling the truth. It is hard for me to believe that he has said I was guilty of the crime." On the heels of this remark, the Negro grew angry. "I haven't liked the way Mr. Smith has acted for the last few weeks," he snapped, apparently referring to the lawyer's attempt to take his fingerprints. "I am ready to make a statement to Solicitor Dorsey. I will tell him everything that Mr. Smith said. I can tell some things against him." Then, in a calm tone, Conley gave utterance to the main point: "I don't care what Mr. Smith says. I am innocent and Mr. Frank is guilty." Finally, however, the most negative commentary came from Tom Watson. In the *Jeffersonian*'s October 8 number, he darkly proclaimed:

> The Leo Frank Case Campaign Opens Again!!!
> Of course, all of us knew that it would.
> The only question was, *Who would Rosser-Arnold-Burns and Haas* use next?
> One W. M. Smith.

With that, Watson accused Smith of selling out to the figure who'd been the source of so much controversy during the last round of hostilities:

> According to his own statement, Smith made a deal with the rascally Burns—Burns the fugitive from justice—that he would help in the Frank case if [the detective] would help in the Nelms case.
> If Smith knew anything that would serve the ends of law and justice, why did he want pay for it in the way of Burns's services in the Nelms case?
> If he already *knew* something that would establish the innocence of the Sodomite, why did he demand a price for it?
> If there had been no Nelms case to trade on, would he have continued to keep his knowledge of Conley's sole guilt to himself?

Having thus thrust in the dagger, the Sage twisted it. For one, he suggested that Smith had never actually represented Conley, referring to him as the Negro's "nominal lawyer." Similarly, he scoffed at Smith's promised findings regarding the murder notes, terming them "frazzled talk" about a long-decided question. Then, knowing that many of his readers had likely missed

recent issues of the *New York Times,* he helpfully noted that Smith's pronouncements had prompted the sheet to resume its one-sided coverage.
"Simultaneously with Smith," he reported, "the Ochs paper has opened up
again." All of which served as Watson's preamble to a stern warning: *"LET
W. M. SMITH BE CAREFUL!"*

The extent to which Watson's attacks on Smith both mirrored and stimu-
lated popular sentiment in Georgia became instantly apparent. Indeed, by
October 8, the lawyer already found himself fending off scores of threatening calls. As he would subsequently put it, anonymous voices promised "to
do me as [they] did Burns at Marietta" and "to wait on me 500 strong."
Meanwhile, a former political ally publicly suggested that Smith be lynched
at downtown Atlanta's busy Five Points. In an October 7 letter to the
lawyer's partner Aldine Chambers (who was out of town), realtor H. F.
Sanders conveyed a sense of the general mood: "Will Smith is the worst
abused man that it has ever been my fortune or misfortune to know. The
condemnations and curses that are heaped upon him by the public is
enough to damn an angel from heaven." Seventy-five years later, Smith's
daughter would recall her father phoning home one day during this week
and asking her mother to bring his gun to the office. She would also recall
falling asleep at night to the cadence of a policeman walking patrol outside
their home. Ultimately, the atmosphere grew so tense that the lawyer sent
his family to live at a small farmhouse north of the city. Then he went into
the papers with yet another broadside. This time, his purpose was not so
much to explain himself as to fight back.

Beneath the de rigueur headlines (CONLEY'S LAWYER DEFIES LYNCHING
THREAT, boomed the *Georgian*), Smith declared:

> It seems absolutely essential at this point that an understanding about
> me should be reached—my stock of folk haven't got "much rabbit" in
> them. Though I am condemned by every citizen of this town, county and
> state as a traitor, a scoundrel, I intend to stick by my guns, figuratively and
> literally. I do not intend to be intimidated by cowardly character assassins.

That said, the lawyer confronted the allegation that he'd betrayed his client
for money, asserting:

> Many believe that I had my price and got it. All can believe that if they
> will. The world is usually so sordid-minded that it is hard to understand
> that divine mercy does let a spark linger in some souls, and that there are
> men in the world who can rise to just such situations.

Plainly, this is how Smith saw himself. Moreover, he could not fathom why others weren't equally receptive to second thoughts. "How our officials can close their minds and rest their hands upon the idea that there is no possibility for further light and study to point out the error [of Frank's conviction] is a new theory to me that human justice is infallible." And it was not just the authorities whose reticence puzzled the lawyer. Addressing all Atlantans, he charged:

> The trouble with the good people of this community is that you haven't enough sand in your public gizzard that is working properly. There are thousands of people in this section who have an intelligent belief in Frank's innocence and are afraid of the howl of a bunch of curbstone theorists who never even saw the inside of the pencil factory and who, if called upon, can give no intelligent reason for their belief.

Having thereby fired shots over the bow not just of Beavers, Lanford and Dorsey but of the citizenry at large, Smith drew a line in the sand:

> Just tell the folks that there is one man on the job who does not intend to be bluffed. Whatever it takes to bear a man's part I have got it. This is not bragging, but just a plain cold statement. I am doing business at the same old stand, not much business, but what I have I am there to attend to.
>
> Whenever any of the boys start my way with the rope, kindly suggest that they would do well to first inquire as to my record as a "sharpshooter" from the Adjutant General's office or of any shooting gallery in the city of Atlanta, and ease it to them that my specialty is rapid-fire work at moving targets . . . Counsel them as the Sage of McDuffie does me: "Be careful."

Heartfelt but self-righteous, soaring but vainglorious, Smith's defiant remarks were nothing if not provocative. And though they doubtless galvanized Frank partisans, in the end they chiefly served to goad Tom Watson into hurling an even more brutal return volley. This time, the weapon was one of the nastiest in the Sage's arsenal—ridicule. Mocked the banner atop the *Jeffersonian*'s October 15 edition:

> The Frank Case Brings in Another Horse—
> A Smaller One Than Usual

"As long as a donkey refrains from trying to make music, one never knows what his bray may sound like," Watson began, "but the moment he tries to waste his sweetness on the desert air, we know that another ass is in our midst. Poor little William M. Smith!" And it only got worse. In a line-by-line analysis of the lawyer's last statement, Watson did everything but hoot and hiss. Referring to Smith's boast that his inlaws didn't have "much rabbit" in them, he noted:

> By this, he means that he is brave, fearless, pugnacious, bellicose, combative, courageous, dauntless, heroic, war-like.
> The rabbit runs away, as Burns fled from Marietta, but Smith is a horse of another color, and Smith will never run.
> Thus we have a picture of Smith drawn by Smith himself, and we know that he possesses sand.
> We know it because Smith says so—and if Smith doesn't know, who does?

Regarding Smith's claim that he'd been motivated not by the prospect of financial gain but by a "spark of divine mercy," Watson assayed:

> As an unworthy part of "the world" which Smith has such a poor opinion of, I take off my hat, right now, and apologize to Smith for being alive.
> I don't feel that any ordinary human being has any real right to be inhaling the same air with Smith.

Then, feigning sympathy for Frank's longtime counsel, the Sage inquired:

> Where were Reub Arnold, Luther Rosser and Haas, Haas & Haas when Smith was giving out [this] idiotic card?

His adversary thus derided and dispatched, Watson raised what to him was the main issue: "The pure little Gentile victim is dust in the grave, while the Sodomite who took her sweet young life basks in the warmth of Today, the be-flowered pet of newspapers, lawyers, detectives and philanthropists." And he posed the main question: "Is there never to be an end of the Frank case? Is he the one criminal for whom the laws, the courts, and the people must make an entirely new system?"

The ferocity of Watson's fusillade shook Smith, but he could not have been surprised by it. He was, however, caught off guard by criticism that came concurrently from another quarter—the bar. Though Smith believed that he'd positioned Jim Conley out of legal danger, hence fulfilling his professional obligations, his fellow practitioners were not so certain. Many felt that even if the Negro could not be tried for Mary Phagan's murder, he could be tried for perjury, itself a serious crime. Yet even more significant, the consensus was that no matter the circumstances, for a lawyer to turn against a client was simply unconscionable. Locally, the forum for such sentiments was the annual Atlanta Law School Banquet, which happened to be taking place at the Winecoff Hotel in October. There, Robert Troutman, a recent graduate of Columbia University Law School who was in the process of forming what would become a top silk-stocking firm, articulated the prevailing view of Smith, telling his audience:

> Among the important principles that should be sustained by the bar is the principle that a lawyer should stick by his client through thick and thin after he has accepted a case. He has no right to parade his opinion one way or another as to his client's guilt. A lawyer is not retained to express any opinion or belief. He is retained to provide his client all legitimate means of defense.

Nationally, the forum was the *New York Times Magazine,* which framed the debate with the headline: SHOULD A LAWYER BETRAY A CLIENT TO SAVE INNOCENT MAN? Notwithstanding the paper's advocacy of Frank's cause, its editors gave prominent play to the criticisms of Smith voiced by the eminences interviewed. True, several accorded the Atlantan the benefit of the doubt. Harlan Fiske Stone, dean of Columbia University Law School and a future chief justice of the United States Supreme Court, maintained that as long as Smith had not acted based on anything revealed to him in confidence by Conley, he was governed only by "personal consideration and conscience" and therefore had been free to speak. Others, however, believed that Smith had erred. D. Cady Herrick, formerly a New York trial judge, dismissed the notion that a lawyer could arrive at an independent assessment of someone he'd represented. "Facts found on investigation by the attorney are usually based on talks with his client," he contended. "The investigation would never have been made if it were not for the relation of lawyer and client. I cannot see that there is any distinction as far as the seal of silence is concerned." Francis W. Aymar, a professor at New York University Law School, was even firmer:

> I think that the client should have the right to come with absolute freedom to his lawyer and discuss his case in all its phases, even to the extent of confessing guilt for the crime, and that the client should be protected in all the statements he makes. I believe it to be unjust to the client to permit the seal of silence to be removed from the lawyer's lips under any circumstance.

Thus it was that as autumn, with its morning frosts and evening wood smoke, came to Atlanta, Smith found himself a maligned and embattled man. As he made his way each day between home and his downtown office, he would walk briskly, sticking to the middle of the sidewalk—the better to frustrate would-be assailants intent on either grabbing him from an alley or pulling him from the curb into a slowly moving car. Passing acquaintances received only a nod. And as a last resort, there was the pistol, now tucked constantly in a jacket pocket. Yet the lawyer had few regrets. "Regardless of public conjecture," he informed a reporter, "there is a personal conscious-ness of which I am proud. The same spirit for the right that led me to dis-charge my duty for Conley drove me to learn the truth about this crime." Years later, Smith's son would add: "You know, Dad felt responsible for Frank's conviction—as responsible as Dorsey. So once he'd realized his error, he was adamant about seeing the thing through." Just what the effort would entail depended on the rulings soon to be handed down by the Geor-gia Supreme Court. Should that body uphold the lower courts, Frank's counsel intended to make great use of the lawyer. Declared Leonard Haas:

> If the decisions are adverse to Frank, there will be but one other course open—application for a pardon or commutation before the governor and the pardoning board. Then it will be possible for us to present Mr. Smith's evidence.

SEVENTEEN

Cause Célèbre

Though the envelope that arrived at Leo Frank's cell on a cold morning the first week of December 1914 bore a postmark from the unprepossessing town of East Orange, New Jersey, its contents could not have been more fabulous had it been stamped "Marrakesh" or "Kathmandu." "I want to tell you a few things that are going to happen," began the letter from the noted muckraker Christopher Powell Connolly, an East Orange resident. *Collier's Weekly,* he announced, would devote parts of two upcoming issues to his 18,000-word article on the factory superintendent's case. Moreover, the influential magazine intended to distribute the piece to 10,000 newspapers "with permission to print in full." Connolly, like his famous confrere Lincoln Steffens, generally took sides in what he wrote, and in this instance he had aligned himself with the defense. As he declared up top: "What I want to do is to have this whole situation reopened in such a way that it will be tried by an audience composed of the people of the United States, prepared to listen calmly to its presentation and to your absolute vindication on the facts."

Had Connolly stopped here, Frank, who was beginning his second winter of incarceration in the Fulton County Tower, would have had ample reason to rejoice, but there was more. "I have in mind a public protest meeting in Carnegie Hall in New York—a dignified meeting and not a Northern or sectional meeting at all, but a meeting in which we can get some Southern men of prominence to take part, and I will take that meeting in hand and put them over the hurdles of this case. By that time we will have every editor in New York interested and we will see that they are there. The effect ought to be felt and will be felt" across the country.

In sum, Connolly was assuming the position of point man in a soon-to-be launched nationwide public relations campaign to save Frank from the gallows. In closing, he vowed: "I have plans—we all have plans—which cannot all miscarry. Before we get through every man, woman and child in the United States will be interested. This is no exaggeration. There are men behind this proposition who will turn the United States upside down before any harm comes to you."

The choice of C. P. Connolly, as his well-known byline read, to fire the initial shot in what promised to be a noisy and contentious war was exceedingly astute. At 51, the New York–born writer was a combative Irish Catholic who in his early twenties had moved to Montana, studied law under United States Senator Thomas J. Walsh and risen to become the chief prosecuting officer for the city of Butte. Along the way, Connolly had discovered that his true interest lay in journalism, and his new home had given him his first subject—the battles between law and order that occurred in Montana's copper fields during the late 1890s and early 1900s. Connolly's 1906 series on the topic for *McClure's* stirred, as the *New York Herald Tribune* would later report, a "nationwide sensation," rocketing him into the top ranks of the muckrakers. In 1907, he was *Collier's* man at the trial of the International Workers of the World leader William "Big Bill" Haywood for the murder of Idaho governor Frank Steunenberg. In 1911, he represented the same magazine on a bigger story—the proceedings against the McNamara brothers for the bombing of the *Los Angeles Times* building, the case in which Detective William Burns had played a key role. On every assignment, Connolly formed lasting associations with powerful figures (Haywood's prosecutor, future United States Senator William P. Borah, became a friend, as did former president Theodore Roosevelt), proving himself resourceful, ambitious and, within the bounds of his genre's partisan standards, evenhanded.

The selection of such an accomplished and well-connected writer to present Frank's case was no accident. Connolly had been handpicked for the task by Albert D. Lasker. In late September, the Chicago advertising magnate had written Frank to inquire if Connolly—who had recently returned from a reporting foray to Atlanta—had received the information needed for the job. In the following weeks, the condemned man's lawyers maintained a steady correspondence from Atlanta to Chicago and East Orange, apprising Lasker of the project's progress while providing Connolly with copies of the court documents necessary to flesh out his research. Frank's counsel were essentially at the muckraker's beck and call, running down not just stray facts but photographs and—when suitable pictures were unavailable, as was the case with Lucille Frank—booking studio sessions.

Two days after alerting Frank to the imminent publication in *Collier's*, Connolly mailed the galleys of the first installment to Henry Alexander, with instructions that the lawyer forward them. In a cover note, Alexander told the condemned man: "I presume he wants you to return the proof with any suggestion as quickly as possible." Several days later, Alexander departed for New York to review the manuscript of the second installment.

Frank's excitement regarding the *Collier's* stories was immense, leading him to see Connolly as his equivalent of the novelist whose manifesto, *J'ac-*

cuse, alerted the world to the plight of another Jewish martyr, Alfred Drey-fus. "I trust that you may prove to be my 'Zola,' " he wrote Connolly. A grand comparison, yet it also conveyed desperation. This because, in the weeks since William Smith's change of heart made headlines, the legal news had been almost uniformly bad.

On October 14, Frank and his allies were dealt a severe blow. Roared the *Georgian*'s page-one banner:

LEO FRANK LOSES

The Supreme Court of Georgia had unanimously upheld Judge Benjamin Hill's denial of the extraordinary motion. The decision was unambiguous:

> In view of the nature of the alleged newly discovered evidence on the basis of which an extraordinary motion for a new trial was made, and the strong counter showing made by the State in regard to it, there was no abuse of discretion on the part of the trial judge in refusing to grant a new trial, nor was there error in overruling the motion on any of the grounds set out therein.

Frank's supporters tried to remain positive. "I don't think you need feel at all discouraged," counseled one, adding that the Tye-Peeples motion on the constitutional issue arising from Frank's absence from court at the reading of the verdict offered a greater chance of victory. Still, all involved knew that a door had closed. As the *New York Times* observed: "This was Frank's fifth attempt to obtain a retrial or an annullment of the verdict."

On November 14, the defense suffered another reversal. Boomed the *Journal*'s page-one banner:

LEO M. FRANK LOSES LAST FIGHT IN STATE SUPREME COURT

Georgia's highest judicial body had unanimously upheld Judge Hill's ad-verse ruling on the constitutional issue raised by the Tye-Peeples motion. While the court concurred with the defense's claim that Frank should have been present to receive the jury's decision, it ultimately agreed with Hugh Dorsey's contention that his lawyers had not only signed off on the arrange-ment but had failed to challenge it in a "timely manner." Using the same language the solicitor had used in his oral argument back in June, the jus-tices found:

It would be a trifling with the court to allow one who has made a motion for a new trial on over 100 grounds . . . and [had] the motion heard by both the superior and the supreme courts and after a denial by both courts of the motion to now come in and by way of a motion to set aside the verdict include matters which . . . ought to have been included in the motion for a new trial.

Where a motion for a new trial is made, the defendant must set out all that is known to him at the time or by reasonable diligence could have been known by him as grounds for a new trial . . .

We know of no provision in the constitution of the United States or of this state . . . which gives an accused person the right to disregard the rules of procedure in a state and demand that he shall move in his own way and be granted absolute freedom because of an irregularity (if there is one) in receiving the verdict. If an accused person could make some of his points of attack on the verdict and reserve other points known to him . . . to be used as grounds for further attacks on the verdict, there would be practically no end to a criminal case.

Frank and his allies could no longer mask their disappointment. "Well, I had expected the court to be with me this time," the condemned man told reporters gathered outside his cell at the Tower. The following morning, the *New York Times* noted: "An appeal to the Supreme Court of the United States is now all that stands between the prisoner and death except Executive clemency."

On November 20, the Frank camp received its next setback—the Supreme Court of Georgia refused to certify a writ of error that would facilitate a United States Supreme Court review of the ruling on the Tye-Peeples motion. The justices were simply "not impressed with the construction placed upon their previous decision" by the prisoner's counsel, reported the *Journal.*

Still, several routes over which Frank's case could reach the nation's highest tribunal remained open. Accordingly, Henry Peeples and Henry Alexander left Atlanta by train late on the twentieth, checking in the next day at Washington's new Willard Hotel, two blocks from the White House. The lawyers, joined by the American Jewish Committee's Louis Marshall, then took a taxi to the New Hampshire Avenue home of Supreme Court Justice Joseph R. Lamar, a native of Augusta, Georgia, and the circuit justice for the Fifth Judicial Circuit, of which Atlanta was a part. To support the contention that Frank's absence from court when the jury returned its verdict had violated his constitutional rights, they submitted a brief that cited as a precedent a dissenting opinion penned years before by Lamar himself in which he'd argued that in a murder case where the defendant had not been present to receive an adverse decision, the conviction should have been set aside. The meeting broke up after an hour and a half, with the justice agreeing to take the application under advisement, but ultimately he found that the issue was one of state law and unworthy of review. On November 23, Lamar denied the request, declaring:

> Frank made a motion for a new trial in which the fact of his absence . . . from the courtroom was not made a ground . . . The Supreme Court of Georgia, among other things, held that under the laws of Georgia and the practice of its courts, a motion for a new trial is a proper method by which to attack a verdict rendered in the prisoner's absence . . . the ruling involves a matter of state practice and presents no federal question.

Frank received these grim tidings with growing apprehension. Though friends surrounded him in his cell, his voice trembled when he told the press: "I thought I deserved a chance. I don't know what will be done now."

On November 26, Frank's lawyers referred their application for review to a second Supreme Court justice—Oliver Wendell Holmes, Jr., the legendary Yankee who had been thrice wounded in the Civil War and was by 1914 a towering figure in legal circles. This time, Alexander alone delivered the presentation, reasserting the points made before Lamar and bolstering them with a summary of the trial that emphasized that his client's absence from court at the reading of the verdict resulted from hostility that had permeated the proceedings:

> Several times during the trial, a crowd inside and outside the courtroom applauded when the State scored a point . . . On the last day of the trial, after the case had been submitted to the jury, a loud and boisterous crowd of several hundred people were standing on the street in front of the Court House. The crowd cheered the State . . . Indeed, such demonstration finally actuated the court in making the request of defendant's counsel, Messrs. Rosser and Arnold, to have defendant and the counsel themselves be absent at the time the verdict was received in open court, because the Judge apprehended violence to defendant and counsel and the apprehension of such violence naturally saturated the minds of the jury so as to deprive the defendant of a fair and impartial consideration of his case, which the Constitution of the United States . . . entitled him.

After an hour's contemplation, Holmes, like Lamar before him, declined to issue the sought-after writ. Asserted the justice: "I am bound by the decision of the Supreme Court of Georgia. The motion to set aside came too late." The adverse ruling notwithstanding, Holmes entertained misgivings about what had transpired in Atlanta. Thus elsewhere in his opinion, he declared:

> I understand that I am to assume that the allegations of fact in the motion to set aside are true. On these facts I very seriously doubt if the petitioner (Frank) has had due process of law—not on the ground of his absence when the verdict was rendered so much as because of the trial taking place in the presence of a hostile demonstration and seemingly dangerous crowd, thought by the presiding Judge to be ready for violence unless a verdict of guilty was rendered.

After an unending series of defeats, this was an exceptional triumph for the defense. Declared the front-page headline atop the next morning's *New York Times:*

JUSTICE TO FRANK DOUBTED BY HOLMES

Inside, the paper that had been at the forefront of the fight for nearly a year editorialized:

> From the lips of Justice Holmes, for the first time in the proceedings taken after conviction, we have an expression of interest in the human considerations of this case. Justice Holmes deserves the highest commendation for this human departure from the dry legal formula . . . In this utterance, Justice Holmes gives expression to the thought that is in the minds of the whole public outside of Atlanta. By these words we are confident he has saved the life of an innocent man condemned to death because of the clamor of a community that seemed to have gone mad through passion and prejudice.

Holmes's remarks regarding the atmosphere in which Frank was tried prompted an outpouring of comment. The *Baltimore Sun,* the *Milwaukee Sentinel,* the *Houston Chronicle,* the *Washington Star,* the *Philadelphia Inquirer,* the *New York World* and dozens of others weighed in. The consensus was that the genuine issue had been lost in a maze of procedural minutiae. Asserted the *Boston Journal:* "If the man has not had a fair trial he should have one. The technicalities of law must not be permitted to supersede justice." The state that many held responsible for this upside-down thinking was also roundly criticized. Asked the *Louisville Courier-Journal:* "Do the people of Georgia realize that the mob spirit of Atlanta is about to send a man to execution whose guilt has been by no means proved?" Then there were the discourses on race. Hard upon its initial leader, the *New York Times* declared: "What is mysterious is that the people of Atlanta, when they found out the only evidence against Frank, a white man of upright life and spotless record, was given by a dissolute negro of known criminal tendencies, did not realize that a grave mistake had been made." Finally, there was a puzzlement, best expressed by the *Albany* (New York) *Knickerbocker Press,* over what was now to be done:

> Is it not an amazing commentary upon our judicial system that an asso-
> ciate justice of the United States Supreme Court "seriously doubts if Frank
> has had due process of law" and yet there is no means at hand by which
> "due process" may be had?

In a lengthy statement released the day after Holmes issued his opinion and carried in full by newspapers in Atlanta and New York, Leo Frank sounded many of the same themes. "Can it be that the law, and our system of its administration, is so inexorable that truth and innocence may never be heard after the die is cast?" he asked. "Is the door forever closed and the way barred?" Relatedly, he asserted that the justices who'd overruled his various appeals had not only never considered the evidence in the case but that the twelve men who did consider it had been terrorized into their ver- dict. "Only in one trial was I pronounced guilty, and that was by a jury sur- rounded by an atmosphere reeking with prejudice and mob violence." The condemned man followed this observation with a jab at his adopted home- town: "It is strange to me that a community that boasts of such a dynamic force for good as the 'Atlanta spirit' should so bloodthirstily desire the undoing and annihilation of a human life." All of which led to one of those perorations that in the months since Frank began making pronouncements had become increasingly common:

> That my vindication will eventually come I feel certain. Whether I will
> live to see it, I cannot tell. I am human enough to want to live to see it, for
> it is my right and due. But I may not. I may suffer death. Still, one thing is
> sure. The truth cannot be executed. Vindication may be long in coming, but
> it will come. With this knowledge, death itself has little terror for me.

On November 30, in the midst of the resurgent optimism sparked by Holmes's comments, Frank's counsel once more appeared before the United States Supreme Court. The request was again for a writ of error, yet this time it was made not to one justice but to the entire court. The occasion also marked the emergence of a lawyer who had heretofore kept his involvement in the background—Louis Marshall. With the enthusiastic support of the condemned man's chief financial backer ("I am glad that Mr. Marshall is taking hold of the matter," Albert Lasker had recently written Frank), the American Jewish Committee president had, in truth, assumed full control of the defense. Looking back over the past weeks, he informed Henry Alexander: "One of the misfortunes of this case lies in the fact that there have been too many counsel and that they do not work in unison." Worse, these representatives were at least partially to blame for the multiple setbacks. "The federal question could only be discovered" in the requests made to Lamar and Holmes "by the aid of a high-power magnifying glass," Marshall scolded Alexander.

The defense's new application to the United States Supreme Court was supported by briefs written by both Alexander and Marshall that while addressing distinct aspects of the case dovetailed into a coherent whole. Alexander argued that the right to be present throughout a trial simply could not be waived. His point: Despite Lamar and Holmes's initial determinations, a federal matter was at stake. Marshall, playing to the doubts expressed by Holmes in the section of his opinion concerning the environment in which the proceedings occurred, maintained that "the mob" outside the building where Frank was tried "paralyzed the judicial function." The result: "The duly constituted authority, at the most critical moment of the trial, surrendered its judicial powers." The court, he averred, was "coerced by threats of violence into denying a right protected by the Constitution."

Four days after the defense reapplied for a writ of error, as national press attention was rising, Tom Watson returned to the fray. "Leo Frank as a Regular Newspaper Contributor," read the page-one banner atop the *Jeffersonian*'s December 3 number, beneath which the Sage proclaimed:

> Never before in the history of this country has any convicted criminal been given the freedom of the daily papers that Frank has enjoyed.
>
> It is a lonesome week when we are not regaled with several columns of old hash, freshly warmed over by this filthy and murderous Sodomite.
>
> Simultaneously with the appearance of this stuff in the Georgia papers, it appears in the Northern papers which are owned by rich Jews.
>
> The Baltimore *Sun,* owned by Abells; the New York *World,* owned by the Pulitzers; the *Times* owned by Ochs seem to receive Frank's statements by telegraph at the same time that he hands out copy to the dailies in Georgia.

Watson's ire regarding the distribution given to Frank's utterances was as nothing compared to his disdain for their content. Regarding the assertion that no appeals court had considered the evidence in the case, he declared:

> Good God! What an arrant falsehood!
>
> The defendant *always* alleges that the verdict was strongly and decidely against the evidence.
>
> Therefore, the Supreme Court *had* to pass on the evidence. The Supreme Court *did* pass on the evidence. And the Court *did* say that the evidence was sufficient to sustain the verdict.

Then there was Watson's contempt for the opinions articulated by the newspapers themselves. Honing in on a view expressed most baldly by the *New York Times,* he observed:

> In the Frank case, the great point emphasized by the Jewish papers is that the main witness against Frank was a *negro!*
>
> It seems that negroes are good enough to hold office, sleep in our beds, eat at our tables, marry our daughters, and mongrelize the Anglo-Saxon race, *but are not good enough to bear testimony against a rich Jew!*

The implicit racism of many of the defense's allies was, of course, a fat target, but Watson did not stop there, indulging in his own appeal to prejudice by quoting from a book by Edward A. Ross entitled *The Old World and the New:* "The fact that pleasure loving Jewish businessmen *spare Jewesses, but PURSUE GENTILE GIRLS* excites bitter comment." Whereupon he exclaimed:

> God in Heaven! If Ross had the Frank case in mind, he could not have hit it harder.

On December 7, less than a week after Watson's reemergence, the United States Supreme Court rejected the defense's latest request for a writ of error. There was no opinion, just a one-word decision: "Denied." Yet when the news reached Frank's cell, he reacted calmly. After all, there was offsetting reason for cheer. As Henry Alexander had written him a couple of nights before:

> I expect to hear . . . that the motion for leave to file the petition for the writ of error has been granted. But even if not, I think we have the fight whipped anyway. Connolly's articles will upheave the country.

C. P. Connolly's two-part article on the Leo Frank case in the issues of *Collier's Weekly* for December 17 and December 23 was everything Connolly had predicted it would be and all the defense could have wished for. The first piece opened with a two-page layout dominated by a photograph of Frank in high collar, suit and tie, clasping a cigar in his hand in the manner of a young titan of industry. This was no murderer, the writer declared at the outset, but a "shy, nervous intellectual" who "looks through his prison bars with the eyes of the stoic." Nonetheless, the police had charged the poor man with Mary Phagan's murder, and Atlanta had demanded his conviction and now sought his execution. The reason: "Politics, prejudice, and perjury."

The most poisonous of these influences, asserted Connolly, was prejudice. "In certain parts of the South," he wrote, "there are those who harbor the medieval picture of the fire-breathing, murderous Jew portrayed by Marlowe" — in *The Jew of Malta,* a play thought to have inspired *The Merchant of Venice.* Georgians had applied this stereotype to Frank, maintained the muckraker: "On the last day I was in Atlanta I went to the office of one of Frank's lawyers to say good-by. The telephone rang. 'If they don't hang that Jew, we'll hang you,' came the message." This phrase — "If they don't hang that Jew, we'll hang you" — would now enter the popular consciousness, with many of the condemned man's supporters claiming that it had been chanted by crowds at the trial.

If prejudice led to the initial suspicion of Frank, it was politics, argued Connolly, that led to what he termed the frame-up. The hostilities between the newspapers and the police department, the stresses inherent in a city whose institutions had not kept pace with its growth — the writer pointed out how these factors had played a part. He was most persuasive, however, on the role of the Pinkerton Detective Agency. Quoting from a new affidavit by L. P. Whitfield, the Pinkerton operative who'd always doubted Frank's guilt and had eventually gone to work for the defense, he reported that early in the probe Harry Scott, the firm's second in command and Frank's nemesis, had remarked: "Unless the Jew is convicted, the Pinkerton Detective Agency [will] have to get out of Atlanta."

Which left perjury. Calling on his years as a prosecutor, Connolly highlighted the contradictions in Jim Conley's affidavits and trial statements, proclaiming: "Frank was convicted solely on Conley's testimony. Without it, there was no case." Then, in the second installment of his piece — which was illustrated by a photograph of the pencil factory and portraits of Luther Rosser and Reuben Arnold — he essentially put the Negro in the dock. First, he assailed the state's theory of where Mary Phagan had been murdered:

There was found four corpuscles of "blood"—a mere iota—on the second floor [of the plant]. The girl was brutally handled and bled freely, not only from the wound in her head but from other parts of her body . . . There were cinders and sawdust in the girl's nose and mouth, drawn in in the act of breathing . . . Her face had been rubbed before death into these cinders—yet Conley swore that he and Frank carried the body in a "crocus" sack into the cellar.

Next, he asserted—as the defense had long held—that the murder had occurred in the basement:

Mary Phagan went down the stairway that noon . . . she was in plain view, with her silver mesh bag in her hand, of this semi-intoxicated, lustful, improvident, and impecunious negro who lay concealed all that morning in the shadow of a pile of packing boxes at the foot of the stairway . . . At the foot of the stairway was an elevator shaft which led to the . . . cellar, and alongside of this elevator shaft was also a trap door—the "hole" referred to in one of the "murder notes."

And what did Connolly make of the notes? Borrowing from the studies of Alexander, Smith and Berry Benson, he wrote:

The purpose of the notes . . . was to *divert* suspicion, which would be immediately defeated by the handwriting itself, which was not Mary Phagan's . . . Frank would have known that instantly, but Conley was capable of no such logic. He placed the pencil and the notes and the pad by the body to *make people believe Mary Phagan had written the notes in the cellar.* He thought that the police would recognize it as a negro's crime, and he makes the notes describe a negro. He knew that the crime occurred in the basement, and so he picks on the man [William Nolle] who was employed down there. He never dreamed of the storm of prejudice that would swirl around Frank and make it so easy for him to say, and be believed, that Frank had dictated the notes.

The muckraker closed his case against Conley—and his piece—with an insight revealing that Frank's lawyers, after months of groping to comprehend the relevance of the unsavory evidence that had recently been dubbed "the shit in the shaft," had made a critical breakthrough:

There was a substance found at the bottom of the elevator shaft on Sunday which had been left there on Saturday morning. This is undisputed. It is Conley's own testimony. If the elevator had gone into the basement that

Advertising magnate Albert D. Lasker
(Corbis)

Detective William Burns
(Corbis)

The interior of the Georgia State Prison Farm in Milledgeville, 1915
(Corbis)

Adolph S. Ochs
(Hulton Archive)

William Randolph Hearst
(Hulton Archive)

The Jeffersonian

Vol. 12, No. 34   Thomson, Ga., Thursday, August 26, 1915   Price, Five Cents

"The Wages of Sin is Death."

"DINAH, the daughter of Jacob . . . went out to see the daughters of the land; and when Shechem, . . . *prince of the country*, saw her, *he took her, and lay with her, and defiled her.*

And it came to pass, on the third day, when they were sore, two of the sons of Jacob, Simeon and Levi, . . . took each man *his sword,* and came upon the city (of the prince), *and slew all the males.*

And they slew Shechem "(and Hamor, his father) with the edge of the sword, and took Dinah out of Shechem's house.

The sons of Jacob came upon the slain, and spoiled the city, because *they had defiled their sister.*

And all their wealth, and all *their children* (little ones) and *their wives* took they captive."

And when Jacob whimpered his fears that the Cannanites and Perizzites would combine against the few Jews, and kill them, Jacob's bold sons sternly answered their father:

"*Should he* (Shechem) *deal with OUR SISTER, as with an harlot?*"

(Genesis, 34th chapter.)

Rabbi Wise, of New York, announced death against every member of the Vigilance Committee which *executed upon Leo Frank the sentence the Law had three times pronounced* in the court room; and which the Sheriff would have executed, *had not one of Frank's own lawyers illegally commuted his sentence.*

Rabbi Wise fiercely demands that every official connected with our Prison establishment, be sent to the penitentiary for life.

Rabbi Wise, Nathan Straus, and the Jewish pettifogger, Louis Marshall, demands that I be indicted for *murder.*

Mary Phagan was *not* Jacob's daughter, you see.

Mary Phagan was not the sister of Jacob's sons, you see.

Mary Phagan was nothing but a Cannanite; and the Jewish prince, therefore, had a right to take her and defile her—*the young prince who slept in a blue silk night gown,*

when the sons of the Cannanites came upon him.

The sons of Jacob did not accuse Shechem of violence to their sister. Dinah appeared to be willing. She was continuing to live with the prince. He had not struck her in the face, knocked her against a crank handle, rendered her unconscious, and then choked her to death with a cord.

Dinah made no complaint: Dinah evidently meant to remain with the prince.

Hamor, the father of the young prince, went to Jacob, and pleaded with the patriarch, *urging him to give Dinah to Shechem in honorable marriage.*

Shechem himself went humbly to Jacob, and begged for Dinah in marriage.

All the reparation that any man can make, after such a sin, *Shechem earnestly offered to make.*

With deceit in his heart (the Jewish writer of Genesis says so) Jacob gave his consent to the marriage, upon condition that all the young males of the city of Hamor and Shechem be *circumcised.*

By the highest court of earth, Leo Frank's trial was pronounced legal and fair.

By the highest court in Georgia, the evidence was declared to be sufficient to support the verdict of the jury.

By the judicial department of our State government, Frank's guilt had been ascertained, and the death penalty imposed.

By one of his own Lawyers, the verdict and the decisions were all brushed aside.

BY THE PEOPLE, that void act of Frank's lawyer was ignored, *and the sentence carried out.*

The Law forfeited this man's life, for a horrible crime, *and he has paid.* That's all.

Now let outsiders attend to their own business, AND LEAVE OURS ALONE.

The condition was complied with: "every male was circumcised;" and then it was that the Jews, without any trial at law, without any sentence of any court, fell upon the people whom they had craftily thrown off their guard; and these Jews wreaked indiscriminate slaughter upon young and old, male and female, innocent and guilty.

They slew the old father, Hamor, who had gone to Jacob and pleaded for peace, reconciliation and atonement.

They robbed every dweller in the city, taking the cattle, the crops, and the wealth stored in the houses.

They took the innocent wives of the innocent men whom they had put to the sword.

They took these innocent wives into captivity, to become the slaves and the concubines of the Jews.

They took "the little ones"—the boys and girls—to make servants of them, and to use the girls as Eastern lust has always used helpless women.

There's the record! GO READ IT, RABBI WISE! Go and read it, Nathan Straus!

Your own scribes wrote it; and for more than two thousand years you have held it to be sacredly true.

Did your God sanction that vengeance, visited upon a man and his people, *because of the defilement of one consenting Jewess?*

You say that He did: you say that He blessed Jacob greatly, *and you are exceedingly fond of naming your sons after Simeon and Levi, the sons of Jacob, who did this thing.*

What about it, Rabbi Wise?

What about it, Nathan Straus?

Have you one code for a Jewess, and another for a Gentile girl?

Tell us! We believe that you have; and that you have secretly and powerfully organized to enforce it.

We believe that *your law* exempts the Jew who defiles the Gentile maiden.

We believe that *your law* permits the libertine Jew to use *our sister,* as an harlot.

If you haven't that kind of law in your

(CONTINUED ON PAGE TWO.)

FRANK VIRTUALLY CONFESSED. CEASED TO CLAIM INNOCENCE.

WHEN the Vigilantes went into Frank's room, at the State Farm, and told him they had come for him, he did not seem greatly surprised, and he made no outcry.

He was led out by four men, making no resistance.

He was not roughly treated. If the Sheriff had been in charge of the execution, the proceedings could not have been better conducted.

He as not bumped down the stone steps, as Northern papers have stated.

He was not "tortured" with questions, or in any other way.

Twice, in the seven-hour automobile ride of 170 miles, he was asked if he killed Mary Phagan.

He did not answer.

Not once, in all that long ride to death, did he protest his innocence.

When day overtook the Vigilantes, and they decided to execute the sentence of the Law two miles short of Mary Phagan's grave, he was again asked if he killed her.

Again he was mute!

Then he was asked if he wanted to make any statement, and he answered, "No!"

Later, and as if speaking to himself, he used an expression which showed that he preferred to die silent, rather than bring shame upon his people.

A confession could not save him, and could only bring additional grief upon his family.

He stoically closed his lips, and paid the penalty which the Law demanded.

He did *not* die protesting his innocence

to the last, as the Northern papers, and the Hearst papers state.

The most significant feature of his conduct, during that seven hours' ride, through the darkness and silence of night, was, that he did not once remonstrate with the Vigilantes, and did not once say to them—as he had been saying so often for two years— "I am innocent."

He was guilty; and his conduct at the last corroborates the official record, which I have carefully summarized and will present to the public in Watson's Magazine for September.

That number, read in connection with the August issue, makes up the record which will, for all time to come, prove how Big Money endeavored to defeat Justice in Georgia—*and met a Waterloo.*

The Jeffersonian, August 26, 1915

Governor John Slaton hung in effigy outside Atlanta the week
after he commuted Leo Frank's sentence, June 1915
(Georgia Department of Archives)

Long view of the lynching (WBJHMA)

Frontal view of the lynching
(Joe McTyre Collection, Alpharetta, Georgia)

Close-up of the lynching
(Georgia Department of Archives)

A celebration of the lynching in Marietta's town square
(Corbis)

CIRCULATION Yesterday, Tuesday 58,210

THE ATLANTA CONSTITUTION

CIRCULATION LAST SUNDAY 49,167

Vol. XLVIII.—No. 64.   ATLANTA, GA., WEDNESDAY MORNING, AUGUST 18, 1915.—TWELVE PAGES.   Daily and Sunday, carrier delivery, 12 cents weekly. Single copies on the streets and at all news stands 2 cents.

MOB'S OWN STORY IN DETAIL

Section of Big Crowd Waiting to View Frank's Body

Photo by Francis E. Price.
Some of the thousands of men, women and children gathered at the funeral parlors of Greenberg & Bond, and between 2:30 in the afternoon and 7 o'clock in the evening they filed past the body.

How Plans Were Formed And Put Into Execution Without Slightest Hitch

THOUSANDS VIEW BODY

Men, Women and Children March Past Casket in Undertaking Parlors---Crowd Grows Threatening When Refused Permission to See Body---Remains Taken to Brooklyn at Midnight Following Services in Chapel.

After having been viewed by many thousands of men, women and children as it lay in the undertaking parlors of Greenberg & Bond, the body of Leo M. Frank is now en route to Brooklyn, where the funeral exercises will be held. On the same train are Mrs. Frank, Alexander Marcus, her brother-in-law; Rabbi David Marx and several other friends of the family.

Although it was first attempted to prevent the public from seeing the body of the dead man, the threatening nature of the crowd which gathered at the undertaking parlors led to the decision that it would be best to admit the public, under police supervision.

Full details of the laying of the plans for the removal of Frank from Milledgeville and their successful culmination were disclosed Tuesday.

STORY OF HOW MOB LYNCHED FRANK.

"The public will never know the identities of the 25 brave and loyal men who took into their own hands the execution of a law that had been stripped from them by Governor Slaton. I would not advise inquisitive authorities or persons to try to reveal them. They are as zealously banded together now, and as relentless, as the moment they invaded the state prison."

This was the statement of a citizen of Marietta to a reporter for The Constitution Tuesday afternoon. He was thoroughly aware of the movements of the lynching clansmen, of the process of organization, of their plans, and of their painstaking system of advance preparations. He would neither admit nor deny that he was a member of the mob.

"The men who hanged Leo Frank, the murderer of Mary Phagan, did not go about it with a spirit of lawlessness nor vindictiveness. They felt it a duty—a duty to their state and commonwealth, a duty to the memory of Mary Phagan, whom all Cobb county loved, and whose memory is cherished in every household in the hills you see over there to the west.

FIRST PLANNED FOR MONTHS AGO.

"They would have lynched him more than a month ago if some one hadn't got careless and permitted a 'leak.' Governor Harris was apprised of the plans and ordered the militia to be in readiness. That was the day when the county police were scouting in the edge of Fulton and Cobb counties on the lookout for automobiles from Marietta.

"Governor Harris and the military authorities no doubt received widespread censure for this apparently unnecessary action, but if the truth were known it gave Leo Frank at least one month of grace he would not have received from the hands of the men who were about to go to Milledgeville for him.

"Ever since the day Governor Slaton commuted the sentence of Frank this morning's hanging has been in process of formulation. Minute and definite plans were drawn, and there was not a missing thread from the fabric of the perfected scheme when the twenty-five men set out early last night on their journey to Milledgeville.

PROMINENT MAN CHOSEN AS LEADER.

"Meetings were held in a spot so conspicuous that you would be astonished to hear its name called. A leader was chosen, a man who bears as reputable a name as you would ever hear in a lawful community. He was a man respected and honored. Hundreds of men would obey him—the twenty-five would have gone through hell and high water with him.

"The chosen twenty-five (although this wasn't the entire number available) were men whose worth was known, collectively and individually. I doubt that you would find anywhere a body of men more loyal, faithful, obedient and determined. They were resolved to bear whatever burdens arose as though it fell upon them individually, and to go through with their plans at any cost.

"They were business-like, as well as determined. Like business ventures, they would not go into it without first knowing every detail

Purposely unidentified man holding
a photograph of the lynching
and an oak branch at Mary Phagan's
grave, summer 1915
(Marietta Museum of History)

Frank's casket being removed from his parents' home, August 20, 1915
(Corbis)

Lucille Frank, near collapse, being escorted to the funeral
(Corbis)

Anti-lynching editorial cartoon, *New York World*, August 18, 1915

Herbert Clay shortly before his death, summer 1923
(Courtesy Eugene Herbert Clay, Jr.)

Judge Newt Morris (left) and H. N. Randolph, McAdoo
delegates, on a cruise of the New York harbor during the 1924
Democratic Party convention (Corbis)

Lucille Frank, circa 1950
(WBJHMA)

Tom Watson shortly before his death
(Southern Historical Collection, The Library of the
University of North Carolina at Chapel Hill)

William Smith, "The Revenant," circa 1945
(Courtesy Walter Smith)

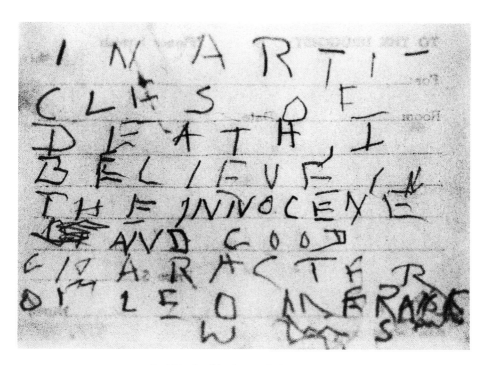

Smith's deathbed note, February 1949
(Courtesy Charley Smith)

Smith with prospective students at the Fort Smith School, circa 1946
(Courtesy Walter Smith)

Saturday noon [as the Negro had sworn], it would have been crushed. It was crushed when the elevator was operated on Sunday. This is a physical fact that cannot be argued away, and which unimpeachably disproves Conley's story.

The defense's response to the *Collier's* presentation was, predictably, ecstatic. In a late-December letter to Connolly, Frank termed the pieces "bully," requesting "two or three dozen for distribution here at the jail." The condemned man was equally delighted that the stories, as promised, were widely reprinted across the country. The *New York Times*, for instance, gave them nearly a full page.

The response from Tom Watson was, just as predictably, condemnatory. Boomed the headline atop the *Jeffersonian*'s December 17 number: "Another Campaign of Big Money Begins: C. P. Connolly." Watson was furious that the muckraker had quoted no one connected to the prosecution. Furthermore, he was outraged that Connolly presented as fact many debatable claims, among them that Frank had been convicted solely on Jim Conley's testimony. Such liberties prompted Watson to begin his own review of the case, adducing details damning to the condemned man. What most infuriated Watson, however, were the outside forces that were *"spending half-a-million dollars to save the rich Jew from the legal consequences of premeditated and horrible crime."* Referring to the wide distribution given to the *Collier's* articles, the Sage proclaimed:

> Big Money is now using C. P. Connolly as its megaphone. C. P. Connolly is flooding the country with literature, finely gotten up on glossy paper and illustrated by a cut of the horribly sensual face of Leo Frank. The purpose is to divide public opinion, create mawkish sentiment and manufacture a sympathy which will influence the authorities.

In mid-December, the defense inaugurated a final push to get Frank's case before the United States Supreme Court. Adding urgency to the effort was the fact that in the wake of the ultimate defeat of the application for a writ of error, Judge Benjamin Hill had set January 22, 1915, as a new execution date. It could all be over in another month.

On December 17, Frank's Atlanta counsel, acting at the behest of Louis Marshall, filed a petition for a writ of habeas corpus before Judge William T. Newman of the United States District Court of the Northern District of Georgia. The petition drew innovatively upon the Fourteenth Amendment, which was adopted during Reconstruction to protect the newly freed slaves from state interference with their fundamental rights as citizens. However, the amendment's broad language ensuring "due process" and "equal protection" for all persons offered the possibility of wider application. Unlike the precisely defined writ of error, the habeas corpus remedy could trigger an inquiry into the legality of one's loss of liberty. As of 1914, the ability of a federal court to use such powers to upset a state court criminal conviction was unresolved. Thus it was that on December 19, when Henry Alexander and Henry Peeples presented oral arguments before Newman, they devoted their energies to defending the validity of the approach. Insisted Alexander:

> This matter involves one of the gravest questions that can come before a federal court. To a large extent it is a new question.

Added Peeples:

> We realize, your honor, that on the very threshold here we are met by the question of difference between an application to the United States Supreme Court for a writ of error and an application to this court for a writ of *habeas corpus*. There is a fundamental difference. The jurisdiction of the Supreme Court on a writ of error from a state court is very narrow and restricted. But on a writ of *habeas corpus* the United States district court has the discretion and latitude to examine and determine whether a state court has lost jurisdiction. As I say, the difference is a wide one and a fundamental one.

Simultaneous to the filing of its petition in United States District Court in Atlanta, the defense redoubled its effort to win support for Frank in the court of popular opinion. The *Collier's* pieces, as expected, had introduced the case to the entire nation. "Outside the state of Georgia," Albert Lasker wrote a friend who'd inquired as to the articles' impact, "the press of the United States, including the leading papers of every city in the South, are editorially agitating public sentiment for the unfortunate Frank. Daily, hundreds of papers are editorially crying that Frank's execution would amount to judicial murder." Not surprisingly, the sheets leading the charge were in New York. The *World* was now wholeheartedly in the defense camp. So, too, the *Herald.* More significant, William Randolph Hearst's flagship, the *Journal* (following in the footsteps of his Atlanta property), had also aligned itself with the condemned man. "If Frank's life is saved," the chief's roving editorial eminence, Arthur Brisbane, wrote Lasker in late December, "Frank will owe [it] not in least to any one of the lawyers you have paid so liberally but to W. R. Hearst, a man of real power and of a kindness of heart that is not appreciated."

The groundswell had started, and Frank's allies were doing everything within their abilities to see that it spread across America. Yet critical as the

Collier's articles and the exertions of such kingmakers as Lasker and Hearst were to the process, it was Adolph Ochs who ultimately pushed the hardest. December 1914 found the *New York Times* in the midst of an all-out drive of the sort it had never undertaken before. Only three days during the month did the paper not publish a major article on the Frank case. Some of its stories, particularly if there was a new development, strove for balance, but by and large, Ochs's sheet was more interested in disseminating propaganda than in practicing journalism. Beneath such headlines as LAWYERS UNITE FOR FRANK, FRIEND'S PLEA FOR FRANK, GEORGIANS URGED TO PLEAD FOR FRANK and ATLANTA'S MOB SPIRIT, the *Times*'s news department presented a shrill and one-sided picture of the facts. The paper turned over eight columns to William Burns to promulgate his theories of the Phagan murder, sans comment from Hugh Dorsey and without acknowledging the detective's partial responsibility for his troubled sojourn in Georgia. The editorial page hammered the message home as well. In five lengthy pre-Christmas institutionals (GEORGIA'S JUSTICE PECULIAR, boomed one topper; INNOCENCE NOT NOW THE ISSUE, another) the *Times* committed its influence to the task of creating an atmosphere conducive to a favorable decision on the defense petition now before the federal court. While the paper's overseers seemed vaguely cognizant that it might not be politic to tar all Georgians with the same brush ("Anti-Jewish prejudice had influence upon some thoughtless minds in Atlanta, but there is not the slightest reason to suppose that the intelligent people of the city were affected by it," conceded one leader), the overriding intention was to arouse indignation and stimulate action.

By the third week of December, the outrage generated by the *Collier's* articles and the daily pronouncements in the *Times* had started to make itself manifest. From Philadelphia came news of a planned mass meeting at the Academy of Music to discuss Frank's conviction and to agitate for justice. Similar sessions were scheduled in other northern cities, among them Chicago, where in announcing their intentions, organizers caught the spirit of the moment: "The Leo M. Frank case can be reckoned among the cause celebres of the world."

The spectacle of it all struck such a jarring note in Georgia that it was not just Tom Watson who protested. In a wire to Adolph Ochs, Thomas Loyless, the moderate editor of the *Augusta Chronicle,* inquired: "Why have the *Times* and other publications so owned and controlled attempted to make so much out of this Frank case? You slander the people of Georgia when you undertake to make it appear that Frank's race or religion had anything whatsoever to do with his conviction."

Yet however heavy-handed the publicity campaign had become, from the perspective of those calling the shots, events dictated no less. For one,

Judge Newman, without even hearing from Hugh Dorsey, had denied the petition for a writ of habeas corpus, declaring:

> This matter has been tried in the state courts. The state supreme court held that it did not present a federal question, or, if one had been presented, that it should have been embodied in the motion for a new trial.
>
> This decision was taken before the justices of the United States Supreme Court, and Justices Lamar and Holmes held that it was for the states to determine their method of practice . . . The status of the case seems to be the same here . . . In view of this, I have not the jurisdiction nor the power to grant the writ.

At a subsequent hearing in Atlanta on December 21, the picture darkened further. In a bitter speech opposing a defense motion seeking Newman's certification for an appeal to the United States Supreme Court, Dorsey brutally attacked the foundation of Frank's position:

> We abundantly disposed of this allegation of mob violence before Judge Roan at the time Frank made his motion for a new trial, and we satisfactorily met the allegation before every court in which it has been urged. We showed by witnesses that none of the alleged demonstrations in the court room during Frank's trial and none of those alleged to have occurred in the streets outside the court house ever came to the attention of the jury.

The solicitor then lashed out at the condemned man's lawyers, declaring that the only explanation for Holmes's comments regarding the hostile environment in which the trial occurred was that the facts had been misrepresented to him. Shortly thereafter, Newman rejected the motion for certification.

In response, Henry Alexander took issue with Dorsey's allegation that he had, in effect, lied to a Supreme Court justice. "I challenge the statement emphatically," he told reporters. "It is unfair to charge that Frank is seeking favorable action by warping the facts." But be that as it may, the condemned man's lawyers had no choice but to return to the nation's capital to make a last-ditch application to an individual who'd already turned them down once.

At 8 A.M. on the day before Christmas, Louis Marshall stepped off a train at Washington's Union Station, and by 10 he was again walking through the front door of Joseph R. Lamar's New Hampshire Avenue home. But where at the presentation of the petition for a writ of error the American Jewish Committee president had played merely a supporting role, he was now Frank's sole representative, the decision having been made that Alexander would remain in Atlanta to prepare an application for executive clemency should Marshall's mission fail. For an hour, Frank's lead counsel made an impassioned argument as to why Lamar should over-rule Judge Newman. To begin with, he cited the points elucidated a month earlier, asserting that the trial court had lost jurisdiction when the defendant was not present for the reading of the verdict. Then, referring to a new 32-page brief, he adduced the various reasons why the petition for a writ of habeas corpus confronted the Supreme Court with a genuine federal issue, one that not only justified a hearing on Frank's behalf but offered the tribunal an opportunity to decide a significant constitutional question with implications for the entire country. Finally, Marshall bluntly mentioned the reams of publicity that had been accorded the case, making the claim that should the Supreme Court fail to consider Frank's plea, the American people would lose confidence in the body as a fair and impartial broker. As he later informed his Georgia counterparts: "I made an *argumentum ad hominem* and told [Lamar] that the question involved had attracted so much interest that it meant as much to the Court, and to public confidence in the administration of justice, as it did to Frank. I flatter myself that it made an evident impression." Shortly after 12, Marshall emerged into the early afternoon of a preholiday city emptying by the minute as government employees rushed home. Around 4, he received a call from Lamar saying that there would be no decision for at least several days. While a light note in the justice's voice left Marshall "somewhat encouraged," he briefly contemplated going over his head to Chief Justice Edward White. But after weighing the move, he rejected it, telling a friend: "It might come back to Lamar's ears and he might resent my action." Hence with dusk falling, Marshall returned to the station. "Good cheer to Frank," he wired Atlanta before departing. Yet for all the lawyer's optimism, as his train sped through the night toward New York, he pondered a somber Latin phrase—*hoc opus, hic labor est,* this is the hard work.

Christmas fell on a Friday in 1914, and over the weekend that followed, Frank and his supporters awaited Lamar's decision. For the condemned man, though buoyed by the presence at the Tower not just of Lucille but of his parents, who were in Atlanta visiting, the hours ticked by with excruciating slowness. "It is hard for me to see just which way . . . my vindication will come," he wrote C. P. Connolly. To which the *Collier's* correspondent gamely replied: "My dear Leo, I don't blame you for feeling doubtful. You must remember, however, that the seed is now being planted in your favor. You will hear from this in good time. I believe you will get some kind of hearing."

Monday, December 28, dawned cold and cloudy in Atlanta, with Frank's fate still up in the air, but at midday, Henry Alexander received phenomenal news. Soon enough, the story was on the wires, and extras were on the streets. Screamed the *Journal*'s gigantic banner:

FRANK APPEAL GRANTED

Echoed the *Georgian:*

FRANK WINS APPEAL TO SUPREME COURT

Justice Lamar had concurred with Marshall's contention that a vital constitutional issue was at stake. His ruling:

> The Supreme Court of the United States has never determined whether on a trial for murder in a state court, the due process clause of the federal Constitution guarantees the defendant a right to be present when the verdict is rendered.
>
> Neither has it decided the effect of a final judgement refusing a new trial in a case where the defendant did not make the fact of his absence when the verdict was returned a ground of the motion . . .
>
> Nor has it passed upon the effect of its own refusal to grant a writ of error in a case where an alleged jurisdictional question was presented in a motion filed at a time not authorized by the practice of the state where the trial took place.
>
> Such questions are all involved in the present case, and since they have never been settled by any authoritative ruling by the full court, it cannot be said that there is such a want of probable cause as to warrant the refusal of an appeal. That being true, the certificate should be given and the appeal allowed.

Frank's wife, mother-in-law and parents were with him at the Tower when word came of Lamar's ruling. Soon thereafter, friends began arriving, and between smiles and tears, an impromptu party commenced. Noted one writer: "The cell of Leo Frank looked like the scene of a big reception this afternoon and tonight." The calmest person present was, characteristically, the one with the most to celebrate. In part, the condemned man's subdued reaction reflected the weeks of uncertainty through which he'd just passed. "His face betrayed the strain of the past month," reported the *Georgian*. Eventually, however, Frank's spirits lifted. In a comment alluding to the hope that events would start to go his way, he told the press: "It is a long lane that has no turning."

From David Marx's perspective, all credit went to Louis Marshall. "I feel that I have a right as well as a privilege to express to you my appreciation for the service you are rendering every Jew in the land," the rabbi wrote the lawyer. Meanwhile, Frank distributed laurels to the men who'd given his plight notoriety, creating the climate in which Marshall had worked. "In assuring you of my deep appreciation of the stand you have taken in my case," he wrote Adolph Ochs on January 1, "may I not extend to you my heartfelt good wishes for a happy New Year? I feel that a more thorough understanding of the issues in the case among the people throughout the United States has been brought about to a great extent by the space you so kindly have given to it." In a letter to Albert Lasker composed on the same day, the condemned man—while making sure to thank the advertising magnate—reiterated his praise for the publisher of the *New York Times*. Lasker concurred, responding:

> I quite agree with you that Mr. Adolph Ochs, through his espousal of the "cause of an innocent man" largely made possible the progress we have made.

Yet despite the plaudits and the renewed confidence, Frank and his supporters well understood that they had not achieved a victory so much as been given an opportunity, and a fragile one at that. Hugh Dorsey had immediately announced that he would fight the appeal vigorously, and he'd asked for an expedited hearing. The case would be on the Supreme Court's February docket. In brief, the defense faced another life-and-death battle. And like those in the past, it would be fought in multiple arenas. As the condemned man wrote C. P. Connolly on New Year's Day: "I feel that the missionary work to enlighten the people of the true aspects of this case must not be relaxed."

During the early weeks of 1915, both Frank and his allies used every avenue to get their version of the story before the American public. On January 6, A. B. McDonald of the *Kansas City Star* became the first in a continuing series of national newspaper reporters to arrive in Atlanta for a sit-down interview with the now all too loquacious man in the Tower. The resulting piece advanced the same conclusion as *Collier's*—Frank had been railroaded. Hand in hand with the favorable factual presentations came a bumper crop of like-minded editorials. Predictably, many of them appeared in the *New York Times*. Typical was a lengthy essay by a deputy New York police commissioner published in the paper's magazine. Headlined, FRANK IS INNOCENT, SAYS GEORGE S. DOUGHERTY, the article concluded that "no testimony of fact or circumstance warranted Frank's conviction." Ochs's paper was not, however, alone. William Randolph Hearst's morning *New*

York American joined in, as did the satirical magazine *Puck* (published by Nathan Straus, Jr., son of the Macy's Department Store baron), which inaugurated its commentary with a cartoon depicting the states of the union as passengers in a touring car driven by Uncle Sam riding to the rescue of Frank just as Georgia was about to string him up. And as if such productions weren't enough, the condemned man continued his own career as a polemicist. "Do you care to make a statement in your behalf to be printed in our newspaper?" asked Victor Morgan, the editor of the *Cincinnati Post.* The answer was yes. In the task of fulfilling this assignment and others like it, Frank was aided substantially by his wife. Every evening, Lucille departed her husband's cell following their regular visit carrying a folder containing his handwritten pronouncements and his replies to the increasing number of letters arriving from well-wishers. Then, night after night at home, she sat at an Underwood typewriter she had purchased several weeks earlier at the Fielder and Allen Office Supply Company. The next morning, the condemned man's crisply typed position papers and correspondence, all bearing the initials "Mrs. LMF," would go back to the Tower for his signature, then by mail to the far reaches of the country.

The impact of this latest wave of publicity was, once more, mixed. Outside Georgia, the perception that the state and its citizens were involved in an anti-Semitic persecution of an innocent man became universal. Commenting on the reaction to A. B. McDonald's piece, Jacob Billikopf of Kansas City wrote Albert Lasker: "Few articles which have appeared in the *Star* in recent years have created such a furor." But inside Georgia, the perception that the nation and its Jewish-owned newspapers were involved in the persecution of a state and its people further hardened. Predictably, Tom Watson did the most to promulgate the view. Under such page-one banners as "The Continued Campaign of Slander Against the State of Georgia in the Frank Case," the *Jeffersonian* devoted its January and February issues to deriding the arguments of Frank's "millionaire backers." Citing comments printed by the *Times,* the *World* and—particularly galling since Nathan Straus, Sr., was a native Georgian—*Puck,* the Sage proclaimed: "This campaign of lies, abuse, defamation and race hatred gets worse and worse. It must be costing the Chosen People a lot of money." Had Watson been the sole local proponent of these opinions, they might have dissipated, but again, he was not. In mid-January, former Georgia governor Joseph Brown, in his first public remarks on the subject, took to pages of the *Augusta Chronicle* to inquire: "Are we to understand that anybody except a Jew can be punished for a crime?" There were, to be sure, people in the state who did not harbor such thoughts, but they generally remained silent. As the *Kansas City Star*'s McDonald had observed:

The managing editor, associate editor, city editor, assistant city editor and court reporter of an Atlanta newspaper said to me they knew Frank was entitled to a new trial; his trial was not fair.

"Then why don't you say so?" I asked.

"We dare not; we would be accused of being bought by Jew money," they answered.

No one was better attuned to the deepening religious and regional polarities in the Frank affair and the role the outside press played in exacerbating them than Louis Marshall. "Apparently nothing that may be written will, under present conditions, affect public sentiment in Georgia" in a positive way, he advised the condemned man in a despairing January 20 letter. Yet bemoan this fact though he did, the American Jewish Committee president was no longer of a mind to urge fellow Jews to keep quiet, much less ask his client to cease giving interviews. Marshall understood that Supreme Court justices read the *New York Times* and could be influenced by a national hue and cry. With the case headed back to the capital, he made the calculated decision that continuing coverage by crusading northern newspapers was of greater strategic value than not.

Shortly after 2 P.M. on Thursday, February 25, the clerk of the United States Supreme Court in Washington called the case now known as *Frank* v. *Mangum,* so identified because under law it was Fulton County sheriff Wheeler Mangum who had deprived Frank of his liberty. A crowd had turned out to hear the oral arguments, packing the gallery. Louis Marshall, no stranger to the historic room with its green marble columns, spoke first:

> This court has said that there must be a trial before a competent tribunal. A competent tribunal is one that holds the scales of justice impartially, that is not swayed by fear or favor. Here, the trial was marked by prejudice and hostility. Jeers at counsel for Frank were permitted when they lost a point. The crowd almost trespassed upon the jury box, hanging over the jury box, and their whispers were heard throughout the courtroom. Applause greeted the Solicitor General when he appeared at the seat of justice. Finally, the court asked counsel to meet him in private conference, and then, upon the insistence of the court that the prisoner might be torn from the sanctuary of the court and lynched by a mob if he was present when the verdict was returned, counsel consented to his being absent. The jury was left to return its verdict to the prosecuting officer and the mob. They knew what that meant.

Marshall had thus summarized the factual basis for the appeal. When he attempted to go further, the nine justices—who gazed down from high-backed leather chairs behind a raised platform—began, as was their custom, to pepper him with comments and questions. Indicating that he believed the defendant's waiver of his presence at the ultimate moment was, as the state had contended, an inconsequential irregularity, 57-year-old Mahlon Pitney, a New Jersey Republican who had served in Congress, declared: "We have said that a court may abolish trial by jury, and I do not see why a state may not abolish one of the incidents to a jury trial."

Replied Marshall: "The right is a Constitutional right. It is part of the right to be heard."

Whereupon Chief Justice White, a jowly former United States senator from Louisiana who had fought for the Confederacy, asked: "Is it your argument that in a jury trial where the accused is not present, he has not been heard and the trial has been illegal and he must go free?"

Again, Marshall was brief and firm: "The right to be heard includes the right to be present at the final stages of the trial as well as the earlier stages."

Unsatisfied, White pressed the issue, inquiring where in the United States Constitution he might locate such a right. Additionally, he asserted that from his reading of the evidence, Leo Frank had actually been heard at length, particularly in his unsworn statement. Then the chief made an observation that appeared to suggest he felt the matter was more properly one of local practice. In Louisiana, he said, Roman law still prevailed and juries returned majority instead of unananimous verdicts. Do you think, he demanded, that this invalidates all jury verdicts in my state?

Having run into a strong headwind, Marshall changed course, broaching the other premise upon which the defense's application rested—Frank's trial had been poisoned from the outset by the threat of hostilities. No sooner had the lawyer made the assertion than Oliver Wendell Holmes, Jr., encouragingly interjected: "I am free to confess that point is one that impressed me very much." On the strength of this endorsement, Marshall elucidated the disruptions that had marked the proceedings. Yet disturbing as the litany of offenses sounded, Pitney was not convinced, wanting to know whether the state had contested the allegations and whether the Georgia Supreme Court had considered and dismissed them. Before Marshall could answer, he received another assist from Holmes, who declared that if what the condemned man's counsel said was true, "it wouldn't matter if twenty courts had passed on the matter." Nonetheless, Frank's lawyer was obliged to concede that the lower courts had, in fact, ruled against the defense's claims regarding the atmosphere in which his client had been tried, although in the last minutes of the day's session he declared that

Luther Rosser and Reuben Arnold had "misapprehended the procedure in the early stages," depriving the appeals court of a full accounting of the details.

Friday morning saw Marshall again getting resistance from Chief Justice White, who expressed concern that if the Supreme Court found for Frank, "any man under sentence in a state court could come to the supreme tribunal for a writ."

"I do not so consider it," said Marshall. "Here is a case involving a question of due process of law. It is a case where there is no dispute as to the facts."

That said, Marshall stressed what to him was a significant distinction. He was not asking the body to set aside Frank's conviction but to order a new trial. As he'd informed Henry Alexander several days before:

> If the judges [are] confronted with the proposition that the adoption of our views would mean the unconditional discharge of Frank whether guilty or innocent, they would struggle very hard against such a conclusion. On the other hand, if they are satisfied that Frank did not have a fair trial and that by adopting our jurisdictional theories they can accord him a new trial, that would be in conformity with modern tendencies in the administration of the criminal law, and would go far toward preparing the way for a favorable reception of our theories.

After Marshall conveyed this vital point to the justices, he threw himself upon their mercy, concluding: "Unless we have a remedy here, we are helpless."

Once Marshall sat down, the state—which was represented in this forum not just by Hugh Dorsey but also by Georgia attorney general Warren Grice—took issue with almost every point the defense had adduced. "There was no coercion of the prisoner," insisted Grice. "It was simply the case of a kind-hearted judge suggesting to counsel that their client remain absent." The state's chief prosecutor then disparaged the claim that an underlying bias had infiltrated Frank's trial: "There was no public prejudice against the defendant at the opening of the trial. Such feeling as was aroused against him was aroused by the character of the evidence as the trial progressed." Moreover, on the few occasions during the proceedings when outbursts occurred, Grice added, Judge Roan promptly put them to a halt.

Dorsey devoted his turn before the tribunal to reiterating the contentions made by Grice and to advancing the view that the disturbing picture of the trial painted by Marshall was an exaggeration. He termed the defense lawyer's assertions "an enlargement upon the truth." Then, repeating the charge he'd made before Judge Newman, the solicitor alleged that in their petition for the writ of habeas corpus, Marshall and Henry Alexander had suppressed the fact that the state courts had upheld the prosecution's claim that no adverse impact resulted from the alleged hostilities during the Frank proceedings. Dorsey concluded by citing precedents supporting a defendant's right to waive his presence at the reading of a verdict.

In short, utterly divergent accounts had been placed before the court. As a consequence, it announced that it would reserve its decision, meaning that there would be no ruling for at least a month, maybe longer. Both the defense and the state appeared to have advocates on the nine-member panel, but neither side speculated publicly as to how the justices would vote. As for Leo Frank, he was optimistic. "I am hopeful of winning," he wrote C. P. Connolly shortly after the hearing. "I feel very hopeful of a favorable decision."

During the weeks in which the Supreme Court deliberated, the Frank case stayed very much alive in the nation's prints. Of the many pieces seeking to exonerate the condemned man, the most prominent ran in the March number of *Everybody's Magazine,* which like *Collier's* was a primary outlet for muckrakers. Beneath the headline "Did Leo Frank get JUSTICE?," Arthur Train, a New York assistant district attorney who traveled in elite social circles, concluded that "as a matter of logic, the evidence points indubitably to Conley rather than to Frank." True, Train saw some merit in the state's theories. Moreover, he was repulsed by the condemned man, noting: "Many of his supporters admit that he is shrewd, cold, egotistical. He is even suspected of rather enjoying the limelight in which he finds himself." Still, the writer believed that the facts relied upon by the prosecution just didn't add up. "Why should Frank seek assistance from an unreliable and perhaps treacherous negro merely to take the body down in the elevator?" he asked. "Why should he wish to leave a clue as to his confederate's identity by having him write two notes? Or why, if the notes were written upstairs, and the body taken down in the elevator, did Frank tell the negro to write that 'he push me down that hole'? Why 'hole' at all? And what became of the purse and the money?" So persuasive was Train on all of this that the *New York Times*—as it had done with C. P. Connolly's articles—reprinted excerpts, then followed up with a major editorial, declaring: "Like every other investigator of this remarkable case not subject to local prejudice and excitement, Mr. Train has reached the conclusion that Frank is innocent."

Not surprisingly, Tom Watson simply could not let such pronouncements pass. Responding to the *Everybody's* piece as well as to several other recent stories (particularly one that appeared in Joseph Pulitzer's *St. Louis Post-Dispatch*), the banner stripped across the *Jeffersonian's* March 25 issue proclaimed: "The Leo Frank Case Still Raging in Northern Papers." In the accompanying text, Watson scored the "outsiders who cannot or will not weigh the facts which prove Frank's terrible crime." There also now appeared in the Sage's remarks a new and menacing tone. After wrapping up a list of the evidence against Frank, he warned:

> If Frank's rich connections keep on lying about this case, SOME-THING BAD WILL HAPPEN.

On April 19, the United States Supreme Court, by a seven-to-two vote, upheld Judge Newman's denial of Frank's petition for relief. In a dense and lengthy decision written by Mahlon Pitney, the lopsided majority found against the condemned man on every point. The conservative justice, who broadly interpreted "due process" in rulings invalidating progressive state laws designed to protect workers, was content to leave "due process" in the hands of the state when it came to the rights of criminal defendants. Summing up, Pitney declared:

> Frank's allegations of hostile public sentiment and disorder in and about the courtroom improperly influencing the trial court and the jury against him have been rejected because found untrue in point of fact upon evidence presumably justifying that finding and which has not been produced in the present proceeding. His contention that his lawful rights were infringed because he was not permitted to be present when the jury tendered its verdict has been set aside because it was waived by his failure to raise the object in due season when fully cognizant of the fact.
>
> In all of these proceedings the state, through its courts, has retained jurisdiction over him and accorded to him the fullest right and opportunity to be heard according to established modes of procedure and now holds him in custody to pay the penalty of the crime of which he has been adjudged guilty.
>
> In our opinion, he is not shown to have been deprived of any right guaranteed to him by the Fourteenth Amendment or any other provision of the Constitution or laws of the United States. On the contrary, he has been convicted and is now held in custody under "due process of the law" within the meaning of the Constitution. The judgement of the District Court refusing the application for a writ of *habeas corpus* is affirmed.

Devastating as Pitney's opinion was, the court was not of one mind. Oliver Wendell Holmes and Charles Evans Hughes, a former governor of New York who in just a few months would resign to run as the Republican presidential candidate against Woodrow Wilson, then return to the court as chief justice, vigorously dissented. In an elegant opinion penned by Holmes but which read as a joint product as a result of Holmes's suggestion to "put *we* for I throughout," the two declared:

> Whatever disagreement there may be as to the scope of the phrase "due process of law," there can be no doubt that it embraces the fundamental conception of a fair trial with opportunity to be heard. Mob law does not become due process of law by securing the assent of a terrorized jury. We are not speaking of mere disorder, or irregularities in procedure, but of accounts where the processes of justice are actually subverted. In such a case, the federal court has jurisdiction to issue the writ . . .
>
> Supposing the alleged facts to be true, it is our duty to declare lynch law as little valid when practiced by a regularly drawn jury as when administered by one elected by a mob intent on death.

Frank was smoking a cigarette when a *Georgian* reporter arrived at the Tower with the bad news. Initially, the condemned man could not speak. After a moment, though, he said, "I am very much disappointed." Then he began to pace the tiny enclosure that for so long had been his home and where, just two days earlier, he had turned 31. "I will never suffer the death penalty," he declared between puffs. "Truth will ultimately prevail." The reporter wondered whether the prisoner was referring to the next step in the battle, an appeal for executive clemency. Yet before Frank could respond, his wife appeared. Unlike at previous dark moments, Lucille was now composed. As the visitor withdrew, she approached her husband's cell and reaching her hands between the bars pulled him to her, kissing him on the cheek.

EIGHTEEN

Commutation

The morning after the United States Supreme Court delivered its adverse ruling, Leo Frank's lawyers, in a dramatic bit of stagecraft revealing that they had long been ready for such an eventuality, announced that they were in possession of a letter written by Judge Leonard Roan in which he both reasserted his misgivings as to the condemned man's guilt and urged executive clemency for him. Under any circumstances, this revelation would have generated headlines, but what made it a sensation was the fact that the document's author was dead. The fatigue and sense of malaise that had plagued Roan prior to Frank's trial had turned out to be a prelude to a fatal diagnosis—cancer. By late 1914, the disease had spread, and he was confined to the Berkshire Hills Sanitarium in North Adams, Massachusetts. There, in December, as both his and Frank's options were rapidly diminishing, the jurist dictated his final thoughts on the matter to a secretary, who then typed them up on the sanitarium's stationery. They read:

> Gentlemen: After considering your communication asking that I recommend clemency in the punishment of Leo M. Frank, I wish to say that at the proper time I shall ask the prison commission to recommend and the governor to commute Frank's sentence to life imprisonment . . .
>
> It is possible that I showed undue deference to the opinion of the jury in this case when I allowed their verdict to stand. They said by their verdict that they had found the truth. I was still in a state of uncertainty, and so expressed myself. My search for the truth, though diligent and earnest, has not been so successful. In the exercise of judicial discretion, restricted and limited according to my interpretation of the decisions of the reviewing court, I allowed the jury's verdict to remain undisturbed. I had no way of knowing it was erroneous.
>
> After many months of continued deliberation, I am still uncertain of Frank's guilt. The state of uncertainty is largely due to the character of the negro Conley's testimony, by which the verdict was evidently reached . . .
>
> The execution of any person whose guilt has not been satisfactorily

proved to the constituted authorities is too horrible to contemplate . . .
Hence at the proper time I shall express and enlarge upon these views
directly to the governor and the prison commission. However, if for any
cause I am prevented from doing this, you are at liberty to use this
letter at the hearing.

No sooner had the existence of Roan's statement been made public
("the voice from the tomb," the defense christened it) than Frank's lawyers
gathered at Leonard Haas's office in the Fourth National Bank Building, an
Italianate skyscraper on Peachtree Street in downtown Atlanta. In attendance were Leonard and Herbert Haas, Henry Alexander and the two men
whose conduct of the trial had increasingly come under fire, Luther Rosser
and Reuben Arnold. Long into the evening, the group debated a difficult
choice: whether to apply for a full pardon for their client or, following the
late judge's lead, to seek merely a commutation of the death sentence.
Though all present were, in the *Journal's* estimation, "fully confident that
Frank was innocent," they ultimately chose the lesser goal. "This course,"
the paper reported, will be pursued because "the attorneys feel that in the
face of the adverse action of the various courts of appeal they could hardly
hope for a pardon."

The following day, when several of the lawyers who had attended the
previous night's meeting arrived at the Tower to present their plan, they
ran into an unexpected road block—Frank would not agree to it. "I am not
asking for mercy," he snapped. "I am innocent and have been unjustly
convicted. What I want is justice." In response, Alexander and the others
argued that a commutation, far from constituting an admission of guilt,
would buy the prisoner "the opportunity for time and future developments
to prove his innocence." More soberly, they added that they believed this
tack offered the only chance of success. Ultimately, Frank concurred, and
he and his counsel began drafting a petition. Written over the condemned
man's signature, it concluded:

> I am absolutely innocent of the crime of which I was convicted. My
> death would neither avenge it, nor punish the real perpetrator. I have
> no personal knowledge of the crime other than the facts related by me in
> my statement made at the trial. Beyond these facts, I know no more than
> any other person who was present in the court room and heard the evi-
> dence.

Once the application was notarized, it was submitted to the proper authorities. The date was April 22, 1915.

On the surface, the events that would now unfold were explicitly prescribed by law. Following the return to Georgia of the mandate from the United States Supreme Court, a new execution date would be set, and the state Prison Commission, a three-man body that supervised Georgia's penal institutions and served as its pardon and parole board, would hold a hearing. After deliberations, the commission would issue a recommendation to the governor, who would then conduct his own hearing. Typically, the governor reached the same conclusion as the Prison Commission, but not always. In such instances, final authority was vested in the executive.

On another level, the road ahead was murky, with the identity of the key player in the process up in the air. Because Frank's appeals had taken so long to wend their way through the courts, what a year before had been the near certainty that any application for a pardon or commutation would go to John Slaton was now no certainty at all. In just a few weeks, Slaton would step down, making way for the newly elected Nathaniel E. Harris. Reported the *New York Times* in its May 3 edition:

> The case may be handled by Governor Slaton, but it is doubtful. His term expires in June, and it is believed that the Prison Commission will not have completed consideration of the case by that time. In fact, it is believed that the commission will not begin consideration of the case until some time in June. In that event, Governor-elect Harris will pass on the case.

Thus Frank's lawyers found themselves facing two perplexing questions. First, which of the executives would be more likely to spare their client's life? Then, once the initial determination was made, what mechanism could be set in motion to assure that Frank's petition reached the governor's office when the right man was in place?

While it was a safe bet that Slaton, due to his partnership with Rosser and his connections with Atlanta's elite, would be the defense's pick to pass on Frank's application, the choice was not a foregone conclusion. The sitting governor was not on good terms with all of the condemned man's supporters. Several months earlier, in response to a request by Frank that the *Journal* lobby his cause to Slaton, editor James R. Gray replied: "The governor is not friendly to this paper. If we should urge him to pardon you or commute your sentence, I believe it would have an effect directly opposite to what we wish." Also arguing against putting the matter before Slaton was his having made it known that he hoped to avoid any conflicts of interest. As the *New York Times* reported: "It is understood that Governor Slaton would prefer the case to go to Harris. The Governor's attitude is due to the fact that he is a member of the law firm which defended Frank." Finally, the condemned man's lawyers simply liked Slaton's successor. Sixty-nine-year-old Nat Harris, a Confederate veteran and longtime judge from Macon, was regarded as warmhearted and fair-minded. In fact, the incoming governor's reputation was such that some thought he was the better candidate. Observed the *Times:* "It is an open secret that Frank and his friends would prefer Harris to make the final disposition of the case."

Yet the crosscurrents and gray areas notwithstanding, in the end, initial impressions were correct — Slaton was the man the defense ultimately wanted to decide Frank's fate. For one thing, the governor's remarks on the topic had been consistently evenhanded. When asked by reporters how he would handle the petition should it come to him, he had asserted: "I shall be guided solely by the merits of the case and my own conscience. The question is this: If Leo M. Frank is guilty, he ought to be hanged. If he is not guilty, then he ought to be saved." Moreover, Slaton had made a point of declaring that the prisoner's religion would have no bearing on his thinking. "Frank shall not be a victim of injustice because he is a Jew. I don't want the impression to go out that the governor of Georgia could not give justice to a Jew. My own personal feelings toward the Jewish people may be judged from the fact that Mr. Phillips, my law partner for nineteen years, is a Jew." Meantime, Harris, while also vowing impartiality, had tailored his comments to a different constituency. "You can just say this for Nat Harris that if the matter of dealing executive clemency is to be considered by him, the entire outside world will not be taken into consideration. It is entirely a Georgia matter, and if I am to consider the case I shall consider it with the interests of Georgia at heart." Finally, though, it was not what Slaton and Harris were saying to the press that tipped the balance but what those inside the highest echelons of Frank's camp were hearing privately from an informed source. In early May, Arthur Brisbane, William Randolph Hearst's freewheeling second in command, told Louis Marshall that, as one writer later put it, "Frank would have a better chance to live if Governor Slaton, rather than his successor, received his appeal." Marshall believed this conclusion to be accurate. After all, not only were Hearst and Slaton politically allied, but Brisbane had for months been in close contact with Albert Lasker concerning the case.

Just because Frank's supporters wanted Slaton to pass on the commutation application did not mean that it would work out that way. If anything, as news accounts had indicated, the timing seemed to favor the matter ending up on Harris's desk. Traditionally, the United States Supreme Court did not forward mandates to the lower courts until 30 days after making a ruling, meaning that the soonest the case could be returned to Georgia was

May 19. By that juncture, the Prison Commission's regular monthly meeting would have concluded. The body's next scheduled session was set for June 7, fewer than three weeks before Slaton's term expired. Unless exceptional steps were taken, the man the defense deemed most likely to show Frank mercy would not have the opportunity to do so.

Which was why on May 5, Louis Marshall asked the Supreme Court for the immediate release of the mandate in Frank's case. The high tribunal sometimes acceded to such requests when they came from the losing party in an action, and this was one of those times. When reporters in Atlanta sought Henry Alexander's comment on the move, he professed surprise. "We have just been notified of the step taken in the Supreme Court," the lawyer contended. "Frank's local counsel were not advised that the step was to be taken." That said, Alexander did his best to make it sound as if the defense had no preference in the matter. "Those representing Frank's application before the Prison Commission and the governor have no desire to hasten or retard the hearing before either the commission or the governor. They wish and expect the application to take the usual and ordinary course." But despite such a statement, there was nothing usual and ordinary about what had just transpired—the mandate was coming back to Georgia a critical fourteen days early.

At 11:35 on the morning of May 10, Leo Frank emerged from a door behind the bench of Judge Benjamin Hill's courtroom in Atlanta's handsome new Fulton County Court House. At the condemned man's side were Leonard and Herbert Haas, Henry Alexander, Luther Rosser and Reuben Arnold. Beaming up from a seat at a table situated in front of the packed gallery was Lucille. Once more, an execution date was being set, and once more, Frank used the moment to address not just those within his hearing but the larger audience beyond:

> Again, I stand before you. Again, I can but reiterate that I am innocent of the murder of Mary Phagan. I have absolutely no knowledge of that tragic occurrence.
>
> My execution will not avenge Mary Phagan's death. A life will have been taken for a life, but the real culprit will not have paid the penalty. I will suffer for another's crime.
>
> My trust is in God, who knows that my protestations of innocence are the truth. At some future date the whole mortal world will realize it.

With that, the condemned man was done, and Hill set June 22 as the date. Throughout her husband's remarks, Lucille had retained her composure, but upon hearing the judge's words, she placed a handkerchief over her eyes and bit her teeth into her lower lip. Frank, however, never wavered. Back at the Tower, where Sheriff Wheeler Mangum immediately drove him, he lingered for a moment on the street smoking a cigarette and talking to his parents, who'd just arrived in town and would stay for the duration. Before disappearing into the stone lockup, he kissed his mother and smiled. Still, there was no doubt that the burden had started to weigh on him. It showed in his face, which one reporter described as "noticeably pale," and in a new written statement, which his lawyers distributed shortly after the hearing and in which he said: "I am fully alive to the fact that my position is most precarious. It's a situation which is so far removed from anything that my life and mental attitude could have bespoken. It is so hideous, but at the same time so unreal, so incongruous." Still, there was a glimmer of hope. As the *Journal* noted in its account of Hill's hearing: "With the fixing of June 22 as the date of execution, it became certain that Governor Slaton would be called upon to pass upon the case. Governor Slaton does not go out of office until Saturday, June 26."

Even as the defense was inaugurating its last round of legal maneuvers, it was also launching its final publicity push. The campaign began on a glorious spring afternoon when Geraldine Farrar, who was in Atlanta participating in the Metropolitan Opera's annual Southern season, walked into the Fulton County Tower. At 33, the blue-eyed, black-haired diva was the most highly acclaimed soprano in America—her portrayal of Cio-Cio-San in Puccini's *Madame Butterfly* had recently thrilled New York audiences. As if this weren't enough, she was on her way to becoming a movie star. As Farrar's fans, called "Gerry-flappers," already knew, she would soon travel by private train car to Hollywood. There, Samuel Goldwyn would cast her in *Maria Rose* opposite another rising talent, dashing Wallace Reid, and Cecil B. DeMille would direct her in his groundbreaking epic *Joan, the Woman*. For the moment, though, something else was on the performer's mind. "One of my great anticipations," she told a reporter when discussing her trip to Georgia, is "to visit Leo Frank."

Farrar almost stopped short while ascending to the Tower's oppressive cell block. "I had the sensation of nausea, and I wanted to turn back," she later remarked. But after spending just a few minutes with Frank, she added, "the disheartening influence of the dark place left me." Declared the diva:

> There is nothing in his outward appearance to be so impressive. It is his intellect that counts. You would perhaps hardly notice him in a crowd, but

when he speaks you sit and listen. I strove as hard as I could to look upon him from a completely unprejudiced standpoint, but all the while my conviction of his innocence grew upon me, and I finally resigned myself to total faith in him.

Frank, his wife, who was making her regular late-day call, and their famous visitor spent an hour together chatting. As it happened, when Leo and Lucille were courting, they had seen Farrar perform, and they remembered the experience happily. They also discussed the great concert halls of Europe, most of which the singer had played and many of which Frank knew. All the while, Farrar, aside from just listening, made mental notes about everything from the condemned man's attitude toward death ("He has no more idea of dying than I have. Even now, he is studying for his future") to the manner in which he and Lucille related:

> There is poignant pathos in the grief of his wife. Her hand went through the bars to rest on his all the while we chatted. Deep down in her heart there is sorrow untold, but when he takes hold of her fingers and glances into her eyes a smile brightens her face.

As dusk neared, Farrar bid the couple farewell and emerged to meet the press. "One might hear everything that could possibly be considered a detriment to Frank's case," she said, "but to sit and talk with him would convince even the most callous of his innocence." After making a few similar comments, Farrar went to a telegraph office, where she dashed off a wire to the *New York Times*. In it, she gave a description of all she had seen and felt while unequivocally stating her belief that the condemned man was incapable of murder. As a result, newspaper readers not just in Atlanta but in the North as well awakened the next morning to a new type of propaganda. Now, instead of a lawyer or magazine writer speaking out on the case, it was the beautiful creature Samuel Goldwyn decreed the nation's most glamorous woman. Proclaimed the *Constitution*'s above-the-fold topper:

Leo Frank An Innocent Man
Declares Geraldine Farrar
After Visit to Tower Cell

In the wake of Farrar's widely reported endorsement — and in reaction to the Prison Commission's announcement that it would take up the commutation petition at a special May 31 session — the pro-Frank drumbeat intensified. Though there was a lull after the May 7 sinking of the Cunard liner *Lusitania* by a German submarine, as front pages brimmed with accounts of the tragedy (1,200 dead, many of them American) and its repercussions which made the United States's entry into the conflict that would become World War I nearly inevitable — the very vastness of the chaos rising up from Europe in the end acted only to increase interest in the factory superintendent's fate. When explaining why the New York–based Women's Peace Society had turned its attention from the fighting overseas to the battle coming to a head in Atlanta, Mrs. Desmond Adams, the group's secretary, revealingly stated: "We first thought of trying to stop the war, but that seemed impossible" and hence "we focused our attention on matters at home, and the life which it seemed ought to be saved was that of Leo M. Frank."

And so somewhere in America on every day of May 1915 someone was either circulating a petition asking that Georgia authorities commute Frank's death sentence, making a speech demanding the same or from the pulpits of both temples and churches praying for divine intervention. New York City was predictably a hotbed of such activity. At the corner of Sixth Avenue and Twenty-third Street beneath a giant banner urgently emblazoned DO IT NOW. SIGN PETITION TO SAVE LEO FRANK, lines formed around the block. The goal was to obtain one million signatures to forward to Atlanta, and toward that end organizers not only manned booths but dispatched school children armed with pencils and sheaves of copy paper to surrounding neighborhoods. Louis and Rose Perlman of 120 West Twenty-fifth Street, ages seven and eight, collected 1,500 names in one day. Seven-year-old Sadie Garfinkle of 237 Seventh Avenue gathered 100 signatures in under 30 minutes. Across the river in Brooklyn, members of the Leo Frank Committee were engaged in similar work, as were those in another group in uptown Manhattan at Seventh Avenue and 126th Street. All the while, the big guns of the city's journalistic, business and religious establishments pounded home the need for such labors. The *New York Times* published seven pro-Frank editorials during the month. William J. Wollman, director of the J. S. Bache Brokerage, lent his voice to the fight. So did Stephen S. Wise, the rabbi of the Free Synagogue, who on May 17 told an overflow audience at Carnegie Hall: "I do not ask the liberation of Frank at this time. But until he is proved guilty, he ought not to die." Echoing Wise's plea were Dr. Madison Peters of the North Baptist Church on Eleventh Street in Greenwich Village and Dr. Edward Young of the Bedford Prebyterian Church in Brooklyn.

New York was not the only city where men and women took to the streets and the lecterns to rally support for Frank. In Chicago, following mass meetings at the Powers Theater and the Auditorium Hotel, Lester Bauer, secretary of another Leo Frank Committee, declared May 24 Leo M. Frank Day. By way of preparation, volunteers carrying petitions canvassed the Loop and outlying suburbs collecting signatures to send to Atlanta.

Within a week, 400,000 had committed their names to the cause. Meantime in Boston, thanks to the lobbying of Alexander Brin, a 21-year-old reporter for the *Boston Traveler,* the agitation was, if anything, even more vigorous. All month long, the paper published daily coupons addressed to Governor Slaton. They read: "The undersigned believe that there is strong doubt as to the guilt of Leo Frank. We hereby respectfully petition you to commute his sentence." By May 26, the *Traveler's* drive had generated 200,000 signatures and stirred so much interest that a capacity crowd thronged historic Faneuil Hall to hear a lineup of revered New Englanders ask Georgia officials to spare the condemned man's life. For the most part, the addresses were sober and thoughtful, but one was confrontational. To raucous cheers, Boston's colorful mayor, James M. Curley, roared:

> We want to say to Tom Watson from Faneuil Hall that every man in the United States is entitled to justice without distinction of race or creed or color. And we want to say that the organ of Tom Watson is a disgrace to newspaperdom.

Simultaneously, Frank's supporters were undertaking a letter-writing campaign. Most of the notes and telegrams to John Slaton came from ordinary citizens, but thanks to the efforts of such powerful allies as Albert Lasker, Julius Rosenwald and C. P. Connolly, Georgia's governor received messages from United States senators representing Connecticut, Idaho, Illinois, Louisiana, Mississippi and Texas as well as the governors of Arizona, Louisiana, Oregon, Michigan, Mississippi, Pennsylvania, Texas and Virginia. (Two national figures who rejected overtures to participate were the former presidents William Howard Taft, who turned down a plea from Rosenwald, and Theodore Roosevelt, who said no to Connolly.) By May 18, a mammoth box on Slaton's office floor was spilling over with mail. Ultimately, the governor received more than 100,000 requests asking him to spare the factory superintendent's life.

The climax of the Northern crusade on Frank's behalf came the last week of May when delegations from Chicago and Boston, one headed by John O'Connor, chief justice of the Cook County Criminal Court, the other by former Massachusetts governor Eugene Foss (who owned B. F. Sturtevant, where Frank had apprenticed after graduating from Cornell), arrived in Atlanta bearing massive crates of petitions requesting clemency for the condemned man. Combined with those shipped via railroad express from New York (two trunks full) as well as such cities as Los Angeles, Cincinnati and Omaha (where newspapers had printed coupons similar to those that appeared in the *Boston Traveler*), the petitions contained over two million signatures. As the date for the Prison Commission hearing approached,

America seemed to be speaking as one. As United States Senator John W. Kern of Indiana put it in a May 28 telegram to Slaton:

> I beg you to spare this man's life. He will die a martyr in the estimation of millions of American citizens if you permit him to be executed.

And it wasn't just Northerners who advocated clemency. In fact, as the nationwide campaign was hitting high gear, many of the Georgia institutions that a year earlier had supported Frank in his extraordinary-motion fight again rallied to his side. Twice during the week before the Prison Commission hearing, the *Atlanta Journal,* its troubled history with Governor Slaton notwithstanding, called for mercy. In its initial leader ("Commute Frank's Sentence to Life Imprisonment," declared the headline), the paper asserted that the framers of Georgia's constitution had invested the executive with the pardoning power for precisely such cases as this one, "where all ordinary legal processes had failed." That said, it reiterated the claim that the trial had been conducted in a poisonous atmosphere. Then, citing William Smith's change of heart, it charged that "the depraved and drunken negro" was Mary Phagan's killer. And as for the pro-Frank clamor from the North, the sheet applauded it as a heartfelt outpouring:

> Localities and groups are often moved by gusts of sentiment to intercede in a condemned prisoner's behalf, but that is not the source or character of this appeal. A few hundred or a few thousand impressionable persons here and there could be swayed by mere pity, but when hundreds of thousands of people in every part of the United States reach the same conclusion and urge the same request, we may be sure that they act upon a solemn conviction.

Also rejoining the fray was the Confederate veteran Berry Benson, William Smith's mentor, whose essay pointing to Jim Conley as the author of the murder notes was now available in pamphlet form. And there were new advocates as well. Colonel Pendleton Brewster, one of Hugh Dorsey's partners; Hooper Alexander, United States district attorney for the northern district of Georgia; Robert C. Alston, former president of the Georgia Bar Association; the Reverend C. B. Wilmer, rector of St. Luke's Episcopal Church; and the lawyer Arthur Powell each endorsed clemency. So, too, did the *Augusta Chronicle*'s Thomas Loyless. Averred the editor:

> I stand for commutation of the death sentence to one of life imprisonment. In this way, it seems to me, we might best live up to our state's motto—"Wisdom, Justice, Moderation."

Yet in the end, most Georgians believed that Frank should pay the ultimate penalty, and the man who reinforced that view was, of course, Tom Watson. Calling on his vaunted skills as both a lawyer and a polemicist, the Sage used the spring issues of the *Jeffersonian* to level new charges of misconduct against the defense, deliver what amounted to another closing argument for the state, repulse the attacks against Georgia's courts by the "millionaire Jews" and their press agents and order the Prison Commission and the governor to stick to their guns.

Regarding Judge Leonard Roan's letter seeking clemency for Frank, Watson all but branded it a forgery:

> The letter from Judge Roan pretends to have been written December last.
>
> In December, 1914, the Judge was in such a terrible and agonizing condition that an operation taking away his jaw and almost the whole side of his face had to be performed.
>
> In December, the sufferer could not hold a pen.
>
> He certainly could not have prepared such a letter as Frank's lawyers presented *without assistance.*
>
> This is the blackest feature of the defensive methods, blacker than the attempt to bribe witnesses and to suppress evidence.

As to why Frank's lawyers were resorting to such trickery, Watson maintained that it was because the truth could not sustain them. Though he raised once more the topic of the hair and blood evidence and Monteen Stover's testimony, Watson came down hardest on the character issue. "What sort of man is Leo Frank?" he asked. His answer:

> In the official record are the names of more than a dozen white girls and ladies who swore in open court that *Frank's character* for lewdness, lasciviousness, immorality WAS BAD!
>
> Could Hugh Dorsey have drummed up a dozen white women *of so good a character the defendant's lawyer did not question them* to testify that the reputation of any respectable man of Atlanta is *bad?*
>
> The evidence of white witnesses establishes the fact that Frank lusted after *this* little Gentile girl Mary Phagan.

Then there was Watson's reaction to the latest onslaughts from outsiders he regarded, at best, as misinformed:

> In behalf of Frank, Governors of States are importuned to meddle with our affairs; school children sign monster petitions; Ladies' Peace Societies

fall into line; and mass meetings are held in Chicago and elsewhere, and these Northern "mobs" gathered from the promiscuous elements of city life pass resolutions about a case of which they know nothing, except what is excitedly stated by some inflammatory speaker who has never himself seen the official record . . .

Woe unto God-fearing fathers and mothers who are trying to raise pure girls when such a man as Frank can become the romantic hero of theatrical money seekers like Geraldine Farrar.

Finally, Watson honed in on the upcoming hearings. "It is embarrassing to the majority of Georgians that John M. Slaton is a member of the law firm to which Frank's leading attorney belongs," he remarked in the *Jeffersonian*'s May 27 number. The governor's untenable position thereby stressed, the Sage issued an edict — and a warning:

> The Governor of Georgia should consider—
> (1.) That if the Law is not allowed to take its course in the Frank case, we might as well abolish the Law and save all future expense of similar mockeries of Justice;
> (2.) That a commutation of sentence will be tantamount to a pardon, and he had just as well sign the one as the other;
> (3.) That if the Prison Commission or the Governor undertake to undo — in whole or in part — what has been legally done by the courts that were established for that purpose, *there will almost inevitably be the bloodiest riot ever known in the history of the South.*
> Consequently, the Prison Commission and the Governor, in such a contingency, would be directly responsible in morals for whatever lives were lost.
> Shall one malefactor suffer the just punishment of the law after his legal conviction has been upheld in all the courts, State and Federal, or shall we have wild disorder and perhaps the loss of scores of innocent lives because of this most wicked and most criminal convict?
> It is up to the Prison Commission and the Governor.
> If I were the bosom friend and legal adviser of every one of these officials, I would say—
> *LET THAT TREE LIE WHERE IT FELL!*

By 9:30 A.M. on May 31, a tensely quiet crowd filled the corridors outside the prison commission meeting chambers on the third floor of the state capitol in downtown Atlanta. Inside, the 100 chairs allotted for spectators had long been taken. Seated together at the front of the gallery were Leo Frank's parents and Lucille, who wore a simple black dress accented by white trim. Arrayed behind adjoining desks at the head of the room were the three commissioners. Chairman Robert E. Davison was a 60-year-old lawyer from the East Georgia hamlet of Woodville. Eugene Leigh Rainey, bow-tied and dapper, published a weekly paper, the *Dawson News*, in the southwest corner of the state. Mustachioed Thomas E. Patterson was a 46-year-old lawyer from the middle-Georgia town of Griffin.

Though Henry Alexander and Leonard Haas were present, Frank's case would be in the hands of yet another new lawyer—William Schley Howard, a former prosecutor from a rural judicial circuit east of Atlanta who had also served two terms in the United States Congress. Schley Howard, as everyone called him, was a widely respected advocate. He was also well liked. The lawyer had been selected for this difficult task over several nationally known practitioners. From the perspective of Albert Lasker, who was again footing the bill, Tom Watson's criticism of outside interference had made it vital that a popular local deliver the condemned man's final plea.

Howard began his presentation by reading aloud Judge Roan's letter endorsing the commutation of Frank's sentence. "It is the most precious document in the case. It is a new lease on life for Leo M. Frank," he declared upon finishing. Then, in hopes of both maximizing the letter's impact and silencing those critics who maintained that it was a fabrication, the lawyer recited a letter submitted by the late judge's closest in-law, Dr. J. T. Roan of rural Jessup, Georgia:

Judge L. S. Roan was my brother, and during March, 1914, he visited me in my home. He discussed the case and trial with me. I do not undertake to quote his words, but the following are a few of the impressions which were made upon me by his conversation.

The impressions were that a spirit of mob violence permeated the whole atmosphere of Atlanta and even entered the court room and manifested itself in various ways.

The impression also that I received was that Frank had accounted for every moment of his time on the day of the murder, except a few minutes, and that in the morning and afternoon Frank kept a very intricate set of books in perfect shape, and he could not conceive that a man of Frank's disposition could have done this had he committed the crime.

He further left upon me the impression that the evidence itself taken as a whole left grave doubt in his mind as to Frank's guilt and that in passing upon the motion for a new trial, he only considered the errors of law and did not pass upon the evidence. He was very sure that the supreme court would grant Frank a new trial and that this would be better for Frank than for him to do it.

Taking my brother's conversation as a whole, I am sure he must have entertained grave doubt as to Frank's guilt.

Howard next provided the commissioners with a number of documents whose contents reinforced the view that Frank's application for clemency was founded upon his innocence. Among the submissions were such predictable items as the dissenting opinions from the Georgia and United States Supreme Courts. Also included were a few surprises, the most newsworthy being the Annie Maude Carter letters, which were tendered in typed duplicate that made for easier comprehension, and the reports of the physicians who after examining Frank for signs of deviancy had given him a clean bill of health. Then there was a new item — a study of the murder notes by Albert S. Osborn, a New York–based handwriting expert. Though Osborn's "psychoanalysis," as he termed it, covered some of the same ground as had the works of Benson and Smith, it did isolate one fresh peculiarity — the notes were written in the third person. For documents purporting to have been composed by a girl in her death throes, this was odd. To Osborn's thinking, Frank would not have committed such an error. "An intelligent man should realize at once that to be most effective the note[s] should be in the first person." The less sophisticated Conley, he believed, wrote them alone.

Howard also made sure that the commissioners heard directly from eminent citizens who supported clemency for Frank. During the daylong hearing (the afternoon session was moved to the general assembly chambers to accommodate the demand for increased seating), speakers representing such Georgia cities as Savannah, Dalton and Brunswick pleaded for the condemned man's life. Appearing as well were several of the Northerners who'd come South bearing petitions. Former Massachusetts governor Foss vouched for Frank's character while his employee the feminist Mary Delaney Fisher begged for mercy in the name of the nation's women and Marshall Field's Department Store chairman T. N. Higginbotham intoned: "Don't leave the Frank case for history to correct. Correct it and make judicial history."

Schley Howard interspersed the personal testimonials and pleas with readings from the letters of various others advocating clemency. Legally, the best informed correspondent was Fulton County's blind coroner, Paul Donehoo, who asserted:

> Personally, I have never made up my mind that Mr. Frank is guilty. On the contrary, there is so strong a doubt lingering in my mind on the point that I should feel very badly indeed to stand by and see him hanged. When

I examined him at the Mary Phagan inquest, he was more than necessarily open and this spirit on his part has always appealed to me as entirely inconsistent with the theory of his guilt.

Emotionally, the writer who made the most impact was Lucille Frank. Her letter was less a plea than a rebuttal to the nasty rumors that had been circulated regarding her home life and her failure to visit her husband when he was first taken into custody. Lending poignancy to her words was the fact that as Howard read them, she sat in the front row sobbing.

> Our marriage has been exceedingly happy and has never been marred by the slightest cloud. Leo was regarded and loved by my parents as a son, and was always courteous, gentle and most respectful in his relations with them . . .
>
> When my husband was first arrested on this charge and was detained at police headquarters, I hurried to Decatur Street, accompanied by my father and brother-in-law. I was not allowed to go up to my husband and remained in the office of the probation officer, from whence my friends prevailed upon me to return home. Being assured that my husband would be released at any moment, I remained at home, but as soon as it became apparent that he would be detained indefinitely I went to him immediately and have been going to him every day since.

A chorus of beseeching voices thus raised, Howard took a moment to summarize his final documentary submission—William Smith's study of the murder notes. The 100-page report expanded upon the lawyer's headline-grabbing insights into Jim Conley's speech and writing patterns. Spelling, grammar, repetition of adjectives, favorite verb forms—every element was fully fleshed out. "In this article," Smith contended, "I show clearly that Conley did not tell the truth about those notes." Then, he declared: "I swear to you that I believe Leo M. Frank to be innocent. With all the earnestness and seriousness of my life, I appeal to you not to let him die."

Hard upon the presentation of Smith's report, Howard commenced his closing argument. Though he was brief, he nonetheless made a handful of crucial points. First, picking up on Smith's study, he asserted: "It can be shown by the letters Conley wrote to Annie Maude Carter in prison that Conley was the sole author of the death notes found beside the body. The mind behind the murder notes belonged to the hand that wrote them." This fact alone, the lawyer insisted, "is sufficient to warrant commutation." That said, Howard sought to counter the opinion advanced by Tom Watson that neither the prison commission nor Governor Slaton possessed the legal right to intercede:

> The power to pardon comes from our English ancestors. It is commensurate with the power of the king, and it is still as big in Georgia as it is in England. The power of pardon is the exercise of an act of grace . . . The execution of this power does not discredit the courts, neither does it put its exponents in an attitude of antagonism or hostility toward the courts. The power to set aside a statutory procedure, such as has preceded us in the Frank case, is a power with which you and the governor have been entrusted directly by the people.

Having appealed to the commissioners' nobler instincts, the lawyer concluded by appealing to their baser ones, in the process framing the decision before them in the same terms that Rosser and Arnold had framed it for the jury:

> This case has not a parallel in judicial appeals in this state. Conley has been credited rather than us, and we have been doubted. That is the sum of the entire case. Never before in the history of this state has there been an instance where such a low, vicious negro has been believed against the character and testimony of exemplary whites.

Thereupon, Howard sat down. While Hugh Dorsey had submitted a letter to the Prison Commission objecting to the commutation of Frank's sentence, he had skipped the hearing, vowing to make his stand later before the governor. Hence when Chairman Davison asked the audience if anyone wished to speak for the opposition, he was met by silence.

Any thought that the defense would have not just the last but the only word before the Prison Commission was short-lived. A mere two hours after the board's hearing ended, hundreds of men and women fervently opposed to clemency for Frank began to gather twenty miles to the north of Atlanta in Mary Phagan's hometown of Marietta. "Mass meeting Monday night," declared the handbill that had been distributed throughout the community over the weekend. "Object: to protest against commutation of the death sentence of Leo M. Frank." By 7:30, nearly 1,000 people were assembled inside the Cobb County Courthouse, a vast space illuminated by gaslights and dotted by signs forbidding the consumption of that messy staple of Southern cuisine, peanuts.

The first speaker, newly elected state legislator John Tucker Dorsey (a distant cousin of the Fulton County solicitor), kicked off the evening with a bellowing war cry: "Let him hang!" The extended applause that greeted this ejaculation made it plain that though Mariettans had remained quiet about the Frank case during the months since Detective William Burns was driven from their midst, they continued to seethe regarding what they, like Watson, saw as the efforts of wealthy and influential Northerners to frustrate justice. Following Dorsey to the lectern was the banker Moultrie Sessions, who in an address that was ostensibly a paean to the legal system argued that the factory superintendent's execution would send a strong message that the courts could be trusted, thus discouraging those who would resort to the extralegal alternative—lynch law. Finally, however, it was Fred Morris, a respected Cobb County lawyer and, more important, a former University of Georgia football phenom, who summed up the collective mood:

> Mary Phagan was a poor factory girl. What show would she have against Jew money? When they found they couldn't fool the people of Georgia, they got people from Massachusetts, New York and California to try and raise trouble. Well, we throw the advice of these outsiders back in their teeth. To hell with what they think.

At night's end, a motion was adopted to send a delegation to Atlanta the next day to express Marietta's views to the Prison Commission.

Accordingly, at 10 A.M. on Tuesday, June 1, fourteen well-known Cobb Countians trooped into the same third-floor capitol hearing room where, just a few hours before, Schley Howard had begged for Frank's life. The contingent included not only John Tucker Dorsey and Fred Morris but Marietta mayor E. P. Dobbs; Bolan Glover Brumby, scion of a famous Georgia family and president of a prosperous furniture manufacturer; Cobb County ordinary Gordon Gann; *Marietta Journal* editor Josiah Carter, Jr.; former Cobb County sheriff William J. Frey; and Elmer Phagan, little Mary's uncle. An illustrious group, made more so by the presence of Herbert Clay, solicitor general of the Blue Ridge Circuit (which included Cobb County) and son of the late Alexander Stephens Clay, who had served Georgia in the United States Senate from 1896 until his death in 1910.

"We think the law in this case should take its course," declared Clay, who led off. "Something has been said about prejudice and an unfair trial, but we believe the evidence shows Frank guilty. People outside of Georgia who have read biased, I might say subsidized, accounts of this case have been urging you to commute. But if you commute this sentence, capital punishment might as well be abolished. If the extreme penalty should be enforced, it is in this case."

Clay was followed by Fred Morris, who asserted that the "people of

Cobb County want to see the law enforced impartially on the rich and poor alike."

At this, Commissioner Thomas Patterson interjected that what was at issue had nothing to do with Frank's wealth but with the possibility that he might be innocent. Read Judge Roan's letter, he urged.

In response, Morris expressed the now widely held view that the letter was a forgery, adding that even if it wasn't, its author had expressed nothing new.

Yes, he did, Patterson rejoined. "A doubt as to his own action."

The last Cobb Countian to speak was John Tucker Dorsey. "The voice from the tomb" that he wanted the commissioners to hear did not belong to Judge Roan but to another recently deceased Georgian: "W. J. Phagan, Mary Phagan's grandfather, a noble citizen who went to his grave with his mind fully made up as to the guilt of Leo M. Frank."

After Dorsey returned to his seat, Chairman Davison brought the hearing to a close.

During the eight days the Prison Commission deliberated, the mood inside the defense camp remained almost unanimously hopeful. Dozens of well-wishers congregated from morning to night in the hall outside Frank's cell at the Tower. Friends like Milton Klein, Rabbi David Marx, Dr. Benjamin Wildauer and Sam Boorstin were constant presences, as were Lucille and all the family members. The lawyers, particularly Henry Alexander and Schley Howard, also frequently stopped by. So, too, did William Smith. Frank jotted the name of every visitor in a leather diary he'd recently begun keeping, a volume in which no one received more mentions than a newcomer who had established himself as the cause's most vociferous cheerleader.

The *Boston Traveler*'s Alexander Brin had journeyed south to cover the doings of the Massachusetts delegation. When his fellow New Englanders returned home, he remained. The young reporter's dogged faith in Frank's innocence and his enthusiasm in expressing the same filled a void that had been left when C. P. Connolly, in the wake of his failed attempt to enlist Teddy Roosevelt's support, dropped out of contact. (As the climax approached, the muckraker checked in to a spa in Battle Creek, Michigan. "I did not write," he later confessed, "because I did not have the courage.") Throughout the first week of June, Brin repeatedly interviewed Frank, scoring a string of front-page scoops. "I spent fully two hours with Frank in his cell yesterday," declared a typical offering. "You cannot spend an hour with this quiet, brave man without becoming deeply impressed with his sincerity.

Everybody who goes out from his presence feels about him as I did." While Brin caught some of the factory superintendent's stilted manner ("He refers to himself as 'Frank' just as if he were a spectator in the tragedy of which he is the principal"), his pieces were otherwise consistently laudatory. "There is nothing sorrowful, nothing sullen, nothing cringing about Frank," the reporter wrote. "His conscience is clear. He is serene."

Hand in hand with the *Traveler*'s glowing accounts of Frank's steadfastness, other Northern papers were unabashedly predicting victory. Reported the *New York Times:* Defense lawyers "are optimistic as to the outcome of the hearing on the petition. It will not be at all surprising if the three commissioners vote unanimously in favor of commuting." Echoed the *New York Tribune:* "It is authoritatively stated that the commission will recommend commutation. Two commissioners, it is said, were ready to vote for commutation at the close of the hearing last Monday. The two are governed by Judge Roan's letter, in which he expressed doubt as to Frank's guilt."

Yet even as Frank's allies were reassuring the nation—and themselves—that they were on the verge of a great triumph, the forces within Georgia opposed to clemency were not only gaining strength but making themselves loudly heard. At 8:30 P.M. on Saturday, June 6, a crowd of approximately 2,500 assembled on the Washington Street steps of the state capitol to protest against commutation. The main speaker, the Reverend A. C. Hendley of the Capitol View Baptist Church, denounced outside interference in the case. Following his address, the gathering adopted a resolution pointedly upholding trial by jury. Meantime, at a stand on the event's periphery, a sales agent took subscription orders for the *Jeffersonian,* which had recently revealed that Robert Davison and Thomas Patterson were the commissioners leaning toward clemency. Cautioned Tom Watson:

> Let Davison and Patterson have a care. They are walking on the edge of an abyss.

In the end, however, the most telling indicator of where a majority of Georgians stood at this juncture came in a statement involving not Leo Frank's fate but Jim Conley's. As it so happened, it was during the prison commission's deliberations that the celebrated Negro, after serving ten months of his one-year sentence for acting as an accessory after the fact in the Phagan murder, was released from the Bellwood prison camp. The prospect of Conley wandering the streets of an overwrought Atlanta prompted a Northern observer to worry that he might be lynched. Yet when this emissary from above the Mason-Dixon line voiced his concern, he received a reply that not only brought him up short but summarized local opinion. " 'Lynch him?' exclaimed a native Georgian. 'Never in a thousand years.' "

Word that the Prison Commission had by a two-to-one vote declined Leo Frank's petition for the commutation of his death sentence reached the Tower late on the morning of Wednesday, June 9. "Is it possible? Is it possible?" Frank asked. Within minutes, Lucille and Rabbi Marx arrived, followed by other in-laws. "Tears flowed freely from the eyes of all," Alexander Brin observed.

After the many positive prognostications, this unexpected turn of events was devastating for Frank, and for the first time in months he found himself practically mute. As a consequence, he looked to his friend Milton Klein to shield him not only from the predictable requests for comment but from a crush of casual sympathizers. "Mr. Frank has nothing to say right now," Klein told a crowd in the Tower's lobby." The next morning, the condemned man wrote Albert Lasker:

> The decision of the Prison Commission was a blow . . . I don't know why I am chosen to go through this ordeal.

Under Georgia law, the Prison Commission was not required to explain its reasoning in instances where it chose not to recommend clemency. Hence, the two-man majority of Eugene Rainey and Robert Davision said nothing. The sole public comment came from the lone commissioner to support commutation. Despite having been singled out by Tom Watson, Thomas Patterson released a lengthy dissent. In it, he attacked the state's case, asserting that Jim Conley "had the highest motive for placing responsibility for the crime on Frank—that of self-protection." To send a man to death "on the testimony of an accomplice, when the circumstances of the crime tend to fix the guilt upon the accomplice" was unconscionable. Ultimately, though, Patterson's protest was merely that. As the *Constitution* flatly noted: "Governor Slaton now becomes the final authority of the case."

There can be little doubt that in his heart, John Slaton wanted no part of the Leo Frank affair. His decision, whichever way it went, would offend thousands while overshadowing the accomplishments of a governorship that had seen Georgia's debt refinanced at an advantageous rate and taxes reduced. Moreover, the timing was horrendous. Early June at Slaton's 75-acre estate, Wingfield—a rolling expanse of woodlands and rose gardens north of Atlanta in Buckhead—was an interlude of lawn parties and outdoor theatrical productions presided over by the dramatically inclined first lady, Sallie. This year, the highlight was a staging of *The Gift,* an impressionistic retelling of the Pandora's box story starring society belles in the roles of Terpsichore, Cleo and Calliope and featuring interpretive dances. To spend the closing days of one's term absently immersed in such firefly-lit scenes was surely preferable to taking up a clemency proceeding that not only involved a matter of life and death but threatened to open an all too real Pandora's box of sectional and religious strife. Yet this is what it had come to.

At 9:00 A.M. on Saturday, June 12, Slaton walked into the packed anteroom of his capitol office in downtown Atlanta and called the final hearing on the Frank case to order. Hugh Dorsey was present, as were Henry Alexander, Schley Howard and the rest of the defense team, which now included another new lawyer, Manning Yeomans, a homespun figure from Southwest Georgia hired to placate hostile rural Georgians.

In hopes of scoring big at the outset, Schley Howard opened the hearing by attacking one of the claims at the core of the prosecution's case—Conley's contention that he and Frank had used the factory elevator to transport Mary Phagan's body from the office-floor scene of the crime to its resting place in the basement. More likely, he informed Slaton, the Negro, after waylaying the girl in the plant's lobby, had employed the oft-mentioned scuttle hole as the point of entry to the lower level. "A man such as Conley could very readily have gone down that ladder and when his shoulders and arms were free above could have drawn her body towards him." To back up this theory, Howard played his ace, introducing the subject of an odiferous piece of evidence whose relevancy had previously been addressed publicly only in *Collier's,* and there but obliquely. That evidence: the so-called shit in the shaft. Declared the lawyer:

> You have got this from Conley: That morning [Saturday, April 26, 1913] his bowels moved. He went around and in front of and inside the elevator shaft on the basement floor had a passage of his bowels. Now you have in evidence by other witnesses that when these people [the responding officers] came Saturday night, they find that human stool in the bottom of that elevator shaft untouched. But that Sunday, in running the elevator down, the investigators smashed into the stool, and the smell of it revealed its existence. Now mark you, if they [Frank and Conley] had brought the body down in the elevator on Saturday it would have smashed the excrement then.

Where in the past, Frank's lawyers had caught Conley in little lies, ones he blithely admitted, here, for the first time in an official forum, they had apparently caught him in a big lie, one that cast doubt on his entire testimony.

As Slaton pondered the significance of what he had just heard, Howard, displaying a keen sense of theatrics, moved off in another direction. By his count, the state's case, excluding the charges made by Conley, boiled down to nineteen elements. Frank was the last person to admit having seen Mary Phagan alive; he sent Newt Lee away from the factory on the afternoon of the murder; he was nervous the morning the body was discovered; he changed his mind as to whether Lee had punched the time clock correctly; supposed blood spots and hair purported to have come from little Mary's head had been discovered in the plant's metal room—the lawyer ticked them all off. Then, with a sweeping gesture of his hand, he proclaimed:

An explanation may be given of every one of these alleged instances against Frank more consistent with his innocence than any guilt.

Whereupon Howard, knowing that he would be permitted to expand on his views in the coming hours, ceded the floor to a group of citizens who held a far different position than his.

The contingent from Marietta was headed by the town's best-known citizen, former governor Joseph M. Brown, although the same man who'd started the ball rolling before the Prison Commission did so here. "I don't care to make any extended argument in this case," began Herbert Clay, "but I want to say this to your excellency. The people of Cobb County feel that a jury has passed on this case, the higher courts have passed on it, and in view of the fact that no new evidence has been discovered, it is not right to ask your excellency to commute the sentence." That said, Brown took the floor. Urging his successor to obey both the state's law and God's, he asserted:

When a governor is asked to set aside a judgement and correct all the courts, he is asked to change our Constitution and laws and to make mercy instead of justice. Let me call your attention to the fact that the word mercy is not in the Constitution of Georgia, and nowhere in the Bible is it used as having the right to defeat justice.

Brown concluded by reiterating a point Moultrie Sessions had made at the gathering in Cobb County, in the process issuing what sounded like an ultimatum:

Now in all frankness, if your excellency wishes to insure lynch law in Georgia, if you wish to hopelessly weaken trial by jury in Georgia, you can strike this dangerous blow at our institutions and our civilization by retrying this case on the identical evidence upon which all the courts have adjudicated it. If you defeat the law, the people of this state see no reason for jury trials. In its bearing upon the future, this is the most important case any living man in Georgia has had under review. One law for all, or no law at all. Now, which shall we have?

On the heels of the Mariettans' stern blasts, the governor recessed the hearing until Monday.

During the brief weekend hiatus, the pressure both from without and within Georgia increased. A number of national figures added their names to the already lengthy register of those supporting clemency. Most prominent among them was the vice president of the United States, Thomas R. Marshall. Also signing on were a dozen leading magazine and newspaper editors, including Herbert Croly, editor of the *New Republic;* C.P.J. Mooney, editor of the *Chicago Tribune;* Mark Sullivan, editor of *Collier's;* R. E. Stafford, editor of the *Daily Oklahoman;* and D. D. Moore, editor of the *New Orleans Times-Picayune.* Finally, there was another private appeal from a man who had long been in Frank's corner. Declared William Randolph Hearst in a lengthy letter to Slaton:

> I have heard you say that any man could do the right thing in an ordinary situation, but the test of a really great and genuine man was to be able to do the right thing in an exceptionally critical and important situation.
>
> I feel that you, as the governor of a great state, should rise above all smaller matters, above all the mistakes of the friends of Frank, above all the antagonism of his enemies and deal with this question as the Great Judge will eventually deal with us.
>
> Commutation to life imprisonment will prevent the possibility of a great mistake being made, a mistake which could never be rectified, a mistake which if made would involve you and Georgia in everlasting and unavailing sorrow and regret.

Closer to home, the wind blew the other way. No sooner had Slaton adjourned Saturday afternoon's session than a crowd once again formed on the Washington Street steps of the state capitol. The high point of the protest came when the famed hillbilly musician Fiddlin' John Carson, his Stradivarius reproduction in hand, stepped to the fore to debut a new work. Sung to the tune of an old standard, "Charles Giteau," "The Ballad of Mary Phagan" expressed the sadness and grievances of most Georgians, emotions only heightened by the mournful bowing and harshly sweet voice of the artist:

Little Mary Phagan
She went to work one day;
She went to the pencil factory
To get her little pay.

She left her home at 'leven
When she kissed her mother good bye;
Not one time did the poor child think
She was going there to die.

Leo Frank he met her
With a brutely heart we know.
He smiled and said, "Little Mary,
Now you go home no more."

He sneaked along behind her
Till she reached the metal room.
He laughed and said, "Little Mary,
You've met your fatal doom."

She fell upon her knees,
To Leo Frank she pled.
Because she was virtuous
He hit her across the head.

He killed little Mary Phagan,
Was on one holiday,
And called for old Jim Conley
To take her body away.

He took her to the basement,
Bound hand and feet;
Down in the basement
Little Mary lay asleep.

Newt Lee was the watchman;
When he went to turn the key,
Down in the basement
Little Mary he could see.

He called for the officers—
They locked him in a cell—

The poor old innocent nigger
Knew nothing for to tell.

Come all of you good people,
Wherever you may be,
Supposing little Mary
Belonged to you or me?

Her mother sits a-weeping,
She weeps and mourns all day.
She prays to meet her baby
In a better world some day.

Judge Roan passed the sentence,
You bet he passed it well;
Solicitor Hugh M. Dorsey
Sent Leo Frank to . . .

Carson played the ballad again and again, as if by repeatedly chanting its somber lyrics, he could consecrate Georgia's seat of government, influencing the direction of the hearings that would presently resume there.

On Monday, it was Hugh Dorsey's turn, and he opened with an assault on the defense's assertion that Frank had not received a fair trial. Sounding a theme that he'd initially articulated during his closing argument before Judge Roan, the solicitor charged the factory superintendent's lawyers with raising the issue only after realizing they were losing the battle. If the climate in which the proceedings took place was prejudiced, he asked, why hadn't Luther Rosser and Reuben Arnold sought a change of venue? Why hadn't a single Georgia Supreme Court justice ruled favorably on the point when Frank advanced it in his motion for a new trial? The answer: The allegation was false. True, many Northerners, among them the dissenting justices of the United States Supreme Court, believed the contention, but Dorsey attributed this fact to the "assiduously disseminated claim appearing in the papers throughout the nation to the effect that spectators in the audience arose and cried out to the jury, 'Hang Frank or we will hang you.' " Addressing Slaton, he declared: "Your excellency, the record shows that at no time from the beginning to the end of the trial did anybody cry out against Frank or offer to do him harm."

Dorsey then undertook to rebut the petition's other main assertion—the one holding that the condemned man was innocent. The solicitor turned first to the character charges against Frank, which he reminded Slaton would have been inadmissible had not the defense opened the door. Then he mentioned the fact that Rosser and Arnold had failed to cross-examine the girls who'd testified to the factory superintendent's reputation for lasciviousness, adding that the lawyers had good reason for refraining: "The state was ready to show specific acts of misconduct." That said, he led the governor through the circumstantial evidence that he believed demonstrated Frank's interest in Mary Phagan, recalling such details as his alleged refusal to give Helen Ferguson her pay the day before the crime.

With that, the stage was set for a recapitulation of Conley's allegations, yet Dorsey, reacting to Schley Howard's earlier dismissal of those elements of the state's evidence not provided by the Negro, instead undertook a bold program. He would leave out Conley's testimony altogether. "Eliminate Jim Conley," he told Slaton, and the case against Frank was still overwhelming. The solicitor started by naming the witnesses who'd sworn that neither the blood nor the hair found in the factory's metal room the Monday after the crime had been present at quitting time the Friday before. Then, he attacked what he termed "the minute alibi the defendant attempted to palm off on the jury" regarding his activities on the afternoon of the murder. The fact of Monteen Stover's arrival at Frank's empty office shortly after 12:00 P.M. was, of course, the most damaging particular. But Dorsey also saw significance in a previously unremarked-upon discrepancy in the reasons the superintendent had provided for not attending an Atlanta Crackers baseball game later that day. At the coroner's inquest, Frank testified that he'd begged off due to the inclement weather, yet in his statement at the trial, he maintained it was because he'd yet to finish work on the company's financial sheet. The truth, argued the solicitor, was that he had needed the time "to make some disposition of the body of the girl."

Which brought Dorsey to the topic of Frank's actions on the Sunday Mary Phagan's remains were discovered. From his failure to answer the responding officers' initial phone call to his home, to his skulking at the morgue, his behavior, Dorsey said, had been suspicious. Specifically, the solicitor cited the irreconcilability of Frank's much remarked upon nervousness and his apparent attempt to seem offhanded by mentioning that he was wearing a blue suit. "Why trembling if so indifferent?" he asked. "Answer: Guilty."

From here on out, Dorsey argued, Frank had only dug himself in deeper. For starters, on the Monday after the murder, he'd told Pinkerton detective Harry Scott that James M. Gantt was infatuated with Mary Phagan, when on Sunday he'd told Black he didn't know the girl. Then there was the fact that cord of the sort that had been used to strangle little Mary was kept in abundance near where the state argued the crime occurred—the second-floor metal room. Most persuasively, the superintendent, despite knowing that Conley could write, had not suggested early on the Negro as a possible author of the murder notes.

No, Dorsey informed Slaton, the state did not need Conley's testimony to convict Frank. The other evidence was sufficient. So much so that clemency should not be granted. Declared the solicitor in closing:

> I am not lacking in mercy, but I have been moved to appear here before you because I am solicitous that the laws shall be, as the Constitution of our state declares, impartially and completely administered. I am fearful that if the verdict of juries in plain cases, as I conceive this to be, shall not be carried out against the influential as well as the friendless, it would be an incentive to lawlessness in our state, the consequences of which no man can calculate, and I am unwilling even passively to be a party to the encouragement of such a situation.

In the wake of Dorsey's presentation, Slaton ordered a two-hour recess. He had decided to make a field trip to the grim granite structure at the center of the mystery. Accompanied by the solicitor, the police department's lead investigator, Detective John Starnes, and Schley Howard, the governor toured all the relevant parts of the National Pencil factory. In the office, he examined the desk where the murder notes were allegedly written. In the metal room, he inspected the lathe handle around which the hair purported to have come from Mary Phagan's head had been discovered. And in the basement, he familiarized himself with both the spot where the girl's body had been located and the elevator shaft bottom in which the feces that now figured so large in the defense's argument had been deposited.

Starting Monday afternoon, Schley Howard would dominate the hearing's remaining hours. The lawyer began by reiterating his contempt for those elements of the state's case that Hugh Dorsey contended were sufficient to convict Frank even if Conley's charges were dropped:

> What does it matter that Frank was nervous on the morning when he was called out of his home? What does it matter what he did when he heard the telephone bell ring about three o'clock? What does it matter that he shivered and shook as he went in the early morning from his home down to the undertaker's, where the dead body lay? What does it matter that he looked furtively, if at all, on the body of the dead girl? They are only mental states, absolutely compatible with a perfectly innocent construction.

Howard then turned his guns back on Conley. Some of what he had to say—particularly a lengthy explication of the evolution of the Negro's pretrial affidavits—was, no matter how critical, unsurprising. Equally predictable was another descent into racism. Regarding what he saw as a key motive in Conley's attack on Mary Phagan, the lawyer stated:

> Who but that knows the negro knows that the prize above life itself to him is the privilege of debasing a white woman.

All this aside, there was much that was inspired and new in Howard's presentation. For one, he surmised that a heretofore largely unremarked upon item that had been found by the responding officers next to little Mary's body—her handkerchief—pointed to Conley as the killer. "Ladies carry their pocket handkerchiefs in these mesh-bag purses," he remarked. "I do not know whether this girl had hers there or not, but this is certain: We did not see the purse or the money. If that handkerchief was in that purse, the person that got the purse, if they had been [as] indifferent about the purse as they were about the handkerchief, could have left the purse." Even more illuminating were the lawyer's insights into Conley's most damning allegation against Frank, the charge of perversion. As Howard saw it, the Negro, possibly encouraged by the investigating officers, had sensed the need to add a provocative detail to his testimony that would explain the opposing judgments of the medical experts as to whether the Phagan girl had been raped:

> I believe that someone undertook to graft [onto] Conley's story the very commonplace idea that as a Jew Frank had been circumcised and he was in that respect "unlike other men." In the eyes and mind of a man like Conley, a man who had been circumcised and to that manner transformed, became different from other men.

Bluntly put, the widely held view of Frank as a deviant very likely sprang from a crude, anti-Semitic mischaracterization of the bris ritual's disfiguring impact on the Jewish male member, one that perforce altered sexual practices.

Though the Atlanta papers did not run the most titillating aspects of Howard's analysis, news nevertheless spread, further piquing the interest of an already avid public. When the hearings reconvened Wednesday morning following a one-day break to allow Slaton to fill a speaking engagement, the governor's anteroom was thronged. Nearly a hundred spectators, many of them women, elbowed their way inside while a dozen or so diehards stood atop chairs pulled up to the door.

Schley Howard planned to concentrate on the authorship of the case's most significant clues—the murder notes. He opened by acquainting Slaton with the reports, most of them introduced the previous spring during the extraordinary-motion battle, suggesting that the notes were written not, as the state maintained, in Frank's office, but in the basement. Then he broached the subject of William Smith's study of the notes' language. But before he could get going, he was interrupted by the governor.

Indicating that he wasn't happy with several of Howard's earlier pronouncements, Slaton asked for a more thorough explanation as to why the hair found on the metal room lathe and the blood spot located nearby did not implicate Frank. In response, the lawyer adduced both some familiar facts—Dr. Harris's admission that the strands he took from Mary Phagan's head during the autopsy did not match those twined around the lathe and Dr. Smith's testimony that the spot in question contained only a few corpuscles of blood—and a fresh theory. After much consideration, the defense had concluded that the two-and-a-half-inch wound little Mary had suffered to her scalp could not have been inflicted by the action of Frank knocking her into a freestanding machine of approximately her height. Declared Howard:

> There was never blood on that poor child's dress above her waist. Her clothing has shown no blood above the waist. This blood, if it had been from a lick struck while she stood erect, while the surging arterial blood flowed in her body, would have flowed its silent flow in buckets and would have spoken an eternal truth.

Next, Slaton asked to hear from Howard and Dorsey on a topic he'd been unable to get out of his mind since Frank's counsel introduced it at the opening session—the shit in the shaft. Specifically, the governor wanted to know whether the elevator always hit bottom when descending into the basement or whether it could be stopped above the ground. If the latter was so, it called into question the defense's thesis that the fresh mound of excrement mashed on Sunday controverted Conley's claim that he and the superintendent had used the lift to move Mary Phagan's body.

"Your excellency," replied Dorsey, "this was a disputed point of the record. If the elevator had gone down at the time Conley and Frank used it, it would not necessarily have gone to the ground. You can stop it anywhere. You can stop it an inch from the bottom, and if it was stopped there it would not have mashed that substance."

Howard, of course, took the opposite view, backing it up with quotations from the trial transcript that when uttered had seemed irrelevant but in this new context could not have been more telling. "Here it is," the lawyer said after thumbing through a thick document. " 'The elevator hits the dirt at the bottom.' That is Conley's statement. Darley says, 'There is nothing to stop it except when it hits the bottom.' Rogers testifies, 'It stops itself when it gets to the bottom.' "

The discussion having thus ended in disagreement, Slaton directed Howard to return to the day's initial subject—the murder notes. The lawyer spent an hour elucidating the many similarities William Smith had found between the language of the notes and that of the Annie Maude Carter letters. In Howard's words, Smith's report provided a "mathematical demonstration" that the murder notes were the mental property of Conley.

The notes, of course, constituted the pivot around which the Frank case turned, and now that they were under discussion, Howard offered one last hypothesis, this one intended to suggest what had led Conley to tell the police that Frank had dictated them to him. After setting the scene at headquarters, he declared:

> The detectives had Conley in a room and said, "You have lied about writing; you can write. Take this pencil and you write." They made him write the very words of the notes. That is the experience Conley actually passed through and where the idea got readily in his mind that the act of a mere amanuensis would exonerate him from the blame, and then it was that he related how Frank dictated [them] to him.

From Howard's perspective, the transparent falsehood of Conley's claim that Frank had dictated the notes provided the perfect ending point.

The burden John Slaton bore became literally apparent Wednesday evening when he and his executive secretary, a young lawyer named Jesse Perry, walked out of the capitol carrying several boxes of transcripts, legal briefs and other documents. After packing the material into a car, the two drove to Wingfield. There, in quiet and solitude, the governor would study the record and decide Frank's fate. With the execution set to take place in six days, time was short. Accordingly, he got right to work. Midnight found him sitting in the estate's library, going over evidence and jotting down notes.

From early Thursday morning until midday Saturday, Slaton and Perry kept at it, toiling among tables piled high with records and affidavits. The two left Wingfield but once. Friday afternoon, they drove back to Atlanta, halting before the looming National Pencil factory. The outing had a single purpose. Reported the *Constitution:*

> Primarily the trip to the factory building was made to test the elevator on which Conley swore he and Frank transported the body to the basement from the second floor. The governor wished to satisfy his mind whether the elevator was adjustable in speed or descended to the bottom of the shaft precipitately.

The only other known interruptions in Slaton's labors went unnoted by the press. Yet they, too, were vital. As William Smith would later write: "I had two private interviews with Governor Slaton, in which I gave [him] possession of many important facts and urged the commutation of Mr. Frank's sentence."

During the period in which the governor deliberated, Leo Frank entertained scores of visitors at his cell in the Fulton County Tower. The men and women who had been with him from the beginning were now, at what could well be the end, with him still. His brothers-in-law Charles Ursenbach and Alex Marcus, his cousin-in-law Jerome Michael from Athens, Dr. Benjamin Wildauer, Charles Wolfshiemer, Milton Klein, Sam Boorstin, the Haases and Henry Alexander all dropped by repeatedly. So, too, did Anne Carrol Moore, formerly the librarian at Brooklyn's Pratt Institute, who, despite her new life as assistant director of the New York Public Library's main branch, had such warm memories of the scholarly boy she'd once tutored that she'd come to Atlanta to lend her support. Most days, Frank and Lucille took lunch alone, and every evening, his parents were there to say good night. Since his setback before the Prison Commission, the condemned man had rallied emotionally. Noted the *Georgian:* "To all appearances he retained his usual good spirits." Still, the prospect of the gallows—which occupied an interior courtyard at the Tower—was now imminent and made to seem even more so by Slaton's response to a question put to him on Friday as to whether he'd reached a decision. "No," he replied, then added: "The judgment of the court should cause the prisoner to prepare for death." That afternoon, Leo sent Lucille to a bookstore, from which she returned bearing a novel titled *The Little Shepherd of Kingdom Come.*

It was around noon on Saturday in the library at Wingfield that Slaton made up his mind. The remainder of the day and much of the night was given over to the preparation of what would ultimately be a nuanced 29-page document. Writing with several audiences in mind, the governor began by acknowledging the widely divergent opinions the Frank affair had generated:

> This case has been the subject of extensive comment through[out] the United States and has occasioned the transmission of over 100,000 letters from various states requesting clemency. Many communications have been received from citizens of this state . . . opposing interference with the sentence of the court.

Having thus in essence acknowledged that his decision would be unpopular with one group or the other, Slaton set about defending Georgia's honor against outsiders "who have not read the evidence and who are unacquainted with the judicial procedure in our state." The governor took issue with most of what had been published about the Frank trial in the Northern press. The factory superintendent was not, he asserted, tried by a mob, adding that "if the courtroom manifested its deep resentment toward Frank, it was because of the revelation of [facts] that in any community would excite unbounded condemnation." Nor, he declared, had the evidence been insufficient to sustain a guilty verdict. "Those giving expression to this utterance," he repeated, "have not read the evidence and are not acquainted with the facts."

That said, Slaton adduced a dozen pieces of evidence "that to any reasonable person" would tend to incriminate Frank. The ordering of Newt Lee from the premises at 4:00 P.M. on the day of Mary Phagan's murder, the unprecedented phone call to Lee later that same evening, the defense's failure to cross-examine the character witnesses who'd testified as to the factory superintendent's reputation for lasciviousness—the governor cited these and other elements that gave him pause. And on top of all of it were the allegations made by the state's star witness. "It is hard to conceive that any man's power of fabrication of minute details could reach that which Conley showed, unless it be the truth."

Had providence stilled Slaton's hand Saturday evening, his decision, as it then read, would have given every indication that he intended to let Frank's execution proceed. But three thousand words into the document, the governor returned to the crucial question: "Did Conley speak the truth?" The power of his story notwithstanding, Slaton had concluded that the answer was a resounding no. There were many factors that led him to this determination, but two stood out, and he addressed them at length, beginning with the shit in the shaft:

One fact in the case, and that of most important force in arriving at the truth, contradicts Conley's testimony. It is disagreeable to refer to it, but delicacy must yield to necessity when human life is at stake.

The mystery of the case is the question as to how Mary Phagan's body got into the basement. Conley testified that he and Frank took the body down in the elevator on the afternoon of April 26th, 1913 . . .

Conley testified that on the morning of April 26th he went down into the basement to relieve his bowels and utilized the elevator shaft for the purpose.

On the morning of April 27th at 3 o'clock when the detectives came down into the basement by way of the ladder, they inspected the premises, including the shaft, and they found there human excrement in natural condition.

Subsequently, when they used the elevator, which everybody admits only stops by hitting the ground in the basement, the elevator struck the excrement and mashed it, thus demonstrating that the elevator had not been used since Conley had been there.

If the elevator was not used by Conley and Frank in taking the body to the basement, then the explanation of Conley cannot be accepted.

As to how the governor could be certain that the majority view holding that the elevator always hit the ground was correct, he cited his private Friday trip to the factory, where he said he tested and retested the lift personally. Each time, it touched bottom.

The other convincing element for Slaton was William Smith's study of the murder notes, and he enumerated a number of the similarities Smith had discovered between the grammar and diction of the notes and the grammar and diction of Conley's other known written and spoken utterances. They included the frequent use of the words "did" and "Negro," the employment of the term "make water" to mean "urinate," the use of the word "play" as a synonym for "intercourse" and the reliance on compound adjectives. Stated the governor: "Conley was the real author of the murder notes."

There was much else that Slaton believed demonstrated a reasonable doubt as to Frank's guilt. He accepted, for instance, the argument that Monteen Stover arrived at the factory on the day of the murder before Mary Phagan, thus invalidating the significance of this key witness's testimony. Additionally, he felt there was no truth to Conley's charge of perversion against Frank, adopting Schley Howard's position that "the only reason Conley had to make such a suggestion is that someone may have told him Jews were circumcised."

By way of ending, Slaton offered a legal rationale for commuting Frank's sentence to life imprisonment, asserting that contrary to the claims of those who opposed the action, there was sufficient new evidence not introduced at the trial, principally Dr. Harris's revelations concerning the hair he'd taken from Mary Phagan's head at the autopsy and the Annie Maude Carter letters. Moreover, there was Judge Roan's posthumous letter. Ultimately, however, the governor knew that the decision was his, therefore he concluded:

> The performance of my duty under the Constitution is a matter of my conscience. The responsibility rests where the power is reposed. I can endure misconstruction, abuse and condemnation, but I cannot stand the constant companionship of an accusing conscience, which would remind me in every thought that I, as governor of Georgia, failed to do what I thought to be right.

Sunday dawned giving every indication that it would be another day without resolution. The headline atop the front page of the *Georgian* was: SLATON STILL DELVING INTO FRANK PAPERS. Thus the principals in the case busied themselves with their regular activities, unaware that the governor had made his determination. At the Tower, the familiar crush of friends and family members descended on Frank, wishing him well while nervously fearing the worst. The afternoon passed, then the supper hour. At 9:30, the condemned man retired, ignorant of his fate.

Frank was asleep when around 11:30 a deputy appeared at his cell and told him to get dressed. Sheriff Mangum had just received a call from the office of the Prison Commission, which had itself just been notified by Slaton, who all day had sat on the news, believing that in the present climate, the safest course was to transfer the reprieved man to the state prison farm in Milledgeville in the dead of night. The plan was to catch a 12:01 train to Macon, and the rush was so great that Frank had no time to gather his possessions or pack. He dressed in six minutes, whereupon he and two deputies walked out the Tower's front door and through Atlanta's deserted streets without encountering a soul. At Terminal Station, they were met by Mangum, who'd gone ahead to purchase tickets, then descended to the platform and boarded a coach car on which one or two passengers registered a look of recognition before nodding off.

At 2:44 A.M., the Central of Georgia train pulled into the Macon station. There, Frank and the deputies waited while Mangum rented a car for the remainder of the trip to Milledgeville. Though Frank seemed enormously relieved, there was something taut and frantic in his eyes during the drive through the empty countryside. "There were cars following us," he later told a reporter. Yet this was not so. The journey was uneventful, the pursuing automobiles merely figments in the mind of a tired and scared man. Around 5:00, just as day was breaking, the party reached its destination. There, behind a fence, inmates clad in stripes were moving through the faint gray light. "I had begun to think I wouldn't get to see this place," Frank remarked shortly after pulling up to the main building.

Monday morning, Atlanta awakened to the cries of newsboys shouting FRANK'S SENTENCE IS COMMUTED BY SLATON. By 10:00, swarms of people were milling about everywhere, bringing the city to a virtual halt. Though some of these citizens surely approved of the governor's decision, the majority did not. In response to a query regarding the public mood, Mayor Jimmy Woodward wired the *New York World:* "The larger part of the population believes Frank guilty and that the commutation was a mistake."

Around noon, an excited throng burst into Slaton's office, but the governor, exhausted from the weekend's travails, had not come in, and the crowd drifted back onto the capitol lawn. Shortly thereafter, an unidentified man, graying and gaunt, mounted the building's steps and, gazing over the packed mass of humanity, bellowed: "Who will follow me?" To enthusiastic cheers, this latter-day Danton then led the multitude into the senate chamber, which was soon filled to overflowing and where long into the afternoon speakers took turns denouncing the state's chief executive.

Across town at city hall, like-minded orators were whipping up a far more unruly crowd. Among the some 5,000 gathered here, many were spoiling for fights, and as the day progressed, there were numerous arrests, the most dramatic being that of a plainclothesman who had joined in the protest and who, after being rebuked for doing so, slugged Chief James Beavers in the face. The officer was stripped of his gun and badge and promptly carted away in a patrol wagon, but the incident was hardly reassuring.

While it's doubtful anything John Slaton could have said would have placated the populace, at midday he summoned the press to Wingfield. Still in pajamas, eyes dull and swollen from lack of sleep, the governor was nonetheless clearheaded. "All I ask is that the people of Georgia read my statement and consider calmly the reasons I have given for commuting Leo M. Frank's sentence," he urged. "Feeling as I do about this case, I would be a murderer if I allowed that man to hang. I would rather be ploughing in a field than to feel for the rest of my life that I had that man's blood on my hands." Adding that he was convinced Jim Conley had killed Mary Phagan, the governor ended the conference by releasing his commutation order, enabling editors to get the lengthy document into late editions. Boomed the *Journal*'s page-one banner: SLATON GIVES REASONS FOR COMMUTING FRANK.

Yet no matter how compelling the governor's rationale, most Atlantans were unmoved. As night fell, the speechifying continued, especially downtown at Five Points, where at 8:30, to cries of "Pay the Governor a Call," a throng of about 4,000 set out on foot toward Slaton's mansion.

The route to Buckhead runs six miles straight up Peachtree Street, but the mob was undeterred by distance or, at first, by the police, bulling through several roadblocks. To hoots and hollers and honking horns, the men stopped only to break into a hardware store in search of guns and to steal bricks and other potential weapons from a couple of construction sites. At the midway point, fifty mounted officers led by Chief Beavers made a stand, turning back hundreds. Still, nearly 2,000 got through, storming on toward their destination.

Wingfield, situated as it was on wooded acreage and set far back from Peachtree near its intersection with Pace's Ferry, made an attractive target. Due to the vehemence of the day's earlier protests, the Fulton County police had done their best to fortify the place, barricading the drive with barbed wire and stationing a squad of officers and deputized citizens around the perimeter. But after receiving word of the crowd's size, the governor, who was waiting up with friends—among them Henry Alexander, counsel to Frank—realized that the preparations were inadequate and declared martial law, mobilizing the state militia's Fifth Regiment.

The mob had been outside Slaton's mansion no more than a few minutes when the troops arrived and with fixed bayonets took up position. Initially, the demonstrators rained stones and bottles on the guardsmen, injuring the major in command and several others. But following this barrage, the militia swung into action, driving the throng back down Peachtree. Though the mob remained defiant, taunting the troops with a pointed version of the ditty "I Didn't Raise My Boy to Be a Soldier," it was shortly in full retreat. By midnight, the threat had been quashed.

The danger, however, had not passed. In fact, as soon as this group had fled there was a report that 200 Mariettans were approaching from the north, necessitating the deployment of troops to the rear of the governor's property. That the Cobb Countians were en route should have surprised no one, as Marietta's sentiments in the matter were well known and if anything, its response to Slaton's decision had been more violent than Atlanta's. The town had hanged the governor in effigy on the courthouse square, emblazoning an attached placard: "John M. Slaton, King of the Jews and Traitor Governor of Georgia." The likeness was then pulled down and torched beneath the community's monument to its late hero, Senator Alexander Stephens Clay. What happened next was apparently even uglier, although the *Marietta Journal* glossed over the details, maintaining: "We feel it best that some incidents not be mentioned." Despite having built up such a head of steam, the Mariettans thought better of taking on the militia and stopped just shy of Slaton's estate.

While no other sorties were launched against Wingfield this night, it was not for lack of hostility. Georgia fairly throbbed with rage. In the middling city of Columbus, a mob hanged Slaton in effigy, riddling a figure labeled "Governor Slaton, the Traitor" with countless rounds of ammunition. In the rural community of Woodstock, there was a similar display. And in the county-seat town of Newnan, a crowd strung up effigies of both Slaton and Frank, set them afire, then dragged them behind a car through the streets. In only a day, the governor had become the second most reviled man in the state.

For all of Monday's turmoil, Tuesday dawned peacefully in Atlanta. By noon, Governor Slaton was ensconced in his office at the capitol, the halls packed not with protesters but with favor seekers and well-wishers. The atmosphere was at once unabashedly political—with several key patronage positions to fill before stepping down at week's end, Slaton remained a potent figure—and surprisingly buoyant. Save for the *Constitution,* which in keeping with its pro-Dorsey stance had refrained from commenting on the commutation, the city's newspapers had rallied around the governor, praising him for his "manly" decision and predicting that in time, he would be vindicated.

Proclaimed the *Journal:*

Whatever individuals may think as to the guilt or innocence of [Frank], a majority of them recognize in this remarkable case an element of doubt so huge and staggering that the mind recoils from contemplation of the extreme penalty of the law inflicted upon this unfortunate man. It is this irresistible and irrepressible doubt that Governor Slaton has recognized. The governor has shown wisdom and courage in his performance of an act of simple justice.

Declared the *Georgian:*

Had the Governor desired to proceed along the line of least resistance and do the easy thing, he might have resisted his conscience and let this defendant go to his death upon the scaffold, but the Governor could not in good conscience do that. It was not for him to weigh the political consequence of an act of this sort—and be it said to his credit, he did not. It was only for him to do his duty. The Georgian believes that Governor John M. Slaton deserves the commendation of the people of Georgia.

Then there were the hosannas from the national press. Now with the *San Francisco Call,* Harold Ross, after noting that there was "strong religious prejudice against Frank," wrote:

> Governor Slaton, realizing the large element of existing doubt, was duty bound to save him from the gallows. His act will receive the endorsement of the American people, with a notable exception perhaps in his own state.

Added the *New York Times:*

> Governor Slaton feels that because of this act he must live in obscurity the rest of his days. His view is too narrow. He quite misunderstands what awaits him. If he but look beyond the boundaries of the State of Georgia, he can know and feel to how high a place he has raised himself in the esteem and admiration of the whole country. Had Georgia sent Frank to the gallows, the good name of the State would have been blackened and its people would have been under reproach. Governor Slaton has saved Georgia from herself. He has made his name illustrious.

Yet even as editorialists sang Slaton's praise, martial law remained in effect within a half-mile radius of Wingfield, where the Fifth Regiment had pitched tents and thrown up machine gun nests, digging in as if preparing for a siege. The militia's continued presence underscored the fact that no matter what the papers—especially such pro-Frank sheets as the *Journal,* the *Georgian* and the *Times*—might say, their utterances were irrelevant to most Georgians. The only voice to which the people listened belonged to Tom Watson.

The first postcommutation issue of the *Jeffersonian* hit the streets Thursday, and for sheer demagogic genius, it eclipsed everything Watson had heretofore produced. To begin with, he prefaced its page-one fulmination with a verse from that fiercest biblical prophet, Jeremiah, wherein the Lord, decrying "a wonderful and horrible thing committed in the land," asks: "Shall not My soul be avenged on such a nation as this?" Having thus intimated his purposes, Watson then summoned the faithful. And he did it by summoning the ghosts in whom they believed. "Once, there were *men* in Georgia," he roared, "men who were afraid of nothing save to do wrong; men who sprang to arms and went to death on a bare question of *principle.* The sons of those men carried the tattered Stars and Bars farthest up the heights of Gettysburg; met the first shock of battle at Manassas; led the last charge at Appomattox." Inexorably, the Sage was resurrecting the past, rekindling its buried passions, preparing his congregation to view what had occurred not merely as a miscarriage of justice but as an affront to the South. Only after stoking the fires did he finally thunder:

> *Our grand old Empire State HAS BEEN RAPED!*
>
> Like the Roman wife of old, we feel that something unclean, something unutterably loathsome has crept to bed with us, and befouled us during the night: and that while the morning has come again, it can never, *never* restore our self-respect.
>
> *We have been violated, AND WE ARE ASHAMED!*

The despoiler, of course, was John Slaton:

> After the hue and cry which the Burns Detective Agency and the Prostitute Press has kept up for more than a year, Governor Slaton turns out to be the dead fly in the ointment, the weak joint in our armor, the vulnerable heel that lets the fatality enter our body politic.
>
> Judge Roan could not be moved; our Supreme Court could not be swayed; the United States Supreme Court could not be stormed; the lowly work people, whose evidence perhaps took the bread out of their mouths, could not be bullied or bribed.
>
> Our system stood, like Jackson . . . it was a stone wall.
>
> At last, *one partner got before the other—ROSSER BEFORE SLA-TON—and the one partner gave what the other partner wanted.*
>
> If there was ever a time when Slaton should have proved his manhood, it was when he was occupying so ambiguous a position.
>
> *Either his firm should have withdrawn from the case, or he should have withdrawn from the firm.*

The governor, though, was not the sole transgressor. As Watson never tired of asserting, there had been "dark places" all along, and for the hundredth time, he took his readers through the litany of offenses, among them "the attempt to get William Smith to fix the crime" on Jim Conley. Yet the commutation decision remained the unforgivable sin, for behind it, Watson saw not just a perfidious alliance between partners but the influence of those well-heeled sons of David who, he charged, controlled Slaton:

> Jew money has debased us, bought us, and sold us—and laughs at us.
>
> Bought and sold! Cried off at the auction block, and knocked down to Big Money!
>
> *ONE LAW FOR THE RICH, AND ANOTHER FOR THE POOR!*

What Georgians can now deny it?

Mary Phagan, pursued and tempted, and entrapped, and then killed when she would not do what so many other girls had done for this Jewish hunter of Gentile girls.

There she lies at Marietta, unavenged by the Law!

And her pursuer and murderer, spirited out of Atlanta, *unshackled,* and taken in his natty new suit and patent leather shoes, on *a Pullman palace car,* to the State Farm, *FROM WHICH AN ESCAPE WILL BE ARRANGED FOR HIM IN LESS THAN THIRTY DAYS!*

The Haas Finance Committee and its cooperative organizations do not intend that Frank shall be punished at all, for the rape and murder he committed on the Gentile girl.

In their eyes, she was legitimate prey; and with their Unlimited Money and Invisible Power, they have established the precedent *in Georgia* that no Jew shall suffer capital punishment for a crime committed on a Gentile.

In the name of God, what are the people to do?

This, of course, was the question, and Watson's counsel—which he had presaged at the outset by invoking Jeremiah and delivered now as a call to arms—would change history:

> Hereafter, let no man reproach the South with Lynch law: let him remember the unendurable provocation; and let him say whether Lynch law *is not better than no law at all.*
>
> What Rosser and Slaton have together done nullifies the Code, abolishes the courts, and plunges us into administrative anarchy.
>
> Shall my soul not be avenged on a such a nation as this?
>
> *A WONDERFUL AND HORRIBLE THING IS COMMITTED IN THE LAND.*

A day after Watson's broadside appeared, reports began to circulate that a group of 150 Mariettans known as the Knights of Mary Phagan had met at the child's grave and vowed "to 'get' Slaton and Frank, no matter how long it takes." All three Atlanta papers ignored these rumblings, but the *New York Times* flatly asserted: "There seems to be little doubt that such a body has been formed."

Who faced the greater initial danger from this fraternity was abundantly plain. Getting Frank would require breaking into the Milledgeville state prison farm, which following the arrival of its celebrated new inmate had been reinforced with extra guards and ammunition. Boasted the *Macon Telegraph:* "The prison is too secure to ever brook outside violence, for approach to the buildings would be fraught with untold danger. Death would be the toll of any man, or set of men, who would defy the defenses." The *Telegraph*'s hyperbole aside, few would have disputed its analysis—Frank was beyond the easy reach of those who wished him harm.

Another possibility was that the Knights—or others of their ilk—might seek retribution against Georgia's Jews as a whole. Since the commutation, Atlanta and Marietta had been deluged with red-lettered flyers promoting a boycott of Jewish-owned businesses. *"AMERICAN GENTILES,"* the leaflets advised, *"IT IS UP TO YOU."* More ominously, an organization calling itself the Marietta Vigilance Committee had posted threatening notices on the doors of the little town's handful of Jewish merchants. They read:

> You are hereby notified to close up this business and quit Marietta by Saturday night, June 26, 1915, or else stand the consequences. We mean to rid Marietta of all Jews by the above date. You can heed this warning or stand the punishment the committee may see fit to deal out to you.

Yet unsettling as these developments were, an indiscriminate assault on the state's Jews also appeared unlikely. In fact, upon hearing that such sentiments were abroad, Hugh Dorsey telegraphed his Cobb County counterpart, Herbert Clay, urging him to use his "good offices to pacify the people and prevail upon them to permit these merchants to remain . . . As you and I know, this kind of thing should not be done." In response, Clay not only promised to take the appropriate steps, but the Marietta Board of Trade—in the persons of Josiah Carter, Jr., Moultrie Sessions and garage owner Jim Brumby—agreed to back him up. Though the board members felt compelled to state that "Leo Frank should have been hung" and that the governor had "outraged justice," they endorsed restraint: "We beg our citizens to still stand for law and order, and not punish innocent people for the wrongs of others."

The choice, then, was clear. If vengeance was to be meted out, it would almost surely be meted out against John Slaton, most likely on Saturday amid the pageantry attendant to Nat Harris's inauguration as Georgia's new governor. As the *New York Times* reported:

> Preparations have been made for a great anti-Slaton demonstration at the capitol. Railroad men report that unusually large crowds are coming to the inauguration from the country towns and rural districts, and the prophets assert that the crowds will be here for the purpose of showing their disapproval of Governor Slaton's action. If the inauguration pass[es] without incident, a bountiful crop of rumors will have come to naught.

John Slaton's last day in office began just after 2 A.M. when a mob of 200 well-armed men launched the week's second assault on his estate by firing on a sentry. What followed more nearly resembled a brawl than a battle, as elements of the Fifth Regiment, after raking the woods with an admonitory return volley, plunged into the darkness, knocking heads and rattling teeth. Wisely, the raiders soon turned tail, most of them escaping. But 26 were placed in custody (among them Mary Phagan's uncle D. R. Benton, of Cobb County), and in a search of the immediate area, guardsmen found a potentially lethal cache of dynamite caps and fuses.

Around dawn, Slaton emerged from his mansion to look over the prisoners, who were being temporarily detained in his stables. The sight of these men—whose ages ranged from 16 to 46 and whose number included butchers, bricklayers and even a couple of realtors—deeply distressed the governor. "He stood still for a moment," guardsmen who were present later recollected, then turned with an expression on his face that suggested "his heart was breaking." Until this moment, Slaton had underestimated the people's outrage. Yet for all that, he hastened downtown to his office at the capitol, where after spending the morning addressing his final correspondence, he and Sallie hosted an informal reception for the leaders of the legislature and assorted salons, among them one of the Mariettans who had so vociferously opposed the commutation of Frank's death sentence, retired governor Joseph Brown.

At the appointed hour of noon, Slaton and his guests made the short walk to the hall of the house of representatives, where the memberships of the joint legislative bodies, along with scores of dignitaries and functionaries, had convened. Observed the *Constitution:* "The gallery was crowded to its utmost standing room capacity, and hundreds crowded about the doors." Outside on the capitol lawn stood hundreds more.

The inauguration ceremony itself, save for an eruption of hisses that greeted Slaton when in accordance with tradition he presented the state seal to Nat Harris, actually proceeded smoothly. But once the transfer of power had been completed and the former governor and his successor emerged arm in arm from the house chamber, the atmosphere degenerated. "I could see people on the stairs and in the vestibules gnashing their teeth, shaking their heads, and exhibiting various evidences of hostility," Harris later wrote, adding that Slaton gripped his arm so tightly it turned blue. Though the two men briefly ducked into a conference room, there was no escaping the inevitable and soon enough, they appeared on the capitol steps, where to angry shouts of "Lynch him," they descended between columns of soldiers toward a waiting car. It was then that the attempted assault occurred. As Harris subsequently remembered:

Governor Slaton entered the automobile first and just as I was preparing to follow him a strong, rough looking man darted from the crowd holding in both his hands a large piece of iron pipe about five feet long and an inch thick. He raised this to strike the ex-Governor over my head and shoulder. He could not have reached him without hitting me. Instantly Major Polhill Wheeler, who was in command of a battalion of the National Guard . . . seized the hands of the man . . . and turned aside the blow, saving Governor Slaton and myself from a terrible injury or perhaps death.

In the wake of this incident, Slaton—who was widely believed headed to New York later in the afternoon—was whisked to Terminal Station, scores of protestors not far behind on foot. Yet while the ex-governor's car did stop at the depot, he didn't get out. Instead, following a brief pause, his driver darted beneath a canopy of viaducts that carried street traffic—and the throng—above the tracks. By the time men shouting "Where's Slaton?" started boarding departing trains, their quarry was sitting down to a luncheon in his successor's honor at the Ansley Hotel several blocks away.

This was, by all rights, Nat Harris's moment, but when the gathering's host asked Slaton to say a few words, he obliged, delivering a statement that few who heard it soon forgot:

> Honest people may disagree with me, an honest man, but we realize that we must be measured by our consciences. Two thousand years ago another Governor washed his hands of a case and turned a Jew over to a mob. For two thousand years that Governor's name has been accursed. If today another Jew were lying in his grave because I had failed to do my duty I would all through life find his blood on my hands and would consider myself an assassin through cowardice.

Shortly thereafter, armed guards escorted the former governor back to Wingfield.

As it turned out, the reports of John Slaton's departure for New York were merely premature. On Monday—following yet another night during which troops and marauders exchanged gunfire in Buckhead—the ex-governor and his wife left Atlanta on Southern Railways. Upon arriving in Manhattan the next evening, they checked in to the Waldorf-Astoria. There, Slaton—after dropping by the barbershop for a shave and fortifying himself with one of the hotel's renowned and potent Star cocktails—met the press, which accorded the "fine, big, upstanding Southerner" the sort of welcome usually reserved for war heroes. So solicitous were the questions, so exuberant the camera flashes, that Slaton was soon expounding on every aspect of the case. Regarding his authority to intervene, he vowed: "It was my duty to correct the errors the courts themselves could not correct." Regarding his probe of the murder, he asserted: "I left no stone unturned." But it was Slaton's recounting of a private drama attendent to his moment of decision that attracted the most attention. As the *New York World* reported:

> He told an interesting story of how he first let it be known that he was going to save Frank's life. He and Mrs. Slaton were in their library. He had been deliberating for hours. He turned to his wife and said:
>
> "Dear, my conscience and my mind will not allow me to send that man to the gallows. It may mean my own life, and it probably will mean my political life if I commute him, but I'm going to do it. What do you say?"
>
> Mrs. Slaton (Sallie Grant, she was, granddaughter of old Governor James Jackson of Georgia, who fought six or eight duels) didn't hesitate. She replied instantly, putting her arms about him: "All right, Jack, never mind the consequences, let's commute!"

After the news conference, Slaton and his wife stepped out for a night on the town with their most enthusiastic journalistic patron, William Randolph Hearst. The first stop was the New Amsterdam Theater, home of the Ziegfeld Follies. Then it was on to a dinner party at the publisher's West End Avenue apartment.

For the Slatons, this was the start not just of a triumphant New York visit (several mornings later, they generated a flurry of news stories by appearing at the downtown courtroom where Harry K. Thaw, murderer of the architect Stanford White, was attempting to demonstrate that he was sufficiently sane to forgo continued incarceration) but of a summer-long vacation. Following a week in Manhattan, they would repair to the Adirondacks, then travel to Chicago and on to Alaska via the Canadian Rockies. From there, they would journey to San Francisco. After taking in the Pan-Pacific Exhibition, they would hop down the coast to San Simeon, where they would once again be the guests of Hearst. Finally, they would sail to Hawaii. All in all, they would be gone three months, long enough, they hoped, for tensions at home to subside.

NINETEEN

Marietta

Around the time the Slatons departed Georgia, a number of powerful Mariettans filed into a building on or just off the town square.
The exact location is a mystery, although as someone who was
apparently there put it later, the spot was "so conspicuous you would be
astonished to hear its name called." Which was fitting, for the men in attendance were conspicuous, too. Undoubtedly, most of the individuals who
appeared before the Prison Commission to argue against the commutation
of Leo Frank's death sentence were present. And several of the so-called
Knights of Mary Phagan were present as well. In the end, however, the only
names that matter belong to the men who emerged from the session as the
leaders: Eugene Herbert Clay, John Tucker Dorsey, Fred Morris, Bolan
Glover Brumby, former governor Joseph M. Brown, and Judge Newton
Augustus Morris. They were the ones who would answer Tom Watson's call.
They were the ones who would set the fatal machinery in motion.

The plan was staggeringly audacious—to abduct Frank from the state
prison farm in Milledgeville, transport him across multiple jurisdictions
back to Marietta, then hang him in plain view. Notwithstanding the fact that
lynchings occurred with grim regularity in Georgia during the teens (there
would be 22 of them in 1915), and regardless of the undeniable truth that a
majority of the state's populace would rejoice should Frank perish in this
manner, such an undertaking would be fraught with difficulties. Unlike
most prospective victims, this one was not some hapless Negro incarcerated
in a county jail protected, at best, by an indifferent deputy with a shotgun
across his lap. He was a white man who counted among his allies the most
influential lawyers in Georgia and the entirety of the national press, and he
was housed in a state penitentiary strongly garrisoned and newly bristling
with arms. Moreover, Warden J. E. Smith answered to three prison commissioners, who in turn answered to Governor Harris, who in the wake of Slaton's leavetaking had not only declared the Frank case "a matter of past
history" but had issued a clear warning to potential vigilantes: "I am fixed in
my belief that no one, however aggrieved he may feel himself to be, has the
right to take the law in his own hands." Then there were the inherent logis-
tical hurdles. Almost none of the 150 miles of road that separated Milledge-

ville from Marietta were paved, and the most direct route ran through Atlanta, a city where Frank boasted a substantial number of supporters.

Yet despite the many obstacles, if ever there was a group that could pull off such a scheme, this was it. Politically, each of the Mariettans was exceedingly well connected, not just in Atlanta but throughout Georgia. Socially, they were equally impressive, with entrees via marriage or business into many of the state's best families. Financially, the story was the same. But in the end, the intangibles carried the most weight. To a one, these individuals were renegade spirits. Authority, unless it was their own, was an affront to them, the prospect of outraging the whole of Jewry and Yankeedom an allure. Simultaneously, they felt duty-bound to administer the sentence that they—like Tom Watson—believed Slaton had illegally set aside. The men were, in short, as self-righteous as they were intractable. Consequently, they would be able to steal the light even as they summoned the dark.

By far the most charismatic of the Mariettans was Herbert Clay. At 34, the oldest son of Georgia's late United States senator was a man of great accomplishments and even greater excesses. That Clay was loved in Cobb County as much for the one as the other, while on the surface a contradiction, was in fact unsurprising, for he was the prince of this rural realm, and what he achieved, its people celebrated, and what he got away with, they relished.

Clay's achievements spoke for themselves. At 29, he had been elected mayor of Marietta. At 30, he had married the former Marjorie Lockwood, a Montgomery, Alabama, belle whose beauty and ambitions rivaled those of her slightly younger Montgomery contemporaries, Tallulah Bankhead and Zelda Sayre. And at 31, he had been elected solicitor general of the Blue Ridge Circuit, which made him the state's chief prosecuting officer from the Fulton County line north to the Tennessee border. In 1910, in a glowing assessment of Clay's potential, the *Constitution* reported: "He is wide-awake, genial, full of energy, liberal and absolutely devoted to the best interests of Marietta and her people. 'A chip off the old block,' he will be heard from further in the not far future."

But plain as Clay's promise surely was, what those in Cobb County—and for that matter most Georgians—first thought of upon hearing his name were his outrageous escapades, for in his personal life he was a thoroughgoing scandal and had been since boyhood. With the senator away for months at a time in Washington, Herbert, his sister Evelyn, and their brothers—Lex, Frank, Ryburn and Lucius—had been raised by their mother, Francis White Clay, in a substantial two-story frame home that to this day dominates Atlanta Street south of the town square. Francis Clay was the soul of piety and propriety, and whenever the children passed through the downstairs parlor, it was all "yes ma'am" and "no ma'am" and "if you please." But once they reached their second floor domain—which nominally served as their sleeping quarters but was in truth a cross between a clubhouse and a saloon—they indulged in innumerable vices. As Clay's son, Eugene Herbert, Jr., would reflect decades later: "Everybody was spoiled by Grandmother. They were told they were the best in the world and grew up without restraint. Grandmother thought there was discipline. But there was no discipline. Only manners."

At the turn of the century, Herbert entered the University of Georgia, an institution that he seemed to regard as merely a bigger and more diverting stage upon which to frolic. In short order, he went out for the football team, joined the Bulldog Club, and made himself a fixture at dances in both Athens and Atlanta. The dances, which usually featured ragtime bands, were inevitably triumphs for Clay, who quickly developed a reputation as a swain. Sandy hair swept back from his brow, eyes brimming with merriment or devilry, lips turned up in a teasing half smile, he was the sort around whom girls fairly quivered. Years afterward, a woman who was acquainted with Clay at the university said simply: "He was the most attractive man I ever met." The school yearbook, *The Pandora,* summed up Clay's sophomore year by pronouncing him "A Social Success," while the student newspaper, *The Red and Black,* cryptically denominated him "He with the pretty eye."

Yet for all Clay's charms, there was a heedless, self-destructive quality to his sojourn at the university. He drank improvidently and fell behind academically. Worse, when inebriated, he became unruly, posing a threat to himself and others. During the fall of 1901, he was dismissed from the football team for unspecified "training violations." Shortly thereafter, he was found wandering the streets of Athens firing a pistol into the air. Before he could do any harm, he was subdued, but the administration was not amused and expelled him. The spring of 1902 found him at Mercer University in Macon, where he completed his undergraduate and law degrees.

In any young man's life, expulsion from school would be a signal event, and so it was for Clay, but not in the way one might have thought, for at least publicly his family did no more than wink. In fact, the senator, upon enrolling son Lex at Georgia, made light of the episode, remarking famously: "The University ruined Herbert, and now I'm sending Lex here to ruin the University."

Senator Clay's statement—its bravado notwithstanding—seems on a deeper level willfully fatalistic, and by 1915, it could easily have been viewed as a sadly prescient epitaph for the entire family. Lex, far from ruining the university, had been dismissed for drunkenness, and while he was nobody's fool, he had become a perpetually besotted presence on the Marietta square. Meantime, Frank—who had graduated from West Point solely because President William Howard Taft had expunged an embarrassment of demerits from his records—had contracted syphilis while stationed in the Philippines and, after being discharged in San Francisco in the fall of 1914, had disappeared. Three months later, in an episode reported on the front page of the *New York Times,* Frank had turned up dazed and disoriented by the side of a road in Louisiana. Herbert had brought him home to Marietta. And as for Evelyn, she'd developed, in her hairdresser's words, "a little bit of a reputation." The former Lucille Sessions, whose banker father was among the Mariettans who spoke at the Prison Commission hearing, was blunter: "She had big bosoms and people talked about her." And the former Laura Margaret Hoppe, Bolan Brumby's niece, was blunter still: "Bolan told me, 'Now, Margaret, you must not go with Evelyn Clay anymore. Everybody will think you're just as bad as she is.' "

As the summer of 1915 began, the Clay clan appeared to be imploding, yet Herbert—despite his inclination for strong drink—was, if anything, at the top of his form, widely admired and genuinely effective as a prosecutor. Seventy-two years later, Luther Hames, a superior court judge who in the 1930s practiced with several of Clay's former partners, recalled: "He was a powerful politician. He knew every voter by name. He paid the poll tax for people." Lex Jolley, during the late teens Clay's law clerk, concurred: "He was just a likeable fellow. A terrific personality. He had a way of convincing people." This persuasiveness stemmed in part from the fact that Clay's sins diminished the distance between his lofty station and those lower elevations inhabited by the folks. Like a groggy Irish lord, he seemed to rule not from above but from below. Yet finally, his pull was rooted in the old-fashioned bedrock of leverage, for as solicitor general, he was one of the most influential men in North Georgia, the man who decided whether to pursue a prosecution or let it drop, whether to bust a bootleg still or look the other way. As longtime *Marietta Journal* associate editor Bill Kinney—who has lived his life in the shadow of the Frank case and as a young man knew many of the Cobb Countians who participated in the events of 1915—would subsequently observe: "All those involved owed Clay personal favors."

The member of the core group of Mariettans who most nearly rivaled Clay in sheer magnetism was John Tucker Dorsey. But where Clay's intoxicating allure owed something to rotting southern gentility, Dorsey's hit you between the eyes like a bolt of white lightning. Reared in the Georgia mountains, John Tuck—as his friends called him—was, at 37, an emerging star at the bar and in politics. Like his distant cousin Hugh down in Atlanta, he appeared to be going places fast. Yet in appearance and demeanor,

Dorsey was still very much a backwoods figure. Big and bearish, face dominated by a cleft chin, wide mouth, and a perpetually cocked left eye, he came across as both shrewd and capable of violence—and he was.

John Tucker Dorsey was a killer. In 1905, in the town of Gainesville 50 miles northeast of Marietta, he bludgeoned a man to death during a drunken argument. According to court documents, the crime, while not premeditated, was vicious:

> The accused and the deceased, on the night of the killing, were both drinking, and it appears that they had some controversy about taking a drink of whisky . . . The accused had with him a billiard cue, cut down so that it was used as a walking stick . . . The stick . . . was the large end of a billiard cue, cut about four feet long and an inch or more in diameter at the larger end. The deceased used an insulting epithet to the accused and menaced him by drawing his hands from his pockets and holding them in a fighting attitude. It does not appear that the deceased had any weapon. The accused thereupon struck the deceased with the billiard cue and knocked him down. The deceased arose and struck the accused several licks, apparently with his fists and the accused again struck the deceased with the billiard cue, knocked him down and rendered him unconscious. From the effects of these blows the deceased died the following day.

Dorsey, as it turned out, was convicted twice of manslaughter—the second time because the first verdict was overturned due to judicial error. After then losing on appeal, he served a brief sentence on the Cobb County chain gang, where shackles dug so deeply into his ankles that he was scarred for the length of his days.

To say that John Tuck was repentant wouldn't be entirely right, as in later years, he would tell cronies that by calling him a son of a bitch, his victim had sufficiently provoked him. Nonetheless, there can be no doubt that after doing his time, John Tuck had put the incident behind him, taking his rightful place as one of Marietta's premier trial lawyers—at one point, he won 10 consecutive murder cases. To have Dorsey in your corner was to have a man whose every phrase and gesture were calculated to carry the day. As his son Jasper subsequently recalled:

> He was a character. Had he wanted to make a profession out of being a preacher or an actor, he could have done either with great success. He enjoyed trying cases in the courtroom where his talents and histrionics could be brought fully to bear. He could go from outrage at the malefactions of some individual or witness . . . to where he had the homiletic qua-

ver in his voice. He could be as charming as a dancing master one minute and raise his voice in a shout in another. He was great before a jury.

And Dorsey was great before the voters as well. In the fall of 1914, he was elected to his first term in the legislature, which in the end was why he was so crucial to the task now at hand.

During the last week of June 1915—which happened to be not only the week Frank's death sentence was commuted but the week the general assembly convened—John Tuck traveled to Atlanta to take his seat. A few days thereafter, Speaker William H. Burwell did the freshman legislator the unusual honor of appointing him chairman of the House Penitentiary Committee. The *Constitution* noted the appointment with wonder, observing: "From time immemorial the chairmanship has been filled by selection from the big timber of the legislature." Other than having served on the chain gang himself, Dorsey had no qualifications. But notwithstanding such fine points, the Mariettan suddenly found himself in a position to wield considerable influence over not only Warden J. E. Smith and all those who labored at the state prison farm but the three commissioners to whom they answered.

If Clay and Dorsey were the rapscallions in the group, Fred Morris was the Eagle Scout. Like the two others, he was a lawyer, and like Dorsey he was, at 39, serving his first term in the legislature. But there the similarities ended. The son of J. G. "Gid" Morris—a Confederate veteran and prizewinning farmer—Fred had been reared in the Cobb County countryside, a dark-haired, nut-brown boy equally at home in the woods with a rifle or on a river with a rod. But nowhere was he more at home than on an athletic field. Dazzlingly swift and strong, he had enjoyed a storied three-sport career at the University of Georgia, starring at end for Coach Pop Warner's varsity eleven, playing baseball and running track.

After a brief stint in Atlanta as a newspaperman, Morris had returned to Marietta to practice law, taking on both criminal and corporate clients, among them the mighty Central of Georgia Railroad. Yet even as he grew in professional stature, a large part of Morris remained the brave, fleet-footed boy darting through the gloaming, across the gridiron, down the cinder track. Until his mid-thirties, he captained Cobb County's division of the state militia, and during the 1906 Atlanta race riots he saw action. In 1912, when two Negroes in neighboring Forsyth County were accused of raping a white woman—an accusation that led to the banishment of all blacks from the county—he represented one of them, even though he cared nothing for the Negro race's plight. And when the Boy Scout movement began, he organized the Marietta troop. These were the things a man did. So now he also did what a man did—lent his glory, his honor, his racing heart to the mission. Fred Morris gave the plot legitimacy.

So, too, in a different way, did Bolan Glover Brumby. At 39, Bolan was the scion of a fabled family. Arnoldus Brumby, founder of the Georgia Military Institute—located, during the Civil War, in Marietta—had educated many Confederate soldiers, among them Bolan's father, James Remley Brumby. The war was cruel to James Brumby, claiming the lives of one brother and, in his mind, his grief-stricken mother. As a consequence, he returned home both destitute and bitter. Yet after trying his hand at several enterprises, he launched a furniture-manufacturing concern whose signature piece—a slat-backed, cane-bottomed rocking chair—became not just a huge seller but an emblem of Southern hospitality. From Atlanta to New Orleans, no front porch was complete without a Brumby rocker.

Thereafter, the Brumbys took success as a birthright, and by 1915, numerous members of the connection had attained it. Cousin Richard B. Russell (born Richard Brumby Russell) would soon take a seat on the Georgia Supreme Court, while his son, Richard B., Jr., would within several years embark on a political path that eventually led to the United States Senate. Meanwhile, down in Florida, nephew Otis Brumby was editing a newspaper (the *St. Petersburg Times*) of which he was a part owner. And nephew Tom Brumby had recently wed Cordelia Gray, daughter of the *Atlanta Journal* publisher James R. Gray.

Yet driven and accomplished as so many of them were, the Brumbys shared another, darker trait: a proclivity to feud, especially among them-selves. In fact, due to a dispute over a now forgotten issue, Richard Brumby Russell disassociated himself from the family, legally changing his name to Richard Brevard Russell. A falling-out between brothers James and Tom—whom James had brought into the furniture business—was even nastier. The upshot: Tom gained control of the Brumby Chair Company (and its profitable rocker), while James was forced to start over.

True to character, James Brumby got his new venture—the Marietta Chair Company, which produced furnishings in the mission style—quickly on its feet, thanks in part to the fierce exertions of his manager and vice president, Bolan Brumby. Bolan, whom the *Constitution* described in 1910 as "one of North Georgia's most successful businessmen," was the very image of arrogant Southern aristocracy. High forehead, wide-spaced eyes, aquiline nose, defiant mouth, he stormed through life quarreling with friends and smiting foes. As an old friend remembered years later: "He was wild and daring."

Though Bolan was known to flare up over almost anything, nothing angered him more than Northerners. Considering the fact that he marketed his furniture above the Mason-Dixon Line—stores from Boston to San Francisco featured Brumby pieces—such hostility may at first seem incomprehensible. But in the house where Bolan was reared, "Yankee" was a dirty word. In fact, as late as 1929, James Remley Brumby, in a history written for his children, cried: "Oh that murderous War. How I wish I could forget all about it and from my heart forgive those murderers." Later in the same history, Brumby described a time after the war when he had considered moving to Mexico "to get from under the U.S. Gov't. which I hated—have not yet learned to love it."

And neither had Bolan Brumby. By helping to plan Frank's demise, this volatile son of Dixie was in essence launching a rearguard action in the Civil War.

Undoubtedly, the most revered of the men who had decreed death for Frank was Joseph Brown. The former governor, of course, had never censored himself when it came to his opinions regarding the case. Indeed, during his remarks at the clemency hearing, he had tacitly endorsed a lynching. Yet what role Brown now played is open to speculation. The best theory is that he served as the group's link to Tom Watson. While no documents survive to confirm the connection, it is certain that Brown was beholden to the Sage, for had it not been for Watson's work in Brown's 1908 gubernatorial campaign against Hoke Smith, the Mariettan never would have been elected. As C. Vann Woodward notes in *Tom Watson, Agrarian Rebel:*

> The business manager of the *Jeffersonian* proposed to Brown that, provided enough extra papers were ordered, he would print a "campaign issue" that would be "a document of tremendous force." He added: "In making you this offer we are practically giving you the advantage of a thorough campaign organization." The offer was accepted. The itemized bill presented by the *Jeffersonian* to Brown, presumably covering all services during the campaign, amounted to $2,674.10 in payment for 82,500 extra copies of the paper and fifty-one two-months subscriptions.
>
> At the primary election in June . . . Joseph M. Brown was nominated by a small majority of 12,000.

Simply stated, Brown had purchased victory from Watson. In monetary terms, the former governor had satisfied the debt, but in a larger sense, he remained under obligation. Thus, if Watson had a man in Marietta, it was almost surely Brown. And as the *Marietta Journal*'s Kinney unequivocally asserts, the ex-governor was among those who conceived the mission to Milledgeville.

It was, in its way, an extraordinary group. Yet had it not been for Judge Newt Morris, it would have been lacking in the raw nerve essential to the task under consideration. Where Herbert Clay and John Tucker Dorsey were drunk with the idea of lynching Frank and would attempt to intoxicate both their fellow Cobb Countians and the officials in Milledgeville with the same wine, Morris was coldly sober. Where Fred Morris (Judge Newt's distant cousin) thought that the men were doing their "duty as citizens," the judge entertained no illusions. Where Bolan Brumby was refighting the war, Morris was engaged in a battle for the here and now. And where Governor Brown was servicing an old account, Morris was amassing political capital for future use. Quite simply, for Judge Newt Morris, this was an opportunity.

At 46, Judge Newt, as he was generally called, was Marietta's most intimidating public figure. Though not a physically imposing man, he was rarely crossed, and one look at his severe visage suggested why. Lips turned down beneath a thick mustache, cheeks easily flushed, he appeared quick to anger, and he was. But it was his eyes—gray, flinty, opaque—that bespoke his true nature. Pragmatic, calculating, ruthlessly self-disciplined, Judge Newt did not blink at anything. As the former Lucille Sessions, whose father often did business with Morris, put it: "Judge Newt always came out on top."

Ever since arriving in Marietta fresh from the University of Georgia Law School in 1893, Morris—a native of adjacent Cherokee County—had aggressively sought to elevate himself both on the stump and financially. First elected to the legislature in 1897, he soon rose to the speakership, and in 1904, his fellow assemblymen presented him with a singular token of their esteem: a mahogany gavel fashioned from a piece of stair rail taken from Washington, Georgia's Heard House, where during the terrible spring of 1865, a fleeing Jefferson Davis had conducted the Confederacy's last cabinet meeting. After seven years in the legislature, Morris was appointed a Democratic Party committeeman, and in 1909, he was elected judge of the Blue Ridge Circuit. Three years later, when Cobb County native William Gibbs McAdoo came to Georgia to champion the presidential campaign of his father-in-law, Woodrow Wilson, it was Morris who'd introduced him to cheering throngs.

As Judge Newt had ascended politically, so, too, had he made hay, but not through his law practice. Rather, Morris ran a side business as a property developer and contractor, and from it, he earned enough money to obtain a fine home, Sugar Hill, near the square. Though Morris Construction was known for doing quality work, Judge Newt was regarded as a sharp operator. James T. Anderson, Jr., for six decades Marietta's Chevrolet dealer, recalled that whenever his father, a wealthy Cobb County farmer, engaged Morris's outfit, he kept his canceled checks for fear Judge Newt might sue for nonpayment. Deveraux McClatchey, Jr., an Atlanta lawyer with Cobb County roots, also knew something of Morris's dark side, having once fought him in court. Years later, McClatchey grumbled: "I try not to hate anyone, but I come close with him. I'm sure he had no principles." Harold Willingham, a Marietta lawyer and ex-legislator, offered a more colorful verdict: "He was a fourteen-karat son of a bitch with spare parts."

That Judge Newt could simultaneously occupy a position of the highest esteem and the greatest scorn in Marietta—that he could be at once respected and reviled—was not dissimilar to the manner in which Herbert Clay could be an object of tongue wagging yet retain power. In short, just as Clay was the town's prince, Judge Newt was its boss, and the populace regarded him with a kind of nervous awe. Indeed, the parallels between Clay and Morris—the men who, in the end, were the most crucial to the plan afoot—went deeper, in that both were shaped by early experiences that convinced them they could get away with nearly anything. In Clay's case, that experience was his expulsion from the University of Georgia, which, whatever inconvenience it caused him, was ultimately dismissed with a shrug. In Morris's case, the experience was not so well known—at least not in Georgia. Though most Mariettans were aware that Judge Newt, prior to attending law school, had spent a little time out west, few had ever heard why he came home. Which was just as Morris desired it, for the story was not the sort a judge would want to get around.

The date was 1889, and the place was the high-desert town of Lancaster, California. While actually located in northern Los Angeles County, Lancaster is east of the San Gabriel Mountains, the last divide between the West of tumbleweeds and the West of ocean breezes. In Lancaster, Joshua trees, not citrus groves, punctuate the endless vistas. In the winter, there is snow; in the summer, blistering heat. The Mojave is only a few miles distant. Yet in the 1880s, Lancaster beckoned, for the nearby hills held rich deposits of gold and borax, and the sprawling landscapes were perfect for grazing cattle. With an uncle—Mace Mayes, member of a respected Marietta clan— already in residence, Newt, who was twenty years old, had gone there to seek his fortune.

By the time Morris arrived, Mayes had established himself as one of Lancaster's leading citizens. Not only was he a partner in both a saloon and a butcher shop, but he had been elected constable. Mayes took care of his nephew, making a place for him at the butcher shop and pinning a badge on him to boot. (Soon enough, Deputy Morris attracted headlines by trailing a jewelry thief to Bakersfield.) Eventually, young Newt became a justice of the peace, moonlighting as a salesman for the Antelope Valley Real Estate Agency.

Yet respectable appearances notwithstanding, Mace Mayes and Newt Morris were apparently involved in some shady dealings. As David Earle, staff anthropologist at the Lancaster Museum, stated years later: "It's widely believed that Mace Mayes and Newt Morris were in the cattle-rustling business. That's what all the oral histories say, and I think there's a fair case that Mayes and Morris got their hands on cattle for which they did not have title." The men's actions, Earle added, are open to varying interpretations. In one, the two can be viewed simply as Georgia boys who got caught up in local politics, which had a South-versus-North flavor. In the other, they must be judged more harshly. But regardless, there's no disputing the fact that the pair's activities in Lancaster came to an ugly conclusion.

In the summer of 1891, Newt Morris was accused of attempted murder in the shooting of M. H. "Rony" Crane, like himself a former deputy constable. As the *Los Angeles Times* reported it, Morris allegedly bushwhacked the man, firing at him with both barrels of a double-barrel shotgun through a window of his uncle's saloon. Though badly wounded, Crane survived, primarily because at the time of the incident, he'd been holding a thick copy of the *California Penal Code* and it had partially deflected the shells. From his hospital bed, Crane told the district attorney that Morris was a "bitter" enemy and that moments before the shooting, "he heard the clicking of a gun hammer and on looking up saw Morris." On July 17, Morris was charged with "wilfully, unlawfully, feloniously and with malice aforethought" assaulting "a human being with . . . intent to kill" and transported to Los Angeles, where the preliminary hearing would be held.

For five mid-August days in a downtown courtroom crowded with not only spectators but reporters (the fact that Crane's life had been saved by a law book provided an irresistible angle), both sides argued their cases. Through the testimony of several Lancaster merchants and a vaquero named Porfirio Valencia, the prosecution methodically established that Morris had ready access to a double-barrel shotgun and had been seen lurking outside his uncle's saloon the night of the incident. The state's star witness, however, was Crane himself, who calmly identified Morris as his assailant. Then it was the defense's turn. After introducing the fact that Crane initially named someone else as the shooter, Morris's lawyers argued that the wounded man had falsely accused their client because several months previous, he'd arrested Crane for horse stealing. Finally, the defense put up two teenage girls as alibi witnesses, both of whom swore that young Newt was with them at the time of the shooting.

After a week of testimony, Judge L. Stanton decided there was sufficient evidence to bind the defendant over, and on August 18, he ordered that Morris stand trial in Los Angeles Superior Court. Bail was set at $3,500.

Accounts of what happened next differ. According to anthropologist Earle, Morris—fearful of both conviction and the exposure of his other illicit activities—skipped out on his bail. According to documents on file at the Los Angeles County courthouse, however, charges were inexplicably dropped. Either way, Morris hung up his spurs and returned home.

By 1915, of course, what had transpired in California was 2,000 miles and nearly a quarter of a century behind Morris. Yet the incident can't be dismissed as a minor indiscretion, for it reveals a man capable of violence who may have believed himself above the law.

Newt Morris was a devious and brassy character. As he aged, his tactics grew more sophisticated, but the motivation was always the same—to remove those who stood between him and the object of his desire, and the object of his desire in 1915 was control of Georgia's Democratic Party. That such was the case, there can be no question. Indeed, at the party's 1914 convention in Macon—in an incident that was an echo of the past and a precursor of the future—Judge Newt had ambushed someone else. The victim this time: John Slaton. The governor, who had never made any secret of his hope to serve in the United States Senate after finishing his term, had won that summer's primary. But because he had not received a majority of the votes, the contest had been thrown onto the convention floor, where Thomas Hardwick, the second-place finisher, mounted a forceful challenge. The fight's most heated battles involved the seating of competing slates of delegates. Which was where Morris, a member of the credentials committee, took aim. Reported the *Constitution*, Judge Newt sat Hardwick men over Slaton men, which of course was politics. But as Slaton delegates later told it, Morris went further, luring those he could not deny credentials into hotel rooms stocked with whisky. By the fourteenth ballot, a sufficient number of Slaton supporters had been waylaid that Hardwick was at last nominated. In the wake of this triumph, Judge Newt had moved on to bigger game. Though he clearly believed that Leo Frank was guilty (in 1913, at the Phagans' request, Morris had quietly offered his counsel to the then besieged Hugh Dorsey, who had just as quietly declined), it seems plain that he now saw Frank less as a murderer than as an emblem of his opponents' power. If he could pull off the mission to Milledgeville, he would destroy the Slaton wing of the Democratic Party, leaving the Watson wing forever in his thrall.

While many of the organizers' activities in the days following their first meeting remain mysterious, there's little doubt that they devoted most of the time to selecting the men who would carry out the actual raid on the prison farm. For all their zeal, the planners never intended to make the trip themselves. They had too much to lose. As Emory University history professor Judson Ward, a Marietta native who as a boy knew many of the individuals involved, subsequently asserted: "The power structure would not touch anything like this with their hands." Instead, Clay and the others would delegate the job to a cadre of enthusiastic loyalists composed along military lines. Of the men who would make up the group, none were more vital than those who would serve as the lieutenants. Once the mission got under way, they would exercise complete control. Consequently, they were chosen first. Their names: George Daniell, Gordon Gann and Newton Mayes Morris—Judge Newt's double first cousin, generally known as Black Newt.

Like the men who picked them, the field commanders were all strong-willed characters. But more important, they were all members of Marietta's petit bourgeois. Which, of course, was perfect. Beneath the elites who were calling the shots yet above the poor dirt farmers and laborers who would serve as foot soldiers, they would obey when ordered, lay down the law when required.

George Daniell was the proprietor of a jewelry shop on the north side of the Marietta square. The store, which had a cast-iron clock out front, was a favorite gathering place, and many old-time Mariettans believe the planners met there. Daniell himself, at 45, was a stout, florid, gabby fellow who was "into everything" in Marietta from politics to the Rotary Club. Most particularly, he was into hillbilly music, and by 1915, he was making quite a name for himself as the leader of a band that played at dances and warmed up political rallies.

Gordon Gann was, at 36, an ambitious lawyer and something of a pro-tégé of Judge Newt. The two had once shared offices. In 1914, Gann had been elected Cobb County ordinary, which placed him in charge of probate court and put him in touch with most everyone in town.

Both Daniell and Gann were popular figures. Yet just as the organizers would have lacked sufficient gall had it not been for Judge Newt, the lieu-tenants would have lacked sufficient grit had it not been for Black Newt.

Black Newt—an apt moniker for the leathery-complected, rakish Morris—was, at 37, following in the footsteps of his fairer-skinned and more distinguished relative. Like Judge Newt, he operated in several spheres. In his official guise, Black Newt ran the Cobb County convict camp—the chain gang. Consequently, he was responsible for paving and maintaining roads and highways. His workforce consisted of two forty-man crews transported to job sites in wheeled cages. These rolling contraptions served not merely as modes of conveyance but as the prisoners' living quarters. Years later, Narvel Lassiter, Black Newt's nephew, recalled: "He'd pull the cages by team or truck. They'd have a caravan and set up and do work in one section of the county. I hate to think of the sight of those people." Pistol holstered to his leg, bullwhip coiled on his shoulder, Black Newt watched over his charges from horseback. "If they didn't walk the chalk line, he'd get with 'em," James W. Lee, fiddle player in George Daniell's band, remembered years afterward. "He'd spank 'em down there on the chain gang." So proficient was Morris with his bullwhip that he was sometimes also known as Whipping Newt.

When not at his day job, Black Newt served as the foreman of his cousin's Morris Construction Company. The setup was inspired. Judge Newt used his connections to win jobs, then Black Newt used his expertise and a gang of Negro laborers to do them. As Bob Garrison, another of Black Newt's nephews, subsequently recalled: "Black Newt had mules, wagons and a scoop that would hold two yards of dirt. He dug lakes and foundations for houses." By 1915, Black Newt was doing well enough to have built a comfortable two-story home on Atlanta Street just down from the Clays' place.

Yet in the end, the relationship between the two Newts was rooted in more than money. Like the ties that bound most of the Mariettans who got caught up in this thing, those that connected the cousins involved history. As Black Newt's son, Paul Morris, later explained: "In 1898, my daddy was running a liquor still with Judge's brother. Charlie was Judge's brother. And the judge found out the still would be raided and bought them a train ticket and they went to Texas. My daddy stayed a year, and Charlie never came back." After this, Paul Morris added, "Anything Judge wanted to do, my dad would do it." And what Judge Newt wanted Black Newt to do in the summer of 1915 was lead the mission to Milledgeville.

Once the men who would captain the party were chosen, the organizers wasted no time drafting those who would serve in the ranks. Though they were not brazen, neither were they terribly secretive. As a Mariettan who was too young at the time to be considered for duty but old enough to see the wheels go round later stated: "They'd go to a man's office and talk to him or . . . see a man on the job and talk to him. A man in the shop where I worked was involved. I think there were four in my building who were going." Added one of the leaders: "The organization of the body was more open than mysterious. It was more on the order of a plain, 'open-and-shut' business proposition."

By this point, the planners knew exactly what they were looking for. At the top of the list were lawmen, especially deputy sheriffs, whose duties included transporting prisoners to the state farm and who thus not only possessed relationships with prison personnel but knew the roads between Marietta and Milledgeville. Almost equally coveted were men who boasted particular skills that might be needed either during the trip or at the penitentiary. Thus automobile mechanics, telephone linemen, electricians, doctors and explosives experts were avidly recruited. Finally, there was a demand for raw muscle — men who could stand and fight.

Also by this point, the planners knew exactly what they were not looking for. As the *New York Times* reported: "The lynchers would have with them no men of lawless character or bad reputation. The lawless and the violent men of Cobb County were not permitted to know what was going on." While this stricture applied across the board and was meant to keep anyone who might compromise the scheme at a distance, it was aimed at one specific individual: Robert E. Lee Howell, the sawed-off bantam who in 1914 had assaulted William Burns and might have killed him had not Judge Newt packed the detective into a car and raced him out of Marietta. Though Howell would have relished a role, the planners, true to their word, told him nothing.

The organizers' exacting criteria notwithstanding, they had no trouble finding the 25 men they believed the job required. For one thing, a majority of Mariettans, like a majority of Georgians, had been so utterly blinded by Tom Watson's poison that they fervently believed Frank was a monster. Moreover, and again thanks to Watson, most Mariettans believed Frank had escaped death because he had exploited his Judaism. "No Jews ever pay for the crimes they commit," a Mariettan subsequently declared in explaining why an in-law participated. Finally, though, the men who threw themselves into the scheme were motivated by neither bloodlust nor anti-Semitism. Rather, they felt obliged to accept an urgent and weighty responsibility. Here again, of course, their minds had been twisted by Watson, but as Dorothy Smith, the daughter of Lawrence Haney, one of the party, put it years later: "This was something my father felt he had to do. He was not proud, but he was not ashamed."

The prospective participants sought only two pledges from the organizers. One, they wanted a fair assessment of the risks. "They would not go into it without first knowing every 'lay of the ground,' " a planner told the *Constitution*. Two, they wanted some assurance they would not be prosecuted afterward. While the organizers could not guarantee there would be no danger, they promised to exert their considerable influence in Atlanta and

Milledgeville. As for the courts—Herbert Clay and Judge Newt were the courts.

And so the 25 signed on. Some would serve in supporting roles. Jim Brumby—who not only owned a garage but was Bolan's brother—would service the cars. L. B. Robeson, freight agent at the Western and Atlantic Railroad, would lend his Stutz Bearcat. Marietta Mayor E. P. Dobbs would also lend his car. Former sheriff William Frey would tie the noose. Banker Robert A. Hill would provide incidental funding. And as for the rest—they intended to speed through the night to Milledgeville. Sheriff George Swanson and Deputies William McKinney and George Hicks, taxi driver Cicero Dobbs (and his Overland Sixty), farmer D. R. Benton (the Phagan girl's uncle and one of those arrested during the assault on Slaton's home), farmer Horace Hamby, mule trader "Coon" Shaw, and Dr. C. D. Elder all said yes. So did the young Burton brothers, Emmet and Luther, both strapping and brave. So did the redheaded electrician "Yellow Jacket" Brown, who would ride his motorcycle. And so did Dorothy Smith's father, farmer Lawrence Haney, who one day would dictate the names of all involved to Dorothy and her sister, Golmer, who, in turn, would place them in the family Bible.

These were men, one of the planners told the *Constitution,* "whose worth was known collectively and individually, who were resolved to bear any burden and to go through with their plans at any cost."

TWENTY

Milledgeville

Leo Frank awakened to his new world sick in body and tormented in mind. "Picture a frail figure," wrote the first national reporter to reach Milledgeville following the commutation, with "a face pinched, drawn and colorless. The ridge of the high-bridged nose is sharp, the eyes and eyebrows stand out like ink splotches in the parchment-like whiteness." Emotions, the *New York Tribune*'s John J. Leary added, chased one another swiftly across Frank's visage. One moment, his smile conveyed a "yearning, bashful appeal." The next, his "mouth twisted itself into an ugly sideways grin—the snarl the running wolf throws back at its pursuers." When Leary stood to depart, Frank "took the hand held out to him within both of his—the frantic, wiry grip of a child in the dark."

Though Frank was not so ill that he was confined to bed, any thought that he might soon be put to work in the fields alongside his fellow inmates was quickly abandoned. Suffering from nausea, a cold contracted during the frantic night flight from Atlanta and what the *Macon Telegraph* termed a "nervous breakdown caused by the terrible strain which he has undergone in his long fight to escape the gallows," he spent his initial days in Milledgeville shuffling in and out of the prison hospital, where he was under a physician's care. As he wrote Lucille his second morning on the farm: "After that which I have gone through it will take some time before I gain my poise and physical balance."

For all of Frank's ailments, however, it was clear from the outset that he was grateful his life had been spared and hopeful that he would find peace. "It has indeed been an ordeal for both of us my darling," he confided to Lucille, "but in time both of us will be happy."

Improbably enough, the state prison farm provided a conducive setting for Frank's physical and emotional recovery. Though much about the institution—particularly its wards for Negro and female inmates—had long been regarded as inadequate, its shortcomings were not of a sort that seemed likely to affect white male prisoners. Spread out over four thousand acres two miles northeast of Milledgeville, the place—if one could ignore the armed guards and barbed-wire fencing—was actually lovely. The crops (mostly corn and cotton) were terraced into the rolling landscape, while tall pines lined the roads. Anchoring the property was the dormitory to which Frank had been assigned. A massive L-shaped redbrick affair fronted by a columned portico and topped by incongruously graceful gun towers, the building contained offices for the warden and a bookkeeper, a library, and open barracks that housed the bulk of the prisoners, who bedded down on army cots arranged in parallel rows. Erected just four years earlier, the structure was considered a showpiece. Reported the *Macon Telegraph:*

> The main building is a credit to the [prison] commission. There isn't a jail in Georgia more sanitary; in fact, it would be a model jail that would equal it in this respect. In it are some conveniences, the modern showers for instance, that are lacking in many a Georgia home. Beyond a doubt, some of the people in that prison are in better living surroundings than they were before they went there.

The *Telegraph* was not alone in giving the facility glowing reviews. The *New York Tribune*'s man was equally impressed:

> Outside the Milledgeville farm is well kept in appearance. Inside, it is light and airy. None of the strange odors that assail one in New York prisons are here. The place was clean and sweet tonight after three hundred men had entered fresh from their work in the fields.

Contributing significantly to the prison farm's relatively benign atmosphere was the fact that most of the some 1,000 men and women incarcerated here were either aged, infirm (one ward housed tuberculars) or products of privileged backgrounds. To be sure, there were dangerous characters at Milledgeville, but the state sentenced the bulk of its able-bodied offenders to chain gangs, where they labored building highways under the likes of Black Newt Morris. Consequently, the prison farm was regarded as a soft snap. The inmates ran the gamut from Aunt Rhody Ann Meeks, an ancient, pipe-smoking black woman who rode around the place in a little horse-drawn wagon, to Dr. J. W. McNaughton, the South Georgia physician whose unsuccessful 1913 appeal of his murder conviction had been a factor in the one-month delay of Frank's trial. Prior to Frank's advent, Milledgeville's most illustrious prisoner had been the seventy-year-old Bill Miner, who in his heyday as a train robber in the 1870s coined the phrase "Hands up!"

Presiding over this institution were two vastly different men. At 35,

Warden J. E. Smith was considered an innovative administrator, though he had no training in criminology, having previously worked in the turpentine business in Alabama. Strong-jawed and solidly built, he boasted a reputation, in one reporter's estimation, as "quick, nervy, fearless and experienced." Upon Frank's arrival, it was Smith who had aggressively increased security.

Of equal dignity to Smith was the farm superintendent, J. M. Burke. In his mid-fifties, the rugged, sun-bronzed Burke was a veteran of the state correction department, which, far from being a recommendation, made him a part of the only recently discredited past. Not until 1910 had Georgia done away with the last vestiges of its infamous convict lease system, whereby the state rented offenders to industrialists, chiefly brick manufacturers and coal mine owners. The arrangement had proved profitable for everyone except the convicts, who were routinely mistreated. The full extent of the abuse had not emerged until 1908, when, during legislative hearings, the official ostensibly charged with inspecting workplaces for safety violations testified. That official was Burke. As the *Constitution* reported:

> "Every time I went into the coal mines I found men who had been hurt by falling slate," Burke told the committee. Then he laughed.
>
> "Did you ever go down into the Durham Coal mines to ascertain the cause of so many injuries?" asked the chairman.
>
> Witness laughed and stated he once went 100 yards into the Durham mines, but found so much mud and water therein he came out. He laughed again.
>
> "Convicts under the care and protection of the state are forced to work in these mines, are they not?" asked a legislator.
>
> "Oh, yes sir," was the answer of Inspector Burke, who again laughed.
>
> Asked if he had ever gone into the mines at the Lookout Mountain Coal and Coke Company to see what caused the crippling of so many men, Inspector Burke said he had not. Again he laughed, this time apparently in surprise that such a question should be asked.
>
> "I would have had to go down on my hands and knees and crawl in to inspect that mine," he told the chairman.
>
> Subsequently, Burke added: "I never did inquire why so many men were whipped."

Burke's testimony had helped to sound the death knell for the convict lease system, although professionally he'd suffered no reversals. Around Milledgeville, however, the locals regarded him as a "pretty rough character."

That Frank realized his well-being would depend largely on the actions of Warden Smith and Superintendent Burke was evidenced by the fact that from the beginning, he did all he could to curry favor with the men. In fact, if his letters, which were censored by prison authorities, are any indication, he shamelessly flattered them. "The warden is some fine fellow," he wrote Lucille early on. "I know you will like him." Several days later, describing a meeting with Smith and Prison Commissioner Robert E. Davison (who had, of course, refused to interfere with Frank's death sentence), he informed Lucille: "This morning, I had a talk with Judge Davidson [sic] . . . and the warden. They are both my friends and will do all in their power for my best interest." And it wasn't just to his wife that Frank praised his captors. To Luther Rosser, he wrote: "The warden and his staff here are very kind to me. I know I shall get along nicely with them." To Sears and Roebuck Chairman Julius Rosenwald, he asserted: "I am in an environment which, through the kindness of the Warden and his staff, has been made as liveable as circumstances will permit." And to Manning Yeomans, the country lawyer who'd joined his team at the end, he wrote: "The Warden and his staff have treated me white."

Exactly how Smith, Burke and the staff—which consisted chiefly of inmates whose good behavior had earned them trusty status—regarded Frank's efforts to ingratiate himself cannot be said, but there can be no doubt that within days after arriving in Milledgeville, the celebrated new prisoner had accumulated the trappings of a life that while not luxurious was, by the standards of most penal institutions, remarkably plush. Through a judicious use of funds (Lucille sent her husband a $5 check that first week), Frank quickly exchanged his prison-issue grass mattress for one made of cotton. Meantime, thanks to a Milledgeville friend of his uncle Moses named Roy Alford, he acquired towels, washcloths, soap and a razor and was thus soon able to write Lucille: "I shaved this a.m. Look real human." Also thanks to Alford, who had married into one of the town's best families and lived in a Victorian home frequented by local gentry, Frank met many of the area's leading citizens, most of whom sympathized with his cause and several of whom brought him gifts, ranging from bags of citrus fruit to boxes of peaches. Not surprisingly, Frank's family, Atlanta friends and supporters across the country were even more generous. His brother-in-law Alex Marcus sent a sateen work cap. His lawyer, Leonard Haas, sent an Ingersoll watch and a mirror. (Of the timepiece, Frank wrote his wife: "It's a beauty, much too fine for my present environment.") Temple member George Gershon (a member of the grand jury that indicted Frank) contributed a box of fifty cigars. The New York Public Library's Anne Carroll Moore mailed books. And this was just for starters. Before no time, Frank's assigned footlocker overflowed with tins of crackers and sardines and packs of cigarettes and Beechnut gum. Most extravagant, however, was the retailer Charles Elya's shipment of phonograph records, which over Lucille's objection ("Do not get all classical records," she wrote her husband. "Get some that will appeal to all"), included primarily works by Caruso and Geraldine Farrar. Frank played the discs on a Victrola in the warden's office.

Predictably, the improvement in Frank's surroundings was accompanied by a corresponding improvement in his health, and by the end of his first week in Milledgeville, he was assigned chores, as he phrased it, "commensurate with my present physical condition." Awakening each morning at four, he donned striped jersey and pants and joined a cleaning detail comprised of the prison's frailest inmates. After several hours scrubbing floors, the men washed up and sat down to a breakfast of biscuits, eggs and buttermilk. Then they worked a second shift, after which they took dinner. Just a few days into this routine, in a letter to Herbert Schiff, his old colleague at the pencil factory, Frank sounded like a man on the mend:

> I am feeling much better. My cold has almost disappeared. My appetite is good and my face is filling out and my color is coming back. I have been given some light work about the building. This puts an edge on my appetite. The sanitary conditions here are good. The atmosphere here is healthy. I am sleeping like a top.

Frank's work schedule, despite the early hours, left him plenty of time to himself, and he spent most of it at a table in a small room adjacent to Warden Smith's office. There, with green rows of corn visible through a window in front of him, he wrote letter after letter. Composing on either lined Montag notebook paper or prison stationery, Frank worked until his hand cramped. "I wrote 14 letters this a.m.," he boasted to Lucille one day. The next, he exclaimed: "This letter is only the 16th I have written today!" Many of these were perfunctory responses to pieces of mail from strangers, but those addressed to people who'd contributed significantly to the cause could hardly have been more heartfelt. To Anne Carroll Moore, Frank wrote:

> Your letter of 6/28 brought to me its message of cheer and inspiration. I was so glad to hear from one whose helpful friendship meant so much to me during those last trying hours in the "Tower." It was the voice and presence of the long-ago—infusing spirit and exhorting manhood . . .

To the mother of his lawyer Henry Alexander, he wrote:

> I wish to again assure you how deep is my affection and how profound my respect for your illustrious and noble-minded son. You and Mr. Alexander

may well be proud of him. He has been to me more than counsel or friend.
He has been a brother, and I treasure his association most highly.

However, it was to Luther Rosser—who had been widely criticized for mis-
handling the defense—that Frank directed his most thoughtful words:

> I want to assure you how deep is my respect for you as a man and attorney.
> I am not in this predicament because of anything you did or did not do.
> My misfortune is the result of a "system" coupled with ignorance and chi-
> canery.

In short, Frank felt profoundly indebted to all those who had supported
him, and before many days were out, he had dispatched notes to everyone
from John Slaton and Albert Lasker to Oliver Wendell Holmes.

Yet as Frank, a National Pencil Company pencil in hand, sat looking out
over the prison farm, he could not resign himself to the fact he would spend
the rest of his life in the place. Thus in his letters to those closest to him, he
invariably raised the idea of reopening the fight for exoneration. With
Rosser, he backed into the subject:

> The sunshine and atmosphere here are great. I have plenty of opportu-
> nity to view plant life and my observation in the crimino-psychological
> field is practically limitless.
>
> Still "stripes" and the environment of a penal institution, while interest-
> ing in their way, pall upon the vision of an innocent man. Physically, I am a
> part of it; spiritually, I am totally foreign. Yet as the old saw has it, "ad astra
> per aspera." It cannot last for always.

With Anne Carroll Moore, he was more direct:

> This is the breathing spell in the present phase of my life to gain the
> strength and reserve for the spurt to freedom, vindication and that honor
> which is justly and rightfuly mine.

No sooner had Frank articulated his intention to begin the war anew than
a general willing to lead the armies into battle arrived at Milledgeville in the
person of the filmmaker Hal Reid. Armed with a camera and tripod and
accompanied by a crew, Reid—who had been in Atlanta at the time of the
commutation and shot footage of both the rioting and of Governor and Mrs.
Slaton at home—had come to make an authorized documentary movie.

Over the last days, Frank had been besieged by requests of every sort
from individuals who hoped to exploit his tale. Linton Starr, an *Atlanta*

Journal reporter who had befriended Frank early on, wanted the prisoner to "write your own story on . . . trip to Milledgeville." Charles Lincoln, the managing editor of the *New York World,* asked Frank to "write anything you want." How to respond to such overtures had engendered disputes among Frank's advocates. Herbert Haas was dead set against further public comment, fearing that more attention would only increase animosities. "Let me caution you against giving out interviews," he admonished Frank. "A friend of ours advised us today that interviews from you were appearing in Northern and Eastern papers . . . I think you should not do this." Meanwhile, Albert Lasker, who after all was in advertising, counseled the opposite. Frank was himself of two minds. At first, he'd written Lucille: "It would be well for the case to be given little or no publicity for a while. I little thought folks could be so rabid and prejudiced, not to say bloodthirsty." Yet in the same letter, he'd asked how the *New York Times* was covering the latest events and told his wife to instruct Herbert Haas to "get Ochs to deadhead" the paper to him. The next day, Frank had issued a request for gratis copies of another sheet that had championed his cause, directing Lucille: "Remind Herbert to see Gray about sending me the Atl. Journal." In part, Frank's fascination with the press sprang from his belief that he owed his life to the sensation it had created. But it was also true that the sight of his name in print mesmerized him. As the *Times* assistant editor Garet Garrett recorded in his diary, no less a supporter than Ochs had "once said that Frank would feel cheated if he did not have a chance to make a speech from the scaffold." In the end, then, it was little wonder that Frank leaped at the opportunity to have not just his saga but his face presented on screen— particularly when the presenter, as was the case with Hal Reid, intended his work to rally the troops.

Reid set up his equipment in the warden's office. Though he posed Frank both alone and talking with Smith, for many of the shots he put himself front and center with his leading man—for he, too, was a celebrity. Which was another reason why Frank had assented to this venture.

James Hallek Reid was at the height of a career that had started on the stage, veered into journalism and, in 1910, progressed into the movies, at first on camera, then behind it. In just five years, the 55-year-old filmmaker had compiled numerous credits, scripting such works as *Kaintuck* and *Indian Romeo and Juliet,* directing an adaptation of *The Deerslayer* and—of vital interest to Frank—directing and producing an anti-death-penalty feature entitled *Thou Shalt Not Kill.* Reid's greatest contribution to Hollywood, however, was his son, Wallace, who was presently filming *Maria Rose* with Geraldine Farrar and was on his way to becoming the brightest star on the Paramount lot. Frank had found yet another powerful propagandist.

Reid shot in Milledgeville for just a day, then packed up his camera and raced to New York, where after developing his film, he hosted a screening at the Palace Theater for an audience of one—Rae Frank. This was a critical command performance, as in essence Reid was submitting the initial footage from his movie to its subject's mother for approval. Lights dimmed, voices fell silent, and—as Mrs. Frank subsequently wrote her "dear boy"— the images came alive:

> First you were talking with Mr. Reid; then you were standing talking to . . . Warden Smith, he turned and looked out of the window and pointed, you took a forward movement and looked out of the window also, nodding your head in assent as if you were saying, "Yes I see." Then there was a picture of you looking at an open book as if reading; that was all there was of you. There was also the Gov's home, and he and his wife talking together, and one picture where they enter their auto and go to town, also each taken alone.

Though the movie was plainly in rough form, Rae Frank liked what she saw. Later that day, Reid telegraphed Herbert Haas:

> FRANK SENIOR SAW PICTURES POSITIVELY DELIGHTED SHE POSES
> FOR ME TOMORROW SHE WISHES MRS LUCILLE TO POSE ALSO PLEASE
> CONSULT LARGEST PICTURE EXCHANGE THERE ENGAGE MOVING
> PICTURE CAMERA MAN SUPT HIS MAKING PICTURE OF HER HAVE HIM
> TURN OVER TO YOU THE BOX CONTAINING FILM AFTER TAPING IT
> SECURELY AND SEND IT COD ALL EXPENSES TO MY OFFICE.

To shoot Lucille, Reid's cameraman would have to travel to the college town of Athens, where over the Fourth of July weekend she had begun a long visit with her merchant uncles, Bud and Simon Michael. Lucille had undertaken the trip in hopes of raising her spirits. Though overjoyed that her husband's life had been spared, since the commutation she had lapsed into a listless depression. As she'd written Leo his first week at the prison farm: "You know, honey, it seems as if every day is Sunday—I'm so lonesome, with no place to go, but home." To the extent that he could, Leo had attempted to cheer her, replying: "Rest up and get back to your poise of health and mind." He'd been more demonstrative in a later letter, declaring: "It is a joy and pleasure to have so good-looking a wife as you are and I think you will improve right along now that the harsh strain is over." However, Lucille had not improved, and at Leo's urging, she had decided to spend several weeks away.

The Michael brothers' adjoining Prince Avenue mansions held many fond memories for Lucille. She had, of course, stayed with her uncles in the spring of 1909 after accepting Leo's marriage proposal, and she now hoped to rediscover something of that happy girl. "This is certainly a lazy life," she confessed to Leo early on. "After breakfast, which I . . . eat alone, because I get up late, I write a few letters, then we have dinner at 12—after which there's nothing to do but nap and bathe and dress." Once out of bed, Lucille often beguiled the hours arranging Victrola records for a "private concert" or joined Aunt Em and several Athens matrons in the parlor for a rubber of bridge. Sometimes she ventured downtown to the family department store, then rode back with Uncle Bud in his car. After supper, she read or, exhibiting an interest in the occult, conducted "seances at letter writing" with her cousins.

But try as Lucille might, she could not recover overnight from a two-year siege of sadness and worry. Her reserves had been severely taxed, and the world remained threatening in big ways and small. The Fourth of July holiday, for instance, filled her with dread. As she wrote Leo: "It has poured all day, and I hope that the same weather prevailed in Atlanta. I had a kind o' idea that the ruff nex might erupt tonight when they should be filled with booze and the spirit of independence." Then there was the fear that she might say something in public that would spark even greater hostility against her husband. Thus, when she was invited to the Athens Country Club, she declined.

The pressure never relented, and as she had done her entire life, Lucille responded by overeating. That was why, when she learned a film crew was en route to Athens, she panicked. "The 'movie man' will be here tomorrow to take my pictures," she wrote Leo the night before. "I'm certainly all up in the air about it. I'm so fat and ugly. Gee! I hate to think about me on canvas; don't you?"

Such self-loathing on Lucille's part, so at odds with the resolve she'd displayed during the dark months just past, suggests what a toll the whole awful affair had exacted. Still, by the next day, she was ready to face the camera, and for the better part of the morning, she worked hard to comply with the filmmaker's directive that she "talk and show animation." In fact, as soon as the crew departed, she began to fret that she might have succeeded too well in depicting herself as sunny and carefree. As she immediately wrote Leo:

> I just had my "movies" made. I certainly hope they will be good. Don't you? . . . I think this, tho'—if they are calculated to do *you* personally any good, they should show you and me together . . . Now to show you down there, and me away from you animated and lively, will not arouse much sympathy, I'm afraid. I started to write Mr. Reid, but tho't I'd put it up to you.

These misgivings did not concern Reid, who, far from seeing any problem, was delighted with the footage his men took in Athens, and Lucille, in turn, was comforted and relieved. To be again contributing to the exoneration of the man she consistently addressed as "my angel," "my heart" or "my own" was all the tonic she required. As she had written Leo his first week in Milledgeville:

> Everyone is so happy that you are going to have the chance that we have prayed for to prove your innocence to all the "doubting Thomases." Of course the *world* as a whole knows you are guiltless, but you *must be* vindicated.

Yet even as Leo Frank and his supporters were preparing to resume the struggle, the Mariettans who had decreed Frank's death were initiating their plot's most cunning manipulation, one that if all worked as planned, would render the prison farm defenseless by making its officials answerable not to Governor Nat Harris but to them. The tool the conspirators would use in attempting to pull off this coup had been provided them shortly after Frank's arrival in Milledgeville when the state legislature—whose anti-Frank leanings were such that it had only barely defeated a motion to open its session with a reading of Tom Watson's postcommutation paean to Judge Lynch—appointed a special delegation to conduct an inspection of the prison farm. The body's charge was to investigate a reported typhus outbreak, but after a mere 24 hours on the scene, its members had moved far beyond the original scope of the job. Just how far became apparent when upon returning to Atlanta, they released their findings.

PAROLE PRISONERS OR TAKE CARE OF THEM, COMMITTEE REPORTS, boomed the headline atop page one of the *Journal*'s June 30 editions. STATE FARM IMPROVEMENTS ASKED, echoed the next morning's *Constitution*. Some of the facts supporting these headlines were genuinely new and alarming. Since January, three inmates had indeed died of typhus. Equally disturbing was the discovery that the institution was dumping raw sewage upstream from the aquifer that supplied water to both the prison and the city of Milledgeville. Finally, though, most of the revelations involved the sorry state of the place's dormitories for Negro and female prisoners and thus were not revelations at all, as the legislature had long known of and ignored such realities. Nonetheless, the delegation members acted as if they'd unearthed a fresh scandal, proclaiming:

> We will not attempt to explain conditions in detail, but your imagination can supply all that is necessary when we inform you that there are 140

negro men incarcerated and crowded into one room of an old wooden barn 50 by 150, and absolutely no sewerage facilities. To say nothing of health requirements, in case of fire in this building, these prisoners would have to be allowed to burn to death or escape and become an awful menace to the surrounding country. There are 129 colored women prisoners in one room 30 by 100—adjoining the white female ward and only separated by a wall with a door leading from the whites to the colored, and sanitary conditions here are worse.

If anyone in the Georgia press was disturbed by either the staleness of the allegations (no matter how shameful the facts) or the timing, they kept quiet about it. Indeed, the special delegation's report ignited the predictable round of journalistic indignation. The *Constitution* ran a front-page photo essay depicting various "deplorable conditions" at the farm. The *Journal,* meanwhile, editorialized against the same wretched circumstances, intoning, "Georgia is too great a state and her people are too proud to suffer the neglect of her prisoners. The state owes a peculiar obligation to those who are incarcerated at the prison farm, and that duty is to conserve the health, life and morals of the inmates."

Hard upon the outbreak of the controversy, the legislature increased the pressure on the prison authorities by ordering several members of the State Board of Health (among them, Dr. Henry F. Harris) to Milledgeville to determine whether the scientific data supported the preliminary findings. As it turned out, the medical men were actually harsher in their assessments. "Prison Farm Conditions 'Absolutely Disgraceful' Declares Health Board," blared the headline atop the July 8 *Constitution.* What gave these findings their urgency was both the specificity of the details ("The feces and urine are deposited in buckets kept in the overcrowded sleeping quarters, and these buckets are emptied at irregular intervals") and the implications of the conclusion. Prison officials, the physicians asserted, should be indicted for "criminal neglect."

Just that quickly, the careers of Commissioners Patterson, Rainey and Davison and Warden Smith and Superintendent Burke had been put at risk. At first, Commissioner Davison tried to counterattack. "We have known all along of the deplorable conditions at the farm," he told reporters, reminding them that in each of the past three years, the legislature had turned down the commission's requests for appropriations to build not just a "new wing for the negro convicts similar to the wing occupied by the white convicts" but a sewage plant. Yet in the end, he and the others found themselves at the mercy of the newly appointed chairman of the legislature's penitentiary committee: John Tucker Dorsey of Marietta. In announcing his intentions to travel to Milledgeville to clean up the mess, Dorsey declared:

> We are going to vary the custom of the past. Heretofore, the committee has made these inspection trips between sessions of the legislature. By investigating conditions now and determining upon the improvements and reforms to be instituted my committee can make its recommendations to the legislature while it is still in session which will afford an opportunity to institute the needed changes without undue delay.

The nerviness of it all was extraordinary, suggesting that Dorsey's coolest lynching brethren, particularly Judge Newt Morris (who had, of course, once been speaker of the Georgia House) and former governor Joseph Brown, were choreographing the strategy. Not that these men left fingerprints. Now was the time for misdirection and stealth. Save for the chosen few, no one was to know, and apparently no one did. The only interest Frank's lawyers expressed in any of this indicates they took the story at face value. As Henry Alexander wrote Frank the day the news broke:

> I trust that you will be able to guard yourself against the danger of typhoid fever which is reported as prevailing at the State Farm. Let us know if there is anything that we can do about this. I can send you some solid alcohol and a burner with which to boil your water if you desire it.

While the scheme intended to open the prison farm's gates from within was unfolding, Tom Watson was bombarding Georgia with another fusillade of verbiage. Having called the tune, he was now creating the climate in which the Mariettans could play it out to its conclusion.

AFTERMATH OF SLATON'S TREACHERY IN THE FRANK CASE, trumpeted the page-one headline atop the *Jeffersonian*'s July 8 issue, beneath which Watson, seizing on the ex-governor's much quoted remarks regarding the participation of his wife, Sallie, in the commutation process, mockingly inquired:

> Was Sally [*sic*] the real commuter, after all? And was it Sally Fanny Grant who annihilated both the juries and both the Supreme Courts?
>
> Slaton cannot complain of the mention of his wife's name. *It was he who slopped over in New York and divulged the private conversation which took place in his country palace.*
>
> Slaton told the New Yorkers that Sally threw her arms around him and answered—
>
> *"Jack, let's commute!"*

So you see, we were unusually blessed in having two gubernatorial judges to retry the Frank case, and to upset all the courts; one was Chief Justice Jack, and the other was Associate Justice Sally.

Watson's disgust with the Slatons, however, was mild compared to his increasing contempt for the "Rich Jews" who, as the *Jeffersonian*'s July 15 banner declared, "Continue to Defame the People and the Courts of Georgia." The "Jerusalem friend" who merited the nastiest reproof was R. H. Macy & Company chairman Nathan Straus. By the Sage's lights, Straus had committed two unpardonable offenses. First, he'd told the *"New York Hebrew American"*—as Watson now referred to Hearst's morning New York paper—that he'd never been prouder of his native state than when its governor commuted Frank's death sentence. Then he had encouraged Nathan Jr. to publish an article in *Puck* asserting that Frank's vindication would not be won until "Thomas Watson, the very embodiment of the beast in looks, manners, and conduct" was behind bars. Watson retaliated by giving conspicuous play to what he billed as an anonymous letter:

Atlanta, Ga. July 9th 1915

Dear Sir:

I note that one Nathan Straus claims to be a Georgian, and puts a great deal of stress upon that fact.

About one year ago, I spent some weeks in New York, and you know that this same Nathan Straus owns a very large retail store on the corner of Broadway and Thirty-fourth street, and that he also conducts a big restaurant on the eighth floor of the building. Mr. Straus owns the building and the merchandise. I was greatly surprised on entering this restaurant, which is a very large one, to find that negroes were being served at regular tables, and that white girls were compelled to wait on them.

I mean that they have a large number of white girls who serve as waitresses, and that it is not infrequent to see a bunch of negroes go into this restaurant that belongs to Nathan Straus and take any table they choose and be served by white girls.

This condition does not exist in any first-class hotel or boarding-house in the city of New York, outside of this store. I would not write you concerning this matter except for the fact that I want the Southern people to know the kind of place Mr. Straus is conducting.

"I am, yours very truly,
        ATLANTA."

Straus, of course, was not the only Jew whose conduct in the affair had incensed Watson, and he also assailed the *Times*'s Ochs, the *World*'s Pulitzer and the *Boston Traveler*'s Brin. Indeed, so furious was the Sage at Frank's coreligionists that he concluded this diatribe with one of his most provocative discourses to date:

> The question is—
> *Do the rich Jews want to create among the Gentiles of this country the same deep dislike which they have created everywhere else?*
> There must be some general cause for the universal feeling against the Jews in Spain, in France, in Russia, in Poland, and in Hungary.
> *What is that cause?*
> Why is it that all Caucasian races, in the Old World, are "prejudiced" against the Jew?
> Having had no such "prejudice" ourselves, we have freely welcomed the immigrant Hebrew, and given him a *National House of Refuge.*
> If they destroy the friendly relations that have always existed between us, where do they expect to go?
> If they continue their rancorous and villainous abuse of the people who wanted Leo Frank punished for his awful crime, they will raise a tempest which they cannot control.
> *Do they want it?*
> Is this lewd, loathsome murderer worth the price?

The *Jeffersonian*'s readers thus put wise to the Jews—and the Jews thus put on notice—Watson yet again reviewed the evidence against Frank: the bloody shirt "planted" at Newt Lee's, the strands of "Mary's" hair discovered on the factory lathe and Monteen Stover's "damning" testimony.

In the end, though, Watson was less concerned with the past than with the future, for as he saw it, Frank's supporters would now conspire to get Jim Conley *"TO TAKE THE WHOLE CRIME UPON HIS SHOULDERS."* As it was written in the *Jeffersonian*:

> Conley is out and Conley is poor and Conley loves liquor and Conley can be made to see ghosts and Burns can use on Conley one of the negro detectives and one of the negro "witch doctors" that Burns boasts of using to scare negro witnesses in railroad cases.
>
> As soon as [Burns] thinks it safe to recommence his infamous operations, you will see the Atlanta dailies blossom out into 2-inch headlines, as they did when William M. Smith announced that *he* would expose his client and show the world that the negro alone committed the crime.
>
> There will be a "confession" from Jim; and Jim will be following Slaton's trunks on the way to the Setting Sun, and the filthy Sodomite will dis-

appear from the State Farm to resume his pursuit of little Gentile girls in cities remote from Atlanta.

By mid-July, Watson was in continuous eruption. It was as if a fissure had opened up inside his brain from which malevolent lampoons, bigoted maunderings, special pleadings, paranoid fantasies and, to give him his due, the occasional stinging insight or perversely pithy utterance convulsively geysered. Not surprisingly, numerous Georgians responded approvingly, among them many who had previously shunned the Sage but had lately become converts because, explained one, "his was the only paper in Georgia that protected our State from the slanders of the Northern press." The *Jeffersonian*'s circulation, which prior to the beginning of its anti-Frank crusade just over a year earlier had stood at 25,000, was now nearing 87,000. As C. Vann Woodward would later note, stacks of Watson's sheet "melted like snowflakes" in Atlanta, Savannah, Columbus and Augusta, while in small towns eager crowds met incoming trains bearing the latest issues.

Such was the atmosphere when John Tucker Dorsey arrived in Milledgeville the morning of July 12. Accompanied by a large contingent of legislators, and by Commissioners Rainey, Davison and Patterson, the penitentiary committee chairman made a show of performing his official duties. He inspected the prison farm's Negro and female dormitories and its sewage disposal site. Then he interviewed inmates, among them an unwitting Leo Frank. ("The Prison Committee of the State Legislature were here today," Frank wrote Lucille. "I met many of the representatives and spoke to them.") Afterward, Dorsey repaired to the warden's office to confer with Smith, Superintendent Burke and the commissioners—the men whose cooperation was essential if the lynch party was to avoid an armed confrontation with the guards.

Dorsey's meeting with the prison officials was almost surely marked by discord. While Burke, if his behavior during the convict lease hearings is any indication, was unlikely to have opposed the Mariettans' scheme, and while Davison and Rainey had already voted once against clemency, Patterson and Smith were different stories. Patterson, of course, had championed Frank's cause during the prison commission hearings. And as for Smith, the courtesy he had shown Frank was evidently genuine. As his daughter Rebekah, an Atlanta lawyer, recalled 82 years later: "My father believed Frank was innocent."

Yet whatever the conflicting sympathies among the men who sat across from Dorsey, they were united by a single reality—each of them could be politically and personally ruined if held responsible for the prison farm's shortcomings. As the penitentiary committee chairman was uniquely suited to make plain to them, they could either protect Frank and endanger their livelihoods, even face prosecution, or at the appointed hour they could instruct guards to look the other way and retain their positions.

Following several hours of negotiations, some sort of agreement was reached. Upon emerging from the session, Dorsey unequivocally absolved the prison officials of any culpability in the matter that had putatively brought him to Milledgeville. "Conditions at the farm are deplorable," he told a *Journal* reporter, but "the prison commission should be exonerated of any blame. For the last four years, they have called attention to these conditions in writing, and they have predicted an epidemic of typhoid fever. But they cannot install a sewage system and a pure water supply without money. The legislature alone is to blame for its niggardly and stingy policy."

For Herbert Clay, Fred Morris, Bolan Brumby, Governor Joe Brown and Judge Newt Morris, this was extraordinary news—the lynch party would be given safe passage into and out of the prison farm. During the past weeks, the band of 25 had made a trial run between Marietta and Milledgeville, learning which roads were passable while greasing the palms of various sheriffs. Cars were gassed, guns loaded, alibis (something about a fishing trip) concocted and resolves firmed. Black Newt and company were ready, and before day's end they would receive their orders. Barring an unanticipated eventuality, Leo Frank would be dead in 36 hours.

Sometime early on the morning of July 13, a telephone rang at the headquarters of the Georgia state militia in Atlanta. According to Adjutant General J. Van Holt Nash, the guard's commanding officer, the voice on the other end of the line belonged to "an authoritative source in Marietta" calling to report that an "organized crowd" of Cobb Countians was "preparing to travel in automobiles tonight to Milledgeville." As one of the lynching brethren afterward confessed, "a leak" had occurred. This was the unanticipated eventuality.

The official response to the intelligence was swift and forceful. Nash wired Macon, ordering three militia companies to muster at the armory. Meantime, a Central of Georgia train was put in readiness at the Macon station. Simultaneously, Governor Nat Harris, whom Nash had also notified, was directing the captain of Milledgeville's guard unit to call out his troops. And Fulton County sheriff Wheeler Mangum, who'd been alerted as well, was dispatching deputies to patrol the roads between Atlanta and Marietta.

Confronted with this show of force, the Mariettans aborted their mission, whereupon a peculiar calm descended on Georgia, one during which the state's power structure refused to address the magnitude of what had nearly transpired. Yes, the story made the front pages. And yes, the custodians of law and order made the expected noises. "If anyone thinks they can go to Milledgeville or even the adjacent vicinity and start something without encountering the military, they'll be sadly mistaken," vowed General Nash. But in the main, the actual facts of the matter went unreported. Neither the *Georgian* nor the *Journal* devoted more than two inches to the episode, and while the *Constitution*'s account was somewhat longer, it stressed that all was now "quiet as usual." The prize for circumvention, however, went to the *Macon Telegraph,* which discounted the threat altogether, declaring: "The entire affair appears to be based on a 'rumor' which seems to have no head."

The reasons for the general unwillingness to confront the truth were various and tangled. At first, Frank's lawyers and his allies in the press seemed simply dumbstruck. Then, once the shock wore off, they decided that to speak out at this point would do nothing but provide fodder for Watson. Thus they told themselves that the militia's decisive action had put the fear of the Lord in the individuals who'd been behind the plot. As Henry Alexander confided to Frank a day after the news broke: "I am hoping that things are quieting down."

Meanwhile in Marietta, the men whose best laid plans had been thwarted possessed their own motives for keeping mum. Most obviously, they wanted to avoid implicating themselves. More significant was this: They were not going to jeopardize another try at a later date, for far from being cowed by the guard, they were outraged. Indeed, some of them were so furious at having been denied satisfaction that they came close to demonstrating on the town square. "While the parties were on their way to the courthouse," Governor Harris later revealed, "somebody was kind enough to say: 'We had better go slow about this matter; an investigation will result and the truth will come out and the truth will show that the Governor was right [to intervene].' So the meeting was abandoned."

Yet quite apart from the conflicting factors that led all involved to clam up, there was finally a simpler explanation for the silence. Before anyone could address what had nearly happened in Milledgeville, something did happen there.

The afternoon of Saturday, July 17, found Leo Frank in cheerful conversation with his wife. Lucille had arrived in Milledgeville three days earlier, and she'd spent several hours at the prison farm each day since. Though the couple had devoted some of the time to pondering the menacing portents, they'd passed most of it gossiping and laughing. Lucille had gone on and on about her in-laws. "If I ever saw an overgrown boy," she'd written just before leaving Athens, "it's Uncle Bud. He's the limit. I'll tell you more when I see you." In the same vein, Leo had talked endlessly about his perennial bachelor friend Milton Klein, who'd recently astounded everyone in their circle by marrying, and about his sister, who earlier in the summer had given birth to her second child. And so the visit had proceeded. For a moment, it was as if there had been no murder, no trial, no outcry, and they were back in Atlanta, secure in their small world. As Frank put it at week's end in a letter to Anne Carroll Moore: "You know how comforting and pleasurable it is to me to have my wife near."

Around 6 P.M. Saturday, Lucille returned to the rambling white farmhouse on the edge of the prison grounds where she was staying as the guest of Superintendent Burke, leaving Leo to eat with his fellow inmates, then retire to his cot, which was located near the front of the barracks. At 9, lights dimmed. A trusty posted at the door kept watch inside, while an armed guard stood sentinel outside.

Shortly after 11, a convicted murderer named William Creen—whose bunk was four removed from Frank's—called to the trusty, asking permission to speak to him. Permission granted, Creen rose to his feet carrying what looked to be nothing more than a folded newspaper and made his way toward the door. When he reached Frank's side, he halted, gazed down at the sleeping man, who lay on his right shoulder, then, without warning, struck. Driving a knee into Frank's chest to pin him to the mattress, Creen drew a butcher knife from its hiding place and raked it across his victim's throat with a quick, jerky sweep.

Leo Frank's scream awakened the dormitory, and the lights stammered on to reveal a confusing and gory scene. Creen, who remained on top of the startled man, was preparing to strike a second blow, while Frank, both arms outstretched, blood spurting from his neck, was attempting to fend off his assailant. For a second, the pair remained so embraced. Then the trusty, assisted by several inmates, wrestled Creen to the floor. A moment later, medical help appeared in the persons of two other inmates.

J. W. McNaughton and L. M. Harris, both doctors, needed but one look at Frank to recognize the severity of his wound. Seven and a half inches in length, it ran from beneath his left ear to the other side of the Adam's apple. Unless they acted, Frank would die right there, so they picked him up and carried him to the nearby prison hospital. There, McNaughton identified the most immediately life-threatening injury: a severed external jugular vein.

By the time Dr. Guy Compton, the prison physician, arrived from his home in Milledgeville some fifteen minutes later, McNaughton had completed the tricky task of ligating the jugular. Yet even at that, Frank had lost so much blood that the first thing Compton did was insert an IV and start a saline drip. Then he operated. Luckily for Frank, neither his windpipe nor his carotid artery had been cut, though both had been laid bare. Still, it took two hours for the physician, assisted by McNaughton and Harris, to close the opening, then dress a nasty wound to the right hand suffered during the scuffle. Throughout, Frank remained conscious. "Am I going to die?" he asked at one point. Replied Compton: "We don't know." To which Frank stoically rejoined: "If I am going to die, I am not afraid. Nothing stands between me and God."

Not long before sunrise, Compton—accompanied by the Macon doctors W. A. Little and Harry Moses, who had been called in to consult—emerged to issue a statement to the press. The procedure had been a success, but Frank was in critical condition. Any number of complications ranging from blood poisoning to hemorrhaging could prove fatal. To assist in the patient's care, Lucille would soon summon Dr. Howard Rosenberg, the family physician, from Atlanta.

Sunday dawned with William Creen chained by his feet to a post at the rear of the barracks. Reedy and mustachioed, he presented both a pathetic picture and a puzzle.

From the outset, opinions varied as to Creen's motivations for attacking Frank. Of all the prison farm's inmates, he was one of the few who could truly be called a pathological killer. Reputedly responsible for several deaths for which he was never tried and admittedly the slayer of a man in an incident that was ruled self-defense, the 42-year-old Creen was serving a life sentence for the 1913 murder of a South Georgia insurance agent. He had shot his victim between the eyes solely because the man had asked him to stop cursing a group of boys. Initially, Creen had attempted to avoid prison by pleading insanity. A couple of years earlier, while working on a construction crew erecting a bridge over the Chattahoochee River, he'd taken a bad fall, suffering a concussion. He "hadn't been right since," argued his lawyer. A panel of alienists, however, declared Creen competent to stand trial, although following conviction he was judged too feeble for the chain gang and sentenced to Milledgeville. Even so, Warden Smith had instructed guards to refrain from angering Creen. He wasn't the sort one wanted to get worked up—unless, of course, it was with a purpose in mind.

Thus the conflicting theories. One maintained that Creen was demented and had acted alone. The other held that he was demented but had functioned as "the tool of others." Either way, in the hours following the incident, all anyone could say for certain was that he'd stolen a knife from the prison kitchen (at first, the press erroneously reported that the implement had been used to slaughter hogs) and slipped it past the guards. That this was the extent of the credible information was due in large part to Creen himself who, after telling a *Journal* reporter, "I only wish that I had had more strength," announced he would not speak again unless granted an audience with Governor Harris.

Though the attack on Leo Frank occasioned banner headlines, the reaction—at least from newspapers that had heretofore been in the victim's camp—was both spotty and irresolute. Neither the *Georgian* nor the *Journal,* each displaying the same paralysis that had seized them following the stillborn raid on the prison, uttered a word editorially. Meanwhile, the assault brought to the surface deep internal divisions at the *New York Times.* On July 19, Garet Garrett noted in his diary: "We almost shudder, not at the cruelty of Frank's situation, but at the pathetic, tragic necessity of keeping up the talk about it . . . Mr. O[chs] must know that the Times has printed altogether too much Frank stuff." Yet over the objections of those around him, Ochs, his faith in Frank's innocence undiminished, directed one of Garrett's colleagues to "write something." The result:

> The latest development in the case of Frank, who is believed by thousands of his fellow countrymen to be a cruelly persecuted man, will stir the public sympathy and increase the amazement and regret that the unreasonable show of public feeling against him in Georgia has caused. While bravely serving his sentence, he is set upon by a fellow-convict, armed with a murderous weapon such as no dangerous prisoner should be permitted to handle at any time. This man, Creen, has a record of three murders. He was clearly a dangerous convict, one with a passion for killing. That he should have been allowed freedom of movement in prison speaks ill for the discipline at Milledgeville; that he should have had a chance to secrete a sharp knife for use in his premeditated attack seems incredible. To look for the motive of Creen is not necessary. He was a man of murderous instincts, and though a prisoner and nominally under strict surveillance he had an opportunity to gratify them.

Deliberate and dutiful, this was not so much condemnation as it was testimony to the harsh reality that after a year and a half of beating the drum, many *Times* staffers felt enough was enough.

Ultimately, a few pro-Frank publications—among them the *New York World* and the *New Republic*—would speak out strongly. Yet for the most part, there was simply the muffled sound of partisans in retreat.

The editorial response from publications that had no use for Frank was, on the other hand, unanimously forceful. It was also astonishingly hostile, an antagonism heightened by the fact that in the attack's immediate after-math, the *Macon Telegraph* printed an interview with a newly released convict who accused prison officials of coddling their famous inmate. According to George Johnston, who'd been sent up for theft, Frank "was treated over there as though he was the warden's brother, just on a little social visit. No guy with money ever goes to work on that place, friend. They lie around and have an easy time. They live pretty well, those with money. Take Frank, for instance. He's had a big roller top desk moved in and he spends the whole day writing at it and working on his own business, I guess." Johnston's charges, though they conveyed an underlying truth, were false in their particulars (Frank, of course, did perform duties, while the sole desk on the premises belonged to Warden Smith), and the *Telegraph* eventually ran a correction. But by then, it was too late, the allegations having been reprinted by papers across Georgia, usually with accompanying commentaries. One of the ugliest of them appeared in the *Cherokee Advance*, a weekly published just up the road from Marietta in Canton, another hotbed of anti-Frank sentiment. Not only did the *Advance* reproach the wounded man for the privileges he'd allegedly received before the assault, it reproached him for the quality of medical care he'd received in its wake:

> The fight between Creen and Frank is one thing, the treatment accorded Frank after the accident is quite another. We are told that there is no discrimination in the treatment of prisoners in good standing at the state farm whether he be a rich Jew or whether he be an unfortunate wretch without a penny in the world. The daily news from Milledgevile tells us that Dr. Compton, prison physician, has consented to take personal charge of Frank's case at all times. He has associated with him Dr. Rosenberg, Frank's family physician, of Atlanta, Dr. Harris, a prisoner at the farm, and Dr. McNaughton. The dispatches add that two noted doctors from Macon were rushed to Milledgeville shortly after the cutting.
>
> This treatment is quite at variance with that received by other inmates.
>
> The *Advance* is in no sense bloodthirsty and is certainly always anxious and willing to give first aid to the injured, but we are not convinced that Leo Frank should be shown any more consideration than hundreds of other poor unfortunate wretches who—if we are to believe reports—are simply dying by inches in a horrible hole without money and without friends.

Heartless as such remarks were, no country editor was going to beat Tom Watson at his own game. For the Sage, this most recent incident offered up a gift coveted by all demagogues: a bit of information—or, better, misinformation—that can be twisted to one's own ends. In the present instance, that godsend was the inaccurate initial report that Creen's knife had been used to slaughter swine. Watson employed the falsehood to taunt Jews in general and Macy's chairman Nathan Straus (whose son's magazine had again lambasted Watson) in particular. Proclaimed the *Jeffersonian*'s July 22 leader:

> Note: The butcher-knife used had been in operation during the day *killing hogs.*
>
> Nathan Straus can make a memorandum of *that.*
>
> Kosher!

Contemptuous and derisive, these few lines cut, in their way, more savagely than Creen's blade, violating not a body but a faith.

As the final, sun-blasted days of the Georgia July receded, Leo Frank lay coughing and shivering in the prison hospital. Initially, with his temperature at 102 degrees and his wound puffy and seeping, his physicians had been guarded, terming his condition "very, very serious." Yet even as early as Sunday afternoon, Dr. Compton told his patient, "You have a good chance." To this, Frank, his voice barely audible, his senses dulled by opiates, had replied: "I must live. I must vindicate myself."

Frank's recovery was not, though, going to be easy. As his first visitors—among them Henry Alexander, Rabbi David Marx, Lucille's uncle Bud and several members of the press—discovered, he was extremely weak. Observed the *Journal*'s Linton Starr:

> Frank recognized one correspondent by holding out his bandaged right hand. He smiled bravely and called the correspondent's name. The whispered greeting started his cough and he was permitted to say nothing further.

Nonetheless, just 72 hours after the attack, Frank was strong enough to be moved from the prison hospital to the small room next to the warden's office where he'd previously conducted his correspondence. Here, monitored by doctors and watched over by Lucille, he would convalesce in a bed set up for that purpose. Precluding any unexpected complications, reported his physicians, Frank would pull through, and the credit, they agreed, belonged to a fellow convict, one who'd once before helped buy time for him. As Dr. Rosenberg freely acknowledged: "Dr. McNaughton saved Frank's life."

The same day most Georgians learned that Leo Frank would survive ("Frank's Condition Steadily Improving," read the *Constitution*'s banner), John Tucker Dorsey waded into a packed conference room at the state capitol in Atlanta for a meeting of the House penitentiary committee. At the top of the agenda were a number of legislative resolutions demanding that the Prison Commission investigate whether William Creen had acted alone or at the behest of others. From Dorsey's vantage, no good could come of any inquiry that raised the specter of an outside conspiracy. Hence, shortly after he gaveled the session to order, he tabled the resolutions, ceding the floor to an ally who introduced a motion to give the penitentiary committee the authority to conduct the probe. Dorsey threw his weight behind the proposal, for if it was enacted, he could at least run the show, shielding himself and others from exposure. Not that he allowed as much for public consumption, contending instead: "To let the commission do the investigating means that we turn the case over to their own jury." Yet despite Dorsey's efforts, his committee—the majority believing the law left them without recourse—voted 14 to 9 against him. Several hours later, Chairman Davison announced that at week's end, he and his commissioners would journey to Milledgeville. The next morning, Governor Harris declared that he would accompany the men.

To the lynching brethren, Dorsey's failure to take control of the Creen inquiry constituted another setback. Now, in just five days, a group of newly emboldened prison commissioners and, more ominously, the governor, would be at the prison farm asking questions. Yet Herbert Clay, Judge Newt Morris, former governor Brown and the others were not about to be deterred. Animated by the same convictions that had spurred them from the start and too deeply enmeshed to back down, they intended to see this thing through until the end.

Thus it was that the Cobb Countians undertook to wire the Creen investigation. As they'd done in the past, they would generally operate behind the scenes. Yet there's no doubt as to the cards they held. Nor is there any doubt as to the identities of those against whom they would play them.

At this juncture, Governor Harris presented the greatest stumbling block in the Mariettans' path. Not only had he helped derail the initial raid, he had come out early on against vigilantism. All this notwithstanding, the governor wasn't the insurmountable barrier to prejudice and violence that he seemed. To begin with, it was Harris's perceived unwillingness to give Frank a fair shake that had set off the scramble to convene the clemency hearings prior to the expiration of Slaton's term. Moreover, since taking office, Harris had already proved that he was unwilling to place himself between a group of influential toughs and a terrorized Jew. The relevant incident had occurred in the little municipality of Canton. There, a mob said to have included the mayor and the sheriff had ordered merchant Sam Cohen to get out of town. When Cohen didn't oblige, the rowdies smashed in his storefront. Later, they tied a stick of dynamite to his door. It was then that a gentile friend of Cohen's beseeched Harris to intercede:

> We believe it is time that strenuous steps were being taken to investigate this matter and place the blame on the guilty parties.
>
> It is the general opinion that men higher up in Canton are at the head of this gang of law breakers and we believe that this Jew is entitled to protection and the peaceable pursuit of his trade as well as others here in town, and we want to implore you to take immediate action to clear up this outrage and prosecute the guilty parties.

Through his secretary, Harris replied:

> Governor Harris duly received your special delivery letter of July the seventh, and at the same time had a call from Mr. Cohen . . .
>
> Under the Constitutional limitations, the Governor must act in cases of this kind according to certain specified forms.
>
> If you can furnish sufficient evidence to the effect that the Sheriff and Mayor are in a conspiracy to intimidate Mr. Cohen, or to do him violence, the matter could then be taken before the Grand Jury or presented to the Legislature.
>
> If you will lay the evidence upon which your belief is founded, as expressed in your letter, before the Governor, he will be glad to suggest the proper procedure.

Harris's message couldn't have been much clearer—Cohen and his would-be savior were on their own.

But even if Governor Harris had been made of sterner stuff, the lynching brethren would have possessed ample reason to believe they could bend him to their collective will, for they had ties to him via both the ballot box and a son-in-law. For starters, Harris never would have been elected had it not been for Tom Watson. At a pivotal moment of the 1914 campaign, the Sage had endorsed Harris, and just as former governor Brown remained hostage to a similar favor, so, too, did he. Ultimately, though, the Cobb County boys were linked to Harris through family—the governor's youngest daughter, Fannie, was married to Herbert Clay's best friend. Campbell Wallace, Jr., was secretary of the state's powerful railroad commission, and he and the former Fannie Harris lived around the corner from the Clays. As leading members of Marietta society, the couples regularly mixed, often entertaining together. It was all quite cozy and, for Leo Frank, terribly inauspicious.

Splendid a hand as the Mariettans held, they couldn't just strong-arm a governor, and in the days leading up to the investigation into the Creen incident, they applied pressure only obliquely. They would not be so subtle when it came to those other potentially troubling individuals—the prison commissioners. Bluntly put, they would attempt to buy them. Which was why during this same week, John Tucker Dorsey asked the legislature to appropriate $30,000 for the construction of a sewage plant and new dormitories for Negro and female inmates at the prison farm.

Governor Harris spent the night before the inquiry at his family home in Macon, making the short trip to Milledgeville early the next morning with Commissioner Rainey, Adjutant General Nash and John Tucker Dorsey. Commissioners Davison and Patterson, who'd arrived a day before, and Warden Smith met the men at the train station, and by 6:15, they were all sitting down to a country breakfast at Superintendent Burke's house.

Significantly, the statehouse types invited the numerous reporters gathered at the prison farm to cover the probe to eat with them. For those calling the shots, the care and feeding of these boys—who included the *Journal*'s Starr, the *Constitution*'s Ned McIntosh and a young scrapper named John W. Hammond, who ran a one-man Atlanta bureau serving the *Macon Telegraph* and the *Augusta Chronicle*—was paramount. This was not a time to take the press for granted.

The first order of business was to familiarize Governor Harris with the penitentiary. As he'd never before visited the place, the idea was not without merit. Yet from the outset, the undertaking itself felt scripted. In fact, whether the investigators were touring barracks or tromping over the grounds, they met with encounters that seemed designed to make the story other than what it was. At the tubercular ward, for instance, a group of emaciated inmates begged Harris for pardons so they "could go home to die." The reporters could not take notes fast enough. Even more piteous—and more diverting—was six-year-old Bessie Stripling's plea to the governor. As the men approached the main dormitory, the girl, whose father was serving a life sentence, ran up to Harris, tugged at his sleeve and asked: "Won't you please turn my papa loose? He is sick and there is nobody to work for us at home." Visibly moved, the governor patted the child on the head and promised to grant her wish.

In the end, however, Creen could not be avoided, and around noon, the delegation was shown to the cot to which he was now chained.

> "Creen, have you told your story?" asked Harris.
> "No," Frank's assailant replied.
> "Are you ready to tell it now?"
> "Yes, I'll tell it to you."

And that, as John W. Hammond pointedly observed, "was the entire extent of the 'open' investigation." The rest of the inquiry would be held behind closed doors.

The parts of the probe that mattered, then, were conducted free from reportorial scrutiny. As armed guards stood watch outside the warden's office, Harris and Nash alone questioned Creen. After an hour or so, the man was led away, and the prison commissioners rejoined the group. After debriefing Warden Smith, the party made its way to the room where Frank was recovering. The intention was to quiz him, too, but as he was still having trouble speaking, the investigators could do no more than observe doctors dress his wound.

When it was all over, the governor reconvened the newspapermen and announced the inquiry's findings: Creen had acted of his own accord, motivated not by outside forces but, oddly enough, by opposition to them. "He said he had heard a great deal of talk by the people in the prison of the danger that would come to the place if Frank was kept here," Harris asserted. "He said he knew from what he had read from the papers that there was danger of an attack on the place by a mob; that if the attack was made the mob would shoot through the windows and a lot of people would be killed; that the guards would shoot at the mob and there would be a lot of killing on both sides. He said he thought that over and came to the conclusion that it would be his duty to save the people here from danger."

With that, Governor Harris was finished with the task that had brought him to Milledgeville, yet there was one other matter to address. Like every other official who'd inspected the prison farm that summer, he was appalled by its many inadequacies, and in closing, he vowed to ask the legislature to appropriate a hefty $50,000 for improvements.

From John Tucker Dorsey's perspective, the day could hardly have gone better, and the headlines atop the next morning's Atlanta papers were better still. GOVERNOR TOUCHED BY THE SAD PLIGHT OF MANY CONVICTS, declared the *Constitution*. GOV. HARRIS TO ASK $50,000 FOR BUILDING AT THE STATE FARM, roared the *Journal.* In sum, the reporters downplayed the investigation, preferring instead to emphasize Harris's humane response to the inmates' benighted living conditions. True, there was no reason for the press to doubt the governor's determination that Creen had been an independent operator. Frank's assailant *was* too unstable to have been enlisted by a conspiracy. Still, the *Constitution*'s account didn't even mention the inquiry until an inside page. And as for any discussion of the plot actually afoot, it went unrecorded.

There was, however, one dissenting voice, and it belonged to John W. Hammond. In a dispatch that dominated front pages in both Augusta and Macon, Hammond noted:

> So far as what caused the attack on Leo M. Frank by William Creen is concerned, whether or not there were surrounding circumstances which might have thrown a different light on what the public knows or has read of the affair; why Creen was so situated that he should be able to smuggle a knife into the sleeping quarters of a lot of convicts, I know no more now than I did before I came to Milledgeville. In fact, if there was any investigation of the attack on Leo M. Frank at the state farm today, I can't say of my personal knowledge.
>
> I am sorry that I can't write other—concerning the "investigation"—than that it was a frost. There wasn't any investigation as the public would expect an investigation to be; there wasn't anything brought out, as the public naturally expected would be.
>
> In the end was there reason to promise the public an "investigation"?

Upon returning to Atlanta, the various state officials who had participated in the Creen inquiry vigorously attacked Hammond's piece. Asserted the governor: "My reason for not allowing the press to hear Creen's statement" was that he "stated positively that he would tell his story to no one except the governor." Meanwhile, Prison Commission chairman Davison dismissed the article as "absurd."

Yet even had the authorities said nothing, it's unlikely that the story would have prompted much of an uproar, for in the wake of the investigation there was no longer anyone at the capitol with both the power and the inclination to look into Hammond's charges. Indeed, there was now no longer anyone with the power and the inclination to forestall the lynching brethren.

Whatever Governor Harris may have thought of Frank prior to visiting the prison farm, he left disliking the man. Though there were immediately rumors to this effect—among them, a pernicious and utterly unfounded one circulated by Watson maintaining that "Creen told Governor Harris he cut Frank because Frank had tried to sodomize *him*"—it would be ten years before Harris confirmed them in print. In his memoirs, he revealed the determining moment:

> I went into [Frank's] room while the doctor was dressing the wound. The gash extended from ear to ear and was so frightful in appearance that I wondered at his being alive. While the doctor was washing the wound Frank coughed, and I asked the doctor immediately, with a good deal of sympathy in my voice: "Won't that wound attack his lungs before it heals?" When I asked this, Frank laughed—a queer sort of laugh—a laugh that showed, at least to me, a hard, careless heart, and the doubt, which I had about his guilt, was lessened greatly, as I heard the laugh, and looked into his face.

Though there is no evidence that Harris's negative impression of Frank led him to endorse the Mariettans' plan, there was no need for him to endorse it. All he had to do was stay out of the way.

General Nash also seems to have departed the prison farm resigned to the inevitable, chiefly because Harris was. Not only had the governor just reappointed Nash as head of the state militia, but the governor's oldest son, Walter, served as the general's liaison to the legislature. In short, the sole Georgians authorized to order out the guard in the event of a raid on Milledgeville were a yoked team, one for which others held the reins.

Finally, just four days after the Creen probe, the general assembly signed off, too, approving a $30,000 appropriation for the prison farm. Plainly, many of the legislators were blind to the hidden agenda here. The money would, after all, pay for much-needed brick and mortar. But in truth, the vote marked the denouement of the intrigue that had begun over a month earlier with John Tucker Dorsey's appointment as chairman of the penitentiary committee. The conspirators had succeeded in getting the state to finance what would now come to pass. Georgia was going into the lynching business.

Having twice been reprieved, first by a besieged governor, then by a physician convicted of murder, Leo Frank believed he owed his life to nothing less than divine intervention. "Thanks be to God, I am recovering nicely," he began an early-August letter to Dan Lehon, the Burns detective who'd nearly met his own demise investigating the case. "It was indeed providential that good medical help was so near at hand. At that, the doctors say my recovery is marvelous. Surely, God has let me live and aided me in this dark hour for a brighter day, which must be near at hand."

Though Frank was still being attended by three physicians, his wife had now largely assumed day-to-day responsibility for his care. Lucille, who'd taken up residence at the Alfords', arrived at the prison farm early each morning and was ushered into the room adjacent to the warden's office where Leo continued to recuperate. There, after bathing and feeding her husband, she sorted through his correspondence, deciding which merited a personal reply and which could be answered with a mimeographed letter. Then, she sat by his bed, holding his hand. "Mrs. Frank has been, in this painful ordeal, my ministering angel," the wounded man confided to Lehon.

Unbeknownst to Leo, once Lucille was done with her nursing duties, she spent the day's remaining hours working as his ambassador. In this, she was following the instructions of Herbert Haas, who after it was certain that Frank would live had written her:

> In as much as Leo is at the farm, you must continue to do all in your power to win the friendship and kindness of those who are in charge, not for the purpose of getting anything beyond what is Leo's due and right, but in order that there may be no hesitancy about his getting it. It . . . depends on you, and I have every confidence in your ability to handle well the situation. Do not let Leo read this letter.

Lucille also handled another extremely sensitive matter—Leo's finances. Fearful of calling attention to the fact that her husband's medical care was being underwritten by northern Jews, she paid doctors from her own account, which Herbert Haas replenished whenever Albert Lasker mailed a check. Haas, who'd been the most cautious of Frank's lawyers, was so intent on disguising the actual source of this funding that when Lucille used a Yiddishism for money in a communication to him, he forcefully rebuked her:

> Please, in the future, do not write on a postal card anything like the word "muzzumah." You cannot be too careful.

By this point, though, one word on the back of a postcard wasn't going to increase the anti-Semitism rampant in Georgia—especially not with Hal Reid's movie premiering in New York.

Prosaically entitled *Leo M. Frank and Governor Slaton,* the picture was both a documentary and a distortion. Here were the first moving images of the dramatis personae of the tale that had so long captivated America. Yet vivid as the shots were, there was no effort at balance, no mention of troubling facts or of Slaton's conflict of interests. In other words, this was just the movie its subject had wanted—and exactly the one New Yorkers wanted to see. Extolled *Variety*'s critic: "Remarkable." Hoping to capitalize on the extensive coverage the case had received, the Loew's chain promoted the picture as THE MILLION DOLLAR PUBLICITY FEATURE! and booked it into eight theaters, including ones at Lincoln and Greeley Squares and on Avenue B.

Yet however favorably Yankees reacted to Reid's movie, the sole Southern reviewer whose opinion counted—Tom Watson—viewed it as yet another insult. Had the Sage confined his commentary to the picture's lack of objectivity, his critique would have been justifiable, but instead, he once again vented his animus against Frank's coreligionists. "Why Do They Keep Up the Big Money Campaign Against the People and the Courts of Georgia?" asked the headline atop the August 12 *Jeffersonian,* beneath which Watson scornfully explained:

> There is a Moving Picture circuit controlled by Marcus Loew.
>
> Marcus is doubtless a worthy descendant of Moses.
>
> Like most gentlemen from Jerusalem, Marcus loves money, and never knows what it is to get enough.
>
> Marcus is advertising Jack Slaton as an asset in his business, and is evidently expecting to coin many ducats thereby.
>
> Perhaps the rich Jews believe that they are entitled to get some of their money back—the money which gave Burns a front-page display for more than a year and then gave Slaton an army and a war-zone of his own.
>
> Marcus Loew advertises in *The Billboard* his new attraction, which he aptly terms,
>
> *"The Million Dollar Publicity Feature."*

Israel's true ends thereby further enumerated, Watson brought his peroration to a resounding—and familiar—finish:

> Let the rich Jews beware!
> *THE NEXT JEW WHO DOES WHAT FRANK DID IS GOING TO GET EXACTLY THE SAME THING THAT WE GIVE TO NEGRO RAPISTS!*

This same week, former governor Joseph Brown—in a position paper published in the *Macon Telegraph*—echoed the Sage's clarion call: The time had come for "the people to form mobs."

Monday, August 16, dawned oppressively hot in Milledgeville—by midday, the temperature had hit 90 degrees inside the prison barracks. Yet despite the weather, Leo Frank's spirits were soaring. Nearly a month had passed since Creen's attack, and the patient was well on his way to a full recovery.

Sitting at the table in the room next to the warden's office, wearing only a white, monogrammed nightshirt, he wrote *Collier's* C. P. Connolly:

> I have gained and am gaining right along in strength. My appetite is good and I sleep well. I can move my head and neck (within limitations) reasonably well for the time being and this will improve a whole lot in the course of a few weeks. My wound is all healed except in one little place where drainage still obtains. This also will be healed in a few days. In time, I think I will be all right again.

The prognosis out of the way, Frank devoted the remainder of the letter to the topic that prior to the knifing had loomed largest in his mind: the cause. Connolly's connections in New York publishing and politics were extensive, and Frank wanted to know everything, asking whether he'd spoken to Hal Reid or seen his movie ("He thought he could help") or read the latest *Puck* ("They sure stick it to Watson"). He also requested a favor. Connolly's *Collier's* articles had been published in hardback as *The Truth About the Frank Case,* and Frank hoped he would send Warden Smith ("a friend") an autographed copy.

Overjoyed to be once again engaged with the outside world, Frank wrote several other cheerful and inquisitive letters on this long, hot day. "How do you view the recent changes, unrest and present situation in Atlanta?" he asked Dr. Benjamin Wildauer. "I get the Journal daily but it is hard for me to glean anything therefrom. I know you are posted on the 'inside.' "

Undoubtedly, Frank understood the level of antipathy abroad in Georgia. In her last letter, his mother had written him:

> T.W. . . . is not ashamed nor afraid it seems to me; he has a criminal mind and perverted brains. There are . . . others in the same boat with him.

Yet he'd persuaded himself that the hostility would soon end, and that the fight for exoneration would resume. Indeed, he'd just received fresh ammunition from William Smith in the form of a box containing copies of Berry Benson's pamphlet arguing that Jim Conley had authored the murder notes and was thus Mary Phagan's killer. As Frank informed Dr. Wildauer, he was already putting the pamphlets to use:

> I am doing "missionary work" with them in Milledgeville . . . Bill wanted them given away.

Late in the afternoon, Lucille dropped by for a long visit. Tuesday, Leo was scheduled to rejoin the general prison population, and the two would have fewer chances to see each other. That notwithstanding, there was reason for happiness, and around five, Lucille returned to the Alfords', her heart lifting as well.

Not long after Frank's wife left, the prison commissioners arrived at the prison farm from Atlanta. Ostensibly, Rainey, Davison and Patterson had come to discuss the construction about to begin on the place. But in fact, they were there to do the lynching brethren's bidding, for even as dusk was descending, seven automobiles were racing south through the Georgia countryside toward Milledgeville.

Under the command of Black Newt Morris, George Daniell and Gordon Gann, the chosen 25 had departed Marietta during the afternoon on a staggered schedule so as not to attract attention. At a prearranged location, the drivers had reconnoitered and from there on, the group stuck together. Each of the vigilantes carried a rifle and a pistol; some wore goggles. Wire cutters and a box of explosives rode in one car, a thick manila rope with the noose already knotted in another.

Around nine, the cars reached the outskirts of the prison farm, where the electrician, Yellow Jacket Brown—who'd spent the past several days scouting about Milledgeville on his motorcycle noting the location of phone lines—was waiting. Shortly thereafter, phones throughout most of the town went dead.

TWENTY-ONE

The Lynching of Leo Frank

The roar of seven automobiles, headlights dimmed, tearing up the long prison farm drive so distressed a trusty named F. J. Turner that, as he later put it, he "exhausted every available energy and effort to prevail upon the night watchman in charge, Mr. Hester, to send Mr. Frank out the back way, under guard, as he would be protected." Hester, however, improbably rejoined that the vehicles carried joyriders, thus during the crucial seconds it took the cars to reach Superintendent Burke's house, he did nothing. When the lead car rolled to a halt and armed men bounded out, Turner was "then dead certain that it was a mob," and he again implored Hester to move Frank, but again to no avail. Shortly thereafter, Burke answered an insistent rapping on his door. As he subsequently related: "When I passed the threshold, two strong men grabbed me and in an instant snapped handcuffs on my wrists. Four others stood guard over me, two with shotguns and two with heavy pistols, and I was marched up to the penitentiary building." In the meantime, the rest of the party had proceeded to Warden Smith's home. There, roughly the same scenario was enacted, although once divested of his prized pump-action shotgun, Smith was allowed to remain with his terrified wife under the watchful eye of Lawrence Haney.

Though the Mariettans were entering what was ostensibly hostile territory, they approached the prison's barbed-wire-entangled gate with a bravura suggesting that they expected cooperation. Only two wore masks, and no one betrayed any anxiety. Yet lest anyone think they actually were paying a social call, they kept their guns trained on Burke, and upon reaching the entrance, they got busy with their wire cutters. Afterward, Tom Lawlater, the trusty encharged with the keys, told a reporter: "I saw they meant business, and there was nothing for me to do but open the gate."

Just that easily, then, the vigilantes were behind the walls. In the dark, the compound presented something of an obstacle course. But not only were the men carrying a map of the grounds, an insider had put them wise to the fact that Frank had yet to be returned to the general population. So after assuring a few startled prisoners that they meant them no harm, a designated contingent dashed up the steps of the main building, heading directly to the room adjacent to the warden's office where the star inmate was billeted and where they encountered their only resistance. This from a trusty who extinguished an oil lamp beside Frank's door.

"Come here with a match," a voice barked.

"I haven't got one," replied the trusty.

"Well, you had better get one damned quick," the voice insisted, its owner unholstering his pistol.

The lamp was immediately relit.

The group found Frank awake but still in bed, wearing his monogrammed white nightshirt. When he asked if he could dress, he was pointedly informed that where he was going, he wouldn't need clothes. He was then handcuffed and escorted to the stairs. There, two men took him by the arms, two by the legs and another by the hair, dragging him outside and throwing him into the rear of one of the waiting cars. As Frank, moaning from the rough treatment, stared up at his captors, they dangled the thick manila rope they'd carried with them in his face.

With that, the Mariettans' work at the farm was finished. As they piled back into their automobiles, one of their lieutenants announced that they intended to take Frank to Cobb County and hang him over Mary Phagan's grave. On the heels of this declaration, Burke asked to be uncuffed, but when told he'd have to accompany the party, he retorted, "Damned if I go anywhere with you." Whereupon someone fitting the description of Black Newt Morris (the *Georgian* reported that he brandished a whip) bellowed, "All right, boys; make for the swamps," and the seven cars, lights now blazing, sped off. All told, the vigilantes had needed but ten minutes to abduct the nation's most celebrated prisoner. Astonishingly, not a shot was fired. The only hitch was that in their haste, they'd forgotten Haney, the man assigned to cover Warden Smith. Hence no sooner had the automobiles turned onto the highway than two turned back, stopping at the warden's residence just long enough to reclaim their lost lamb. Then they were gone for good.

In the raid's immediate aftermath, Burke was joined in the prison yard by Smith and Commissioners Davison, Rainey and Patterson, and with varying degrees of sincerity, they went through the motions of mounting a response. But even if each of the men had been in earnest, they would have been unable to take action, for as they quickly discovered, the phone lines into Milledgeville had been cut. Similarly, the gas line of Smith's car had been slit. Eventually, some Negro inmates awakened the farm bookkeeper, who found a vehicle in working order and drove into town with the news—yet here, too, Yellow Jacket Brown had done his job, severing not just the phone lines leading to the homes of state militia captain J. H. Ennis and Baldwin County sheriff S. L. Terry but all except one of the long-distance lines connecting Milledgeville to the outside world. That lone line led to Augusta. Thus around midnight—two hours after the lynch party had departed—a bulletin was finally transmitted, and officials in counties that lay on the direct route between the farm and Marietta were alerted. Soon, Fulton County deputies were patrolling the highways leading into Cobb County from the south, and reporters were making their way to the cemetery where little Mary was buried.

By this juncture, of course, the caravan bearing Leo Frank had disappeared into the night, although not as utterly as its leaders had hoped. At the Little River, an unbridged stream ten miles north of Milledgeville, the vigilantes lost precious time when they were unable to locate the home of a ferry operator. But far from panicking, the men used the delay to cut phone lines at surrounding country stores and fire rounds of ammunition into the woods. The salvos were heard throughout the area, diverting an initial posse from Milledgeville and prompting early reports—bannered atop the *Georgian*'s first extra—that Frank had been shot to death. Yet such wasn't the case, for once the group finally negotiated the river, they pressed ahead at a steady clip, their charge sitting quietly between young Luther and Emmet Burton in the second car, his shirt luminous among the galluses and wool hats.

After barreling through Eatonton, the birthplace of Joel Chandler Harris, the Mariettans plunged north into the backroads briar patch of such rural counties as Jasper, Newton, Walton and Barrow, all the while keeping far to the east of Atlanta. It remains unclear whether this had always been the intended route or whether the group's leaders changed on the fly, responding to a tip from some sympathizer along the way who alerted them to the fact that the main arteries were being watched. Whichever, the choice was inspired, allowing the men to outflank any pursuers. With arrogant impunity, they raced over 100 miles through the cotton fields of middle Georgia, their passage witnessed only by the random darkened farmhouse, evidenced only by the cloud of red dust billowing in their wake.

Somewhere during the trip, the occupants of Frank's car briefly engaged him in conversation. Citing a source whose bona fides were "beyond all question," the Associated Press later reported its gist:

"Is there anything you would like to say before your execution?"

At first there was no reply. Then, slowly and perhaps painfully, the recently wounded man shook his head.

"No," he said. The word was scarcely audible above the throb of the engine.

For a long time following the only sound was that of the automobiles. Then Frank was asked if he had killed the Phagan girl, and the captors say he made no reply. This question was not repeated again until near the journey's end, and again, it is said, there was no reply. The final interrogation was:

"Is there nothing you wish to say?"

"No."

These four questions constituted the sole conversation in the death car as it sped along the miles which were steadily bringing Frank nearer to Cobb County.

Despite its roundabout route and one breakdown—Gordon Gann's car had to be abandoned by the roadside—the party made excellent time, and about daybreak it reached Alpharetta, 20 miles northeast of Marietta, which meant it would be approaching its destination as if returning not from Milledgeville but from the North Georgia mountains.

Exactly what happened in Alpharetta—in 1915, the seat of now-defunct Milton County—is uncertain. Subsequently, Judge Newt Morris and a young protégé from Canton named John Wood contended that since the Blue Ridge Circuit Court was slated to convene there later that morning, they simply happened to be up and about when the group came through. Even 75 years after the fact, Herman Spence, during the 1930s Wood's law partner, was offering this version of events: "John Wood went out and took a walk and in the course of the walk met some cars and there was a sheeted figure in the middle of one, and he was convinced it was Leo Frank. He went and got Newt Morris." Maybe so, but if the long-accepted story is true, Judge Newt and Wood were early risers, for the men transporting Frank hit town around 6:00 A.M. A more likely scenario is that Morris and Wood had awakened at that hour for the purpose of joining the party on the last leg of its trip. Regardless, the two—traveling in Wood's Model T—weren't far behind the group as they left Alpharetta, tore through Roswell, then turned onto Roswell Road, along which they proceeded until they reached Frey's Gin, where Leo Frank's journey would conclude.

Though Frey's Gin was two miles east of Marietta, there can be little doubt that the vigilance committee—the vow to hang Frank above Mary Phagan's grave notwithstanding—had always intended to lynch him here. Later, there would be talk suggesting that fear of being caught by the rising sun had prompted the party to pull up shy of its objective, but like so much that would come out of Cobb County, such talk was calculated to obscure the truth. And the truth was that the gin belonged to the man—former sheriff William Frey—who had tied the noose. Moreover, waiting at the site was a piece of furniture essential to the job: a table. Finally, the location was not without its symbolic resonance, in that it faced the Benton homeplace where little Mary, prior to moving to Atlanta, had lived and where her kin-folk still resided.

Frey's Gin was surrounded by a grove of trees, and it was into this small woods that Frank's captors marched him. The doomed man, his bare toes sliding over moist grass, never faltered. According to the most authoritative report, "he behaved throughout with a calmness and dignity and an utter lack of panic." After walking 200 feet, the group stopped before a sturdy oak, and someone looped the business end of the manila rope over a high limb. Meantime, the table that would serve as the platform was put into position.

While these preparations were being made, Frank apparently asked for and was granted permission to write a note to Lucille, jotting a few sentences in a foreign language some thought to be Yiddish but was almost certainly German. Then—speaking either in response to a specific question or to himself; the accounts vary—he uttered what amounted to a final statement: "I think more of my wife and my mother than I do of my own life." The remark's authenticity is evidently indisputable. (Although as one reporter noted: "In telling this story it must be remembered that we have not Frank's version and never will have it. We have only the lynchers' word for it.") Its meaning, however, is ambiguous. Whether, as admirers subsequently asserted, Frank was voicing a noble sentiment, or, as detractors countered, he was skirting the truth for fear of devastating his family, no one can say. As it had been in the beginning, so it was at the end.

With soft morning sunlight dappling down through the late-summer foliage, the vigilantes blindfolded Frank, bound his feet together, cinched a khaki cloth around his exposed lower torso, lifted him onto the table and placed the noose over his head. After agreeing to return Frank's wedding band to Lucille, a man identified in most reports as simply "the leader" pronounced the court's sentence and kicked over the table. The time was 7:05. The man was Judge Newt Morris.

The first witnesses to arrive on the scene—or so the cover story had it—were William Frey, a friend of Frey's from Augusta named Walter Yaun, *Marietta Journal* editor Josiah Carter, Jr., and merchant Gus Benson. Supposedly, Frey and Yaun had been in his yard picking peaches when the caravan hurtled by, and though the ex-sheriff said he caught a glimpse of Frank and suspected "something was doing," he claimed that he initially did nothing. In fact, Frey said he changed clothes and ate breakfast before driving into Marietta. There, he maintained, he met Carter, who informed him the cars never made it to the cemetery, and Benson, who told him he'd seen them turn "on the road there by your gin." Only then, Frey said, did he realize a lynching might have occurred on his property. Only then, he said, did he return home, walk into the grove, and spy the body. "Yonder it is," Frey said he exclaimed, and for all his account's bald-faced absurdities, yonder it indeed was.

Leo Frank, head snapped back, chin resting in the noose's bottom coil, dangled from above. Though half an hour had elapsed since the deed was done, his body was still warm, for unlike those wretches dropped through the gallows' trapdoor in a putatively humane hanging, Frank had not died instantly. Rather, he had slowly suffocated, struggling so ferociously he'd ripped open his neck wound. Blood oozed down his shirtfront. As the *Constitution* would grimly note: "He undoubtedly flayed the air."

By the time Frey wandered into his woods, all of Georgia and, for that matter, much of America, was awaiting word of Frank's fate. Not only had Atlantans awakened to front-page headlines (SPEEDING MOB SEIZES FRANK, boomed the *Georgian*); so, too, had the inhabitants of most every other city in the land. Intoned the *New York Times:* LEO M. FRANK KIDNAPPED AT NIGHT FROM GEORGIA STATE PRISON FARM BY ARMED MEN IN AN AUTOMOBILE. Nowhere, however, was interest more avid than in Marietta, where agitated locals had been congregating on the square since dawn. It was to this audience that an allegedly anonymous source—speaking by phone to Deputy Sheriff Hicks, who had himself made the trip to Milledgeville—broke the news: "Leo Frank's hanging to a limb down here near Frey's Gin. Retribution!" And so the spectacle began.

From Marietta, from neighboring farms and villages, and finally, from Atlanta, they came. Observed the *Atlanta Journal*'s Rogers Winter:

> They swarmed the road from both directions. They seemed to rise up out of the ground, so fast they came. The automobiles came careening, recklessly disregarding life and limb of occupants. Horse-drawn vehicles came at a gallop. Pedestrians came running.
>
> The vehicles stopped in the road at the grove and soon packed the road and overflowed into the fields. As the vehicles would stop, their occupants would jump out and run to the grove, bending forward, panting, wild-eyed.
>
> Women came. Children came. Even babes in arms.

By 8:30, over one thousand people had gathered, and scores more were arriving each minute.

Initially, at least, the gawkers conducted themselves with a degree of restraint. Noted the *Georgian*'s O. B. Keeler:

> In a terrible way it was like some religious rite. Watching the curiously reverent manner of those people, a manner of thankfulness and of grave

satisfaction, it was borne in with tremendous force what the feeling must be on those Cobb County men and women toward the man who they believed had slain Mary Phagan.

The journey to Frey's gin was a sort of dreadful pilgrimage.

"I couldn't bear to look at another human being, hanging like that," said one woman. "But this—this is different. It is all right. It is—the justice of God."

Among the men there was evident a grim and terrible satisfaction.

"They did a good job," was the comment, spoken in many tones, but with a curious inflection that was always the same. "A good job."

Yet however solemnly the crowd at first comported itself, however content most seemed merely to gaze upon Frank's body as if it were a gaffed tarpon, the prize catch, the prospect that things could get out of control quickly became apparent. As the numerous photographs taken that morning suggest, the gamut of emotions ranged from jubilation to rage to something approaching sexual rapture. In the background, boys tossed straw boaters. To the side, rambunctious sorts jostled for better vantage. Up close, a couple fervently embraced. And in front, a slack-jawed young man clung to Frank's distended blue hand. Commented Rogers Winter:

> A horrible sight met the eyes of the people who were first to arrive at the grove, and a still more horrible sight met the eyes of the later arrivals, who found not only the body swaying but surging around it a closely packed mass of men whose excitement was something fearful.

That Frank's inanimate form inspired near hysteria was hardly surprising, for of all the tribal rituals by which the white South asserted itself, none released more primitive energies than a lynching. And of all the men who ever wound up at the end of a lynch mob's rope, few conjured as many explosive associations as this one. Murderer, sodomite, Jew, Yankee—these were fighting words to everyone gathered at Frey's Gin. Seventy-eight years later, Narvel Lassiter—who was 9 in 1915 and whose mesmerized visage peers out from just behind the tree in several of the lynching pictures—distinctly recalled making a connection between the blood seeping from Frank's neck wound and the Watson-spawned rumor that Creen had inflicted the wound in response to Frank's homosexual advances. "Granddad told me a lot about it," said Lassiter, "and he knew a lot." Others leaped to even uglier conclusions. As the cloth girdling Frank's waist was only loosely tied, his genitals were, from several angles, visible. In the eyes of beholders unaware that death by hanging causes the extremities to engorge with fluid, here was the livid root of the victim's degeneracy.

The longer Frank's body hung at Frey's Gin and the larger the throng—which would eventually approach 3,000—grew, the more likely it became that some final atrocity would be committed. Already, in fact, the bolder lads had cut off the dead man's shirtsleeves. Then they'd knifed away the rope that had bound his feet. Though the majority of people, contended one writer, opposed "Apache-like barbarities," they were unwilling to counter the "rough element." They would go where they were led.

Such was the atmosphere when Robert E. Lee Howell—the truculent, hard-drinking firebrand who'd been so conspicuously excluded from the lynch party—announced his arrival on the scene by discharging the contents of his pistol into the air. Bareheaded, coatless, his eyes blazing, Howell was, by all accounts, in a frenzy, and after pushing his way through the crowd, he threw up his hands, clenched his fists and shaking them at Frank's body began to chant: "Now we've got you! You won't murder any more little innocent girls! We've got you now!! We've got you now!!!"

Howell's effect on the assembled multitude was galvanic, and the multitude, in turn, galvanized Howell. "Every once in a while when he paused," reported Rogers Winter, "some man in the crowd would give a yell, and the crowd would join in the yell, and it would get higher and higher, and the sound of it would fill the little grove and echo back and forth. These demonstrations seemed to fan the fury of the man by the body. His gesticulations became more violent, his raving words came faster and faster from his mouth, pouring out of him like a torrent."

The moment had come, and Howell wasn't going to be denied a second time. Again addressing himself directly to Frank's body, he proclaimed: "They won't put any monument over you! They are not going to get you! They are not going to get a piece of you as big as a cigar!"

It was at this juncture that Judge Newt Morris returned to Frey's Gin.

"Hear me, men," Morris pleaded after clambering atop a tree stump. "Citizens of Cobb County, listen to me, will you?"

A hush fell over the grove.

"Whoever did this thing," he began.

"God bless him, whoever he was!" Howell interjected.

"Whoever did this thing," the judge again began, patting the wild man on the head as if he were a fractious child, "did a thorough job."

"They shore did," echoed the throng.

"Whoever did this thing," Morris repeated, "left nothing more for us to do. Little Mary Phagan is vindicated. Her foul murder is avenged. Now I ask you, I appeal to you, as citizens of Cobb County in the good name of our county, not to do more. I appeal to you to let the undertaker take it."

No sooner had the judge uttered these words than Howell exploded. "We are not going to let the undertaker have it!" he shrieked. "We are going to burn it! That's what we are going to do! Come on, boys! Let's burn the dirty thing!"

"Men," Morris forcefully rejoined, "don't do anything to this body. Let the undertaker have it. The man has a father and a mother and whatever we think of him, they're entitled to have the body of their son. Men, I appeal to you for the good name of our county. Let all who favor giving the body over to the undertaker say, 'Aye.' "

A chorus of "ayes" rang out.

"Now, let all who oppose it say, 'No.' "

"No!" Howell alone importuned.

After a show of hands ratified the verdict, Morris jumped to the ground and dashed to the rear of the crowd, calling for the undertaker, whose horse and wagon happened to be standing by.

What occurred next was hideous and confusing. Even as two Negroes who worked for the undertaker drove the wagon into the grove, someone laid a sharp blade to the lynch rope, and Frank's body tumbled to the earth with a thud. On impact, the throng rushed forward, Howell in the lead, until the dead man appeared to vanish. Eventually, the Negroes reached him with their wicker basket. "Bring the body on, men," shouted Morris. "Bring it on. Quick, for God's sake." But there was no room to maneuver, so the judge wedged his way into the pack, holding it at bay just long enough for the pair to get a grip. The Negroes, however, managed only a couple of steps before Howell reached out and struck at the basket, upending it and spilling Frank's remains once again onto the hard red clay.

Later, people would shake their heads as they tried to fathom Howell's rabidness. Just a mean cuss, they reckoned. Just low-down, no matter his high birth. And that was part of it. Yet in the end, Robert E. Lee Howell—namesake of one great man, cousin of another—was driven as much from without as from within. Marietta boy, Tom Watson supporter, somehow more—not less—than his confreres, he was the quintessential native son. Georgia now spoke through Howell as he raised a boot high above Frank's corpse.

"Again and again," wrote the *Journal*'s Rogers Winter, "as a man grinds the head of a snake under his heel, did the man drive his heel into the face of Leo M. Frank, grinding the black hair into the dirt and dead black leaves until the crowd, stricken silent and motionless, could hear the man's heel as it made a crunching sound."

"Stop him, for God's sake, stop him!" Morris cried. Yet as the judge understood, he alone possessed the necessary moral authority, and after reaching Howell's side, he expended all of it, begging him to halt. Whether Morris got through to the man no one knows, but he did distract him long enough for the Negroes to recapture the body, stagger to the wagon and pull away.

The rig barely made it to the National Cemetery that marks Marietta's eastern city limits before it was overtaken by several automobiles—among them John Wood's Model T, Judge Newt riding shotgun. With what looked like half the throng from Frey's Gin in pursuit on foot, the prospect of further mutilation seemed imminent, and at the first chance, Morris jumped out of the car, climbed up on the seat of the undertaker's wagon and seized the reins. At a wide spot in the road, Wood again pulled alongside, and in one deft move, the judge leaped to the ground, jerked the basket containing Frank's remains into his arms and placed it across the Model T's backseat. "Now, John," Morris roared after climbing back in beside him, "drive like hell to Atlanta." And with Rogers Winter—a heretofore unheralded city hall reporter whose scintillating account of the morning's events would be transmitted by the Associated Press to the four corners of the earth— perched on the running board, that's what he did. Wrote Winter:

> Opening wide his throttle, Attorney Wood poured into his motor everything it would hold.
>
> By his side, with drawn face and gleaming eyes, Judge Morris strained forward, peering through the dust, waving his arms and shouting for automobiles to make way.
>
> Crosswise of the tonneau, the end of it projecting a foot or more on each side of the car, jostled and swayed the undertaker's long basket with the dead body inside.
>
> Down the road toward Atlanta sped the car, and up the road toward Marietta sped automobiles loaded with men going like mad to see the body.
>
> The car with the body gave the cars with the sightseers just enough room for the end of the basket to miss a collision, and the cars with the sightseers gave equally as little room for the car with the dead man.
>
> Low over the road hung an endless roll of dust, and through this dust the three men in the death car would dimly see cars coming one after another, a procession of them, all speeding like racers; and the death car would swerve a little to the right to pass them, which made the basket jostle and sway and rattle, while the sightseers flashing past would wave their hands and shout hoarse shouts as they raced northward to Marietta to see the body hanging in the grove.

At Smyrna, a crossroads community south of Marietta, Wood stopped long enough for Winter to duck into a phone booth and call Atlanta's Greenberg & Bond Funeral Home, which agreed to dispatch a motor hearse, then the party resumed its journey down through the valleys of Cobb, across the broad Chattahoochee and into town. At the corner of Marietta and

Ashby on the capital's northwestern outskirts, the mortuary's machine was waiting. "In a mad haste," reported Winter, "the basket was shoved into the undertaker's funeral car," and out of the executioners' hands. It was almost noon.

And so Leo Frank was returned to Atlanta, but he would not rest in peace—not yet. Though the undertakers made every effort to conceal the body, word quickly leaked out, and within an hour, hundreds had found their way to the hiding place—the funeral home garage. Amidst threats to break down the doors, Police Captain L. S. Dobbs (who two years before as a lowly sergeant had not only been among the men who answered Newt Lee's call but had discovered the murder notes) ordered a squad of 40 mounted officers to escort the remains to the establishment's chapel, which was two blocks distant. Shortly thereafter, the public was admitted.

For five hours this swelteringly hot August afternoon, Leo Frank's battered corpse, the cheeks crushed from the impact of Howell's boot heel, lay on a makeshift bier in Greenburg & Bond's front hall. Though the sight proved too ghastly for a few (several elderly ladies collapsed), most reacted "without so much as a look of horror." Upon exiting the funeral home, people lingered on the streets, talking excitedly and, as quickly as labs could print them up, buying pictures taken at Frey's Gin before the body was cut down. All the while, newsreel cameramen from Pathé and Mutual ground away. By dusk, more than 15,000 men (among them Frank's initial nemesis, Detective John Black), women and children had borne witness to the lynching brethren's work.

Meantime in Marietta, a fresh crowd had formed on the town square. There, Fiddlin' John Carson—whose new ballad had attained enormous popularity since its debut two months before—was sawing away on his Stradivarius reproduction, his thin nasal voice carrying the doleful tune and warning lyrics out over the sea of work-weary faces and into the red clay hills beyond:

Little Mary Phagan
She went to town one day;
She went to the pencil factory
To get her weekly pay.

She left her home at eleven,
She kissed her mother goodbye;
Not one time did that poor girl think
She was going off to die.

Leo Frank he met her
With a brutely heart and grin;
He says to little Mary,
"You'll never see home again."

I have an idea in my mind,
When Frank he comes to die,
And stands examination
In that courthouse in the sky.

He'll be so astonished
To what the angels say,
How he killed little Mary
Upon that holiday.

Judge Roan passed the sentence;
He passed it very well;
The Christian doers of heaven
Sent Leo Frank to hell.

Carson played the ballad again and again until finally folks tired of it, and he broke into *That Old Time Religion,* which was good enough for them.

TWENTY-TWO

Burial

That Thursday morning, Pennsylvania Station teemed with lawmen. Uniformed officers guarded the entrances. Plainclothes detectives circulated throughout the lobby. But it was at the great steel-girdered balcony overlooking the platforms where trains arrived and departed that the New York police had concentrated their forces, sealing off the gate that opened onto the stairs leading down to Track Six. Southern Railway's #36 from Atlanta, which was bringing Leo Frank's remains home for burial, was due at 6:00, and the possibility that the body's arrival might occasion violent demonstrations was all too real.

For the past two days, New York—and, for that matter, Chicago, San Francisco and dozens of other northern and western cities large and small—had witnessed an unbridled outpouring of grief and condemnation. "A world at war will pause from its awful work long enough to shudder at this deed of darkness," Rabbi Stephen S. Wise had predicted upon hearing of Frank's death, and so it had.

First had come the lamentations, particularly from recent Jewish immigrants to New York, who'd imagined that they had left persecution behind in the shtetls of the Ukraine and the ghettos of Warsaw. Reported the *New York Tribune:* "Always emotional, the East Side received the news as though a great hand were squeezing its heart dry." Doleful crowds gathered outside the offices of Yiddish papers such as the *Warheit* and the *Forward,* while on street corners solitary mourners wept. Across from Seward Park, noted one reporter, "a bent old woman like the sculptured figure of sorrow" rocked to and fro whispering: "Tot-tot! Leo is dead."

Soon enough, however, the dirges had given way to denunciations. Terming the lynching "a stain upon our country," American Jewish Committee president Louis Marshall declared: "Georgia is now on trial in the forum of civilization." Meantime, Macy's chairman, Nathan Straus, thundered: "The lynching of Leo Frank is a disgrace." And it wasn't just Jews who voiced such sentiments. Organizations ranging from the American Bar Association to the Illinois Federation of Colored Women's Clubs passed resolutions castigating Georgia, while individuals ranging from the president of the National American Woman Suffrage Association (who viewed the lynching as a "shameful" by-product of chivalry) to Booker T. Washington (who saw the crime as the inevitable fruit of a society that permitted the "promiscuous lynching of black men and women") issued fierce rebukes. So, too, did John Slaton, who, from San Francisco, where he was taking in the Pan-Pacific Exhibition, decreed: "Every man who engaged in the lynching should be hanged, for he is an assassin." In the end, former president William Howard Taft might well have been speaking for the country as a whole when, stepping off a train in Salt Lake City to attend a convention, he told reporters: "The lynching of Leo Frank was a damnable outrage. There was no excuse, no mitigating circumstances to justify the action of the Georgia mob. An action like that makes a decent man sick."

Amplifying and reinforcing the feeling abroad in the land, the nation's press had also vehemently decried the lynching, its editorialists lambasting Georgia—and Dixie—with the sort of vituperations usually sparked only by a deadly act of foreign aggression. Pronounced the *Akron Beacon-Journal:*

> A more unspeakable outrage was never perpetrated than was this infamous butchery. There are bad people in hell who would not only have regretted it, but who would turn away from it in horror. The plain fact is that Georgia has everlastingly placed a smirch of ineradicable barbarism across its once fair escutcheon. Georgia is a good place for every decent man and woman to stay away from.

Charged the *San Francisco Bulletin:*

> Georgia is mad with her own virtue, cruel, unreasoning, blood-thirsty, barbarous. She is not civilized. She is not Christian. She is not sane.

Concluded the *Chicago Tribune:*

> The South is barely half educated. Whatever there is explicable in the murder of Leo M. Frank is thus explainable. The South is a region of illiteracy, blatant self-righteousness, cruelty and violence. Until it is improved by the infusion of better blood and better ideas it will remain a reproach and a danger to the American Republic.

The *New York World,* meantime, expressed its disapproval with an editorial cartoon depicting Georgia as a gun-toting harridan brandishing a torch that burns with the words LYNCH LAW, while in the background a silhouetted figure dangles from a tree. And as for the *New York Times,* it acidly proclaimed:

The State of Georgia should either apprehend the murderers of Leo M. Frank and punish them according to its laws, or its people should honor them by election to the chief judicial offices in their gift. Any half-way course will be a cowardly evasion. Either the lynchers of Frank faithfully represent public opinion in Georgia or they do not represent it. If Georgia approves lynching, then honors bestowed upon the lynchers would attest to the shameless courage of the Georgia public and its willingness to defy public opinion in the other States of the Union.

All of which explains why when Southern's #36—running twenty minutes late—finally rumbled into Pennsylvania Station, the police let only a few people onto the platform, among them a handful of newspapermen and Negro porters and the family members who'd come to claim the dead: Rudolph Frank and Otto and Marian Stern.

Practically the first person off the train was Lucille Frank, and while she was thickly veiled, those awaiting her saw at once that she was in a state of near collapse. Not that this was any wonder, for Lucille had not slept since being awakened some 55 hours earlier with the news of Leo's abduction. Once the worst had been confirmed, she'd immediately thrown herself into the tasks attendant to an unexpected death. Tuesday morning had seen her everywhere in Milledgeville, settling accounts with various merchants, answering telegrams of condolence, arranging for Leo's belongings to be collected from the prison farm and bidding goodbye to the Alfords. Only after completing these jobs had she allowed her uncle Bud—who'd driven down from Athens—to chauffeur her home, where more chores awaited. Various well-meaning friends had already begun planning an Atlanta funeral, but native Georgian though she was, Lucille was not about to let her husband's remains be interred in a state that had brought him to such a hideous end. Consequently, she had taken charge of the arrangements, tending to details right up to midnight when unassisted and showing no serious effects of her ordeal, she had boarded her train. Yet over the course of the long trip north, Lucille's strength had ebbed, and when she spotted Leo's father, sister and brother-in-law she at last broke down, sobbing: "It's over. It's all over now."

Huddled there on the nearly empty platform, Lucille and her in-laws momentarily appeared lost and alone. But within minutes, they were joined by Rabbi David Marx, Alex Marcus, Henry Alexander and Herbert Haas, all of whom had also come up from Atlanta. As hugs and handshakes were exchanged, Rudolph Frank excused himself from this tight group and made his way slowly down the length of the train to the express car. When an officer attempted to block his path, he pointed to a simple green pine box wedged amid a jumble of baggage and in a voice still thick with his native

Germany choked: "Let me— Let me— Can't you see— I'm that boy's father." Thereupon the guard relaxed, and for the next few minutes the grieving man stood by as his son's casket, the attached death certificate mislabeled "Leo *Moses* Frank," was loaded onto a cart and thence into an elevator for transport to a waiting hearse.

Once the hearse's doors had been shut and the living had climbed into taxicabs, a police motorcycle escort led the vehicles out of Pennsylvania Station's Thirty-first Street exit and past several hundred onlookers who stood respectfully behind barricades. Then, it was north onto Seventh Avenue, east onto Thirty-second Street and finally south onto Fifth Avenue for the ride downtown to the Manhattan Bridge and across the East River. When the caravan reached Brooklyn, the taxis headed toward the Franks' Underhill Avenue home, while the hearse, its outrider and a trailing car of reporters proceeded to an Atlantic Avenue mortuary, where an undertaker would spend the afternoon reconstructing the dead man's features, repairing the damage done by Robert E. Lee Howell's boot heel.

Leo Frank was buried early Friday morning at Mount Carmel Cemetery in the Cypress Hills section of Queens, his remains accompanied to the grave by immediate kin and some 30 invited friends. Both the hour and the limited number of mourners had been dictated by the family, who after Thursday had seen enough of crowds. No sooner had the cabs transporting Lucille and the others from Pennsylvania Station pulled up at 152 Underhill than the crush had started. Eventually, somewhere between 5,000 and 10,000 curious souls—among them old Jews from the neighborhood, mothers pushing baby carriages, newsboys hawking extras, kids on a lark, a perambulating hurdy-gurdy man, even an unidentified Negro intellectual who coolly told the press he'd come for no other reason than to see how whites endured a circumstance usually reserved for members of his race—had made their way to the three-story graystone between Sterling and Prospect Places. Though a squad of officers from the Grand Avenue Precinct had enforced order, the bereaved had virtually been held captive in their own house all day. Not until 11 P.M., when the throng began to dwindle, had the undertaker been able to bring Frank's body home, the pall bearers carrying the shiny black coffin that had supplanted the pine box from Georgia into the parlor amid the chalky explosions of the newspaper photographers' flashes.

Daybreak had found still more New Yorkers congregating outside 152 Underhill—as of 8:30, the number totaled 800. Consequently, Rabbi Marx had conducted the funeral as soon as possible. The ceremony, though wrenchingly emotional (Rae Frank several times called out for her boy), was mercifully brief, and once the tearful in-laws had filed by the open casket for a last look into the face that had been brother, son, husband, they had climbed into limousines and departed for the graveyard. At Mount Carmel, both Marx and Dr. Alexander Lyons—the rabbi at Brooklyn's Eighth Avenue Temple, Leo's childhood synagogue—read prayers, after which, as Lucille softly sobbed and Marian Stern stared away in glassy silence, the casket was lowered and Marx and Rudolph Frank recited the Kaddish. When the final words had been intoned, the survivors turned from their loved one's lily-and-aster-heaped resting place and walked to their cars.

Thus was the body of Leo Frank committed to the earth, yet for those who had endlessly championed his innocence, there would be no surcease. Even as the gravediggers were at work, back across the East River in Manhattan, an agitated throng had been assembling. The setting was Cooper Union, which had long been booked on this date for a conference to address the persecution of European Jewry and hence provided the perfect forum to explore instead avenues of redress against the persecutors of one specific American Jew.

Though the New York police were once again out in force, they were unprepared for either the crowd's size—an estimated 20,000—or its emotional intensity. Crying Jews surged into the historic old meeting hall, quickly filling it to capacity and, after the doors were closed, breaking in the lobby windows. The overflow spilled onto Third Avenue for two blocks in each direction, and not until the event's organizers agreed to send out representatives to speak to the masses left standing on the sidewalks did the threat of riot subside.

The various ideas bandied about inside Cooper Union, coming as they did between frenzied expressions of sorrow and animosity, were initially hard to categorize, but over the course of several hours, two opposing schools of thought emerged. The first held that the responsibility for meting out justice to Frank's lynchers fell entirely to the state of Georgia. This was the view of the event's chairman, Nathan Straus, as well as that of J. S. Bache's William J. Wollman (the Wall Street broker who had backed the commutation fight), the American Jewish Committee and the editorial pages of the cause's leading New York propagandists—the *Times*, the *World* and the *Journal*. While these individuals and institutions vigorously advocated the arrest and punishment of the guilty parties ("The State of Georgia must prosecute all the murderers," roared Straus), they believed they should not participate directly in the effort lest they provoke resentment among the very authorities they hoped to spur to action.

The infuriated multitudes had not, however, come to Cooper Union to hear talk of restraint. They had come to receive their marching orders, and in this, they were not disappointed, for most of those who spoke felt that only by bringing outside pressure forcibly to bear could they induce Georgia officials to mount a thorough investigation. Among the orators articulating such a position were the financier N. Taylor Phillips and New York City's education commissioner, Joseph Barondess. During a lengthy fulmination frequently interrupted by cheers and applause, Phillips asserted:

> Our people do not live in this country because of the favor of any man. We have shed our blood for this nation. Fellow Jews, you will never get justice, you will never receive your lawful due, unless you fight for it soul and body, day by day.

Barondess, meanwhile, brought the faithful to their feet by invoking the name of the era's exalted Jewish martyr—Captain Alfred Dreyfus. In France, a nation "not as far advanced as ours," he boomed, Dreyfus had ultimately been exonerated of spying accusations and restored to his military rank. Why was it, Barondess then asked, that in the United States, putatively the land of religious freedom, Leo Frank had met so far worse a fate? The answer could not have been more unsettling—or more galvanizing:

> The Jews of America are not organized. They are weaklings. Come, rise.

With that, the crowd stood and in the Hebrew tongue of its fathers prayed for strength.

The Cooper Union convocation was just the first of several such assemblages—among them one at Boston's Faneuil Hall that drew a crowd of eight thousand and sparked rhetoric "equalled in radicalism only in the days before the Civil War." Taken together, these rallies signaled that Northerners in general and Jews in particular intended to do what they could to apprehend Leo Frank's killers. And while there was no overarching plan, no coordinated effort, action commenced along several fronts. In New York, in Chicago and even in Hoboken, New Jersey, newspaper editors and businessmen inaugurated reward funds, the richest of which earmarked $20,000 for any member of the lynch mob who turned state's evidence. Meantime, in the Midwest and New England, boycotts were organized. Urged the *Boston Traveler:*

> To the degree that a humane public can rebuke the State of Georgia by refusing to have any part of her unholy people's products, they will do so. Anything made or grown in Georgia will bear a sinister brand and be

suggestive of lynchings, and it ought to be, and doubtless will be, left untouched.

In response to such calls (the *Milwaukee Free-Press* proposed complete "commercial, social, and political ostracism"), at least a scattering of merchants stopped stocking Coca-Cola, and the president of Chicago's Police Patrolman's Association announced that his officers would no longer honor prisoner extradition requests from Atlanta as "Georgia was not capable of self government." New York congressman Isaac Siegel, reacting to a widespread demand that the federal government prosecute the man many held liable for Frank's murder, offered legislation to ban Tom Watson's *Jeffersonian* from the mails.

Finally, however, there were those who, while welcoming the bounties and sanctions, endorsed a more aggressive approach, proposing what amounted to a guerrilla mission behind enemy lines. Toward that end, two New York–based groups—one headed by the Brooklyn suffragette Bella Newman-Zilberman, the other chaired by Judge Edward Swann of Manhattan's Special Sessions Court and Harry Schlacht, president of the East Side Protective Association—had raised sufficient funding to hire a number of private detectives, and within days the city's papers were reporting that these "young men had left New York for Marietta to hunt down the twenty-five members of the lynching party."

For all the morbidly orgiastic convulsions that rocked Georgia in the immediate wake of the lynching, by the time Leo Frank's body was laid to rest, a tensely watchful hush had descended on the state—most especially on Marietta. "I've been asked if I found Marietta quiet after the lynching," wrote the *New York Tribune*'s John J. Leary, once again the first national reporter on the scene. "I did. It was as quiet as a dynamite factory; so quiet that it seemed as though a healthy sneeze would start an explosion." Upon arriving in town, Leary momentarily feared that he himself might constitute that sneeze. No sooner had he parked than another car pulled in behind his, blocking him in, and a couple hundred men who only seconds before had been whiling away the hours on the courthouse lawn gathered round. Yet after Leary stated his business, the sea parted and he walked unmolested across the square to the offices of the *Marietta Journal,* whose editor, Josiah Carter, Jr., was expecting him. As for the idlers, they returned to their idling, or the appearance thereof, just as Marietta reassumed the mantle of tranquillity. Which, of course, was exactly as the lynching brethren desired it. A placid surface had to be maintained, but so, too, did a coiled sense of menace. As the *New York Times*'s Charles Willis Thompson, who fetched up in Cobb County shortly after Leary, described it:

> Marietta today is in a mood of braced purpose and resolve. Every stranger who comes into town is under observation the moment he arrives. The surveillance is not obtrusive, but it is unmistakable. [The town's] mood is one of determination to protect the men who, in its eyes, executed the law after it had been trampled on. It is resolved that not a hair on their heads shall be harmed.

The process whereby Marietta—primarily in the persons of the individuals who'd orchestrated events thus far—would endeavor to conceal the identities of the lynch party members and, by so doing, attempt to frustrate any effort to get to the bottom of the crime itself, had actually begun even as Fiddlin' John Carson was serenading the masses the day of the hanging.

The first order of business had been to get the men who'd made the trip to Milledgeville to some safe haven where they could unwind. Though all of the vigilantes believed in the righteousness of what they had done, the undertaking had exacted a toll—both physically and emotionally. Seventy-five years later, Lawrence Haney's oldest daughter, Golmer, who was 5 that summer, would vividly recollect her father's homecoming from Frey's Gin. "I remember waking up early in the morning, and he was crying and my mother was crying," she recalled, adding: "I'm sure my dad felt bad about it. He was a human being." What was done, though, was done, and eventually, Haney had silently trudged into the fields behind his place, where he'd thrown himself into the numbing work of pulling corn. Elsewhere around Cobb County, similar scenes had played out. Hence that same afternoon, the 25—along with a couple of the mission's masterminds—were again on the move. Their destination: a rustic fish camp owned by the party's coleader George Daniell on the Etowah River in the hills north of town. There, the participants could not only collect themselves but compare notes.

Meantime back in Marietta, several of the lynching brethren had set up what amounted to a press office. Its purpose: to discourage the numerous Atlanta newspapermen who'd descended on the town from asking too many questions while simultaneously planting misleading information with these same gentlemen. That the effort was successful, there can be no doubt, as the following morning, Atlantans—and, for that matter, New Yorkers, Bostonians and residents of every other city whose papers picked up the resulting stories—awakened to a surfeit of threats, taunts and fabrications. "The public will never know the identities of the 25 brave and loyal men who took into their own hands the execution of a law that had been stripped from them by Governor Slaton," one of the mouthpieces told the *Constitution.* "I would not advise inquisitive authorities or persons to try to reveal them." That said, this same spokesman, in a remark clearly intended for the amusement of his fellow conspirators, teased would-be investigators with a cryptic clue, declaring that the lynch party's leader bore "as reputable a name as you would ever hear in a lawful community." While those on the outside could only puzzle at this statement, for those on the inside, it was easily and comically transparent. The leader plainly referred to, Black Newt Morris, bore a reputable and lawful name indeed—that of his cousin Judge Newt.

From the outset, then, the Cobb Countians delegated to hold the world at bay had gone about the task with characteristic impudence. At times, in fact, they had indulged in outright ridicule. In a telegram to Detective William J. Burns, Marietta's police chief jeered: "Leo Frank lynched here. Come quick and help investigate." Such cracks notwithstanding, the prevailing attitude was one of care and caution. When the *Atlanta Journal,* in its first edition the day of the lynching, reported that on the previous night, Marietta lawmen had been unable to account for the whereabouts of a number of cars, Mayor E. P. Dobbs—who, not incidentally, owned one of the machines in question—had gone right to work composing a bold refutation. Thus beneath the headline, MARIETTA OFFICIALS DIDN'T KNOW OF MOB, the *Journal*'s late editions carried the following item:

> I desire in the interest of justice and truth to say that the Marietta and county officials had no knowledge of any automobiles leaving Marietta last night nor were they apprised of the return of any machines today.
>
> None of the officials had any intimation of such an undertaking until the body was found about two miles from the city this morning.
>
> E. P. DOBBS, MAYOR.

Yet for all their early successes, the lynching brethren understood that it would take more than a few disingenuous comments to the press to cover up a crime of this magnitude. Not only did they face threats from without, but they faced them from within, for the overwhelming reaction of Dixie's elites had been, if anything, more censorious than that of their Northern counterparts. GEORGIA'S SHAME! the headline atop the *Constitution*'s initial postlynching editorial had cried, beneath which the organ of the New South, after calling for the punishment of the slayers, sadly observed:

> For the first time, perhaps, since the murder of Mary Phagan, those convinced of the innocence of Leo Frank as well as those who believe in his guilt share a common view: That Georgia herself has been tied by the neck and dragged through the mud.

Not surprisingly, the *Journal* had gone even further, bitterly proclaiming:

> If this lynching, which by the way, is the ninth that has occurred in Georgia within the last eight months, is condoned by reasonable authorities, who can say how frequent and swift will be the lynchings to follow? Let us face the stark and terrible issue now, or resign our State to the unbridled instincts of the jungle.
>
> As the chief custodian of the State's honor and law, it is the Governor's solemn duty to probe this crime to its blackest bottom and to exhaust every resource at his command to see that the guilty are punished and the State's integrity vindicated. If Governor Harris does nothing else during his entire administration but does this in just completion, he will have rendered his State immortal service and will go into history among the bravest and great men of his time.
>
> It is a straight-out issue between law and anarchy. Let Georgians choose for themselves.

And it wasn't just Atlanta's newspapers that had condemned the crime. The *Macon Telegraph,* the *Savannah Press,* the *Columbus Enquirer*—all had raised their voices in protest, as had such influential regional organs as the *Louisville Courier-Journal,* the *Richmond Times-Dispatch* and the *Jackson Clarion-Ledger.* The editors of these sheets had demanded action, and if the word of Georgia's governor was to be believed, action they would get. Speaking from the South Georgia town of Fitzgerald, where on the morning of the lynching he had been attending a reunion of Confederate veterans, Nat Harris declared:

> I am greatly shocked and aggrieved, and I do not believe that the people of Georgia will at all approve of this action. I am sure that it will hurt Georgia greatly everywhere, and I am extremely sorry that it occurred.
>
> It can be taken for granted that I will use my every power to see to it that the members of this mob receive fitting punishment for their crime. I will see to it that the authorities of the county in which the crime occurred receive every help at the disposal of the state.

With that, the governor had boarded a train back to Atlanta, where he promised to take personal charge of the investigation.

Nat Harris's vow to pursue Leo Frank's executioners signaled the beginning of the official probe into the lynching, a probe that in short order was backed up by a $1,500 state reward and endorsed by the *Georgian* and the

Atlanta Chamber of Commerce. Yet from the start, most observers could do little but shake their heads at the inquiry's prospects. In the same dispatch that contained his description of Marietta's determination to repel all comers, the *New York Times*'s Charles Willis Thompson reported:

> Nobody talks seriously of the investigation Governor Harris is promising, and there are very few who believe there is the slightest chance of any of the murderers being put to any grave trouble, much less punished. They are known to many of the citizens of Marietta, who would die rather than reveal their knowledge or even their suspicion.

Closer to home, the *Macon Telegraph* advanced the same conclusion:

> There are of course to be investigations—the usual thing presumably. It is said every effort will be made to apprehend these men. Doubtless they can be apprehended—doubtful they will.

Several factors contributed to the general skepticism that greeted Harris's pledge. For one, in the wake of the governor's return to Atlanta, the *Journal* reported that despite having been awakened in the wee hours of Tuesday morning with the news of Leo Frank's abduction, he had refused to call off his scheduled trip to the Confederate veterans' reunion in Fitzgerald, boarding a train that departed Terminal Station at 7 A.M.—the approximate time of Frank's death. Few disclosures could have spoken more powerfully: Regardless of statements to the contrary, Harris wanted to put as much distance between himself and this awful mess as possible. That such was the case was hardly a surprise, as the governor could not but have realized that if he looked too deeply into the crime, he would come face-to-face with information he did not want to know or already knew and wanted to forget. Though no names had been divulged, the fact that the lynch party and its organizers had included Georgians of the first rank was immediately and everywhere a foregone conclusion. Observed the *Times*'s Thompson:

> The word mob does not seem descriptive, for these men did not display the ordinary characteristics of a mob. Lynching mobs are usually composed of riff-raff, but this one consisted of leading citizens in the community, men prominent in business and social circles.

Yet even had Harris been inclined to take on the lynching brethren, the popular support that would have been necessary for him to proceed simply did not exist. While Georgia's principal newspapers and the standard-bearers of Southern capital and industry were clamoring for him to act, they did not speak for the poor dirt farmer or factory girl. As Atlanta mayor Jimmy Woodward—who, like John Slaton, was in San Francisco attending the Pan-Pacific Exposition but, unlike the former governor, supported the lynching brethren's doings—put it in an inflammatory after-dinner address to the California State Assessors' Association: "Seventy-five percent of the people of Georgia are convinced that the man lynched Monday [*sic*] night committed the deed, and they are on the ground and ought to know." To that 75 percent, of course, Tom Watson was the final authority, and while the crime had occurred just before the *Jeffersonian*'s weekly deadline, he had nonetheless managed to get a boxed item that spoke directly to his constituency onto the front page:

> In putting the sodomite murderer to death, the Vigilance Committee has done what the Sheriff would have done, if Slaton had not been of the same mould as Benedict Arnold. Let Jew libertines take notice. Georgia is not for sale to rich criminals.

Little wonder that the *Macon News*, which had denounced the lynching, was ultimately moved to advise:

> The less said about the matter from now on the better. Frank no longer lives; those who wanted vengeance at least should be satisfied, and it will be better for everybody concerned to let the Frank case rest forever.

An inquiry had been promised, however, and an inquiry there would be. In fact, there would be several, the first of which convened in Nat Harris's Atlanta office the Thursday after the lynching. Though presided over by the governor, this session would be conducted by the men who according to Georgia law were charged with probing crimes that occurred on prison farm property—the prison commissioners Robert Davison, Eugene Rainey and Thomas Patterson.

From the viewpoint of the many anguished souls in and out of Georgia who, while incredulous that Leo Frank had been carried away without the necessity of breaking a lock or firing a shot, were ignorant of the Prison Commission's complicity in the crime, this opening round in the investigative process offered reason for hope. In the days since the lynching, some genuinely significant evidence had emerged from Milledgeville. The *Georgian*'s William Flythe had been the initial reporter to reach the prison farm, and he'd developed the intelligence that the person who cut the phone lines into town prior to the abduction was a redheaded, motorcycle-riding electrician—a description fitting that of the man who'd done the job, Yellow Jacket Brown. Hard upon this newsbreak, the Hearst paper's competitors had also scored coups, the *Journal* reporting that the handcuffs that had been used on Superintendent J. M. Burke—now in the prison commission's possession—bore factory serial numbers through which their purchasers could well be traced, the *Constitution* reporting that before speeding into the night with their captive, someone in the vigilance committee had thoughtfully returned Warden J. E. Smith's valuable pump-action shotgun to his office. And these were just the items that had made it into print. Because the 25 had conducted themselves so openly during the raid, many penitentiary employees and inmates were in a position to provide promising leads. Indeed, within hours of the crime, the trusty F. J. Turner had posted a letter to Lucille Frank naming Cobb County deputy sheriff William McKinney as one of the party members.

The clues and witnesses necessary for the Prison Commission to have pursued a close examination into what had transpired in Milledgeville were, in short, available. Yet any expectations that the body actually was going to pursue such an examination evaporated shortly after the inquiry began when Governor Harris announced that due to the sensitive nature of the matters under consideration, the proceedings would be conducted behind closed doors. From the outset, the commissioners—like the governor—had wanted nothing more than to make the incident go away. As a matter of fact, no sooner had news of Frank's death hit the papers than Rainey and Davison had publicly absolved prison personnel of any culpability in the crime. Proclaimed Rainey: "I do not see how the prison officials at Milledgeville could have done anything Monday night to save Frank." (In response, a grateful Warden Smith had told the *Journal:* "I am very glad the prison commissioners were here when the attack occurred.") Yet even taking these sorts of unmistakable signals into account, the brazenness with which the three-man authority now behaved was breathtaking. After meeting for no more than an hour, the commissioners simply departed, leaving Harris to announce the investigation's outcome to the press. Based on what Davison and the others had just told him, the governor asserted, the guards in Milledgeville never had a chance. To have put up a fight would have been "suicidal." There had been only one choice—to capitulate to the mob. That said, Harris, in a statement that flatly contradicted the boasts of two months earlier regarding the prison farm's impregnability, declared:

> The building at the State Prison Farm is not a penitentiary in any sense of the word. It is designed primarily as a place to detain prisoners. There are very little, if any, facilities for resisting an attack from the outside.

Though he went on to reassure the reporters that he would do all in his power to bring the guilty to justice, the governor made it clear that not only would he not divulge any evidence he had discussed with the commissioners but that the body's work was done. The primary responsibility for delving into the lynching would fall to the chief prosecuting officer of the jurisdiction in which it had taken place.

The Saturday following the lynching, Herbert Clay strode into the same office where just two days earlier the prison commissioners had washed their hands of the affair. In the honeyed tones of a natural-born charmer, he assured Nat Harris that he would "exert every effort" within his power as solicitor general of the Blue Ridge Circuit to "detect the members of the mob that lynched Leo M. Frank." Though the Atlanta papers contented themselves with merely reporting this development, the deeper implications did not go entirely unnoted. Scoffed one North Georgia weekly:

> Herbert Clay announced that he intends to ferret the mystery to the bottom. Can you imagine what a terrible sifting of sand there will be when Herbert gets to the bottom.

But even had no one spoken, there can be little chance that any Georgian who'd witnessed the events of the past months would have mistaken Clay's appearance on the stage for other than what it was. After all, he had led the Marietta delegations that argued against the commutation of Frank's death sentence before both the Prison Commission and Governor Slaton. Yet here he was vowing to pursue the parties who'd accomplished the thing he'd so volubly advocated, the thing he'd surreptitiously helped to bring about. The idea was absurd on its face, intimating that the proceedings to come—the coroner's inquest and the grand jury hearing—would constitute the cruelest sorts of judicial farces, the final articulations of the lynching brethren's contempt for those who'd been aligned with Frank.

Unlike most farces, the ones Herbert Clay would orchestrate were meant to serve a dual purpose. True, if everything went as planned, they would mock justice, but more important, they would simultaneously immunize the members of the vigilance committee against justice. Consequently, there could be no breaking of ranks, no slips.

At first blush, the coroner's inquest would hardly seem to have demanded Herbert Clay's attention. Cobb County coroner John Booth was a member of the original Ku Klux Klan, inducted into the fraternity during Reconstruction by the original grand wizard, Confederate general Nathan Bedford Forrest. For the 75-year-old Booth, the Frank lynching recalled the sort of work he and his hooded comrades had pursued half a century before. As he told the Associated Press, he admired the vigilance committee's "precision and secrecy." Small surprise, then, that few placed much stock in his vow to probe the crime vigorously. Predicted the *Constitution:* "The inquest verdict will surely be death at the hands of unknown parties."

Still, the lynching brethren could not be too careful, and when exactly one week after Frank was found hanging at Frey's Gin Coroner Booth convened his hearing, he quickly ceded the Cobb County Courthouse floor to the lawyer whom Herbert Clay had picked to question witnesses—state representative John Tucker Dorsey. Standing at Dorsey's side was another member of the Marietta bar, this one selected by the Cobb County Commission—Gordon Gann. The inquest would be conducted by one of the crime's architects, assisted by one of the lynch party's commanders. And as for the coroner's jury itself, it included mob member Coon Shaw and was chaired by Dr. W. H. Perkinson, a close friend of Judge Newt Morris.

The impresarios who produced and directed this spectacle knew how to put on a show. To the amused satisfaction of several hundred shirtsleeved or overalled spectators gathered inside the courthouse and the uncomprehending dismay of thousands beyond Georgia's borders following through the newspapers, the players acted out their parts with conviction and flair. So well scripted were the vignettes that at one point, Dorsey confidently waltzed witness Gus Benson—the merchant who'd seen the lynch party turn into Frey's Gin—right up to the edge of a revelation:

> "You say you saw at least one of the men step from one of the automobiles that had turned off the main road at the Frey gin?"
>
> Benson moved a little nervously in his chair.
>
> "Yes sir," he replied.
>
> The acting prosecutor paused, and then shot out:
>
> "Who was he?"
>
> "I do not know."
>
> There was an audible relaxation in all parts of the courtroom.

For the most part, however, the questioning progressed less dramatically. Asked if he'd discovered Frank's body, former sheriff William Frey testified that he reckoned he had. Asked if he'd instructed the Marietta police to investigate the crime, Mayor E. P. Dobbs said of course. Shortly before noon, after quizzing a dozen witnesses, Dorsey and Gann turned the case over to the jurors, who, as expected, found only that Frank "came to his death by being hanged by the neck." As to who might have done such a thing, they were at a loss. Not that Dr. Perkinson and the others gave the matter much thought. They returned their verdict following three minutes of deliberation.

Before Herbert Clay could ring up the curtain on the investigation's last act, he had to deal with a potential problem—the grand jury foreman, James T. Anderson. In the words of the veteran *Marietta Journal* associate editor Bill Kinney, Anderson was "soft on lynching." Over 70 years later, James T. Anderson, Jr.—who was 12 in 1915—would remember his father walking out of a Fiddlin' John Carson concert in Marietta that long-ago August after the musician, who'd continued to capitalize on Frank's death, struck up his signature ballad. The elder Anderson, respected member of the community though he was, disapproved of what the community had sanctioned and wanted no part of it.

The behind-the-scenes manipulations that ensued during the days leading up to the grand jury hearing can only be surmised, but their results, scrawled across a document submitted to the Cobb County clerk of court, remain on file for all to see. Herbert Clay removed Anderson as the jury foreman, replacing him with the Marietta banker who'd helped to fund the mission to Milledgeville—Robert A. Hill. The solicitor also got rid of one more juror, replacing him with another fellow conspirator—Bolan Glover Brumby.

One of the very few Mariettans who might have done the lynching brethern legal harm was thus shunted aside. Yet even at this juncture, the men masterminding events were not about to let down their guard. On the morning of September 1, H. L. "Snax" Patterson—who several months earlier had succeeded Newt Morris to the judgeship of the Blue Ridge Circuit Court—took his place behind the bench in the Cobb County Courthouse and, looking down on the grand jurors, issued a remarkable charge:

> It has been published broadcast over the world that a lynching has recently occurred in Cobb County. It is your duty to make a thorough and complete investigation of that, as it is of all crimes when brought to your attention. Your oaths bind you to honestly, fairly, and impartially make an investigation of it, but it is not your duty to assume the role of secret service men, the role of detectives. You were not selected in the capacity of private detectives but as grand jurors of your county, and your work is that of grand jurors and not the work of secret service men.
>
> Now, gentlemen, you will retire and enter upon the discharge of your duties.

Thereby relieved of the responsibility to do anything more than a cursory job, the jurors took up the case.

Over the course of two days, Herbert Clay, assisted by John Tucker Dorsey, presented 35 witnesses—among them the three prison commissioners and the omnipresent Mayor Dobbs—to the grand jury. The testimony, of course, was privileged, not that the outcome was ever in question.

As the retired superior court judge Luther Hames, who during the 1930s was John Dorsey's law partner, subsequently revealed: "Seven members of the lynch party were on the Grand Jury." Accordingly, Clay emerged from the courthouse the afternoon of September 2 carrying presentments that over the signatures of Hill and Brumby concluded:

> We have been unable to connect anybody with the perpetration of this offense or to identify anyone who was connected with it, although we have investigated the information furnished us by officers and other parties. To this end we have subpoenaed and examined witnesses in an effort to disclose the perpetrators of this crime, but none of these witnesses could identify any of the parties. We have done our best to do our duty and ferret out this crime, and regret to report that we find it impossible to indict anyone.

Considering the tumultous hue and cry generated by the news of Leo Frank's lynching, the silence that greeted word of the Cobb County grand jury's decision was staggering. Yes, a few northern papers expressed shock. Roared the *Boston Post:*

> The Cobb county grand jury reported Thursday that it had been unable to find enough evidence to indict anyone for the lynching of Leo M. Frank.
> Is Georgia in America?

But by and large, the press, particularly the Atlanta press, said nothing. Neither the *Journal,* the *Constitution* nor the *Georgian* ventured even a comment on the perfunctory finale to the affair that had captivated the city for two and a half years. "The newspapers unite in asserting that publicity ought not now to be followed up," Luther Rosser noted in an early-September letter to his still-vacationing partner, John Slaton. Local editors told Rosser that "the public mind [was] so inflamed that publicity [would] amount to nothing except to further ferment the present disorder." This was undoubtedly true. Yet in the end, various forms of self-interest played a greater role in dictating the hands-off policy. At the *Journal,* any urge to pursue the story or criticize the grand jury would have to have been weighed against the fact that publisher James R. Gray's daughter was married to the first cousin of a Mariettan who'd helped to plan the crime—Bolan Brumby. At the *Constitution,* nothing could be written because publisher Clark Howell's first cousin was the Mariettan who'd danced a jig on Frank's face—Robert E. Lee Howell. (So sensitive were Atlanta publications to Howell's part in things that his name did not appear in any of their accounts.) At the *Georgian,* further coverage was checked by a substance thicker than blood—money. Due to the sheet's lobbying for the commutation of Frank's death sentence, it had lost a substantial number of readers and suffered a corresponding decline in advertising revenue. As the former Hearst reporter Herbert Asbury would later observe in the *American Mercury:* "Thousands who had been our friends turned on us. Everywhere we heard mutterings about 'the damned *Georgian.*' " Consequently, the paper simply dropped the matter, resuming instead the crusade against child labor it had been waging that long-ago April weekend when Mary Phagan was found dead in the basement of the National Pencil factory.

The muteness of Atlanta's newspapers, however, was not nearly as astonishing as the muteness of the newspaper that was almost solely responsible for transforming the Frank affair into a nationwide cause célèbre — the *New York Times.*

Initially, Adolph Ochs, though outraged at the crime, had attempted to see it in a philosophical light. As he'd entered the conference chamber of his paper's Forty-third Street tower for the staff's first editorial meetings after the lynching, he had carried himself, in Garet Garrett's observation, with "an air of reconcilement." While the publisher had never stopped believing in Frank's innocence, he had also never warmed to him as a human being. Noted Garrett in his diary: "I'm sure at last it was a relief to Mr. O. to have him lynched and out of the way . . . I have felt for some time that he secretly despised Frank." Thus it was that during these early sessions with his top men — among them the editorial page editor, Charles R. Miller, and the acting managing editor, Frederick Birchall — Ochs had encouraged a dispassionate debate. "We discussed . . . whether the Jews were interested in Frank as a Jew or as an innocent," Garrett recalled. That topic led to an exchange regarding Frank's possible guilt, a subject that prompted consideration of the sexual aspects of the Phagan murder and as it happened introduced the issue of "whether or not Jews are more libidinous than other people." This matter, Garrett wrote, was touched upon only lightly but was "remarkable for having been mentioned at all."

Yet soon enough, Ochs's detachment gave way to anxiety, and he was questioning everything he'd thought and done since becoming involved in the Frank case. This period of introspection was occasioned by two extraordinary pieces of writing, the first of which was by Charles Thompson, in Garrett's estimation the only *Times* reporter to have written "honestly about the sentiment of Georgia and not what the Times was supposed to want . . . Mr. O. didn't like it, of course, and yet he knew it was true, and had to be printed. There was no help for it."

Published beneath the headline FRANK LYNCHING DUE TO SUSPICION AND PREJUDICE, Thompson's lengthy analysis adduced three primary reasons for what had taken place in Marietta on August 17:

First—The belief that the Jews of the country, hitherto not the object of any hostility or dislike, had banded themselves together to save a criminal because he belonged to their race and religion and thus ranged themselves in opposition to men of other races and religions. Against this belief no argument was effective, no denial was listened to.

Second—The bitter resentment over what everybody in Georgia to whom this correspondent has talked calls "outside interference": and this does not mean only the "interference" of the New York newspapers by a long shot, though Tom Watson has done his level best to make it appear that the New York newspapers are attempting to govern the State of Georgia.

Third—And this is the thing which turned the smoldering fire into a raging flame and maddened men who were merely angry—it is believed from one end of the State to the other that Governor Slaton was Frank's lawyer and pardoned his client after every court had upheld that client's conviction. The ignorant believe Slaton was bribed, or that at best he received as Frank's lawyer a share of the fee paid to his firm; the more intelligent believe that he was merely influenced in his judgement by the fact that Frank was his firm's client.

Thompson's reporting deeply troubled Ochs. Heretofore, the publisher had regarded his role in the Frank affair as that of a crusader, never really considering how it all might have appeared from a Georgian's perspective. More significant, Ochs had not previously paid much attention to the rumblings from within that the *Times,* by continually highlighting news tending to exonerate Frank and persistently editorializing on his behalf, had overstepped its bounds. It was on this point that the publisher felt most vulnerable, and it was to this point that the other piece of writing that would so unnerve him was explicitly addressed.

In the lynching's immediate aftermath, Ochs had ordered his staff to distribute the *Times*'s initial editorial denouncing the crime to all of Georgia's daily papers. The hope had been that the sheets would reprint the scorching broadside, but there had been no takers. In fact, W. T. Anderson, editor of the antilynching *Macon Telegraph,* had been so alarmed by the publisher's thinking that he had immediately wired him back. In his diary, Garrett paraphrases the wire's contents:

> The message . . . said that for the sake of the Times and Mr. O., it [the *Telegraph*] would not print the editorial as requested to do, and for the sake of the decent people of Georgia and especially for the sake of the Jews in Georgia would Mr. O. not stop this offensive propaganda. It was

the outside interference of the Jews, led by the Times, that had made it necessary to lynch Frank. The Jews in fact were responsible for what had happened to him.

The next morning, the *Telegraph* would give prominent play to an eloquent
restatement of these sentiments:

> As it now stands [in Georgia], Israel itself stands indicted and is the
> object of a great deal of indignant anger, but the individual Israelite is
> liked and respected.
>
> Against the race generally there is, however, a sentiment of anger, a
> proneness to denunciation, which is just at the present in *quiescent status
> quo.*
>
> If among the outside newspapers generally there is any attempt at sus-
> tained denunciation of this state, Thomas E. Watson will, with a quick
> eagerness, accept what he will consider a gage of battle thrown at his feet,
> and he will answer in kind—more than in kind.
>
> Watson will be answered in kind, and so it will go on until the time will
> come when he will tell the people of the State of Georgia that the rich Jews
> of the nation have bought up the press of the Republic to vilify and black-
> guard and defame the State of Georgia in revenge for the killing of Leo M.
> Frank. And when that charge is brought it will be passionately and plausi-
> bly presented—and Georgia generally will believe it.
>
> What will follow such a charge? Anti-Semitic demonstrations? Cer-
> tainly. Anti-Semitic riots? Probably. Actual violence to Jewish citizens?
> Possibly.
>
> The men responsible are the Strauses, the Ochses, the Pulitzers and
> other leading Jews of New York and the East generally. These men now
> hold the comfort, safety, peace and happiness of the Jews of Georgia in the
> hollow of their hands.

Following so quickly upon Thompson's dispatch, the Macon paper's reaction had shaken Ochs to his core, awakening in him not just the realization
that he might share some of the blame for Frank's fate but the fear that by
aligning himself so thoroughly with the poor man he had endangered the
Times itself, coming perilously close to identifying the sheet in the public
mind as the one thing he'd never wanted it to be—"a Jewish newspaper."
Consequently, when the publisher had appeared at a subsequent editorial
conference, he'd struck Garrett as wan and subdued, and the ensuing
debate was sobering. Some in the room argued that the *Telegraph*'s wire
was "but a kind of intimidation," maintaining that if Ochs believed Frank

innocent, he should continue demanding editorially that Georgia prosecute the murderers. Others, among them Garrett, advanced the opposite view:

> I said we should consider a few simple facts. Mr. O. was the most promi-
> nent newspaper publisher in the country. He was a Jew. The Times had
> printed more stuff for Frank than any other newspaper and [had] a special
> correspondent in Georgia. It was clear what a great many people would
> make of those facts. Also, it was clear, and we needn't deny it any longer,
> that a majority of the people of Georgia approved of the law having been
> taken into the hands of the mob because they believed money had been
> used to thwart the forms of justice.

After listening intently to the back-and-forth, Ochs rendered his judg-ment—the *Times* would drop the Frank case. Wrote Garrett:

> Mr. O. . . . has really a remarkable gift of putting himself in the other
> man's place. He said that if he were a Georgian he would have resented the
> outside interference. Also, he could see how it looked to a great many peo-
> ple that Gov. Slaton, law partner of the man who defended Frank, should
> have commuted his sentence. It was very hard really to meet the argument
> that Frank had received every legal consideration, which undoubtedly he
> had . . .
> So perishes a great enthusiasm, for the sake of The N.Y. TIMES.

And so perished something of the certitude that had long been integral to Ochs's self-conception. The experience had been shattering, and for several days thereafter he stayed home—in Garrett's phrase, "nursing his nerves."
  Which was why when the Cobb County grand jury audaciously closed the books on the Frank case, the *New York Times* said nothing.

With the abdication of the press, the last credible threat to the vigilance committee ceased to exist. While several northern Jewish organizations would continue to agitate for action, they would fail to agree on a plan and hence do nothing. And as for the private detectives dispatched to Georgia by the Brooklyn sufragette Bella Newman-Zilberman and her New York allies, they would prove equally ineffectual. Arriving in Cobb County dis-guised as day laborers, this group of apparently amateurish hawkshaws instantly set off alarms. Reported the *New York Herald:*

> MARIETTA—Eight men whose conduct aroused suspicion and who did
> not give satisfactory explanations of their presence here were rounded up

last night, placed in a box car attached to a freight train ready to leave and sent away. The car was guarded until the train left the town limits.

Since Leo M. Frank was lynched here several persons whose business in the town was not known have been invited to leave.

The lynching brethren had achieved everything they had set out to achieve. And they had been assisted by a final bit of subterfuge, one accomplished through the unwitting agency of two reporters looking for a positive angle in what had otherwise been a bleak story.

The newsmen responsible for Judge Newt Morris's universal lionization were unlikely dupes. Indeed, as they had shown not just in their coverage of the lynching but in their understanding of the deeper social forces at play, the *New York Times*'s Charles Thompson and the *New York Tribune*'s John Leary were keen observers. Since joining the *Times* in 1899, the 44-year-old Thompson—a lawyer by training—had distinguished himself first as the paper's Washington bureau chief, then as the editor of its book review and finally as a roving political writer who also penned editorials. Along the way, he had scored numerous exclusives, among them a world-beating account of a battle between Allied and Chinese forces in Peking during the Boxer Rebellion. Meantime the 40-year-old Leary was also a formidable figure. One of the *Tribune*'s most astute national correspondents, he would win the 1920 Pulitzer Prize for his coverage of violent labor unrest in the coal fields of West Virginia.

Neither man, however, was a match for Newt Morris, who by virtue of having rescued Leo Frank's body from the howling mob was prime feature material. Both Thompson and Leary sought Morris out, and he granted each writer generous interviews. The resulting articles put the judge on a pedestal. Describing his dramatic address to the throng at Frey's Gin, Thompson enthused:

> Morris is a wonderful stump-speaker, one whose voice has that mellow and magical quality which captures a crowd and who knows the art of touching the ignorant as well as that of appealing to the intelligent. He has a persuasive and arresting intonation and the power at the moment of being all things to all men.

On the same topic, Leary was equally effusive:

> Morris is not a big man physically, but he gives the impression of quiet power, of being a man who is sure of himself at all times. In a way, his face seemed familiar, but I could not recall him. That night after my work had been finished, I placed the resemblance.

In person, he is the double of Bat Masterson, clean-cut, lithe and alert, who twenty or more years ago kept Western bad men in order.

Having thereby elevated Morris to Olympian heights, each reporter advanced identical conclusions. Declared Thompson:

Judge Newton A. Morris is the hero of one of the most dramatic events in the whole strange history of the Frank case. He is the only hero of the Frank lynching.

Echoed Leary:

And there is the story of the trip, in the picture of which there is one outstanding figure—that of a soft-spoken, youngish man in Marietta at whose words mobs drop their prey—Judge Newton A. Morris of Cobb County.

No sooner had these accounts been put on the wires than papers everywhere began running their own encomiums. From Philadelphia to San Francisco, editors paid tribute to Judge Newt. The *New York Herald* splashed a shot of him pleading with the crowd at Frey's Gin atop its front page. Other sheets did likewise. Even to the end, then, the conspirators cast their spell, burying the truth of what had happened in Cobb County as surely as Frank's remains had been interred in Queens. Pronounced one Northern daily:

"Newt" Morris's part in Georgia's tragic episode should be conspicuously held up to view and emphasized. Morris represented not merely himself. He represented the better angel of all our natures.

TWENTY-THREE

Recessional

In early September, Lucille Frank returned to the Georgia Avenue home where she and Leo had spent most of their married days. Awaiting her was a stack of condolence letters, most from high-placed Atlantans. Wrote Mrs. Sig Montag, the wife of the National Pencil Company's majority stockholder: "My heart aches with you and for you." Celeste Parrish, supervisor of the city's Department of Education, vowed that she was one of the South's "many Christian women who have never wavered in their belief in your husband's innocence." One by one, the new widow answered these notes, invariably concluding: "My dear one lives and will always live in the hearts of those who loved him and to whom it is a labor of love to strive to clear his name." This, she had decided, would be her life's mission.

Two weeks after Leo's death, Lucille was in constant pain, her sense of loss manifesting itself in headaches and nausea. Friends counseled everything from brisk morning walks, to immersion in classical music, to swearing off chocolates. None of it helped. Which left a seemingly endless stream of empty hours punctuated only by periodic attempts to contact Leo through psychic mediums, one of whom, speaking via a "spirit father" in Oklahoma City, quoted the dead man as saying: "Get all out of life that you can. I am sorry I had to leave you." What solace Lucille found in these putative messages from the beyond is impossible to say, although she did take comfort from a more tangible offering from her late husband, his wedding ring. True to Frank's last request, the lynching brethren had seen to it that the ring (a plain gold band engraved "L.S. to L.M.F., Nov. 30, 1910") was delivered to the *Georgian*'s O. B. Keeler, who lived just off the square in Marietta, with instructions that he forward it. While the reporter pounced on the scoop that had literally been placed in his hands (beneath a triple-deck, front-page screamer, he wrote: "If ever an object was charged with tragedy, it is the wedding ring of Leo M. Frank. And it was in my pillow last night"), he dutifully fulfilled his part.

For Lucille Frank, a lifetime's worth of suffering had been compressed into a few months, and she found herself, though a mere 27 years old, weighed down with what felt like the sorrow of the ages. Her psyche had been deeply bruised, her opinion of humanity irrevocably darkened. To make matters worse, nearly everyone in Atlanta's Reform Jewish community had been similarly affected, none more so than its spiritual bulwark, David Marx. In a mid-September letter to the New York Public Library's Anne Carroll Moore, the rabbi confided: "I [am] not enjoying the best of health, and I am deficient in bodily vigor. My mind, at times, feels weary." That said, the man who had once dismissed the notion that anti-Semitism was endemic in Georgia laid the blame for what had transpired on the anti-Semitism endemic in Georgia. "You can never kindle a fire out of non-flammable material," he declared. "Watson is possible because he had the material to play upon—ignorance, religious hatred, pharisaism [and] theological pride." The hostility that culminated in Frank's death, he averred, had been "simply fanned into expression." For the Washington Street community, this was, in sum, a period of painful reassessment. And as for the world outside the few blocks surrounding the Temple, there was either silence ("Strange to relate, the 'N. Y. Times' does not carry anything these days," Rae Frank wrote Lucille)—or worse.

Inflammatory as the *Jeffersonian*'s earlier pronouncements had been, they actually paled compared to its postlynching pyrotechnics. Beginning with his final August issue and continuing through September, Tom Watson lit up the skies with so many rhetorical flares and girandoles that all of Georgia appeared suffused in their lurid glow. For starters, under the sizzling page-one topper "The Wages of Sin Is Death," he amplified upon his view that Frank's killing had been a legal execution: "A Vigilance Committee, instead of the Sheriff, carried out *a sentence which remained in effect. In the eyes of the law, THE COMMUTATION DID NOT EXIST.*"

That said, Watson excoriated Frank's principal supporters, his intention being to use this moment to drive them permanently from the field. One of his main targets was John Slaton. After repeating the allegation that the "vagabond governor" had been "bribed by the Jews," he encouraged him to continue his travels in the Pacific:

> Maybe when he reaches Honolulu, he will think of Rangoon, and take the road to "Mandalay, where the sun comes up like thunder from China across the bay."
>
> It might seriously impair his health if he were to return to Georgia.

Watson also singled out Atlanta's newspapers. Mocking the headline with which the *Constitution* had editorialized against what happened in Marietta, he roared:

"Georgia's Shame" is that the Jew advertiser and the Jew banker *throt-tled the Atlanta papers.*

"Georgia's Shame" is that Atlanta's dailies have betrayed the State.

Most persistently, Watson bombarded the local and national Jewish leaders who had banded together to save one of their own. Addressing the lawyers who'd supervised fund-raising efforts for Frank, he declared: "MESSERS. HAAS, Your Gold Calf stands discredited. YOU AND YOUR METHODS ARE UNIVERSALLY DESPISED." Addressing Stephen A. Wise, he inquired: "Oh, Rabbi Wise! Is your soul never wroth when a Jew defiles a gentile? We believe that *your law* permits the libertine Jew to use *our sister* as a harlot." All of which served as a preamble to a fiery warning to any son of David who might be contemplating vengeance:

> The assassination of myself would be a signal for a bloody outbreak against the Jews.
>
> The outbreak would not be confined to Georgia.
>
> This country has never had riots against the Jews, as all European countries have had; *but the same causes,* if they exist *here, will produce the same results as elsewhere.*

Scattered throughout the *Jeffersonian*'s renewed attacks on Frank's allies were highly colored accounts of how the factory superintendent purportedly met his end. The purpose of these unverifiable reports was to further justify the Cobb Countians' actions. Beneath the August 26 banner FRANK VIRTUALLY CONFESSED; CEASED TO CLAIM INNOCENCE, the Sage asserted:

> When day overtook the Vigilantes and they decided to execute the sentence of the law, [Frank] was asked if he killed the girl.
>
> *He was mute!*
>
> Then he was asked if he wanted to make any statement, and he answered, "No!" Not once did he say as he had been saying so often for two years, "I am innocent."
>
> He was guilty; and his conduct at the last corroborated the official record.

On September 9, Watson reiterated this contention, insisting that "Frank closed up stoically, *and made no protest of innocence.*" On September 16, he announced that he had learned that Frank, when asked to tell the truth about Mary Phagan's murder, remarked, THE NEGRO TOLD THE STORY! meaning, of course, that Jim Conley's version was accurate. Finally, on September 30, Watson provided what for his tens of thousands of readers would be the definitive word on the matter, informing them that as Frank "swung into eternity," he could be heard to implore, "God forgive me."

Distorting and disparaging as the *Jeffersonian*'s portrayal of Frank's behavior at Frey's Gin was, not everything Watson published in the fall of 1915 could be dismissed as demagoguery. His ongoing critique of the defense team ("I never did think that Luther Rosser and Reuben Arnold amounted to much as criminal lawyers.") and his continual twitting of Slaton for conflict of interests (HE WAS ONE OF FRANK'S LAWYERS) appealed to a far wider segment of Georgia's populace than outsiders could have known. So did his remarks on child labor. As he noted in his September 9 issue:

> Mary Phagan was not fourteen years old.
> The National Pencil Factory, owned by Frank's people, fought our Child Labor bill, fiercely, and helped to kill it—and, in God's mysterious way, it cost the Superintendent his life!

Then there was his September 30 exposure of how the *New York Times*'s coverage of the Frank case had been compromised by its business manager Louis Wiley's dealings with such partisans as Albert Lasker.

Still, in all, the *Jeffersonian*'s performance in the aftermath of Frank's death was sulfurous and brutal. In a midautumn salvo directed at Georgia's Jews en masse, Watson proclaimed: *"You have blown the breath of life into the Monster of Race Hatred; and THIS FRANKENSTEIN, whom you created at such enormous expense, WILL HUNT YOU DOWN!"* That the Sage was in a very real sense describing himself was apparently not something of which he was consciously aware.

Considering the great triumph that Leo Frank's lynching represented both for those who'd pulled it off and for Tom Watson, the likelihood that anyone from within Georgia might at this pass arise to repudiate what had occurred in Marietta and rebuke the Sage seemed all but nil. Yet Thomas W. Loyless of the *Augusta Chronicle* did exactly that. The editor was, of course, already on record as having favored the commutation of Frank's sentence. Moreover, his newspaper had not only published Berry Benson's arguments pointing to Conley as Mary Phagan's murderer but John Hammond's skeptical account of Governor Nat Harris's summer visit to the prison farm in Milledgeville. Nonetheless, in a signed September 12 broadside headlined SLATON OR WATSON—WHICH? Loyless undertook an altogether more difficult—and lonely—task. His purpose: "To render a service to my state, which still lies bleeding and torn, humiliated and disgraced before the world, as a result of the most devilish plot that was ever hatched."

At the outset, Loyless asserted that the rabidness rampant in Georgia during the past weeks had convinced him of the unfairness of Frank's trial: "I know, now, the mob had charge of his case from beginning to end. The jury was influenced by public clamor."

One of the chief justifications for clemency thus restated, Loyless mounted an aggressive defense of the man he regarded as the lone hero of the piece—John Slaton. As he saw it, any clear-eyed reading of the political, fiscal and cultural realities at play in Georgia at the time the matter came before the governor gave the lie to Watson's claim that in commuting Frank's sentence Slaton had sought to enrich himself. Rather, the editor wrote, "every logical, selfish reason argued for the gallows." As evidence, Loyless ticked off a list of the difficulties the governor had to have foreseen that the decision to spare Frank's life would cause him:

> Frank's commutation meant personal danger and great embarrassment to both Slaton and his family.
> Commutation of Frank's sentence meant virtual political suicide. Slaton's political ambition was his chief passion, and his prospects were the very best.
> Commutation of Frank's sentence could not redound to Slaton's pecuniary interests, but on the contrary would injure them.

Yet despite all of this, the editor added, Slaton "refused to pass the case on to his successor, because he felt that to dodge it would amount to cowardice; he commuted the sentence because he thought it was his duty to do so. You find such examples of courage and fidelity to duty in books, but rarely if ever in real life."

By way of bolstering his contention that Slaton, far from seeking profit in granting Frank clemency, had actually acted selflessly, Loyless leveled an explosive allegation. "About a week before Slaton rendered his decision," he charged, "Tom Watson sent Governor Slaton word through a mutual friend that if the governor would let Frank hang, he (Watson) would be Slaton's 'friend for life,' and that it would result in Slaton becoming United States senator next time and the master of Georgia politics for twenty years to come. Of course, Slaton spurned the suggestion—for it meant that he should sacrifice a human life for the sake of his political ambition. I dare Watson to deny this, for I have the proof of it in my possession, and he knows the man by whom I can prove it."

The force of this allegation was undeniable, and on its strength Loyless embarked on an overview of Watson's many well-known career setbacks (the congressional defeat of 1892, the vice presidential loss of 1896) and low points, arguing that his anti-Catholic campaign of 1911 and 1912 had not only made him "the most thoroughly discredited man in Georgia" but had cost the *Jeffersonian* readers. Prior to "seizing on the Frank case" he had, in short, been in dire straits. With that, Loyless turned the tables on the Sage, proclaiming that it was he who had achieved financial gains from recent events. Watson, he wrote, had "abused and aroused, assailed and slandered" for just one reason — "the cash that flows into his coffers from the publication of this vile stuff." Asserted the editor:

> Watson has three controlling passions — BITTERNESS born of political disappointment; EXAGGERATED EGO, causing him to seek notoriety in any and every way possible; and AVARICE — money being to him the greatest god of all.

Then, addressing Georgians as a whole, Loyless posed what he saw as the key question: "Why have we made him the guardian of our public conscience?"

For Leo Frank's beleaguered and bereaved family and friends, Thomas Loyless's singular effort to, in his words, "lead the people back to the light of reason" appeared little short of a miracle. David Marx made certain that the dead man's northern supporters, as well as his mother, received copies. The Reverend C. B. Wilmer, rector of Atlanta's St. Luke's Episcopal Church and a supporter of Slaton's commutation decision, used his sermon the following Sunday to praise the *Chronicle* editor and to assert that Georgians who continued to take their cues from Watson were "worshipping false gods." The most eloquent statement of appreciation, however, came in a September 28 letter to Loyless. Wrote Lucille Frank:

> My heartfelt thanks for your brave conduct. Your article is the first ray of sunshine from darkness, sorrow and tragedy, covering a period so long that it seems to have been an eternity. It has been so cruel that long ago I decided that life itself is a delusion — a fearful mockery. How I thank you!

Lucille's letter to Loyless marked more than just a private moment of vindication. Because she went on to address several significant topics and because the editor, after obtaining her blessing, stripped her letter across the front page of the *Chronicle*'s October 1 editions, it opened a second front in the paper's campaign to restore Georgians to their senses. Lucille's initial point was both poignant and direct:

I am a Georgia girl, born and reared in this State and educated in her schools. I am a Jewess; some will throw that in my face, I know, but I have no apologies to make for my religion. I am also a Georgian, an American, and I do not apologize for that, either. I sat beside Gentiles in school, they were my playmates, and I loved them; many of my most intimate girlhood friends are Christians. My brother-in-law is a Christian and his loyalty and fidelity in this terrible ordeal has been as staunch as that of anyone of my own religion.

That said, the widow made her only recorded comment regarding the lynch party members and, without naming the chief instigator, the men who had egged them on:

I only pray that those who destroyed Leo's life will realize the truth before they meet their God—they perhaps are not entirely to blame, fed as they were on lies unspeakable, their passions aroused by designing persons. Some of them, I am sure, did not realize the horror of their act. But those who inspired these men to this awful act, what of them? Will not their consciences make for them a hell on earth, and will not their associates, in their hearts, despise them?

While Lucille's letter constituted the most visible weapon in the *Chronicle*'s counterattack, others contributed behind the scenes. None more so than William Smith. In late September, the lawyer initiated a correspondence with Loyless designed, in his words, "to help you in your fight." As he declared at the outset: "In reading the *Jeffersonian,* I find [it] teeming with misstatements of fact and I will take the liberty of calling your attention to same from time to time. You will stop Watson only when you check him on the FACTS of the Frank case. And if you will dog his steps every week, and call attention to the inaccuracies of his publication, YOU ARE BOUND TO CRUSH HIM AND HIS LAWLESS WORK." Hence when in early October the *Jeffersonian* repeated the charge that the murder notes attempted to implicate Newt Lee in Mary Phagan's death and thus bore the sign of Frank's authorship, Smith wrote the editor that the notes in truth attempted to finger factory fireman William Nolle and thus pointed to Conley as their author. Similarly, when the *Jeffersonian* made the claim that prior to Slaton's executive clemency hearing the defense had told a potential associate counsel that commutation was a "sure thing," Smith worked up a response contending that no such communication had occurred.

For Loyless, the submissions from Smith served both to fortify his resolve and to replenish his arsenal of ideas, and as the fall of 1915 wore on, the *Chronicle* fired away at a wide range of targets. Boomed the headlines:

A SHAME TO HAVE OUR LAWS SO TRAMPLED UPON, MAKING GEORGIA SAFE
AND SANE AGAIN and, most gleefully, PLACES WHERE SALE OF *JEFFERSO-*
NIANS SLUMPED MORE THAN HALF LAST WEEK.

At the same time the *Chronicle* was attempting to stir up some homegrown indignation, forces from outside Georgia that had either been
aligned with Frank or were outraged by his fate were also showing signs of
life. At the behest of Louis Marshall, United States attorney general
Thomas Gregory was preparing to prosecute Tom Watson on the grounds
that his articles calling for the lynching constituted obscenity. As a result of
his anti-Catholic diatribes, the Sage had previously faced such charges, winning acquittals. This time, however, the justice department planned to try
Watson in a jurisdiction outside Georgia, thereby increasing the odds of
conviction. Meanwhile, Governor Nat Harris—who at the conclusion of the
prison commission's investigation into the lynching had repaired to his
summer home in Tennessee to recover from a never specified illness—had
returned to Atlanta to find his desk cluttered with letters from Northern
detectives and lawyers proposing methods for ferreting out members of the
lynch party. Typical was the suggestion of Benjamin A. Richmond, former
district attorney of Cumberland, Maryland, who suggested sending an operative to Marietta who would "mingle freely with the people, sympathizing
with the deed." Eventually, he predicted, his man would obtain "the admissions of a great many parties."

Yet for all the *Augusta Chronicle*'s editorializing and all the threats of
legal action, there was at this date never much danger that Tom Watson
would be silenced or the truth regarding the lynching conspiracy exposed.

For Watson, after having successfully stared down the likes of Adolph
Ochs and William Randolph Hearst, fending off Thomas Loyless amounted
to child's play. In a series of published responses in which he never referred
to Loyless by name, calling him instead either "the little jackass" or "the
near-Catholic editor," the Sage repudiated each of the *Chronicle*'s charges.
Regarding the claim that he'd tried to bribe Slaton, he said that to the contrary he'd merely sent a messenger to the governor with the following
instruction: "You tell Jack Slaton to stand like a man against all this outside
pressure in the Frank case, and to uphold the Courts and the Law, and I will
stand by him." To the allegation that he'd been in the Frank case for the
money, he rejoined that since the *Jeffersonian* was the only Georgia paper
willing to tell the truth about the story, the people had supported it, and his
income had deservedly increased. Then, throwing his haymaker, Watson
declared that it was the *Chronicle* that had entered the fray on a for-profit
basis, asserting that its editor, like so many others, had sold his news
columns to "the carpetbagger brotherhood who have been the vampires of
the South and grown rich on the toil of Gentiles." In short, Watson con-

tended that the Haases, Luther Rosser and Slaton himself were behind the "fusillade on the *Jeffersonian.*" And what had they accomplished by it?

> *They have simply reopened the Frank case,* chunked up every brush-heap of passion, and thrown fresh fuel on every fire that was dying down.

No sooner had Watson tendered these accusations than death threats against Loyless began pouring into the *Chronicle.* Declared a typical correspondent: "We are with Tom Watson and when he calls for help, we are coming 50,000 strong and some more of Frank's kind will swing."

The United States attorney general, of course, presented a bigger problem for Watson, but here again the job wasn't anything he couldn't handle. "I tell the Attorney General to his teeth," the Sage asserted at a mass meeting, "you cannot remove me from the Southern district of Georgia. If I have to give up my life for having incurred the savage hatred of the rich Jews, it will be given up right here in the same region where my ancestors gave up theirs." That said, Watson dispatched an envoy to Governor Nat Harris to request that he petition Gregory to drop the proceedings altogether. Years later, Harris, referring to this envoy as simply a "prominent gentleman," would write:

> The gentleman stated to me that he had just come from Mr. Watson and had been directed to say to me that if I would prevent such a step being taken he would give me his earnest support for re-election to any offices that I might seek.

After securing the governor's assent, the prominent gentleman telephoned Watson. Recalled Harris: "Mr. Watson expressed his gratification." In the wake of this meeting, the governor traveled to Washington to see the attorney general. In Harris's telling, Gregory was incredulous:

> "What kind of politicians have you got in Georgia?" demanded the Attorney General. "When you come to me you always denounce Mr. Watson in unmeasured terms, and yet when I propose to silence him or punish him . . . you come here and take his part and urge me to let him alone. Why is this?"
>
> I did not answer him according to the inquiry, but contented myself with telling him that I wanted him to let Mr. Watson alone for the sake of the honor of my own state and the people.

The truth was more complicated. As previous events had shown—and as the governor's reaction to the prominent gentleman's offer attested—

Harris was hostage to his political ambitions. Moreover, his connections to several of the lynching brethren left him vulnerable to suasion. As Luther Rosser wrote the still-vacationing John Slaton:

> Our Governor is certainly a wonder. The oyster's backbone is a steel rod compared to his. I have no idea that the old man will live out his term. The worry of [all of this] will certainly cost him his life.

Not that Harris was the only compromised Georgian. Shortly after the governor departed Washington, the state's entire congressional delegation, save for Senator Thomas Hardwick, appeared in Gregory's office to make the same request: Drop the case against Watson. Which was what the attorney general did. Despite the protests of Louis Marshall, the Sage would escape prosecution.

Which left just a few last details. In response to the raft of letters from private detectives who'd hatched plans for investigating the lynching, newly elected Georgia attorney general Clifford Walker produced a finding declaring that there was "no fund which could be legally applied to such purposes." All offers were rejected. Meantime, in the two towns where the truth was known, payoffs were helping to assure that lips remained sealed. In mid-September, $30,000 in construction contracts were awarded for the expansion and modernization of the prison farm. Reported the *Milledgeville Union Recorder:* "The new 'L' to the main building will be about the first of the work to be undertaken. The building will give a dormitory space practically double that at the farm now." The state, in other words, had fulfilled its obligation. Similarly, near the end of fall, the 25 Mariettans who'd carried out the crime also received a bonus, albeit from a private source. As Lawrence Haney's daughter, Dorothy, would subsequently recall: "A few months later, Daniell Jewelry gave everyone a set of silverware for 'a job well done.' My sister still has some of it. All the men who went received this."

Leo Frank's allies had been vanquished, his killers protected and paid. More than that, however, in the deeper war over Georgia's future—the one whose forces had been so starkly arrayed on April 26, 1913—the past appeared to have triumphed, and it had done so in a way that would make itself felt for the next fifty years.

The first call for a revival of the Ku Klux Klan came on the front page of the *Jeffersonian*'s September 2 edition. Commenting upon the "sectional and racial hatred poured upon the South" by Frank's supporters, Watson proclaimed:

The North can rail itself hoarse, if it chooses to do so, but if [it] doesn't quit meddling with our business and getting commutations for assassins and rapists who have pull, *another Ku Klux Klan may be organized to restore HOME RULE.*

Like so many of Watson's utterances, his appeal for a new Invisible Empire struck a deep and mystic chord among many Georgians. Though the hooded fraternity had not been active in the state for half a century (Nathan Bedford Forrest's Klan had officially disbanded in 1869), it was not forgotten. As the historian Charlton Moseley notes in his study *Latent Klanism in Georgia, 1890–1915:* "Forty years after Reconstruction the Ku Klux Klan [remained] alive in the minds and folklore." Moreover, on January 8, 1915, the storied white-robed Knights had ridden again, this time at the Los Angeles premiere of D. W. Griffith's *The Birth of a Nation.* Subsequently, the movie, based on Thomas Dixon's best-selling novel *The Clansmen,* had been showing to both great protest and great acclaim at theaters in the Northeast. Due to the stereotypic manner in which *The Birth of a Nation* portrayed its black characters, the NAACP had attempted to block wider distribution. Yet the allure of the film's narrative (young Klansman Ben Cameron saves Dixie from carpetbaggers while avenging the death of his sister at the hands of a Negro brute) and the power of its cinematic innovations (armies of sheeted figures sweep across the screen as if come to life) carried the day. Declared one critic: "If there is a greater picture, may we live to see it." The success of *The Birth of a Nation* was assured when Griffith and Dixon arranged a private screening in the White House Blue Room for Dixon's old college classmate, Woodrow Wilson. When the lights went up, the president famously remarked: "It's like writing history with lightning, and my only regret is that it is all so terribly true." The Atlanta opening was set for December 6.

The climate in which a reconstituted Ku Klux Klan might take wing was, in short, perfect. Enter William Joseph Simmons. At 35, the self-styled Colonel Simmons was a failed Methodist preacher from Alabama who in 1915 was in Georgia working as an organizer for the Woodmen of the World lodge. An inveterate fraternalist whose jacket lapels drooped from the weight of Knights Templar and Masonic pins, he was tall, redheaded, deep-voiced and consumed by grandiose ambitions. Yet to date, he had not discovered his true calling. All this changed when within weeks of Frank's lynching, Colonel Simmons—after being struck by a car on an Atlanta street corner—was for a time confined to bed. During his convalescence, the Colonel, who claimed as a young man to have envisioned ghostriders galloping across the American sky, decided to inaugurate a new Klan. On

October 16, he filed a petition with Georgia's secretary of state seeking a charter for the organization of which he would be imperial wizard.

Thirty-four men, reputedly among them several who'd made the trip to Milledgeville, signed Simmons's petition, and on the evening of November 23, Thanksgiving eve, they met at Atlanta's Piedmont Hotel for what was to be a historic event. Awaiting the party was a chartered bus, but because the night was blustery, only fifteen hardy souls clambered aboard for the drive to Stone Mountain, where after hiking up to the granite summit, they found a giant pitch-and-kerosene-soaked wooden cross that the Colonel had put into position earlier in the day. The site chosen for this glorious moment was spectacular—and not just because it could be seen for miles in every direction. Stone Mountain was owned by the the Venables, the family who had built the structure that housed the National Pencil Company. That was the name carved over the factory door. Among those who went to the mountaintop on November 23 was 13-year-old James Venable, who many years later would himself become imperial wizard. Whatever the forces that had claimed Leo Frank, one could make a case that they were indigenous to the bedrock of Georgia, that they were darkly and primally of the South. Which was why what was kindled here on this evening, while constituting a beginning, seemed ancient and immemorial. As Simmons would subsequently write:

> Suddenly I struck a match and lighted the cross. Everyone was amazed. And thus that night at the midnight hour while men braved the surging blasts of the wild wintry mountain winds bathed in the sacred glow of the fiery cross, the Invisible Empire was called from its slumber of half a century to take up a new task and fulfill a new mission for humanity's good.

With the coming of 1916, Leo Frank's Atlanta family members and supporters found themselves either burrowing into deep internal recesses or scattering to distant cities.

For Frank's German-Jewish intimates who chose to remain in Atlanta, a shying away from any outward manifestations of their Judaism became the order of the day. Alan Marcus, Leo and Lucille's nephew, was a boy at the time. He would later recall: "We became introverted. We would hardly go out of the house. My father had practically to give away part of his business, Marcus Clothing Company. It became Marcus & Holley, 62 Peachtree Street. He sold to a non-Jewish person. Why would he have sold?"

The desire among Atlanta's Reform Jews to find safety by immersing themselves more deeply into the city's gentile majority was epitomized by the behavior of David Marx. Despite the rabbi's initial impulse to blame Georgia Christians for Frank's demise, within a few months he had reversed course and was again making every effort to align his congregation with those same Christians. "He believed," said one Temple member, "that the closer the Temple got to the churches, the better off we were." In his study of Southern Jewry, *The Provincials,* Eli Evans conveys the gist of the rabbi's thinking:

> The lynching had a profound impact on Marx . . . he reacted the only way he knew . . . He became [an even more] starkly powerful force for assimilation . . . He forbade the singing of Hatikva, the Jewish anthem of hope, as a "song of looking back"; he attacked the idea of the Jewish state from the pulpit; he refused to use wine or a canopy in wedding ceremonies.

Though Marx stopped short of becoming a self-hating Jew, there can be no doubt that he did all that he could to make his flock less conspicuous, so much so that he often cast aspersions on the ritual-heavy practices of Atlanta's growing Orthodox Jewish population. "The stories of [Marx's] efforts to blame the Orthodox community for the anti-Semitism that led to the lynching," notes Evans, left a bad taste that lingered for a generation.

Not all of the Atlanta Jews who'd backed Frank were willing to stay in the city under such conditions. Among the most conspicuous to depart was Samuel Boorstin, the young lawyer who in the spring of 1914 had played a role in putting together the extraordinary motion and had grown close to the condemned man. During the spring of 1916, Boorstin, who was of Russian extraction, moved with his wife and their 2-year-old son, Daniel, to Tulsa, Oklahoma. Eight decades later, Daniel Boorstin, the author of several noted works of history and for many years Librarian of Congress, said that while his father was always tight-lipped about his reasons for leaving, the precipitating event had occurred after the lynching when thugs bashed in the windows of a bank owned by his brothers-in-law. Quiet acquiescence offered no guarantee of safety. It was better to start anew elsewhere.

Also departing Atlanta in the spring of 1916 was the woman who had suffered worst of all. As early as late fall of the previous year, Lucille Frank had contemplated fleeing the scene of her sorrow. For a while, she had considered going to Chicago and had corresponded with a college there about enrolling in the study of architecture. Ultimately, however, she had accepted an offer from her brother-in-law, Charles Ursenbach, to take a position as manager of a women's ready-to-wear shop he was opening in Memphis, Tennessee. Lucille's feelings upon her leavetaking appear to have been hopeful. On February 9, her mother-in-law wrote her:

My dear child Lucille, I want to wish you all kinds of *luck*. If Chas's venture is successful, it will be up to *you* only as to whether you are valuable to him and incidentally to yourself.

However, there could be no denying that the still-grieving woman would forever carry within herself a knowledge of life's capriciousness. As her mother-in-law pointedly added: "Each of us is, in a great measure, 'master of our destiny,' *barring accidents.*"

For a number of Frank's Christian allies, the dislocations, though lacking any element of religious hostility, were equally wrenching. While by the end of 1915 John Slaton had returned to Atlanta, accepting the view, spelled out by Luther Rosser, that "there is no organized force that would seek to do you harm," his stay was brief. Early in 1916, he and Sallie joined numerous other notables as guests on Henry Ford's *Peace Ship,* the oceangoing yacht on which the automaker crossed the Atlantic in the hope of persuading European leaders to forgo war. When Ford's efforts, which were widely regarded as naive, failed, the Slatons came back to Atlanta, but again only for a few months. The former governor took a job with the Red Cross, and for the duration of the Great War, he and his wife resided in Romania, preferring life on the embattled continent to that at home.

Whatever upheavals the Slatons endured, they were mild compared to those experienced by Thomas Loyless. On the heels of the editor's clash with Tom Watson, much of downtown Augusta, the *Chronicle* building included, was destroyed by fire. The disaster strained Loyless both physically and financially. Worse, he was beginning to lose his eyesight. By 1919, he had written his last editorial for the paper and was soon out of journalism altogether, taking a position as manager of a down-at-the-heels spa and resort in Warm Springs, Georgia. For a man who had once run a major daily newspaper, 15 dilapidated cabins and a 46-room hotel built around a pool and mineral bath must have represented a comedown, although Loyless tried not to look at it that way. He and his backer, the philanthropist George Foster Peabody, dreamed of creating a rehabilitation center for polio victims. Which was why shortly after accepting the job, Loyless traveled to the North. Franklin D. Roosevelt, Woodrow Wilson's assistant secretary of the navy, had contracted the disease and was seeking a facility in which to undergo treatment. During Roosevelt's first stay at Warm Springs, Loyless helped to oversee the regimen whereby the patient tried to regain feeling and strength in his withered legs. Eventually, the men became close, and as Roosevelt improved, he gave his new friend much of the credit. Loyless did not, however, live to see Roosevelt grow strong enough to return to politics, much less ascend to the White House. Two years after the future president began visiting Warm Springs, the sole newspaperman to mount a sustained protest against the lynching of Leo Frank was dead of cancer.

Like Loyless, William Smith found himself in a tailspin during the early months of 1916. The lawyer's phone essentially stopped ringing, as old clients forsook him and new ones failed to materialize. Soon, he abandoned his office in downtown Atlanta's gleaming Hurt Building for more humble quarters on gritty South Forsyth Street. "Dad hung in there trying to make a living," said his son Walter, "but he'd committed professional suicide by trying to save Frank." Half a year after the lynching, Smith still carried a pistol.

In the summer of 1916, hoping both to economize and to change his surroundings, Smith moved his family to a farmhouse he owned on Chickamauga Avenue in an as yet undeveloped section west of Atlanta. That fall, Mary Lou, despite having given birth to the couple's third child a few months earlier, took a job as an assistant at a new public kindergarten. Ultimately, Smith's efforts to rebuild a life in Georgia came to naught. "Dad told me he was so disheartened and disgusted that he said, 'I'll never practice law again,' " Walter Smith recalled years later. "He felt the system didn't work." Smith, despite his many efforts for the defense, continued to blame himself for the final outcome. "A major part of the whole thing was regret, remorse and an extreme feeling of guilt," said Walter Smith. "As Dad would say, he'd rendered Conley 'impervious to cross-examination.' "

In 1917, his prospects in Atlanta nonexistent and his faith in the law all but destroyed, Smith quit his practice and left the city, making his way to Virginia, where he took a job as an assistant shipfitter at the Newport News Ship Building and Dry Dock Company. Shortly thereafter, he migrated to an adjacent military base, where he worked as a carpenter building hay barns. Meantime, Mary Lou and the three children moved back to the family's Lucile Avenue home in Atlanta's West End section, where they lived off the rent paid by an ever shifting collection of boarders, the proceeds from the sale of the Chickamauga Avenue property and the few dollars Smith managed to send back from time to time.

For Smith, 1917 went by in a haze of labor and movement. Once again, he was a tramp alumnus, though now it was not a lark. By 1918, he was in New York City, where he accepted a job with the William Burns Detective Agency. What Tom Watson would have made of such a fact can only be imagined, but as Walter Smith subsequently put it: "Dad needed the job." Smith was assigned full-time to the Morse Dry Dock Company at the end of Fifty-sixth Street in Brooklyn. The Great War made the massive shipbuilding facility a prime target of espionage. "The people he worked with thought he was a timekeeper," remembered his daughter, "but he was working really in security to protect the yard from Germans." The Morse company was so pleased with Smith that it ultimately hired him away from

Burns, affording him the financial security to bring his family to New York. By the year's end, Smith, Mary Lou and the children were living in an apartment on Brooklyn's Sixth Avenue.

While Smith continued to be a valued employee at Morse and Mary Lou found work teaching at a New York probationary school, she felt lost in the big city. When the Atlanta Public Schools offered her a position, she jumped at the opportunity, rushing home with the children. Once again alone, Smith began to consider resuming his chosen profession. "Dad decided he'd trained as a lawyer and that he'd practice," recalled Walter Smith.

In the spring of 1920, Smith passed the New York bar and Mary Lou, her one-year teaching commitment in Atlanta fulfilled, sold the Lucile Avenue home and its furniture, packed up the china and returned to New York. As an enticement, her husband had purchased two lots in a still-sylvan section of Staten Island. During their first months in the Westerleigh neighborhood, the Smiths lived in a one-room tar-paper shack heated by a potbellied stove. "It was really roughing it," remembered Walter Smith. Meanwhile, Smith, with the help of a couple of laborers, dug a foundation, poured concrete and began framing a new house. By the winter of 1920, the two-story clapboard dwelling at 149 Mountain View Avenue was finished. Around the same time, Smith accepted a job at McLaughlin & Stern, a New York City real estate law firm at 15 William Street just off Wall Street, where he would work as an associate for a straight salary. For him at 40, a partnership seemed out of reach. Smith had regained his belief in the law, yet as his son later reflected: "Dad had made up his mind he never again wanted to take a criminal case. So he drew up contracts, visited clients. Real estate law is complicated in New York, and he found it satisfying." Occasionally, sitting on the porch of their Mountain View house, Smith and his wife would share their regrets about ending up so far from home and everything familiar to them. No one knew how to fry chicken in New York, much less prepare beaten biscuits. Yet any nostalgia the two felt for Atlanta was tempered by their awareness of the reality of what they'd been through there and a shared conviction that the injustice visited upon Leo Frank bespoke an ingrained and intolerable small-mindedness. In fact, they had a phrase for it, one Mary Lou had coined during her brief attempt at repatriation. "When Mother got off the train at Terminal Station," her daughter recalled, "she said, 'Atlanta looks squished.'" By this, Mary Lou did not mean that the capital of the New South appeared compact. She was speaking figuratively. "It all tied in to the Frank case," explained her daughter. The Smiths saw Atlanta as a place whose people had failed to measure up in a dark hour, who had shrunk from the truth. The diminution was one of the collective heart. How could they ever go back?

Though few came right out and said so, Georgians in general and Atlantans in particular found life in the aftermath of the Frank affair to their liking. The slogan "a return to normalcy" would not enter the lexicon until Warren Harding's 1920 presidential campaign, but it perfectly describes the atmosphere. Long-standing views had been affirmed, and the evidence appeared across a broad spectrum. For one thing, there was the tolerant, indeed amused, reaction to the further escapades of the drama's Negro hero.

Around 1 A.M. on November 1, 1915, Jim Conley was arrested along with ten other men and women in Atlanta's Vine City neighborhood at what the *Georgian* termed a "disorderly house." The next morning, he was arraigned in police court. However, there, as the *Journal* dryly reported, "instead of drawing a fine, Jim drew a bride." This unusual resolution arose from Conley's stated desire to marry one of the seductresses with whom he'd been apprehended. To this, Judge George Johnson not only assented, but when Conley professed to have insufficient funds to buy a license, the magistrate passed the hat, contributing a large share of the money from his own pocket. Then, in the presence of a crowd of lawyers and gawkers, Johnson performed the ceremony, pronouncing James Conley and Mary Glover man and wife. On the way out the door, the groom begged reporters, "Don't write me up, for God's sake. I've been in the papers enough." But, of course, his request fell on deaf ears. And this was just the beginning.

Throughout the remaining weeks of 1915, the first months of 1916 and, in fact, much of the next three years, Jim Conley would remain almost constantly in the news. Only now, the stories would chart a rapid spiral downward. On November 7, six days after his wedding, the new husband was picked up, in the *Journal*'s phrase, for "bride beating." Several weeks later, he was arrested for the same offense. On February 13, 1916, the *Constitution* allowed that "Conley is 'in again' for wife beating." Hard upon this spree, the man whose testimony had doomed Leo Frank was charged with public drunkenness, then vagrancy. By 1918, Conley, in one writer's estimation, had "spent more time in jail than out of it" since Mary Phagan's murder. And the worst was still to come. At 12:30 A.M. on January 13, 1919, during an attempted break-in at a West Side Atlanta drugstore, the Negro was shot in the chest by the proprietor, who had been lying in wait following a burglary several nights before. After a lengthy stay at Grady Hospital, Conley stood trial in superior court, where investigating officers testified that he had not only been in possession of tools useful in breaking and entering when apprehended but that he was suspected in 31 prior incidents. The jury quickly voted to convict, and Judge John Humphries pronounced a sentence of 20 years, whereupon Conley, far from looking stricken, burst into laughter. Cracked a court attaché: "He figures the governor will pardon him out—the son of a gun."

By any measure, it had been a tawdry sequence of events, yet far from inspiring Atlantans to rethink their opinions, Conley's postlynching misadventures served to preserve the predominant view. To wit: Jim was an ignorant, drunken lowlife incapable of manufacturing a complex story designed to implicate Frank in little Mary's murder. Though a minority thought differently (one lawman who met Conley in 1918 called him "the smartest criminal [I've] ever come in contact with"), the verdict was all but unanimous—the authorities had been right about this Negro.

At the same moment Jim Conley was beginning his descent, the two white Georgians most responsible for Leo Frank's fate were beginning a corresponding ascent. The process started with a spring 1916 visit by Hugh Dorsey to the home of Tom Watson. Shortly thereafter, the Fulton County solicitor general announced his candidacy for governor, at which point the Sage, forsaking his pledge of just a few months earlier, denounced Nat Harris, who was seeking reelection, as a Slaton man. In his endorsement, Watson termed Dorsey "the fearless Solicitor General who won the great fight for LAW AND ORDER, and the PROTECTION OF WOMANHOOD, in the Frank case," adding: *"The Jeffersonian is for him tooth and nail."*

Predictably, Dorsey, who played to the electorate's anti-Jewish leanings ("The attitude of the Hebrews in the Frank case," he told gatherings, "has demonstrated the fact that the successful prosecution of a Hebrew is regarded as a persecution"), was swept into office. Moreover, a number of other Watson-backed proposals and candidates were also successful. Not only did the state Democratic Party adopt a platform plank condemning all attempts on the part of the United States government to extradite Georgia citizens for trial, but Atticus Henslee, the Frank juror whom the defense had accused of anti-Semitic bias in its initial appeal, was elected to the Prison Commission. In his endorsement of the former buggy salesman, the Sage wrote: *"He is* THE JUROR *who was so outrageously* DENOUNCED BY LUTHER ROSSER IN THE FRANK CASE! *Henslee stood firm and true."*

For Watson, this was a time of triumph. Politically, the only goal that now eluded him was elective office of his own. Little wonder, then, that in 1920 he announced his candidacy for the United States Senate seat held by his sworn enemy, Hoke Smith. There was, however, another aspirant—Hugh Dorsey. During the campaign, which played out against a backdrop of postwar anxiety regarding aliens and "Reds," Watson and Dorsey took sharply delineated positions. (Hoke Smith, who tacked to the center, soon fell hopelessly behind.) Dorsey, who was supported by the American Legion, championed Woodrow Wilson's call for a League of Nations to adjudicate international conflicts. Watson, who was supported by the Ku Klux Klan, opposed the League, but in a twist, he became a voice for civil liberties, railing against the efforts of Wilson's new attorney general, Mitchell Palmer, to imprison laborers and immigrants suspected of harboring communist sympathies. In fact, the Sage was so outspoken on the matter that as he crisscrossed Georgia, he often referred to the farmers who met him in one hamlet after another as red-clay Bolsheviki. Though some might have found the Watson of 1920 a far cry from the one who'd attacked Leo Frank, he believed that he was merely continuing his battle for the workingman. By the campaign's end, he was drawing vast crowds, and his victory was a foregone conclusion. After years in the wilderness, Watson was back. And as for Dorsey, he retained the job of governor until June 1921.

Incongruously enough, Dorsey, though never wavering in his belief in Frank's guilt, was Georgia's most progressive governor of the time. Concerned by a plague of violence that met the state's black veterans as they came marching home from war, he authored a groundbreaking 1921 study entitled "A Statement as to the Negro in Georgia." Under such headings as "The negro lynched," "The negro held in peonage" and "The negro subject to individual acts of cruelty," he detailed 135 incidents of racial injustice that had occurred over a two-year period, declaring: "If the conditions indicated by these charges should continue, both God and man would justly condemn Georgia." Dorsey did not, however, stop here. In a series of sweeping proposals, he outlined legal remedies whereby the governor could dispatch state police officers to potential trouble spots and convene grand juries to investigate lynchings. Not surprisingly, the responses to Dorsey's ideas varied widely. At an interracial conference in Atlanta, he won the support of many who'd spoken out against him during the Frank affair, including the *Georgian*'s James B. Nevin, the Reverend C. B. Wilmer and Rabbi David Marx. But at mass meetings throughout the state, the populace at large condemned him. Roared a typical *Constitution* headline: DORSEY PEONAGE PAMPHLET SCORED. When his program came before the legislature it was defeated. Nonetheless, his thinking on the topic was ahead of its time, and so it remained. In fact, as a Fulton County Superior Court judge during the 1930s, Dorsey was at the center of a critical First Amendment case that enabled him to make another enlightened decision. A 19-year-old Negro named Angelo Herndon had been convicted of distributing communist literature on the steps of the Atlanta post office. He was represented by a young lawyer named Elbert Tuttle, who was a Cornell student during the Frank trial. "I took the Herndon case to Hugh because I wanted to give him a chance to pay his debt to society for what he'd done to Leo Frank," Tuttle recalled years later in his chambers at the Fifth District United States Court, from whence during the 1960s he'd presided over the desegregation of many of the South's schools. Tuttle's instincts were correct: Dorsey ruled that Georgia had denied Herndon his right to free speech. The United States Supreme Court subsequently concurred.

Watson, meanwhile, continued to stand defiantly at the barricades. Not that there weren't anomalies here, too. In the fall of 1921, during a debate in Washington over the senatorial candidacy of Henry Ford, who had been disseminating virulent anti-Semitic literature through a journal called the *Dearborn Independent*, the Sage proclaimed:

> Henry Ford is editing a paper devoted to war upon the Jewish race — not some criminal Jew, convicted or unconvicted — but upon the whole race — the race that produced Moses, Solomon, David . . . and Jesus Christ. All Christendom rests upon a Book, and that Book is the Book holding the creed of a Jew. Nevertheless, Henry Ford condemns the whole race, forgetting that in all our wars the Jew has fought side by side with the Gentile, forgetting that the soundest principles of democracy and good government and catholic humanity are to be found in the sacred parchments of the Jews, forgetting . . . that Jews compose music that will perhaps outlive the Pyramids . . . I doubt the senatorial fitness of a man who indicts a whole race because of the faults of some of its black sheep.

Watson's criticism of Ford was doubtless sincere. In the end, however, it indicated no real change. (To him, the automaker was just another Yankee industrialist.) More typical was his reaction to a congressional inquiry, also in the fall of 1921, into Klan-related violence. Bursting into a capitol hearing room, Watson positioned himself at the side of the probe's main witness, Imperial Wizard Simmons, vowing to protect him from "any attacks from anybody." Shortly thereafter, in reply to a question from a fellow senator as to whether he himself was a member of the Invisible Empire, the Sage proudly allowed that back home, he was regarded as "the King of the Ku Klux." Which would be how he was remembered. Suffering from asthma and the afflictions of old age, Watson died in Washington of a cerebral hemorrhage on September 26, 1922. At his funeral in Georgia, the most impressive floral arrangement was an eight-foot-high cross of red roses sent by the Klan.

And so the Sage was gone, but through the 1920s, his hooded legatees would accrue power and influence — and not just in Georgia. From the Klan's white-columned Imperial Palace in Atlanta, Kleagles, as its salesmen were known, spread the message to "White, Gentile, Protestant, American Citizens," who in turn paid a $10 fee for insignias and robes. By 1923, Imperial Wizard Simmons was ensconced in a mansion, Klan Krest, and membership totaled over a million, a number that included Georgia's new governor, Cliff Walker, who eight years before as Nat Harris's attorney general had produced the finding that forbade the expenditure of state funds to investigate Leo Frank's lynching.

The Klan reached its apogee as a political force during the summer of 1924 when it nearly seized control of the national Democratic Party. True to form, the movement began in Georgia when the grand dragon of the local realm instructed delegates to the state convention in Atlanta to choose delegates to the national convention in New York pledged to the Klan's presidential candidate—William Gibbs McAdoo. The result: 85 percent of those selected to attend the gathering at Madison Square Garden were either members of or in sympathy with the Invisible Empire. Upon reaching New York, the Georgians found many kindred spirits; the Klan presence was so pervasive that its leaders took a floor atop the Hotel McAlpin. The convention's fiercest fight was over a proposed platform plank condemning political secret societies and pledging the party "to oppose any effort on the part of the Ku Klux Klan to interfere with the religious liberty or political freedom of any citizen because of religion, birthplace or racial origin." Klan delegates rallied against the plank, and polling was conducted in a hostile atmosphere. Notes one historian: "Fist-fights were started. State standards were broken." In the middle of the ultimately successful battle against the plank was a Georgia delegate who nine years before in an oak grove outside Marietta had kicked over the table that led to the Invisible Empire's reemergence. That man was Judge Newt Morris.

As the years began to pass, Leo Frank's supporters all but stopped speaking publicly about the case. For those who stayed in Atlanta, coexistence with their victorious opponents demanded as much. Though this was true for everyone, it was more true for Luther Rosser, whose son, Luther Jr., was, of course, married to Hugh Dorsey's sister, Sarah. "The only way the relationships in the family survived is that no one ever discussed the subject," Rosser's grandson Tom Shelton later recalled. Following Rosser's death from a heart attack in 1923, the topic remained taboo. "We shared Christmases with the Dorseys through the 1930s," added Shelton, "and as a consequence we just didn't talk about it—it was too close."

The reluctance of Frank's gentile allies to address the topic sprang merely from discomfiture, but for members of Atlanta's German-Jewish elite, the silence had about it an added air of repression and dread. Decades afterward, Clarence Feibelman, who as a teenager had attended the trial and subsequently went to work for the Montag Paper Company, recalled: "It was a subject that wasn't talked about at all. We didn't want to revive a nightmare." Leonard Haas's widow, Bea, echoed this view: "The Jewish community was scared to death and kept a low profile." Herbert Haas's son Joseph, who practiced law with his father for nineteen years, concurred: "My father never wanted to talk about it. He never got over the horror of it.

It was just a terrible thing that happened in his life." Charles Wittenstein, general counsel to the Southern office of the Anti-Defamation League, an organization that was founded in 1913 and came into its own primarily as a result of the Frank lynching, put the Temple congregation's feelings into perspective: "The attitude of the older Jews was 'leave it alone.' What was behind it was a fear that if the case was reopened, they'd experience the [same] kind of anti-Semitism again."

The Atlanta Jewish community's determination to quell conversation about the Frank case, and, most especially, to keep further mention of it out of the newspapers, revealed itself again and again. The first and most dramatic incident occurred in 1922 when a young Dutch reporter expressed interest in revisiting the matter. Shortly after landing a job at the *Constitution,* Pierre Van Paassen immersed himself in the records at the Fulton County Courthouse. There, he discovered what seemed to be critical new evidence—Frank's dental X rays and photographs of Mary Phagan's body "showing teeth indentures." Confirming long-standing speculation, Van Paassen later wrote: "The murdered girl had been bitten on the left shoulder and neck before being strangled." What was truly startling, however, was this: "The photos of the teeth marks on her body did not correspond with Leo Frank's set of teeth . . . If those photos had been published at the time of the murder . . . the lynching would probably not have taken place." Filled with youthful enthusiasm, the reporter secured his editor's permission to undertake a series intended, as he'd subsequently put it, to "establish Frank's innocence and rehabilitate his memory." Then came the hurdles. Upon consulting Frank's friend and lawyer Henry Alexander, Van Paassen was told to back off. "The Jewish community still felt nervous about the incident. If I wrote the articles old resentments might be stirred up . . . It was better, Mr. Alexander thought, to leave sleeping lions alone." Joining the chorus of naysayers were several unnamed rabbis (David Marx undoubtedly among them) who "actually pleaded" with Van Paassen's editor to cancel the assignment. Reporters meet such resistance every day, but what followed was unusual. "Lay off the Frank case if you want to keep healthy," read the unsigned note Van Paassen presently received. Shortly thereafter, as he was driving home one morning, "a large automobile" pulled up beside his and forced it "into the track of a fast-moving street car coming from the opposite direction." Van Paassen escaped injury, but his vehicle was demolished. Badly shaken, he dropped the story. Nonetheless, all of it—the apparently telltale photographic and X-ray images he saw at the courthouse, the insistent lengths to which some Atlanta Jews went to dissuade him from going forward—remained vivid in his mind throughout a career that saw him rise to the top of Parisian journalism. In his 1964 memoir *To Number Our Days,* Van Paassen devoted as much space to his brief and nearly fatal attempt to revive interest in Leo Frank as he did to some of the European personages who stood center stage in his later life.

Through the succeeding generations, Atlanta's Jews remained committed to the view that the less said about the Frank case, the better. During the 1940s, when the lawyer Arthur Powell, a supporter of Slaton's commutation decision, published a book in which he tantalizingly asserted that he was "one of the few people who know that Leo Frank was innocent," he was restrained from revealing his hand by the intervention of his law partner, Max Goldstein. The nature of the information Powell possessed is unclear (the consensus is that it further implicated Jim Conley), but whatever it was, there is little doubt as to what happened to it. Following Powell's death, Goldstein—believing that it would only inflame the feelings of those in disagreement—destroyed it.

The thoroughness with which Atlanta's Jews succeeded in banishing the Frank case from public discourse might suggest that they had also succeeded in banishing it from their collective consciousness. But that was not so. In truth, the efforts made to expunge all mention of the topic offered proof of just how firmly it remained foremost in their minds. The outer silence existed in direct proportion to an inner awareness, and nothing better illustrates the point than an ongoing obsession of Henry Alexander's. Even as the lawyer had been discouraging Pierre Van Paassen from opening old wounds, he had himself been assiduously seeking information about men and women involved in the affair. In fact, from 1916 until the early 1950s, the lawyer amassed scores of clippings. Some of the stories—among them, a series of 1921 articles detailing the indictment of Monteen Stover for participating in a badger scam in which she enticed married men into hotel rooms, then allegedly bribed them on threat of exposure—must have proved satisfying, offering further evidence of how disreputable many of the prosecution witnesses had indeed been. Other pieces—a 1919 account revealing the death of the longtime *Constitution* reporter Britt Craig from pneumonia shortly after taking a job at the *New York Sun;* a 1925 story reporting the death of Frank's mother—enabled Alexander to close the books on various of the tale's leading figures. Then there were the dispatches that could not have helped but gall, most especially one from 1933 reporting Governor Eugene Talmadge's extension of a full pardon to William Creen, the prison farm inmate who'd slashed Frank's throat several weeks before the lynching. There were also numerous articles regarding the further careers of a number of Mariettans—Herbert Clay, for one—indicating that Alexander possessed a strong inkling as to who was responsible for Frank's execution. In the end, the most poignant item in the lawyer's file was a photograph taken either while he was a student at the University of Georgia or shortly thereafter showing him and his roommate, Hugh

Dorsey, chatting amiably while leaning against a tree trunk at a picnic. In 1943, upon learning that Dorsey would be present, Alexander had refused to attend the fiftieth reunion of his University of Georgia class. Yet he held on to the picture, for it provided an image of what life had been like for Atlanta's Jews before the lynching.

Not surprisingly, there was another group of Georgians who maintained a strict silence about the Frank case. In the index to a 1935 history of Marietta entitled *The First Hundred Years,* the victim of the town's most notorious crime merits but a single dry entry: "Frank, non-resident." Along with a few other similarly discreet but prideful communal acknowledgments—in the 1920s, the trunk of the oak tree at Frey's Gin received a commemorative whitewashing, while during the same period one of the sleeves of Frank's nightshirt was framed and put on display behind the bar of a roadhouse a few miles south of the lynching site—this was it in terms of public recognition. Recalled *Marietta Journal* associate editor Bill Kinney: "You can't imagine what it used to be like around here. Just the mention of the case would cause people to admonish you."

Yet the inexpressible truth was that for the Mariettans involved the lynching constituted a defining event. For nearly half a century, the political, financial and social course of the town would be influenced by what had transpired at Frey's Gin. Leo Frank was, in brief, forever a resident.

The Mariettan who benefited most immediately from the lynching was Judge Newt Morris. Reelected to the judgeship of the Blue Ridge Circuit in 1916, he would retain that position until 1920, then assume the chairmanship of the Marietta school board. His successes on the national political stage continued at the 1928 Democratic Party convention (he was chairman of the Rules and Order of Business Committee) and again at the 1932 gathering. In 1934, Morris reset his sights on big game—Franklin D. Roosevelt. Responding to the president's attempt to secure another term for Georgia Democratic committeeman John S. Cohen, managing editor of the *Atlanta Journal,* the judge wired party chairman James A. Farley: "You may save him now, but the loyal Georgians will beat hell out of him in 1936. Georgia Democrats are red-blooded Americans capable of running their own affairs without outside interference." Ultimately, Morris contracted rheumatoid arthritis, and for the last several years of his life, he was practically immobile. Still, thanks to the ministrations of his Negro manservant, he was a presence on the Marietta square until shortly before his death in 1941.

John Tucker Dorsey reaped similar rewards as a result of his role in the lynching. After completing his term as the legislature's prison committee chairman and receiving a full pardon from his distant cousin Governor

Hugh Dorsey for his youthful murder conviction, he succeeded Herbert Clay as solicitor general of the Blue Ridge Circuit, thereby assuring that the group responsible for the events at Frey's Gin retained control of the prosecutor's office. After returning to private practice, Dorsey was reelected to the statehouse, where he became connected to the Gene Talmadge machine. During the 1950s, he would serve as Cobb County ordinary and on the board of Marietta's Larry Bell Park. Late into his days, John Tuck remained a big, gruff, respected figure. At a fish camp he owned on the Coosawattee River near Ellijay, 50 miles north of Marietta, the town's bucks gathered every summer to play cards and drink corn liquor — to become, in the words of one of them, men.

Numerous members of the Brumby family likewise prospered in the wake of the lynching. True, the two family members most directly involved in the crime — brothers Bolan and Jim — did not remain in Georgia. In the late teens, Bolan Brumby moved to Clearwater, Florida. Jim Brumby, who spent the war years as Marietta's mayor, left in 1921 to take a job as city manager in Ocala, Florida. Yet it was also in 1921 that Otis Brumby, scion of the family's other branch, sold his interest in the *St. Petersburg Times* and returned home to start a new paper, the *Cobb County Times,* which in 1951 merged with the *Marietta Journal.* Fifty years later, a Brumby still presided over not just the *Journal* and a string of profitable suburban weeklies but the Brumby Chair Company, manufacturer of the famed rocker, five of which sat on the White House's Truman Balcony during the presidency of fellow Georgian Jimmy Carter.

Though the powerful men who helped to arrange, then cover up, Frank's lynching ultimately gained the most from their handiwork, some of those who played lesser parts profited as well. In return for his funding of the raid, the banker Robert A. Hill was not prosecuted when he subsequently shot and killed his son-in-law. One of the last to draw on this same account was the farmer Lawrence Haney. Like many of the men who made the trip to Milledgeville, Haney spent the 1930s and '40s working in patronage jobs. For a while, he helped Black Newt Morris run the Cobb County chain gang, then he served on the Marietta police force. Haney's final such position was night security guard at the city's Larry Bell Park during the 1950s. By this point, he had become an occasionally drunken presence who sometimes threatened park patrons. His behavior was so unpredictable that a young park board member tried to have him fired. Prior to the necessary review session, this naive reformer believed he controlled three of the board's four votes. There was one outstanding vote — it belonged to John Tucker Dorsey. No sooner had the meeting to decide Haney's fate started than Dorsey threw his weight behind his loyal underling, instantly assuring that he retained his employment. As Bill Kinney, who was the board member who'd sought Haney's removal, later put it: "There was one thing that J. T. Dorsey would not tolerate—anyone messing with old man Lawrence Haney."

Of all the beneficiaries of the Frank lynching, the one who went furthest was the one whose role, save at the end, remains obscure. Whether John Wood did any more than serve as the wheelman, helping Judge Newt Morris race Frank's body from Marietta to the Atlanta city limits, will probably never be known. However, it is a certainty that thereafter Wood rapidly achieved power and renown. In 1916, he was elected to the state legislature. In 1921, he was elected solicitor general of the Blue Ridge Circuit, succeeding John T. Dorsey. Following four years as North Georgia's chief prosecutor, he won Newt Morris's old job as judge of the Blue Ridge Circuit, a position he would hold until 1931, when he was elevated once again, this time to a seat in the United States Congress, representing Georgia's Ninth District. In 1934, Wood suffered a rare setback, losing in the Democratic primary. He returned home, where for the next ten years he prospered as a defense lawyer. In 1945, Wood was returned to Congress. Back in Washington, he was appointed to the House Un-American Activities Committee, of which he would become chairman in 1950. Among his protégés was a brash young California congressman assigned to his committee—the future president Richard Nixon. During HUAC's 1953 investigation into communist activity in Hollywood, it was Wood who subpoenaed Lillian Hellman to testify, thereby inadvertently engendering the playwright's oft-quoted demur. In a letter to Wood, the author of *The Little Foxes* declared:

> I am not willing . . . to bring bad trouble to people who, in my past association with them, were completely innocent of any talk or any action that was disloyal or subversive. I do not like subversion or disloyalty in any form, and if I had ever seen any, I would have considered it my duty to have reported it to the proper authorities. But to hurt innocent people whom I knew many years ago in order to save myself is, to me, inhuman and indecent and dishonorable. I cannot and will not cut my conscience to fit this year's fashions.

And so life progressed for the better part of the lynching brethren. Yet there was a small contingent for whom the weight of it all proved burdensome. In several instances, in fact, reverberations from the events at Frey's Gin may have sent participants to an early grave.

Though Herbert Clay would remain solicitor general of the Blue Ridge Circuit until 1918, within two years of Frank's death he was in trouble. His difficulties began, at least publicly, at 12:30 A.M. on May 19, 1917, when he allegedly accosted a 26-year-old nurse as she walked across the Marietta town square. According to Bobby Lou Greer, Clay "grasped her by the arm and insulted her." The next evening, Mrs. Greer, who that morning had demanded an apology, met her well-known assailant as he was emerging from a movie theater.

> "I have been waiting all day for that apology," she announced by way of greeting.
> "I am ready to apologize now," came the reply.

In the end, however, no apology was tendered. Rather than give Clay a chance to exercise his charm, Mrs. Greer lashed out at him with a buggy whip she had been holding in her hands. All told, she struck eight blows. Roared the headline atop the next day's *Georgian:* WOMAN USES HORSE-WHIP ON SOLICITOR GEN. CLAY.

On the surface, the encounter with Bobby Lou Greer was of a piece with the other outrageous escapades to which Clay had been linked since his brief but disruptive tenure at the University of Georgia. Yet on a deeper level, the incident indicated a new lack of restraint, one suggestive not of a man trying to get away with as much as possible but of one begging to be caught. And there would be more.

On a Sunday night sometime later in 1917 or early in 1918, Clay checked in to Dave Jarrett's Hotel, a celebrated lodging house in the little mountain town of Ellijay, where the Blue Ridge Circuit was set to hold a week of court. The docket was full of cases, yet rather than retire early, Clay and the lawyer with whom he was rooming, John Tucker Dorsey, stayed up until all hours drinking. As Dorsey's longtime partner, Luther Hames, later related: "Dorsey told me that when Herbert drank, he got loose bowels. Anyway, he took a shit in bed and tried to roll Dorsey into it. That's where the fight started." The next thing anyone knew, Dave Jarrett was pounding on the door of another guest, Newt Morris.

> "Judge," the hotelier screamed, "you've got to do something about those damn lawyers. They've shit all over their room, in the bed clothes."
> "Bring me the bill and I'll pay it," a furious Morris responded. "Then burn the bed clothes."

The story quickly became a staple of after-hours conversation among members of the Marietta bar. More significant, it ruined the solicitor's relationship with Morris, who now grew to disdain and possibly fear him. If Clay's lack of control was such that he'd leave a stinking mess for the judge to clean up, what guarantee was there that in a similar moment of insobriety he would not divulge the story of Frank's lynching? Reflecting on the subsequent tension between the men at the heart of the conspiracy, Luther Hames observed: "Judge Newt Morris and Herbert Clay were terrible enemies."

Another result of Clay's loutish behavior was that his marriage came apart. Marjorie Lockwood Clay had put up with more from Herbert than most women would have. Not only was there his drinking and carousing, but there was her apparent disgust regarding his involvement in the events at Frey's Gin. Marjorie's father was Montgomery's top society architect, and she had been raised in a home free from anti-Semitism. According to Bob Gamble, senior architectural historian for the Alabama Historical Commission, "Mr. Lockwood was the darling of the Jewish community." In 1919, Marjorie was granted a divorce and custody of Eugene Herbert, Jr.

Living with his mother and dangerously overweight (the once handsome rake had ballooned into a bloated 40-year-old with a 54-inch waist), Clay nevertheless did his best to carry on in the old style. And to some degree he succeeded, winning election to the Georgia Senate in 1920, then securing the body's presidency, which in effect made him the state's lieutenant governor. Clay never lost his ability to use his ebullience to get himself out of jams. In late 1921 or early 1922, he demonstrated as much following an incident that saw him forced to walk home through downtown Marietta wearing only his underwear after nearly being caught in flagrante delicto with a neighbor's wife. Rather than despair, Clay, accompanied by several clergymen, appeared the next day on the square in front of the statue of his revered father and asked for forgiveness. As those who were there would later recount, he declared: "I have befouled another man's nest." He was reelected to the senate by a large majority.

For all of this, however, Clay's life was careering toward a terrible conclusion. On a January night in 1923, a young Marietta girl named Annie Gober who was a passenger in Clay's car was killed just south of town when he swerved to avoid oncoming traffic and she was tossed through his windshield. Though no charges were filed against Clay, the accident fit into the larger careless pattern. The end came at 3 A.M. on Friday, June 22, when Clay was found dead in a room at an Atlanta hotel. A coroner's inquest ruled that death resulted from "fatty degeneration of the heart." The truth, however, was evidently different. "Clay was killed when a whore hit him over the head with a liquor bottle," Luther Hames asserted years later. Advancing another theory was Clay's son, who maintained that his father was murdered by the Ku Klux Klan. The basis for this view is twofold. First, Clay had attacked the group in the state senate. Second, his besotted unreliability was a threat not only to the lynching brethren but to the hooded fraternity. Whichever, there's now no way of knowing. As Herbert Jr., citing his family's preference for decorum at all costs, would later put it: "My grandmother covered up everything."

While Clay was the most prominent of the conspirators to meet an ugly and premature end, he was not the only one. Just before noon on March 10, 1925, 58-year-old William Frey, the man who'd knotted the rope and on whose property Frank was lynched, shot himself to death in front of a corn crib on his farm, not far from the hallowed oak tree. Years later, a Marietta historian asserted that Frey's death "was not thought to be related to the Frank matter but to concern over his health, which declined dramatically after a stroke in September, 1924." Still, following so closely upon Clay's death, the suicide struck a chord. As Deveraux McClatchey, Jr., whose father was one of Clay's pallbearers, would subsequently say: "My dad said everyone involved suffered a violent death."

In truth, Clay and Frey were the exceptions. Nonetheless, several others involved in Frank's lynching lived their final days in fear. As Otis Cheatham, a railroad conductor who in the summer of 1970 nursed George Daniell, one of the mission's field lieutenants, through his last illness, recalled: "He was kind of scared; I don't know what of, but he had a pistol by his bed."

Another of the participants spent his concluding years consumed by a different concern — that of exposure. After retiring from Congress in 1955, John Wood was nominated by President Dwight D. Eisenhower to a three-year term on the Subversive Activities Control Board. Both of Georgia's United States senators supported the nomination. However, at a hearing before a subcommittee of the upper chamber's Judiciary Committee, witnesses testified that not only had Wood been a member of the Ku Klux Klan during the 1920s but that as chairman of HUAC, he'd derailed an investigation into the group. After quoting a statement in which the former congressman referred to Klan affiliation as "an old American custom, like illegal whiskey drinking," Civil Rights Congress Secretary William J. Patterson, in words that must have made Wood, who was present in the room, wince, brought up another "old American custom," declaring:

> Five thousand lynchings have taken place in the South, a large part of them in Georgia. No lyncher has ever been brought to justice, nor have I heard Mr. Wood open his mouth on one occasion where these acts of violence were taking place.

By way of concluding his argument that Wood's nomination should be rejected, Patterson accused him of being "a racist and an anti-Semite." Such charges presented a powerful threat to the former congressman's prospects. And while at a second hearing, Wood mounted a vigorous defense — contending that he'd dropped out of the Invisible Empire following just one meeting, prosecuted Klan members while solicitor general of the Blue

Ridge Circuit, and never blocked a HUAC probe of the group—his nomination was dead.

Finally, a handful of those involved in Frank's lynching confronted, to lesser and greater degrees, the painful truth. For two men, the awareness eventually dawned that they'd been exploited by the conspiracy's leaders. "My dad definitely thought he'd been used," Lawrence Haney's daughter, Dorothy, recalled. And Black Newt Morris's son, Paul, said: "My mother never did like Judge Newt, because anything Judge wanted to do, my dad would do it. Daddy did all the work, and Judge got all the money."

In any last analysis, Haney and Black Newt's late-in-life recognitions hardly amounted to admissions of wrongdoing. For a couple of others, however, there was genuine remorse. "Fred Morris agonized over it for years," recalled Bill Kinney, speaking of the lawyer and Boy Scout leader who'd done so much to legitimize the plot. "He had it on his conscience until the day he died." While clearing out Morris's desk following his death, Luther Hames found one of the famous photographs of Frank's body hanging at Frey's Gin. "I told Fred's widow that I wanted it," the judge remembered years afterward. "But she wouldn't let me have it. She tore it into a thousand pieces. She said, 'This has caused us enough grief.' " If possible, Luther Burton, the young man who'd served as muscle on the trip to Milledgeville, felt even deeper regret. Though massive in size and rough in appearance, Burton, who for much of his adult life ran a coal yard, was generous of spirit. "When I grew up," recalled Moultrie Sessions's daughter, Lucille, "if you were late paying for the coal, it didn't matter." During the Depression, added another old-time Mariettan, "a local shoe store went out of business, and Luther went in and bought the stock for $500, then gave the shoes to people who didn't have any." It was perfectly in character, then, that Burton, who outlived everyone else involved in the lynching, would ultimately conclude that he'd sinned. "He was guilt-ridden about it," observed Bill Kinney. "First, he believed he'd broken the law. Then, in taking another man's life, he believed he'd broken God's law." In 1973, cognizant that his days were dwindling down and convinced, in Kinney's words, that he was "going to hell," Burton sought out Cobb County Superior Court judge James Manning and confessed not only his part in the crime but the names of everyone else involved and many of the conspiracy's particulars. Before the year was out, Burton was dead.

Shortly after Burton's death, Jim Manning, who was himself getting on in years, spent an evening with Bill Kinney. During the course of the visit, the judge told the editor—who was a nephew of the lynch party member

Cicero Dobbs—everything that Burton had told him. Ever since boyhood, Kinney, the community's discouragement notwithstanding, had been fascinated by the Frank case. As a fledgling reporter, he'd gleaned bits and pieces of the story. Later, through his friendship with in-laws of Lawrence Haney, he'd been allowed to read the list of participants that the old farmer had secreted in the family Bible. The revelations Manning passed on all but completed the picture. As much as anyone could know what had happened at Frey's Gin, Kinney now knew. Yet this dark truth, far from setting the editor free, engendered a kind of paralysis. As he later phrased it: "I have a delicate situation." What Kinney meant is that nearly 90 years after Frank's demise, he found himself in possession of information that, no matter how newsworthy, would shock and sadden a generation that by and large had grown up in ignorance of its predecessors' responsibility for an awful deed. Everywhere the editor looked, he saw them. Walking across the square was "Coon" Shaw's son. Enjoying a drink at the country club was Governor Joseph Brown's grandson. It was all so intimate. Moreover, the children had inherited the earth. John Tucker Dorsey's son, Jasper, became chief executive officer of Southern Bell Telephone. General Lucius Clay, Herbert's younger brother, was military governor of Germany following World War II, in which role he oversaw the Nuremberg trials of Nazi war criminals, signing the death warrants of Hermann Goering, Martin Bormann and the others convicted of atrocities. (According to Herbert Jr., who also served in Berlin, Lucius Clay knew of his sibling's role in the Frank lynching, but it did not affect his judgments.) The lawyer Chuck Clay, Herbert's nephew, was for many years chairman of Georgia's Republican Party. And Bolan and Jim Brumby's second cousin Otis Jr. was publisher of the *Marietta Journal.* For Kinney, this last fact loomed largest. "I will never be able to write honestly about the lynching, because I have to live with these people," he said one morning in the 1990s. "I can't take the Brumbys' money for all these years, then stab them in the back." Other than the occasional veiled reference to this conspirator or that in the editor's widely read Saturday column, there would be no cleaning of the slate. The silence continued.

With the curtains of fog and iron already tightly drawn in Georgia by the 1920s, the Atlanta Lucille Frank returned to from Memphis six years after the lynching seemed, at least on the surface, tranquil and settled. The old hostilities were hidden away, so much so that when the 33-year-old widow took a job at the glove counter her brother-in-law managed at that bastion of female sophistication, J. P. Allen, she would regularly wait on the wives and children of various of the lynching brethren—she unaware of their connection to her husband's death and they unaware, too. Recalled Lucille

Morris Suhr, the daughter of Judge Newt Morris, who became a frequent customer: "She was charming and nice. I felt so sorry for her."

Living at first with her sister, Rosalind, and her husband, Charles Ursenbach, in a house in the old Washington Street neighborhood and then, midway through the decade, moving—as so many in Atlanta's German-Jewish community at the time did—to fashionable Druid Hills, Lucille Frank, at least in appearance, had reclaimed her place in life. Always well dressed (although usually in black) and now wearing distinctive horn-rimmed glasses, she played bridge almost every weekend with a tight group of matrons of the approximate same age. At home, she read literature and history, listened to the Saturday-afternoon radio broadcasts of the New York Metropolitan Opera and kept up a friendly competition regarding word derivations with her teenage nephew Harold Marcus. "She and Harold were always trying to stump each other," remembered Harold's younger brother, Alan.

Yet the outward display of poise and grace notwithstanding, Lucille's emotional state was more fragile than in the crime's aftermath. "She was a problem, a burden," recalled Alan Marcus. Added Alan's wife, Fanny: "She was always looking for an argument. She was antagonistic. You'd go right, she'd say left. She wanted love, but she did not know how to give."

Conversation regarding the source of Lucille's suffering was verboten. If the topic of Leo's death came up, she responded with uncontrollable emotion. "When you mentioned Marietta—just name it—she boiled," Alan Marcus remembered. "She would say, 'I just don't talk about it.' " And worse than the anger were the tears. In the 1940s, when the news broke that Arthur Powell believed he could establish Frank's innocence, the *Constitution* sent a young reporter named Celestine Sibley to see Lucille. "When I told her what I wanted, she just started crying," Sibley remembered some 50 years later.

For the most part, the family shielded Lucille from painful reminders of her great tragedy, a task made easier by the care and wealth of the widow's brother-in-law, Charles Ursenbach. Upon his wife's death, Ursenbach moved himself and Lucille into the luxurious Briarcliff Hotel on Ponce de Leon Avenue in Northeast Atlanta. Soon, Lucille was able to quit her job at J. P. Allen and enjoy the use of a four-door La Salle sedan in which Ursenbach's Negro driver chauffeured her to her bridge games and other appointments.

Ultimately, all the whispering and the tiptoeing around the truth forced Lucille more deeply into a shell. "Lucille was an extremely depressed person," remembered Dr. James Kauffman, an internist who began treating her in 1952. "There were psychiatrists, of course, but she wouldn't agree to see one." Instead, she brought her problems to Kauffman. "I saw her many times," he recalled. "She somatized her complaints. She had chest pains, headaches. When I think of her, I think of depression." At that, Kauffman paused, then added: "Leo may have been killed, but she served a life sentence."

By the mid-1950s, Lucille was living at the Howell House, one of Atlanta's first air-conditioned apartment buildings. Now in her mid-60s, her illnesses were no longer only in her mind. Suffering from hardening of the arteries, she spent her days walking gingerly from her unit, where she grew lilies and violets on the balcony, to the lobby, where she whiled away long afternoons talking with other tenants. Much thinner than during her twenties ("Her doctor told her she had a beautiful body," recalled Fanny Marcus. "She needed to hear that. She'd never been complimented enough"), she was a woman with a sad half smile and bitter memories. "To sum up her being," declared Alan Marcus, "she was pretty, strong, hurt." Lucille died on April 23, 1957, from heart disease. When Alan and Fanny cleaned out her bedroom, they found photographs of both Leo and his grave, the wedding ring that the lynchers had returned and, said Fanny, "a lot of letters written to Leo long after his demise."

Lucille's funeral was held at Atlanta's Patterson Funeral Home, after which her body, as she had requested, was cremated. It was her wish that her ashes be scattered in a public park, but a city ordinance forbade the practice, so the small box containing them was stored on a back shelf at the mortuary, where it was all but forgotten.

The years following Lucille's death marked another uneasy period for Atlanta's Jewish community. The trouble started on October 12, 1958, when the Temple—recently moved to an imposing Palladian structure on a mansion-lined section of north Peachtree Street—was badly damaged in a racist bombing. Arrests were eventually made, but the defendants—one of whom was represented by James Venable, who'd grown up to become not only the Klan's imperial wizard but a well-known lawyer—were acquitted. For the graying sons and daughters of Israel who'd lived through the Frank affair, it all seemed frightfully familiar. Thus it was that when an official from Patterson's called the Marcuses in either late 1962 or early 1963 and told them that they needed to make a decision regarding the disposition of Lucille's ashes, they panicked. The last thing they wanted was any sort of public ceremony that might expose the community to scrutiny or attack. After retrieving the box containing his aunt's remains, Alan placed it in the front trunk of his sporty red Corvair Manza and once more tried to forget. "I rode those ashes around in the car for six months," he remembered. Finally, in the predawn grayness of a morning in mid-1964, Alan picked up his brother and drove downtown to Oakland Cemetery, passing through its somber gates and over its tree-shaded alleys until he reached the Jewish section. There, kneeling on the moist grass and using garden tools, the two dug a grave between the stones topping the resting places of Lucille's parents, Emil and Josephine Cohen Selig. The Marcuses worked quietly and quickly, careful not to draw attention to themselves. Though the sky all around them was fingered by glass and steel skyscrapers—evidence that in the conflict that had claimed Leo Frank, it was the future that was now ascendant—they were oblivious. Following a brief prayer, the men set the box containing Lucille's ashes in the hole, replaced the sod and drove away, leaving this Georgia girl among her people, unmarked but not alone.

TWENTY-FOUR

The Revenant

Early one morning in the fall of 1948, William Smith walked into the clerk's office of the Fulton County Courthouse in downtown Atlanta and picked up certified copies of a number of records pertaining to his representation of Jim Conley three and a half decades before. Then the 69-year-old lawyer strolled north through a city that in many ways bore as little resemblance to the hustling state capital of 1913 as he bore to the ramrod-straight young man who in those days had practiced here. Bursting with veterans just back from World War II and awash in new money, Atlanta was poised for the great boom that would finally transform it into a modern metropolis. Smith, meanwhile, had aged markedly. Shoulders stooped and hair a flinty gray, he was a figure from the rapidly receding past. More worrisome, over the last several months he'd experienced health problems that had started with fatigue and blurred vision and progressed inexplicably and, for someone who'd so prided himself on his rhetorical ability, maddeningly to a paralysis of the vocal cords. The lawyer's doctor believed he'd suffered a series of small strokes, but whatever it was, it had filled him with a heightened sense of urgency. As he'd recently told his son Walter, in one of the notes penciled in capital letters that now served as his sole form of verbal communication: "LIFE AND LIFETIME ARE OF MUCH VALUE, FAR BEYOND OUR CONSIDERATION."

Accordingly, once Smith reached the Carnegie Library just off Peachtree Street, he quickly got down to work on what was only the latest of several ambitious projects—a memoir of his involvement in the Leo Frank case. With bound volumes of the Atlanta newspapers from the summer of the trial before him and the documents he'd just obtained at the courthouse tucked into his brief case, the lawyer let his mind drift back to his first dealings with the Negro whose testimony had convicted the factory superintendent and around whom his own existence had pivoted. Entering his thoughts in a brown Montag notebook, he wrote:

MY MOVES FOR CONLEY

    I. Worked with state in establishing Frank's guilt.
      (a.) Then believed in Frank's guilt.

(b.) It's easy to mentally swing with the tide of public thinking.

(c.) Prepared jury list.

(d.) Prepared briefs of law at trial.

(e.) Prepared Conley physically, mentally for witness stand.

(f.) Made Conley available for city police, for Pinkerton detective and for Solicitor General.

(g.) Cultivated friendly attitude with Solicitor General and Police and Pinkerton.

(h.) Barred everyone else from access to Conley.

As these jottings indicate, Smith's ideas were still in the incubation stage. Though he'd decided to focus on the events surrounding his shift of allegiance from the prosecution to the defense and while he'd picked a title— "A Competent and Compellable Witness"—that reflected his continuing desire to lay to rest the resulting charge that he'd betrayed his client, he had yet to begin the necessary spadework. The transcript alone would require a week to read. At the thought of such labor, the lawyer shut his eyes in exhaustion. He would get back to it, he told himself, after lunch.

The dining room of the Piedmont Hotel was a place where the Old South met the New, where politicians from outlying towns mingled easily with salesmen from national manufacturing concerns. Smith felt comfortable here. So much so that after his meal, he settled into an overstuffed chair in the lobby and watched the comings and goings of the diverse clientele, an occupation that he could enjoy all afternoon. In fact, when a former acquaintance sat down beside the lawyer and failed to recognize him, he decided to have a few laughs. He started by passing the man a note asking if he was "a Davis." Subsequently, Smith recorded the ensuing dialogue:

HE SAID "YES." THEN I ASKED HIM IF HE WAS A RAILROAD MAN, AND HE SAID "YES." I ASKED HIM IF HE WAS THE SON OF AN EX-SHERIFF NAMED DAVIS. HE SAID, "YES." AFTER EACH QUESTION, HE ASKED ME WHO I WAS. AND I WOULDN'T TELL HIM. HAD A LOT OF FUN OUT OF IT.

But notwithstanding the reviving energies that this exchange suggests, the lawyer did not return to work, waiting instead for his son—who was now launching his own law practice in Atlanta—to stop by and drive him to his house in the northern suburbs. Shortly after reaching home, Walter Smith asked his father why he hadn't gone back to the task at hand. Came the sad but honest reply:

I'M WEAK. TO SIT IN A STRAIGHT CHAIR AT THE LIBRARY OR EVEN FOR A SHORT TIME AT THE TABLE JUST WEARS ON THE LITTLE STRENGTH I HAVE.

For Walter Smith, his father's acknowledgment of his waning powers only confirmed what he already knew—the book was going to be an uphill climb. Still, it was one that the younger man believed had to be attempted. Like so many who'd been entangled in the Frank case, William Smith was tortured by unresolved emotions. While Walter anguished at the prospect of watching his father struggle, he felt there was something the older man wanted to get on paper. At the same time, there was something he wanted from his father—an explanation, not so much for the decisions of 35 years earlier but for the effects those decisions had on both the man who made them and the people who loved him.

Though the Frank case—in the form of notecards William and Mary Lou had used during their painstaking 1914 study of the murder notes, a dog-eared copy of the Brief of Evidence and even a few letters from the factory superintendent—had always been a presence in the Smiths' Staten Island home in the 1920s and 1930s, it was rarely a topic of conversation. In a busy house where both parents were embarking on new lives while simultaneously raising three children, too much else was happening to dwell on events that with every passing year seemed more remote.

Once settled on Mountain View Avenue, Smith and Mary Lou had set out to remake themselves. For Smith, the goal was to gain true proficiency in real estate law. All those battles in the criminal courts of Atlanta had not prepared him for clause-and-codicil-riddled rental agreements, zoning regulations and quit-claim deeds. Hence after putting in a long day at McLaughlin & Stern, he would spend his evenings at home studying—and taking care of the children. Beginning in 1922, Mary Lou was continually enrolled in night school. First, she earned a bachelor's degree in English at New York University, then a master's degree in English at the same institution, whereupon she migrated uptown to Columbia. There, she obtained her master's in education. By the late 1920s, she was teaching English at Staten Island's Tottenville High School.

Given the demands of work and family, neither husband nor wife had much time for outside pursuits. Still, there were off days, and when they came, Smith devoted himself to two long-standing interests. For one, the lawyer spoke frequently at temperance meetings. After years of eschewing drink, he not surprisingly viewed the passage of the Eighteenth Amendment in 1919 as a moral victory.

During this same period, Smith also took to the hustings to promote his other great cause—social and legal equality for American Negroes. As the featured speaker at the 1924 Fourth of July celebration held by his neighborhood association—the Westerleigh Improvement Society—Smith, after indulging in the expected flourishes about America's many freedoms, went off, as was his wont, in an altogether unexpected direction, telling the hot-dog-and-hamburger-sated audience:

> We boast of our freedom, we boast of our constitutional guarantees to every man, regardless of race, color or previous conditions of servitude, yet we must admit that the Black American is forced to appeal to our National Government for protection, for even his very life, and against the mobocracy of White Americans, who set up stakes upon which to burn him or who take his life at the end of a lyncher's rope.
>
> State Governments, administered by White Americans, are powerless or unwilling to protect him . . . We find that oath-bound, sometimes hooded and masked organizations exist, raising the flaming cross of Christ as the banner of racial hatred. Our officers of the law have failed in the discharge of their duties in the face of these hooded bigots; our juries, sworn to deal out justice to murderers, have forsworn their oaths at the demand of these masked assassins.
>
> As a Southern man, the son of a Confederate soldier, I say that the Black Man in America is here to stay. His standards of life, he is elevating; his children, he is educating; his voice he is making heard in every profession and calling; his wisdom, he is contributing even to the councils of the nation. Now, through the courage of our people, Black and White Americans can and must move forward, hand in hand, as brothers.

As had been the case back in Georgia, Smith did not limit his activities in behalf of Negroes to mere words. Shortly after his Westerleigh speech, he went to Brooklyn to see the Reverend Henry Hugh Proctor, now the pastor of the Nazarene Congregational Church. The two had much to discuss—old times in Atlanta, their mutual acquaintance Jim Conley—but the main purpose of the lawyer's visit was to invite his friend to become the first black clergyman to address his Staten Island church. Proctor accepted. Meantime, Smith also tried to knock down a higher racial barrier. Responding to a membership invitation from American Bar Association president Charles A. Boston, he wrote:

> It would be a pleasure for me to sign this application and forward same as requested, and I would be delighted to be a member of the American Bar Association, but for the fact, very clearly indicated upon the form of application which you wish me to sign, that Association membership is based upon a discrimination . . . both because of color and of race, and that my signing such an application would be an implied agreement on my part to accept membership on such basis.

As a native-born American, a white man, a Southerner by birth and rearing, and a member of the Sons of the Confederacy, I believe that the day has passed in this land when so distinguished an association as the National Brotherhood of Lawyers can honorably yield to any discrimination upon which the Constitution and Laws of our Nation have placed a no uncertain ban and as to which the racial facts of professional life in America demonstrate its lack of justification . . .

While I appreciate greatly your personal courtesy indicated in your offer to endorse my application for membership in the Association, I must deny myself the privilege . . .

The day is coming when I will be able to avail myself of your kind offer to endorse my application. That day is not far distant. It will be when the American Bar Association makes personal and professional character, not race and color, its sole qualification for membership. That day cannot be long delayed. We have traveled too far onward and upward toward higher things for it to be otherwise decreed.

Smith's willingness to go against the grain regardless of political or professional considerations remained, in short, as strong as ever. There was, however, one matter on which he continued to censor himself during this period—the Frank case. Not that he didn't come close to addressing it. In the spring of 1929, *Liberty*—the self-proclaimed "Weekly for Everybody," whose mixture of sensationalistic journalism, celebrity profiles and hardboiled fiction made it a worthy rival to the *Saturday Evening Post*—invited readers to submit solutions to any of ten real-life mysteries, among them the murder of Mary Phagan. The prize: publication in the magazine and a $500 payment. For Smith, the contest was tantalizing. Here was a chance not just to lay out the case against Jim Conley before a national audience but to justify his own much debated conduct. Yet with the opportunity came risks. Old hostilities could be reignited, while such friends as Hugh Dorsey, who despite all that had passed between them had written a letter of recommendation to the New York bar when Smith resumed practice, could be hurt. After much agonizing, the lawyer embarked on what appeared to be a safe course of action, penning his theory of the crime in his daughter's voice, then submitting the resulting 12-page manuscript under her byline. In its way, the idea was inspired. As a girl, young Mary Lou, now a senior at Barnard College, had, of course, been at her parents' side as they conducted their reinvestigation in the summer of 1914. "I can recall, as if it was yesterday, the trip my father and mother made with me and my older brother through the pencil factory in an effort to test Conley's story in the light of the physical facts found at the scene of the crime," Smith had her recollect. "I rode on the elevator into that dark basement of death." Such passages provided the perfect hook for a compelling account of everything from Smith's findings regarding the authorship of the murder notes to Dorsey's failure to inform either the defense or the jury that the hair taken from little Mary's head during the autopsies did not match that found on the plant lathe where the prosecution argued that she'd been killed. In fact, the resulting piece was so well crafted that it won the *Liberty* competition. At which point its true author became apprehensive. Along with his initial concerns about the potential negative impacts were new ones about the fitness of using his daughter as a front to discuss what was still a controversial subject. Which was why at the eleventh hour, Smith had Mary Lou withdraw the article. Later, and in his own name, he assured himself, he would do something with the material.

During the 1930s, as the Great Depression clamped down, Smith and his wife pushed themselves hard. Mary Lou rose rapidly in the New York City school system, by mid-decade becoming head of the McKee Vocational High School English department. Meanwhile, Smith was eventually elevated to a partnership at McLaughlin & Stern, and—thanks to the lobbying of his partner Martin Lippman—found himself frequently back in the courtroom. As Lippman, in a note to one of the firm's clients, put it:

> I believe that Mr. Smith, if permitted to sum up this case, would without doubt satisfy the jury that we are right . . . I do not care how eloquent or convincing Mr. Shapiro [opposing counsel] is, I say that he is no match for Smith in summation. I say, without hesitation, that if I were in your position (and I regard myself as a pretty fair trial lawyer), I would unhesitatingly permit Smith to sum up this case in preference to myself. He is a born orator, he knows and understands this situation very keenly, it lives and throbs in him, and I am satisfied that he can make the jury feel just as he does.

Though not everyone at the firm was so sanguine about the lawyer ("He was a dreamer, not a rainmaker," partner Frederick Ballen later recalled), Smith used the connections that resulted from his newfound status to benefit financially, buying control of a bond issue for a hotel and real estate development. Thanks to the reviving economy of the early 1940s, the sale was a success, earning him a handsome commission. After years of struggle, he was well fixed.

With his bank account flush, Smith could have eased into retirement. He and Mary Lou had not only survived a terrible ordeal, but they had prospered. And the children seemed headed toward productive lives. Their oldest son, Frank, was enrolled in premed at the University of Southern

California and fronting a swing band—Frank Smith's Rajahs of Rhythm. Their daughter, Mary Lou, was pursuing a law degree at the Brooklyn Law School. Walter was preparing to enter Duke University.

Yet despite how much there was for Smith to revel in, despite his vows to live in the future, there was something profoundly unsettled in him, some nagging anxiety stemming from his actions in the Frank case. This anxiety, wed to the lawyer's lifelong inclination to take on worthy causes, would give birth to a grandiose dream.

Walter Smith first heard of his father's plan to move the family back to the South when he was a senior at Duke. During a visit, the older man spoke of how much he missed the region, then articulated an ambitious plan in which he wanted his son's assistance. The goal: to start a free school for impoverished Appalachian children in the lovely little town of Dahlonega, where nearly half a century before Smith had attended North Georgia College. As the lawyer saw it, the institution would provide its students with both a solid educational foundation and the military discipline he'd valued as a boy. In a nod to this last purpose, he'd already decided upon a name— the Fort Smith Academy.

For Walter Smith, who, unlike his father, was a skeptical sort and, moreover, enjoyed an occasional snort of bourbon, the prospect of devoting his life to good works, of turning his back on the things of this world before he'd experienced them, could not have been less appealing. While he never flatly rejected the offer, he took refuge first at Columbia University, where he earned his master's degree in English, then at the *Atlanta Journal,* where he worked as a reporter, and finally, at the onset of World War II, in the United States Navy.

In spite of Walter's resistance—indeed, in spite of the resistance of all the children—William Smith made a good start of it. The site of approximately 700 acres, which he acquired parcel by parcel over a period of several years in the late 1930s and early 1940s, was surpassingly beautiful. Nestled in the Yahoola valley nine miles north of Dahlonega, the land had once been home to a Cherokee princess, Trahlyta, who was buried nearby. Redbuds, dogwoods and pines marched up the gentle mountain slopes, while a creek wandered through the emerald bottoms. Rhododendrons were everywhere. On summer evenings, a blue mist settled upon the horizon. In winter, the air was crisply clear, with an occasional spray of snow.

At the same time that Smith was putting together the Fort Smith property, he was using his New York law office to raise funds and solicit supplies. From some quarters, the responses were positive. One of Smith's partners pledged $5,000, an in-law who worked at the publishing house of Macmillan & Company provided 3,000 books, and Axel Sturdel, formerly the trumpet player in Frank Smith's band and by this point Tommy Dorsey's arranger, also sent a check. Others, however, were less receptive. John D. Rockefeller, Jr., whom the lawyer ran into in Manhattan one day, brushed him off. Same thing with Borden Dairies, which answered a 1944 request by Smith for a calf from Elsie for the school's working farm by informing him that the trademark milk cow's offspring were pledged to the war effort.

Still and all, Smith was optimistic. So much so that shortly after he and Mary Lou moved to Dahlonega in the fall of 1944, he upped the ante by purchasing two of the town's most fabled institutions. Situated just off the courthouse square, the Smith House (the founder was no relation to the new owner) was known throughout the South for both its rustic mountain rooms and its "family style" meals, where patrons sat together at long wooden tables piled high with bowls of collards, black-eyed peas, okra, green beans, sweet potatoes, corn bread and, even in bad times, never fewer than three meats. Just around the corner from this landmark in a barnlike frame building whose front door was arched by luxuriant honeysuckle vines stood the offices of the lawyer's other acquisition—the *Dahlonega Nugget,* circulation 840. Despite its limited press run, the newspaper, which took its name from a gold strike that had occurred in the town in the early 1800s, exerted an outsize influence. Its former editor, J. B. Townsend, was a favorite of that avid student of the American language H. L. Mencken, who frequently reprinted his homespun editorials in the pages of the *American Mercury.* Townsend's brother—known simply as Uncle Goley—remained on staff as publisher emeritus and, more critical for a sheet whose type was still set by hand, compositor.

Smith had bought in to the heart of Dahlonega, and he'd done so because the Fort Smith Academy was only part of his dream. At the Smith House, he hoped to re-create the graciousness with which he'd been raised. In the *Nugget,* he would expound on his notions of *communitas* and *civitas.* And if one day the locals began referring to him in the old style as "the Colonel," he would take it not so much as his due but as a sign that after all the years away, he'd been welcomed home.

Initially, everything went well for Smith and Mary Lou in Dahlonega. Early each morning, they drove the nine miles from their temporary quarters at the Smith House to the Fort Smith compound to supervise construction. The first building to go up was a small but sturdy one-room building reminiscent of a country schoolhouse that would function as the school's library. Once the roof was on and the shelves were in place, Mary Lou spent hours there creating a card catalog for what had become a sizable and varied collection of books. To the inside front binding of each volume, she affixed a bookplate that contained the Fort Smith Academy's Latin motto—*Non Sibi Sed Aliis,* Not for Ourselves but for Others. It was by this philosophy that she and her husband intended to live out their days. Next came the headmaster's residence, where the couple would live. A handsome frame structure with gabled eaves, a stone chimney and a roomy front porch, it sat on a terraced shelf of land looking down on the prospective location of the campus.

Late afternoons found the Smiths back in Dahlonega at the *Nugget*'s tiny office. When not helping Uncle Goley set type for such hot items as the dates of upcoming revival meetings, get-well wishes to ailing citizens and tips on proper crop rotation, Smith wrote the weekly editorial, which ran at the top of page 2. From the outset, it was clear that North Georgia journalism would no longer speak in the folksy voice of J. B. Townsend. In the initial leader, which appeared on January 19, 1945, the new editor wrote:

> We believe that we have a well-behaved, hard working and appreciated Negro citizenry. We shall advocate for them and for improvement in their living, working and civic conditions and of educational operations for their children.

Save for this mildly shocking assertion, there was little else in Smith's inaugural utterances to worry the homefolks. Coming out foursquare for "our churches, our college, our schools, our lodges and all of our uplifting institutions" was hardly revolutionary. Smith's New York background aside, most Dahlonegans welcomed both the messenger and the message. And besides, they reminded themselves, the newcomer was a wealthy man. Not only was he in a position to enrich them through work at Fort Smith or at his other businesses, but rumor had it that in the tradition of a benevolent southern squire, he was already proving a soft touch for humble townspeople with aspirations of their own. Little wonder that after just a few weeks, the city council asked Smith to serve as city attorney. It would be an honor, he replied.

Inevitably, Smith's honeymoon ended. However, it did so not because of the *Nugget*'s editorials regarding Dahlonega's black populace or some other far-reaching issue but because of those that addressed a topic that mattered even more in the town—pigs and chickens. As it happened, the winter of 1945 found Dahlonega in an uproar regarding a referendum set for March 30 that would determine whether homeowners could continue to keep swine in their yards and operate commercial chicken houses in residential neighborhoods. In a February 23 broadside headlined MOVING FORWARD, Smith jumped in on the side of the reformers. "Did you ever see a clean hog pen?" he asked. "At their best, they are bound to be centers of filth, stench, of fly breeding and of rat feeding. Our hog-raising citizens are certainly maintaining dangerous menaces to public and private health." As for the chicken houses, Smith declared: "Our citizens simply object to the construction of these unsightly structures, the increased fire risk, the noises and odors. Every home in their vicinity is depreciated in value. We have reliable information that other such structures are soon to be erected in our city. A few men, no matter how excellent citizens they may be, should not enjoy privileges so destructive of the health, happiness and comfort of our citizens generally."

Not surprisingly, numerous Dahlonegans disagreed with Smith. In fact, the negative response to the *Nugget*'s anti-urban-livestock editorial was so great that the paper introduced a new column called BOTH SIDES for the sole purpose of handling protests and complaints. Yet Smith was not deterred. In the weeks leading up to the referendum, he hammered away, presenting information establishing the relationship of animal waste to the spread of typhus and discussing the negative economic impact an outbreak of the disease would have on the town. His solution: Move the offending operations to specifically zoned locales where they would have minimal effect on the physical well-being of the human population. "We do not desire to run the town," he concluded. "We are perfectly willing that the voters run the town. It just so happens we are the present owners of the *Nugget* [and] we are charged with the duty and responsibility as newspaper folks of presenting facts."

On the appointed date, Dahlonegans went to the polls where, in what the *Nugget* termed "an orderly and well-managed election," the referendum passed by a substantial majority. The crusading editor had won his first battle. But in the process, he had lost the war. At its April 6 meeting, the city council fired Smith as city attorney. Moreover, several of the town's leading lights—men who just a few months earlier had enthusiastically greeted the newcomer—began to disparage him to others of their station. Recalled longtime Dahlonega resident Frances Jones: "John Moore was a prominent citizen, and he kept cows in his yard a block from the square and [Smith's editorials] made him mad. And he had a lot of friends." Never one to back down, Smith reacted to his dismissal as city attorney by terming it "a baby act." As for those who were speaking out against him, they were just "venting personal spleen." Beneath the public bravado, however, Smith was deeply wounded, not so much by the nasty squabble itself but by the fact that it revealed that his fantasy of an idyll in the Georgia mountains where after so many years in exile he could live among his own people in harmony and understanding was exactly that—a fantasy. Just a few months later, he sold the *Nugget* to Frances Jones. Then, on March 15, 1946, he divested himself of his other in-town property. In its article announcing the Smith House's sale, the *Nugget* reported: "Mr. Smith plans to continue with his school project for underprivileged children, Fort Smith. Fort Smith's goal is to give a complete education, including college, to the children placed there."

And so several of Smith's illusions had been swept away, but his greatest aspiration abided, and all through 1946 and 1947, he fought to see it realized. One morning a week, he worked out of an office in Dahlonega. Recalled Nell Young, who served as his secretary: "He wrote letters to donors, wealthy people, saying he was going to build the school." The rest of Smith's time was spent at Fort Smith. There, a crew of laborers recruited from the neighboring hollows constructed a sawmill. Once the mill was up and running, Smith supervised the harvesting of trees from the surrounding woodlands. Within a few weeks, 40,000 board feet of lumber stood piled beside the dirt road that ran through the place. Sitting on his porch at night with Mary Lou, the would-be educator could close his eyes and almost see the school: committed teachers, yearning students and maybe someday his own grandchildren, all here in this pristine setting, seeking after knowledge.

Sometime during the first few months of 1948, Walter Smith, back from the war and finishing law school in Atlanta, perceived all at once what his father did not—there would never be a Fort Smith Academy. In fact, save for the headmaster's house and the library building, none of it would ever get off the ground. In one of those shattering moments where a child abandons his illusions and looks at a parent in all of his human fallibility, Walter Smith looked at William Smith and realized:

> He was an old man obsessed with a dream he couldn't accomplish. He'd become so devoted to this that he'd lost all sight of reality. He'd spread the word around that he had all these plans—he told everyone he would do it. They thought he was a millionaire. In truth, he didn't have the money to pull it off. It was, I hate to say it, pathetic.

By Walter's estimate, his father had sunk over $100,000 into his dream, most of it tied up in the land and some, bearing out the scuttlebutt around Dahlonega, loaned for a song to poor bets. No money was coming in from investments and none from donors. Yet even had the financial picture been rosier, the prospects still would have been hopeless, for almost overnight Smith had grown ill. Exhaustion, eyestrain, aches. Soon would come the loss of voice. Recalled Walter: "He was mentally sharp, but he had no strength. He was a sick man."

Walter's assessment of his father's situation was harsh but realistic, yet it was not unsympathetic, for he knew that the dream of Fort Smith was rooted in the central scarring drama of the older man's life—the Leo Frank case. Through all the years, William Smith had carried a never-ending burden of guilt regarding both the fatal consequences of his actions at the start of the affair and the personal costs of his actions at its conclusion. Even three and a half decades later, he shuddered that he had not seen through Jim Conley. Which was one of the reasons, his son believed, why he'd undertaken an impossible task. As Walter observed: "Dad was trying to make amends for what he felt was the worst mistake of his life—getting sucked in by this liar." Yet there was another element as well. Though William Smith never regretted changing loyalties in the midst of the fight, believing that he'd not only acted in good conscience but had completed his obligations to his client, he did regret the impact that change had on himself and his family. For all practical purposes, they had been driven into the wilderness, forced to leave their beloved South. Even as a young man, Smith had, of course, stood apart in the region. Yet Georgia had made him. He was as much alumnus as tramp. And like so many native sons, he'd wanted the same for his sons and daughter. Remembered his youngest: "Much of the dream for the school grew out of his hopes for us. He thought we'd be together."

Walter Smith's understanding of all of this ultimately prompted him to urge his father to find a new purpose. Psychologically, the Fort Smith Academy, no matter how noble in concept, represented a monumental skirting of the actual issue. On the other hand, a book on the Leo Frank case—one that not only told the story of a husband and wife working together to exonerate a condemned man but related the consequences those efforts inflicted on themselves and their family—might lead somewhere. Such a work could be the ailing man's gift to himself and his children.

Thus it was that at least a couple of times a month during the summer and fall of 1948, William Smith would make the trip from Dahlonega to Atlanta, spending the days downtown at the courthouse or in the library, while bunking at night with Walter. Despite his mysterious illness, he threw himself into "A Competent and Compellable Witness." This, finally, was what he was meant to do, and he'd long known it. In fact, in a 1944 letter to former governor John Slaton, with whom he'd kept in touch, Smith had declared:

Some day it may be that I shall commit to writing in a more or less permanent form the complete story of this unfortunate matter, insofar as the facts may then be within my grasp. My intimate knowledge and relationship to the entire matter somewhat places me under a duty and a responsibility. I feel that I am duty-bound to make a careful and comprehensive contribution to the vindication of the memory of Mr. Frank . . . Any such effort should be very thoroughly presented. My contribution to this end, I feel sure, would be read with the deepest interest and with rare appreciation by our thinking fellow Georgians. It may be that I shall be spared long enough to discharge this duty.

In the end, however, Smith would not be spared. Though he did get a few words on paper, they displayed neither the incisiveness of the 100-page study of the murder notes he'd prepared 34 years before nor the dramatic intensity of the article he'd penned under his daughter's byline 14 years later for *Liberty*. "Mr. Frank's lead counsel was Luther Z. Rosser," he wrote in a typical passage. "He asked no favors. He gave no quarter. He battled everybody in his way. He was the 'knock down and drag out' type. It is my humble judgement that if Mr. Reuben R. Arnold, who was later retained, had first gone to the police station, Mr. Frank would never have been charged." It was all like that. Not that this was so surprising. By late autumn of 1948, Smith's condition had deteriorated. The final diagnosis was amyotrophic lateral sclerosis, Lou Gehrig's disease. Paralysis of the vocal cords is a not uncommon symptom.

On a frigid morning in February 1949, William Smith departed the Fort Smith property for the last time. Up the unpaved lane, past the pile of ice-rimed lumber—which two years after it had been cut still stood on the grounds—then onto U.S. 19, he and Mary Lou rode. At the wheel of the green Chevrolet Bel-Air was Lee Jerrard, one of the locals who'd worked on the place. He was doing the couple another courtesy—driving them to the hospital in Atlanta.

Down to Dahlonega, around the square, past the Smith House and the *Nugget* the car sped, proceeding south through Dawsonville, Cumming and Alpharetta. Soon the suburbs appeared, then Atlanta. Walter, who was waiting at Crawford Long Hospital, greeted his parents with as much hope as he could summon, but it did no good. As they waited for a nurse to complete the admission forms, father turned to son and on a pad of paper wrote: "JUST TELL HER I'VE COME HERE TO DIE." It was a fact. The paralysis had spread to the windpipe and diaphragm.

By noon, Smith was in an oxygen tent in a private room, and calls were going out to the other children—Frank, now practicing medicine in Portland, Oregon, and Mary Lou, still in New York. Through it all, the dying man remained alert, using the time left to him to put his thoughts on paper. Mostly, he addressed unfinished business—unpaid debts, insurance policies, outstanding bills. Writing in clipped, telegraphic bursts, he pushed each message through an open crease in the clear plastic to Walter. It went on like this for several hours. At a certain point, however, Smith was gripped by a larger idea. Laboriously, he printed a long sentence in block letters. Then, with a flourish, he scrawled his signature. Walter instantly grasped the note's importance, understood that it was at once a crystallization of the thoughts that had been meant for the book, an offering to the family and, because of the legal construction, an appeal to some unknown court. These were not just last words but a final argument. They read:

IN ARTICLES OF DEATH, I BELIEVE IN THE INNOCENCE AND
GOOD CHARACTER OF LEO M. FRANK.
W. M. Smith.

Soon thereafter, Smith was dead. Several days later, he was buried in a cemetery a mile from Fort Smith. For the next 27 years, his wife would live on in the house overlooking the Yahoola valley. Almost until the end, she kept the little library, the only part of the dream that had taken physical shape, open to the public. Few patrons visited, but she did not seem to worry. As she had learned, people could not be forced to see the truth. They had to come to it on their own.

Epilogue

On a winter afternoon three days before Christmas 1983, 85-year-old Alonzo Mann walked slowly across the lawn of the Georgia capitol in Atlanta. When he reached the statue of Tom Watson that stands at the western entrance to the seat of government, he paused. Then Leo Frank's former office boy—now a stooped, white-haired gent in a worn topcoat—headed up the capitol steps. On a summer day 70 years earlier, Mann had failed to tell the factory superintendent's trial jury what he believed to be the truth: Frank did not murder Mary Phagan. On Saturday, April 26, 1913, Mann had barged into the National Pencil Company lobby and seen Jim Conley toting the girl's body.

For a lifetime, Mann had carried his secret with him. At first, he said he was too scared to repeat it—hence his barely audible testimony during the proceedings against Frank. When he grew older, he claimed to have told a few people, yet they ignored him. But finally, he had found someone who would listen. One year before this gray holiday afternoon, Mann had sat down with lawyer John J. Hooker, a debonair financier and unsuccessful Tennessee gubernatorial candidate, who had agreed to take his deposition.

"I opened the door to the National Pencil Company and walked in," Mann informed Hooker in a soft, sure voice.

"What time was that?"

"I think it was a little after 12:00. I looked up to the right, and there was Jim Conley with a girl in his arms and she was limp. He looked around at me. He couldn't reach me. He says, 'If you tell anything about this, I'll kill you.' So I turned around and went out the door and went home."

Hooker took a deep breath. Then he began to read from an affidavit Mann had given to the *Tennessean* in Nashville (*Tennessean* reporters Jerry Thompson and Robert Sherborne had published the first newspaper account of Mann's story on March 7, 1982).

" 'He had the body of Mary Phagan in his arms,' " Hooker read.

"Yes, he had the body of a young lady in his arms," Mann answered.

" 'She appeared to be unconscious or perhaps dead.' "

"That's right."

Hooker paused. Then he asked, "Now, Mr. Mann, when you got home, what did you tell your mother?"

"I told my mother what happened, and she says, 'Don't say anything about it because we don't want to get involved in it.' "

Mann obeyed his mother's request. He was that terrified of Conley, and his parents were that terrified of the hostility their son might attract if he came forth. Now, he informed Hooker, he was obsessed by another fear: He was afraid that he was going to carry the burden of not speaking out to the grave.

This was the crux of Mann's statement, and it became the foundation for an application for a posthumous pardon for Frank filed by Charles Wittenstein, southern counsel for the Anti-Defamation League, and Dale Schwartz, a fellow Atlanta lawyer. For a year, the members of the Georgia Board of Pardons and Paroles pondered the request. Finally, on this December day, they had reached a decision.

The reopening of the Frank case prompted not only local and national headlines (GIVE LEO FRANK A DESERVED PARDON, declared the *Constitution*), but an NBC television movie starring Jack Lemmon in the role of a courageous John Slaton. (The film ignored the inconvenient fact of the governor's partnership with Luther Rosser.) The development also resurrected long-submerged hostilities between the descendants of key figures in the affair. Joining in vociferous opposition to a pardon were Harvard-educated lawyer Tom Watson Brown, the populist's great-grandson; Hugh Dorsey, Jr.; Jasper Dorsey, son of lynching planner John Tucker Dorsey; and Mary Phagan Kean, niece and namesake of the victim. As a consequence, the Board of Pardons and Paroles deliberated in an atmosphere that echoed the one in which the various courts had labored seven decades before.

There were also other parallels, chief among them the murkiness of the evidence, which over time had not surprisingly grown even more impenetrable. Dramatic as Alonzo Mann's late-in-life assertions were, they added little of probative value. Both the prosecution and the defense had all along agreed that Conley carried Mary Phagan's body, the difference being that Hugh Dorsey maintained he had done so in the role of accomplice, while Rosser and Reuben Arnold countered that he was the principal. True, Mann's story, by placing Conley in the factory lobby, did give the lie to the Negro's contention that he'd used the elevator to transport the remains, but far from being a revelation, this assertion merely corroborated what the so-called shit in the shaft had indicated a lifetime before. In other words, the central riddles remained unresolved, and any opportunity to cast new light on them was negligible.

Most daunting, Jim Conley's final whereabouts were unknown—not that there hadn't been sightings. By the early 1930s, after serving half of his 20-year sentence for armed robbery, the Ebony Chevalier of Darktown had returned home. In 1933, Elmer R. Gould, a 20-year-old Clark College student, stopped at the Capital City Laundry on Mitchell Street to apply for work. "I saw a man transporting clothes out of a truck," recalled Gould. "I asked him if he had a job. And he said, 'What's yer name?' And I said, 'Elmer.' And he said, 'See da boss, El-more.' He was always stretching everything out. That was Jim Conley." Gould was employed to sweep up in the afternoons, and thus began a relationship that lasted for seven years. During this time, as Gould moved on to pursue a master's degree at Atlanta University, he worked regularly with Conley, becoming familiar enough with him to know that while he was living with Mary—the woman he'd married when both of them were hauled into court shortly after Frank's lynching—he'd taken back up with Lorena Jones, his common-law wife from before the trial. "I got the idea that Jim was involved with a lot of stuff," said Gould. "He would drink and carouse. He was always on the phone to some woman explaining why he hadn't been where he was supposed to be." The pattern continued at downtown's Luckie Street YMCA, where Conley, after taking a position as head of the maintenance department, hired Gould. "Jim had an office in the basement of the Y, a room with a cot in it. I suspect he slept there some nights. He always left through a gate in the basement that opened onto the alley. Things were always going on— women, numbers running. Jim hung with a tough group. The men were all big gamblers, and Jim carried a pistol in a holster." At no point during Gould and Conley's acquaintance—which ended when the younger man took a teaching position in a rural Georgia school district—did Conley ever confess to murdering Mary Phagan. "All the time I knew Jim," remembered Gould, "he'd tell me, 'El-more, I didn't do a thing—only guilt I had was helpin'.' "

Another, more remarkable sighting of Conley occurred in the 1930s when 14-year-old Anna Belle Phagan, Mary Phagan's niece, emerged from a Bellwood grocery store to see a Negro in conversation with little Mary's stepfather, John W. Coleman, and brother, Joshua. So surprised was Anna Belle, Joshua's daughter, by the scene that she exclaimed, "Dad, what are you doing with that nigger?"

Her father said, "Do you know who this is? This is Jim Conley."

"He's the one who killed Aunt Mary," she replied.

"No, I didn't have anything to do with it," asserted Conley.

With that, the group escorted the celebrated Negro to the Phagan home and invited him inside for a visit. "They talked for about an hour," recalled Anna Belle one afternoon in the late 1980s as she sat in a small apartment overlooking the Georgia Tech campus in Northwest Atlanta, not far from her old neighborhood. "My dad was nice to Conley. I remember Conley saying he wanted a drink of whisky. I don't think Dad gave him one. But I do believe he gave him a little bit of money."

The last recorded appearance by Conley took place on October 20, 1941, when he was arraigned in police court on charges of public drunkenness and gambling. STAR WITNESS IN FRANK CASE ARRESTED HERE, roared the *Constitution*'s headline. "Conley said he had been living a quiet life," the paper reported. "He refused to talk about the Frank case." Whereupon the most infamous black Atlantan of his time vanished from public view. There is no death certificate on file for Conley at the Georgia Department of Vital Records, although in the 1970s, one of his old gambling buddies informed Elmer Gould—by that point one of the first black instructors at suburban Atlanta's Briarcliff High School—that Jim "had passed." Added Gould: "Jim is probably buried in the country, some rural church. Or he could have been given a pauper's burial. The undertaker probably got stuck with the cost of disposing of him."

Conley's disappearance from the scene was not the only factor complicating the Board of Pardon and Paroles' attempt to delve back into the Phagan mystery. Also gone were the state's files. In 1947, an Atlanta lawyer and writer named Allen Lumpkin Henson visited Hugh Dorsey in his office to discuss the possibility of writing about the case. "Magazines all over the country keep on distorting the facts," Dorsey told Henson before directing his attention to a large cabinet packed with the documents and pieces of physical evidence that had factored so large during the summer of 1913. "Every scratch of the pen, including my notes and memoranda made during the trial" were there, the former solicitor remarked. Not long after this meeting, Dorsey was dead. Seventeen years later, his oldest son, James, wrote historian Leonard Dinnerstein: "During the years since my father's death I am afraid that any old papers which he might have preserved have been lost or destroyed." As a result, the men looking into the matter in 1983 were unable to apply the tools of contemporary forensic science to such items as Frank's dental X rays and the photographs of the bite wounds supposedly covering Mary Phagan's body. Simply put, the argument would never move beyond that of Conley's word versus Frank's.

All of which, of course, invited renewed speculation regarding the enduring enigma of Frank's vexing conduct in the wake of Mary Phagan's murder and at his trial. While the Board of Pardons and Paroles was considering the posthumous pardon application, a never before circulated letter written in the winter of 1914 by the factory superintendent to a Cornell classmate surfaced. In the letter, which is addressed to John Gould, a Detroit automotive engineer, Frank makes his only known admission that he mishandled himself during the initial months of his ordeal. "My dear Gould," he wrote, "in April 1913, outrageous trouble overtook me like a bolt from the blue. The charge was so preposterous that at first I treated the matter disdainfully, it was all so foreign and far removed from my most fantastic conception or thought." That concession made, Frank went on to lay the blame for what had transpired where his supporters laid it. "The public, so easily aroused here in the South, conceived a vicious animosity and vindictive hatred toward me, aided and abetted by racial prejudice and getting the man higher up. Discretion and intelligence was thrown to the winds and unreasoning mob rule took its place."

Revelatory though Frank's comments to John Gould are, they fail to address the many allegations of sexual impropriety that played such a large role in his conviction. Could all the stories of misconduct have been fabrications? Or was there some element of truth to the charges, one that while far from making Frank a murderer haunted his conscience and compromised his ability to mount the sort of righteous defense that would have carried the day?

The missing evidence and the continuing puzzles notwithstanding, the Board of Pardons and Paroles did possess one new source of insight — John Slaton's commutation order. That document, which contains William Smith's interpretations of the murder notes and Schley Howard's theories regarding Conley's allegations of perversion, strongly suggests Frank's innocence. Still, even when combined with Mann's statement, the information did not justify overturning the conviction. Decreed the board:

> After exhaustive review and many hours of deliberation, it is impossible to decide conclusively the guilt or innocence of Leo M. Frank. For the board to grant a pardon, the innocence of the subject must be shown conclusively. In the board's opinion, this has not been shown. Therefore, the board hereby denies the application for a posthumous pardon for Leo M. Frank.

Predictably, the adverse decision prompted editorial consternation. In one of the more reasoned critiques, *Constitution* political editor Frederick Allen, while agreeing that the evidence presented to the board was insufficient to the purpose, bemoaned the fact that the state continued to ignore the larger issues. "By today's standards," Allen wrote, "Frank did not receive a fair trial." The board "should have sent a strong signal that the state of Georgia did not condone anti-Semitism."

In 1986, Charles Wittenstein and Dale Schwartz filed a second application with the Board of Pardons and Paroles, one that rather than seeking to absolve Frank of Mary Phagan's murder asked the state to admit culpability in his demise. This time the board responded favorably, finding that Georgia had denied the factory superintendent his constitutional rights by failing to ensure his safety while he was incarcerated at the prison farm in Milledgeville. Asserted the *Journal:* LEO FRANK PARDON DECISION A VICTORY FOR ALL GEORGIANS.

Yet tragically, there will never be a resolution to the Frank case. The underlying tensions are too great. Had the murder of Mary Phagan not happened when it did, it would have been merely another atrocity. Yes, there would have been headlines, and yes, there would have been anguish and gall. But after the dead were buried and the ritual of justice enacted, life would have resumed, and slowly the numbing years would have proceeded until only a few could remember, and even they but dimly. That is not, though, what occurred. The ghosts still clamor to be heard and the trial refuses to end and the sons refight their fathers' battles and like a transfiguring scar, the events that made up the saga have grown ever more vivid. Many swear they know why this is so, and they speak of Jews and injustice and the vengeful magistrate—Judge Lynch—who presided at the end. These arguments all have their merits, but they ignore the conflict that was there to begin with, the conflict between the future and the past that was dramatized so audaciously on April 26, 1913, the conflict that transformed murder into myth.

Notes

Abbreviations for Notes

AC   *Atlanta Constitution*
AChr   *Augusta Chronicle*
AG   *Atlanta Georgian*
AHC   Atlanta History Center
AJ   *Atlanta Journal*
AJA   American Jewish Archives
BOE   Brief of Evidence, In the
       Supreme Court of Georgia,
       Fall Term, 1913
BT   *Boston Traveler*
BU   Brandeis University Archives

CTrib   *Chicago Tribune*
GDA   Georgia Department of
       Archives
Jeff   *Jeffersonian*
LAT   *Los Angeles Times*
MT   *Macon Telegraph*
NYH   *New York Herald*
NYT   *New York Times*
NYTrib   *New York Tribune*
PR   Pinkerton Reports, on file at the
       American Jewish Archives

1. April 26, 1913

3 Though descriptions of how Mary Phagan spent the morning hours of April 26, 1913, appear in the April 28 editions of all three Atlanta newspapers, the most accurate and concise presentation of the information can be found in the interviews Detective L. P. Whitfield conducted with Fannie Coleman and Ollie Phagan: PR, May 2, 1913, pp. 1–3.

3 "exceedingly well-developed": Fannie Coleman in PR, filed by W. D. Mac-Worth, May 13, 1913, p. 25.

3 "Well, Myrt I don't know": Mary Phagan to Myrtle Barmore, in Hutch Johnson, "The Leo Frank Case" (master's thesis, Florida State University, 1966).

4 Accounts of Mary Phagan's background appear in the April 28, 1913, editions of all three Atlanta newspapers as well as in her mother's testimony at Leo Frank's trial: BOE, p. 1.

4 *"My pa ain't no millyunaire"*: "My Pa," originally published in *Successful Farmer,* reprinted by *AC,* May 14, 1913.

5 the average workweek lasted 66 hours: Leonard Dinnerstein, *The Leo Frank Case* (New York: Columbia University Press, 1968), p. 7.

5 *Journal of Labor* reported four thousand requests: ibid., p. 8.

5 In 1905, 2,414 . . . died: Franklin Garrett, *Atlanta and Environs* (Athens, Ga.: University of Georgia Press, 1969), vol. 2, p. 559.

5 they'd staged their own musicale: *AJ,* April 2, 1913; Gene Wiggins, *Fiddlin' Georgia Crazy* (Urbana: University of Illinois Press, 1987), pp. 48–49.

6 THINKS GEORGIA TREATS: *AG*, April 26, 1913.

6 "Georgia is the only state": ibid.

6 "little girl in the mill town": *AC*, June 4, 1913.

6 "A Funeral by Lamplight": *AC*, editorial, IMPOSING UPON, May 4, 1913.

6 "Our principles": *AC*, April 27, 1913.

7 "the awful curse": *AC*, April 28, 1913. Alexander McKelway would later blame Mary Phagan's murder on Georgia's failure to enact child labor laws. See GIRL'S DEATH LAID TO FACTORY EVILS, *AG*, April 30, 1913.

7 " 'Thy Kingdom come' ": *AC*, April 27, 1913.

7 "in America today": *AG*, May 5, 1913.

8 "a hundred dull red eyes": C. Vann Woodward, *Tom Watson: Agrarian Rebel* (New York: The Macmillan Company, 1938), p. 351.

8 "Old Man Peepul . . . the Standard Oil Crowd": ibid., pp. 351, 357.

8 "fat old dago . . . voluptuous women": ibid., p. 433.

8 "in the Valley of the Shadow . . . Your Uncle T.E.W.": ibid., pp. 431, 433.

9 2,719½ gross of new pencils: BOE, Defendant's Exhibit 3, p. 254 and Defendant's Exhibit 4a, p. 257.

10 "Largest Manufacturer of Disinfectant": *Atlanta City Directory 1905*, p. 60.

12 "first white female child": David Marx, "History of the Jews of Atlanta," *Reform Advocate*, November 4, 1911.

12 For a thorough history of both Atlanta's Jewish community and the Hebrew Benevolent Congregation presided over by David Marx, see Steven Hertzberg's authoritative *Strangers Within the Gate City* (Philadelphia: Jewish Publication Society of America, 1978), pp. 19, 40, 115.

12 "The Germans . . . shook their heads": Eli N. Evans, *The Provincials* (New York: Atheneum, 1973,), p. 276.

12 "Marx would have been": ibid., p. 278.

12 "He [Marx] was trying to say": ibid.

13 formed the Standard Club: Garrett, *Atlanta and Environs*, vol. 2, p. 481.

13 "a five o'clock town": Eleanor Ringel, interviewed by author, summer 1986.

13 "the permanent rank": *AJ*, April 27, 1913.

13 $357,000 for prime commercial lots: *AC*, April 27, 1913. Converted to 1999 dollars, the property would have sold for $6,050,847.

13 "cubist gowns . . . cubist walk": *AG*, May 14, 1913.

13 displaying . . . "September Morn": *AJ*, June 14, 1913.

13 campaign to raise the city's population: *AG*, June 9, 1913.

14 "We have . . . put business": Henry Grady, in Thomas Daniel Young, Floyd C. Watkins and Richard Croom Beatty, *The Literature of the South* (Glenview, Ill.: Scott, Foresman, 1968), p. 478.

14 "the bitterness of defeat": *AC*, April 27, 1913.

14 composed a piano trilogy: *AG*, June 23, 1913.

15 "I frankly and freely confess myself": *AG*, June 29, 1913.

15 John Slaton and Luther Z. Rosser: *AC*, April 27, 1913.

15 embroiled in a battle in Rabun County: *AG*, May 25, 1913. (Rosser's co-counsel, Alex King, was one of the founders of King and Spalding, Atlanta's most influential law firm: *The First Hundred Years*, authorized history of King and Spalding, Atlanta: privately published, 1985, p. 87.)

15 "one of the greatest scenic wonders": *AG*, May 25, 1913.

15 "once Georgia was largely attractive": *AG*, April 27, 1913.

15 "The most beautiful sight": C. Vann Woodward, *Origins of the New South* (Baton Rouge: Louisiana State University Press, 1951), p. 418.

16 grand finale performance of . . .

Tosca: AJ, April 26, 1913, and *AC,* April 27, 1913.

16 "A Week of Wonders": *AJ,* April 27, 1913.

16 a red-nosed dandy: *AC,* April 27, 1913.

17 "The majority of them": *AJ,* April 26, 1913.

2. Look Out, White Folks

18 "a white woman has been killed": *AG,* April 30, 1913.

18 "I rubbed the dirt and trash": ibid.

19 "Look out, white folks": *AC,* April 28, 1913.

19 "I did not see the body.": *AG,* April 30, 1913.

19 "By raising the skirt": Executive Clemency Hearing transcript, pp. 144–45.

20 "said he wood love me": Murder Note #1, BOE, State's Exhibit Y.

20 "put it off on" . . . "White folks, that's me": *AC,* July 30, 1913.

21 "that negro hire down here": Murder Note #2, BOE, State's Exhibit Z.

21 "a white man's nigger": *AG,* July 29, 1913.

21 "You did this": *AJ,* April 30, 1913.

21 "[At] almost three o' clock": *AG,* April 30, 1913.

22 " 'Figuratively' speaking": *AC,* October 27, 1914.

23 My account of the anxiety at Mary's home the night of April 26 is taken largely from the testimony of her stepfather, John W. Coleman, at the coroner's inquest: *AG,* May 1, 1913.

24 Detective John Black's background is well detailed in "How Detectives Trailed Clues in Phagan Murder Case": *AC,* July 27, 1913.

25 most "immaculate attaché": *AC,* April 27, 1913.

25 "suave and polite": ibid.

25 "Is this Mr. Frank" . . . "I'll send a car": statement of Leo Frank, BOE, p. 202.

25 "Has anything happened at the factory?": testimony of W. W. Rogers, BOE, pp. 11–12.

25 "His voice was hoarse": testimony of John Black, BOE, p. 17.

26 "extremely nervous": testimony of W. W. Rogers, BOE, p. 12.

26 "I asked them what the trouble was": statement of Leo Frank, BOE, p. 202.

26 "a drink of whisky": testimony of W. W. Rogers, BOE, p. 12.

26 "Mr. Rogers and Mr. Black differ with me": statement of Leo Frank, BOE, p. 202.

27 "the face of the dead girl": *AJ,* July 30, 1913.

28 "I stood right in the door": statement of Leo Frank, BOE, p. 203.

28 "saw Leo M. Frank as he looked": Harold W. Ross, *San Francisco Call,* June 23, 1915.

29 "Yes, Mary Phagan worked here": testimony of W. W. Rogers, BOE, p. 13.

30 "It seemed to be caught": statement of Leo Frank, BOE, p. 204.

30 "When we started down the elevator": testimony of N. V. Darley, BOE, p. 32.

30 "a great deal stronger": statement of Leo Frank, BOE, p. 204.

30 "fresh mound of human excrement": testimony of W. W. Rogers, BOE, p. 15.

32 they had been "borrowed": The next day, the *Journal* scooped the *Constitution* and the *Georgian* with a front-page photograph of the "long tall black" note: *AJ,* April 28, 1913.

32 "unless one looked directly at the body": *AG,* April 30, 1913.

33 the "tired and angry" victim: *AG,* April 28, 1913.

33 when he'd called out, "Hello, Mary": ibid.

33 "I couldn't keep my eyes off her": *AC,* April 28, 1913

33 "That's the man": *AG,* April 28, 1913.

33 "was reeling slightly": *AC,* April 28, 1913.

34 the day's dwindling hours: statement of Leo Frank, BOE, pp. 206–9.

34 Ty Cobb: *AC,* April 27, 1913.

3. Extra, Extra

35 "got a picture of her on the slab": McLellan Smith, April 1964, Washington D.C, interviewed by Leonard Dinnerstein, AJA.

35 "showing her in street dress": *AG,* April 28, 1913.

35 doctored morgue mug shot: W. A. Swanberg, *Citizen Hearst* (New York: Schribner, 1961), p. 234.

35 MRS. COLEMAN PROSTRATED: *AG,* April 28, 1913.

35 "a little playful girl": ibid.

35 "The poor baby": ibid.

35 "young girls working everywhere": ibid.

36 NEIGHBORS OF SLAIN GIRL: ibid.

36 GRANDFATHER VOWS VENGEANCE: ibid.

36 "I'd help lynch the man": ibid.

36 "Standing with bared head": ibid.

36 "a little laboratory work": Herbert Asbury, "Hearst Comes to Atlanta," *American Mercury,* January 1926, p. 88.

37 "It wasn't raining": ibid. p. 90.

37 "Who Is This Man?": *AG,* April 28, 1913.

37 "$500 REWARD": ibid.

37 "EXCLUSIVE Information Leading to the Arrest": ibid.

37 The *New York Journal* printed 40 extras: *Citizen Hearst,* p. 189.

37 NEW STRANGLING ARREST: *AG,* April 28, 1913, afternoon edition.

37 ARRESTED AS GIRL'S SLAYER: ibid., home edition.

37 GANTT ARRESTED: ibid., night edition.

38 "in modern parlance, a wow": Asbury, "Hearst," *American Mercury,* January 1926, p. 90.

38 celebrated both occasions: *Citizen Hearst,* p. 343.

38 "not newspapers at all": ibid., pp. 192–93.

38 "To be a Hearst reporter": ibid., p. 233.

39 "Everything is quiet": ibid., p. 127.

39 THE WARSHIP *MAINE*: *New York Journal,* February 17, 1898.

39 "ruthless, truthless newspaper jingoism": *Citizen Hearst,* p. 162.

40 Hearst offered Watson a job: C. Vann Woodward, *Tom Watson: Agrarian Rebel* (New York: The MacMillan Company, 1938), p. 356.

40 "Bill Zimmer's Hen Call": *AG,* February 17, 1912.

40 Circulation figures for the *Georgian, Journal* and *Constitution* from William Curran Rogers, "A Comparison of Coverage of the Leo Frank Case" (master's thesis, University of Georgia, 1949).

41 For further understanding of the political rivalry between the *Constitution* and the *Journal,* see Dewey Grantham, Jr.'s, *Hoke Smith and the Politics of the New South* (Baton Rouge: Louisiana State University Press, 1958).

41 CRIME WAVE SWEEPS CITY: Asbury, "Hearst," *American Mercury,* January 1926, p. 88.

42 "This Is Why Atlanta's Electricity Must Be Cheaper": *AG,* February 12, 1912.

42 "Be An Optimist and Hitch Your

Wagon to the Star of Atlanta's Destiny": ibid.

42 "familiar with the South and Georgia": Asbury, "Hearst," *American Mercury,* January 1926, p. 88.

42 "finest staff of any paper": De-Witt Roberts, "Anti-Semitism and the Leo Frank Case," report for the Anti-Defamation League, c. 1950.

42 "Had not Hearst owned the *Georgian*": Asbury, "Hearst," *American Mercury,* January 1926, p. 89.

43 Hearst had feted the Slatons: *AG,* April 20, 1913.

43 Hearst's roving surrogate: Asbury, "Hearst," *American Mercury,* January 1926, p. 89.

43 a Coates screamer: Don C. Seitz, *Joseph Pulitzer: Liberator of Journalism* (New York: Simon & Schuster, 1924), pp. 241–42.

43 tooling around Manhattan: W. A. Swanberg, *Pulitzer* (New York: Scribner, 1967), p. 279.

43 "slumbered peacefully": Asbury, "Hearst," *American Mercury,* January 1926, p. 89.

44 "knowing little if anything of the South": ibid.

44 "played the case harder": ibid.

44 the *Constitution* . . . devoting just a column and a half: *AC,* April 28, 1913.

44 "They couldn't verify half the *Georgian*'s stories": Asbury, "Hearst," *American Mercury,* January 1926, p. 88.

44 GOD'S VENGEANCE: *AJ,* April 28, 1913.

4. Onward, Christian Soldiers

46 "some white substance": testimony of R. P. Barrett, BOE, p. 27.

46 "I had used that machine": ibid.

46 "It's Mary's hair": *AJ,* April 28, 1913.

47 Beavers pulled a bottle of alcohol from his pocket: ibid.

47 "blood stains leading from the lathe": *AG,* April 28, 1913.

47 "murdered in the metal room": *AJ,* April 28, 1913.

47 The detectives' suspicions of Gantt are recounted in the *AC, AG* and *AJ,* April 28 and April 29, 1913.

48 "a squad of detectives and criminal experts": *AC,* April 29, 1913.

48 "Newt Lee has been saying something": statement of Leo Frank, BOE, p. 209.

48 "He was rubbing his hands": *AG,* April 30, 1913.

48 "Go out and have a good time": testimony of Newt Lee, BOE, p. 2.

48 "Chief Lanford will tell you": statement of Leo Frank, BOE, p. 209.

49 "Hello boys, what's the trouble?": ibid.

49 "If it's clothes they want": Luther Rosser Shelton, interviewed by author, November 14, 1991.

49 "I am going into that room": statement of Leo Frank, BOE, p. 210.

49 My account of Frank's meeting with Chief Lanford and Luther Rosser is taken from reports in all three Atlanta newspapers, the transcript of Frank's April 28, 1913, deposition for Lanford (BOE, State's Exhibit B, pp. 243–45), and the transcript of Frank's August 8, 1913, statement at his trial (BOE, pp. 174–220).

50 "came in between 12:05 and 12:10": Frank's deposition for Lanford State's Exhibit B, BOE, p. 243.

50 "I paid her and she went out": ibid.

50 "What's the matter": ibid., p. 244.

50 "after I give him the keys": ibid.

51 "talking to Newt Lee was J. M. Gantt": ibid.

51 "Why, it's preposterous": statement of Leo Frank, BOE, p. 210.

51 "showed them my underclothing": ibid.

51 "every article of clothing": ibid., p. 211.

52 "a ceaseless procession": *AG,* April 29, 1913.

52 "Come along dearie": *AJ,* April 29, 1913.

52 "two random investigations": ibid.

53 "The police place no belief": *AJ,* April 28, 1913.

53 "Strange Notes Increase Mystery": *AG,* April 28, 1913.

53 "detectives worked diligently": *AC,* April 29, 1913.

53 "a kaleidoscope": *AJ Magazine,* May 18, 1913.

54 Until 1931, recruits were issued a badge: Herbert Jenkins, *Keeping the Peace* (New York: Harper and Row, 1970), p. 1.

54 relying instead on a network of "lock boxes": Cliff Kuhn, interviewed by author, July 17, 1989.

54 In 1915, the force arrested 11,787 Negroes: Annual report of the Atlanta chief of police, 1915.

54 The portrayal of the Wood-Winbush police brutality scandal is taken from accounts appearing on consecutive days in the *Atlanta Journal* during the first week of December 1910.

55 "whitewash committee": *AC,* August 10, 1911.

56 The best portrait of the "restricted district" appears in a series of articles in the *Atlanta Georgian* between September 24 and 27, 1912.

56 This section's overlord was a dashing rogue named Charles C. Jones: *AG,* September 26, 1912.

56 "having a high old time": *Dahlonega Nugget,* June 15, 1900.

56 "There are many who say": *AG,* September 25, 1912.

57 The influence of the Men and Religion Forward Committee is elucidated in chapter four of Martha Tovell Nesbitt, "The Social Gospel in Atlanta: 1900–1920" (Ph.D. diss., Georgia State University, 1975) and in Cliff Kuhn, *Living Atlanta* (Athens, Ga.: University of Georgia Press, 1990), pp. 188, 248.

58 "When the Woodward administration went into office": *AG,* September 26, 1912.

58 "The action of Chief Beavers": *AG,* September 24, 1912.

58 "It was a bad mistake": *AG,* September 25, 1912.

58 "Dramatic Suicide Marks Clean-Up": ibid.

58 "This is the end": ibid.

59 "I'm enforcing the law": *AG,* September 24, 1912.

59 The most complete account of Chief Beavers's triumph appears in the *Literary Digest,* May 3, 1913.

59 had decreased "fully one-third": *AJ,* June 9, 1913.

60 "It is useless to detain me": *AC,* April 30, 1913.

60 $1,000 REWARD: *AC,* April 29, 1913.

60 was conducted in a weathered . . . church: *AG,* April 29, 1913.

61 "We pray for the police": *AC,* April 30, 1913.

61 "Goodbye, Mary. Goodbye": ibid.

61 PASTOR PRAYS FOR JUSTICE: *AG,* April 29, 1913.

62 "preferably a Pinkerton detective": for a reliable sketch of the Pinkerton agency's practices, see Carl Sifakis, *The Encyclopedia of American Crime* (New York: Facts on File, 1982), pp. 569–70.

62 "assist the city detectives": statement of Leo Frank, BOE, p. 211.

63 "John Black [seems] to suspect me": testimony of Harry Scott, BOE, p. 22.

63 "He [Frank] stated": ibid., p. 23.

63 "I told him [Scott] something": statement of Leo Frank, BOE, p. 214.

64 " 'I know what's the trouble' ": *AC,* April 29, 1913.

65 THREE HANDWRITING EXPERTS: *AJ,* April 29, 1913.

65 "Through its own investigations": ibid.

65 "trying to point suspicion at Newt Lee": *AJ,* July 31, 1913.

66 "a little piece of material of some shirt": statement of Leo Frank, BOE, p. 215.

66 "distinct odor of blood": ibid.

66 "how a chief of police should conduct himself": *AC,* April 30, 1913.

67 "If you are the murderer": *AC,* April 30, 1913.

67 "I was humiliated and distressed": *AG,* June 15, 1913.

67 Lucille was downstairs "weeping bitterly": *AC,* April 30, 1913.

67 "humiliation and harsh sight": statement of Leo Frank, BOE, p. 219.

67 "made light of the evidence": *AJ,* April 29, 1913.

67 "We have sufficient evidence": *AC,* April 30, 1913.

68 "Newt, you haven't got long": ibid.

68 "LEE'S GUILT PROVED!": *AG,* April 29, 1913.

68 "I swear 'fore God I didn't do it": *AC,* April 30, 1913.

68 "innocent as a babe": ibid.

69 "Lee was badly frightened": *AJ,* April 30, 1913.

69 "In that room was detective Scott": statement of Leo Frank, BOE, p. 216.

69 "They put Newt Lee into a room" ibid., pp. 216–17.

70 "for about ten minutes": testimony of Harry Scott, BOE, p. 24.

5. A Good Name, a Bad Reputation

71 "Was Factory Used as Rendezvous?": *AJ,* May 1, 1913.

71 NUDE DANCERS' PICTURES: *AG,* April 29, 1913.

72 "immoral purposes": *AC,* May 1, 1913.

72 "frolics were secretly held": ibid.

72 "Under our present condition of morals": *AG,* April 29, 1913.

73 "bright [and] quick witted": *AC,* May 1, 1913.

73 "She began talking about Mr. Frank": ibid.

73 he described how he'd waited in vain for Mary: ibid.

73 "her parents feel an inward fear": Arthur Powell, *I Can Go Home Again,* (Chapel Hill, N.C.: University of North Carolina Press, 1943) p. 287.

73 FRANK TRIED TO FLIRT: *AC,* May 1, 1913.

74 "not easily diverted from the point at issue": *AJ Magazine,* April 11, 1937.

74 "I would not be holding this jury if I were satisfied": *AG,* May 2, 1913.

75 "John Black and I then made an investigation": PR, filed by Harry Scott, May 1, 1913, p. 1.

76 "I met Helen Ferguson and secured a statement from her": PR, filed by L. P. Whitfield, May 6, 1913, p. 10.

76 "I was on duty at the parcel check room": PR, filed by F.C.P., May 4, 1913, p. 6.

77 "Going back to Friday, April 25th": ibid., p. 7.

77 WITNESSES POSITIVE: *AJ,* April 29, 1913.

77 "to the home of Miss Lena Barnhardt": PR, filed by Harry Scott, May 8, 1913, p. 16.

77 "The National Pencil factory was closed": PR, filed by L. P. Whitfield, May 5, 1913, p. 8.

78 "when talking to some of the women": PR, filed by F.C.P., May 9, 1913, p. 19.

78 "I went to Mrs. Holmes' house": PR, filed by F.C.P., May 8, 1913, p. 16.

79 "Leo Frank, the superintendent and general manager": *AC*, May 2, 1913.

80 "Chess Notebook No. 1": contains 30 pages of chess gambits, the Leo Frank Collection, AHC.

80 "I liked to make him blush": *AG*, June 15, 1913.

81 "She inclines to that perfect brunette type": ibid.

81 "Gibbs: $10.00, lining: $2.80": Leo Frank collection, AHC.

82 "cases of 'love at first sight' ": *AG*, June 15, 1913.

82 Lucille's valentine, Leo Frank collection, AHC.

82 "Tho' I have not heard so": This and the other letters that Leo Frank wrote Lucille Selig in June 1909 are in the Brandeis University Archives.

84 "was artistic with quantities of smilax": *AJ*, December 1, 1910.

85 Katie Butler's comments appear in an interview by Dr. Levering Neely of Atlanta, summer 1986. In an interview by the author on October 2, 1998, Frank's niece, Catherine Smithline, confirmed that Lucille suffered a miscarriage.

85 "many husbands in the world as good as Leo": *AG*, June 15, 1913.

85 Paul Donehoo expounded on his view of the coroner's function to Medora Field Perkerson in the *Atlanta Journal Magazine*, April 11, 1937.

86 "this little girl who was killed came up": *AJ*, May 6, 1913.

86 "She asked if the metal had come": PR, filed by Harry Scott, Defendant's Exhibit 92, BOE, p. 306.

87 "Frank . . . startled his audience": *AC*, May 6, 1913.

87 FACTORY SUPERINTENDENT'S STATEMENTS: *AG*, May 6, 1913.

87 LEO FRANK INNOCENT: *AC*, May 6, 1913.

88 " 'Do you know Leo M. Frank?' Donehoo began": The coroner's interrogation of the three witnesses appears in *AC*, May 9, 1913.

89 "Sensational Statements Made at Inquest": ibid.

6. Skulduggery

91 Dr. Henry Fauntleroy Harris's credentials and background are best summarized in his obituary, "DEATH HALTS HUNT FOR CANCER CURE": *AJ*, March 18, 1926.

91 PHAGAN GIRL'S BODY EXHUMED: *AG*, May 5, 1913.

92 "The investigation has been hesitating": *AG*, May 1, 1913.

92 "He seemed pleased with our progress": *AC*, May 2, 1913.

92 "Dorsey is probably the only man": *AJ*, May 5, 1913.

93 "the burden of convicting": *AG*, May 1, 1913.

93 hair taken by Dr. Hurt . . . "has been lost": *AJ*, May 7, 1913.

93 "A chart was made of the cuts and bruises": *AC*, May 8, 1913.

93 "The fingerprints on the body": *AG*, May 7, 1913.

93 "the crime that was taken for granted": ibid.

93 "wounds about the chest and shoulders": *AC*, May 9, 1913.

94 Dorsey's defeat in the Applebaum case is discussed in MRS. J. A. APPLEBAUM ACQUITTED: *AC*, April 26, 1913.

94 Dorsey's defeat in the Grace case is discussed in DORSEY UNAFRAID AS HE FACES CHAMPIONS OF THE ATLANTA BAR: *AG*, August 1, 1913.

94 "an unusual negro": The Tanner case is covered in *AJ*, December 3, 1910.

95 "Old friends come home in the evening": William Smith, "The Most Unforgettable Character I've Met,"

manuscript in author's possession, circa 1947.

96 Hugh Dorsey, Jr., gave an overview of his father's past in an interview by the author on December 3, 1984; background information is also available in JUDGE R. T. DORSEY BREATHES HIS LAST: *AJ*, February 3, 1909, and HUGH M. DORSEY NEW SOLICITOR GENERAL: *AG*, October 26, 1910

96 the coroner's jury . . . recommended: *AC*, May 9, 1913.

96 "Have you discovered any positive information": *AG*, May 11, 1913.

97 "I wonder if they're all asleep in there?": *AC*, May 11, 1913.

97 "horrible false details": *AG*, May 11, 1913.

97 "I cannot help but sympathize": by the Old Police Reporter, ibid.

97 "sensational and misleading" reports: *AC*, April 30, 1913.

98 POLICE HAVE THE STRANGLER: *AG*, April 29, 1913.

98 "Foster Coates made a blunder": Herbert Asbury, "Hearst Comes to Atlanta," *American Mercury*, January 1926, p. 90.

98 "said the *Georgian* had called Frank guilty": ibid.

98 "aroused the community": *AJ*, April 30, 1913.

98 "the storekeepers . . . rubbed their hands": Asbury, "Hearst," *American Mercury*, January 1926, p. 92.

99 BUSINESS MEN PROTEST: *AJ*, May 30, 1913.

99 THE SUPREMACY OF THE LAW!: *AG*, May 1, 1913.

99 "Coates . . . was riding wild": Asbury, "Hearst," *American Mercury*, January 1926, p. 92.

99 "The merchants began withdrawing their advertisements": ibid.

100 W. A. Swanberg comments on Hearst's willingness to alter his editorial positions in *Citizen Hearst* (New York: Scribner, 1961), p. 425.

100 "I went to the pencil factory that Saturday": *AC*, May 10, 1913.

101 Dorsey hired "the world's greatest detective": *AJ*, May 10, 1913.

101 "He [the solicitor] has some mighty good men": *AC*, May 11, 1913.

101 "The squad at headquarters are not inferior": *AC*, May 14, 1913.

101 "I have not been able to satisfy myself": *AJ*, May 12, 1913.

102 "the crime was committed in the basement": *AC*, May 14, 1913.

102 "struck upon the back of the skull": ibid.

102. "a secret conversation between two attachés": *AC*, May 20, 1913.

102 BURNS CALLED: *AG*, May 12, 1913.

103 "the greatest detective certainly": as quoted by Gene Caesar in *The Incredible Detective: The Biography of William J. Burns* (Englewood Cliffs, N.J.: Prentice-Hall, 1968), p. 188.

103 "more suggestive of a successful salesman": ibid., pp. 14–15.

103 "I gladly welcome Mr. Burns": *AC*, May 18, 1913.

103 "The girl was lured": *AC*, May 20, 1913.

104 "one entirely overlooked before": *AC*, May 19, 1913.

104 "We have overlooked nothing": *AC*, May 21, 1913.

104 With witnesses . . . behaving as "if they were under instructions": *AC*, May 25, 1913.

105 For an overview of the Charles W. Morse case, see Carl Sifakis, *The Encyclopedia of American Crime* (New York: Facts on File, 1982), p. 503. For information on Thomas B. Felder's role in the case, see "Felder Calls on Taft For Morse's Parole": *AJ*, August 11, 1911.

105 For insight into Thomas B. Felder's ties to Atlanta society, see "Mayor Admits Dictograph Is Correct": *AG*, May 24, 1913, wherein Felder discusses his wife's leadership of the Atlanta Players'

Club. For an overview of Felder's connections to the city's bar owners and houses of prostitution, see FELDER DENIES PHAGAN BRIBERY: *AG*, May 23, 1913.

106 "The affiant, while at the police station": *AJ*, May 23, 1913.

108 "what I say to you is strictly confidential": *AJ*, May 21, 1913.

108 "Do you think Frank murdered that girl?": *AJ*, May 24, 1913.

109 "Did you tell Tom Felder": *AJ*, May 25, 1913.

110 Colyar was one of the subtlest knaves ever to hit Atlanta: See "Career of A. S. Colyar Reads Like Some Story in the Arabian Nights," *AC*, May 24, 1913.

110 COL. THOMAS B. FELDER DICTOGRAPHED: *AJ*, May 23, 1913.

110 "FELDER IS THE MOUTHPIECE": *AJ*, May 25, 1913.

110 "the issue is now": Felder's self-defense is covered in *AC*, May 25, 1913.

111 "there is no police plot to protect Frank": *AJ*, May 25, 1913.

111 "Mr. Felder . . . had begun to 'bombard' the public": *AC*, May 27, 1913.

111 "Like Some Story in the Arabian Nights": *AC*, May 24, 1913.

112 "probably no man in Tennessee": ibid.

112 "Now isn't Colyar a fine specimen": *AC*, May 25, 1913.

112 "He [Colyar] may be a crook": *AJ*, May 25 1913.

112 "be stripped naked and ridden through Atlanta": ibid.

112 "This is a helluva family row": *AJ*, May 27, 1913.

112 "Felder does not, nor has he at any time": *AC*, June 11, 1913.

113 "Once Felder charged Newport Lanford with favoring Frank": *AG*, June 10, 1913.

114 "Mrs. Coleman also stated": PR, filed by L. P. Whitfield, May 2, 1913, page 3.

114 "I don't want you to see the girl": *AC*, May 11, 1913.

114 signed by a madam named Nina Formby: *AC*, May 23, 1913.

115 "I asked Miss Mills what she knew": PR, filed by W. D. MacWorth, May 14, 1913, p. 27.

115 "Extraordinary passion goaded on this man": Hugh Dorsey, *Argument of Hugh M. Dorsey at the Trial of Leo Frank* (Atlanta: Johnson-Dallis Company, 1914) p. 74.

115 Some of what went on during the . . . hearings leaked: *AJ*, May 25, 1913.

116 the grand jury was comprised: *AJ*, May 28, 1913.

116 "State Faces Big Task": *AG*, May 28, 1913.

117 "It is regarded as likely that the defense will claim": ibid.

117 "Should the State be able to prove": ibid.

7. A Clean Nigger

118 "Jim Conley isn't a cornfield negro": *AC*, August 3, 1913.

118 "On Saturday, April 26, 1913": James Conley's statement to John Black and Harry Scott, May 18, 1913, BOE, Defendant's Exhibit 36, p. 281.

119 "with a kind of African drawl": *AC*, August 3, 1913.

119 "He was dead drunk": *AG*, May 27, 1913.

120 "This woman is not my wife": Conley's statement to Black and Scott, May 18, 1913, BOE, Defendant's Exhibit 36, p. 281.

120 "Like a great dumbbell": W.E.B. Du Bois, "The Negro South and North": *Bibliotheca Sacra* 62 (July 1905).

120 "the smell of money": John Dittmer, *Black Georgia in the Progressive*

Era (Urbana: University of Illinois Press, 1977), p. 12.

120 "Negro Monte Carlos": *AJ*, August 3, 1913.

121 "a score of negro merry-makers": *AC*, April 2, 1913.

121 of 14,045 cases tried in 1900, 9,500 involved blacks: Dittmer, *Black Georgia*, pp. 88–89.

121 "Being of that vast class of society": *AJ*, July 20, 1913.

121 " 'dat ain't no cocaine,' " *AC*, November 2, 1910.

122 "to do so would mean their complete ruin": Dittmer, *Black Georgia*, pp. 88–89.

122 one of the region's first Jim Crow ordinances: C. Vann Woodward, *The Strange Career of Jim Crow* (New York: Oxford University Press, 1955), p. 99.

122 "the practice hit a peak between 1880 and 1900": Dittmer, *Black Georgia*, p. 131.

122 My account of the 1906 Atlanta race riot is largely taken from John Dittmer's excellent *Black Georgia in the Progressive Era*, pp. 123–31. Also helpful in understanding the riot is Mark Bauerlein, *Negrophobia* (San Francisco: Encounter Books, 2001).

122 TWO ASSAULTS, THIRD ASSAULT, FOURTH ASSAULT: Dittmer, *Black Georgia*, p. 124.

123 "The whites kill . . . good men": ibid., p. 128.

123 25 Negroes were dead: ibid., p. 129.

123 "who commit the unmentionable crime": *AG*, August 25, 1906.

124 My account of John D. Rockefeller's influence upon elite Atlanta blacks is taken from Taylor Branch's magisterial *Parting the Waters* (New York: Touchstone Books, 1989), pp. 27–68.

124 On April 1, 1913, several hundred well-dressed Negroes: *AJ*, March 29, 1913, quarter-page ad.

125 Born a slave, Herndon had opened his eponymously named barbershop shortly after arriving in Atlanta in 1882: Dittmer, *Black Georgia*, pp. 37–38.

125 "When you saw him walking down the street": Kathleen Adams, interviewed by author, February 26, 1988.

126 "Reverend Proctor was a teacher in his pulpit": ibid.

126 "having exclusive mulattoes in their society": *Atlanta Independent*, October 23, 1915.

126 "Mulattoes as a group": Dittmer, *Black Georgia*, p. 62.

127 "when Martin Luther King [Sr.] came to town": Kathleen Adams, interviewed by author, February 26, 1988.

127 "Our church is the mother of Atlanta University": Henry Hugh Proctor, *Between Black and White* (Boston: The Pilgrim Press, 1925), chapter 8.

127 "a disgrace to civilization and unfit for cattle": Dittmer, *Black Georgia*, p. 147.

127 In the late 1890s, Jim had attended Mitchell Street Elementary: *AG*, August 4, 1913. Source for material on Ara Cooke: *Atlanta University General Catalogue, 1867–1929* (Atlanta, 1929), p. 57. Source for material on Alice Carey: *Annual Circular and Catalogue of Spelman Seminary* (Atlanta, 1893), p. 31. Carey (whose name in sometimes spelled without an "e") was later the influential director of the Auburn Avenue branch of the Atlanta Public Library.

128 "To the best of her recollection": PR, filed by W. D. MacWorth, May 16, 1913, p. 29.

128 Subsequently, Frank would claim: statement of Leo Frank, BOE, p. 218.

128 "Mr. Holloway stated": PR, filed by W. D. MacWorth, May 16, 1913, p. 29.

128 "look into a drawer in the [office] safe": ibid., p. 30.

129 "The handwriting appears to be identical": ibid.

129 "Conley jumped up from behind the washstand": ibid.

129 "We were unsuccessful": PR, filed by Harry Scott, May 18, 1913, p. 33.

129 "a negro wearing a green derby hat": ibid.

130 "we've got the deadwood on you": AC, July 13, 1913.

130 "White folks, I'm a liar": ibid.

130 " 'I didn't do it,' Jim swore": ibid.

131 they took him to a basement-level isolation cell: ibid.

131 "Boss, I wrote those notes": AJ, May 24, 1913.

131 "On Friday evening before the holiday": Statement of James Conley, May 24, 1913, BOE, Defendant's Exhibit 37, pp. 282–83.

132 "false in every detail": AG, May 26, 1913.

132 "put through such a severe cross-examination": AJ, May 26, 1913.

132 "Conley wrote the notes": ibid.

132 "Conley's delay in making his confession": AG, May 27, 1913.

132 "No theory that has placed the responsibility of the crime upon Frank": AG, May 24, 1913.

133 "absurdities in its structure": AG, May 27, 1913.

133 "gaining information against Frank": AG, May 28, 1913.

133 "as if they are convinced he committed the murder": AJ, May 29, 1913.

133 "Conley grew weak, lost appetite": AC, July 13, 1913.

133 SUSPICION TURNED TO CONLEY: AG, May 28, 1913.

134 "I make this statement, my second statement": Statement of James Conley, May 28, 1913, BOE, Defendant's Exhibit 38, pp. 283–89.

136 "had practically cleared the mystery": AG, May 28, 1913.

136 "their most material witness": AC, May 29, 1913.

136 "Now the theory of the crime we entertain": AJ, May 29, 1913.

137 "Three responsible officials": AG, May 29, 1913.

137 "Little if any credence": AJ, May 29, 1913.

137 Luther Rosser had taken the train to rugged Rabun County: AG, May 26, 1913.

138 "Detectives who pin faith to the negro's story": AC, May 30, 1913.

138 "I wish they would let me face Mr. Frank": AJ, May 31, 1913.

138 "I waited for him downstairs": Statement of James Conley, May 29, 1913, BOE, Defendant's Exhibit 39, pp. 289–91.

140 CONLEY SAYS HE HELPED FRANK: AC, May 30, 1913.

140 "The negro's affidavit": AJ, May 30, 1913.

140 "they considered the negro's final affidavit proof conclusive": AC, May 30, 1913.

141 "I feel like a clean nigger": AC, May 31, 1913.

141 "when he whistled to you twice?": This part of Jim Conley's account is from AG, May 30, 1913.

141 "When I got back here, I got scared and hollered to Mr. Frank": ibid.

142 "He [Frank] picked up her feet": ibid.

142 "I took her body out of the elevator": ibid.

142 "Show us the way you left the girl's body": ibid.

142 "You can't help but believe him": ibid.

142 "Frank climbed up this ladder": ibid.

143 "Mr. Frank sat down in his swivel chair": This part of Conley's account is from AJ, May 30, 1913.

143 "He told me to come out of the wardrobe": ibid.

143 "He handed me this pad and then told me to write": ibid.

143 "Have you been abused or threatened by the officers": ibid.

143 CONLEY TAKEN TO FACTORY: ibid.

144 "Conley appeared perfectly composed": AG, May 30, 1913.

8. A Tramp Alumnus

145 CONLEY LAYS BARE PHAGAN CRIME: *AG,* May 30, 1913.

145 the true sponsors of this get-together were not especially concerned with Conley's fate: William Smith, autobiographical notes, circa 1940, pp. 29–30. (Smith's notes, on which much of this chapter is based, were provided to the author by Smith's son Walter. They were written in the third person, apparently as a curriculum vitae in narrative form as part of a job application. For clarity's sake, I have transcribed them into the first person when quoting directly.)

145 "he ain't paid me nuthin' yet": *AC,* May 31, 1913.

146 "ratification of my employment": *AC,* October 4, 1914.

146 "Practically my entire communication at that time": ibid.

146 "The girl must have been dead for about 15 minutes": *AJ,* May 31, 1913.

147 "only such officials as were approved by me": *NYT,* October 5, 1914.

147 "a sincere effort to protect Conley": ibid.

147 "In a very short time, I became convinced": Smith, notes, pp. 29–30.

148 "I sacrificed the compensation I was to receive": *NYT,* October 5, 1914.

148 "penniless and friendless": Smith, notes, p. 32.

148 "No white man killed Mary Phagan": *AC,* May 31, 1913.

148 "great influence and unlimited financial means": Smith, notes, p. 32.

148 "shared the view of the prosecuting attorney": ibid., p. 30.

148 "My justification for this course": ibid., p. 32.

148 "in the early part of my career": ibid., p. 17.

149 "exercise that extreme care and caution which a prudent man would exercise": "Georgia Railway & Electric Co. v.

Rich," *Georgia Reports,* March, 1911 term, p. 498.

149 "We are not unaware of the trying situation": ibid.

150 "handle the matter with great care": Smith, notes, p. 19; details of the Merritt case are presented in "Merritt v. The State," *Georgia Reports,* March 1910 term, p. 263.

150 "a reasonable doubt of Roger Merritt's guilt": Smith, notes, p. 20.

150 Smith details his relationship with Proctor in his autobiographical notes, pp. 20–22.

150 Proctor left the plan's implementation to Smith: Smith, ibid., pp. 19–20.

151 "Out of this war": *AChr,* April 29, 1912.

151 Smith gives an overview of the Intercollegiate Oratorical Contest on page 6 of his autobiographical notes. The contest is also described in the November 3, 1900, editions of the *Atlanta Constitution* and the *Atlanta Journal.*

152 "The Negro Problem": Smith, notes, p. 6.

152 "a fair and just deal for the 'Brother in Black' ": ibid.

152 "The South's Contribution to the American Republic": *AC,* October 30, 1898; *AJ,* October 31, 1898.

152 "not tarnished by those vilifying flings": Smith, notes, p. 6.

152 "Educate the negro, and you spoil a good field hand": Eli N. Evans, *The Provincials* (New York: Atheneum, 1973), p. 144.

152 The description of Smith's personal appearance and demeanor is taken from the author's June 22, 1987, interview with his daughter, Mary Lou Smith Allen, and from numerous interviews with his son Walter. Details regarding his early legal cases come from Thornton et al. *v.* Jackson, executor, *Georgia Reports,* October 1907 term, pp. 700–704; Hendrix *v.*

Elliott, *Georgia Reports*, March 1907 term, pp. 301–4; Wright, Williams and Wadley *v.* Brown, sheriff, *Georgia Reports*, October 1909 term, pp. 389–90; Sharp *v.* The State, *Georgia Reports*, March 1910 term, pp. 605–7.

153 "to eventually become the Solicitor General": Smith, notes, p. 27.

154 "one of the biggest public demonstrations": *AJ*, May 29, 1908.

155 Smith had plunged into deeper waters: Smith, notes, pp. 12–13.

155 Smith was an avid joiner: Smith, notes, pp. 10–11.

156 Information on Smith's courtship of his wife and their subsequent relationship comes from the author's June 22, 1987, interview with the couple's daughter, Mary Lou Smith Allen.

156 "beautiful Southern queens": William Smith, "The Turning of a Hundred Years," in the University of Georgia student magazine, *The Georgian*, March 1901, p. 155.

156 Information regarding the Smiths' Atlanta home life comes from numerous interviews over a ten-year period with their youngest son, Walter.

157. "half rations of an inferior grade, sleeping in jails": Smith, notes, p. 8.

157 "a prejudice against the 'stars and stripes' ": William Smith, "A Tramp Alumnus," *The Georgian*, April 1902, p. 245.

157 From Montreal, he shipped as a deckhand on the steamboat *Hamilton* to Toronto: Smith, notes, p. 9.

157 "cutting cane on a sugar plantation": Smith, "A Tramp Alumnus," p. 247.

157 "seen something of America before settling down": Smith, notes, p. 7.

157 "Chinese, dagoes and negroes": Smith, "A Tramp Alumnus," p. 247.

158 "learned a great deal about his fellow Americans": Smith, notes, pp. 9–10.

158 "Georgia is on the war path!": Shelby Foote, *The Civil War* (New York: Vintage Books, 1986), vol. 1, p. 16.

158 "Resolved that the Interference with Strikes": *The Red and Black,* University of Georgia student newspaper, April 12, 1901.

159 "The Northern states with their better educational facilities": Smith, "The Turning of a Hundred Years," *The Georgian*, March 1901, p. 156.

159 "Negroes will be banished": ibid., p. 157.

159 "vase in which roses have once been distilled": ibid., p. 159.

160 My account of Dora Smith's death comes both from interviews with Walter Smith and from the *Augusta Chronicle,* August 26, 1897.

160 "dulled his youthful experience of grace": *AChr*, February 22, 1889.

160 "The Triumph of Individualism": *AC*, November 3, 1900.

160 "I made application to a number of prominent law firms": Smith, notes, p. 10.

9. Skirmishes

162 "the severest sort of grilling": *AG,* June 2, 1913.

163 "I don't know a thing about it": *AJ,* June 9, 1913.

163 "Both men are employees": *AC,* June 4, 1913.

163 "I will not talk": ibid.

164 COOK'S SENSATIONAL AFFIDAVIT: *AG,* June 4, 1913.

164 "fully as startling": Minola McKnight's statement is taken from *AC,* June 5, 1913.

164 "Sunday, Miss Lucille said": ibid.

165 "I don't know why Mrs. Frank didn't come": ibid.

165 "When I left home": ibid.

165 "Incoherent Statement": *AG*, June 4, 1913.

165 "The affidavit is nearly all hearsay": *AJ*, June 4, 1913.

166 "Did you sign": *AG*, June 5, 1913.

166 "I ain't got no lawyer": ibid.

166 "Luther Z. Rosser maintains his sphinxlike": *AJ*, June 9, 1913.

166 "Luther Z. Rosser maintains his usual": *AC*, June 3, 1913

167 "The action of the Solicitor General": Lucille Frank's open letter appears in *AG*, June 5, 1913.

167 "My husband was home": ibid.

168 "I have been compelled": ibid.

168 "I know my husband": ibid.

168 "Minola McKnight": *AJ*, June 5, 1913.

168 "I have read the statement": *AG*, June 5, 1913.

169 "urging him to take steps to prevent": *AJ*, June 6, 1913.

169 "If the Phagan tragedy": *AC*, June 7, 1913.

169 "To be strictly truthful": *AG*, June 8, 1913.

170 "I think fairness to Mr. Frank": *AG*, June 7, 1913.

170 "no saint": *AG*, June 15, 1913.

171 "He ever has been": ibid.

171 "Mr. Dorsey and the detectives": *AC*, June 8, 1913.

171 "a very ordinary, ignorant": *AC*, June 11, 1913.

171 "out of his head": *AJ*, June 10, 1913.

171 "Conley made one statement": *AC*, June 11, 1913.

172 "This negro is not to give any": ibid.

172 "police petting": *AG*, June 11, 1913.

172 "made passionately insane": *AC*, June 3, 1913.

174 "protest . . . farce": *AJ*, June 13, 1913.

174 "That the detectives should wish": This and the account of Jim Conley's release and rearrest are from *AG*, June 13, 1913.

174 "Well, Jim": ibid.

175 "I didn't want to get out": ibid.

175 My account of the deal made by Hugh Dorsey and William Smith is drawn from Smith, notes, p. 30.

176 My portrait of Reuben Arnold is taken from his father's obituary, ALL ATLANTA MOURNS DEATH OF COL. ARNOLD: *AJ*, July 15, 1914, and details provided by his son, Thomas, in a lengthy letter to the author dated August 23, 1989.

177 "The sting of Reuben Arnold": *AC*, August 7, 1913.

177 "I hazard not a thing": *AG*, June 22, 1913.

178 "Gentlemen, some months ago": *AJ*, June 26, 1913.

178 SHE REALLY POSTPONED: ibid.

179 NEW PHAGAN EVIDENCE: *AG*, July 9, 1913.

179 pointed "more strongly than ever": ibid.

179 "At the trap door": PR, May 15, 1913, p. 27.

179 "We then secured": ibid., p. 28.

180 "I was in Atlanta": *AG*, July 13, 1913.

181 "We place the utmost reliance": *AG*, July 10, 1913.

181 MINCEY'S OWN STORY: Mincey's account appears in *AG*, July 14, 1913.

182 "I stopped and got into": ibid.

183 "thoroughly disgusted": ibid.

183 "I sincerely doubt": ibid.

183 CONLEY IN SWEATBOX: *AG*, July 11, 1913.

184 "Although evidence was constantly piling up": Herbert Asbury, "Hearst Comes to Atlanta," *American Mercury*, January 1926, p. 91.

184 "If it can be shown": *AG*, July 13, 1913.

184 "It would be unusual": *AG*, July 20, 1913.

185 "went over the head": *AC*, July 19, 1913.

185 "The meeting's only purpose": *AG*, July 19, 1913.

185 "an unseen force": *AJ*, July 19, 1913.

186 "Jim Conley has been dealing": *AC*, July 19, 1913.

186 "If the grand jurors": ibid.

186 "The Grand Jury": *AG*, July 20, 1913.

187 "gratification of his professional pride": ibid.

187 "It is appropriate": ibid.

187 "The Solicitor General": *AG*, July 21, 1913.

188 "I am requested": ibid.

188 "It made absolutely no difference": *AG*, July 22, 1913.

188 "midnight seances": Leo Frank, "Leaflet No. 7," June 3, 1914, on file at the New York office of the Anti-Defamation League.

189 "to make Conley impervious": Walter Smith, interviewed by author, July 8, 1986.

10. Prosecution

190 A preliminary note on sources. During the 1960s, the transcript of the Leo Frank trial disappeared from the records room of the Fulton County Courthouse. The only official record of the proceedings now extant is the Brief of Evidence, a digest of testimony vetted by the state and the defense and used during the appeals process. While authoritative, the brief, owing to the fact that the lawyers' questions do not appear in it, contains just one side of the trial's back-and-forth. Fortunately for posterity, the newspapers of the time published virtually verbatim coverage of important legal proceedings. By mid-afternoons throughout July and August of 1913, the *Atlanta Journal* and the *Atlanta Georgian* were on the streets with editions containing every word uttered at the morning sessions. The next day, Atlantans awakened to copies of the *Atlanta Constitution* containing every word uttered at the afternoon sessions. I have drawn exhaustively on these accounts to present the battle that was the Frank trial. Where inconsistencies exist, I relied on the brief as arbiter. For the most part, however, the newspaper coverage is solid. In the trenches for the *Journal*

were Harold W. Ross, Harllee Branch and Charles Phillips, Jr. From the *Georgian* were Archie Lee, William Flythe, James Keeling and John Minar. The *Constitution* was represented by Sidney Ormond, Vernon Stiles and Britt Craig. These men, generally writing without bylines, produced thousands of inches of copy. Their words live on in my trial chapters. For brevity's sake, I have cited only selected passages. Otherwise, my notes for "Prosecution," "Defense" and "Verdict" would run to scores of pages.

190 "Hardly once during this morning": *AJ*, July 28, 1913.

190 "The men and girls": ibid.

191 "probably will be the coolest": *AG*, July 28, 1913.

193 "If there was any fear": ibid.

193 "Frank looked quickly": *AC*, July 29, 1913.

194 "Not infrequently": *AG*, July 28, 1913.

195 "Of the many juries": *AC*, July 29, 1913.

195 "The jury apparently": *AG*, July 29, 1913.

196 When court reconvened: There

were no opening statements in the Frank trial. The proceedings simply began with Dorsey's examination of Mrs. Fannie Coleman.

196 "Many spectators": *AJ,* July 29, 1913.

196 "During [Mrs. Coleman's] mental suffering": *AC,* July 29, 1913.

197 "as though a barber had passed a razor": ibid.

198 "The positive way in which little Epps": ibid.

199 "dem big lawyers": *AG,* July 29, 1913.

201 "Diagram of Phagan Murder": ibid.

201 "Has you ever seed one whut's been hit": ibid.

202 "reminded me much of a big mastiff": *AG,* July 30, 1913.

204 "The defense expects to show": *AG,* July 29, 1913.

204 "We've got to commence": *AJ,* July 29, 1913.

205 "the groundwork for their theory": *AG,* July 29, 1913.

206 "smiled an applause as gracious": ibid.

206. "Seasoned courthouse officials": *AC,* July 30, 1913.

206 "The negro appeared": *AJ,* July 29, 1913.

206 "As for the examination of Newt": *AG,* July 30, 1913.

206 "Time and again": ibid.

207 "Will Conley be as nimble-witted": ibid.

210 "Lawyers must wear coats": *AJ,* July 30, 1913.

212 FRANK LAUGHS FOR FIRST TIME: *AG,* July 30, 1913.

212 "Arms akimbo, glasses firmly set": ibid.

213 "In the elevator shaft": BOE, p. 15.

216 GIRL'S STORY: *AG,* July 30, 1913.

216 "Defense to Claim": *AJ,* July 30, 1913.

219 "The detective's features flushed": *AG,* July 31, 1913.

221 "Our contention is": *AJ,* July 31, 1913.

221 "saw what I expected": *AG,* July 31, 1913.

222 "Collapse of Testimony": ibid.

222 "Detective John Black": *AJ,* July 31, 1913.

222 DEFENSE RIDDLES: *AC,* July 31, 1913.

223 "When Wednesday's session": ibid.

223 "There is a feeling": *AG,* July 31, 1913.

226 "Scott refused": ibid.

227 "Scott proved": *AJ,* July 31, 1915.

229 "Barrett made probably the best": *AG,* July 31, 1915.

229 "He admitted that the blood": *AJ,* August 1, 1913.

230 "The state fared better": *AG,* August 1, 1913.

234 "I made an examination": BOE, p. 49.

234 "It is perfectly plain sailing": *AC,* August 2, 1913.

236 "I discovered no violence": BOE, p. 46.

236 "Her hymen was not intact": ibid., p. 47.

236 STATE ADDS LINKS: *AG,* August 2, 1913.

237 "Gentlemen, it has been said": *AJ,* August 2, 1913.

237 "turned a liberal hose": *AC,* August 3, 1913.

237 Hugh Dorsey describes William Smith buying new clothes for Conley in his closing argument: *Argument of Hugh M. Dorsey at the Trial of Leo Frank* (Atlanta: Johnson-Dallis Company, 1914), pp. 131–32.

237 "The State HAS definitely shown": *AG,* August 2, 1913.

238 "The questions to be thrashed out": *AG,* August 3, 1913.

238 a World Series baseball game: *AJ,* August 4, 1913.

240 "with the voice of a young teacher": ibid.

240 "with an expression of pathetic pleading": *AG*, August 4, 1913.

241 "He says, 'Well, that one you say' ": BOE, p. 55.

242 "strained forward in their seats": *AG*, August 4, 1913.

242 "Apparently . . . they were willing": *AC*, August 6, 1913.

243 "The negro forgot nothing": *AG*, August 4, 1913.

243 "Jim's story was so completely": *AJ*, August 4, 1913.

243 "Jim Conley has upset traditions": *AG*, August 5, 1913.

244 "Wise lawyers in the courtroom": *AC*, August 5, 1913.

246 "the vilest and most amazing": *AJ*, August 4, 1913.

246 "The crossing of Conley": *AG*, August 5, 1913.

246 "a painted-cheek girl": *AC*, August 5, 1913.

249 "This man, as your honor knows": *AJ*, August 5, 1913.

249 "Don't you know a nigger never had sausage": *AG*, August 5, 1913.

250 "During Mr. Rosser's questioning": ibid.

252 "When a recess was ordered": *AJ*, August 5, 1913.

252 "The value of this evidence": *AC*, August 5, 1913.

253 "There is no use in getting wrought up": *AC*, August 6, 1913.

253 DEFENSE MOVES TO STRIKE: *AJ*, August 5, 1913.

253 "his hopeless task": *AG*, August 5, 1913.

254 "As to how that dung came to be in the shaft": BOE, pp. 72–73.

254 "Did you meet a man named Mincey": *AC*, August 6, 1913.

255 "He moved uneasily": *AG*, August 6, 1913.

255 "Would Judge Roan rule for the state": *AC*, August 7, 1913.

256 "Jim . . . don't you say a word": *AJ*, August 6, 1913.

257 My account of the method whereby William Smith received his $40 payment is taken from the lawyer's autobiographical notes, p. 30, and WILLIAM SMITH TELLS WHY HIS OPINION HAS CHANGED, *AC*, October 4, 1914.

257 "I have serious doubts": *AC*, August 7, 1913.

257 "a riot of applause": ibid.

257 ROAN'S RULING HEAVY BLOW: *AG*, August 7, 1913.

258 Conley's story was "a ragtime composition": ibid.

258 "Arnold failed to develop": *AC*, August 7, 1913.

259 "Every single thing": *AG*, August 6, 1913.

260 "If the story Conley tells": ibid.

11. Defense

261 THE UNDOING OF CONLEY: *AG*, August 8, 1913.

261 "the biggest element in the case": ibid.

261 "Not one in a hundred": *AC*, August 8, 1913.

261 "Further than this witness": *AG*, August 7, 1913.

262 "Childs's testimony if believed": ibid.

263 "He was chewing his lips": BOE, p. 81.

264 "Scott's statement created": *AC*, August 8, 1913.

265 "looked a bit too short": *AG*, August 8, 1913.

266 "If the testimony": *AG,* ibid.

268 "Defense Will Seek to Show": *AC,* August 9, 1913.

270 "partly spoiled": *AG,* August 9, 1913.

272 "Under the heading 'Material Costs' ": BOE, pp. 88–89.

274 "Saturday was by far": *AC,* August 10, 1913.

274 "As all interest centered": *AG,* August 10, 1913.

277 "The human tongue could not produce": BOE, p. 161.

277 "the best the defense": *AC,* August 12, 1913.

279 "a sturdy farmer": *AC,* August 13, 1913.

279 "He was frightened": *AJ,* August 12, 1913.

280 "a direct contradiction": *AJ,* August 13, 1913.

282 "It's the most unfair thing": *AC,* August 13, 1913.

284 "with emphasis": *AJ,* August 13, 1913.

286 "No, nor you either . . . Gentile dog . . . Christian dog." According to the *Atlanta Constitution* of August 14, 1913, Rae Frank said simply, "No, nor you either." Hugh Dorsey, in his closing argument, reminded the jurors that Mrs. Frank had called him "a dog": Hugh Dorsey, *Argument of Hugh M. Dorsey at the Trial of Leo Frank* (Atlanta: Johnson-Dallis Company, 1914), p. 2. The *New York Sun* for October 12, 1913, reports that Mrs. Frank used the term "Christian dog."

287 MOTHER OF FRANK DENOUNCES: *AC,* August 14, 1913.

290 "For a minute or two": *AJ,* August 14, 1913.

290 "The loyalty with which Frank's instructors": *AC,* August 15, 1913.

291 "Dewey Hewell has been brought": *AC,* August 16, 1913.

291 "The only use we would have had for Mincey": *AC,* August 23, 1913.

294 "perfectly composed": *AC,* August 16, 1913.

294 "Dear Uncle": BOE, Defendant's exhibit number 42, p. 294.

295 "The examination of Rae Frank": *AG,* August 17, 1913.

296 "Miss Jackson's testimony": *AC,* August 17, 1913.

297 "the defense unquestionably": *AG,* August 17, 1913.

297 "It is unique in the annals": ibid.

297 "Many people are arguing": ibid.

299 "I married in Atlanta": BOE, p. 195.

299 "My duties . . . were": ibid., p. 175.

299 "picture his every movement": *AG,* August 17, 1913.

299 "No one came into my office": BOE, p. 176.

299 the earnestness one can imagine: *AJ,* August 19, 1913.

300 "Of all the mathematical work": BOE, p. 178.

300 "The first order": ibid.

300 "Starting here with order 7187": ibid., p. 184.

301 "To the best of my knowledge": ibid., p. 186.

302 "Now, one of the most intricate": ibid., p. 195.

302 "One of the tricks of the trade": ibid., p. 191.

302 "This sheet, the financial": ibid., p. 195.

303 "Gentlemen, I was nervous": *AG,* August 18, 1913.

303 While discussing his anxiety at the sight of Mary Phagan's body, Frank also addressed his behavior when the Atlanta police arrived at his home the morning of the murder, his actions later that day while visiting the pencil factory and his contacts with the investigating officers prior to his arrest. These comments are quoted in my second chapter, "Look Out, White Folks,"

and in chapter four, "Onward, Christian Soldiers."

304 "The date I was taken": BOE, p. 219.

304 "grilled the negro": ibid., p. 217.

304 "I did not speak": ibid., p. 218.

304 "Gentlemen, I know nothing": ibid., p. 219.

305 "Very few in the courtroom": AG, August 19, 1913.

305 "There will be those": ibid.

12. Verdict

306 "would be embarrassing for ladies": AG, August 19, 1913. Despite Dorsey's request, both Mrs. Franks remained in the courtroom.

306 "unprintable": ibid.

306 "sprang a sensation": AJ, August 19, 1913.

307 "I was present when Minola": BOE, pp. 226–27.

308 STATE IS HARD HIT: AC, August 20, 1913.

311 WOMEN ARRAIGN: AG, August 20, 1913.

312 "In reply to the statement": BOE, p. 243.

313 "They had the right to inquire": AJ, August 21, 1913.

313 "It may seem strange": ibid.

314 "You doubtless have read": ibid.

314 "It was because": ibid.

315 "The idea that Jim": ibid.

315 "a fellow named Mincey": ibid.

316 "God grant that we can get away": AG, August 21, 1913.

316 "This man Kendley": AJ, August 21, 1913.

316 "I tell everybody": ibid.

317 "What did it amount to?": AJ, August 22, 1913.

323 "Gentlemen, take a look at this": AC, August 23, 1913.

324 "Conley is a plain, beastly, drunken": AJ, August 22, 1913.

324 "They got a dirty, black": ibid.

325 "There's Professor Starnes": AG, August 22, 1913.

325 "Professor Scott would say": ibid.

325 "My friend Hooper said": AJ, August 23, 1913.

326 "If you, as white men": AG, August 22, 1913.

326 "The gentlemen have abused": AC, August 23, 1913.

326 "Gentlemen, do you think that I": ibid.

327 "I honor the race": AG, August 23, 1913.

327 "This great people": AC, August 23, 1913.

327 "Now gentlemen, put yourself": Hugh Dorsey, Argument of Hugh M. Dorsey at the Trial of Leo Frank (Atlanta: Johnson-Dallis Company, 1914), p. 26.

328 "What business did this man have": ibid., p. 27.

328 William Smith discusses organizing the pro-Dorsey demonstration on the courthouse steps in William Smith, "My Views as to the Death Notes," introduction, p. 2, John M. Slaton Collection, GDA.

328 "absolute decorum": AG, August 23, 1913.

328 "unspoken fear": AChr, August 26, 1913.

329 "Oscar Wilde was an Irish knight": Dorsey, Argument, p. 31.

329 "Up goes your alibi": AG, August 23, 1913.

330 "I know enough about human nature": Dorsey, Argument, p. 43.

334 "Only the limitations": AC, August 24, 1913.

334 "The real reason": *AChr,* August 26, 1913.

335 "a white hot philippic": *AG,* August 23, 1913.

336 "Gentlemen of the jury": Dorsey, *Argument,* pp. 99–100.

336 "Did you make an earnest": ibid., p. 103.

336 "Like a dog to his vomit": ibid., p. 111.

337 "I tell you, gentlemen": ibid., p. 121.

337 "This cabbage proposition": ibid., p. 123.

337 "So far, not a word": ibid., p. 130.

338 "The defense's failure": ibid., p. 139.

338 "Gentlemen, every act": ibid., pp. 145–46.

341 "the cry of guilty took winged flight": *AC,* August 26, 1913.

341 "The solicitor reached no farther": ibid.

342 "Mrs. Frank huddled closer": ibid.

342 My source for the number of *Georgians* printed on the day of Frank's conviction is the *Atlanta Georgian* of August 26, 1913.

343 "It is ordered and adjudged": *AJ,* August 26, 1913.

343 "The trial which has just occurred": *AG,* August 26, 1913.

343 "The jury heard none of the cheering": ibid.

343 JIM CONLEY, THE EBONY CHEVALIER: *AG,* August 7, 1913.

344 "Well, boss, dem niggers": ibid.

13. Appeals in and out of Court

345 "Oh, please take me away": *AC,* August 26, 1913.

345 "The long case": *MT,* August 27, 1913.

346 "I would like to enlist": David Marx to Louis Marshall, August 30, 1913: Leonard Dinnerstein, *The Leo Frank Case* (New York: Columbia University Press, 1968), p. 74.

346 "Mr. Ochs is a non-Jewish Jew": Garet Garrett diary, courtesy Richard Cornuelle, June 30, 1915, p. 59.

346 resisted pleas to take the lead: Susan E. Tifft and Alex S. Jones, *The Trust* (Boston: Little, Brown and Company, 1999), pp. 94–95. Tifft and Jones present a thorough study of Ochs's ambivalent view of his Judaism.

346 "a Jewish newspaper": Garrett diary, August 21, 1915, p. 94.

346 attorney-at-large for the Jewish people: Morton Rosenstock, *Louis Marshall: Defender of Jewish Rights* (Detroit:

Wayne State University Press, 1965), p. 27.

347 "always talking too much about Jews": ibid., p. 40.

347 "The correspondent . . . reported": Garrett diary, August 26, 1915, p. 96.

347 "horrible judicial tragedy": Louis Marshall to Joseph L. Magnes, September 5, 1913: Leonard Dinnerstein, "Leo Frank and The American Jewish Community," p. 6, manuscript at AJA.

347 "a second Dreyfus affair": Marshall to Irving Lehman, September 9, 1913: Dinnerstein, *The Leo Frank Case,* p. 74.

348 "It would be unfortunate": Marshall to Milton Klein, September 9, 1913: Dinnerstein, "Leo Frank," p. 6.

348 "There is only one way of dealing": Marshall to Lehman, Dinnerstein, *The Leo Frank Case,* p. 75.

348 "Frank's religion precluded": *American Israelite,* September 26, 1913.

348 "great regret": Marshall to Adolph

Kraus, September 27, 1913, Dinnerstein, "Leo Frank," p. 7.

348 "may not only subside": ibid.

349 CELL NOW LIKE LIVING ROOM: AC, August 28, 1913.

349 My description of Frank's exercise routine is drawn from DESPITE DEATH SENTENCE, AJ, August 28, 1913, and FRANK LOOKS TO HEALTH, AG, September 1, 1913.

349 "There is no suggestion": AG, August 29, 1913.

350 JURORS JOHENNING AND: AJ, October 1, 1913.

350 "Johenning had a fixed opinion": Amended Motion for a New Trial, p. 135, on File at the Georgia Department of Archives.

350 "Henslee was prejudiced": ibid., p. 134.

350 My account of the barbeque for Frank jurors is taken from PLENNIE MINER IS HOST AT JOYOUS BARBEQUE, AG, September 14, 1913.

350 "I know that he's guilty": Amended Motion for a New Trial, defense affidavits, p. 5, on file at the Georgia Department of Archives.

350 "I am glad they indicted": ibid., p. 3.

351 "I believe Frank is guilty": ibid., p. 2.

351 "The charges that the jury": AG, October 3, 1913.

351 "the charges are bosh": ibid.

351 "Henslee's prejudice": AG, October 6, 1913.

351 My summary of the affidavits recounting the exposure of Frank jurors to pro-prosecution sentiments during the trial is drawn from the *Atlanta Journal* of October 4, 1913, and from the Amended Motion for a New Trial, defense affidavits, pp. 8–10.

352 "took hold of one of the jurors": Amended Motion for a New Trial, defense affidavits, p. 6.

352 "unless they brought in a verdict of guilty": ibid., p. 13.

353 "hang this man on the dotting of an 'i' ": AG, October 22, 1913.

354 "pronounced and continuous applause": ibid.

354 "I can give my opinion": AG, October 23, 1913.

354 "which the jury heard": AJ, October 23, 1913.

355 "I did not know how A. H. Henslee": Amended Motion for a New Trial, State affidavits, p. 23, on file at the Georgia Department of Archives.

356 "As illustrating the attitude": ibid., p. 48.

356 "The club has among its members": ibid., p. 51.

356 "because the said Mack Farkas": ibid., p. 49.

356 "express himself in a way": ibid., pp. 23–27.

356 "of the same race and religion": ibid., p. 40.

357 "I did not at any time": ibid., p. 28.

357 "It takes thirteen jurors": Reuben Arnold, *The Trial of Leo Frank, Reuben R. Arnold's Address on the Motion for New Trial* (Baxley, Ga.: Classic Publishing Company, 1915), p. 9.

358 "that has reflected": ibid., p. 10.

358 "Argument was lost": ibid., p. 12.

358 "Was ever a case heard": ibid., p. 13.

358 "he saw his own life": ibid., p. 16.

358 "Left alone . . . the negro spread out": ibid., p. 15.

358 "They took his story": ibid.

358. "merely to prejudice": AG, October 25, 1913.

359 "If Leo Frank is hanged": ibid. Inflammatory passages such as this one were edited out of the version of Arnold's argument published in book form. I have restored them from the contemporary newspaper accounts to show the full ex-

tent of the bitterness among opposing counsel.

359 "Your honor . . . the state's case": Arnold, *The Trial of Leo Frank,* p. 28.

361 NEXT TRIAL MAY BE HELD: *AC,* October 26, 1913.

361 "improbable and ridiculous": *AG,* October 27, 1913.

362 "If the verdict of guilty": *AJ,* October 28, 1913.

362 "The people were not aroused": *AG,* October 28, 1913.

362 "the people in the streets": ibid.

362 "eloquent tongued": ibid.

363 "Your honor said": ibid.

363 "As God is in the heavens": *AG,* October 29, 1913.

363 "What does Mr. Dorsey mean": *AJ,* October 29, 1913.

363 "the brand of Cain": *AG,* October 29, 1913.

363 "Dismiss from your mind": ibid.

364 "was greater than": *AG,* October 31, 1913.

364 "Impressed by the portentousness": ibid.

364 "Gentlemen, I have thought": ibid.

364 "Judge Roan has put": *AG,* November 1, 1913.

365 "Judge Roan displayed": the *Brunswick News* as quoted in *AG,* November 6, 1913.

365 "It was none of Roan's business": the *Waycross Herald,* November 5, 1913.

365 "Our Supreme Court has held": Herbert Haas to Louis Marshall, October 31, 1913, as quoted in Dinnerstein, *The Leo Frank Case,* p. 79.

365 My account of the crucial meeting at Temple Emanu-El is taken from the minutes of the American Jewish Committee, p. 180, November 8, 1914.

365 "the case of Leo M. Frank": ibid.

365 My figures on the cost of Frank's defense are drawn from Dinnerstein, "Leo

Frank," pp. 9–11, and Dinnerstein, *The Leo Frank Case,* p. 199.

366 "It would be most unfortunate": Louis Marshall to William Rosenau, December 14, 1914: Dinnerstein: "Leo Frank," p. 8.

366 JEWS FIGHT TO SAVE LEO FRANK: *New York Sun,* October 12, 1913.

366 "Atlanta is probably freer": ibid.

366 "Prejudice did finally develop": ibid.

366 "resolving to take no action": minutes of the American Jewish Committee, p. 180, November 8, 1914.

367 My portrait of Albert D. Lasker is drawn from John Gunther's biography *Taken at the Flood* (New York: Harper and Brothers, 1960).

367 "He detested anti-Semitism": ibid., p. 78.

367 "I thank you and your father": Leo Frank to Albert D. Lasker, December 18, 1913: Julius Rosenwald Papers, University of Chicago Library.

367. "When Mr. O. returned": Garrett diary, August 26, 1915, p. 96.

368 "Your honors would not believe": *AG,* December 15, 1913.

368 "If there were errors": *AG,* December 16, 1913.

368 "The jury may have thought": ibid.

368 "There was nothing much gained": *AG,* December 17, 1913.

368 "The court will proceed": ibid.

368 "The words of his judgment": *AG,* December 11, 1913.

368 "From timidity": ibid.

369 "It is not the office": Brief of the Defendant in Error, October 1913 term, Georgia Supreme Court, p. 95.

369 "We submit": ibid.

369 "Our contention in this case": ibid., pp. 73–76.

369 "unless it appears there has been": *AC,* February 18, 1914.

369 "The general rule": ibid.

370 "material and relevant": ibid.

370 "the condition of the body": ibid.

370 "This court will not interfere": ibid.

370 "calculated to prejudice": *AJ*, February 17, 1914.

370 "No fixed plans": *AC*, February 18, 1914.

370 "Ole Marster" *AJ*, February 17, 1914.

14. Brightness Visible

371 "seemed to reach": *NYT*, March 6, 1914.

371 "My trial, my accusation, my rebuffs": ibid.

371 "When I informed the solicitor": *AJ*, February 20, 1914.

372 "He knew the truth": *AG*, February 22, 1914.

372 "The solicitor, in his zeal": ibid.

372 Harris was merely offering an "opinion": *AG*, February 20, 1914.

372 "had lost none of its strength": ibid.

372 he "did not see Mr. Leo M. Frank": *AG*, February 22, 1914.

372 "If they were at such pains": *AG*, March 4, 1914.

373 "I now state": *AJ*, March 4, 1914.

373 "Just stick to that": ibid.

373 TESTIMONY DOCTORED: *AG*, March 4, 1914.

373 SPLIT COURT DENIES: *NYT*, February 18, 1914.

373 "committed the *Times*": Garet Garrett diary, courtesy Richard Cornuelle, August 26, 1915, p. 96.

373 EVIDENCE FOR FRANK HIDDEN: *NYT*, February 21, 1914.

373 RETRACTS EVIDENCE: *NYT*, February 23, 1914.

373 WOMAN ADMITS SHE LIED: *NYT*, February 26, 1914.

374 FRANK CONVICTED BY PUBLIC CLAMOR: *NYT*, March 2, 1914.

374 "certain persons who are interested": *NYT*, March 4, 1914.

375 "in the Frank case to the finish": *NYT*, March 5, 1914.

375 DETECTIVE PROMISES: *AG*, March 4, 1914.

375 "work day and night": W.C.G. to Julius Rosenwald, March 4, 1914 (Julius Rosenwald papers, the University of Chicago Library Department of Special Collections).

375 "Mr. Lasker's secretary": ibid., March 9, 1914.

376 Approaching the bench: Frank's statement and the reaffirmation of his sentence appear in *AJ*, March 7, 1914.

377 "It is a terrible thing": *AG*, February 26, 1914.

377 "If I had been guilty": *AC*, as reprinted in *NYT*, March 9, 1914.

377 "I am obliged": *AJ*, March 15, 1914.

377 "The Truth Is on the March": *NYT*, March 6, 1914.

378 "He was drunk": *NYT*, March 2, 1914.

378 SAYS CONLEY MOLESTED HER: ibid.

378 "the strongest connecting links": *AC*, March 6, 1914.

378 "I spoke to him": ibid.

378 "The statements of Mrs. Miller and Mr. Lefkoff": ibid.

378 "The truth continues on the march": *AC*, March 7, 1914.

379 "It seems to the writer of this article": Henry Alexander, "Some Facts about the Murder Notes in the Phagan Case" (privately printed pamphlet in possession of the author), p. 7.

379 "We had an old Negro woman": L. O. Bricker, "A Great American Tragedy," *Shane Quarterly*, April 1943.

379 NEW EVIDENCE: *AJ*, March 8, 1914.

380 "The simplest explanation": *NYT*, March 9, 1914.

380 "They will have to change": ibid.

380 "old duplicate pads": ibid.

380 "I hope Solicitor Dorsey rests": ibid.

381 "We'd printed all this stuff": Harllee Branch, interview by his grandson, Harllee Branch III, in Atlanta, October 1962. (By courtesy of Harllee Branch III.)

381 "Frank Should Have a New Trial": editorial in *AJ*, March 10, 1914.

382 "Frank should have a new trial": *NYT*, March 16, 1914.

382 "The fact that Frank is a Jew": ibid.

382 "Even among the people": *NYT*, March 15, 1914.

383 "The Frank Case": *Jeff*, March 19, 1914.

383 "For many years": ibid.

383 My account of Watson's animus for Hoke Smith is taken from C. Vann Woodward, *Tom Watson: Agrarian Rebel* (New York: The Macmillan Company, 1938), pp. 386–89.

384 "desire to bring disgrace": ibid., p. 413.

384 *"Who is paying for all this?"*: *Jeff*, March 19, 1914.

384 "Does the *church* invade": ibid.

384 "Does a Jew expect": ibid.

385 "Conley had nothing": *NYT*, February 25, 1914.

385 "If the law didn't demand": *AG*, February 24, 1914.

385 "the only way": ibid.

385 The best portrait of Burns's conduct and demeanor while in Atlanta appears in "How Will I Solve the Phagan Murder Mystery? By Common Sense, Says Burns": by Angus Perkerson, *AJ Magazine*, March 22, 1914.

386 "I have no doubt": *AJ*, March 16, 1914.

386 "I know the people": *AJ*, March 23, 1914.

386 "I will throw open to Burns": *AC*, March 17, 1914.

386 he examined the crime scene: *AJ*, March 16, 1914.

386 "easier than I expected": *AG*, March 19, 1914.

387 "contact with abnormal people": *AJ*, March 16, 1914.

387 "savage instinct": *AC*, March 20, 1914.

387 BURNS IS CERTAIN: *AG*, March 22, 1914.

387 BURNS SAYS HE CAN SOLVE: *NYT*, March 19, 1914.

387 Detective Burns Says He Soon Can Prove: *CTrib*, March 19, 1914.

388 For an overview of Lasker's efforts to recruit noted Americans to Frank's cause, see John Gunther, *Taken at the Flood* (New York: Harper and Brothers, 1960), p. 88.

388 "protest against the execution": *NYT*, March 26, 1914.

388 AN INNOCENT MAN: *NYT*, March 15, 1914.

388 "Frank, the highly educated": ibid.

389 "the strongest ever filed": *NYT*, March 28, 1914.

389 "joined in the immoral conduct": Dalton's comments appear in the extraordinary motion for a new trial, filed with the brief of evidence at the Georgia Supreme Court, pp. 31–34.

390 "baby you ought not never said anything": This and the following quotations are from Jim Conley's letters to Annie Maude Carter, Slaton papers, GDA.

391 "beyond a peradventure": *NYT*, April 27, 1914.

391 William Burns's descriptions of Mary Phagan's carefully cut underclothing constitute the fifth amendment to the extraordinary motion for a new trial, filed with the Brief of Evidence at the Georgia Supreme Court, p. 65.

392 "After examining the clothes": *AJ*, April 8, 1914.

392 "specialists on nervous diseases": ibid.

392 "Frank was normal": *NYT,* April 9, 1914.

392 "acts of perversion": *AG,* April 12, 1914.

392 "I am not so hard up": ibid.

392 "The state of Georgia": *AG,* April 24, 1914.

392 "Police department today": William Burns to Adolph Ochs, April 24, 1914, William Breman Jewish Heritage Museum.

393 ABSOLVE FRANK: *NYT,* April 25, 1914.

393 "Does the State of Georgia Deserve": *Jeff,* April 19, 1914.

393 "stage-lecturing sleuth": *AG,* March 21, 1914.

394 "I asked Mr. Burns": Herbert Haas to Albert Lasker, April 17, 1914, *AJA.* By the date of Haas's appeal to Lasker for more money, the Frank defense had spent approximately $80,000, which

converted to 1999 dollars would total $1,333,000. Before it was all over, Lasker would put $100,000 into the fight, making his contribution alone $1,666,000 in 1999 dollars.

394 "I hate to be compelled": ibid.

394 "Believe me": Albert Lasker to Herbert Haas, April 20, 1914, *AJA.*

394 "ought to give at least $10,000": Albert Lasker to Louis Wiley, April 20, 1914, *AJA.*

395 For an overview of Louis Wiley's influence at the *New York Times,* see Susan E. Tifft and Alex S. Jones, *The Trust* (Boston: Little, Brown, 1999), pp. 89–90.

395 Wiley mailed a copy: Louis Wiley to Jacob H. Schiff, *AJA,* April 22, 1914.

395 "During Christmas week": *AG,* April 24, 1914.

396 "One of the men said": ibid.

396 "mixed up in the situation": ibid.

396 "A fair trial is what I want": *AG,* April 26, 1914.

15. Darkness Falls

397 "Sentiment is as keen": Herbert Haas to Albert Lasker *AJA,* April 30, 1914.

397 "How Much Longer": *Jeff,* April 23, 1914.

398 "just handing money out": *AJ,* May 4, 1914.

398 "a cowardly lie": *AG,* April 30, 1914.

398 "We want nothing to do with him": ibid.

398 "On Thursday, April 23": *AG,* April 28, 1914.

399 "Since the state": ibid.

399 "The Frank Case; the Great Detective": *Jeff,* April 30, 1914.

400 "You not only expressed": *Jeff,* April 2, 1914.

400 "Tom Watson is a lighthouse": ibid.

400 HORRIBLE MISTAKE: *AC,* May 1, 1914.

401 My depiction of Marietta's agricultural, industrial and financial underpinnings in 1914 is taken from MARVELOUS MARCH OF MARIETTA, *AC,* November 27, 1910, and MARIETTA—THE GEM CITY OF GEORGIA, *AC,* May 10, 1914.

401 For a thorough account of the Great Locomotive Chase, see Shelby Foote, *The Civil War* (New York: Vintage, 1986), vol. 1, pp. 377–78.

402 "define his position": *NYT,* April 8, 1914.

402 "I have promised to beat you": *AJ,* May 2, 1914. My portrait of Robert E. Lee Howell is drawn from interviews with his kinsman, Hill Huffman, on October 24, 1990, and February 3, 1992.

402 "walked down the back streets": *AG*, May 2, 1914.

402 "The great detective ran": *Jeff*, May 7, 1914.

402 "level-headed citizens": *AC*, May 2, 1914.

403 "Bob Howell's hand": *NYT*, August 20, 1915.

403 "I do not care to go behind": *AJ*, May 1, 1914.

403 "If nothing added to nothing": ibid.

404 "the Jews" would get him: ibid.

405 "mixed up in the case": ibid.

405 "She knew Frank's relations with women": ibid.

405 "Well, I've got Carrie Smith": ibid.

405 "live with Monteen Stover": ibid.

405 "improper proposals": ibid.

405 "not like other men": ibid.

406 "Defense Affidavits Forged": *AG*, May 1, 1914.

406 ANGRY CROWD: *AJ*, May 1, 1914.

406 "Oh, I merely want to ask": *AC*, May 2, 1914.

406 "Do you profess to be able": This question and the following pages of Q&A between Dorsey and Burns and Arnold and Burns are taken from DETECTIVE BURNS GRILLED BY DORSEY FOR OVER AN HOUR, *AJ*, May 2, 1914, and BURNS IS FIERCELY GRILLED BY SOLICITOR, *AG*, May 2, 1914.

410 "Judge Hill allowed": Herbert Haas to Albert Lasker, *AJA*, May 2, 1914.

411 "You will take the rope": *AJ*, May 4, 1914.

412 "I can't tell a lie like that": ibid.

412. "They said Frank": ibid.

412 "Jimmy tried to kiss me": ibid.

412 "No trash, books or papers": ibid.

413 "personally positive": ibid.

414 "That was truth on the run": *AG*, May 4, 1914.

414 "I have on several visits": *AJ*, May 4, 1914.

414 "come out and declare": ibid.

416 "She broke down": *AJ*, May 5, 1914.

417 "Epps told us": *AJ*, May 6, 1914.

417 "who in the least understands": ibid.

418 "Your honor, let this point": ibid.

418 "You could not hunt": ibid.

418 "Credibility of witnesses": ibid.

418 "familiar with the vernacular": *AC*, May 7, 1914.

419 "three physical facts": *AJ*, May 6, 1914.

419 "Those notes show": ibid.

419 "I had expected": *AG*, May 6, 1914.

419 "The trial of Leo M. Frank": *NYT*, [May 8, 1914].

419 "We are busy at work": *AC*, May 7, 1914.

419 "disgusted at the farcical methods": Louis Marshall to Louis Wiley, May 5, 1914, *AJA*.

420 "I know that the lawyers": ibid.

420 "I am afraid the whole business": Samuel Untermeyer to Louis Wiley, May 5, 1914, AJA.

420 "The Frank Case: What Does It Reveal": *Jeff*, May 14, 1914.

421 "He did not waive": *AJ*, April 16, 1914.

421 "nothing but a trifling": *AC*, June 6, 1914.

421 "Our motion is founded": ibid.

422 Minola McKnight was knifed: *AC*, June 15, 1914.

16. A Change of Heart

423 "published one of his hands": *NYT*, August 2, 1914.

423 "fronting on the ocean": Leopold Haas to Leo Frank, July 24, 1914, AHC.

424 "He wanted my promise": *NYT*, October 4, 1914.

424 "For some reason": Mary Lou Smith, "How, by Whom, and in What Way Was Mary Phagan Murdered,"

manuscript, 1929, p. 3. Carbon copy in author's possession.

424 "something held back": *AC,* October 4, 1914.

424 "He would not let me know": ibid.

424 "I have always felt": ibid.

425 *Le Chiffre Indéchiffrable*: Berry Benson to Daniel S. Lamont, U.S. Secretary of War, October 26, 1896, Benson Papers, Southern Historical Collection, University of North Carolina Library.

425 "The harder the problems": Berry Benson, *Five Arguments in the Leo Frank Case* (Augusta, Ga.: privately published, 1915), p. 2.

425 "with some interval of time": ibid., p. 7.

426 "If Frank had dictated": ibid., p. 6.

426 "there is not a white man": ibid., pp. 2–3.

426 My portrait of Colonel James Perry Fyffe is drawn from "Col. Fyffe Laid to Rest with Honors": *Chattanooga News,* January 21, 1926, and "Death Claims Col. J. P. Fyffe, Noted Soldier": *Chattanooga Times,* January 20, 1926. In a January 8, 1914, letter on file at the AJA, Louis Marshall wrote to Adolph Ochs regarding Fyffe's employment.

426 "This Chattanooga newspaper man": Walter Smith, interviewed by author, July 8, 1986.

427 "Let us examine sacredly": William Smith, "My Views as to the Death Notes," frontispiece to introduction. On file in the John M. Slaton Collection at the Georgia Department of Archives, this 100-page legal sheet document, compiled over a several-month period in late 1914 and early 1915, presents the results of Smith's independent investigation into Jim Conley's involvement in Mary Phagan's murder. Because its pages are not successively numbered, I have broken the study down by subject into the following three sections: introduction, main text and language test.

427 "My father bent over": Smith, "How, by Whom," p. 8.

427 "My father could not believe": ibid.

427 "I can understand": *AC,* October 4, 1914.

428 "My mother screamed": Smith, "How, by Whom," p. 8.

428 "forced to smile": William Smith, "My Views as to the Death Notes," main text, p. 6, GDA.

428 "resolved to play": ibid., pp. 7–8.

429 "densely ignorant": ibid., p. 1.

429 "This man here, by these notes": Hugh Dorsey, *Argument of Hugh M. Dorsey at the Trial of Leo Frank* (Atlanta: Johnson-Dallis Company, 1914), p. 65.

430 "page 936: 'Alright, I will do' ": Smith, "Death Notes," language test, p. 13.

430 "i don't care . . . but i *did* not know that you": ibid., p. 14.

430 "I [was] swept into the truth": *AC,* October 4, 1914.

431 "compellable witness": ibid.

431 the Smiths were left with 40 nouns: Smith, "Death Notes," language test, pp. 1–42.

431 My account of the Smiths' working methods is drawn from a June 22, 1987, interview with their daughter, Mary Lou Smith Allen, who was present in the house when they conducted their study, and from numerous interviews with their son Walter, who spoke frequently with his father regarding the process.

432 Take the word "long": Smith, "Death Notes," language test, pp. 30–31.

432 the word "down": ibid, pp. 35–37.

432 Consider the phrase: ibid, p. 27.

432 "living in the South": ibid.

433 "page 954: '*I went to*': ibid, pp. 38–39.

433 the Smiths had enumerated: ibid, p. 42.

433 95 percent were monosyllabic: Smith, "Death Notes," main test, pp. 17–18.

433 compound adjectives: Smith, "Death Notes," language test, pp. 33–35.

433 "Any sane man": ibid., pp. 18–19.

434 "In a personal interview": ibid, p. 2.

434 "gave me a scratch pad": James Conley, statement of May 24, 1913, BOE, Defendant's Exhibit 37, p. 282.

434 "Dad told me": Walter Smith, interviewed by author, June 12, 1987.

435 "Conley was wary": ibid. Berry Benson refers to the fingerprint scheme in a September 15, 1914, letter to Leo Frank on file at the AHC.

435 "I have never ceased": AC, October 3, 1914.

435 "Frank Not Guilty, Believes Conley's Lawyer": ibid.

435 CONLEY IS GUILTY: AG, October 3, 1914.

436 CONLEY, NOT FRANK, CALLED SLAYER: NYT, October 4, 1914.

436 "The unfortunate publicity": AC, October 4, 1914.

436 "Reading the official record": ibid.

436 "I know Daisy Hopkins": ibid.

437 "upon a comparative study": ibid.

437 "With the loyal and enthusiastic": AG, October 3, 1914.

437 "It is unnecessary": NYT, October 4, 1914.

437 "his honest opinions": ibid.

437 "Attorney Smith's announcement": NYT, October 4, 1914.

438 "The state stands": NYT, October 5, 1914.

438 "Only a few days ago": AJ, October 3, 1914.

438 "I haven't liked the way": NYT, October 6, 1914.

438 "I don't care what": NYT, October 4, 1914.

438 "The Leo Frank Case Campaign": Jeff, October 8, 1914.

438 "According to his own statement": ibid.

439 "LET W. M. SMITH BE CAREFUL!": ibid.

439 "to do me as [they] did Burns": AG, October 8, 1914.

439 "Will Smith is the worst abused": H. F. Sanders to Aldine Chambers, October 7, 1914, Aldine Chambers papers, AHC.

439 Mary Lou Smith Allen recalled the anxiety in the household following her father's public change of heart in her June 22, 1987, interview with the author.

439 CONLEY'S LAWYER DEFIES: AG, October 8, 1914.

440 "Brings in Another Horse": Tom Watson's attack on Walter Smith is from Jeff, October 15, 1914.

442 "Among the important principles": AC, October 31, 1914.

442 SHOULD A LAWYER BETRAY: NYT Magazine, October 11, 1914.

443 "Regardless of public conjecture": AC, October 4, 1914.

443 "Dad felt responsible": Walter Smith, interviewed by author, July 8 and September 4, 1986.

443 "If the decisions are adverse": AC, October 5, 1914.

17. Cause Célèbre

444 "I want to tell you a few things": This and the following quotations are from Christopher Powell Connolly's letter to Leo Frank, November 28, 1914, AHC.

444 My portrait of C. P. Connolly is drawn from David Mark Chalmers, The Social and Political Ideas of The Muckrakers (New York: The Citadel Press, 1964), pp. 26–32. For more on Connolly, see J. Anthony Lukas's Big Trouble (New York: Simon and Schuster, 1997), pp. 677–78.

445 a "nationwide sensation": *New York Herald Tribune*, November 9, 1933.

445 Not only did Albert Lasker guide Connolly in his coverage of the Frank case, but he met with *Collier's* editor Mark Sullivan to discuss the story: Albert Lasker to Leo Frank, November 30, 1914, AHC.

445 "I presume": Henry Alexander to Leo Frank, November 30, 1914, AHC.

446 "my 'Zola'": Leo Frank to C. P. Connolly, December 3, 1914, AJA.

446 LEO FRANK LOSES: *AG*, October 14, 1914.

446 "In view of the nature": *AC*, October 15, 1914.

446 "I don't think you need": C. P. Connolly to Leo Frank, October 20, 1914, AHC.

446 "Frank's fifth attempt": *NYT*, October 15, 1914.

446 LEO M. FRANK LOSES LAST FIGHT: *AJ*, November 14, 1914.

447 "It would be trifling": *NYT*, November 15, 1914.

447 "Well, I had expected": *AJ*, November 14, 1914.

447 "An appeal to the Supreme Court": *NYT*, November 15, 1914.

447 "not impressed": *AJ*, November 20, 1914.

448 "Frank made a motion": *AJ*, November 26, 1914.

448 "I thought I deserved a chance": *NYT*, November 24, 1914.

448 "Several times during the trial": *NYT*, November 27, 1914.

448 "I am bound by the decision": ibid.

449 "I understand that I am to assume": ibid.

449 JUSTICE TO FRANK DOUBTED: ibid.

449 "From the lips of Justice Holmes": ibid.

449 "If the man": *Boston Journal*, as reprinted in the *New York Times*, December 1, 1914.

449 "Do the people of Georgia realize": *Louisville Courier-Journal*, ibid.

450 "What is mysterious": *NYT*, December 5, 1914.

450 "Is it not an amazing": *Albany Knickerbocker Press*, as reprinted in the *New York Times*, December 1, 1914.

450 "Can it be that the law": *AJ*, November 22, 1914.

450 "That my vindication": ibid.

451 "taking hold of the matter": Albert Lasker to Leo Frank, November 12, 1914, AHC.

451 "One of the misfortunes": Louis Marshall to Henry Alexander, December 1, 1914: Leonard Dinnerstein, "Leo Frank and the American Jewish Community," p. 16, manuscript at AJA.

451 "The federal question": ibid., p. 18.

451 "paralyzed the judicial function": *NYT*, December 2, 1914.

451 "coerced by threats": ibid.

451 "Leo Frank as a Regular": *Jeff*, December 3, 1914.

451 "Never before": ibid.

452 "What an arrant falsehood!": ibid.

452 "the great point": *Jeff*, ibid.

452 "pleasure loving Jewish businessmen": ibid.

452 "I expect to hear": Henry Alexander to Leo Frank, December 4, 1914, AHC.

453 The first piece opened: Quotations from Connolly's first article are from *Collier's*, December 17, 1914.

453 In the second installment: Quotations from *Collier's*, December 23, 1914.

455 "two or three dozen": Leo Frank to C. P. Connolly, December 23, 1914, AJA.

455 "Another Campaign of Big Money": *Jeff*, December 17, 1914.

456 "This matter involves": *NYT*, December 20, 1914.

456 "We realize, your honor": ibid.

456 "Outside the state of Georgia": Albert Lasker to Jacob Billikopf, December 28, 1914: Dinnerstein, "Leo Frank," p. 13.

456 "If Frank's life is saved": Arthur

Brisbane to Albert Lasker, December 28, 1914, AJA.

457 LAWYERS UNITE: *NYT,* December 21, 1914.

457 FRIEND'S PLEA: *NYT,* December 18, 1914.

457 GEORGIANS URGED: *NYT,* December 12, 1914.

457 ATLANTA'S MOB SPIRIT: *NYT,* December 6, 1914.

457 GEORGIA'S JUSTICE: *NYT,* December 16, 1914.

457 INNOCENCE NOT NOW: *NYT,* December 2, 1914.

457 "Anti-Jewish prejudice": *NYT,* December 13, 1914.

457 "The Leo M. Frank case can be reckoned": *NYT,* December 22, 1914.

457 "Why have the *Times* and other publications": *NYT,* December 10, 1914.

458 "This matter has been tried": *NYT,* December 20, 1914.

458 "We abundantly disposed": *AJ,* December 21, 1914.

458 "I challenge the statement": *AC,* December 22, 1914.

459 "an *argumentum ad hominem*": Louis Marshall to Haas, December 24, 1914, Julius Rosenwald papers, the University of Chicago Library, Department of Special Collections.

459 "It is hard for me to see": Leo Frank to C. P. Connolly, December 23, 1914, AJA.

459 "My dear Leo": C. P. Connolly to Leo Frank, December 27, 1914, AHC.

460 FRANK APPEAL GRANTED: *AJ,* December 28, 1914.

460 FRANK WINS APPEAL: *AG,* December 28, 1914.

460 "has never determined": *NYT,* December 29, 1914.

460 "The cell of Leo Frank": *NYH,* December 29, 1914.

460 "His face betrayed": *AG,* December 28, 1914.

460 "It is a long lane": ibid.

460 "I feel that I have a right": David

Marx to Louis Marshall, December 28, 1914, BU.

461 "In assuring you": Leo Frank to Adolph Ochs, *NYT,* January 5, 1915.

461 "I quite agree": Albert Lasker to Leo Frank, January 4, 1915, AHC.

461 "I feel that the missionary work": Leo Frank to C. P. Connolly, January 1, 1915, AJA.

461 FRANK IS INNOCENT: *NYT Magazine,* January 10, 1915.

462 "Do you care to make a statement": Victor Morgan to Leo Frank, December 26, 1914, AHC.

462 "Few articles which have appeared": Jacob Billikopf to Albert Lasker, January 19, 1915, AJA.

462 "The Continued Campaign": *Jeff,* February 4, 1915.

462 "This campaign of lies": ibid.

462 "Are we to understand": *AChr.* December 27, 1914.

463 "The managing editor": *Kansas City Star,* January 17, 1915.

463 "Apparently nothing": Louis Marshall to Leo Frank, January 30, 1915: Leonard Dinnerstein: *The Leo Frank Case* (New York: Columbia University Press, 1968), p. 117.

463 "This court has said": *NYT,* February 26, 1915.

464 "a court may abolish": ibid.

464 "a Constitutional right": ibid.

464 "Is it your argument": ibid.

464 "The right to be heard": ibid.

464 "I am free to confess": ibid.

464 "if twenty courts had passed": ibid.

465 "misapprehended the procedure": ibid.

465 "any man under sentence": *NYT,* February 27, 1915.

465 "I do not so consider it": ibid.

465 "If the judges": Louis Marshall to Henry Alexander, February 19, 1915: Dinnerstein: "Leo Frank," p. 19.

465 "Unless we have a remedy": *NYT,* February 27, 1915.

465 "no coercion": ibid.

465 "no public prejudice": ibid.

465 "an enlargement upon the truth": ibid.

466 "I am hopeful of winning": Leo Frank to C. P. Connolly, March 23, 1915, AJA.

466 "Did Leo Frank get JUSTICE?": The passages quoted from Arthur Train's article are in *Everybody's Magazine,* March 1915, pp. 314–17.

466 "Like every other investigator": *NYT,* February 24, 1915.

467 "The Leo Frank Case Still Raging": *Jeff,* March 25, 1915.

467 "Frank's allegations": *United States Supreme Court Reporter,* October term, 1914, p. 594.

468 "put *we* for I throughout": Merlo Pusey: *Charles Evans Hughes,* Vol I. (New York: The MacMillan Company, 1952), p. 289.

468 "Whatever disagreement": *United States Supreme Court Reporter,* October term, 1914, pp. 595–96.

468 "I am very much disappointed": *AG,* April 19, 1915.

468 "I will never suffer the death penalty": ibid.

18. Commutation

469 "Gentlemen: After considering": *AJ,* April 20, 1915, and *AG,* May 31, 1915.

470 "voice from the tomb": *AG,* May 31, 1915.

470 "fully confident": *AJ,* April 21, 1915.

470 "I am not asking for mercy": *NYT,* April 22, 1915

470 "the opportunity for time": *AJ,* April 21, 1915.

470 "I am absolutely innocent": *AJ,* April 22, 1915.

471 "may be handled by Governor Slaton": *NYT,* May 3, 1915.

471 "The governor is not friendly": James R. Gray to Leo Frank, November 27, 1914, AHC.

471 "It is understood": *NYT,* April 30, 1915.

472 "It is an open secret": ibid.

472 "the merits of the case": *NYT,* November 28, 1914.

472 "Frank shall not be a victim": ibid.

472 "You can just say this": *NYTrib,* May 23, 1915.

472 "Frank would have a better chance to live": Leonard Dinnerstein, *The Leo Frank Case* (New York: Columbia University Press, 1968), p. 117.

473 My account of Louis Marshall's efforts to have the mandate in the Frank case returned to the lower court at an early date is taken from the *New York Times,* May 6, 1915. Also of note are Hugh Dorsey's remarks regarding the standard 30-day waiting period: *AJ,* April 19, 1915.

473 "We have just been notified": *NYT,* May 6, 1915.

473 "Those representing": ibid.

473 "Again, I stand before you": *AJ,* May 10, 1915.

474 "noticeably pale": ibid.

474 "I am fully alive to the fact": ibid.

474 "With the fixing of June 22": ibid.

474 My portrait of Geraldine Farrar's high position in the musical and film worlds in 1915 is informed by A. Scott Berg's *Goldwyn* (New York: Alfred A. Knopf, 1989), pp. 52–54, 59.

474 "One of my great anticipations": The account of Miss Farrar's visit is taken from *AC,* May 1, 1915.

475 she dashed off a wire to the *New York Times: NYT,* May 1, 1915.

475 "Leo Frank An Innocent Man": *AC,* May 1, 1915.

476 "trying to stop the war": *NYT,* May 20, 1915.

476 DO IT NOW. SIGN PETITION: *BT,* May 27, 1915.

476 Accounts of the pro-Frank petition drives in Manhattan and Brooklyn appear in the *New York Herald* of April 25, 1915, and the *New York Times* of May 8, 19, 20 and 23, 1915.

476 The *Times* ran its pro-Frank editorials on May 4, 5, 12, 17, 19, 23 and 26, 1915.

476 "I do not ask the liberation": *NYT,* May 17, 1915.

476 Accounts of New York Christians rallying to Frank's cause appear in both the *New York Herald* and the *New York Times* of April 26, 1915.

476 My portrait of the pro-Frank petition drive in Chicago and the formation of the "Leo Frank Committee" there is drawn from the *New York Times* of May 13 and 18, 1915.

477 Alexander Brin's involvement in the Frank case is summarized in GEORGIA DENIES PARDON IN LEO FRANK CASE; LATE *ADVOCATE* PUBLISHER EXPOSED INJUSTICE, *Jewish Advocate,* December 29, 1983.

477 "The undersigned believe": *BT,* May 22, 1915.

477 "We want to say": *BT,* May 27, 1915.

477 Pleading ignorance of the evidence, Taft rejected Rosenwald's plea in a May 17, 1915, letter (Julius Rosenwald Papers, University of Chicago Library, Department of Special Collections). Connolly advised Frank that Roosevelt was "not in a position to do anything" in a May 27, 1915, letter, AHC.

477 Slaton refers to the 100,000 requests in his commutation order, p. 1, Slaton Collection, GDA.

477 My account of the arrival of the pro-Frank petitions in Atlanta is drawn from the *New York Times* of May 18, 1915.

478 "I beg you to spare": *NYT,* May 29, 1915.

478 "Commute Frank's Sentence": *AJ,* May 23, 1915.

478 "I stand for commutation": ibid.

Thomas Loyless to the Prison Commission, May 13, 1915, Slaton Collection, GDA.

479 "millionaire Jews": *Jeff,* April 29, 1915.

479 "The letter from Judge Roan": *Jeff,* June 10, 1915.

479 "What sort of man is Leo Frank?": *Jeff,* April 29, 1915.

479 "In the official record": ibid.

479 "In behalf of Frank": *Jeff,* May 27, 1915.

480 "Woe unto God-fearing fathers and mothers": *Jeff,* May 20, 1915.

480 "It is embarrassing": *Jeff,* May 27, 1915.

480 "The Governor of Georgia should consider": *Jeff,* May 6, 1915.

480 My account of the scene at the opening of the Prison Commission hearings is drawn from *AG,* May 31, 1915.

481 My portrait of Robert E. Davison is taken from a November 23, 1996, interview with 80-year-old E. H. Armor of Greensboro, Georgia. My portrait of Eugene Leigh Rainey is taken from *Georgia's Official Register,* a publication of the Georgia Department of Archives and History, compiled in 1927 by Ruth Blair, p. 29. My portrait of Thomas E. Patterson is taken from Lucian Lamar Knight, *A Standard History of Georgia and Georgians* (Chicago, New York: Lewis Publishing Company, 1917), p. 2218.

481 My portrait of William Schley Howard is drawn from "Sidelights on Georgia Politics," *AG,* September 9, 1913, and the *New York Times* of May 30, 1915.

481 "It is the most precious document": *AG,* May 31, 1915.

481 "Judge L. S. Roan was my brother": *AJ,* May 31, 1915.

482 "An intelligent man should realize": *NYT,* May 30, 1915.

482 "Don't leave the Frank case": *AC,* June 1, 1915.

482 "I have never made up my mind": ibid.

483 "Our marriage has been exceedingly happy": *AG,* May 31, 1915.

483 "In this article": William Smith, "My Views as to the Death Notes," introduction, pp. 5–6, Slaton Collection, GDA.

483 "I swear to you": ibid., p. 7.

483 "It can be shown": *AC,* June 1, 1915.

484 "The power to pardon": ibid.

484 "This case has not a parallel": ibid.

484 "Mass meeting Monday night": *AG,* May 30, 1915

485 "Let him hang!": *BT,* June 1, 1915.

485 "Mary Phagan was a poor factory girl": ibid.

485 "should take its course": *NYT,* June 2, 1915.

486 "A doubt as to his own action": ibid.

486 "The voice from the tomb": ibid.

486 Frank's diary, aside from listing the names of visitors, provides comments on the weather, remarks about correspondence, and a series of cryptic check marks of undetermined meaning. The diary is on file at the William Breman Jewish Heritage Museum.

486 "I did not write": C. P. Connolly to Leo Frank, July 10, 1915, AHC.

486 "I spent fully two hours": *BT,* June 5, 1915.

487 "He refers to himself as 'Frank' ": *BT,* June 1, 1915.

487 "There is nothing sorrowful": ibid.

487 "are optimistic": *NYT,* May 30, 1915.

487 "It is authoritatively stated": *NYTrib,* June 6, 1915.

487 The best account of the June 6 protest meeting on the steps of Georgia's capitol appears in the *Boston Traveler* of June 7, 1915.

487 "Let Davison and Patterson": *Jeff,* May 20, 1915.

488 'Lynch him?': *BT,* June 2, 1915.

488 "Is it possible?": *BT,* June 10, 1915.

488 "Tears flowed freely": ibid.

488 "Mr. Frank has nothing to say": *AG,* June 9, 1915.

488 "The decision of the Prison Commission": Leo Frank to Albert Lasker, June 10, 1915, AJA.

488 "had the highest motive": *AG,* June 9, 1915.

488 "Governor Slaton now becomes": *AC,* June 10, 1915.

488 Highlights of Slaton's governorship are presented in his farewell message to the Georgia legislature: *AJ,* June 29, 1915.

488 The summer social season at Wingfield and the staging of *The Gift* is discussed in "Leaders to Be Out in Force to See Pandora's Romance": *AG,* May 30, 1915.

489 The opening of Slaton's hearing is described in "Governor's Rooms and Corridors Thronged," *AG,* June 12, 1915.

489 "A man such as Conley": transcript of Executive Clemency Hearing, p. 22, Special Collections, Robert W. Woodruff Library, Emory University, Atlanta. This transcript, which has never before been quoted from in print, offers an unexpurgated view of many sordid elements of the Frank case and provides a fuller understanding of the evidence that prompted Slaton to commute Frank's death sentence.

489 "You have got this from Conley": ibid., pp 32–33.

490 "An explanation may be given": ibid., p. 40.

490 "I don't care to make": ibid., p. 41.

490 "When a governor is asked": ibid., p. 48.

490 "Now in all frankness": ibid., pp. 58–59.

491 News of the endorsement Frank's cause received from Vice President Marshall appears in *AG,* June 14, 1915.

491 The decision of such powerful journalists as Herbert Croly to join Frank's bandwagon is noted in *BT,* June 8, 1915.

491 "I have heard you say": William Randolph Hearst to John Slaton, June 10, 1915, *AG*, June 29, 1915.

491 The best accounts of the second protest meeting at the state capitol appear in "Another Frank Meeting Held at the Capitol," *AJ*, June 13, 1915.

491 In *Fiddlin' Georgia Crazy* (Urbana: University of Illinois Press, 1987), a biography of Fiddlin' John Carson, Gene Wiggins gives a full recounting of the composition of *The Ballad of Little Mary Phagan*, pp. 19–45. According to Wiggins, Carson probably performed embryonic versions of the song shortly after Frank's conviction. Yet because the newspapers did not initially take notice, his performance of it during the executive clemency hearings amounted to the official debut.

491 "*Little Mary Phagan She went to work one day*": Wiggins, *Fiddlin'*, pp. 35–36. As with many folk songs, there are alternative lyrics. The version quoted here was recorded by Carson's daughter, Rosa Lee, on an Okeh record in 1925, ibid., p. 44.

493 "Your excellency, the record shows": transcript of Executive Clemency Hearing, p. 71.

494 "The state was ready": ibid., p. 89.

494 "Eliminate Jim Conley": ibid., p. 110.

494 "the minute alibi": ibid., p. 109.

494 "to make some disposition": ibid., p. 111.

494 "Why trembling": ibid., p. 126.

495 "I am not lacking in mercy": ibid. This quote is from p. 53 of a long section of the Executive Clemency Hearing transcript missing from the copy on file at Emory University. The document was provided to the author by Hugh Dorsey, Jr.

495 The best account of Slaton's field trip to the National Pencil factory appears in "Gov. Slaton Inspects Pencil Factory," *AG*, June 14, 1915.

495 "What does it matter": transcript of Executive Clemency Hearing, p. 133.

496 "Who but that knows the negro": ibid., p. 149.

496 "Ladies carry their pocket handkerchiefs": ibid., p. 266.

496 "I believe that someone undertook": ibid., p. 187.

496 My account of the throng that packed into the Wednesday session of Slaton's hearing is taken from "Leo Frank's Fate up to Governor, Hearing is Ended," *AC*, June 17, 1915.

497 "There was never blood": transcript of Executive Clemency Hearing, pp. 253–54.

497 "this was a disputed point": ibid., p. 271.

498 " 'The elevator hits the dirt at the bottom,' ": ibid., p. 273.

498 "mathematical demonstration": William Smith, autobiographical notes, p. 37.

498 "The detectives had Conley": transcript of Executive Clemency Hearing, p. 281.

499 "Primarily the trip": *AC*, June 19, 1915.

499 "I had two private interviews": Smith, autobiographical notes, p. 38. Further reference to these meetings exists in an October 1, 1915, letter from Smith to Thomas Loyless, in the author's possession.

499 "To all appearances": *AG*, June 20, 1915.

499 "The judgment of the court": *AC*, June 19, 1915.

499 Lucille returned bearing a novel: *AG*, June 19, 1915.

500 "This case has been the subject": Commutation Order, p. 1, Slaton Collection, GDA.

500 "who have not read the evidence": ibid.

500 "if the courtroom manifested": ibid., p. 3.

500 "Those giving expression": ibid., p. 4.

500 "It is hard to conceive": ibid., p. 7.

500 "Did Conley speak the truth?": ibid., p. 11.

501 "One fact in the case": ibid., pp. 11–12.

501 "Conley was the real author": ibid., p. 20.

501 "the only reason Conley had": ibid., p. 19.

502 "The performance of my duty": ibid., p. 28.

502 SLATON STILL DELVING: AG, June 20, 1915.

502 My account of Frank's transfer from the tower to Milledgeville is taken from the Atlanta Journal, June 21, 1915. Several accounts, including one in the June 22, 1915, New York Times, contend that Frank was sneaked out of the tower in an ambulance. But the concensus supports the Journal's version.

502 "There were cars following us": NYTrib, June 23, 1915.

503 "I had begun to think": AC, June 22, 1915.

503 FRANK'S SENTENCE IS COMMUTED: AC, June 21, 1915.

503 "The larger part of the population": New York World, as reprinted in the Atlanta Constitution, June 22, 1915.

503 "Who will follow me?": ibid.

503 "All I ask": AJ, June 21, 1915.

503 SLATON GIVES REASONS: ibid.

504 My account of the assault on Slaton's mansion is drawn from "March to Governor's," AC, June 22, 1915, and "State Troops Are Still on Guard," MT, June 23, 1915.

504 "John M. Slaton, King of the Jews": NYT, June 22, 1915.

504 "We feel it best": Marietta Journal, June 25, 1915.

505 "Governor Slaton, the Traitor": MT, June 23, 1915.

505 "Whatever individuals may think": AJ, June 21, 1915.

505 "Had the Governor desired": AG, June 22, 1915.

506 "element of existing doubt": San Francisco Call, June 23, 1915.

506 "Governor Slaton feels": NYT, June 22, 1915.

506 "a wonderful and horrible thing": This and the following quotations from Tom Watson appeared in Jeff, June 24, 1915.

506 "Once, there were men in Georgia": ibid.

508 "There seems to be little doubt": NYT, June 26, 1915.

508 "The prison is too secure": MT, June 23, 1915.

509 AMERICAN GENTILES: NYT, June 24, 1915.

509 "You are hereby notified": Dinnerstein, The Leo Frank Case.

509 "good offices": Hugh Dorsey to Herbert Clay, undated document on file in the New York office of the Anti-Defamation League.

509 "Leo Frank should have been hung": This line comes from a June 23, 1915, handbill titled "To the Citizens of Marietta" in the files of the American Jewish Archives.

509 "Preparations have been made": NYT, June 26, 1915.

510 "He stood still for a moment": Nathaniel E. Harris: The Story of an Old Man's Life (Macon, Ga: J. W. Burke Company, 1925), p. 363.

510 'The gallery was crowded": AC June 27, 1915.

510 "I could see people on the stairs": The Story of an Old Man's Life, p. 356.

511 "Governor Slaton entered": ibid., p. 357.

511 "Honest people may disagree": NYT, June 27, 1915.

511 "fine, big, upstanding Southerner": New York World, June 30, 1915.

512 "It was my duty": ibid.

512 "He told an interesting story": ibid.

512 My account of the Slatons' visit to New York is drawn from the *New York Times* and the *New York World* of June 30, 1915, and the *Atlanta Georgian* of July 1 and 2, 1915.

19. Marietta

513 "so conspicuous": *AC*, August 18, 1915.

513 The date and location of every lynching that occurred in Georgia in 1915 can be found in W. Fitzhugh Brundage, *Lynching in the New South* (Urbana: University of Illinois Press, 1993), p. 277.

513 "a matter of past history": *AC*, June 29, 1915.

513 "I am fixed in my belief": ibid.

514 The basic facts of Herbert Clay's background come from his only son, Eugene Herbert Clay, Jr. I interviewed the younger Clay extensively at his law office in Sarasota, Florida, on February 26, 1987, and again over a two-day period in Marietta on October 31 and November 1, 1987.

514 At age 30, he had married the former Marjorie Lockwood: *Montgomery Advertiser*, January 1, 1911.

514 "He is wide-awake, genial": *AC*, November 27, 1910.

515 "Everybody was spoiled": Clay Jr., interviewed by author, February 26, 1987.

515 Clay's participation on the University of Georgia football team is detailed in the *Atlanta Journal* of October 8, 1901, and the *Athens Daily Banner* of October 19 and October 27, 1901. A typical account of his rollicking appearance at dances can be found in the April 6, 1901, edition of *The Red and Black,* the student newspaper. The 1902 edition of *The Pandora,* the student yearbook, lists him as a member of the Bulldog Club.

515 "He was the most attractive man": Zaida Clay Wood, interviewed by author, June 14, 1994.

515 "A Social Success": *The Pandora,* 1901.

515 "He with the pretty eye": *The Red and Black,* February 9, 1901.

515 "training violations": *AJ*, November 29, 1901. Clay's pistol-shooting escapade is mentioned in the 1902 edition of *The Pandora,* p. 117.

515 spring of 1902 found him at Mercer University: student index, Mercer University, p. 99, courtesy Mercer University Library.

515 "The University ruined Herbert": Mrs. Winter Allfriend, 95 years old, granddaughter of James Remley Brumby, interviewed by author, June 7, 1990.

515 Clay Jr. described Lex Clay's dismissal from the University of Georgia in his interview with the author on February 26, 1987.

515 Marietta resident Dorothy Haney Smith, daughter of lynch party member Lawrence Haney, recalled Lex Clay's appearance on the town square in an interview with the author on June 11, 1991.

516 Clay Jr. described Frank Clay's battle with syphilis in his interview with the author on February 26, 1987.

516 dazed and disoriented: *NYT,* January 18, 1915.

516 "a little bit of a reputation": Dorothy Haney Smith, interviewed by author, November 5, 1990.

516 "She had big bosoms": Lucille Sessions Kappes, daughter of the Marietta banker Moultrie Sessions, interviewed by author, November 25, 1991.

516 "Bolan told me": Mrs. Winter Allfriend, interviewed by author, June 7, 1990.

516 "He was a powerful politician": Judge Luther Hames, a 69-year-old Marietta native, interviewed by author, March 9, 1987.

516 "just a likeable fellow": Lex Jolley, an 87-year-old Marietta native, interviewed by author, September 24, 1990.

516 "All those involved owed Clay": Bill Kinney, associate editor of the *Marietta Journal,* interviewed by author, February 23, 1988.

516 "The accused and the deceased": Dorsey *v.* The State, *Georgia Reports,* March 1907 term, pp. 228–37.

517 Bill Kinney gave an overview of John Tucker Dorsey's legal troubles in an October 7, 1992, address at the Marietta Welcome Center monthly meeting, transcript in the author's possession.

517 he would tell cronies: ibid.

517 he won 10 consecutive murder cases: Jasper Dorsey, interview by Thomas A. Scott for Cobb County Oral History Series, No. 16, at Kennesaw State University, October 4, 1989.

517 "He was a character": ibid.

518 "From time immemorial": *AC,* July 4, 1915.

518 Fred Morris's role on the University of Georgia football team is highlighted in the 1895 edition of *The Pandora;* Katherine Morris Hardy, Morris's granddaughter, provided additional information on his athletic successes in an interview with the author on December 16, 1996.

518 My portrait of Fred Morris's business and legal activities is drawn from the column GEORGIA POLITICS NEWS AND VIEWS: *AG,* June 30, 1915.

518 In 1912, when two Negroes: *AG,* October 1, 1912.

518 when the Boy Scout movement began: Mrs. Guy Northcutt, a 92-year-old Marietta native, interviewed by author, December 16, 1996.

519 My account of Bolan Glover Brumby's illustrious ancestors is taken from James R. Brumby, "Sketch of Life of James R. Brumby," June 11, 1929. I was given a copy of the manuscript by Mrs. Winter Allfriend.

519 My portrait of the Brumby furniture business is drawn from Sarah Blackwell Gober Temple, *The First Hundred Years* (Atlanta: Walter W. Brown Publishing, 1935), a history of Cobb County, pp. 406–7.

519 The relationship between the Brumbys and future United States Senator Richard B. Russell is detailed in Karen Kalmar Kelly, "Richard B. Russell: Democrat from Georgia" (doctoral thesis, University of North Carolina, 1979).

519 The Brumbys' connections to the *St. Petersburg Times* and to the family of the *Atlanta Journal* publisher James R. Gray are discussed in "The Brumby Chair Co.," a pamphlet distributed by the company of the same name in 1992.

519 Richard B. Russell's dispute with the Brumbys is addressed in Kelly, "Richard B. Russell."

519 James R. Brumby describes his falling-out with Tom Brumby in his "Sketch of Life of James R. Brumby."

519 Bolan Brumby was "one of North Georgia's most successful businessmen": *AC,* November 27, 1910.

519 "He was wild and daring": Lucille Sessions Kappes, interviewed by author, November 25, 1991.

520 "Oh that murderous War": "Sketch of Life of James R. Brumby."

520 "to get from under the U.S. Gov't": ibid.

520 "The business manager of the *Jeffersonian* proposed": C. Vann Woodward, *Tom Watson: Agrarian Rebel* (New York: The Macmillan Company, 1938), p. 393.

521 the ex-governor was among those who conceived the mission: Bill Kinney, interviewed by author, June 12, 1990.

521 "Judge Newt always came out on top": Lucille Sessions Kappes, interviewed by author, November 5, 1991.

521 Newt Morris's experience as

speaker of the Georgia House is summarized in *AC,* June 30, 1904; his rise to judge of the Blue Ridge Circuit is recounted in "Judge Newt A. Morris Died Today," *Marietta Journal,* September 22, 1941; his work for William Gibbs McAdoo is cited in *AJ,* April 21, 1912.

521 Longtime Marietta resident Bob Garrison gave an overview of Judge Morris's contracting business in an interview with the author on May 28, 1991. I received further insight into the subject from Morris's nephew, Paul Morris, in interviews conducted on May 29, 1991, and September 9, 1992.

522 he kept his canceled checks: 87-year-old James T. Anderson Jr., interviewed by author, June 6, 1990.

522 "I try not to hate anyone": Marietta native Deveraux McClatchey, Jr., interviewed by author, October 18, 1988.

522 "a fourteen-karat son of a bitch": Marietta native Harold Willingham, interviewed by author, September 1, 1990.

522 Lancaster, California, historian and anthropologist David Earle enumerated Newt Morris's business successes in Lancaster in an interview with the author on October 21, 1991.

523 Morris's work for the Antelope Valley Real Estate Agency is mentioned in an ad appearing in *Antelope Valley Times,* August 1, 1889.

523 "in the cattle rustling business": Earle, interviewed by author, November 27, 1996.

523 bushwhacked the man: *LAT,* July 18, 1891.

523 Though badly wounded, Crane survived: *LAT,* August 11, 1891.

523 "he heard the clicking": *LAT,* Aug. 13, 1891.

523 Morris was charged: The People of the State of California *vs.* Newton A. Morris, Los Angeles County Court documents, July 17, 1891.

523 For five mid-August days: *LAT,* August 15, 1891.

524 there was sufficient evidence: *LAT,* August 19, 1891.

524 The dismissal of charges against Morris is noted but not explained in The People of the State of California *vs.* Newton A. Morris, Los Angeles County Court documents. In a November 9, 1996, interview with the author, David Earle asserted that the general view among the citizens of Lancaster was that Morris skipped out on his bail.

524 Judge Newt sat Hardwick men over Slaton men: *AC,* September 1, 1914.

524 My account of Morris's role in waylaying Slaton delegates at the 1914 state convention is drawn from Allen Lumpkin Henson, *Confessions of a Criminal Lawyer* (New York: Vantage Press, 1959), pp. 49–58.

524 in 1913, at the Phagans' request: *AG,* June 23, 1913.

525 "The power structure would not touch": Judson Ward, interviewed by author, June 20, 1987.

525 My portrait of George Daniell and his jewelry store is drawn from the memories of many old-time Mariettans, among them Lucille Sessions Kappes, who talked about him in a September 4, 1992, interview, and Otis Cheatham, who spoke of him in an August 11, 1995, interview.

525 "into everything" in Marietta: Mrs. Guy Northcutt, interviewed by author, December 16, 1996.

525 My portrait of Gordon Gann is drawn from the "Professional Cards" section of the *Marietta Journal,* May 28, 1915.

525 Black Newt ran the Cobb County convict camp: *AC,* May 10, 1914.

526 "He'd pull the cages by team or truck": Narvel Lassiter, interviewed by author, March 31, 1992.

526 "If they didn't walk the chalk line": James W. Lee, interviewed by author, August 14, 1995.

526 sometimes also known as Whipping Newt: Dorothy Haney Smith, interviewed by author, June 20, 1991.

526 When not at his day job, Black Newt served as the foreman of his cousin's Morris Construction Company: Paul Morris, interviewed by author, September 9, 1992.

526 "Black Newt had mules, wagons": Bob Garrison, interviewed by author, May 28, 1991.

526 By 1915, Black Newt was doing well enough: Paul Morris, interviewed by author, September 9, 1992.

526 "my daddy was running a liquor still": Paul Morris, interviewed by author, May 20, 1991.

526 "They'd go to a man's office and talk to him": Carl Abernathy and Myrtle (Barmore) Abernathy, interviewed by Patricia Raybon, February 14, 1973. The record of the interview is in the possession of Dr. Thomas A. Scott of Marietta.

526 "The organization of the body": *AC*, August 18, 1915.

527 "no men of lawless character": *NYT*, August 19, 1915.

527 The author learned of the reasons for Robert E. Lee Howell's banishment from the lynch party in interviews with numerous Mariettans, among them Bill Kinney, James T. Anderson, Jr., and Luther Hames.

577 "No Jews ever pay": the Abernathys, interviewed by Patricia Raybon, February 14, 1973.

527 "something my father felt he had to do": Dorothy Haney Smith, interviewed by author, November 5, 1990.

527 "every 'lay of the ground' ": *AC*, August 18, 1915.

528 My list of lynch party participants was provided by Dorothy Haney Smith and confirmed by her sister Golmer Haney Wilson. It was further augmented by Luther Hames, Lex Jolley and Bill Kinney. The Mariettans named here were at the forefront of the lynching effort, although others also participated.

528 "whose worth was known": *AC*, August 18, 1915.

20. Milledgeville

529 "Picture a frail figure": *NYTrib*, June 25, 1915.

529 "nervous breakdown": *MT*, May 23, 1915.

529 "After that which I have gone through": Leo Frank to Lucille Frank, June 22, 1915, BU.

529 "It has indeed been an ordeal": ibid.

530 "The main building is a credit": *MT*, July 25, 1915.

530 "the Milledgeville farm is well kept": *NYTrib*, June 23, 1915.

530 A history of the state prison farm in Milledgeville and profiles of its more colorful inmates appears in "Where Many Famous Prisoners Have Served Time": *AC*, June 29, 1913.

530 My portrait of Bill Miner is taken from Carl Sifakis, *The Encyclopedia of American Crime* (New York: Facts on File, 1982), pp. 487–88.

531 "quick, nervy": *MT*, June 23, 1915.

531 For an overview of the convict lease system and its last days, see C. Vann Woodward, *Origins of the New South* (Baton Rouge: Louisiana State University Press, 1951), pp. 424–25.

531 "Every time I went into the coal mines": *AC*, August 8, 1908.

531 "pretty rough character": Louis H. Andrews, an 86-year-old Milledgeville native, interviewed by author, November 15, 1995.

532 "The warden is some fine fellow": Leo Frank to Lucille Frank, June 22, 1915, BU.

532 "I had a talk with Judge Davidson": Leo Frank to Lucille Frank, June 29, 1915, BU.

532 "The warden and his staff here are": Leo Frank to Luther Rosser on July 1, 1915, as printed in *NYT*, August 18, 1915.

532 "I am in an environment": Leo Frank to Julius Rosenwald, July 11, 1915, AJA.

532 "have treated me white": Leo Frank to Manning Yeomans, July 9, 1915, AHC.

532 Frank thanks Lucille for a $5 check in a letter to her on June 25, 1915, BU; he mentions his new cotton mattress in a letter to Lucille on July 1, 1915, BU; he describes his new toiletry items in a letter to Lucille on June 23, 1915, BU.

532 "I shaved this a.m.": Leo Frank to Lucille Frank, June 23, 1915.

532 Frank mentions his new cap in his letter to Lucille of June 25, 1915; he speaks of his new watch and mirror in his letter to her of July 1, 1915.

532 "It's a beauty": Leo Frank to Lucille Frank, July 1, 1915.

532 Frank mentions the gift of cigars from George Gershon in a letter to Lucille on July 6, 1915, BU.

533. "Do not get all classical records": Lucille Frank to Leo Frank, July 6, 1915, AHC.

533 "my present physical condition": Leo Frank to Luther Rosser, July 1, 1915, as printed in *NYT*, August 18, 1915.

533 Accounts of Frank's work routine at the prison farm appear in the *Macon Telegraph* of June 23, 1915, and the *New York Times* of June 25, 1915. Frank describes his chores in a June 30, 1915, letter to Lucille Frank, BU.

533 "I am sleeping like a top": Leo Frank to Herbert Schiff, June 30, 1915, AJA.

533 "I wrote 14 letters this a.m.": Leo Frank to Lucille Frank, July 5, 1915, BU.

533 "This letter is only the 16th": Leo Frank to Lucille Frank, July 6, 1915.

533 "Your Letter of 6/28": Leo Frank to Anne Carroll Moore, July 2, 1915, in Francis Clarke Sayers, *Anne Carroll*

Moore, A Biography (New York: Atheneum, 1972), p. 165.

533 "I wish to again assure you": Leo Frank to Rebecca Solomons Alexander, July 15, 1915, William Breman Jewish Heritage Museum.

534 "how deep is my respect": Leo Frank to Luther Rosser, July 1, 1915, *NYT*, August 18, 1915.

534 "The sunshine and atmosphere here": Leo Frank to Luther Rosser, ibid.

534 "This is the breathing spell": Leo Frank to Anne Carroll Moore, July 2, 1915, in Sayers, *Anne Carroll Moore*, p. 166.

535 "write your own story": Linton Starr to Leo Frank, June 22, 1915, AHC.

535 "write anything you want": Charles Lincoln to Leo Frank, June 22, 1915, AHC.

535 "Let me caution you": Herbert Haas to Leo Frank, June 29, 1915, AHC.

535 "It would be well for the case": Leo Frank to Lucille Frank, June 24, 1915, BU.

535 "get Ochs to deadhead" the paper: ibid.

535 "Remind Herbert to see Gray": Leo Frank to Lucille Frank, June 25, 1915.

535 "Frank would feel cheated": Garet Garrett diary, August 18, 1915, courtesy Richard Cornuelle, p. 90.

535 For a description of Reid's film on Leo Frank, see *Variety*, July 30, 1915.

535 My portrait of Hal Reid is informed by Kevin Brownlow's *Films of Social Conscience in the Silent Era* (New York: Knopf, 1990).

536 "First you were talking": Rae Frank to Leo Frank, July 15, 1915, AHC.

536 "FRANK SENIOR": Hal Reid to Herbert Haas, July 4, 1915, BU.

536 "You know, honey": Lucille Frank to Leo Frank, June 24, 1915, AHC.

536 "Rest up and get back to your poise": Leo Frank to Lucille Frank, June 22, 1915.

536 "It is a joy and pleasure": Leo Frank to Lucille Frank, June 28, 1915, BU.

537 "This is certainly a lazy life": Lucille Frank to Leo Frank, July 9, 1915, AHC.

537 "seances at letter writing": Lucille Frank to Leo Frank, July 7, 1915, AHC.

537 "It has poured all day": Lucille Frank to Leo Frank, AHC, July 6, 1915.

537 "The 'movie man' will be here": Lucille Frank to Leo Frank, July 12, 1915, AHC.

537 "talk and show animation": Lucille Frank to Leo Frank, July 13, 1915, AHC.

537 "I just had my 'movies' made": ibid.

538 "Everyone is so happy": Lucille Frank to Leo Frank, June 24, 1915, AHC.

538 a reported typhus outbreak: AJ, July 4, 1915.

538 PAROLE PRISONERS: AJ, June 30, 1915.

538 STATE FARM IMPROVEMENTS: AC, June 31, 1915.

538 "We will not attempt": AJ, June 30, 1915.

539 The Constitution ran a front-page photo essay: AC, July 9, 1915.

539 "Georgia is too great a state": AJ, June 30, 1915.

539 "Prison Farm Conditions 'Absolutely Disgraceful,' " AC, July 8, 1915.

539 "deposited in buckets": ibid.

539. "criminal neglect": ibid.

539 "the deplorable conditions": AC, July 1, 1915.

540 "We are going to vary": AJ, July 7, 1915.

540 "against the danger of typhoid": Henry Alexander to Leo Frank, June 30, 1915, AHC.

540 SLATON'S TREACHERY: Jeff, July 8, 1915.

540 "Was Sally [sic] the real commuter, after all?": ibid.

541 "Rich Jews": Jeff, July 15, 1915.

541 the "New York Hebrew American": ibid.

541 "Thomas Watson, the very embod-

iment": from Puck, as quoted in the Jeffersonian, July 15, 1915.

541 "I note that one Nathan Straus": Jeff, July 15, 1915.

542 "Do the rich Jews want to create": Jeff, ibid.

542 "TO TAKE THE WHOLE CRIME": Jeff, July 8, 1915.

542 "Conley is out and Conley is poor": ibid.

543 "melted like snowflakes": C. Vann Woodward, Tom Watson: Agrarian Rebel, (New York: The Macmillan Company, 1938), p. 442.

543 "The Prison Committee": Leo Frank to Lucille Frank, July 12, 1915, BU.

543 "My father believed Frank was innocent": 77-year-old Rebekah Smith, interviewed by author, December 21, 1996.

544 "Conditions at the farm are deplorable": AJ, July 14, 1915.

544 "an authoritative source": AC, July 14, 1915.

544 "a leak" had occurred: AC, August 18, 1915.

544 Nash wired Macon: AC, July 14, 1915.

545 "If anyone thinks": ibid.

545 "quiet as usual": ibid.

545 "The entire affair": MT, July 14, 1915.

545 "I am hoping": Henry Alexander to Leo Frank, July 14, 1915, AHC.

545 "on their way to the courthouse": Nathaniel E. Harris, The Story of an Old Man's Life (Macon, Ga.: J. W. Burke Company, 1925), p. 366.

546 "an overgrown boy": Lucille Frank to Leo Frank, July 12, 1915, AHC.

546 "You know how comforting": Leo Frank to Anne Carroll Moore, July 17, 1915, in Sayers, Anne Carroll Moore, pp. 166–67.

546 Leo Frank's scream: MT, July 19, 1915.

546 needed but one look at Frank: ibid.

547 "Am I going to die?": *AJ*, July 18, 1915.

547 Not long before sunrise: *MT*, July 19, 1915.

547 Reputedly responsible: ibid.

547 "the tool of others": *AC*, July 19, 1915.

547 the press erroneously reported: *MT*, July 19, 1915.

547 "I only wish": *AJ*, July 19, 1915.

548 "We almost shudder": Garet Garrett diary, July 19, 1915, p. 71.

548 Ochs . . . directed: ibid.

548 "The latest development": *NYT*, July 20, 1915.

549 Frank "was treated over there": *Cherokee Advance*, July 23, 1915.

549 "The fight between Creen and Frank": ibid.

550 "Note: The butcher-knife used": *Jeff*, July 22, 1915.

550 "You have a good chance": *AC*, July 19, 1915.

550 "Frank recognized": *AJ*, July 21, 1915.

550 "Dr. McNaughton saved Frank's life": *AJ*, July 19, 1915.

551 "Frank's Condition Steadily Improving": *AC*, July 19, 1915.

551 "To let the commission": *AC*, July 20, 1915.

552 B. H. Meadows, a fellow resident of Canton, offers a thorough account of Sam Cohen's travails: B. H. Meadows to Governor Nat Harris, July 1, 1915, Harris papers, GDA.

552 "We believe it is time": ibid., July 7, 1915.

552 "Governor Harris duly received": F. R. Jones, private secretary of Gov. Nat E. Harris, to B. H. Meadows, July 10, 1915, Harris papers, GDA.

552 For the background of Harris's political indebtedness to Tom Watson, see Woodward, *Tom Watson*, p. 434.

552 I owe my understanding of the ties connecting Nat Harris to Herbert Clay and Campbell Wallace to former Marietta resident Bob Livolsier, whom I interviewed on July 28 and September 4, 1990. Livolsier undertook a painstaking study of the many social and financial links among various of the lynching brethren. Contemporary newspaper accounts underscore Wallace's prominence in Marietta: *AC*, April 25, 1915, and *AJ*, July 18, 1915.

553 Dorsey asked the legislature: *AJ*, July 20, 1915.

553 Governor Harris spent the night: *AJ*, July 24, 1915; *MT*, July 25, 1915.

553 At the tubercular ward: *AC*, July 25, 1915.

553 "Won't you please turn my papa loose?": *Milledgeville Union Recorder*, July 27, 1915.

554 "Creen, have you told your story?": *MT*, July 25, 1915.

554 that, as John W. Hammond pointedly observed: ibid.

554 "He said he had heard": ibid.

554 vowed to ask the legislature: *AJ*, July 25, 1915.

554 GOVERNOR TOUCHED: *AC*, July 25, 1915.

554 GOV. HARRIS TO ASK $50,000: *AJ*, July 25, 1915.

555 "So far as what caused": *MT*, July 25, 1915.

555 chairman Davison dismissed: *AC*, July 26, 1915.

555 "Creen told Governor Harris": *Jeff*, August 6, 1915.

556 "I went into [Frank's] room": Harris: *The Story of An Old Man's Life*, pp. 366–67.

556 the general assembly signed off: *AJ*, July 29, 1915.

556 "Thanks be to God": Leo Frank to Dan Lehon, August 6, 1915, *AC*, August 18, 1915.

557 "Leo is at the farm": Herbert Haas to Lucille Frank, July 24, 1915, AHC.

557 The handling of Frank's financial needs is described in a letter from Herbert Haas to Lucille Frank, August 2, 1915, AHC.

557 "Please, in the future": ibid.

557 "Remarkable": *Variety,* July 30, 1915.

558 PUBLICITY FEATURE!: *Motion Picture News,* July 31, 1915.

558 Information on screenings of Hal Reid's film appears in an ad in the *New York World,* July 25, 1915, and in "Stirring Pictures of Leo Frank Episodes in Loew Theaters," *New York Journal,* July 24, 1915.

558 "There is a Moving Picture circuit": *Jeff,* August 12, 1915.

558 "Let the rich Jews beware!": ibid.

558 The time had come for "the people to form mobs": *MT,* August 8, 1915.

558 Frank describes the heat at the prison on the last full day of his life in his letter to C. P. Connolly, August 16, 1915, Harry Golden Papers, Public Library of Charlotte and Mecklenburg County, Charlotte, N.C.

559 "How do you view": Leo Frank to Dr. Benjamin Wildauer, August 16, 1915, AJA.

559 "T. W. . . . is not ashamed nor afraid": Rae Frank to Leo Frank, August 14, 1915, AHC.

559 "I am doing 'missionary work': Frank to Wildauer, August 16, 1915.

559 Tuesday, Leo was scheduled: *MT,* August 18, 1915.

560 Yellow Jacket Brown . . . was waiting: *AG,* August 18, 1915.

21. The Lynching of Leo Frank

561 "exhausted every available energy": F. J. Turner to Lucille Frank, August 17, 1915, BU.

561 "dead certain that it was a mob": ibid.

561 "two strong men grabbed me": *NYT,* August 18, 1915.

561 "I saw they meant business": *AG,* night edition, August 17, 1915.

562 "Come here with a match": *MT,* August 18, 1915.

562 The report that the lynchers dangled a rope in Frank's face and announced that they intended to hang him over Mary Phagan's grave appears in *AJ,* August 17, 1915.

562 "Damned if I go anywhere with you": ibid.

562 "make for the swamps": *AG,* night edition, August 17, 1915.

562 The fact that Lawrence Haney was left behind at the prison farm is common knowledge in Marietta and was conveyed to the author in an interview with James T. Anderson, Jr., on June 14, 1990, and confirmed in an interview with Haney's daughter, Dorothy Smith, on May 29, 1991.

562 Details regarding the initial response of the prison authorities and the lone uncut telephone line are drawn from *AG,* extra #2, August 17, 1915, and *NYT,* August 18, 1915.

563 Accounts of Fulton County deputies patrolling the highways leading into Cobb County from the south are taken from *MT,* August 18, 1915.

563 Reports of gunfire at the Little River and Frank's death appear in *AG,* August 17, 1915, first extra.

563 My account of the circuitous route the lynch party took to evade capture is taken from an interview with Lex Jolley on November 1, 1987.

563 "before your execution?": Associated Press, as printed in *AChr,* August 23, 1915.

564 The fact that Gordon Gann's car broke down on the way home is well known in Marietta and was conveyed to the author in an interview with Bill Kinney, February 23, 1988.

564 The fact that Judge Newt Morris was in Alpharetta on the morning of the lynching is reported in *NYT,* August 19, 1915.

564 "John Wood went out": Herman Spence, interviewed by author, November 15, 1990.

564 That former Sheriff William Frey tied the noose used in the lynching was conveyed to the author in an interview with Bill Kinney, September 16, 1986.

565 "with a calmness and dignity": *NYT,* August 19, 1915.

565 That Frank wrote a note to his wife that was later destroyed was conveyed to the author in his interviews with Bill Kinney on September 16, 1986, and reported in "Frank Tried to Write Wife," *New York Journal,* August 18, 1915.

565 "I think more of my wife and my mother": *NYT,* August 19, 1915.

565 "In telling this story": ibid.

565 The story of the promise to return Frank's wedding band to his wife is told in *AG,* August 19, 1915.

565 That Judge Newt Morris pronounced the court's sentence and kicked over the table was conveyed to the author in interviews with Golmer Haney Wilson on May 29, 1991, Dorothy Haney Smith on January 7, 1993, Bill Kinney on January 12 and June 15, 1995, and Dan Cox, executive director of the Marietta Museum of History, on October 11, 2002.

565 The names of the men who first arrived at Frey's Gin and the description of what they found are taken from the *Atlanta Journal* of August 17, 1915, and the *Augusta Chronicle* of August 25, 1915.

565 "something was doing": *AChr,* August 25, 1915.

566 "Yonder it is": ibid.

566 "undoubtedly flayed the air": *AC,* August 18, 1915.

566 SPEEDING MOB: *AG,* August 17, 1915.

566 LEO M. FRANK KIDNAPPED: *NYT,* August 17, 1915.

566 "hanging to a limb": *NYT,* August 18, 1915.

566 "They swarmed the road": *AJ,* August 17, 1915. Winter's account was later reprinted in *Star Reporters and 34 of Their Stories,* edited by Ward Greene (New York: Random House, 1948).

566 "like some religious rite": *AG,* August 17, 1915.

567 "A horrible sight": *AJ,* August 17, 1915.

567 "Granddad told me a lot": Narvel Lassiter, interviewed by author, March 31, 1992.

568 "Apache-like barbarities": *NYT,* August 19, 1915.

568 "Every once in a while": *AJ,* August 17, 1915.

568 "They won't put any monument": ibid.

568 My account of Newt Morris's dialogue with the crowd at Frey's Gin is taken from Rogers Winter's report in the August 17, 1915, *Atlanta Journal* and from eyewitness dispatches appearing in the August 18, 1915, *Atlanta Constitution* and the August 19, 1915, *New York Times.*

569 "Bring the body on, men": *AJ,* August 17, 1915.

569 "as a man grinds the head of a snake": ibid.

571 My account of Captain L. S. Dobbs's decision to admit the crowd to view Frank's body is taken from "Thousands View Body": *AC,* August 18, 1915.

571 "without so much as a look of horror": ibid.

571 My depiction of the celebration outside the funeral home is drawn from "Frank's Body Hidden from Curious Crowds," *AG,* August 17, 1915, and from views of newsreel footage.

571 My portrait of the celebration on the Marietta square and Fiddlin' John Carson's performance there is taken from "Fiddlin' John Plays": *AC,* August 18, 1915.

22. Burial

573 "A world at war": *NYH,* August 18, 1915.

573 "Always emotional": *NYTrib,* August 18, 1915.

573 "Tot-tot! Leo is dead": ibid.

573 "a stain upon our country": *AC,* August 18, 1915.

573 "a disgrace": *New York Journal,* August 18, 1915.

574 "shameful" by-product of chivalry: *NYTrib,* August 20, 1915.

574 "promiscuous lynching": ibid.

574 "Every man ... should be hanged": *NYT,* August 18, 1915.

574 "a damnable outrage": *NYH,* August 19, 1915.

574 "A more unspeakable outrage": *Akron Beacon-Journal,* as reprinted in the *Jeffersonian,* September 2, 1915.

574 "mad with her own virtue": *San Francisco Bulletin,* ibid.

574 "The South is barely half educated": *CTrib,* as reprinted in the *Millidgeville Union-Recorder,* August 24, 1915.

574 LYNCH LAW: *New York World,* August 18, 1915.

575 "apprehend the murderers": *NYT,* August 18, 1915.

575 My account of Lucille Frank's activities in the wake of her husband's death is taken from the *Macon Telegraph* of August 18, 1915, and the *New York Times* of the same date.

575 "It's over. It's all over now": *NYT,* August 20, 1915.

576 "I'm that boy's father": ibid.

576 "Leo *Moses* Frank": ibid.

576 My portrayal of the family's ride from Pennsylvania Station to Brooklyn is drawn from the August 20, 1915, editions of the *New York Times,* the *New York Herald* and the *New York Tribune.*

576 My account of the scene outside the Franks' Underhill Avenue home is taken from the August 20, 1915, editions of

the *New York Times,* the *New York Journal* and the *New York Tribune.*

577 My depiction of the frenzied meeting at Cooper Union is drawn from "20,000 Hebrews Mourn Frank in Cooper Union": *NYTrib,* August 20, 1915.

577 "prosecute all the murderers": *AG,* August 18, 1915.

578 "do not live in this country": *NYTrib,* August 20, 1915.

578 "not as far advanced": *American Hebrew,* August 27, 1915.

578 "equalled in radicalism": undated newspaper clipping, AJA.

578 "rebuke the State of Georgia": *BT,* as reprinted in the *Jeffersonian,* September 2, 1915.

579 "political ostracism": *Milwaukee Free-Press,* ibid.

579 stopped stocking Coca-Cola: *Jeff,* ibid.

579 "Georgia was not capable": *NYTrib,* August 19, 1915.

579 legislation to ban ... *Jeffersonian: NYH,* August 20, 1915.

579 "left New York for Marietta": *NYTrib,* August 19, 1915.

579 "I've been asked": *NYTrib,* August 22, 1915.

580 "a mood of braced purpose": *NYT,* August 19, 1915.

580 "I remember waking up": Golmer Haney Wilson, interviewed by author, October 2, 1990.

580 My account of the lynch party's use of George Daniell's fish camp is drawn from an interview with Bill Kinney on July 25, 1994.

580 "The public will never know": *AC,* August 18, 1915.

581 "as reputable a name": ibid.

581 "Leo Frank lynched here": *NYTrib,* August 19, 1915.

581 MARIETTA OFFICIALS DIDN'T KNOW: *AJ,* August 17, 1915.

581 GEORGIA'S SHAME!: *AC,* August 18, 1915.

582 "which by the way, is the ninth": *AJ,* August 18, 1915.

582 "I am greatly shocked": *NYT,* August 18, 1915.

583 "Nobody talks seriously": *NYT,* August 19, 1915.

583 "There are of course": *MT,* August 18, 1915.

583 despite having been awakened: *AJ,* August 17, 1915.

583 "The word mob": *NYT,* August 19, 1915.

584 "Seventy-five percent": *NYT,* August 18, 1915.

584 "the sodomite murderer": *Jeff,* August 19, 1915.

584 "The less said about the matter": *Macon News,* August 18, 1915, as reprinted in the *NYTrib,* August 19, 1915.

584 Flythe's accounts offer not only the description of a man resembling Yellow Jacket Brown but also the description of a bullwhip-toting lynch party member who resembled Black Newt Morris: *AG,* night edition, August 17, 1915, and *AG,* August 18, 1915.

585 factory serial numbers: *AJ,* August 19, 1915.

585 returned ... shotgun: *AC,* August 21, 1915.

585 deputy sheriff William McKinney was one of the party members: F. J. Turner to Lucille Frank, August 17, 1915, BU.

585 "I do not see how": *AG,* August 18, 1915.

585 "I am very glad": *AJ,* August 18, 1915.

585 would have been "suicidal": *NYH,* August 20, 1915.

585 "not a penitentiary": *AJ,* August 19, 1915.

586 he would "exert every effort": *AJ,* August 21, 1915.

586 "intends to ferret the mystery": *Winder News,* August 26, 1915.

587 "precision and secrecy": *AC,* August 21, 1915.

587 "The inquest verdict": ibid.

587 My account of the coroner's inquest is based on the work of the *Augusta Chronicle*'s John W. Hammond, the reporter who just a month earlier provided the only skeptical depictions of the prison commission's probe of sanitary conditions at the state prison farm. The *Chronicle* was the lone Georgia daily to staff either the coroner's inquest into the Frank lynching or the subsequent grand jury investigation.

587 "step from one of the automobiles": *AChr,* August 25. 1915

587 "came to his death": ibid.

588 "soft on lynching": Bill Kinney, interviewed by author, August 9 and September 24, 1990.

588 his father walking out: Jimmy T. Anderson, interviewed by author, June 14, 1990.

588 My account of the removal of James T. Anderson from the grand jury and the appointment of R. A. Hill and Bolan Glover Brumby to the same body is based on the handwritten jury list on file at the Cobb County Courthouse for the July term, 1915 (the new jurors were sworn in September 1, 1915). The action was corroborated for me by Judge Luther Hames in a 1987 interview.

588 "It has been published": *AChr,* September 2, 1915.

588 My account of the grand-jury investigation is based on the reporting of the *Augusta Chronicle*'s John W. Hammond, September 2 and 3, 1915.

589 "Seven members of the lynch party": Luther Hames, interviewed by author, 1987.

589 "We have been unable to connect": Herbert Clay to Governor Nat Harris, September 7, 1915. Harris papers, GDA.

589 "The Cobb county grand jury": *Boston Post,* September 5, 1915.

589 "The newspapers unite": Luther Rosser to John Slaton, September 1, 1915, Slaton collection, GDA.

589 "the public mind": ibid.

590 "Thousands who had been our friends turned on us": Herbert Asbury, "Hearst Comes to Atlanta," *American Mercury,* January 1926, p. 93.

590 My account of editorial meetings at the *New York Times* in the wake of Frank's lynching is drawn from the comprehensive entries in Garet Garrett's diary, August 18–26, 1915, pp. 90–97.

590 FRANK LYNCHING: *NYT,* August 20, 1915.

591 My account of the *Times*'s attempt to circulate its anti-lynching editorial to Georgia newspapers is drawn from Garrett's diary, August 21, 1915, p. 93.

591 "for the sake of the Times and Mr. O.": ibid.

592 "As it now stands": *MT,* August 19, 1915, as reprinted in the *New York Tribune* of the same day.

592 "but a kind of intimidation": Garrett diary, August 21, 1915, p. 94.

593 "conduct aroused suspicion": *NYH,* August 27, 1915.

594 My account of Charles Thompson's background is taken from "C. W. Thompson Dies, Editor, Reporter": *NYT,* September 9, 1946; my account of John Leary's background is taken from the files of the Pulitzer Prize Selection Committee, Columbia University, New York.

594 "a wonderful stump-speaker": *NYT,* August 19, 1915.

595 "not a big man physically": *NYTrib,* August 22, 1915.

595 "Judge Newton A. Morris is the hero": *NYT,* August 19, 1915.

595 "the story of the trip": *NYTrib,* August 22, 1915.

595 The photograph of Judge Morris pleading with the crowd appeared not only on the front page of the *New York Herald* on August 20, 1915, but also on the front page of the *Atlanta Journal* on August 17, 1915, and in the March 23, 1929, issue of *Liberty* magazine.

595 " 'Newt' Morris's part": undated newspaper clipping, AJA.

23. Recessional

596 "My heart aches with you": Mrs. Sig Montag to Lucille Frank, August 19, 1915, AHC.

596 "many Christian women": Celeste Parrish to Lucille Frank, August 18, 1915, AHC.

596 "My dear one lives": Lucille Frank to Rebecca Solomons Alexander, September 15, 1915, William Breman Jewish Heritage Museum.

596 The various remedies friends prescribed for Lucille are addressed in letters to her from Louise Hendricks on September 19, 1915, and Rae Frank on October 5, 1915.

596 "Get all out of life that you can": C. L. Musgrove to Lucille Frank, August 20, 1915, AHC.

596 "True to Frank's last request": *AG,* August 19, 1915.

596 "If ever an object was charged with tragedy": ibid.

597 "not enjoying the best of health": David Marx to Anne Carroll Moore, September 21, 1915, BU.

597 "You can never kindle a fire": ibid.

597 "Strange to relate": Rae Frank to Lucille Frank, October 5, 1915, AHC.

597 "The Wages of Sin": *Jeff,* August 26, 1915.

597 "Maybe when he reaches Honolulu": *Jeff,* September 9, 1915.

598 " 'Georgia's Shame' ": *Jeff,* August 26, 1915.

598 "Your Gold Calf stands discredited": *Jeff,* September 2, 1915.

598 "Oh, Rabbi Wise!": *Jeff,* August 26, 1915.

598 "The assassination of myself": *Jeff,* September 9, 1915.

598 FRANK VIRTUALLY CONFESSED: *Jeff,* August 26, 1915.

598 "Frank closed up": *Jeff,* September 9, 1915.

598 THE NEGRO TOLD: *Jeff,* September 16, 1915.

599 "God forgive me": *Jeff,* September 30, 1915.

599 "I never did think": *Jeff,* September 16, 1915.

599 ONE OF FRANK'S LAWYERS: *Jeff,* August 26, 1915.

599 "Mary Phagan was not fourteen": *Jeff,* September 9, 1915.

599 his . . . exposure of how the *New York Times: Jeff,* September 30, 1915.

599 *"You have blown the breath of life": Jeff,* September 2, 1915.

599 SLATON OR WATSON: *AChr,* September 12, 1915.

599 "To render a service": ibid.

601 "worshipping false gods": *AChr,* September 13, 1915.

601 "My heartfelt thanks": Lucille Frank to Thomas Loyless, September 28, 1915, BU; *AChr,* October 1, 1915.

602 "to help you in your fight": William Smith to Thomas Loyless, October 1, 1915, in possession of the author, courtesy Walter Smith.

602 "In reading the *Jeffersonian*": ibid., October 2, 1915, carbon copy in the author's possession.

603 A SHAME TO HAVE OUR LAWS . . .: *AChr,* September 19 and 28, 1915.

603 Louis Marshall's efforts to convince United States attorney general Thomas Gregory to prosecute Tom Watson are best detailed in Morton Rosen-

stock, *Louis Marshall, Defender of Jewish Rights* (Detroit: Wayne State University Press, 1965).

603 "mingle freely": Benjamin A. Richmond to Nat Harris, August 19, 1915, Harris papers, GDA.

603 "the little jackass": *Jeff,* September 23, 1915.

603 "the near-Catholic editor": *Jeff,* October 28, 1915.

603 "You tell Jack Slaton": *Jeff,* September 23, 1915.

603 "the carpetbagger brotherhood": *Jeff,* October 7, 1915.

604 "fusillade on the *Jeffersonian*": ibid.

604 *"They have simply reopened the Frank case":* ibid.

604 "We are with Tom Watson": *AChr,* October 7, 1915.

604 "I tell the Attorney General": C. Vann Woodward, *Tom Watson: Agrarian Rebel* (New York: The Macmillan Company, 1938), p. 447.

604 "The gentleman stated to me that he had just come from Mr. Watson": Nathaniel E. Harris, *The Story of an Old Man's Life* (Macon, Ga.: J. W. Burke Company, 1925), pp. 240–41.

604 "expressed his gratification.": ibid.

604 " 'What kind of politicians' ": ibid.

605 "Our Governor is certainly a wonder": Luther Rosser to John Slaton, September 1, 1915, Slaton collection, GDA.

605 The state's entire congressional delegation, save for Hardwick, asked Gregory to drop the case: Woodward, *Tom Watson,* p. 448.

605 "no fund which could be legally applied": Clifford Walker to Nat Harris, August 24, 1915, Harris papers, GDA. The state's decision not to pursue the lynchers ended all possibilities of any arrests, as in 1915, the Federal Bureau, of Investigation had yet to be founded.

605 The release of the $30,000 in prison construction funds is recounted in

the *Milledgeville Union Recorder,* September 7, 1915.

605 "The new 'L' to the main building": ibid.

605 "a set of silverware for 'a job well done' ": Dorothy Haney Smith, interviewed by author, November 5, 1990.

605 "sectional and racial hatred": *Jeff,* September 2, 1915.

606 *"another Ku Klux Klan may be organized":* ibid.

606 Nathan Bedford Forrest: For a succinct account of the reign of Forrest's original Klan, see Wyn Craig Wade, *The Fiery Cross* (New York: Oxford University Press, 1987), pp. 31-33.

606 "Forty years after Reconstruction": Charlton Moseley: "Latent Klanism in Georgia, 1890-1915," *Georgia Historical Quarterly* (fall 1972), pp. 365-86.

606 My portrait of the events surrounding the premiere of *The Birth of A Nation* is drawn from Wade, *The Fiery Cross,* pp. 119-39, and David M. Chalmers, *Hooded Americanism* (Durham, N.C.: Duke University Press, 1991), pp. 22-27.

606 "If there is a greater picture": Wade, *The Fiery Cross,* p. 132.

606 "like writing history with lightning": ibid., p. 126.

606 My portrait of William Joseph Simmons is drawn from Charlton Moseley's excellent "William Joseph Simmons: The Unknown Wizard," *Atlanta History* (spring 1993).

606 The Klan's reorganization was reported under the headline NEW KU-KLUX KLAN GETS CHARTER: *AC,* December 7, 1915.

607 My account of the modern Klan's first cross burning is based on my September 29, 1990, interview with Imperial Wizard James Venable, who was present that night, and on the reporting of Wyn Craig Wade in *The Fiery Cross,* pp. 144-45.

607 "Suddenly I struck a match": Wade, *The Fiery Cross,* p. 145.

607 "We became introverted": Alan

Marcus, interviewed by author, February 26, 1987.

608 "the closer the Temple got to the churches": Eli N. Evans, *The Provincials* (New York: Atheneum, 1973,) p. 278.

608 "had a profound impact on Marx": ibid., p. 277.

608 "blame the Orthodox community": ibid., p. 278.

608 My portrait of Samuel Boorstin's flight from Atlanta is based on a May 4, 2002, interview with his son Daniel and daughter-in-law, Ruth.

608 she had considered going to Chicago: O. C. Miller, American School of Correspondences, Chicago, to Lucille Frank, October 22, 1915, Leo Frank Collection, AHC.

608 My account of Lucille Frank's move to Memphis is based on an October 16, 1986, letter to the author from her nephew Alan Marcus, and on "Mrs. Leo Frank to Open Store": *Brooklyn Eagle,* February 9, 1916.

609 "My dear child Lucille": Rae Frank to Lucille Frank, February 9, 1916, AHC.

609 "there is no organized force": Luther Rosser to John Slaton, September 1, 1915, Slaton collection, GDA.

609 Following the war, the Slatons returned to Atlanta. In 1932, Slaton ran for the United States Senate only to be resoundingly defeated. Yet despite the fact that Georgians as a whole never forgave him for commuting Frank's sentence, the former governor remained a popular figure around Atlanta, practicing law and supervising the state bar exam through the early 1950s. He died on January 11, 1955.

609 My account of Thomas Loyless's postlynching travails is taken from Edward J. Cashin, "Thomas W. Loyless, Responsible Journalist," *Richmond County History* 9, no. 1 (winter 1977), pp. 18-28.

609 My portrait of Loyless's work at Warm Springs and his part in supervising the treatment of Franklin D. Roosevelt is

taken from Cashin, "Thomas W. Loyless" and Ted Morgan, *FDR* (New York: Simon & Schuster, 1985), pp. 274–76.

610 My account of William Smith's difficulties is drawn from his autobiographical notes and from interviews with his son Walter, on July 8 and September 4, 1986, and June 22 and October 1, 1987, and with his daughter, Mary Lou Smith Allen, on June 22, 1987.

610 "trying to make a living": Walter Smith, interviewed by author, July 8, 1986.

610 "he was so disheartened": Walter Smith, interviewed by author, June 22, 1987.

610 "A major part": Walter Smith, interviewed by author, September 4, 1986.

610 "Dad needed the job": Walter Smith, interviewed by author, September 9, 1986.

610 "The people he worked with thought he was a timekeeper": Mary Lou Smith Allen, interviewed by author, June 22, 1987.

611 "Dad decided that he'd trained as a lawyer": Walter Smith, interviewed by author, July 8, 1986.

611 "When Mother got off the train": Mary Lou Smith Allen, interviewed by author, June 22, 1987.

611 "It all tied in to the Frank case": ibid.

612 "disorderly house": *AG,* November 1, 1915.

612 "instead of drawing a fine": *AJ,* November 1, 1915.

612 "Don't write me up": *AG,* November 1, 1915.

612 "bride beating": *AJ,* November 7, 1915.

612 "Conley is 'in again' ": *AC,* February 13, 1916.

612 "spent more time in jail": *Greensboro* [Ga.] *Herald-Journal,* August 2, 1918, William Breman Jewish Heritage Museum.

612 "He figures the governor will pardon him": *Savannah Morning News,*

February 25, 1919. Accounts of Conley's conviction also appear in the *Atlanta Constitution* for the same day and in the previous day's *Atlanta Georgian.*

613 "the smartest criminal": *Greensboro Herald-Journal,* August 2, 1918.

613 My account of Watson's decision to endorse Dorsey is taken from Woodward, *Tom Watson,* p. 448.

613 "the fearless Solicitor General": ibid, p. 449.

613 "The attitude of the Hebrews": Rosenstock, *Louis Marshall,* p. 95.

613 "*He is* THE JUROR": Woodward, *Tom Watson,* p. 449.

613 My presentation of the 1920 senate race between Watson and Dorsey is taken from Woodward, *Tom Watson,* pp. 470–73.

614 "A Statement as to the Negro in Georgia": this remarkable 24-page document, issued on April 21, 1921, was provided to me by Hugh Dorsey, Jr. It is also on file at the Georgia Department of Archives.

614 Dorsey's campaign against lynching was endorsed by such Georgians as Rabbi David Marx at a conference in Atlanta on April 22, 1921. Their resolution was attached to Dorsey's statement as an addendum.

614 DORSEY PEONAGE PAMPHLET: *AC,* May 22, 1921.

614 "I took the Herndon case": Elbert Tuttle, interviewed by author, June 24, 1987.

614 For an overview of the Herndon case and of Tuttle's role in the desegregation of southern schools, see Jack Bass, *Unlikely Heroes* (New York: Touchstone Books, 1981).

615 "Henry Ford is editing a paper": *Congressional Record,* Senate, 1921, pp. 8055–56.

615 Watson's support for Imperial Wizard Simmons during Congressional questioning is discussed in Andrew S. Rice, *The KuKlux Klan in American Poli-*

tics (Washington, D.C.: Public Affairs Press, 1962), pp. 59–60.

615 "the King of the Ku Klux": ibid., p. 60.

615 My account of Watson's death and funeral is taken from Woodward, *Tom Watson*, p. 486.

615 My depiction of the Klan's rise to power in Atlanta during the 1920s is drawn from Wade, *The Fiery Cross*, pp. 153–66.

615 The best account of the Klan's role in the campaign of William Gibbs McAdoo at the 1924 Democratic Party national convention appears in Arnold S. Rice, *The Ku Klux Klan in American Politics*, pp. 74–84.

616 "Fist-fights were started": ibid.

616 Judge Newt Morris's role at the 1924 Democratic Party national convention was described for me in a November 1, 1987, interview with Herbert Clay's former law clerk, Lex Jolley, who recalled listening to the convention proceedings on the radio. Further details can be found in "Georgia Beats Klan Plank," *NYT,* June 29, 1924, which describes Morris's service on the committee on resolutions.

616 "The only way": Tom Shelton, interviewed by author, November 12, 1991.

616 "We shared Christmases": Tom Shelton, interviewed by author, November 2, 1993.

616 "that wasn't talked about": Clarence Feibelman, interviewed by author, November 29, 1984.

616 "The Jewish community was scared": Bea Haas, interviewed by author, June 20, 1986.

616 "My father never wanted": Joseph Haas, interviewed by author, June 20, 1986.

617 "The attitude of the older Jews": Charles Wittenstein, interviewed by author, November 26, 1984.

617 Pierre Van Paassen recounts his attempts to reignite interest in the Frank case in his *To Number Our Days* (New York: Scribner, 1964), pp. 237–38.

618 "one of the few people": Arthur Powell, *I Can Go Home Again* (Chapel Hill, N.C.: University of North Carolina Press, 1943), p. 291.

618 My account of Max Goldstein's destruction of Arthur Powell's allegedly exculpatory evidence is drawn from the correspondence of Max Goldstein and Irving Engle, Harry Golden Papers, Charlotte-McKlenburg Library, Charlotte, NC. On August 5, 1963, Goldstein wrote Engle: "I accept full responsibility for advising Judge Powell to destroy the memorandum . . . it would have merely resulted in renewing the agitation."

618 Henry Alexander's extensive, ongoing file on the Frank case was loaned to me by his son and namesake, University of Oregon philosophy professor Henry Alexander, Jr. It is now in the possession of the William Breman Jewish Heritage Museum in Atlanta.

618 the indictment of Monteen Stover: *AJ,* February 2, 1921.

618 Britt Craig: *AC,* March 19, 1919.

618 the death of Frank's mother: *NYT* January 2, 1925.

618 a full pardon to William Creen: *AJ* and *AG,* August 1, 1933.

619 Henry Alexander, Jr., spoke of his father's refusal to attend the fiftieth reunion of his University of Georgia class in an interview with the author, October 31, 1988.

619 "Frank, non-resident": Sarah Blackwell Gober Temple, *The First Hundred Years* (Atlanta: Walter W. Brown Publishing, 1935), p. 481.

619 Mrs. Lex Jolley, a Marietta native whose grandfather lived near Frey's Gin, spoke of the whitewashing of the lynching tree in an interview with the author on September 24, 1990. Bill Kinney recalled the framed sleeve of Frank's nightshirt on display at the Stonewall Court in an interview with the author on February 23, 1988.

619 "You can't imagine": Bill Kinney, interviewed by author, August 18, 1990.

619 For a thorough overview of Judge Newt Morris's later career, see "Judge Newt A. Morris Died Today," *Marietta Journal,* September 22, 1941. My account of his later days was further enriched by a September 12, 1995, interview with his daughter, Mrs. Sara Kennedy.

619 "You may save him now": *NYT,* October 7, 1934.

619 My account of John Tucker Dorsey's later career is informed by the interview his son, Jasper, gave to Dr. Thomas Scott as part of the Cobb County Oral History Series at Kennesaw State University. Dorsey's political successes are detailed in "Sam Welsch, John Dorsey Win," in the *Marietta Journal,* September 12, 1940. I also learned much on the topic in a March 9, 1987, interview with Dorsey's former partner, Superior Court judge Luther Hames.

620 Longtime Marietta resident Bob Garrison discussed the role John Tucker Dorsey's fish camp played in the lives of Marietta men in an interview with the author on May 28, 1991.

620 My portrait of the Brumby family's subsequent successes is drawn from interviews with Bill Kinney on May 5 and August 8, 1992.

620 Luther Hames discussed the county's failure to prosecute R. A. Hill for murder in his interview with the author on March 9, 1987. Dorothy Haney Smith discussed the murder itself in an interview with the author on July 7, 1993.

620 Bill Kinney spoke of Lawrence Haney's later life in interviews with the author on October 17, 1991, August 8, 1992, and September 13, 1995.

621 "There was one thing": Bill Kinney, interviewed by author, September 13, 1995.

621 My account of John Wood's rise to political power in Georgia is drawn largely from interviews with his former partner, Herman Spence, on November 5 and November 15, 1990. Further details are taken from "John S. Wood Dies at 83," *AC,* September 13, 1968. In a January 7, 1993, interview, Dorothy Haney Smith told me, "I verified that the last name on the list [of lynch party members] was Wood. It was alphabetical."

621 My account of Wood's rise to national power in the United States Congress, his role on the House Un-American Activities Committee and his relationship with Richard Nixon is informed by Walter Goodman, *The Committee* (New York: Farrar, Straus and Giroux, 1968), pp. 173–74, 190, 197 and 272–73. Also helpful is Stefan Kanfer, *A Journal of the Plague Years* (New York: Atheneum, 1973), pp. 127, 141–42, 196–97.

621 "I am not willing . . . to bring bad trouble to people": Kanfer, *Plague Years,* pp. 196–97.

621 Herbert Clay's alleged assault on Bobby Lou Greer is recounted in the *Atlanta Georgian* of May 20, 1917.

622 WOMAN USES HORSEWHIP: ibid.

622 My account of Clay's escapades at Dave Jarrett's Hotel is drawn from my interview with Luther Hames on March 9, 1987.

623 "were terrible enemies": ibid.

623 "Mr. Lockwood was the darling": Bob Gamble, interviewed by author, August 27, 1993.

623 My portrait of Clay's divorce and decline is taken from interviews with Eugene Herbert Clay, Jr., on February 26, 1987, Luther Hames on March 9, 1987, Lex Jolley on September 24, 1990, and Bill Kinney on February 23, 1988.

623 "I have befouled": Luther Hames, interviewed by author, March 9, 1987.

623 Details of the Annie Gober car wreck appear on the front page of the *Cobb County Times,* January 11, 1923.

623 "fatty degeneration of the heart": *Cobb County Times,* June 28, 1923.

623 "Clay was killed": Luther Hames, interviewed by author, March 9, 1987.

623 "covered up everything": Eugene

Herbert Clay, interviewed by author, February 26, 1987.

624 "was not thought to be related": Guide to Marietta City Cemetery by Curt Ratledge (Marietta: privately printed, 1992), p. 43.

624 "everyone involved suffered": Deveraux McClatchey, Jr., interviewed by author, October 18, 1988.

624 "He was kind of scared": Otis Cheatham, interviewed by author, August 11, 1995.

624 My account of John Wood's failed nomination to the Subversive Activities Control Board is drawn from the transcripts of the confidential hearings held by the Subcommittee of the Committee on the Judiciary of the United States Senate on May 10, 1955, and June 21, 1955. Both documents are on file at the National Archives in Washington, D.C. Also helpful in understanding the proceedings were accounts appearing in the *New York Times* on March 5, May 1, and August 5, 1955.

624 "like illegal whiskey drinking": May 10, 1955, hearing by the Subcommittee of the Committee on the Judiciary of the United States Senate, p. 27. This comment was originally reported by syndicated columnist Drew Pearson.

624 "Five thousand lynchings": May 10, 1955, hearing by the Subcommittee of the Committee on the Judiciary of the United States Senate, pp. 27–28.

624 "a racist and an anti-Semite": ibid., p. 31.

625 "My dad definitely thought": Dorothy Haney Smith, interviewed by author, June 20, 1991.

625 "My mother never did like Judge Newt": Paul Morris, interviewed by author, September 9, 1992.

625 "Fred Morris agonized": Bill Kinney, interviewed by author, February 23, 1988.

625 "I told Fred's widow": Luther Hames, interviewed by author, February 24, 1988.

625 "if you were late paying for the coal": Lucille Sessions Kappes, interviewed by author, November 25, 1991.

625 "a local shoe store": Jimmy T. Anderson, interviewed by author, June 24, 1990.

625 "He was guilt-ridden": Bill Kinney, interviewed by author, June 5, 1995.

625 "going to hell": ibid.

625 Bill Kinney described his evening with Jim Manning and his friendship with the in-laws of Lawrence Haney in an interview with the author on February 23, 1988.

626 "I have a delicate situation": Bill Kinney, interviewed by author, September 16, 1986.

626 "I will never be able to write honestly": Bill Kinney, interviewed by author, August 19, 1990. In January 2000, Stephen Goldfarb, a reference librarian at the Atlanta-Fulton County Library, posted the names of a number of members of the Frank lynch party online at www.leofranklynchers.com. His names were taken from a list that found its way to the office of Georgia lawyer Tom Watson Brown, great-grandson of the legendary populist, and later to the Emory University Library. I had seen the same list in 1986 and regarded it as a starting point as opposed to the answer to the question of who lynched Leo Frank. While Goldfarb fleshed out the document with a few biographical details, he did not convey the relationships among the lynch party members or examine the influence they exerted to pull off then cover up the crime. Nonetheless, his internet posting sparked front-page newspaper stories in the *Wall Street Journal* on June 9, 2000, the *Atlanta Journal-Constitution* on June 12, 2000, and the *Washington Post* on June 20, 2000. Yet despite the exposure, the topic still remained taboo in Marietta (the *Marietta Journal* ignored Goldfarb's revelations). More significant, his list, because it lacked context, did not begin to explain how the lynching brethren got away with one of

the most remarkable crimes of the twentieth century.

626 My account of Lucille Frank's return to Atlanta is drawn largely from my interview with her nephew Alan Marcus, on February 26, 1987.

627 "She was charming and nice": Lucille Morris Suhr, interviewed by author, September 28, 1990.

627 My portrait of Lucille Frank's later years in Atlanta is taken largely from interviews with Alan and Fanny Marcus on February 26, 1987.

627 "she just started crying": Celestine Sibley, interviewed by author, January 8, 1986.

627 "an extremely depressed person": Dr. James Kauffman, interviewed by author, June 18, 1987.

628 "Her doctor told her": Fanny Marcus, interviewed by author, February 26, 1987.

628 "To sum up her being": Alan Marcus to author, October 16, 1986.

628 Lucille died on April 23, 1957, Death Certificate #11201, Georgia Department of Public Health.

628 "written to Leo long after his demise": Fanny Marcus, interviewed by author, February 26, 1987.

628 For a full account of the attack on the Temple, see Melissa Fay Greene, *The Temple Bombing* (New York: Addison Wesley, 1996).

628 Alan Marcus revealed the story of Lucille Frank's burial to me in our interview of February 26, 1987.

24. The Revenant

630 My account of William Smith's 1948 work at the Fulton County Courthouse is drawn from interviews with Walter Smith on July 8 and September 4 and 9, 1986.

630 "LIFE AND LIFETIME": William Smith to Walter Smith, autumn 1948, note in author's possession.

630 "MY MOVES FOR CONLEY": William Smith, autumn 1948, copy of ms. in author's possession.

631 My account of Smith's exhaustion and his lunch at the Piedmont Hotel is taken from my interview with Walter Smith on September 9, 1986.

631 "HE SAID 'YES' ": William Smith, autumn 1948, courtesy Walter Smith.

631 "I'M WEAK": William Smith, autumn 1948, courtesy Walter Smith.

632 My account of William and Mary Lou Smith's early years on Staten Island is drawn from interviews with Mary Lou Smith Allen on June 22, 1987, and Walter Smith on July 8 and September-

ber 4, 1986, and June 22 and October 1, 1987.

633 "We boast of our freedom": William Smith, July 4, 1924, copy of speech in author's possession.

633 Smith discusses his ongoing friendship with the Reverend Henry Hugh Proctor and Proctor's sermon at his Staten Island Church in his autobiographical notes, pp. 21–22.

633 "It would be a pleasure": William Smith to Charles A. Boston, July 31, 1931, carbon copy in author's possession.

634 The *Liberty* contest to solve the murder of Mary Phagan was announced in the magazine's March 23, 1929, issue, which contained an overview of the case by Sidney Sutherland entitled "The Mystery of the Pencil Factory": pp. 43–48. The author is in possession of a carbon copy of Mary Lou Smith's prizewinning entry, "How, By Whom and in What Way Was Mary Phagan Murdered?"

634 "I can recall, as if it was yester-

day": Mary Lou Smith, "How, By Whom," p. 7.

634 "I rode on the elevator": ibid., p. 8.

635 Mary Lou Smith Allen discussed her father's decision to withdraw her *Liberty* article in her June 22, 1987, interview with the author.

635 "I believe that Mr. Smith": Martin Lippman to Jerome R. Bennett, Franklin Trust Building, Philadelphia, November 10, 1929, original in the author's possession.

635 "He was a dreamer": Frederick Ballen, interviewed by author, summer 1990.

635 My account of the collegiate careers of Frank, Mary Lou and Walter Smith is taken from William Smith's autobiographical notes, p. 45.

636 My description of the Fort Smith property is based on a visit there on June 19, 1987.

636 My account of Smith's fundraising successes for Fort Smith is drawn from my interview with Walter Smith, on October 1, 1987.

637 Smith wrote to Rockefeller early in his fund-raising effort: William Smith to John D. Rockefeller, April 4, 1942, carbon copy in the author's possession.

637 Borden Dairies rejected Smith's plea near the end of World War II: Cecil I. Crouse, assistant vice president, the Borden Company, to William Smith, June 29, 1944, original in the author's possession.

637 My description of the Smith House's appearance and cuisine is informed by my consumption of many excellent meals there, the first when I was a college student.

637 The outsize reach of the *Dahlonega Nugget* is attested to by the fact that *The American Mercury Reader,* a collection of articles published in 1944, features the mountain witticisms of J. B. Townsend alongside, among other works initially published in the *American Mer-*

cury, William Faulkner's "That Evening Sun Go Down" and F. Scott Fitzgerald's "Crazy Sunday."

638 "We believe that we have": *Dahlonega Nugget,* January 19, 1945.

638 "our churches, our college, our schools": ibid.

638 William Smith's generosity was first described to me in my interview with Walter Smith on October 1, 1987, and subsequently confirmed in an interview on November 5, 1990, with lawyer Herman Spence, who helped the family collect debts following William Smith's death. This is the same Spence who was a law partner with John Wood, who had been a lynch party associate.

638 MOVING FORWARD: *Dahlonega Nugget,* February 23, 1945.

639 BOTH SIDES: *Dahlonega Nugget,* March 23, 1945.

639 "We do not desire to run the town": ibid.

639 "an orderly and well-managed election": *Dahlonega Nugget,* April 6, 1945.

639 "John Moore was a prominent citizen": Frances Jones, interviewed by author, June 19, 1987.

639 "venting personal spleen": *Dahlonega Nugget,* April 6, 1945.

640 "Mr. Smith plans to continue": *Dahlonega Nugget,* March 15, 1946.

640 "He wrote letters to donors": Nell Young, interviewed by author, June 19, 1987.

640 My description of the 40,000 board feet of lumber piled by the road and my portrait of the Smiths sitting on their porch are drawn from my interview with Walter Smith on June 22, 1987.

640 "obsessed with a dream": Walter Smith, interviewed by author, June 22 and October 1, 1987.

641 My account of William Smith's decision to write "A Competent and Compellable Witness" is drawn from interviews with Walter Smith on July 8 and September 4 and 9, 1986.

641 "Some day it may be": William Smith to John Slaton, February 15, 1944, Ernest Rogers Collection, Robert W. Woodruff Library, Emory University, Atlanta.

642 "Mr. Frank's lead counsel": Smith, "Competent Witness," partial first draft in the author's possession.

642 My account of William Smith's departure from Dahlonega and arrival in Atlanta is drawn from my interview with Walter Smith on October 1, 1987.

642 My portrait of William Smith writ-ing messages while confined to an oxygen tent at Crawford Long Hospital is drawn from my numerous interviews with Walter Smith over a ten-year period.

643 "IN ARTICLES OF DEATH": William Smith, February 10, 1949, courtesy Charley Smith.

643 My account of Mary Lou Smith's last years in Dahlonega is drawn from interviews with Walter Smith and from "Mrs. W. M. Smith Rites Held Febru-ary 19," *Dahlonega Nugget,* February 27, 1976.

Epilogue

644 Alonzo Mann's conversation with John J. Hooker and the contents of his affidavit for the *Tennessean* are drawn from Steve Oney, "The Lynching of Leo Frank," *Esquire,* September 1985, pp. 90–104.

645 GIVE LEO FRANK: *AC,* April 26, 1983.

646 Elmer Gould discussed his rela-tionship with Jim Conley in an interview with the author on August 22, 1990.

646 Anna Belle Phagan Cochran re-called meeting Jim Conley in the 1930s in an interview with the author on June 20, 1986.

647 STAR WITNESS IN FRANK CASE ARRESTED: *AC,* October 21, 1941. An account of this incident also appears in the *Atlanta Journal* of October 20, 1941.

647 "Jim is probably buried": Elmer Gould, in his interview with the author on August 22, 1990. In his 1965 book *A Little Girl Is Dead,* Harry Golden wrote that Conley died in 1962. However, he pre-sented no documentation for the asser-tion, and none appears to exist.

647 "Magazines all over the country": Allen Lumpkin Henson, *Confessions of a Criminal Lawyer* (New York: Vantage Press, 1959), p. 75.

647 "Every scratch of the pen": ibid., p. 76.

647 "During the years": James Dorsey to Leonard Dinnerstein, February 6, 1964, AJA.

648 "My dear Gould": Leo Frank to John Gould, October 29, 1914, the *Detroit Jewish News,* April 1, 1983.

648 "By today's standards": *AC,* Janu-ary 3, 1984.

649 LEO FRANK PARDON DECISION: *AJ,* March 12, 1986.

Bibliography

Archives and Libraries

Leo Frank Collection, American Jewish Archives, Cincinnati.

Leo Frank Collection, Atlanta History Center, Atlanta.

Leo Frank Collection, Robert D. Farber University Archives and Special Collections, Brandeis University Libraries, Waltham, Mass.

Ida Pearle and Joseph Cuba Community Archives of the William Breman Jewish Heritage Museum, Atlanta.

Harry Golden Papers, Public Library of Charlotte and Mecklenburg County, Charlotte, N.C.

Julius Rosenwald Papers, University of Chicago Library, Department of Special Collections, Chicago.

Leo Frank Collection, Department of Special Collections, Robert W. Woodruff Library, Emory University, Atlanta.

Ernest Rogers Collection, Department of Special Collections, Robert W. Woodruff Library, Emory University, Atlanta.

Nat Harris papers, Georgia Department of Archives, Morrow, Ga.

John Marshall Slaton Collection, Georgia Department of Archives, Morrow, Ga.

William Russell Pullen Library, Special Collections, Georgia State University, Atlanta.

Supreme Court of Georgia, records room, Atlanta.

Georgia Newspaper Project, main library, University of Georgia, Athens, Ga.

National Archives; Washington, D.C.

Unpublished and Miscellaneous Material

Alexander, Henry A., "Some Facts About the Murder Notes in the Phagan Case." Atlanta, 1914.

Benson, Berry, "Five Arguments in the Leo Frank Case." Augusta, Ga., 1915.

Branch, Harllee, taped interview by Harllee Branch, III, October 1962. Atlanta, courtesy Harllee Branch, III.

Brumby, James R., "Sketch of Life of James R. Brumby," Marietta, Ga., 1929, courtesy Mrs. Winter Allfriend.

Frank, Leo, "Leaflets 1 through 7, May 22 through June 3, 1914." In these leaflets, which are on file at the William Freeman Jewish Heritage Museum in Atlanta, Frank outlines the case for his innocence. They were originally circularized as part of the defense's 1914 campaign to win Frank a new trial.

Garrett, Garet, "Diary." New York, May 5, 1915 through June 7, 1916, courtesy Richard Cornuelle.

Johnson, Hutch, "The Leo Frank Case." Master's thesis, Florida State University, Tallahassee, Fla., 1966.

Kalmar, Karen, "Richard B. Russell: Democrat from Georgia." Doctoral thesis, University of North Carolina, Chapel Hill, N.C. 1979.

Meadows, Carol, "Review of the Leo M. Frank Case, 1913–1915." Undergraduate research paper, West Georgia College, 1967.

Nesbitt, Martha Tovell, "The Social Gospel in Atlanta: 1900–1920." Doctoral thesis, Georgia State University, Atlanta, 1975.

Roberts, DeWitt, "Anti-Semitism and the Leo Frank Case." Report for the Anti-Defamation League, Atlanta, circa 1950.

Rogers, William Curran, "A Comparison of Coverage of the Leo Frank Case." Master's thesis, University of Georgia, Athens, Ga., 1949.

Smith, Mary Lou, "How, By Whom and in What Way Was Mary Phagan Murdered?" New York, 1929, courtesy Walter Smith.

Smith, McLellan, taped interview by Leonard Dinnerstein, April 1, 1964, American Jewish Archives.

Newspapers

Atlanta Constitution

Atlanta Georgian

Atlanta Journal

Augusta (Ga.) *Chronicle*

Boston Traveler

Chicago Tribune

Dahlonega (Ga.) *Nugget*

Los Angeles Times

Macon (Ga.) *Telegraph*

Marietta (Ga.) *Journal*

New York American

New York Herald

New York Journal

New York Sun

New York Times

New York Tribune

Articles

Asbury, Herbert, "Hearst Comes to Atlanta." *American Mercury* (January, 1926): 87–95.

Cashin, Edward J. "Thomas Loyless, Responsible Journalist," *Richmond County History* (Winter 1977): 18–28.

Connolly, C.P., "The Frank Case." *Collier's Weekly* (December 19, 1914): 6–24 and (December 26, 1914): 18–24.

Dinnerstein, Leonard, "Leo Frank and the American Jewish Community," manuscript of AJA.

MacLean, Nancy, "The Leo Frank Case Reconsidered: Gender and Sexual Politics in the Making of Reactionary Populism." *Journal of American History* (December 1991): 917–48.

Moseley, Charlton, "Latent Klanism in Georgia, 1890–1915." *Georgia Historical Quarterly* (Fall 1972): 365–86.

——, "William Joseph Simmons: The Unknown Wizard." *Atlanta History* (Spring 1993): 17–32.

Train, Arthur, "Did Leo Frank Get 'Justice'?" *Everybody's Magazine* (March 1915): 314–17.

Watts, Eugene J., "The Police in Atlanta, 1890–1905." *Journal of Southern History* (May 1973): 165–82.

——, "How Atlanta Cleaned Up." *Literary Digest* (May 3, 1913): 1012–13.

Books

Allen, Frederick. *Atlanta Rising.* Atlanta: Longstreet Press, 1996.

Arnold, Reuben. *The Trial of Leo Frank, Reuben R. Arnold's Address on the Motion for New Trial.* Baxley, Ga.: Classic Publishing Company, 1915.

Bass, Jack. *Unlikely Heroes.* New York: Touchstone Books, 1981.

Bauerlein, Mark. *Negrophobia, a Race Riot in Atlanta, 1906.* San Francisco: Encounter Books, 2001.

Birmingham, Stephen. *Our Crowd.* New York: Harper and Row, 1967.

Branch, Taylor. *Parting the Waters.* New York: Touchstone Books, 1989.

Brundage, W. Fitzhugh. *Lynching in the New South.* Urbana: University of Illinois Press, 1993.

Caesar, Gene. *Incredible Detective: The Biography of William J. Burns.* Englewood Cliffs, N.J.: Prentice-Hall, 1968.

Cash, W. J. *The Mind of the South.* New York: Alfred A. Knopf, 1941.

Chalmers, David M. *Hooded Americanism.* Durham, N.C.: Duke University Press, 1991.

———. *The Social and Political Ideas of the Muckrakers.* New York: The Citadel Press, 1964.

Dinnerstein, Leonard. *The Leo Frank Case.* New York: Columbia University Press, 1968.

Dittmer, John. *Black Georgia in the Progressive Era.* Urbana: University of Illinois Press, 1977.

Dorsey, Hugh. *Argument of Hugh M. Dorsey at the Trial of Leo Frank.* Atlanta: Johnson-Dallis Company, 1914.

Du Bois, W.E.B. *The Souls of Black Folk.* New York: New American Library, 1969.

Friedman, Lawrence M. *Crime and Punishment in American History.* New York: Basic Books, 1993.

Evans, Eli N. *The Provincials: A Personal History of Jews in the South.* New York: Atheneum, 1973.

Fink, Gary. *The Fulton Bag and Cotton Mills Strike of 1914–1915.* Ithaca, N. Y.: Industrial and Labor Relations Press at Cornell University, 1993.

Garrett, Franklin M. *Atlanta and Environs, Volume II.* Athens, Ga.: University of Georgia Press, 1969.

Golden, Harry. *A Little Girl Is Dead.* New York: World Publishing Company, 1965.

Goodman, Walter. *The Committee.* New York: Farrar, Straus and Giroux, 1968.

Grantham, Dewey, Jr. *Hoke Smith and the Politics of the New South.* Baton Rouge: Louisiana State University Press, 1958.

Greene, Melissa Fay. *The Temple Bombing.* New York: Addison-Wesley, 1996.

Gunther, John. *Taken at the Flood.* New York: Harper and Brothers, 1960.

Hall, Jacqueline Dowd. *Revolt Against Chivalry, Jessie Daniel Ames and the Women's Campaign Against Lynching.* New York: Columbia University Press, 1979.

Harris, Nathaniel E. *The Story of an Old Man's Life with Reminiscences of Seventy-Five Years.* Macon, Ga.: J. W. Burke Company, 1925.

Hayes, Arthur Garfield. *Trial by Prejudice.* New York: Covici Friede Publishers, 1933.

Henson, Allen Lumpkin. *Confessions of a Criminal Lawyer.* New York: Vantage Press, 1959.

Hertzberg, Steven. *Strangers Within the Gate City: the Jews of Atlanta.* Philadelphia: Jewish Publication Society of America, 1978.

Hunt, William R. *Front-Page Detective.* Bowling Green, Oh.: Bowling Green Popular Press, 1990.

Jenkins, Herbert. *Keeping the Peace.* New York: Harper and Row, 1970.

Kanfer, Stefan. *A Journal of the Plague Years.* New York: Atheneum, 1973.

Knight, Lucian Lamar. *A Standard History of Georgia and Georgians.* Chicago: Lewis Publishing Company, 1917.

Kuhn, Clifford M., Harlon E. Joyce, and E. Bernard West. *Living Atlanta, An Oral History of the City, 1914–1948.* Athens, Ga.: University of Georgia Press, 1990.

Lindemann, Albert S. *The Jew Accused.* Cambridge, England: Cambridge University Press, 1991.

Lord, Walter. *The Good Years, From 1900 to the First World War.* New York: Harper and Brothers, 1960.

Nasaw, David. *The Chief.* Boston: Houghton Mifflin Company, 2000.

Pomerantz, Gary. *Where Peachtree Meets Sweet Auburn.* New York: Scribner, 1996.

Powell, Arthur. *I Can Go Home Again.* Chapel Hill, N.C.: University of North Carolina Press, 1943.

Rice, Arnold S. *The Ku Klux Klan in American Politics.* Washington, D.C.: Public Affairs Press, 1962.

Rosenstock, Morton. *Louis Marshall, Defender of Jewish Rights.* Detroit: Wayne State University Press, 1965.

Samuels, Charles and Louise. *Night Fell on Georgia.* New York: Dell Publishing, 1956.

Sayers, Frances Clarke. *Anne Carroll Moore, a Biography.* New York: Atheneum, 1972.

Seitz, Don C. *Joseph Pulitzer, Liberator of Journalism.* New York: Simon & Schuster, 1924.

Sifakis, Carl. *The Encyclopedia of American Crime.* New York: Facts on File, 1982.

Smith, Jean Edward. *Lucius D. Clay, An American Life.* New York: Henry Holt and Company, 1990.

Swanberg, W.A. *Citizen Hearst.* New York: Scribner, 1961.

———. *Pulitzer.* New York: Scribner, 1967.

Talese, Gay. *The Kingdom and the Power.* New York: World Publishing Company, 1969.

Temple, Sarah Blackwell Gober. *The First Hundred Years.* Atlanta: Walter W. Brown Publishing, 1935.

Tifft, Susan E., and Alex S. Jones. *The Trust.* Boston: Little, Brown and Company, 1999.

Van Paassen, Pierre. *To Number Our Days.* New York: Scribner, 1964.

Wade, Wyn Craig. *The Fiery Cross.* New York: Oxford University Press, 1987.

Weinberg, Arthur and Lila, ed. *The Muckrakers,* New York, Simon & Schuster, 1961.

Wiggins, Gene. *Fiddlin' Georgia Crazy.* Urbana: University of Illinois Press, 1987.

Wistrich, Robert S. *Anti-Semitism.* New York: Pantheon, 1991.

Woodward, C. Vann. *Origins of the New South.* Baton Rouge: Louisiana State University Press, 1951.

———. *The Strange Career of Jim Crow.* New York: Oxford University Press, 1955.

———. *Tom Watson, Agrarian Rebel.* New York: Macmillan, 1938.

Acknowledgments

As I write this, ninety years have passed since Mary Phagan was murdered, eighty-eight since Leo Frank was lynched. During the last seventeen of those years, I have devoted myself to learning and writing about the two crimes. I never intended to take so long—but I did. Along the way, I benefited from the knowledge and kindness of numerous people. Many have shared their stories, others their homes, some their hearts.

I am indebted to the following people for their insights into Atlanta at the time of the Frank case and in its aftermath: Kathleen Adams, Cecil Alexander, Henry Alexander, Jr., Thomas Arnold, Daniel Boorstin, Harllee Branch, III, Hugh Dorsey, Jr., Norman Elsas, Clarence Feibelman, Franklin M. Garrett, Elmer Gould, Bea Haas, Joseph Haas, Dr. Mark Huey of the Atlanta public school system, Cliff Kuhn, Dr. James A. Kauffman, Alonzo Mann, Alan and Fanny Marcus, F. Levering Neely, Nancy Saul, Dale Schwartz, Luther Rosser Shelton, Tom Shelton, Celestine Sibley, Andrew Sparks, Ken Thomas, Judge Elbert Tuttle, James Venable and Charles Wittenstein.

From the outset, one of my central areas of inquiry was the Frank lynching and its continuing impact on Marietta. Even after nearly nine decades, some people were unwilling to discuss the matter. Many, however, were forthcoming. Among those to whom I am grateful are Mrs. Winter Allfriend, James T. Anderson, Jr., Otis Cheatham, Chuck Clay, Tim Cole, Dan Cox, Bob Garrison, James Bolan Glover, V., Steve Frey, Judge Luther Hames, Katherine Morris Hardy, Hill Huffman, Lex Jolley, Lucille Sessions Kappes, Mary Phagan Kean, George Keeler, Sara Morris Kennedy, Narvel Lassiter, James W. Lee, Bob Livolsier, Deveraux McClatchey, Jr., George Morris, Newt Morris, Jr., Paul Morris, Mrs. Guy Northcutt, James Phagan, Dr. Thomas Scott, Dorothy Haney Smith, Herman Spence, Lucille Morris Suhr, Judson Ward, Harold Willingham, Golmer Haney Wilson and Zaida Clay Wood.

The other Georgia town that provided a location for a main act in the Frank case is Milledgeville. I am indebted to Louis H. Andrews for sharing his deep knowledge of the place and its personalities and to Jake and Sonny Goldstein for getting me into the now defunct state prison farm.

Though Frank was convicted and lynched in the South, northern newspapers gave the story its national prominence. No publication played a greater role than the *New York Times*. My understanding of the *Times*'s coverage owes much to the unpublished diary of Garet Garrett. Garrett, an assistant editor at the *Times,* observed from up close as the paper risked its journalistic integrity in an effort to exonerate Frank. I am grateful to the writer Richard Cornuelle for sharing Garrett's diary with me.

During the course of my labors, I benefited from the insights of several excellent historians, among them Edward Cashin of Augusta State University, David Chalmers of the University of Florida, Charlton Mosely, professor emeritus at Georgia Southern University, and Leonard Dinnerstein of the University of Arizona, whose 1968 book on the Frank case always stood me in good stead. I am also thankful to the late dean of Southern historians, Yale University's C. Vann Woodward, who interviewed many of the principals in the Frank saga when writing his 1938 book, *Tom Watson, Agrarian Rebel,* and shared his recollections of those interviews with me.

I owe an equal debt to a number of skilled archivists, among them Victor Berch of the Robert D. Farber Archives at Brandeis University, Sandy Berman of the Ida Pearle and Joseph Cuba Community Archives of the William Breman Jewish Heritage Museum, Mike Brubaker of the Atlanta History Center, Dale Couch of the Georgia Department of Archives, Linda Matthews of Emory University's Robert W. Woodruff Library, Anne A. Salter of the Oglethorpe University Library, and Jacob Marcus and Fanny Zelcer of the American Jewish Archives.

Among the people who did me random favors over the years, four stand out. Hutch Johnson, who as a graduate student in the 1960s met one of the men involved in Frank's lynching, provided me with a copy of his master's thesis on the topic. Thomas Kunkel, biographer of Harold W. Ross, shared his theories regarding the role the future editor of the *New Yorker* played in the case. Joe McTyre, a former colleague of mine at the *Atlanta Journal and Constitution,* put his love of photography and history to use in helping me to locate some of the pictures that illustrate this volume. David Earle, anthropologist at the Lancaster (Ca.) History Museum, contributed greatly to my understanding of Newton Augustus Morris's sojourn in California.

Unlike many nonfiction books, mine was researched and written without an editorial assistant. As a longtime newspaper and magazine writer, I believe in hands-on reporting. However, as I neared the finish line, I profited greatly from the labor of Jacob Forman, who helped me plow through the complicated accounts of Frank's numerous appellate battles, and Clay Senechal and Casee Maxfield, who helped me piece together the endnotes.

This book would not exist were it not for my literary agent, Kathy Robbins, whose idea it was. Neither of us realized what we were getting into, but luckily for me, Kathy doesn't know the meaning of the word "quit," and the several times I tried to learn it, she dissuaded me as only she can. My editor at Pantheon, Dan Frank, no relation to my protagonist, also played a strong and positive role. Though he inherited the project from its acquiring editor, Linda Healey, he never treated it as an orphan, working tirelessly and imaginatively on its behalf. I am grateful as well to Altie Karper, the managing editor at Pantheon, for her superb copyediting

Whatever this book's failings, they are my own, but there would have been more of them had it not been for the inspired comments of two dear friends. Georgia native Mitchell F. Dolin brought his legal expertise and literary sensibility to the portions of the manuscript dealing with the United States Supreme Court. Scott Kaufer, magazine editor nonpareil, lent his perspicacity to the book as a whole, recalling to its author the only two things that matter in literature — narrative and character.

I could not have survived the emotional toll this book's protracted birthing exacted had it not been for several people. In Georgia, I relied on the companionship of Jim Auchmutey, John English, Robert Coram and Jeannine Addams, Tom Chaffin and Meta Larsson, John Gillespie and Eleanor Ringel, and Frazier Moore, Jr. At home in Los Angeles, I counted on Sean Daniel and Ruth Hunter, Todd S. Purdum and Dee Dee Myers, Tom Beeton, Greg Critser, and my brother and sister in literary arms, Russ Rymer and Susan Faludi. Also key to my coming through this intact was the friendship of Alex S. Jones and Susan E. Tifft and that of Richard Zoglin. So, too, was the encouragement of Robert and Eleanor Oney, my parents. Most significant, my wife, Madeline Stuart, was unstinting in her love for me. She never wavered in her faith. Her spirit, as well as that of my loyal Jack Russell terrier, Jackson, who has been along for thirteen of the seventeen years, kept me sane.

Finally, there are four Georgians who in their different ways cast a light in the darkness. Tom Watson Brown, great-grandson and namesake of the populist firebrand, repeatedly argued the case for Leo Frank's guilt to me. In an era when Frank's innocence is taken as a foregone conclusion, he helped me to maintain an open mind. Eugene Herbert Clay, Jr., son of lynch party planner Herbert Clay, entertained the sort of painful queries most children would never countenance about a parent. As much as I did, he wanted to know what had happened, even if it implicated his father. Bill Kinney, associate editor of the *Marietta Journal,* though he rarely gave direct responses to my questions, provided what for a reporter is actually better—the right questions to ask and the names of the people who knew the answers. Walter Smith, whose father represented Jim Conley, presented me with both a bequest and a challenge. The story of William Smith's change of heart is dramatic and moving, and Walter entrusted me with its telling. At the same time, he demanded that I follow a difficult path. As he put it, my job was to "ascend to the truth." Walter pointed out the summit—I tried my best to reach it.

Index